Printed Reference Material

Handbooks on Library Practice

MEDICAL LIBRARIANSHIP
Edited by Michael Carmel
Librarian, South West Thames Medical Region
0 85365 502 2

SERIALS LIBRARIANSHIP
Edited by Ross Bourne
*Head of Serials Office,
British Library Bibliographic Services*
Boards 0 85365 631 2
Paper covers 0 85365 721 1

UNIVERSITY LIBRARIANSHIP
Edited by J. F. Stirling
Librarian, University of Exeter
0 85365 621 5

PICTURE LIBRARIANSHIP
Edited by Helen P. Harrison
Librarian, The Media Library, The Open University
Boards 0 85365 912 5
Paper covers 0 85365 693 2

PRINTED REFERENCE MATERIAL
Second edition
Edited by Gavin L. Higgens
recently Chief Librarian, BBC Data

Handbooks on Library Practice

PRINTED REFERENCE MATERIAL

SECOND EDITION

EDITED BY
GAVIN L. HIGGENS

LA

THE LIBRARY
ASSOCIATION
LONDON

© The Library Association 1984.
Published by Library Association Publishing
Limited, 7 Ridgmount Street, London WC1E 7AE
and printed and bound by
Redwood Burn Limited, Trowbridge.

All rights reserved. No part of this publication may be
photocopied, recorded or otherwise reproduced, stored
in a retrieval system or transmitted in any form or
by any electronic or mechanical means without the
prior permission of the copyright owner.

First edition 1980
Second edition 1984
Reprinted 1985

British Library Cataloguing in Publication Data

Printed reference material.—2nd ed.
 1. Reference books——Bibliography
 I. Higgens, Gavin L.
 011'.02   Z1035.1

ISBN 0 85365 995 8 (cased)
ISBN 0 85365 776 9 (paper)

Typeset by Input Typesetting Ltd, London SW19 8DR

Contents

Contributors	xv
Preface to the First Edition	xviii
Preface to Second Edition	xxi

GAVIN L. HIGGENS
1. Setting the Scene — 1
Quick reference material	3
Reference material in:	5
PUBLIC LIBRARIES	5
SPECIAL LIBRARIES	6
ACADEMIC LIBRARIES	7
NATIONAL LIBRARIES	7
Important attributes of the reference librarian	8
Assessment of categories of reference material	12
Guides to reference material	16
Evaluation of categories of reference material	17

GAVIN L. HIGGENS
2. The Reference Process — 24
Reference work	25

Contents

The reference process	30
Essential qualities of the good reference librarian	31
The reference interview or dialogue	36
The search	40
Search strategy	44

KENNETH A. WHITTAKER
3. *Dictionaries*   49

Scope	50
Development	51
Uses	52
Dictionary making	55
Examining	56
Evaluating	57
Types and titles	60
GENERAL LANGUAGE DICTIONARIES	60
SUBJECT DICTIONARIES	64
SPECIAL PURPOSE DICTIONARIES	66
TRANSLATING DICTIONARIES	69
Books of quotations	71
Concordances	72
Library provision	73

A. JOHN WALFORD
4. *General Encyclopaedias*   76

Criteria	77
Some major encyclopaedias	87
ANGLO-AMERICAN	87
Junior encyclopaedias	92
Foreign-language encyclopaedias	94
GERMAN	95
FRENCH	96
ITALIAN	99
SPANISH	100
PORTUGUESE	100
RUSSIAN	101

Contents

DENIS J. GROGAN
5. *Subject Encyclopaedias*   107
   Role and content   109
   Arrangement   112
   Indexing   114
   Treatment   117
   Use   119
   Level   121
   Currency and accuracy   126
   Exploitation   127

BARRIE I. MACDONALD
6. *Biographical Reference Works*   131
   Biographical reference process   132
   Assessment of biographical reference works   133
   Universal biographical dictionaries   136
      GENERAL   136
      CURRENT   138
   National or area biographical dictionaries   140
      RETROSPECTIVE   140
      CURRENT   146
   Specialized biographical dictionaries   149
      RETROSPECTIVE   149
      CURRENT   151
   Biography periodicals   157
   Bibliographical guides and indexes to biography   157
      COLLECTED BIOGRAPHIES   157
      INDIVIDUAL BIOGRAPHIES   159
      PORTRAITS   161
      PERIODICALS   161
      PRIMARY SOURCES   162
      SUBJECT BIBLIOGRAPHIES   162

MALCOLM J. CAMPBELL
7. *Directories and other Business Publications*   165
   Topographical directories   167

Contents

Telephone directories	169
Telegraphic address and telex directories	170
General business directories	171
Individual trades directories and buyers' guides	177
Trade name sources	180
Some 'non-trade' directories	182
Professional registers and membership lists	183
Information source indicators	185
Company reports, card services, etc.	188
Discovering directories	192

GEOFFREY WHATMORE
8. *Newspapers and other Material on Recent Events* — 196

Broadcasting reference	197
Newspapers	198
Newspaper indexes	201
News digests	205
News data bases	207
Year reviews	208
Almanacs	210
International year books	212
Press guides	215

MALCOLM J. CAMPBELL
9. *Periodicals and Serials* — 219

History	220
Current problems and further solutions	221
Types of periodicals	223
Reference use of periodicals	225
Current and retrospective bibliography	226
Library catalogues and union lists	230
Keys to periodicals' contents	232
Indexing services	234
Abstract services	239

Contents

C. PETER AUGER
10. *Reports and Theses, Conferences and Symposia, Standards, and Patents*   246
    Reports   247
    Theses   253
    Conferences and symposia   255
    Standards   258
    Patents   262

HAROLD NICHOLS
11. *Maps, Atlases, and Gazetteers*   267
    Selection   269
    General maps   272
    Thematic maps   274
        GEOLOGICAL   274
        LAND USE MAPS   275
        CHARTS   275
        ROAD MAPS   276
    Atlases   276
    General reference atlases   278
    National atlases   279
        ROAD ATLASES   282
    Historical atlases   282
    Early and local maps   283
    Gazetteers   286

JAMES G. OLLÉ
12. *Government Publications*   294
    British government publications   295
    Parliamentary publications   297
        JOURNALS AND HANSARD   299
        LORDS PAPERS, COMMONS PAPERS, AND COMMAND PAPERS   300
        BILLS, ACTS, AND MEASURES   301
        WEEKLY INFORMATION BULLETIN   302
    Parliamentary on-line information system (POLIS)   302
    Non-Parliamentary publications   303

Contents

STATUTORY INSTRUMENTS	304
REPORTS OF COMMITTEES	304
STATISTICAL PUBLICATIONS	305
MISCELLANEOUS	306
White Papers, Green Papers, and Blue Books	306
Changes in the machinery of government	307
HMSO lists and catalogues	307
HMSO's sales service	308
Standing Committee on Official Publications	309
Non-HMSO publications	309
Retrospective bibliographies	312
Reprints	314
Northern Ireland	315
United States government publications	316
OFFICIAL CATALOGUES	317
THE RANGE:	319
Congressional publications	319
Publications of the Presidency	320
Departmental and agency publications	320
Publications of the Judiciary	320
Information excluded from British and US government publications	321

ANGELA M. ALLOTT

13. *Statistics as a Reference Resource: statistical publications and sources*   **324**

International statistics: guides	326
National statistics: guides	330
Regional and local statistics	333
Subject-based guides and bibliographies	337
Non-official statistical publications and sources	342
Historical statistics: publications and sources	345
'Alternative' statistics: publications and sources	348
Classification schemes for statistics—international and national	351
Building the collection: choosing and using	354
PRESTEL: statistical files	359
Building the collection: maintaining the stock	364

Contents

CHRIS E. MAKEPEACE
14. *Local Studies* — 385
- Bibliographies — 391
- Theses — 396
- National records — 398
- Private records — 398
- Local records — 399
- Dating — 402
- Handwriting — 403
- Periodicals — 403
- Newspapers — 403
- Records of Parliament — 405
- Directories — 406
- Census reports — 408
- Biographical information — 410
- Maps — 411
- Photographs — 413
- Ephemera — 414
- Tape recording — 415
- Archaeology — 415

RICHARD H. A. CHEFFINS
15. *Current General Bibliographies* — 423
- National bibliographies — 425
  - USE — 425
  - COVERAGE — 427
  - FREQUENCY — 430
  - CURRENCY — 431
  - FORMS — 432
  - COUNTRIES WITHOUT . . . — 433
- In-print services — 434
- More information about national bibliographies — 435
- Checklist of national bibliographies, related bibliographies, and major in-print services — 435

GEOFFREY GROOM
16. *Bibliographies of Older Material* — 454
- Universal bibliographies — 456

xi

National bibliographies 469
   GREAT BRITAIN 470
   UNITED STATES OF AMERICA 488
   FRANCE 493

J. DAVID LEE
17. Subject Bibliographies 502
General bibliographies with a subject approach 503
Subject bibliographies—selective 506
Subject bibliographies—comprehensive 510
Special library catalogues 511
Current bibliographies 514
Concordances 515
Indexes to periodicals 516
Tracing bibliographies: bibliographies of bibliographies 521
Library problems of bibliographies 525
   Subject bibliography: the future 528

LENA PARTINGTON
18. International Official Publications 534
United Nations 540
UN agencies 542
   INTERNATIONAL LABOUR ORGANIZATION 543
   INTERNATIONAL MARITIME ORGANIZATION 543
   UNITED NATIONS EDUCATIONAL, SCIENTIFIC, AND CULTURAL ORGANIZATION 544
   WORLD HEALTH ORGANIZATION 544
European Communities 544
Community institutions 545
   THE COMMISSION 545
   THE COUNCIL 546
   THE EUROPEAN PARLIAMENT 547
   THE COURT OF JUSTICE 547

Contents

THE COURT OF AUDITORS	548
Organization for Economic Co-operation and Development	552

J. DAVID LEE

19. *Printed Visual Sources* — 563

Visual enquiry work	563
PROBLEMS	564
Sources	566
THE ILLUSTRATED BOOK	567
ENCYCLOPAEDIAS	568
FACSIMILES	569
VISUAL ARCHIVES	569
BIOGRAPHIES	569
PERIODICALS	570
EXTRA ILLUSTRATED BOOKS	570
Standard works	570
Reference works	573
Visual collections	574
Local history	575
Bibliographies and indexes	576
The illustrations collection	578
Further sources: library coverage	580
Copyright	582
Picture researchers	583
Future developments	584

BERNARD HOUGHTON

20. *Online Information Retrieval Systems* — 588

Online information retrieval industry	590
Historical development	593
Terminals and communication systems	596
Information retrieval principles	599
Indexing languages	602
Search strategies and Boolean logic	604
Online interaction	607
Sample search	610
Online costs	613
Benefits of online searching	616

Contents

PETER H. MARSHALL
21. *Videotex Information and Communication Systems* — 622
    - Defining the systems — 622
    - Historical development — 628
    - Videotex systems structured — 630
    - Communication through Videotex — 633
    - Display and presentation — 639
    - Examples — 639
    - Transmission codes — 644
    - Costs — 645
    - Bibliography and further information — 646

KENNETH G. B. BAKEWELL
22. *Indexes* — 651
    - The importance of the index — 651
    - Definitions, and purposes of, indexes — 653
    - Some early indexes — 655
    - What an index is not — 655
    - What should be indexed? — 656
    - Cumulative indexes — 657
    - The long index — 658
    - How many indexes? — 659
    - How to recognize a good index — 660
    - Could indexes replace library catalogues? — 667
    - Indexing societies — 668
    - Awards for indexers — 669

COMPILED BY M. J. FORD
Index — 677

Contributors

ANGELA M. ALLOTT BA ALA
Librarian in charge
Commercial and Technical Library
Sheffield City Libraries

C. PETER AUGER FLA
Laboratory Manager
Lucas Group Research Centre
Solihull, West Midlands

KENNETH G. B. BAKEWELL MA MBIM FLA
Deputy Head
School of Librarianship and Information Studies
Liverpool Polytechnic

MALCOLM J. CAMPBELL ALA
Librarian
City Business Library
Corporation of London

RICHARD H. A. CHEFFINS BA DIPLIB
Bibliographical Services Division

Contributors

British Library, London
formerly Project Officer
IFLA International Office for UBC, London

DENNIS J. GROGAN BA FLA
Head of Department of Bibliographical Studies
College of Librarianship, Wales
Aberystwyth

GEOFFREY GROOM BA ALA
Assistant Librarian
Department of Printed Books
Bodleian Library
Oxford

GAVIN L. HIGGENS FLA *Editor*
recently Chief Librarian, BBC Data,
British Broadcasting Corporation
London

BERNARD HOUGHTON MA FLA
Senior Lecturer
School of Librarianship and Information Studies
Liverpool Polytechnic

J. DAVID LEE FLA
Librarian
BBC Hulton Picture Library
London

BARRIE I. MACDONALD ALA
Librarian
Independent Broadcasting Authority
London

CHRIS E. MAKEPEACE BA ALA
Librarian
Planning Department
Greater Manchester City Council

Contributors

PETER H. MARSHALL ALA
Reference Librarian
Bexley London Borough

HAROLD NICHOLS MA FLA
Senior Lecturer
Department of Library and Information Studies,
Loughborough University of Technology

JAMES G. OLLÉ MA FLA
recently Senior Lecturer
Department of Library and Information Studies
Loughborough University of Technology

LENA PARTINGTON BA DIPLIB ALA
Senior Librarian, Reader Services
Department of the Environment/Department
of Transport Library Services
London

A. JOHN WALFORD MBE MA PhD FRHistS FLA
Editor
Walford's Guide to Reference Material

GEOFFREY WHATMORE FLA
recently News Information Librarian
British Broadcasting Corporation
London

KENNETH A. WHITTAKER MA FLA
Principal Lecturer
Department of Library and Information Studies
Manchester Polytechnic

Preface to the First Edition

The third (and final) edition of INTRODUCTION TO REFERENCE BOOKS, by A. D. Roberts, appeared in 1956. First published in 1948, the book was written because the author considered that existing textbooks on the subject were badly out-of-date. The work was a great success, and I still have on my own shelves a copy of the first edition, which I bought in 1949 when I was a student.

The period since 1956 has been one of great significance in the field of librarianship in general, and in the area of information retrieval and dissemination in particular; it has, in fact, been the period of the 'information explosion', during which a vast amount of reference material has appeared for the first time. Many important and well-established items, which the reference librarian now takes for granted as being an integral part of his stock, had not appeared in print when Roberts produced his final text. Examples which spring to mind include BRITISH TECHNOLOGY INDEX; GUINNESS BOOK OF RECORDS; MCGRAW-HILL ENCYCLOPEDIA OF SCIENCE AND TECHNOLOGY; and WHO OWNS WHOM.

A growing awareness of the need for effective library-based information services has resulted in the establishment of many new libraries, particularly in the fields of industry, commerce, and further education. The number of universities has increased, and some

Preface of the First Edition

30 polytechnics have been created. To deal with the information explosion, many more librarians and information scientists have been needed; extra schools of librarianship have been formed, and larger annual intakes of students accepted. Finally, The Library Association's examinations have been largely replaced by degrees in librarianship, or by postgraduate diplomas in the subject.

In 1976, the Panel of Assessors of The Library Association concluded that there was a demonstrable need for a work which would effectively up-date Roberts. In producing this work, at their request, I have kept Roberts' framework in mind: due account has been taken, however, of subsequent developments such as on-line retrieval, and appropriate space has been allocated to conference proceedings, symposia, standard specifications, patents, reports, statistical materials, and microforms.

The objective has been to provide, for students and researchers; recently appointed reference staff; and practising librarians, working in small information units, with limited stocks, a practical handbook containing:

(a) some general remarks on reference materials, their evaluation, and use;
(b) a consideration of the reference process, including general strategies for dealing with reference enquiries;
(c) a series of succinct chapters, each by an authoritative contributor, dealing with the various categories of reference material.

Each chapter normally consists of a short general/historical introduction, followed by brief descriptions and comparative critical evaluations of individual items, including those, where appropriate, in microform. It concludes with citations and references, numbered sequentially, as in the text; and with suggestions for further reading. It will be apparent that some contributors have provided these suggestions in the form of a narrative, while others have preferred to list items alphabetically, and to add any necessary notes of explanation. Students should examine both methods, and assess their respective merits and disadvantages. The discerning reader will notice that throughout the text there are variations in bibliographical presentation. Although the British Standards Institution

Preface of the First Edition

has published recommendations relating to bibliographical references (BS 1629: 1976), the librarian and the researcher will still encounter such variations; the opportunity has therefore been taken to provide examples in these chapters.

A work of this nature and length cannot, and should not, aim to be comprehensive; as its title states, it is intended to be a handbook: therefore it does not deal in depth with the literatures of special subject fields. Instead, it concentrates on categories of reference material. Fortunately, two excellent surveys of the literature are available—Walford's GUIDE TO REFERENCE MATERIAL, and Sheehy's GUIDE TO REFERENCE BOOKS. The first edition of the British work by Dr Walford was still in the production stages in 1956; in contrast, the American work now edited by Sheehy was originally issued in 1902, and had respectively as its previous editors Alice Kroeger, Isadore Mudge, and Constance Winchell. The present work is in no way intended to duplicate Walford or Sheehy; wherever possible, students and practising librarians should use it in conjunction with one or both of the guides.

In general, a structured approach has been adopted in the writing of this book. There would be little point in presenting a detailed account of the value and contents of such a generally available work as WHITAKER'S ALMANACK, since all of our readers should have access to it, and be able to examine it for themselves. In deciding at what length to write on any particular item, or kind of reference material, we have been guided by its relative importance, and by the extent to which it is likely to be available in small, medium, or large reference systems; we have also taken into consideration the existence of other satisfactory accounts which the student can read to supplement our own description. Where possible, we have taken a first-rate, easily obtainable example, and used this as a criterion against which other examples can be measured.

Finally, I should like to record my grateful thanks to all the contributors, who cheerfully accepted their allotted chapters—and met their deadlines!

GAVIN HIGGENS

May 1979

Preface to the Second Edition

In this second edition the coverage of the subject has been increased by the addition of three new chapters. These deal respectively with printed visual sources, videotex information and communication systems, and indexes.

The chapter on local studies has been retained, since many reference librarians have to administer and exploit collections of local interest, and researchers make extensive use of such source material. Significantly, in 1983, the University of York instituted pilot projects to test a method for the construction of a bibliographic database of printed materials in this general field.

The Editor would welcome any constructive criticism about the contents of PRM, so that future issues may meet, in the best possible way, the needs of its users.

March 1984   G.L.H.

1
Setting the Scene

Gavin L. Higgens

Reference libraries have the longest history of any type of library. They existed in the days of the clay tablet: from such tablets, information could be consulted, and lists of the tablets available were inscribed on the walls of the buildings concerned. Such lists might be regarded as the primitive forerunners of the library catalogues of today. From their beginnings in ancient times, the functions of libraries have not altered significantly; but the format, quantity and content of the materials making up their stocks, and the resultant services which they have been able to offer, have progressively been transformed to the point where the researcher in the United Kingdom, the United States, and elsewhere, today has access to a network of sophisticated information resources.

The world's population has increased enormously in the last hundred years, during which time there has also been an overall expansion of literacy. The consequent literary output has resulted in an unprecedented volume of library materials—the information explosion, to which reference has already been made in the preface. It is the task of the reference librarian to select appropriate material from this vast output, and to exploit it to the best of his ability; the quantity he obtains will depend on the amount of capital and revenue expenditure which he is able to incur.

Setting the Scene

It is now pertinent to ask the question—what exactly *is* a reference library, and what are the materials which it normally contains?

Harrod[1] defines **reference books** as:

'1. Books such as dictionaries, encyclopaedias, gazetteers, yearbooks, directories, concordances, indexes, bibliographies and atlases, which are compiled to supply definite pieces of information of varying extent, and intended to be referred to rather than read through. 2. Books which are kept for reference only and are not allowed to be used outside the building.' He considers **reference materials** to be 'books and other library materials which may not be borrowed for use out of the library, either because their nature is such that they are prepared for brief consultation rather than for continuous reading, or because they belong to a reference collection.'

Collison[2] contends that it would be wrong to define a **reference library** as one from which no material may be removed: 'the true concept of a reference library is rather a collection of written and printed sources to which people may resort for information. It is in fact better to look on the reference library as a living encyclopaedia: itself a summary of the aims and ideas and achievements of mankind which attempts to provide a complete picture of current information on the subjects within its field. From this it may be seen that as long as a reference library is able to provide adequate information on any topic at any given moment, it is reasonable that it should be allowed to lend secondary material whenever it is thought necessary or desirable to do so.'

The fact that these definitions are not entirely in accord with one another is understandable, for reference work is complex, and has many facets. Depending to some extent on its size, a reference library contains many different types of material, each of which is included because it is a source of information, and the *raison d'être* of such a library is to provide a general information and research service to a particular category of people; this category may comprise anything from the general public within a certain catchment area, to a small number of engineers or scientists, concerned with fundamental research, and in a particular establishment.

The larger reference library may well include within its stock: books, pamphlets, reports, newspapers, periodicals, charts, maps,

Setting the Scene

patents, standard specifications, engineering drawings, internally compiled indexes, slides, film strips, canned film, videotapes, gramophone records, music scores, microfilm, microfiche, ultrafiche, cuttings, theatre programmes, architectural drawings, and so on; a full list would encompass all categories of material which act as sources of information.

The reference staff will normally work most speedily, efficiently, and effectively, if the enquiries desk is close to the core collection of **quick-reference** material, for it is from such stock that a high proportion of factual reference enquiries will be successfully dealt with. The quick-reference collection generally includes dictionaries, encyclopaedias, bibliographies, directories, handbooks, glossaries, subject indexes to periodicals, atlases, gazetteers, etc; most of the items concerned are likely to be arranged alphabetically; the user must therefore know, or ascertain, which form of alphabetization (ie word by word, or letter by letter) has been adopted in the compilation of any particular work. It may be argued, of course, that any form of 'broken order', that is, the placing of blocks of material out of the normal classification sequence, is a retrograde step, as it may confuse the library user, and, to a lesser extent, newer members of the library staff. Nevertheless, for the reason already stated, it is frequently encountered.

A competent reference librarian, with a small but judiciously balanced collection of quick-reference stock available to him, is well equipped to provide a good enquiry service to a variety of users interested in many subject fields. He will already have acquired a detailed knowledge of the contents of individual items, and, as new acquisitions arrive, he will scrutinize each one carefully for any peculiarities, good points, and shortcomings. Such a scrutiny needs to be carried out in a systematic manner, and this will be dealt with more fully. (See p 11.)

It is important for the student to remember that, although quick-reference material normally forms the nucleus of a reference library, the majority of the stock, particularly in large public or academic libraries, is likely to be made up of monographs, treatises, bound or microfilmed sets of back issues of periodicals, etc. Thus, while the generally accepted understanding of a true reference work is one which is conceived on the lines of an encyclopaedia, a

Setting the Scene

glossary, or a dictionary, it is preferable to broaden the concept by thinking in terms of an item from which information may quickly and easily be derived. Such retrieval can be achieved only if the contents of the work are rigorously indexed, or if they are scientifically arranged in a recognizable and systematic way; in other words, the reader must be provided with a layout which is evolutionary, chronological, or in an A to Z sequence.

Again, it is important for the student to realize that material laid out in this manner can have a dual function; it may be deemed suitable by the specialist to be read through completely; the reference librarian, on the other hand, may regard it as being entirely acceptable, in design terms, as a reference tool, in which case he will take full advantage of its ordered approach, its line drawings, half-tones, lists, tables, references, citations, statistics, appendixes, and index, to provide him with separate pieces of information.

A word of warning is necessary here. When the librarian requires really up-to-date information in order to answer a query satisfactorily, he will need to treat with due caution any data which he retrieves from book material. **Books**, by their very nature, cannot be produced very rapidly; the text has to be written and edited, proofs checked, the printing process completed, and the sheets cased; by the time the work has been published, much of the information it contains (depending on the nature of the subject matter) may be superseded or obsolescent. In such a case, the reference librarian might do better to consult recently published **articles in periodicals**, which can be issued more quickly, or obtain the necessary information direct from a specialist, or from an organization which has more ready access to the appropriate knowledge, eg an embassy, a research association, or a government department. To alleviate the problem of obsolescence in key reference works—biographical dictionaries may be cited as a typical category—some major reference libraries ensure that these are updated on a day-to-day basis; a member of staff may, therefore, be given the task of scanning newspapers, etc, for important obituaries, new appointments, honours, decorations, and so on, and of amending salient works accordingly. Although such work is bound to be time-consuming, it is, in terms of improved service, a worth-

Setting the Scene

while activity which results in the quick and efficient answering of factual enquiries.

In the early stages of library history, the reference section was the main part of any library; often, in fact, it was the only part, and it formed, for example, an integral part of various monasteries. Subsequently, the position changed, and in the majority of present-day libraries the reference section is likely to be one department of a larger organization, which may have also a lending department, a music department, a record department, a commercial department, and so on. Some of the large central libraries in cities in the United States of America adopt a subject approach, instead of dividing themselves into reference and lending departments. All material in a particular subject field, whether intended for reference purposes or for loan, is brought together. It is selected, acquired, classified, catalogued, administered and exploited by staff who have specialist experience and knowledge of the subject concerned. This system of subject departments has much to recommend it, and it has been adopted by some public and academic libraries in Britain also.

Nevertheless, in most British **public libraries**, reference material is housed separately from material which readers are allowed to take home, although in the smaller branch libraries, the reference section may well be sited in the corner of the lending area, and be administered by the branch librarian and his lending staff. In such branch libraries, the section is likely to consist of basic stock of the quick-reference variety, such as dictionaries, encyclopaedias and directories. Although, as has already been indicated, an adequate proportion of factual queries can be dealt with from such material, branch staff will often need to turn to their lending library stock for supplementary information, thus treating lending items temporarily as reference material. With such a small core collection of reference material available to him, the branch librarian will seldom, if ever, be prepared to let any of it out on loan. Broadly speaking, the size of the reference collection of a public library system tends to be related to the population, both resident and commuter, which the system serves—the larger the population, the more extensive the reference resources are likely to be. However, in London, for example, some boroughs are much more wealthy than others; fur-

Setting the Scene

thermore, acquisition policies may vary widely. On this subject, therefore, it is possible only to generalize. The larger public reference libraries will normally contain many definitive or important works which are also available in the lending department; in most systems, however, only the more exhaustive treatises will be regarded as reference material, textbooks and monographs being available for loan.

Whereas public reference libraries normally regard books as the backbone of their stocks, **special libraries**, for example those serving industrial or commercial organizations, tend to concentrate on periodicals as their major source of information, and to hold many titles with back sets, covering their particular subject fields. The periodicals collection may well be supplemented by relevant patent specifications; reports issued by the library's own organization and by external bodies; engineering, architectural, and other drawings; British and foreign standards specifications; slides, and so on. The reference collection, which will not normally be available for loan, may well comprise technical handbooks; British and foreign dictionaries and glossaries; commercially produced indexes to periodicals; long sets of abstracts journals; subject and general encyclopaedias; technical and trades directories; union lists of periodicals; conference proceedings, etc.

Where adequate funds are available, such libraries, serving large establishments, may well decide to buy duplicate or even multiple copies of heavily used works. In this case, one master copy will be retained entirely for reference purposes, while the remainder may be allocated to the lending shelves, or be seconded on indefinite loan to a particular laboratory, workshop, or office.

In dealing successfully with budgetary control, the reference librarian, in any category of reference service—public, academic, or special—must bear in mind that, whereas the cost of a book (other than annuals), a pamphlet, or a map, is a once-only cost, a subscription to a periodical is an 'on-going' cost which may increase very substantially during the course of a financial year. Furthermore, if he places a standing order for the title, he automatically incurs expenditure each year, and he must make financial allowance accordingly. In recent years particularly, the charges for many periodicals have increased at an alarming rate, and often unpre-

Setting the Scene

dictably; an additional cost will be involved if the librarian decides as a matter of policy to have periodicals bound. He may decide to compromise by binding those well-used titles which are indexed regularly, but to file as 'separates' those which are more ephemeral, are unindexed, or can be obtained in microform.

Retrieval, for reference purposes, of information from periodicals, is complicated by the fact that there is no standardized system for the issuing of indexes for individual titles. Thus some periodicals are indexed annually by their publishers; some may be indexed at other, varying, intervals; and many are not indexed at all. In view of the current-awareness value of this category of reference material, larger libraries may well subscribe to various **subject indexes to periodicals**, which are issued at regular intervals, and which cumulate into annual volumes. Such works will be discussed elsewhere in this volume (see p. 232); all that need be said at this stage is that there is bound to be some delay before any particular article appears in such a subject index. In the case where a reference librarian attaches particular importance to the information contained in specific periodicals, he may well decide to have such titles indexed by one of his staff, in order to obviate any inherent time lag.

University, polytechnic and other academic libraries will normally have a core collection of quick-reference and general reference material, which is not available for loan. In most libraries of this category, material from the rest of the stock will be loaned to students, teaching staff, and other researchers, sometimes for very short periods. If extensive provision of material for undergraduate use is made, separate departments, containing multiple copies of individual textbooks, may be provided for the purpose. People doing reference work in the main library should not need to concern themselves with such departments, as the works these contain will almost certainly be duplicated in the main library's stock; alternatively, works of a more exhaustive nature are likely to be held there.

National and copyright libraries have very large stocks of reference material which are not generally available for loan. Those entitled, under a provision, still in force, of the Copyright Act 1911, to receive free copies of books published in the United

Setting the Scene

Kingdom, are: the British Library; the Bodleian Library, Oxford; University Library, Cambridge; the National Library of Wales; the National Library of Scotland; and Trinity College, Dublin.

The national libraries have reading rooms and map rooms available for reference and research which cannot easily be done elsewhere.

The Reference Division of the British Library may well be considered the reference library *par excellence* of the United Kingdom, and its vast and varied holdings constitute a yardstick by which the holdings of other libraries may be measured:

(a) The Department of Printed Books contains official publications of all countries and periods, and those of inter-government organizations such as the United Nations and the OECD; an open access collection of bibliographies and other reference works in the social sciences; the largest extant collection of Ordnance Survey material; a collection of modern maps of all countries; an historical collection of maps, topographical views, plans, and charts; and an extensive collection of printed music, British and foreign. In addition, the Newspaper Library at Colindale has British provincial papers published before 1800, and newspapers published after 1800 from all countries; while the Library Association Library contains books, periodicals, pamphlets, films, and visual aids relating to librarianship.

(b) The Department of Manuscripts has a large collection of all kinds of books and documents, ranging from Greek papyri to present-day examples, in various European languages. Its material includes autographs of historic or literary interest; manuscript music; maps; plans; topographical drawings; seals; and charters.

(c) The Department of Oriental and Manuscript Printed Books concentrates on the cultures and the languages of the Near and Middle East, Asia, and North Africa, and is noted for its collection of Japanese block-printed books.

(d) The Science Reference Library (previously the National Ref-

Setting the Scene

erence Library of Science and Invention) contains, for reference purposes, what is surely the biggest and most comprehensive collection in the UK of technical literature worldwide. It is particularly strong on periodicals; abstracts journals; British and foreign patents and patent literature; foreign language dictionaries; trade literature; and trade directories. Intended mainly, but not exclusively, for graduate-level scientists, engineers, and technologists, plus patent agents, it provides enquiry and translation services, photocopying facilities, and direct, online access, via computer terminal, to various databanks. In contrast to other parts of the British Library, no reader's ticket is required.

One of the most important attributes of any good professional assistant in a reference service is the **ability to maintain an objective and critical outlook** towards the materials which make up the stock, or to which he or she has access. However painstakingly an item is compiled, its total current accuracy must always be open to doubt, and the older it becomes, the more inaccurate it is likely to be. Wherever possible, therefore, information provided in one source should be compared with that given in one or more other sources, before it is passed on to the enquirer.

Some actual enquiries may be used to illustrate that well-known reference works can vary in the information which they give on a particular point:

(a) When was Artur Rubinstein, the world-famous pianist, born?
Who's who 1977 states that Rubinstein was born at Lodz in January 1888; *Grove's dictionary of music and musicians* (5th ed) gives his birthday as 28 January 1886; yet, according to *Who's who in music* (6th ed), he was born in Warsaw in 1890; the *Encyclopaedia Britannica* gives the same year—1886—as *Grove's dictionary*; while the *International who's who in music* quotes different dates in different editions—the 1975 edition gives 28 January 1889, the 1980 edition 28 January 1887!

In view of this conflicting information, it would be reasonable to suppose that, for some reason, the pianist's birthdate is uncertain, and the validity of this assumption might well be

Setting the Scene

tested as a separate enquiry. However, as far as the existing enquiry is concerned, it is clear that quick-reference material (which in this case may be regarded as a secondary source of information) is unsatisfactory. The next stage is to see whether an autobiography has been written, and if so, whether the date of birth has been quoted. In fact, there is such an autobiography,[3] and the date quoted is 28 January 1887. This date is now used in the most recent editions of *Grove's dictionary*, and of *Who's who*.

(b) What was the total area and population of Pakistan in 1961?

Chambers's encyclopaedia 1966 gives the total area as 364,373 square miles, and the 1961 census population as 75,866,000; it points out, however, that Jammu and Kashmir, Gilgit and Baltistan, Junagadh and Manavadar are excluded from these figures. *Whitaker's almanack* 1953 gives respective figures of 364,737 and 75,842,000. *Statesman's year-book* 1954 gives respective figures of 364,737 and 75,842,165, and provides as a reference source: Davis, K. *The population of India and Pakistan*. Princeton, 1951.

Here again, the reference assistant is confronted with some statistics which tally, and others which are at variance. If the enquirer is in a hurry, he may decide that the figures are good enough for his needs; on the other hand, he may ask for further research to be undertaken, in which case the reference assistant will have to take his address or telephone number, and contact him again later when he has further information available.

Although example (a) refers to biographical reference works, errors do, of course, occur in other categories. Nevertheless, it is important to realize that who's who-type information compiled by questionnaire, or autobiographical information, is not necessarily more authoritative than detail compiled by other means. It is quite possible for a person to supply, either intentionally or inadvertently, incorrect information about himself. Another point to remember is that although two works may appear to differ on the place and date of someone's birth or death, both may in fact be

Setting the Scene

correct, because they are using different nomenclature and different calendars.

Statistical enquiries, such as example (b) need to be treated with care. Dr Johnson contended that 'round figures are always false', while Benjamin Disraeli, no doubt tongue-in-cheek, is alleged to have said 'there are three sorts of lie: lies, damned lies, and statistics'. Despite these strictures, statistics are essential in the modern world of commerce, industry, and science, and reference staff in the various categories of reference service are bound to have a significant proportion of queries which involve them: Chapter 13 has been devoted to them. All that need be said here is that if really accurate statistics are required, for practical or research purposes, the original publication source should normally be used. Consequently, typographical errors resulting from reprinting in reference works, periodical articles, etc, will be avoided; information provided will be more comprehensive; and the original publication may well contain explanatory notes. (For example, the *Demographic yearbook* (New York: United Nations) has used a code of reliability, in which the letter 'u' against a statistic indicates that the relevant figure is unreliable; italics indicate data from civil registers which are incomplete or of unknown reliability.)

Another important attribute of the professional assistant is the **ability to evaluate reference material**. This is particularly important in systems where the staff, as part of its duties, contributes to the overall selection of stock by keeping abreast of new publications in a particular subject field. In the ideal state, that is in the case of a very large staff establishment, it may be possible to appoint a considerable number of subject specialists, each with responsibility for an in-depth approach to stock within a small branch of knowledge; more often, however, the likelihood is that there will be someone responsible for a major branch, approximating perhaps to one of the main classes of the Dewey Decimal Classification, eg the social sciences, applied sciences, language, literature, geography and history. Subject specialists should also be aware of the value and reliability of earlier material in their field.

In the smaller reference system, however, the staff may be expected to deal with materials on all subjects; it must therefore acquire as much 'expertise' as it can, and relate it to the various

Setting the Scene

categories of material which comprise the stock: books, pamphlets, periodicals, newspapers, reports, maps, gazetteers, illustrations, slides, dissertations, manuscripts, etc. Clearly, not all libraries will require all these categories. The emphasis will vary according to the reference demands made on the unit concerned.

Several excellent guides to reference material give critical evaluations and comparisons of existing bibliographies, dictionaries, encyclopaedias, handbooks, etc, in all branches of literature, while similar works have been published which deal exclusively with a particular subject field, eg biology, mathematics, physics, economics, criminology. When a new work or a new edition appears, however, the reference librarian can either wait for an authoritative review to appear in a learned periodical, such as *The Times Literary Supplement, International Affairs*, or *New York Review of Books*, or he can carry out his own investigation; this is a process which takes skill and time. It is not sufficient merely to scan the preface and extracts from sample parts of the text, in order to establish whether statements made are basically accurate and up to date. On the contrary, the librarian must bear in mind that he is allocating part of his annual revenue to the purchase of the item; it is essential, therefore, that it should contain information not already available, or at least have a different approach, from existing stock, and thus be cost-effective. To 'earn its keep', it should be authoritative, comprehensive, and accurate—and be organized in such a way that information can quickly be retrieved from it.

To establish the authority of a new work, the librarian must assess the qualifications of those responsible for its production—the team who planned it, the editor and contributors (or the author), and the publisher; not only should academic or formal qualifications be considered, but also overall suitability for the task. If the writer has already written one or more standard works, his competence is unlikely to be in question; details of an author unknown to the librarian may well be given in the publisher's blurb, but if this is not the case, and the person is not included in any biographical dictionaries or indexes available, some research on his or her credentials may be necessary.

Volumes which contain signed articles should be checked carefully, the object being to see how many of the total are written by

Setting the Scene

individuals of appropriate standing, and how many of the rest are written by only one or two people. Unless a very high proportion is the work of authoritative contributors, the work is unlikely to be acceptable for reference purposes. The experienced librarian or subject specialist is, of course, aware of the comparative quality and professional reputation of the various publishing houses.

When a comprehensive new work is being considered for addition to stock in a large reference service, it should preferably be examined with care by several members of staff with differing specialist knowledge. In the smaller system, where such a complementary evaluation is not possible, the one or more people available will have to undertake bibliographical research in those areas with which they are not familiar. As has already been indicated, information should not be verified simply by making comparisons with other works, but by returning to the primary source; reference volumes may well copy from one another, so that agreement by them on some particular fact, statement, or statistic is not necessarily a guarantee of accuracy.

Unless the editor or publisher makes such a claim, it would not normally be realistic to expect a work to be totally comprehensive in any subject field, for this would mean that it comprised text, and citations or references, on everything known. **To establish the alleged degree of comprehensiveness** of a new book or report, the librarian should study the preface carefully before proceeding to the text itself, as that is where the editor should give a clear, unequivocal statement of the objectives of the book, and of its inclusions; omissions (due to length or agreed policy); coverage—British and/or foreign; emphasis; bias; etc. In reading the preface, the reference librarian and the subject specialist may not necessarily come to the same conclusions, as their viewpoints could be different. The specialist is apt (it could be argued, quite correctly) to make a rigorous assessment of the text by seeing how it fulfils his own requirements, and he will, in particular, be conscious of any omissions or errors; the reference librarian, on the other hand, will be weighing up the pros and cons of buying the volume(s), bearing in mind that, in the public library, he is seeking a balanced treatment which will meet some, at any rate, of the varying requirements of the general public, with their differing levels of knowledge; in

Setting the Scene

the academic library, he will be considering the varying needs of undergraduates, postgraduates, and researchers; and in the special library, he will be concerned with scientists, technologists, accountants, market researchers, etc, who may need similar information, but at different levels and from different points of view.

To establish whether or not a work is properly balanced, and therefore in all probability unbiased, the librarian can analyse it, using various techniques. For example, in the case of a biographical dictionary which purports to be international, entries can be counted to disclose any degree of national bias, and it might well be the case that an item published in the UK would have a high proportion of British people included, whereas an item of American origin would display an imbalance in favour of people from the North and South American continents. Again, an analysis of contributors may be undertaken to see whether they are biased politically or in terms of religion. The actual vocabulary used can also be revealing.

It has previously been mentioned in passing that a reference work should be an item from which information may quickly and easily be obtained. **To establish whether its contents are appropriately organized**, the librarian must check carefully the choice of headings used, and the adequacy of cross-references and the system of indexing. Headings should be clear and self-explanatory, and the index (a *sine qua non* for any self-respecting reference work) should be rigorously checked to ensure that cross-references and references do, in fact, lead to the information they are supposed to lead to. It must be remembered that the enquirer, in using the work, may not immediately think of the right main heading. A reasonable sample of articles should therefore be checked, and synonyms considered; are such additional headings cross-referenced in the text or included in the index? Any alphabetical sequence should also be checked for consistency; if the compiler has inadvertently used different forms of alphabetization (ie word by word, letter by letter) the user may well fail to find what he wants, particularly if the sequence is a long one (eg in a large encyclopaedia); a short sequence of headings, alphabetized in the two different ways, serves to underline the problem:

Setting the Scene

Word by word	*Letter by letter*
New Jersey	New Jersey
New Zealand	News
News	Newspapers
Newspapers	Newsprint
Newsprint	Newton Abbot
Newton Abbot	New Zealand

The librarian has a difficult decision to make when he is confronted with a work which consists mainly of information which he is aware he can obtain easily from other sources. He must then consider whether the remaining information is, *per se*, worth the cost. If it fills a gap in his stock, and passes the test of authenticity by, for example, citing its original sources, it could well be cost-effective. Frequently, the librarian encounters new works which basically contain nothing which is not duplicated elsewhere; however, they may approach a subject from a different, and useful, point of view. He may, perhaps, have an item in stock which gives a list of short-story writers, with, under each author, a list of his works; the new work may provide him with a comprehensive alphabetical list of short-story titles, each title followed by the author's name, and as such, will almost certainly be deemed a useful acquisition.

When a new edition of a work appears, it should be checked carefully, a strict comparison being made with the earlier version. Has it been thoroughly revised; have only a small proportion of articles or sections been up-dated; or is it merely a reprint with a few amendments here and there? Also (and this is important), has much material been deleted in the newer work? If so, the original should certainly be retained. Furthermore, if, since the publication of the earlier version, some other work, covering the same subject field, has been acquired, the librarian should take this into consideration before deciding whether or not to buy.

Not all categories of reference material have bibliographies: dictionaries, gazetteers, atlases, and directories, for example, are not so equipped. Monographs, treatises, biographies, reports, and articles in periodicals normally have bibliographies at the end of each chapter, or as an appendix; where they are provided, they should

Setting the Scene

be checked to establish that the most recent information is quoted. Nothing further will be said at this stage about bibliographies, as they are considered more fully in Chapters 15, 16, and 17.

As has already been mentioned, several excellent **guides** exist, which are very helpful when the librarian wishes to obtain brief, critical and comparative evaluations of existing reference material. Walford's *Guide to reference material* might well be described as the British reference librarians' bible, while Sheehy's *Guide to reference books* is undoubtedly the equivalent for our American colleagues.

Walford gives emphasis to British publications, but is nevertheless international in scope: it aims to provide details of reference books and bibliographies published, in the main, recently, so that librarians may get relevant information when enhancing or revising their stocks; in addition, it acts as an *aide memoire* to students preparing for examinations, and to practising staff undertaking enquiry work in all types of reference library. It is in three volumes; these deal respectively with science and technology; social and historical sciences, philosophy and religion; and generalia, language and literature, and the arts. The third volume includes a cumulated subject index to all three volumes. Items are listed according to the Universal Decimal Classification (UDC), which results in some of them appearing more than once. To assist with critical annotation, comments from various reviewing journals are included. Prices of items are included, but these need to be treated with caution, because of possible subsequent increases.

Sheehy also lists reference books which are fundamental in research work; the Guide acts as a reference manual for the reference librarian, the researcher, and other users of library resources; an aid to stock selection; and a textbook for the student pursuing a systematic study of reference works. The requirements of these types of users are reflected in the organization and make-up of the volume, which gives items which might be included in large general reference libraries. Scholarly works in English and in foreign languages are represented; where there is sub-division by country, the United States is listed first, with other countries following alphabetically. In contrast to the UDC approach of Walford, Sheehy adopts a series of five parts—general reference works; the

Setting the Scene

humanities; social sciences; history and area studies; and pure and applied sciences. Each item is immediately identified by an unique alpha-numeric code, eg AE192, AE193, etc.

Although severely dated now, Malclès' *Les sources du travail bibliographique* is still a useful bibliographical manual. Walford considers that Volume 3, published in 1958, has importance for the specialist in medicine, pure and applied sciences, and that some chapters constitute the best and most detailed guide to the literature of the relevant subjects. It is a pity that this work has not been updated.

For authoritative reviews of new material, the librarian can turn to newspapers and periodicals; some of these, such as *The Sunday Times*, *The Times Literary Supplement*, *British Book News*, and *Choice* (a monthly book selection journal published by the Association of College and Research Libraries—a division of the American Library Association), deal with works in many subject fields. *Choice* is said to review more serious works than any other reviewing medium in the USA: it includes works from American, Canadian, and European publishers. Specialist periodicals, however, such as *The Economist*, *The Lancet*, *New Scientist*, and *National Geographic Magazine*, tend to consider works in their own subject field.

Although general guidelines for the evaluation of reference material have already been discussed, these need to be supplemented by differing assessments, which will depend on the category of material concerned.

In the case of **encyclopaedias**, checks need to be made on whether there is a continuous revision policy; articles and maps are dated; the binding is substantial and will withstand hard wear; paper is of good quality and the typography clear; illustrations, half-tones (some at least of which should be in colour), maps, plans, and diagrams are well produced, of good quality, and relate to the text; the basic work is brought up to date by supplements or annuals. If continuous revision is used, the reference librarian will have to decide on a buying policy, and how often he proposes to replace sets. Often it is preferable to use encyclopaedias for articles which have continuing importance, and to rely on current publications and yearbooks for more recent information and events.

Setting the Scene

Dictionaries provide the librarian with his main source of information about words—their spelling, pronunciation, derivation, and meaning. Large modern dictionaries, however, are encyclopaedic in character—they deal not only with the word, but with the thing represented by the word, and include good illustrations, quotations, and special lists, such as foreign phrases in common use. Before purchasing such an important work, the librarian must ensure that it has been competently edited, and that it is not merely a reprint, with little or no revision. Checks should be made on the extent of the vocabulary; whether technical and scientific terms, obsolete forms, dialect and slang are included; pronunciation is clearly indicated; changes of meaning are shown and appropriate dates given; etymology, synonyms and antonyms included; definitions are clear and concise; quotations, to indicate use, are listed chronologically to illustrate evolution; and abbreviations and special appendices are supplied.

Periodicals, an expensive but absolutely vital part of the stock, particularly in special libraries, need to be assessed according to whether they are erudite research-type journals, or whether they are 'popular'; both categories meet a particular need, and should be represented. Checks should be made on the authority of the editorial board; presence or absence of abstracts at the beginning of each article; up-to-dateness of references and bibliographies; use of statistics; colour or black-and-white illustrations; plates; plans; diagrams; maps; graphs; calculations, etc; advertisements; and indexing arrangements.

Abstracts journals also form a vital part of the stock, providing as they do a key to the contents of periodicals. Factors which the librarian must consider before taking out a subscription include the authority of the sponsoring body; whether the abstracts are written by subject specialists, and are indicative or informative; whether there is comprehensive coverage of periodicals from all countries; what sort of time-lag there is between publication of the original and the appearance of the abstract; and whether there are frequent, cumulative indexes of authors, subjects, patents, etc, as appropriate.

In addition to periodicals themselves, and to abstracts journals, the librarian will require access to **directories or catalogues of**

Setting the Scene

periodicals, which give bibliographical details of each title: publisher, price, coverage, change of title, etc; **union lists**, which give locations of where back sets are available; and **indexes to periodicals** which provide, alphabetically by subject, brief descriptive details of articles which have appeared in the literature. These categories are dealt with in some depth in Chapter 9.

Newspapers are a valuable source of information, both current and retrospective. Daily, or weekly, they highlight international, national, and domestic affairs, with articles on politics, finance, business, people, and events. *The Times* and the *New York Times* have both been indexed for many years; since most daily papers report important events on the same day, the reference librarian with access to one of these indexes will quickly be able to pinpoint articles, on a particular subject, in various newspapers. Obituaries of well-known personalities are a case in point. Purely local articles, obituaries, and editorials, would not, of course, be found in this way. The *New York Times* now has its own computerized databank. In the past, large reference libraries maintained bound files of newspapers, but these caused problems because the poor quality of newsprint resulted in its rapid deterioration. 'Hard copy' has in many cases been replaced, therefore, by files on microfilm.

Many queries can be dealt with satisfactorily by the use of **maps and charts**, which are representations, drawn to scale, of features on the surface of the earth. Large reference libraries will normally have, in addition to a comprehensive selection of atlases and gazetteers, a judiciously balanced collection of British and overseas maps, at scales varying from 1:1,000,000 (eg the *International map of the world*) or smaller, to the large-scale series, produced by the Ordnance Survey, at 50 inches to 1 mile. Many will be topographic maps, showing both natural and man-made features—contours, heights above sea level, lakes, roads, and so on; but there will also be local historical maps; specialized series, eg geological survey, land utilization survey; and, of course, many British and foreign town plans, and maps for the traveller and holiday-maker.

General **directories**, and specialized directories of subjects or particular classes of people, and of societies and institutions, need to be evaluated carefully, for most of them appear annually. The librarian who has a considerable number of such titles on standing

Setting the Scene

order automatically commits himself to significant expenditure at the beginning of each financial year; nevertheless, this category of material is normally a very important part of the quick-reference collection.

Technical reports, patents, standard specifications, theses, and conference proceedings form a vital part of the stock of many special and academic libraries, and they are dealt with in some detail in Chapter 10.

In concluding this chapter, it should be said that reference librarianship is going through a particularly exciting stage. The need for quicker information retrieval is apparent, and it is being met by the use of new processes and methods such as computer output microfilm (COM); by teletext systems such as CEEFAX (British Broadcasting Corporation) and ORACLE (Independent Broadcasting Authority), which use the 'spare' lines on the normal television screen; by viewdata systems, such as PRESTEL (British Telecom), which use telephone connection transmission; and by the development of computer databases (eg PRESTEL) which can be interrogated via remote keyboard terminals. Online retrieval systems are the subject of Chapter 20, and videotex systems are dealt with in Chapter 21.

Readers of this book should be fully aware of the following:

(a) **Microfilm.** Microfilm offers a compact filing system which enables all the information on the original document to be retained. Images may be kept on roll film, which is normally either 16 mm or 35mm wide, or they may be made into a flat format—microfilm jackets, microfilm aperture cards, or microfiche. A typical microfiche packs 200 document images on to a 6 × 4 inch sheet film.

Many makes of microfilm reader or reader-printer are manufactured; these enable individual frames to be viewed and copied. More complex systems allow large stores of information on roll microfilm to be accessed, aided by a computer which handles all the indexing.

(b) **Word processors.** The word processor may be regarded as a

Setting the Scene

logical development of the typewriter, since it combines the basic typing function with a microcomputer dedicated to the manipulation of text. It is able to prepare text on a screen; commit it to memory; and correct or assemble it again to produce the final correct item before this is printed. Information is stored on floppy disks or diskettes, which are removable.

Unfortunately there is at present, in 1983, little standardization between word processors. It is impossible to take a disk from one supplier's equipment and to use it on a machine produced by a different manufacturer; indeed, different processors from the same manufacturer may not be compatible.

Word processors are not designed as data-processing machines. Nevertheless they can generate catalogue entries, and are ideal for the production of bibliographies; abstracts; periodicals and key-word lists; and general administrative tasks such as duty rotas and timetables.

(c) **Facsimile transmission.** The facsimile transmitter scans documents, normally up to A4 size (210 × 297 mm); a remote photocopy is then created at the distant machine. It is very easy to use, and can reproduce handwriting, typescript, and drawings; photographs, on the other hand, fare less well. In 1983 there are no flat bed machines, so pages from books or periodicals have to be photocopied before they are fed into the transmitter.

CCITT, the Consultative Committee for Telephony and Telegraphy, based in Geneva, has laid down three international standards for facsimile machines:

1972:	Group 1	6 minutes per A4 page
1976:	Group 2	3 minutes per A4 page
1980:	Group 3	less than 1 minute per A4 page

Group 2 machines are often compatible with those in Group 3, and there are now some 20,000 installations in the United Kingdom. A UK Facsimile Directory has been produced by

Setting the Scene

the British Facsimile Industry Consultative Committee in conjunction with British Telecom.

(d) **Videodiscs**. Videodiscs are now at an advanced stage of development. In 1983 a single double-sided disc can store 500,000 A4 pages in digital form, or 50,000 A4 images. The Library of Congress in America has what is claimed to be the first computerized system for storing images on optical discs and reproducing them by high-resolution laser printing. The images of more than 200,000 master cards—the equivalent of 140 card catalogue drawers—can be stored on one side of a disc; any one of the images can be retrieved and printed at a rate of 12 copies per second.

REFERENCES AND CITATIONS

1. Harrod, L. M. *The librarians' glossary . . . and reference book.* 4th ed. Aldershot: Gower, 1982. 692–3.
2. Collison, R. L. *in* Landau, T. *Encyclopaedia of librarianship.* 3rd ed. Cambridge: Bowes and Bowes, 1966.
3. Rubinstein, A. *My young years.* London: Cape, 1973. 3.

SUGGESTIONS FOR FURTHER READING

AMERICAN REFERENCE BOOKS ANNUAL
   Littleton, Colorado: Libraries Unlimited, 1970–
   Brief, signed reviews, arranged alphabetically by subject, are evaluative and comparative. A useful selection book for English-language material.

Cheney, F. N. and Williams, W. J. *Fundamental reference sources.* 2nd ed. Chicago: American Library Association, 1980.
   Covers bibliographic, biographical, statistical, and geographical sources of information; dictionaries, and encyclopaedias; the nature of reference/information service; and useful guidelines for the evaluation of atlases, bibliographic reference sources, English-language dictionaries and general English-language encyclopaedias.

Jahoda, G. and Braunagel, J. S. *The librarian and reference queries: a systematic approach.* New York: Academic Press, 1980.

REFERENCE AND SUBSCRIPTION BOOKS REVIEWS
   Chicago: American Library Association. Annual.
   Lengthy evaluations of encyclopaedias, dictionaries, atlases, etc, cu-

Setting the Scene

mulated from the regular RSBR section in the biweekly periodical *Booklist*.

Thomas, D. M., Eisenbach, E. R. and Hinckley, A. T. *The effective reference librarian*. London: Academic Press, 1981.
Considers the identification, evaluation, and maintenance of reference materials, and discusses methods of responding to enquiries. For the library school student and the new librarian.

Video to online: reference services and the new technology. *The reference librarian*, (5/6), Fall–Winter 1982. 1–205.
24 useful American articles dealing with videotex online reference services, and the online search.

Walford, A. J. (ed.) *Walford's concise guide to reference material*. London: Library Association, 1981.
A condensation of the three-volume work, it contains about 3,000 annotated entries, many of which are new.

2

The Reference Process

Gavin L. Higgens

Having looked, in the first chapter, at definitions of such terms as 'Reference library', 'Reference books', and 'Reference materials', we then dealt briefly with the evaluation and use of such materials. In this second chapter, we shall examine the component parts which go to make up a reference information service, and then discuss the Reference process. Subsequent chapters of the book will be devoted to various **categories** of reference material, and to local studies; printed visual sources; indexes and indexing; online information retrieval systems; and videotex systems.

Ever since the time of the ancient Greeks, man, that most intelligent of creatures, has been concerned to communicate with his fellow men; in other words, he has imparted, conveyed, or exchanged ideas, knowledge, information, etc, using speech, writing, or some other common system of symbols. By the middle of the nineteenth century, methods of communication were being transformed as a result of advances in science and technology. The telegraph and the telephone have been followed by other inventions such as wireless radio, telephotography, and teleprinting. The development of popular periodicals and newspapers, motion pictures and broadcasting by radio and television has permitted quick and efficient communication between a small number of individuals and

The Reference Process

large populations. Such media have been responsible for the new phenomenon of mass communication.

Originally, librarianship involved the acquisition, organization, and housing of library materials. The evolution of reference services as a major aspect of librarianship is quite recent; in fact the term did not appear until about 1890. Initially, college and university libraries in both Europe and the United States adopted a conservative approach to reader assistance, while public libraries were often more generous in this respect. It was left to special libraries—those serving industry, government departments, etc—to introduce a liberal approach, with emphasis on the dissemination of information orally; literature searches; evaluation of sources; preparation of reading lists; and preparation of abstracts. Increasingly, however, reference services have been extended to more demanding and scholarly users. In larger libraries of all types, it is now commonplace to have specialized departments, staffed by librarians with appropriate knowledge, covering science, technology, business, history, art, and so on.

Reference work is often referred to as if it were purely and simply the answering of enquiries through the use of reference material. In its widest connotation, however, it may be said to encompass everything which is essential if users' queries are to be dealt with swiftly, efficiently, effectively, and economically. Such processes include:

(a) the selection and acquisition of a sufficient and appropriate collection of books, pamphlets, newspapers, periodicals, maps, atlases, gazetteers, charts, microforms, standards, patents, reports, conference proceedings, stills, etc;

(b) the arrangement, organization, and maintenance of stock, so that it can be used easily and effectively by both staff and enlightened users;

(c) the compilation of a union catalogue of holdings, supplemented by specialized indexes relating to subjects in which the unit is particularly strong;

The Reference Process

(d) general information files giving details of search strategies employed in the answering of queries which are likely to occur again;

(e) in-service training of professional staff to ensure that optimum use is made of all facilities, and that a sense of team-work is fully engendered;

(f) production of printed guides to the library and the service it can offer (ie publicity hand-outs);

(g) adequate sign-posting, so that new users are not bewildered by the possible complexity of the lay-out;

(h) instructional guidance of groups of students, and others, in the use of reference materials, etc.

Furthermore, an efficient reference service, far from relying solely on its own and adjacent lending resources, will make extensive use of outside sources—other library services, embassies, research associations, personal contacts, and outside loans.

Reference material may be bought from library suppliers; from retail shops; or direct from publishers. Some library suppliers concentrate on the provision of book material, while others act as subscription agents for the regular acquisition of periodicals. It is important for the reference library to have good links with these sources of supply, through the Stock Editor, or whoever is responsible for purchases on its behalf. Some annual publications appear regularly at a particular time of the year; the publication date of others may be less regular, however. As annuals form such a fundamental part of the average quick-reference collection, it is essential, if such a collection is to be kept as up to date as possible, for standing orders to be monitored, and any late deliveries immediately chased.

The acquisition of some foreign material can sometimes be a difficult and frustrating process, and long delays may occur before items are received. In the case of subscriptions to American period-

The Reference Process

icals, about three months need to be allowed from the date when the order is placed to the date of receipt of the first issue.

In his selection of stock, the reference librarian does not have to rely entirely on purchases. Almost certainly, bequests or donations will be received from time to time. These will naturally vary in usefulness, but he should make a point of fostering good relations with such donors, by invariably responding with a courteous letter of thanks; where he does not need the material offered, he might well suggest another library system which would be glad to accept it.

The Gift and Exchange Section of the British Library Lending Division (formerly the British National Book Centre, part of the National Central Library) issues regular lists of books and periodicals on a subscription basis. From such lists the reference librarian may request items, on offer from other library sources to fill gaps in his stock, and help complete, for example, back sets of periodical titles. The number of items he receives should normally be in direct proportion to the number of items he offers.

Having achieved a suitable policy of selection and acquisition, the reference librarian must ensure that his stock is adequately classified and catalogued to meet the needs of his staff and his users. The oldest catalogues were manuscripts in book form. During the nineteenth century, however, printed catalogues became common; well-known examples include those of the British Museum, and of the Library of Congress. Card catalogues were introduced in the 1870s, with the object of overcoming the difficulty, inherent in book catalogues, of incorporating new entries; they have been predominant for many years in public and academic reference libraries, but time has revealed their disadvantages; these include the comparatively large amount of space which they take up in smaller libraries, and the difficulty which users have in tracing material from sections which have many sub-divisions, eg 'Union of Soviet Socialist Republics'. To overcome the space and storage problem, some libraries in recent years have adopted COM (Computer Output Microfilm) fiche catalogues, or are making use of MARC (Machine-Readable Catalogue) output on magnetic tape.

A high proportion of reference libraries, both in the UK and in the USA, has adopted the Dewey Decimal System as the system of

The Reference Process

classification, but many special libraries, particularly those strong in science and technology, prefer the Universal Decimal Classification (UDC), despite the inconveniently long class numbers which this method generates on the spines of books. The Library of Congress Classification is popular in college and university libraries, and is now used by some 400 of them, while some special libraries prefer to index their collections by using a thesaurus of key-words. Alternatively, they may use a system of punched cards, which can be sorted by machine or by using a light box. Holes are punched in a particular position to indicate a special feature or aspect, and all cards through which light passes at a particular punched position have that feature or aspect in common.

The various methods of cataloguing and classification are, of course, fully dealt with in other manuals of librarianship. All that needs to be emphasized here is that, whichever methods are adopted in the reference library, the objective is the same—to provide a key to that library's stock, thus ensuring that both library staff and trained users can quickly, effectively, and economically find the information from it that they require, prior to the retrieval of the relevant document or documents.

In cases where the library maintains specialist collections (eg a local collection; series of technical reports), or indexes of some subject of particular interest (eg short stories; poetry), it may well be considered that these need a different format from the main or union catalogue; consequently they will be indexed separately, rather than being incorporated. Additionally, many reference systems keep a general information index of subject enquiries which have been difficult to answer, but which are likely to recur. By documenting the sources from which the answers concerned were finally traced, reference staff ensure that their colleagues will not have to waste time by going over the same bibliographical ground in future. Having gone through the several links in the bibliographical services' chain—selection, acquisition, classification, and cataloguing, the various categories of reference material are now ready to be organized in the most effective way for efficient use by library staff and other users. The majority of the stock may well be on open access, but access to confidential reports, etc, is certain to be restricted.

The Reference Process

The type of equipment used is dependent on the physical requirements of the category to be housed: static adjustable shelving is normally used for books and back sets of periodicals; where, however, a stack is available for less-used material, and the floor loading is adequate, mobile racking (ie units running on rails, and either manually or electrically operated) may be considered preferable, as the total capacity achieved for any given area is so much greater. Several types of unit are available from library equipment manufacturers for the display of current issues of periodicals and newspapers. Vertical filing cabinets are useful for the storage of pamphlets, folded maps, and town guides, and special versions of them are marketed for keeping collections of spool film or cassettes. Plan chests with horizontal drawers may be used for charts, or paper flat maps, but many librarians prefer cabinets which open from the front, and have the sheets suspended on prongs. Lateral filing cabinets may be used instead of the vertical variety for mounted illustrations and newspaper cuttings; while card catalogues can be adapted to house stills and microfiches. This list, selected at random, is not intended to be complete; it does indicate, however, different types of equipment which may commonly be found in various types of reference library.

Inevitably, the newly qualified librarian appointed to a post in a reference system (whether public, academic, or special) will need a period of induction before he or she can make a cost-effective contribution to the information service; ideally, therefore, he should be attached to an experienced member of staff, and work under supervision so that his output can be monitored. It will be of direct and immediate benefit to him if, during his period of in-service training, he is given ample opportunity to browse through the various categories of reference material making up the stock, and to observe the ways in which seniors conduct reference interviews, and formulate and carry out search strategies. At the outset, he should be given any codes of practice or guidelines to various procedures which may exist, so that he can study them in depth.

The reference librarian should ensure that adequate sign-posting and guidance to the service is available; users will thus quickly be able to orientate themselves. A floor plan of the library, placed near the main entrance, is a desirable feature. Clear, concise in-

The Reference Process

structions on the use of the catalogue, and of equipment such as photocopiers and microfilm readers or reader-printers, will help to prevent misunderstanding and misuse, and at the same time engender users' confidence.

A final aspect of reference work which should be given due attention is the training of users in the basic use of the library and of its materials. In the **academic** library, for example, students should receive, at an early stage in their course, lectures on the objectives of the library, and the services which it can offer. A guided tour should be given, and instruction provided in the use of the catalogue. At a later stage, they may well be taught how to search the literature, and to make good use of abstracts journals. This sort of tuition should stand them in good stead in their subsequent careers.

In **special** libraries, where the number of users being served is likely to be substantially smaller, and where many of them will in any case be known individually to members of the library staff, it should be possible to provide personal tuition in the use of abstracts journals, reports literature, standard and patent specifications, conference proceedings, etc.

In **public** reference libraries, groups of students from the United Kingdom and foreign schools of librarianship; from local clubs and societies, should be given guided tours, with descriptions of the various categories of stock, eg the maps collection, the illustrations collection, and of course, the catalogue. Senior staff may also lecture to appropriate groups of people on the facilities available to them, and the sorts of information they can expect to get, from their reference service.

These, then, are some of the main facets of reference work, and when they have been successfully established, the staff are in a strong position to provide a general information and research service—their *raison d'être*—to their users. This information and research service forms the end product of the **reference process**, which may be defined as the aggregate of the stages through which the reference librarian goes in order to answer quickly, effectively, and economically, questions put to him by an enquirer. The process starts with the receipt of the question, and finishes when the answer has been given. As a rider to this, however, it must be said that

The Reference Process

some questions cannot possibly be answered, and that, in some cases, the librarian's response will be to refer the enquirer to some external source of information. Examples of both of these instances will be discussed later in this chapter.

In broad terms, reference enquiries may be divided, for the sake of convenience, into three categories:

(a) the simple, factual enquiry, which requires a minimal reference dialogue, and which can be dealt with very quickly;
(b) the more difficult enquiry, which necessitates a certain amount of reference dialogue and some period for identification and exploitation of resources;
(c) the really complicated enquiry, which may take hours or days of research, and involve both local and external resources.

In the case of (b) and (c), the reference process is likely to consist of a complex interaction between the enquirer, the reference librarian (who acts as an intermediary), and sources of information. It may involve a considerable number of variables: the identification, retrieval, and handling of various categories of bibliographic material; the psychological approach of the user in his formulation of the question; the psychology of the librarian in making his response; and the environmental framework within which the information need is generated.

A simple representation of the normal sequence of the reference process is shown in Figure 1.

The degree of success which a reference librarian is normally able to achieve in answering enquiries of all kinds is a measure of his aptitude for this sort of work, and it is undoubtedly true that many people do not have such an aptitude. What, then, are the essential qualities or attributes of a good reference librarian? Some of the more important ones are certainly:

1. BROAD SUBJECT KNOWLEDGE

This is particularly useful in libraries where staff may be called upon to deal with queries in all subject fields, and where no subject

The Reference Process

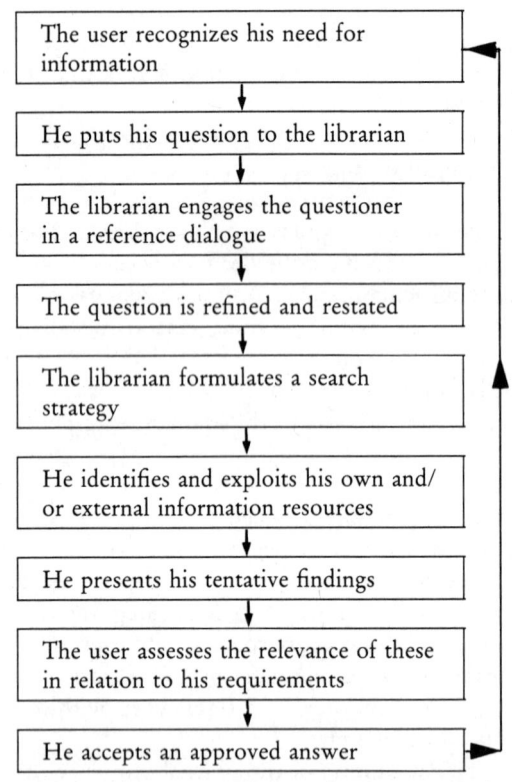

```
┌─────────────────────────────────────┐
│ The user recognizes his need for    │◄─┐
│ information                         │  │
└─────────────────┬───────────────────┘  │
                  ▼                       │
┌─────────────────────────────────────┐  │
│ He puts his question to the librarian│  │
└─────────────────┬───────────────────┘  │
                  ▼                       │
┌─────────────────────────────────────┐  │
│ The librarian engages the questioner│  │
│ in a reference dialogue             │  │
└─────────────────┬───────────────────┘  │
                  ▼                       │
┌─────────────────────────────────────┐  │
│ The question is refined and restated│  │
└─────────────────┬───────────────────┘  │
                  ▼                       │
┌─────────────────────────────────────┐  │
│ The librarian formulates a search   │  │
│ strategy                            │  │
└─────────────────┬───────────────────┘  │
                  ▼                       │
┌─────────────────────────────────────┐  │
│ He identifies and exploits his own and/│
│ or external information resources   │  │
└─────────────────┬───────────────────┘  │
                  ▼                       │
┌─────────────────────────────────────┐  │
│ He presents his tentative findings  │  │
└─────────────────┬───────────────────┘  │
                  ▼                       │
┌─────────────────────────────────────┐  │
│ The user assesses the relevance of these│
│ in relation to his requirements     │  │
└─────────────────┬───────────────────┘  │
                  ▼                       │
┌─────────────────────────────────────┐  │
│ He accepts an approved answer       │──┘
└─────────────────────────────────────┘
```

Figure 1. Sequence of the reference process

specialists are available, eg in many public library systems. Although he should not be expected to be a 'walking encyclopaedia', the assistant with such a broad knowledge will more easily be able to identify the subject field concerned, and thus save valuable time. In special libraries, on the other hand, or in systems with subject departments, an in-depth knowledge of the relevant subject field may be required.

2. ADEQUATE KNOWLEDGE OF REFERENCE TOOLS

Although, during the course of his academic studies, the student should have acquired some familiarity with certain reference items, he should nevertheless take every opportunity, on appointment, to

The Reference Process

browse through the stock, and scrutinize carefully any material he has not previously seen.

3. A KEEN, ANALYTICAL MIND

In practice, it will be found that enquirers seldom phrase their questions properly to begin with. Often, they over-generalize, instead of being specific. Thus, an enquirer may ask: 'Have you any books on railway history?' when what he really needs to know is 'On what date was Paddington Station, in London, officially opened?' Or he may say: 'Where do you keep your atlases?' when the information he actually requires is the latitude and longitude of Reykjavik in Iceland. There are, of course, many reasons for this approach to information. The enquirer may:

(a) prefer to look for the information himself, once he has been guided to the section which he believes (sometimes mistakenly!) to be the right section for his purpose;
(b) feel diffident about involving the librarian with his problem, particularly if the librarian is obviously busy;
(c) feel that he may be made to look foolish, if the question he wants to ask is a simple one;
(d) not wish to show his ignorance;
(e) know what he wants, but find difficulty in putting it into the form of a question;
(f) not really know what he *does* want, and therefore may simply be casting around for ideas. Faced with a question which, in its original form, is too vague, or otherwise unsatisfactory, the librarian has the task of assembling (by judicious use of the reference dialogue) its various facets into a restatement. He is then in a position to formulate his search strategy.

4. ABILITY TO PUT PEOPLE AT THEIR EASE

In special or academic libraries, where there is a captive clientèle, this may not be such a problem, but in public systems, which a

The Reference Process

person may be using for the first time, it is important for the librarian, at an early stage, to establish a suitable *rapport*, not unlike that which a doctor may have with a patient.

5. ABILITY TO COMMUNICATE EFFECTIVELY WITH PEOPLE OF DIFFERING AGES, TEMPERAMENTS, AND ABILITIES

In a university or college library, the librarian may have to deal, in quick succession, with undergraduate or postgraduate students, researchers, and lecturers; in an industrial system, with scientists, technologists and technicians; and in a public system, with teenagers, senior citizens, manual workers, professionals, and so on. He must therefore be adaptable and flexible, and be able quickly to assess the calibre of the enquirer in relation to the sort of question he or she is asking. For example, a person of professional status may require information or guidance not related to his subject field; it does not follow, therefore, that in this particular instance he will want an answer at a highly academic level; on the contrary, he may well be content with a response at an elementary level. Conversely, a young person with a keen interest in astronomy may well have made a special study of the subject, and thus require information at an abnormally advanced level for his age.

6. AN EQUABLE TEMPERAMENT

The tempo in various types of reference library can vary considerably. In a research library, for example, a high proportion of queries may be of the in-depth variety, and speed may not be important; in newspaper or broadcasting libraries, on the other hand, many of them will have to be dealt with very urgently, in order that deadlines are met; staff in such environments may often have several queries on hand simultaneously; it is therefore vital that:

(a) they do not get flustered, but remain 'unflappable';

The Reference Process

(b) in terms of time devoted to each enquiry, they steer a critical path;
(c) in making the decision as to the order in which to answer such enquiries, they must be capable of allocating the right priorities.

7. ABILITY TO DECIDE AT WHAT STAGE IT WOULD BE RIGHT TO CEASE SEARCHING HIS OWN RESOURCES, AND TO TURN INSTEAD TO OUTSIDE RESOURCES

It has already been emphasized in the first chapter that a competent reference assistant, with a small but well-balanced stock, can provide an effective information service; clearly, the larger his stock, the more chance he has of answering a high proportion of queries. In cases where he has plenty of time available, he may well be justified in rigorously pursuing, and eventually tracking down, information within his own database. In such cases, where the query is an abstruse one, he would probably record details in his Information Index. If, however, the enquirer urgently needs an answer, the librarian's duty is to meet that need quickly. His best course, therefore, would be to go to the **primary source**. For example, let us say that an enquirer produces a photograph of a power station, and on the reverse side is the legend 'Greenwich, about 1910'; he has no idea where the photograph came from originally, but urgently wishes to know the station's location; there are no obvious clues to this. Could it be Greenwich, London?—or perhaps Greenwich, New York? A quick check in a world gazetteer, or the index to a good atlas of the world, reveals that there are also places of the same name in Connecticut, Ohio, and Rhode Island. In a small, or even medium-sized unit, the librarian might well establish that none of his encyclopaedias contains an appropriate photograph, and that there are no books in either the reference or lending sections that can provide the information. His instinct tells him that the power station concerned is a British one. A large-scale Ordnance Survey map published in about 1910, and covering the Greenwich area, might well provide the answer, but he does not have such a sheet in stock. The best solution available to him at this point would be to go direct to the most likely

The Reference Process

geographical or subject source, ie the Local Collection of Greenwich Public Libraries; or the library of the organization responsible for power stations—the Central Electricity Generating Board.

The librarian who possesses these qualities is the sort of person who is likely, on a continuing basis, to make a success of the **reference interview or dialogue,** the object of which is:

(a) the establishment of a cordial relationship with the enquirer; this will assist in ensuring that he co-operates fully in helping to solve his problem, and gains confidence in the librarian's ability to be of assistance to him;
(b) clarification and refinement of the question, so that the reference assistant will be able to formulate a search strategy.

The relationship between the librarian and the enquirer is not of such paramount importance when quick, factual queries are being dealt with. For example, the answers to questions relating to the office of a government official, or the spelling of a foreign word, are normally indisputable, and the same material will be used, regardless of what sort of person the enquirer happens to be. Nevertheless, the personal element is still fundamental, and it is important to remember that, if the enquirer was suitably impressed by the way in which his simple query was handled, he is likely to return in the future, when he has a much more abstruse request to make, because his confidence in the librarian's ability will have been engendered.

Help should not, of course, be forced on a reader. Some people prefer to resolve their own problems. Provided that the library has been appropriately organized in the way which has already been described, ie with an adequate catalogue, good sign-posting, etc, an intelligent person accustomed to undertaking research in a library environment may well be able to satisfy his own requirements. Nevertheless, help should always be on hand, should he need it.

The element of **approachability** is important. The librarian in charge of a busy unit should therefore ensure that enough members of staff are available at all times, and that the time-sheet is adjusted so that sufficient assistants are on duty at peak periods. Such as-

The Reference Process

sistants should be accommodated either at individual desks, or at a large enough desk or counter. Enquirers with quick-reference questions should preferably be dealt with separately (at an information desk) from those whose queries are clearly going to take a long time to answer.

Unless the librarian is a subject specialist, he is unlikely to know as much about the subject of a query as does the enquirer; nevertheless, the very fact that he is approached implies a tacit acceptance on the part of the user that the professional knows more about the library, and how to retrieve information from it, than he himself does. In any case, a good reference assistant should *always* allow adequate time for the reference dialogue, and never deal with a question in a perfunctory manner; if he does, he will merely undermine the service, and discourage the enquirer from using it again. The time factor must be a variable; it will depend on a number of things—the type of library, the degree of urgency, staffing conditions at the time, and so on. In most libraries, the majority of interviews are dealt with in *impromptu* fashion, and at a speed consistent with success. Nevertheless, if the librarian begins by creating a friendly atmosphere, the enquirer is likely at once to be put at ease, in which case he will elaborate on his problem. The librarian's role is to aim, by judicious and unobtrusive questioning, to elicit the required information he needs in order to formulate his search strategy; and in doing this, he must constantly remember that it is never safe to work on the assumption that even highly intelligent or well-informed enquirers necessarily know what material is best for their particular needs. He must also be on the watch for vague or ambiguous enquiries, such as 'I want some information on piers (peers?)', and must then establish whether what is required is:

(a) details of peers of the realm;
(b) illustrations, descriptions, or technical construction data on seaside piers—or on moles or breakwaters;
(c) data on the supports of spans of bridges;
(d) data on pillars; or on solid masonry between windows, etc.

No reference assistant can be expected to be omniscient, and there

The Reference Process

will be times when he will need to admit frankly to some degree of ignorance or uncertainty regarding the nature of a query. This may well result in an incipient fall in confidence by the enquirer. If, however, on being enlightened, the librarian can swiftly retrieve some relevant material, he may expect to regain the enquirer's esteem!

The object of the reference interview has already briefly been discussed; by the end of his dialogue with the enquirer, the librarian should have established:

(a) as precisely as possible just what it is the reader wishes to know;
(b) the context of the query, ie why he wishes to know it;
(c) what the reader intends to do with the information once he has got it;
(d) how much the reader knows about the subject already;
(e) whether there is a deadline involved, after which the information will be of no use;
(f) the form in which the information is required;
(g) how much information is required;
(h) whether foreign language material is acceptable, and if so, which languages; and what translation arrangements are needed;
(i) whether information retrieved should relate to any particular period or inclusive dates.

In some cases, of course, the librarian may need to establish other points. While the interview is being carried out, he should, silently, be considering the materials, or categories of material, which might contain the data he seeks, and assessing their relevance to the reader and his needs; and normally, by the time the dialogue has ended, he should be at least well on the way to the formulation of his search strategy. Sometimes, in fact, the search may begin during the interview, in which case the enquirer's response to the material shown him is likely to indicate to the librarian whether or not he is on the right track. Often an enquirer will be satisfied with information obtained from reliable reference sources, but if serious research is being undertaken, it may, as has been previously mentioned, be necessary to go back to the primary source. For example, in a broadcast programme, slipshod research may result in lack of authenticity, and subsequent embarrassment resulting from bad publicity of this in newspapers or periodicals. Similarly, an error of fact in a publication or in a speech may result in a suit for libel, slander, or defamation.

If the librarian has to deal with an enquiry in a subject area with which he is totally unfamiliar, he may well find that even at the end of the interview he is still uncertain how to proceed; he should then work from the general to the particular—the known to the unknown—by getting a definition from a dictionary, or an outline article in an encyclopaedia, a book, or a periodical. Such an article may provide a useful starting-point for the enquirer, while the librarian progresses to phase two of the search.

In conducting the reference interview, the librarian will benefit considerably, and save a lot of time, if he uses open, rather than closed, questions.

Open questions allow the enquirer to elaborate, because he is able to respond as he thinks fit. For example: 'What, precisely, do you wish to know about laser beams?'

Closed questions give the enquirer no freedom to enlarge, because he has to answer either 'yes' or 'no', eg 'Is a black-and-white photograph suitable?'

'Two-choice' questions also inhibit the enquirer, because these involve an 'either, or' response, eg 'Would you prefer English-language or French-language material?'

Once the reference assistant has reached the main part of the interview, he should concentrate on questions which begin with such words as 'how', 'when', 'where', 'why', and 'what', and avoid those beginning 'have', 'will', 'can', 'is', etc. With a query such as 'Where do you keep material on cookers?', the dialogue might well be:

Librarian: It could be in various places. It would be helpful if you could tell me what type of cooker you are interested in, and the sort of information you require.

The Reference Process

Enquirer: Actually, I'm about to move into a new flat, and I want to buy either a gas cooker or an electric one. I've looked at so many types in the gas and electricity showrooms that I'm bewildered by the variety of models, and somehow I'd like to be able to compare them for quality, performance, and so on, before I make up my mind.

By confiding in the enquirer, and asking a couple of open questions, the librarian has immediately established a suitable *rapport*, and learned that:

(a) the enquirer is undecided whether he wants a gas cooker or an electric one;
(b) he has done some basic research already; and
(c) he is looking for comparative specification data.

The librarian's search strategy in this case could well be to check through recent issues of CTI (*Current technology index*), or, if he remembered having seen an actual article, to go direct to it in the appropriate issue of *Which?*, the periodical published by the Consumers' Association.

Some enquiries are phrased in such a way that they cannot categorically be answered. For example, the librarian presented with the question 'How many motorcars will British Leyland Cars produce in 1988?' may well be able to offer a statistical projection, based on certain hypotheses, but clearly, he could not be expected to resolve the question unless its wording were modified. Again, the question 'How long is the Loch Ness Monster?' is not one to which a positive reply can be given, as, despite many contentions, photographs, and a considerable amount of literature, it has never been proved that such a creature exists.

THE SEARCH

Throughout the course of his search, the reference librarian should be careful to ensure that he does not inadvertently overlook any points of access to his database, or any categories of source material

The Search

which could potentially be relevant, or pertinent to the needs of the enquirer. In the case of any complex query, this caveat cannot be over-emphasized; it is also valid, however, in relation to apparently simple questions which prove to be not so simple.

It may, therefore, be said that, when speed of retrieval is essential, a librarian, working as part of an enquiries team, who is aware that:

(a) his enquiry is a difficult one;
(b) he has little immediate knowledge of the subject field;

should, in the formative stage, consult with his colleagues, in case any of them may be better informed, or have dealt with a similar sort of query in the past. The user is, after all, not concerned with how his information is derived, so long as it is accurate. There is, therefore, no professional merit in going unnecessarily over ground which has been covered before.

In the case of a quick-reference enquiry, the librarian will normally think at once of an appropriate source, consult it, and provide an answer. For research-type queries, however, his access points will include the main catalogue; specialized indexes; the information index and file; bibliographies; periodicals indexes; newspaper indexes (eg *The Times*; the *New York Times*), and so on. If he has access to a computer terminal, with a visible display unit (VDU) and/or printer, a vast amount of information, in various subject fields, will quickly be available to him, through commercial databases or database hosts such as Lockheed Dialog; Compendex; Medline; Biosis; Blaise; the *New York Times* databank; Predicasts; etc.

Whether the search involves use of the catalogue, indexes, and bibliographies, or the interrogation of an external database, the searcher must decide on likely subject headings; it would, therefore, be sensible for him to list, in advance, any which seem appropriate, so that he does not inadvertently overlook any. The greater the number of key-words, the broader the search becomes. If the information retrieved is judged by the enquirer to be too general, the librarian will have to select headings which are more specific. As the search proceeds, he will have to decide the order in which

The Reference Process

he proposes to evaluate material disclosed by the catalogue, bibliographies, indexes, etc. Subsequently, each piece of information will have to be assessed in terms of its relevance, and pertinence to the requirements of the user. At the start of a search, the experienced reference assistant will often, automatically, formulate simple equations to provide him with an answer, eg:

dead person + famous Briton = *Dictionary of national biography*;
Pakistan + total population = *Statesman's year-book*;
periodical articles + abstracts + television engineering = *Electrical and electronics abstracts*.

He will be aware, however, of certain information which is not to be found in, say, the DNB, and must therefore know of alternative sources, such as general encyclopaedias; *Who was who*, etc. Similarly, if he were to be asked for a list of articles on some facet of television engineering, with either (a) very brief abstracts, or (b) no abstracts, he might well go to: (a) *Engineering index*, or (b) *Current technology index*.

In any case, he must know where to locate his source material—either he will remember its relative position on the shelves, or its classification, or he will quickly consult the catalogue.

In effect, the search strategy is equivalent to the making of a hypothesis (or the equation previously mentioned), then the checking of its validity. If a complex enquiry is received by letter, the librarian has the opportunity to examine the wording of the question; if there is any element of ambiguity, he will need to telephone or write to the enquirer in order to seek clarification; in the case of a face-to-face dialogue, however, it may be advisable for him to write the question down as clearly as possible. This gives him the opportunity, in consultation with the user, to refine it, and then establish the various key-words which it contains. He may well find, though, that the natural language terms adopted by the user are not the preferred terms in the catalogue, index, thesaurus, or bibliographies. Consequently, he will have to search for relevant synonyms. An added complication is that well-established reference indexing tools use differing subject headings to indicate the same

The Search

subject. The reference assistant, seeking information on Soviet military strength in sources such as *Keesing's contemporary archives*; *Facts on file*; *The Times index*; *New York Times index*; *Current technology index*; *Readers' guide to periodical literature*, etc, will find that the indexing terms used are far from standardized. Also, in making a retrospective search through one title, he may well discover that at some point a preferred term was discarded and replaced by another one.

One of the greatest assets in a reference librarian, during the search process, is **flexibility**. As he proceeds with his strategy, his knowledge of the subject of the enquiry should increase; as a result, he must be prepared to back-track, to side-step, or even to start afresh. Allied to mental agility is the need to keep a list of sources checked, and the relevant results, so that no time is wasted if he has to go off duty before completion of the enquiry, and in consequence has to pass the work over to a colleague.

The experienced librarian is fully aware of the value, in many cases, of the **browsability effect**, and it is because of this effect that he normally prefers to have a personal dialogue with an enquirer, rather than deal with a query by telephone, telex, or letter. In the three latter cases he may answer the question to the complete satisfaction of the enquirer; clearly, however, the answer he gives will be a considered response to the query *as worded*. Unfortunately, this may not have been the ideal wording, since the enquirer may be unsure of what it is he wants to know. If he can visit the library, the reference assistant will be able to offer him, from various sections of the stock, categories of material, to the point where he may well decide that a specific item will better meet his needs than the item or items previously offered in response to his original question.

In formulating his search strategy, the librarian must take account of any constraints imposed by the user. These may include limitations in terms of period, language, level, volume, and time.

The Reference Process
SEARCH STRATEGY

Period

The question 'How many submarines are there in the French Navy?' will only be answered accurately by reference to the very latest sources of information, whereas the question 'How many German U-boats were sunk by the Allies between January 1941 and June 1942?' will be answered from an historical source; in this instance the librarian has been given definite inclusive dates, but frequently the time span is by no means clear. Presented with the query 'I need some information on former President Giscard d'Estaing', the reference assistant will need to establish whether political or domestic detail is sought, and which period of Giscard's life is involved. Once he has determined this, it should be relatively easy to tap relevant sources, assuming that these are available.

One of the main problems facing all but the largest of reference libraries (whether public, academic, or special) is how to retrieve 'current' information, ie information generated up to about a month ago. The answer, for large information services, is the production of **current awareness bulletins**, such as selective abstracts bulletins of articles from newspapers and periodicals; newspaper cuttings; press releases; and diaries of forthcoming events (conferences, exhibitions, etc).

Language

With the possible exception of very large libraries, reference collections in English-speaking countries—the United Kingdom, the United States, Canada, Australia, etc—consist predominantly of English-language material. During his search, however, the reference librarian may well find references—particularly periodical articles—in other languages. In an academic library, or a large special library, this should not constitute a problem, as language specialists may well be available. In public libraries, the assistant will have to establish whether the user can deal with material in French, German, etc, and, if so, at what level. If the user is demonstrably a specialist, or a student, a level may be easily discernable; with a member of the general public, though, the assistant will need to tread warily, if he is not to cause embarrassment.

Sometimes a full translation of an article from a book or a periodical will be required; the librarian should remember that Aslib maintains a list of translators, their languages, and special subject fields. Often, however, sufficient information can be derived from tables, diagrams, and captions, to satisfy a user who does not require an answer in depth. When a translation is needed of a technical or scientific article or report, it may be necessary to have a first version done by a non-specialist, and then to arrange for someone well versed in the appropriate subject field to eliminate any 'howlers'. Clearly, the librarian cannot undertake a meaningful search of material in languages which he is unable to read; the most he can expect to do in this case is to show it to the user who has the necessary comprehension.

Level

When the librarian, in the course of his search, has traced a certain amount of material for his enquirer, he will have to decide how much of it to produce in his reply, and to what extent he should extend the search. Bearing in mind the established needs of the user, he may well reject some items as being too elementary, and others as too advanced; in this case he will have to consider whether to locate further, more suitable, information, thus making a qualitative judgment.

Volume

The amount of material requested may vary from 'everything available' (an unrealistic request if made in a large library, but entirely reasonable in a small unit), via 'enough material to provide a suitable basis for a lecture at a prescribed intellectual level', to the absolute minimum commensurate with an adequate answer. It is essential, therefore, for the reference assistant at an early stage to

The Reference Process

make a quantitative judgment, so that he does not overburden the user with unwanted material.

Time

Normally, quick, factual enquiries present no time problem, even in small units. Difficult, research-type enquiries, however, are a different matter, and the time allocated to them will vary according to the type of library concerned. For example, a technical library serving a research establishment may well be expected to resolve a particular problem regardless of how long the library staff have to be involved. A busy public reference library with only a small staff, however, may have to be fairly rigorous, if it is to keep abreast of all its commitments. Often, of course, the amount of time given will automatically be dictated by the user, if he indicates that he has a deadline, after which information will be of no use to him.

Finally, an important reminder. No reference library can be completely comprehensive, so no reference librarian can be expected to answer, from his own stock, all the queries which he receives. He must constantly remember, therefore, that one of the most important aspects of his work is that he should act, at the appropriate time, as a point of referral. We said, at the beginning of the first chapter, that 'the researcher in the United Kingdom, the United States, and elsewhere, today has access to a network of sophisticated information resources'.

The good reference librarian is the key to that network.

SUGGESTIONS FOR FURTHER READING

Benson, J. and Maloney, R. K. Principles of searching. *RQ*, 14 (4), Summer 1975. 316–20.

Crouch, W. W. *The information interview: a comprehensive bibliography and an analysis of the literature.* Syracuse, New York: ERIC Clearinghouse on Information Resources, 1979. ERIC report. ED-180 501.
A brief analysis of the literature since 1960, for practising librarians, researchers, and teachers.

Further Reading

Davinson, D. *Reference service*. London: Bingley, 1980.
Includes chapters on the reference interview, and on the search for answers.

Galvin, T. J. *Current problems in reference service*. New York: Bowker, 1971.
Thirty-five case histories.

Grogan, D. *Case studies in reference work*. London: Bingley, 1967.
A useful collection of studies, chosen to show how the librarian uses general reference sources—encyclopaedias, dictionaries, directories, bibliographies, and yearbooks—to help solve enquiries.

Grogan, D. *More case studies in reference work*. London: Bingley, 1972.
The 189 enquiries in this complementary volume require use of periodicals, phrase books, books about people and books about places, for their solution. A final section is devoted to 'difficult' queries.

Grogan, D. *Practical reference work*. London: Bingley, 1979.
Includes an excellent introduction to the reference process.

Hillard, J. M. *Where to find what: a handbook to reference service*. Metuchen, New Jersey: Scarecrow, 1975.
A practical guide which lists the most logical and best sources of information on many subjects.

Hillard, J. M. *Where to find more: a handbook to reference service*. Metuchen, New Jersey: Scarecrow, 1977.
Gives added subject headings not covered in the earlier volume, and notes worthwhile additions to subjects already covered.

Hurych, J. The professional and the client: the reference interview revisited. *The reference librarian*, (5/6), Fall–Winter 1982. 199–205.

Hutchins, M. *Introduction to reference work*. Chicago: American Library Association, 1944.
Chapter 3 discusses the reference interview, and Chapter 4 the technique and methods of answering reference questions.

Jahoda, G. and Olson, P. E. Analysing the reference process. *RQ*, **12** (2), Winter 1972. 148–56.
Review of the literature on, and illustrations of, models of the reference process.

Katz, W. A. *Introduction to reference work*. Vol 2. *Reference services and reference processes*. 4th ed. New York: McGraw-Hill, 1982.
Includes excellent chapters on the reference process, the reference interview, and the search. Many flowcharts are given.

King, G. B. The reference interview. *RQ*, **12** (2), Winter 1972. 157–60.
Includes a discussion of open and closed questions.

Knapp, S. D. The reference interview in a computer-based setting. *RQ*, **17**, Summer 1978. 320–4.
Essentials for the search analyst are understanding of purposes, communications, and application of analytical skills.

Linderman, W. B. (*ed.*) *The present status and future prospects of reference information service*. Chicago: American Library Association, 1967.
Contains a useful article—'Broadening the spectrum', by A. M. Rees (pp 57–65), who defines the reference *process*, reference *work*, and reference *service*.

Muñoz, J. L. The significance of nonverbal communication in the reference interview. *RQ*, **16** (3), Spring 1977. 220–4.
Discusses body movements and gestures which indicate the thoughts and emotions of others—head nods, facial expressions, etc. The librarian can help during the interview by avoiding communication signals which inhibit a meaningful dialogue with the enquirer.

Murfin, M. E. and Wynar, L. R. *Reference service: an annotated bibliographic guide*. Littleton, Colorado: Libraries Unlimited, 1977.
Contains 1,258 citations, with descriptive and informative annotations; entries cover the multidimensional aspects of reference service and the reference process. Period covered: 1876–1975.

Rettig, J. A theoretical model and definition of the reference process. *RQ*, **18**, Fall 1978. 19–29.

Rothstein, S. Across the desk: 100 years of reference encounters. *Canadian Library Journal*, **34** (5), October 1977. 391–3, 395–7, 399.

Somerville, A. N. The place of the reference interview in computer searching: the academic setting. *Online*, **1** (4), October 1977. 14–23.

Stych, F. S. Decision factors in search strategy. *RQ*, **12** (2), Winter 1972. 143–7.

Sylvester, E. and Ryder, L. *The reference interview: proceedings of the CACUL symposium on the reference interview ... Montreal 1977*. Ottawa: Canadian Library Association, 1979.
Discusses the reference interview as practised in academic libraries.

White, M. D. The dimensions of the reference interview. *RQ*, **20** (5), Summer 1981, 373–81.

3
Dictionaries

Kenneth A. Whittaker

As the primary aim of most dictionaries is to define words, a particularly appropriate as well as helpful way to begin the study of them is to examine how an authoritative dictionary, the *Shorter Oxford English dictionary*,[1] defines the word 'dictionary'. Its entry is as follows:

1. A book dealing with the words of a language, so as to set forth their orthography, pronunciation, signification, and use, their synonyms, derivation, and history, or at least some of these; the words are arranged in some stated order, now, usually, alphabetical; a word-book, vocabulary, lexicon.

2. By extension: A book of information or reference on any subject or branch of knowledge, the items of which are arranged alphabetically; as a Dictionary of Architecture, Biography, of the Bible, of Dates, etc.

The word dictionary, incidentally, comes from the Latin word 'dictio' meaning a word or phrase.

It can be seen from this definition that the term 'dictionary' is not only applied to books to do with words, but to any book arranged in alphabetical (or dictionary) order. However, a dictionary, to a librarian, is a book that deals mainly, if not wholly, with words.

The kind of book that most often calls itself a dictionary, without

Dictionaries

being one, is the encyclopaedia. A number of encyclopaedias, however, especially subject encyclopaedias, set out to act as dictionaries as well as encyclopaedias, and have, in addition to articles, shorter entries that define terms. Examples of such encyclopaedias are the *Focal encyclopaedia of photography*, and the French *Petit Larousse*, which is both a general encyclopaedia and a general language dictionary.

It has been stated that only quick-reference books to do with words are genuine dictionaries. However, not all such dictionaries call themselves dictionaries, some preferring to call themselves wordbooks, or lexicons, or glossaries, or thesauri, or possibly some other name. The term 'wordbook' is self-explanatory, but a comment is called for on the other three. The term 'lexicon' is derived from a classical Greek word, 'lexikon', meaning dictionary, and is most often applied to dictionaries of ancient languages, such as Liddell and Scott's *A Greek–English lexicon*. The term 'glossary' is most commonly used in the subject dictionary area, as with Harrod's *The librarians' glossary*, and such dictionaries usually explain, not merely define, the words they include. The name 'thesaurus' was used by Roget in 1852 when he published his best-selling *Thesaurus of English words and phrases*. It means a storehouse or treasury of knowledge, and has subsequently usually been used to describe dictionaries, which, like Roget's, arrange words in a classified order, and not in the usual alphabetical one. In recent years, the word 'thesaurus' has become better known as the name given, in information retrieval, to a list of the terms to be used in a particular information retrieval system (especially a computerized system).

SCOPE

Within the limits already laid down, that is, that dictionaries must be to do with words and phrases, the scope of dictionaries is wider than is often realized. Not only are there dictionaries dealing with virtually every language and subject, there are also dictionaries for special purposes such as rhyming, and dictionaries which aim to aid special groups of people such as crossword addicts. There are

Development

also works, which concern themselves with words as literature, rather than with words as language; notably books of quotations, and concordances (these latter do not limit their indexing to the most quotable passages). They have been included in this chapter because they are so closely related to other kinds of wordbooks. The overall scope of dictionaries will be considered further when they are divided into types, and representative and important titles of each type considered.

DEVELOPMENT

The first step towards the compilation of English language dictionaries (to which this section on development will limit itself) was taken in Anglo-Saxon times. It resulted from readers of Latin works jotting down explanations in Anglo-Saxon of some of the more difficult Latin words they encountered. The explanations ('glosses' is the name given to them) were actually placed between the lines, or in the margins, of the books being read. Later, monastic scribes began to extract all the 'glosses' from a manuscript, and to make a list of them. These lists were not at first arranged in alphabetical order, but towards the end of the fourteenth century, alphabetical order became the rule.

The first real dictionary of the English language was published in 1604—Robert Cawdrey's *A table alphabeticall*. The subtitle[2] of this work reveals, however, that its scope was much narrower than that of modern dictionaries, as it read: '. . . containing and teaching the true writing and understanding of hard usuall English words, borrowed from Hebrew, Greeke, Latine, or French, etc.'

Other early English dictionaries also limited themselves to difficult words, and it was not until 1721 that a dictionary was published that included words in common use. This was Nathaniel Bailey's *Universal etymological dictionary*.

In 1755 the great Dr Samuel Johnson published his *Dictionary of the English Language*. The dictionary, as we know it, may be considered to date from this year. Johnson's work was not only influential, but personal, and his character comes out in many of his definitions. My favourite is:[3]

Dictionaries

'LUNCH. As much food as one's hand can hold.'

Dr Johnson believed that dictionaries should lay down the words worthy of use, and so he would not have anything to do with slang expressions, for example. Many dictionary compilers since Dr Johnson have also held his view, which is now called the prescriptive one of a dictionary's function. The view that the purpose of a dictionary is to lay down standards of word acceptability and usage has come more and more under attack in recent times, but it is not dead. The alternative view of the function of a dictionary is the descriptive one, that a dictionary should record words as they are being used (and misused), without passing judgment any more than it has to.

The great dictionaries of the nineteenth century, the *American dictionary of the English language*, first produced in 1828, and the work of Noah Webster; and the *New English dictionary on historical principles*, first published in parts between 1884 and 1928 (now known as the *Oxford English dictionary*), took a middle course between the descriptive and prescriptive viewpoints. In its last edition, however (3rd, Merriam-Webster, 1962), Webster's caused considerable controversy by becoming more descriptive in its approach. But while some differences remain in the opinions held today as to the primary function of these dictionaries, there is no dispute over the increasing need for the major dictionaries to be supplemented by more specialized works, such as technical dictionaries and glossaries. And so the twentieth century has seen an ever swelling number of dictionaries of every size and kind being published, and, of course, being stocked by libraries.

USES

Obviously the uses of a dictionary depend to a large extent on what kind of a dictionary it is, but some general comments are called for, to complement those made later considering the various types of dictionaries. Four broad uses of dictionaries may be distinguished, though there is some overlap between them.

Uses

Quick-reference tool

From the librarian's point of view, this is the important use. A dictionary will indicate the pronunciation, spelling, and meaning of a word. It may also give further information about the word, such as its origin, what part of speech it is, examples of its use, and words related to it. It may, in addition to giving information about words, give all sorts of other useful quick-reference information, such as tables of weights and measures, and how to address people when writing letters to them. Of course, many dictionaries exist to give rather specialized information about words, such as equivalent words in foreign languages. Probably no other type of quick-reference book is consulted as often as the dictionary, and this type of book will be found not only in libraries, but in homes, schools, offices—and even in pockets.

The librarian will use his collection of dictionaries to answer readers who have enquiries such as 'What is the meaning of serendipity?'; 'When do I use the word "unreadable", and when the word "illegible"?'; 'What is the name given to a person who is afraid of heights?'. He may also use his dictionary stock when he has to carry out a literature search, or answer an enquiry on a subject with which he is not familiar. In the latter case he would especially have to do this with enquiries received through the post, as he could not ask the reader for clarification on such occasions.

Sometimes in enquiry work, even though his library has a reasonable stock of dictionaries, the librarian will find that they fail to give him the answer he requires. Before he tries sources of information outside his library, such as ringing up a larger library, he should check various types of books he stocks, which, though not dictionaries, contain information on words. In particular he should check his encyclopaedias (their value as dictionaries has already been mentioned); his standard works (for many, especially those on technical subjects, will be found to contain short subject glossaries); and, if appropriate, the vocabularies in his textbooks relating to foreign-language study.

Dictionaries

Language recorder

Those dictionaries which set out to provide a fairly comprehensive picture of the words of a language or of a subject, especially when they have been compiled from what has been called the descriptive viewpoint, are obviously effective in providing a basic record, for all time, of the words in use when the dictionary was produced. Such dictionaries, after they have been published for some years, also provide an historical record. An historical record is likewise provided by dictionaries like the *Oxford English dictionary*, which set out to trace the development of each word they include, not limiting themselves to current words and usage.

Language standardizer

Probably all dictionaries, not just those produced from a prescriptive viewpoint, act as language standardizers; and, certainly the spelling of English words today is much more standard than it was in Shakespeare's day because, now, unlike then, authoritative dictionaries exist. Incidentally, in the newly developing countries of the world, where the language of an area may be being written down for the first time, dictionaries are being published alongside the first newspapers, books, and other writings in that language. The result is that variations in usage, such as different spellings, are being eliminated before they can start.

For some specialized subjects, attempts are being deliberately made in this country to eliminate variations; the British Standards Institution has issued a series of glossaries, such as its *Glossary of terms relating to work study and organisation and methods* (BS 3138: 1979), with this object in view; and such attempts are also carried out abroad.

Aid to language study

The value of dictionaries during the study of foreign languages is accepted, but their value when one's own language is being studied

Dictionary Making

is sometimes overlooked. And dictionaries like the *Oxford English dictionary* are also used as a quarry for research workers as they delve into specialized aspects of language, literature, and history.

DICTIONARY MAKING

Amongst the research workers just mentioned will be found the compilers of dictionaries, for few dictionaries are made without the study of existing ones. The name given to dictionary making is 'lexicography'. Originally, the compilation of dictionaries was undertaken by one person, or perhaps by a small team of lexicographers. Nowadays, large teams, aided by such devices as the computer, are common. However, there are still today many dictionaries which are small enough to be compiled by a single knowledgeable person.

The steps which the compiler of a dictionary has to take before it is ready for publication usually will be as follows: first he has to bring together a team of helpers; at the same time he will probably consult experts, who will advise him and his team on policies and methods. The second step is the already mentioned consultation of existing dictionaries. Of course, the compiler must stop short of actually copying other dictionaries. The next step is the building-up of a file of information which the compiler thinks will be useful, and which is not easily to be found anywhere else. This file, assembled probably in card form, is built up gradually from searching all sorts of printed material, and possibly through correspondence. Often an important purpose of the file is to give examples of how words, which are to be included in the dictionary, have actually been used. The fourth step is to select, from the information collected, what to place in the dictionary. The material selected for inclusion must then be prepared for the printer, and, when set up in type, proof-read. It took four people a whole year just to check the proofs of merely the first volume of *Harrap's standard German and English dictionary*.[4] Dictionary making, then, is hard work, and, today, it is becoming even more of a challenge, as the ever increasing pace of living has resulted in language changing faster than ever before.

Dictionaries

EXAMINING

It has often been said that most people who consult a dictionary never read the instructions it includes on how to use it. Perhaps this is partly because they do not realize the considerable guidance which is to be found in nearly all dictionaries. Students of reference must, however, know not only about the guidance which dictionaries offer their users, but about all their features. The average dictionary comprises the following five features. In the order they are normally found, they are: Preface; Key to abbreviations; Key to pronunciation; Main sequence of words; Supplementary sequences of words. All need to be examined before any dictionary can be used fully and efficiently.

The **Preface** will indicate the scope as well as the aim of the dictionary. If guidance on how the dictionary should be used is not included in the Preface, a separate 'how to use' feature will be found nearby. The **Key to abbreviations** is a self-explanatory feature, as is the **Key to pronunciation**, though a comment about the latter is necessary: there are two main ways of indicating pronunciation, and neither of them is perfect from the dictionary compilers' point of view. One way is to use an accepted phonetic alphabet; this indicates pronunciation in a scholarly fashion, and so is not always easily understood by the layman. The other way is to re-spell words, using the ordinary letters of the alphabet; this method is more understandable, but also more clumsy.

The **Main sequence of words** is occasionally a classified one, as in the already mentioned *Roget's thesaurus*, whilst there are a number of dictionaries which have more than one alphabetical sequence. Translating dictionaries usually have two sequences; rhyming dictionaries are amongst those which normally have more than two, as they commonly arrange their words by the number of rhyming syllables they contain. However, the vast majority of dictionaries are, of course, arranged in a single alphabetical sequence. Two main methods of organizing any alphabetical arrangement exist: they are word by word (eg New Zealand before and not after Newfoundland) and letter by letter. Many of the larger general English-language dictionaries use the letter by letter scheme prob-

Evaluating

ably because it is the more logical. However, some readers find words more easily when they are arranged word by word.

The content of the entries in the main sequence of a dictionary should be examined to see what each includes. It is surprising how much information a general language dictionary, for example, may give in addition to basic information about its words. It may disclose the origin of them; trace their history; show how writers have used them; give related words and phrases, including synonyms and antonyms; and include cross-references. Furthermore, it will usually indicate words not in common use, or not generally acceptable, by giving them a label, eg *Dialect*; *Slang*; *American*.

Supplementary sequences of words, where they exist, should be obviously listed on the contents pages of dictionaries, but sometimes they may still be missed. Their purpose may be just to update the main sequence, but more usually it is to deal with special categories of words which do not really belong in the main sequence, such as a list of Christian names and their meaning. As well as supplementary sequences of words, encyclopaedic information, such as the names of the Kings and Queens of England, may be found.

EVALUATING

The examination and evaluation of dictionaries go together, as evaluation cannot take place until a thorough examination has been made. The ability to evaluate a dictionary is essential not only for book selection purposes, but for reference work, as enquirers need to be given answers which are from the best available reference books. The evaluation of dictionaries is obviously related to the evaluation of other quick-reference books, and so this section limits itself to just four criteria which are particularly pertinent to dictionaries. They are (in alphabetical order): Authority; Ease of use; Word coverage; and Word treatment.

Authority. The authority of a dictionary is especially determined by who has compiled it, and who has published it. Information about the compiler, his advisers, and his support staff, should be displayed prominently near the front of the dictionary. Beware if

Dictionaries

it is not. However, it is not as easy for the average librarian to judge the precise standing of compilers as it is for him to assess the authority of the publisher because of his knowledge of the book trade. Amongst British dictionary publishers, the Oxford University Press stands supreme, whilst in the United States, the firm of W. & C. Merriam (the publishers of *Webster's new international dictionary*) has a very high reputation. The name Webster is not copyright, and there are poor dictionaries called 'Webster's' published by other American firms. There are several other firms with good reputations, although not all important dictionaries are published by them. Most of these firms will be mentioned when individual dictionaries are considered later in this chapter.

Ease of use. Though dictionaries are seldom really hard to use, they need to be made as easy to use as possible, with each page virtually self-explanatory. However, there needs also to be clear introductory information on the purpose, scope and features of the dictionary, as well as keys to its abbreviations and to its method of showing pronunciation. Dictionaries are easier to use if they have been well designed, with care taken over their legibility and guiding.

Word coverage. It may be possible for subject and special purpose dictionaries to cover their fields reasonably comprehensively without becoming excessively large, but it is impossible for general language and general translating dictionaries to do so. The English language, for example, comprises no less than about half a million words, and so many dictionaries limit their coverage in some way. They may exclude obsolete words; they may exclude words which are only used in specialized subject fields, like medicine; they may exclude words which are only used in a particular locality, for example on Merseyside. However, although most English language dictionaries are select, providing they have a hundred thousand entries, they are adequate.

Many dictionaries consider that they need to supplement their coverage of words with information about people, places, and other encyclopaedia-type material. They are sometimes called encyclopaedic dictionaries. Such dictionaries are useful in the home, where few other reference books exist, but librarians prefer dictionaries which concentrate on word coverage.

Evaluating

A type of word missing from all dictionaries is the newly coined word which has only come into use since the dictionary was published. As librarians often get asked the meaning of new words, it is important that the word coverage of a dictionary is as up to date as possible. As some standard dictionaries are reprinted without being brought up to date, librarians often need to supplement their more comprehensive compilations with smaller but more up-to-date dictionaries. These newer works will also be useful, because they will give the latest meanings of older words—for many words have changed or added to their meanings over the years, eg 'aggravate' now also means 'annoy'.

Two final points on word coverage need to be added. The first is that a few dictionaries, notably the American Thorndike dictionaries, select the words they include on the basis of statistical study of the frequency of use of words. The Thorndike dictionaries, incidentally, are mostly designed for use by children. The second is that the number of words that a dictionary includes can be counted in different ways. Some dictionaries count each of their definitions as separate entries, and so arrive at a coverage total which is really an inflated one. Other dictionaries do not do this, but have a policy of giving derivations separate entries (for example 'glossary' would have its own entry, and not come under 'gloss'). These dictionaries will have less inflated word totals, but they will still be inflated compared with those in dictionaries which include derivations under the basic word-stem.

Word treatment. All dictionaries will set out the information they give about their words in a consistent form and order (which should be explained). It is important to know how any one dictionary treats its words. Does it give their etymology (ie origin and history)? Does it give quotations from literature to support its definitions? Does it include illustrations and diagrams to make its definitions clearer? The amount of information given with each word must, then, be noted, as must the arrangement of the dictionary's most basic information, its definitions. With words which have more than one meaning, either the earliest or the most common will usually be given first. The latter arrangement is the better for quick-reference work.

The quality of a dictionary's definitions is dependent on their accuracy and their clarity. Most dictionary definitions today can be considered reasonably accurate, but their clarity may leave something to be desired. To check accuracy, examine how a dictionary defines specialized words with which you are very familiar; to check clarity, do the same, but also compare a few definitions with those for the same words in other dictionaries.

Final questions to be asked about the word treatment of any dictionary under evaluation are: how does it deal with alternative spellings, and how does it treat words derived from other words? Alternative spellings should be indicated in the entry under the form chosen as entry word, and there should be cross-references from alternative forms. Concerning derivations, most good dictionaries seem to deal with these under the appropriate stem-word, though this practice does make them harder to find.

When dictionaries are evaluated, using guidelines such as the ones just laid down, it will probably be found that Dr Johnson's verdict[5] on dictionaries still holds good: 'Dictionaries are like watches; the worst is better than none, and the best cannot be expected to go quite true.'

TYPES AND TITLES: GENERAL LANGUAGE DICTIONARIES

So far, dictionaries have been looked at overall; they will now be considered type by type, and the important and representative titles commented upon. For comments on a wider range of titles, Walford's *Guide to reference material*, or Sheehy's *Guide to reference books*, should be consulted. But, of course, consulting books which give information on dictionaries is no substitute for examining the dictionaries themselves.

General language dictionaries are often divided into two types, select and comprehensive. The select type may be further divided into three sub-groups: general purpose; children's; and dictionaries for foreigners learning English, for example *Longmans dictionary of contemporary English*.

The general purpose is the most familiar select (or abridged) dictionary, but it is the comprehensive category of dictionary that

Types and Titles: General Language Dictionaries

is most valuable to the librarian, and so receives first attention here. Of course, no dictionary can be fully comprehensive in its coverage of the words of a language, except perhaps one covering a dead language; even the monumental *Oxford English dictionary* (OED) is not all-inclusive; there is also the problem of keeping it abreast of recently coined words.

OXFORD ENGLISH DICTIONARY. Oxford: Clarendon Press, 1933 (corrected reprint with supplement). 13 vols. New supplement in progress.

By far the most comprehensive and detailed English dictionary, it is in a class of its own. It is a pure dictionary, having no encyclopaedic features; but, as its words are treated so as to reveal their history, and with such a wealth of illustrative quotation, this work is a word-encyclopaedia. It was originally published between 1884 and 1928 with the title *A new English dictionary on historical principles*, and the original set of volumes is still in use in some libraries. It is also sometimes described as *Murray's English dictionary*, Sir James Murray being its principal editor. In the last few years a mini-print version (*Compact edition*), easy on the pocket, but not so easy on the eyes, has been issued complete with reading glass. A four-volumed supplement is now three quarters complete, Vol 1 having been published in 1972, Vol 2 in 1976, and Vol 3 in 1982. When complete (probably in 1985), this supplement will replace the original one. This dictionary is remarkable for the quality of its information. However, for quick-reference purposes it cannot be recommended, as its aim is not to give current usage, but to record the development of words. In addition, because it is so large and detailed, it is often hard to find and extract information from it quickly. For quick-reference purposes, one of the abridged versions of this work is more suitable. The *Shorter Oxford English dictionary* is the largest of these abridged versions, and may indeed be classed amongst the comprehensive dictionaries of the English language, as it covers two-thirds of the nearly half million words in the main work, though it gives less information in its entries.

The creation of the *Oxford English dictionary* led to the compilation of other scholarly dictionaries on historical principles,

Dictionaries

probably the best known being the *Dictionary of American English on historical principles*. However, of the dictionaries on historical principles available for foreign languages, one at least, the German *Deutsches Wörterbuch*, is older than the *Oxford English dictionary*. It took over a hundred years, 1854–1960, for this dictionary to complete publication. Also older than the *Oxford English dictionary* is the major comprehensive United States dictionary, Noah Webster's:

WEBSTER'S NEW INTERNATIONAL DICTIONARY OF THE ENGLISH LANGUAGE. 3rd ed. Springfield, Massachusetts: Merriam, 1962.

Unlike the comprehensive dictionaries already mentioned, this one is not on historical principles, but concentrates on current usage. First published in 1828, this dictionary, unlike the *Oxford English dictionary*, has some encyclopaedic features—for example, a section on forms of address. However, the latest edition of Webster's has fewer encyclopaedic features than earlier editions; it also omits many words which were in the previous edition; many libraries still stock the previous one. The current edition of Webster's, though it was criticized when it was published for failing to prescribe correct usage, is of a very high quality, and its usefulness to libraries on this side of the Atlantic is furthered by its indicating British spellings and meanings when they differ from American ones. In 1976 a supplement, entitled *6000 Words*, was published.

Whilst in Britain there is no rival to the *Oxford English dictionary*, in the United States Webster's has several. These will be considered together.

NEW STANDARD DICTIONARY OF THE ENGLISH LANGUAGE. New York: Funk and Wagnall, 1964. 2 vols.

RANDOM HOUSE DICTIONARY OF THE ENGLISH LANGUAGE. New York: Random House, 1966.

AMERICAN HERITAGE DICTIONARY OF THE ENGLISH LANGUAGE. Rev ed. Boston, Massachusetts: American Heritage and Houghton Mifflin, 1975.

Types and Titles: General Language Dictionaries

WORLD BOOK DICTIONARY. Chicago: Field Enterprises Educational Corporation. Annual revision. 2 vols.

Funk and Wagnall's *Dictionary* has been Webster's main rival over the years, but, though as comprehensive (both have about 450,000 entries), it has not been completely revised since 1913, and cannot now be as useful. The other three dictionaries are reasonably up to date, but they are much less comprehensive (in the 200,000 entry range). These large, if only really semi-comprehensive dictionaries, are frequently found in British libraries, perhaps because there are no similar British compilations. All three reach a high standard, and are suitable for school and home, as well as library use. Indeed the *World book dictionary* is basically a large-scale children's dictionary. With the exception of this dictionary (there is a related *World book encyclopedia*, now available online through Compuserve—and also a *World book encyclopedia year-book* which carries a new words section), the other dictionaries under discussion include encyclopaedic information. For example, the *American heritage dictionary* has entries for both people and places, whilst the *Random House dictionary* includes an atlas.

Most libraries stock selective as well as comprehensive dictionaries, except for very selective ones, such as those of pocket size. A reasonably sized selective dictionary will have 40,000 to 120,000 entries, and it might also contain encyclopaedic features, as does the *Oxford illustrated dictionary*. This dictionary, like most encyclopaedic dictionaries, is suitable for use by children, though several good children's dictionaries, including the *Oxford children's dictionary* and *Chambers children's colour dictionary*, are available. Valuable selective dictionaries are:

CONCISE OXFORD DICTIONARY. 7th ed. Oxford: Clarendon Press, 1982.

CHAMBERS TWENTIETH CENTURY DICTIONARY. 4th ed. Edinburgh: Chambers, 1983.

COLLINS ENGLISH DICTIONARY. London: Collins, 1979.

Dictionaries

ENCYCLOPEDIC WORLD DICTIONARY. London: Hamlyn, 1971.

WEBSTER'S NEW COLLEGIATE DICTIONARY. 9th ed. Springfield, Massachusetts: Merriam, 1983.

    The *Concise Oxford dictionary* (COD), a pure dictionary, differs from the more comprehensive members of its family in being a dictionary of current English. Probably the best known of all dictionaries of its size, it has about 75,000 entries; it should be compared with the *Oxford illustrated dictionary*.
    The main rival abridged dictionaries to the Oxford ones are published by Chambers and Collins, being respectively the *Chambers twentieth century dictionary*, which contains more language references and more definitions than any other single-volume dictionary, and *Collins English dictionary*, which offers encyclopaedic features. The *Encyclopedic world dictionary* is a British adaptation of the larger American *Random House dictionary* and is worth contrasting in content and in design with the Chambers work. *Webster's new collegiate dictionary* is American, and the principal abridgement of *Webster's new international dictionary*.

Turning briefly to dictionaries of foreign languages, it should be noted that though such dictionaries are less frequently found in libraries than are translating dictionaries, they complement translating dictionaries by having more detailed entries. Two examples of high reputation are the French *Lexis: dictionnaire de la langue française*, and the Dutch *Groot woordenboek der Nederlandse taal*, by J. H. Van Dale.

SUBJECT DICTIONARIES

In the last section on general language dictionaries, it was possible to mention many important titles; in this one it will only be possible to discuss a few examples. For information on a larger number of subject dictionaries, bibliographies of dictionaries, such as those

Subject Dictionaries

described in the last section of this chapter, should be referred to, or alternatively, appropriate subject literature guides consulted.

Subject dictionaries complement general language dictionaries in two main ways. First, they include highly specialized terms not in general dictionaries (this especially applies in the fields of science and technology). Second, they often have more detailed descriptions of word meanings than those in general dictionaries, commenting on and explaining their terms, not just defining them. Some so-called subject dictionaries are encyclopaedias which incorporate definitions of subject terms. Subject dictionaries, such as Haggar's *Dictionary of art terms*, which are entitled dictionaries of terms, will always be found to be genuine dictionaries.

Some subject dictionaries are aimed at the general public, others at students, the remainder at specialist audiences. Dictionaries in this last category especially can be expected to be prepared by an appropriate body, contain very authoritative definitions, and be regularly revised. A good example of one is the *Meteorological glossary*, compiled by the Meteorological Office. Other good examples of subject dictionaries are:

Harrod, L. M. THE LIBRARIANS' GLOSSARY. 5th ed. London: Gower, 1984.

The best known dictionary of librarianship, and a typical subject dictionary—typical in that some of its entries are long, almost encyclopaedic, and also in that it only gives the spelling and meaning of its words, not other common dictionary information like pronunciation. Compare this dictionary with the much smaller *Glossary of documentation terms* (BS 5408: 1976) published by the British Standards Institution, which, of course, sets out not just to record but to prescribe.

CHAMBERS DICTIONARY OF SCIENCE AND TECHNOLOGY. Edinburgh: Chambers, 1974.

Another typical subject dictionary, but one covering a broad area of knowledge. The successor to *Chambers technical dictionary*, its brief entries are aimed at the layman as well as at the more knowledgeable, and so the work will be found in many libraries. The American *McGraw-Hill dictionary of scientific and technical terms*

Dictionaries

should be compared with it, for the similar contents are packed in a quite different format.

Two subject dictionaries, which are not typical, are also worthy of note simply because each has some unusual feature. Students should look out for such unusual features and think about their value:

Stamp, L. D. GLOSSARY OF GEOGRAPHICAL TERMS. 3rd ed. London: Longmans, 1979.
Exists to bring together definitions given in other books; it often has definitions from several sources (sometimes with comments within an entry).

Gould, J. and Kolb, W. K. DICTIONARY OF THE SOCIAL SCIENCES. London: Tavistock Publications for Unesco, 1964.
Without becoming encyclopaedic, extended commentaries feature in its entries, the normal kind of dictionary definition forming only the first part of them.

SPECIAL PURPOSE DICTIONARIES

Like subject dictionaries, special purpose dictionaries (sometimes called supplementary wordbooks) complement general language dictionaries. They do this in a number of ways, as there are many varieties of them. In the main, they complement by specializing in a class of words which most general dictionaries omit (or are weak on), eg dialect; by specializing in one aspect of language, eg pronunciation; or by approaching words in some special way, eg by their rhyming qualities.

Publications which complement in the first way form a group made up of seven types of dictionary: dictionaries of slang; dialect dictionaries; dictionaries of obsolete words; dictionaries of new words; dictionaries of names; dictionaries of abbreviations; and dictionaries of phrases. Four representative titles in this group are singled out for comment:

Special Purpose Dictionaries

Partridge, E. DICTIONARY OF SLANG AND UNCONVENTIONAL ENGLISH. 7th ed. London: Routledge & Kegan Paul, 1970.

Eric Partridge was a well-known lexicographer, and this is his best known work. An abridged version is available, as a Penguin book, under the title *Dictionary of historical slang*. Australian slang features in Partridge's work, but for American slang the *Dictionary of American slang* by H. Wentworth and S. B. Flexner (New York: Crowell) should be consulted.

Ekwall, E. CONCISE OXFORD DICTIONARY OF ENGLISH PLACE-NAMES. 4th ed. Oxford: Clarendon Press, 1960.

This type of dictionary should not be confused with books, such as gazetteers, which give information on places. It is concerned solely with the history and meaning of place-names. Dictionaries of surnames and Christian names, such as that equally standard work, the *Oxford dictionary of English Christian names*, also exist. (So do ones of eponyms, that is, words like diesel, which originate in a person's name: eg C. P. Auger *Engineering eponyms*, 2nd ed. Library Association, 1975.)

EVERYMAN'S DICTIONARY OF ABBREVIATIONS. Rev. ed. London: Dent, 1983.

This is amongst the better of the many dictionaries of abbreviations available. Libraries should stock several such dictionaries, as they complement one another. Some include signs and symbols; most, as this one, include acronyms, that is, pronounceable words formed from a group of initial letters, eg *Anzac* from Australian-New Zealand Army Corps.

Brewer, E. C. BREWER'S DICTIONARY OF PHRASE AND FABLE. Centenary ed rev. London: Cassell, 1981.

Some dictionaries specialize in phrases of a particular kind, like clichés, or proverbs, but this one is more general; indeed it is not only a dictionary, but an encyclopaedia of literary and historical information. Brewer's famous work is perhaps the most readable of all dictionaries; certainly it needs to be browsed through; features such as its heading *Dying sayings* might otherwise well be overlooked.

Special purpose dictionaries in the second group, that is, those which deal with a specialized aspect of language, comprise five types of dictionary: dictionaries of pronunciation; dictionaries of spelling; etymological dictionaries; dictionaries of usage; and dictionaries of synonyms and antonyms. Two outstanding titles are chosen for comment:

Fowler, H. W. A DICTIONARY OF MODERN ENGLISH USAGE. 2nd ed. Oxford: Clarendon Press, 1965.
This book will be found in many homes, as well as in libraries. The compiler was a famous lexicographer, and his pronouncements on how to use words are respected. First published in 1926, this dictionary was prepared for its second edition by Sir Ernest Gowers of *Plain words* fame. Its entries include one, on the word 'enquiry', that is especially worth examining.

Roget, P. M. THESAURUS OF ENGLISH WORDS AND PHRASES. New ed. London: Longmans, 1982.
Compiled by a doctor after he had retired, and first published in 1852, it is the best known of all dictionaries of synonyms and antonyms, and has been published in a number of versions. Its main sequence is a classified one, because Roget wanted to arrange his entries in the way that would best allow users to find the exact word to fit a thought. Most dictionaries of this kind, though, are alphabetical, as is *Webster's dictionary of synonyms*. Indeed, this work is different from Roget in another way, in that it carefully distinguishes between shades of meaning. Crossword-puzzle enthusiasts find dictionaries of synonyms and antonyms invaluable, though they also use the dictionaries specially designed for them.

The third group of special purpose dictionaries is the one that approaches words in some special way. In fact Roget, because it is classified, approaches words in a special way, and so belongs to this group of dictionaries as well as to the group just dealt with. Most crossword dictionaries belong to this group, as they usually arrange their words by the number of letters in them, whilst reverse-dictionaries also come into it. The reverse-dictionary is of especial interest to the librarian, as it enables enquiries to be answered that would otherwise be very difficult. Indeed, one of the few existing reverse-dictionaries was published by a library, as a result of the library staff's having to compile a file of information to help them solve enquiries that demanded words to fit already known meanings (ie the opposite of the normal dictionary enquiry):

Sheffield Public Libraries. 'ISMS. 2nd ed. City Council, 1972. Rev reprint.

Subtitled 'a dictionary of words ending in -ism, -ology, and -phobia', it reveals, for example, that a morbid fear of fresh air is 'aerophobia'. All that is necessary is a check in its subject sequence under the heading 'Air'.

A recent work which should be compared with the Sheffield one is the *Reverse-dictionary*, compiled by T. M. Bernstein (London: Routledge & Kegan Paul, 1976).

OXFORD-DUDEN PICTORIAL ENGLISH DICTIONARY. Oxford: Oxford University Press, 1981.

An adaptation of a German work, it shows what objects look like. Its classified approach also allows names of objects to be traced if they are not known. Together with the *Oxford-Duden pictorial German–English dictionary* (1980), it replaces the *English Duden* (1960).

TRANSLATING DICTIONARIES

Translating dictionaries, unlike the ones dealt with so far, are not monolingual (or single language); they are either bilingual or multilingual. There are a great number of translating dictionaries published, many of them limited to single subject fields, and so it is usually possible to find one that gives the information needed. It should be pointed out, though, that translating dictionaries do not normally give the meaning of words, just equivalent words in the one or more foreign languages they cover.

Dictionaries

As with general language dictionaries, some translating dictionaries are more comprehensive than others. Where a comprehensive and detailed bilingual dictionary exists for a foreign language, it will be found to be of outstanding use to the librarian, as well as to the scholar, the student, and the translator.

Two examples of such dictionaries, and also an example of a more select one, follow:

HARRAP'S NEW STANDARD FRENCH AND ENGLISH DICTIONARY. London: Harrap, 1972–1980. 4 vols.

The original version of this dictionary was published in the 1930s; it has been both abridged and supplemented, and is now completely revised. A similar multi-volumed work for German is also in course of being published by Harrap, whilst the *Sansoni-Harrap standard Italian and English dictionary*, in four volumes, was completed in 1976.

LANGENSCHEIDT'S ENCYCLOPAEDIC DICTIONARY OF THE ENGLISH AND GERMAN LANGUAGES. London: Methuen, 1962–1975. 4 vols.

The largest completed translating dictionary for German.

CASSELL'S NEW LATIN–ENGLISH, ENGLISH–LATIN DICTIONARY. 5th ed. London: Cassell, 1968.

Single-volumed works, like those in the publisher's series of which this forms a part, will answer the majority of reference enquiries, and will be found in all types of library. Cassell's series has a high reputation, and some of the dictionaries in it (including this one) are also available in an abridged version.

It should be noted that the two sequences of bilingual dictionaries are not always of equal length. In a few bilingual dictionaries there is only a single sequence in fact, as in the *Greek–English lexicon* by H. G. Liddell and R. A. Scott. But this work is still indispensable to students of Ancient Greek.

The second type of translating dictionary, the multilingual or polyglot dictionary, is usually concerned with a single subject, and it is particularly common in the fields of science and technology.

Books of Quotations

The arrangement of multilingual dictionaries is not standard, and an examination of a collection of them will reveal interesting differences. Tabular arrangement, alphabetically by the English words, with the equivalent words following in the foreign languages covered, is one method of arrangement. Separate alphabetical indexes for each foreign language represented will be appended, with such an arrangement. It should be noted that directories with multilingual headings or indexes can be used as polyglot dictionaries, and that they are sometimes both more specific and more up to date than any relevant dictionary.

Among the multilingual dictionaries available are many that form part of a publisher's series, eg:

Clason, W. E. ELSEVIER'S DICTIONARY OF NUCLEAR SCIENCE AND TECHNOLOGY IN SIX LANGUAGES. 2nd rev ed. Amsterdam: Elsevier, 1970.

The six languages covered are English, French, Spanish, Italian, Dutch, and German. Six is a fairly common number for a multilingual dictionary. This series from a Dutch publisher, though mainly on technical subjects, includes *Elsevier's dictionary of library science, information and documentation in six languages.*

Translating dictionaries, like monolingual dictionaries of foreign languages, can obviously present problems of use, at least when they deal with languages which the user does not know; for example, the alphabetical arrangement of words in Swedish puts those beginning with å and ö after z. However, problems of use will, overall, probably be less than expected, and when they do arise, handbooks like C. G. Allen's *A manual of European languages for librarians* can be referred to.

BOOKS OF QUOTATIONS

Books of quotations set out to provide quotations on certain subjects, or by certain authors, and to give sources of quotations; through their indexes they enable half-remembered quotations to be traced. They are frequently used by writers and speech-makers,

Dictionaries

and are also eminently works to be browsed through. Most libraries need to provide a selection of them, as books of quotations complement rather than duplicate each other. This is partly because they include different quotations, but in addition because they are arranged in a variety of ways. The main methods of arrangement are alphabetical by author, and alphabetical by subject. No matter how a book of quotations is arranged, a detailed index to the key-words in its quotations is essential. Books of quotations can be general, like Bartlett's *Familiar quotations*; limited to a single author such as Shakespeare; limited to a single subject, such as religion; or even limited to a single book, such as the Bible. An important general one is:

Stevenson, B. E. HOME BOOK OF QUOTATIONS. 10th ed. London: Cassell, 1974.

Probably the largest book of quotations, it has a particularly good index. American in origin and bias and arranged by subject, like most general books of quotations, it can be used to trace some foreign-language quotations. However, books of quotations published in appropriate foreign countries must be used to trace most foreign material. The *Oxford dictionary of quotations* should be contrasted with Stevenson's, it being British in bias and arranged alphabetically by author.

Sometimes, quotations which cannot be traced in books of quotations will be found elsewhere. Valuable sources are general language dictionaries of the *Oxford English dictionary* type, and dictionaries of phrases. Also of use, of course, are concordances.

CONCORDANCES

Concordances index not just the most quotable passages of a famous author, or book, but every sentence; only unimportant words are omitted. Their comprehensiveness is their particular virtue. Nowadays they are produced with the aid of computers, and so are less arduous undertakings than they once were. Indeed the compiler of the most famous concordance, Alexander Cruden, was

Library Provision

in such a state of mind after he had completed his compilation that he had to be confined in a lunatic asylum at Bethnal Green (from which he managed to escape). Cruden's *Concordance to the Old and New Testaments* has gone through many reprints since it was first published in 1737, though other Bible concordances now exist. Shakespeare is probably the author to have had the most concordances compiled of his work. An outstanding example of these concordances is the *Oxford Shakespeare concordances*, a series of computer-produced titles, which were published by the Oxford University Press between 1969 and 1973.

LIBRARY PROVISION

Though computers are now aiding the compilation of concordances, and indeed dictionaries of other kinds, they have not yet had a revolutionary effect on dictionary provision in libraries. But it would seem that, with the introduction of computer-based online services into libraries, some enquiries concerning words may soon be answered by going to a computer terminal rather than to the shelves. Probably too, microfiche readers (or similar equipment) will be needed to solve such enquiries, as new historical dictionaries may well publish the more specialized parts of their contents only in microform. However, for the moment, the conventional book-form is the one in which dictionaries will be bought. To aid the purchase of them, a number of bibliographical aids are available. Selection aids to general reference books, like *Basic stock for the reference library* by A. J. Walford and C. A. Toase, will, it should be remembered, be of considerable use. Indeed, this work briefly lays down standards for dictionary provision. Also to be remembered are reviewing journals, like *The Times Literary Supplement*; but for foreign and translating dictionaries the more specialist *Bulletin of the Aslib Technical Translating Group* and the *Incorporated Linguist* should be examined; whilst for subject dictionaries the appropriate specialist journals need to be scanned. Amongst the most useful and recent of the bibliographical tools which specialize in dictionaries are:

Dictionaries

Brewer, A. M. DICTIONARIES, ENCYCLOPEDIAS, AND OTHER WORD-RELATED BOOKS. Detroit: Gale, 1979. 2 vols.
   Wide-ranging entries, giving catalogue-type information.

Collison, R. L. DICTIONARIES OF ENGLISH AND FOREIGN LANGUAGES. 2nd ed. New York: Hafner, 1971.
   Some historical information, but only about 2,000 titles dealt with.

DICTIONARIES: AN INDEPENDENT CONSUMER SURVEY. *Good Book Guide*, November 1981.
   Thirty-five general language dictionaries surveyed; fifteen recommended.

INTERNATIONAL BIBLIOGRAPHY OF SPECIALISED DICTIONARIES. 6th ed. Munich: K. G. Saur, 1979.
   Mainly scientific and technical dictionaries.

Kister, K. F. DICTIONARY BUYING GUIDE. New York: Bowker, 1977.
   A book for the public, but recommended also to librarians and student librarians.

Walford, A. J. and Screen, J. E. O. A GUIDE TO FOREIGN LANGUAGE COURSES AND DICTIONARIES. 3rd ed. London: Library Association, 1977.
   Not comprehensive, but evaluative.

WORLD DICTIONARIES IN PRINT, 1983. New York: Bowker, 1983.

REFERENCES AND CITATIONS

1. *Shorter Oxford English dictionary.* Oxford: Clarendon Press, 1959. 1, 544.
2. Cawdrey, R. *A table alphabeticall.* London: I.R. for Edmund Weaver, 1604.

Further Reading

3. Johnson, S. *Johnson's dictionary: a modern selection*. London: Gollancz, 1963. 240.
4. The making of a dictionary. *Books and Bookmen*, October 1963. 31.
5. Johnson, S. *Letters of Samuel Johnson*. Oxford: Clarendon Press, 1952. 3, 206.

SUGGESTIONS FOR FURTHER READING

In addition to the items mentioned below, further reading could well include the relevant chapters in other works on reference material, and in textbooks like Grogan's *Case studies in reference work*.

Alvey, J. Dictionaries and reference books for the translator. *Aslib Proceedings*, **31** (11). November 1979. 521–4.

Douglas, G. H. What's happened to the thesaurus? *RQ*, **16** (1). Winter 1976. 149–55.
A discussion of this type of dictionary.

Hartmann, R. R. K. (ed.) *Lexicography: principles and practice*. New York: Academic Press, 1983.

Hulbert, J. R. *Dictionaries: British and American*. 2nd rev ed. London: Deutsch, 1968.
Wide-ranging, and including information on their use and nature.

Macdonald, A. M. Keeping a dictionary ahead. *Bookseller*, 15 April 1972. 1932–6.
How *Chambers twentieth century dictionary* keeps up to date.

Partridge, E. *The gentle art of lexicography*. London: Deutsch, 1962.
A personal memoir on the subject.

Purchasing a desk dictionary. *Booklist*, **75**. 1 July 1979. 1591–4.

Ulstein, B. The dictionary war. *Bookseller*, 13 June 1981. 2056–60.
Surveys the main publishers now competing for the dictionary market.

4

General Encyclopaedias

A. J. Walford

The *Oxford English dictionary* defines 'encyclopaedias' as '1. The circle of knowledge; a general system of instruction', and '2. A literary work containing extensive information on all branches of knowledge, usually arranged in alphabetical order'. The word encyclopaedia did not form the title or part of the title of a compendium in either ancient or medieval times and only appears in the sixteenth century. Written knowledge was treated systematically as far back as the first century in Pliny the Elder's *Natural history* in 37 books and 2,493 chapters, with an analytical table of contents. The systematic—as opposed to the A–Z—approach continued to flourish in such compilations as Johann Heinrich Alsted's *Encyclopaedia septem tomis distincta*, 1630, in 7 volumes, 35 books and 7 classes, treating of 'everything that can be learned by man by his lifetime'.

The earliest alphabetically arranged encyclopaedia in English was the work of John Harris, first secretary of the Royal Society, in 1704. The eighteenth century, in fact, saw the appearance of several important encyclopaedias. More comprehensive than any previous compilation of its kind was Johann Heinrich Zedler's 64-volume *Grosses vollständiges universal-Lexicon aller Wissenschaften und Künste* (1732–1750; Supplement Vols 1–4: A–Caq. 1751–1754). It also broke with tradition by including entries, as from Vol 18, for the lives of illustrious living persons, and is heavily documented.

Criteria

Ephraim Chambers' *Cyclopaedia; or, An universal dictionary of art and sciences* (1728; 2 vols) is far slighter, excluding historical, biographical, geographical and associated entries, but it did carry numerous cross-references and a prefatory 'analysis of the divisions of knowledge'. Moreover, it achieved a French translation in 1745. To assert, as in *Encyclopedia Americana*,[1] that this translation formed the basis of Diderot's *Encyclopédie* (1751–1780) is to overstate the case. It certainly acted as an inspiration. *L'Encyclopédie*, product of the Age of Enlightenment, was a new concept and the text largely original. It achieved a profound influence on contemporary thinking, for it aimed not merely at providing information but also at shaping opinion; it attacked the Church and contemporary government; it attacked Christianity itself.

The first edition of the *Encyclopaedia Britannica* (1771, 3 vols) consisted of 45 treatises; that on 'Surgery' runs to 238 pages, with definitions of technical terms arranged A–Z, a compromise of sorts between systematic and alphabetical order. The effort to gather together what is fragmentary is evident again in the index volume, Vol 29, of the last British edition of the *Britannica*, 1910–1911—its 'classified list of articles', or, more recently, in the complex 'Propaedia' of the 15th edition, 1974.

So much for the form background. In the twentieth century the volume of information has increased so rapidly in both breadth and depth, that the general encyclopaedia cannot possibly give the answers in the required detail, as it might have done in Zedler's day. Hence the proliferation of multi-volume special or subject encyclopaedias, such as *The new Grove*, or the *McGraw-Hill encyclopedia of science and technology*, apart from single-volumed compendia, not necessarily in A–Z order, eg *The Cambridge encyclopedia of archaeology*.

CRITERIA

In choosing, and using, a modern encyclopaedia, especially if it be multi-volume, certain points must be noted.

General Encyclopaedias

Authority and accuracy

It is usual for the preface to list the names of editor, editorial staff, advisers/consultants and, in particular, contributors, adding the titles of their contributions. The fact that Louis Shores was editor-in-chief of *Collier's encyclopedia* certainly gave it prestige as well as a practical shape. Some encyclopaedias include a statement of the contributors' qualifications or present status, as in *Everyman's encyclopaedia*, or even list their major writings, as in *Collier's*. As a corollary the articles themselves should be signed, but this does not apply to *Everyman's*, even for longer articles.

Authoritativeness can also be linked to the publisher's reputation. Change of publisher in successive editions may not be for the best, although financially imperative. When the *Encyclopaedia Britannica* passed into American ownership with the 14th edition of 1924, the result was basically a revision of the British edition, but with marked differences. The text was drastically cut and rearranged to cater for a changed market, '×' after the original contributors' initials denoting the editorial scissors—not always judiciously applied. Again, the text of a well-known encyclopaedia may be used, with permission, as the basis for international coverage in a national encyclopaedia of another country. The *Grand Larousse encyclopédique* (1960–1964, 10 vols) was so used in the *Grote Nederlandse Larousse encyclopedie* (1971–1979, 25 vols and atlas).

Accuracy in an encyclopaedia is a *sine qua non*. The application of the thirty-year rule for the disclosure of British public documents may clearly alter in detail facts concerning World War II. Reliance on secondary rather than primary sources for authenticity is a not uncommon source of error. The gaps in updating by a continuous part-revision policy that handles only about 10 per cent of the text each year also create unreliability. Katz reports that the *Encyclopedia Americana* now and then falters in the accuracy of its biographical data, although biography entries form 40 per cent of the entire text.[2]

Criteria

Aims and style

For whom is the encyclopaedia intended? Such is the question that encyclopaedias must unequivocally answer in their introductions. A misleading title will raise doubts. What is the intended readership of the *Academic American encyclopedia* when its British reprint is entitled *Macmillan family encyclopedia*? The *Encyclopedia Americana* claims a wide appeal: 'The tens of thousands of articles in the *Americana* serve as a bridge between the world of the specialist and the general reader'. The *World book encyclopedia*, on the other hand, places definite limits on its aims: 'to meet the reference and study needs of students in the elementary school, junior high school, and high school; . . . also as a family reference book'.

Style also needs to be adapted to intended readership. From the preface to *Merit students encyclopedia* we learn that individual articles are designed and written primarily at the grade level at which they are taught. 'Material for the younger student is included at the beginning of an article. As the content of the article is developed, more advanced material is incorporated for the many students who are able to go beyond their grade level.'

It is important that the text of any reference work for young people should not be written in a condescending manner. Some contributors to the earlier editions of *Children's Britannica* were accused by a *Times Literary Supplement* reviewer of 'writing down' to their readers, in that articles by specialists were required to be recast so as to be properly understood by children aged ten.[3] This charge now seems to have been met; in the current edition of *Children's Britannica* the article on aero-engines uses such terms as 'liquid cooled in-line engine'. The 15th edition of *Encyclopaedia Britannica* makes fewer concessions to its readers in its 'Micropaedia'.

Scope and slant

The rapid growth of scientific and technical research has created problems for the multi-volume encyclopaedia that has traditionally given more attention to the arts. The fourth supplement to the

General Encyclopaedias

Enciclopedia italiana, spanning the years 1961–1978, highlights developments in science and technology, eg space stations, in line with advances in the humanities and social sciences.

A national slant in an encyclopaedia may express itself in two ways: 1. The proportion of text, bibliography, illustrations, etc, devoted to the home country and surrounding areas, and to books and other material in the native language, as well as a largely native staff of contributors. This emphasis is wholly understandable, to be respected and made use of in handling reference queries. 2. The slant could involve a nationalistic or partisan interpretation of events and achievements. Thus undue stress may be given, for example, to one country's role in World War II or to the question of sovereignty over the Falkland Islands.

The ideological slant, already noted in Diderot's *Encyclopédie*, is nowhere more pronounced than in *Bol'shaya sovetskaya entsiklopediya* (2nd ed, 1949–1960, 51 vols and index; 3rd ed, 1969–1978, 30 vols), which not only gives the Communist viewpoint regarding events in history, social conditions abroad, theology and much else, but tailors biographical data—and even excision of entries—to match the political climate of the time. In the second edition, the entry for a discredited Beriya was removed in favour of a contribution on the Bering Straits. In the third edition Khrushchev is given a very brief reference, and the contribution on Stalin omits mention of the atrocities committed during his régime. At the opposite pole, ideologically, *Marxism, Communism and Western society: a comparative encyclopedia*, edited by C. D. Kernig (1972–1973, 8 vols), appeared to have few, if any, articles by Marxists or from the Marxist point of view. 'Critical comparison always seems to favour the Western or capitalist point of view.'[4]

A particular religious emphasis, to be anticipated in such a compilation as *The encyclopaedia of Islam*, 1954–   , is also discernible in *Der grosse Duden* (5th ed, 1953–1956, 10 vols) and the shorter *Der neue Herder* (1965–1970, 6 vols and index), which both reflect the Roman Catholic angle.

The scope of a general encyclopaedia may go beyond what is commonly accepted. Several continental sets incorporate the functions of a language dictionary. *Enciclopedia universal ilustrada europeo-americana* (1905–1933, 80 vols in 81; *Suplemento anual*,

Criteria

1914–) swells its total of over 1,000,000 headwords by including definitions of words and terms. *Grand Larousse encyclopédique* (1960–1964, 10 vols) incorporates a dictionary of the French language, from 1600 onwards; and *Brockhaus Enzyklopädie* (17th ed, 1966–1975) devotes a supplementary volume to an illustrated German dictionary, 1976.

A further addition to a set may be an atlas and gazetteer volume. But a good world atlas calls for a suitably large format, hardly shelvable with the encyclopaedia. The *Atlas général Larousse* and *Britannica atlas* are examples. The atlas volume appended to *Meyers neues Lexikon*, is only demy octavo, uniform in format with the text; as a result some maps are cluttered with detail. The 64-page atlas appended to Vol 12 of *Everyman's encyclopaedia* is in the nature of an afterthought, since there is no supporting gazetteer or cross-reference system from the text.

Arrangement

Entries in encyclopaedias are normally arranged A–Z for quick reference, and this inevitably leads to fragmentation of related material, unless there is some attempt at synthesis: adequate cross-references, both within entries and appended to them, 'see' references from non-preferred headwords, an analytical index and a classified list of articles, to iron out inconsistencies. The short-entry policy of *Brockhaus Enzyklopädie*—about 225,000 entries in 20 volumes, ie about 13.5 entries, on average, per page—alleviates only in part the absence of a full index. Similarly, *Everyman's encyclopaedia* (6th ed, 1978, 12 vols) dispenses with an index, the editor claiming that 'comparatively short articles arranged in alphabetical order, backed by an extensive cross-reference system, are the best solution'. This claim is not wholly substantiated.

A further prop to dispersive A–Z order is the classified list of articles, as in *Chambers' encyclopaedia*, vol 15, and the 11th edition of *Encyclopaedia Britannica*, Vol 29. The complex 'Propaedia' volume of *Britannica 3* is much less helpful to users. (The *Britannica 3* separation of c 102,000 quick-reference articles in the Micropaedia from the lengthier entries in the Macropaedia will be discussed later

General Encyclopaedias

on in this chapter.) It is not uncommon for monographic articles in encyclopaedias to be prefaced by an outline contents list of sections.

The alternative to A–Z order of entries is systematic arrangement. Thus, *Encyclopédie de la Pléiade*, 1955– , is a series of 38 volumes on 24 subject areas, each volume/set of volumes having its own editor and index, plus the added advantage of revised editions as necessary. Catering for a younger generation, Mitchell Beazley's *Joy of knowledge* and the out-of-print *Oxford junior encyclopaedia* favour initial systematic arrangement, but the *Oxford junior* reverts to A–Z order within each subject volume, and *Joy of knowledge* adds a two-volume fact index as a corrective and key.

Documentation

Multi-volume encyclopaedias normally provide bibliographies or further reading for at least major articles. Thus *Britannica 3*'s Micropaedia short entries are not documented, unlike the 4,207 extended entries in the Macropaedia. When articles are monographic in length and sectionalized, it is kinder to the user to have bibliographies appended to sections rather than appended in one daunting block. Thus, while the *Enciclopedia italiana* places bibliographies at the ends of sections of lengthy articles (eg 'Italia', Vol 19, pp 693–1051), *Britannica 3* masses its bibliographies (eg 'Judaism, History of', Macropaedia, Vol 10, pp 302–29 in six sections, appends two columns of sectionalized bibliography on pp 328–9).

Not all encyclopaedias have references directly appended to articles, however. *Grand Larousse encyclopédique* places its bibliographies at the end of each volume concerned, where they could well be overlooked. *Collier's encyclopedia* devotes 200 pages of its index-volume to a classified bibliography of some 10,000 very briefly annotated entries that are ingeniously caught up in the index as sub-entries under subjects, persons and places. The *World book encyclopedia* has a comparable practice of adding subject bibliographies/further reading at appropriate points in the index.

The nature of the bibliographies themselves calls for scrutiny. Do they comprise a list of sources used, or of further reading?—

Criteria

by no means the same. Do they include basic periodical articles, documents, iconography (as appropriate), etc, as well as books? Is a running commentary provided, as in *Britannica 3*'s Macropaedia?

Visual appeal

This being the age of colour television, general encyclopaedias have reflected, in varying degrees, the impact of colour. The *New Columbia encyclopedia*—a 'no-nonsense' volume—keeps to infrequent monochrome illustrations and outline text maps, with a factual text set solid. By contrast, the *Grand Larousse encyclopédique* (1960–1964, 10 vols; *Suppléments*, 1968, 1975), with 31,458 illustrations, mostly coloured, and particularly the new *Grand dictionnaire encyclopédique* (1982–   ), excel in the use of colour whenever possible, even for boxed information and step-by-step instructions. Good, authentic colour is indispensable for reproductions of many paintings (eg by Van Gogh, Turner), in botany and zoology, and in depicting scenery, flags, porcelain and the like. Also, the illustrations should be representative of their subjects, whether buildings, towns, or the work of artists, to reflect their different periods/moods. The practice of displaying keyed parts of machinery, implements, vehicles, etc, is followed in most encyclopaedias.

The size of illustrations has some importance. Marginal illustrations are in fashion, but at the cost of size. *Britannica 3* provides, in text, numerous small, column-width photographs that tend to be decorative rather than informative. Town plans that are too small to give names of main streets or location of prominent buildings are a further irritation.

The average user warms to generously sized maps in text. *Britannica 3*'s coloured maps score here. *Everyman's encyclopaedia* has finely drawn black-and-white maps of English counties, but no maps, *in situ*, of France and other countries, while its coloured atlas supplement is heavily printed, at times virtually obliterating place-names. One welcome feature in some American encyclopaedias is the provision of two-page coloured map spreads backed by gazetteers, particularly valuable if all the place-names are caught up

General Encyclopaedias

in the general index. *Collier's encyclopedia* scores heavily here; the *Americana* indexes place-names more selectively.

Quality of index

The ratio of general index entries to text words indexed can be a revealing factor in assessing the quick-reference capabilities of an encyclopaedia. *Macmillan's family encyclopaedia* (1980 ed) has a commendable ratio of about 1:36 (250,000 index entries; 9 million words of text). The *Collier's* index also ranks high, indexing as it does bibliographies, illustrations, and place-names on maps, with an overall ratio of about 1:50 for 21 million words of text. The capabilities of *Britannica 3*'s Micropaedia are less easy to assess since, to the index entries for the Macropaedia, perhaps 250,000, must be added the actual entries in the Micropaedia, given as 102,000.

For young people the index can be enlivened by including basic data entries plus many small marginal illustrations—a fact index or micropaedia of sorts, as in Mitchell Beazley's *Joy of knowledge*. *Compton's encyclopedia*—an Encyclopaedia Britannica Educational Corporation associate product—has an illustrated fact index appended to each of its 26 volumes.

When the publishing programme of a multi-volume encyclopaedia is protracted, as in *Encyclopaedia of Islam* (Vols 1–4, 1954–1980), an interim index becomes highly desirable; hence the index to Vols 1–2 of this special encyclopaedia, compiled by H. and J. D. Pearson in 1979. The need for an interim index became imperative in the case of the *Great Soviet encyclopedia* (1973–1982)—a volume-for-volume translation of the 3rd edition of *Bol'shaya sovetskaya entsiklopediya* (1969–1978, 30 vols).

Book production aspects

A magnifying lens should be at hand for deciphering the tiny print used for the indexes, gazetteers, illustration captions and bibliographies in some general encyclopaedias. This applies to both *Joy*

Criteria

of knowledge and *Grand dictionnaire encyclopédique Larousse* (1982–   ). The latter has a three-column page plus marginal illustrations, and the reduced type size is in sharp contrast to the more ample page, two-column text and sizeable coloured illustrations of *La grande encyclopédie* (1971–1978), the previous Larousse multi-volume set.

The occasional publishing practice of cramming the contents of a general encyclopaedia into a single weighty volume poses problems for the user at the shelves, as well as creating an eventual binding problem. The *New Columbia encyclopedia* (1975), with over 3,000 pages, weighs 10.5 lb. Even worse, the *Random House encyclopedia*, designed for young people, weighs 11.5 lb. Perhaps a lectern should be provided as part of a package deal? Fortunately the English version of *Random House*, the Mitchell Beazley *Joy of knowledge*, is in ten slim volumes, in line with some other junior sets, eg *Children's Britannica* and *New Caxton encyclopedia*. The 1978 *Everyman's*, in easily handled large octavo, is well suited for desk use.

Paper quality is a consideration, particularly with much-used encyclopaedias. If multi-volumed sets have thin paper, like *Britannica 3*, at least use is distributed over 30 volumes. But this does not apply to the flimsy-paper, single-volume *New Columbia encyclopedia*. Colour of paper is a separate issue; we may contrast the greyish-white paper of the *Americana* with the cream-white paper of *Collier's*, to the latter's advantage.

Spine-lettering should be conspicuous, of course, but insufficient attention is paid to the prominence of lettering denoting volume text-coverage—far too small, for example, in *Everyman's encyclopaedia*, deprived, as it is, of an index giving volume number for a particular subject. Only in *World book encyclopedia* is there a serious attempt to provide a volume for each major letter of the alphabet, two volumes for letters C and S. The publisher's urge to provide uniformly sized and paged volumes is understandable, but not at the expense of inadequate volume spine-lettering.

General Encyclopaedias
Up-to-dateness

Multi-volume general encyclopaedias may be kept fairly current in several ways, although a reference librarian will instinctively turn to other more recent sources, particularly for statistical data. Resetting the text of a large encyclopaedia is not undertaken lightly. The *Macmillan family encyclopedia* has run to two editions in as many years (1980, 1982)—an exception to the rule. Where volumes of an encyclopaedia appear at intervals over a number of years, as with Larousse's *La grande encyclopédie* (1971–1978) a shorter, updating—but not superseding—successor, different in style, may be in train (eg the *Grand dictionnaire encyclopédique Larousse*, 1982–   ). A somewhat similar continental publishing policy is pursued by German publishing houses—Brockhaus, Meyer and Herder.

Claims as to the extent of annual text revision and updating vary. The publishers of *Collier's encyclopedia* claim 10 per cent revision, the *Americana* 15 per cent and the *Macmillan family encyclopedia* plans as much as 20 per cent.[5] Continuous revision involves excisions as well as additional pages, lettered 'a', 'b', etc, to avoid major resetting. In theory, a multi-volume set results in a revised, updated edition every decade, but in practice the word 'edition' becomes meaningless; instead we have revised reprints in small issues, keeping the set constantly before the public eye, especially in the USA. 'When a set is more than 5 years old it should be discarded' is Katz's advice to US librarians,[6] but hardly a realistic line in the UK.

The practice of issuing yearbooks as updating supplements to encyclopaedias is not wholly satisfactory. Such yearbooks are usually available only to purchasers of original sets and are best regarded as illustrated surveys of the previous year's events. Think of the tedium involved in searching through the eight volumes of *British book of the year* for later information on a topic covered in *Britannica 3*. An extreme example is the Spanish *Enciclopedia universal europeo-americana* (1905–1933, 71 vols) with its 10 volumes of *Apéndice* and 21 annual supplements. More manageable are the *Enciclopedia italiana*'s four *Appendice*, spanning the years 1938–1978.

Some Major Encyclopaedias

Price factor

The cost of American adult multi-volume encyclopaedias varies considerably, from £1069 for *Britannica 3* (1983 ed.) and $800 for the *Americana* to $450 for *Collier's* and for the *Academic American encyclopedia* (at November 1982 prices). The 1973 edition of *Chambers' encyclopaedia* has been reprinted at $375, and *Everyman's* (1978) sells for £195. For junior encyclopaedias the range is from $469 for *World book encyclopedia* to £124 for *Children's Britannica* and £104 for *Joy of knowledge*. *Merit students encyclopedia* is priced similarly to *Collier's* and, even so, is part of a package deal.

SOME MAJOR ENCYCLOPAEDIAS

A glance at the pages devoted to general encyclopaedias and dictionary-encyclopaedias in Annie M. Brewer's *Dictionaries, encyclopedias and other word-related books, 1966–1974* (1975)[7] mustering some 1,500 titles, shows a preponderance of sets in English. About 500 German, Spanish, Italian and French language titles come next in order of quantity. For the purposes of this survey encyclopaedias in English, German, French, Italian and Spanish, plus Portuguese and Russian, have been selected. Other multi-volume encyclopaedias, such as the *Encyclopedia Canadiana*, that are focused on a single country are not general encyclopaedias in the strict sense.

Anglo-American

The majority of multi-volume general encyclopaedias in English are now published in the USA and not in the UK. This is largely due to the formidable cost of production and marketing. The overhaul of *Everyman's encyclopaedia* for the 6th edition of 1978 must have cost Dent about £1,000,000[8]—and that without the adjunct of an index volume. Sales promotion is an important factor in the highly competitive US market. Encyclopaedia production there is

General Encyclopaedias

largely vested in four publishing concerns: the Encyclopaedia Britannica Educational Corporation, Chicago; Grolier Inc, New York (for *Encyclopedia Americana* and *New book of knowledge*); Field Enterprises, Chicago (for *World book encyclopedia*); and Macmillan Educational Corporation, New York (for *Collier's* and *Merit students encyclopedia*).

The three most used American sets are the *Encyclopaedia Britannica* (1974 edition), *Encyclopedia Americana*, and *Collier's encyclopedia*, all of them pursuing a continuous revision policy, supported by yearbooks.

The ENCYCLOPAEDIA BRITANNICA, most widely known of English-language encyclopaedias, began as an Edinburgh publication—like *Chambers' encyclopaedia*, about a century later—in 1765, as weekly parts, with completion in 1771 as three volumes. In it the arts and sciences were 'digested into distinct treatises or systems. The various technical terms, etc, are explained as they occur in the order of the alphabet'. This approach has been continued, with some modifications. The 9th edition (1875–1889, 24 vols, plus index) was acclaimed as standing in the forefront of the scholarship of its time, with contributions by leading contemporary men of letters. The 10th edition (1902) added 11 supplementary volumes, Vol 35 being a very detailed index with 600,000 entries. The 11th edition (1910–1911) was the last to be published in the UK, by the Cambridge University Press. Vol 29 comprised a detailed index 'containing considerably more than 500,000 headings', and included all place-names on the Emery Walker maps, a model of its kind. A classified list of articles and list of about 1,500 contributors and their principal articles follow the index. The 12th edition (1922) added three volumes, mainly on World War I, and the 13th (1926) provided a further three volumes that viewed the world scene in better perspective.

The *Britannica* passed into American ownership in 1929, half of the editorial staff and contributors being American. The '14th edition' was based on the 11th, but tailored—as we have noted—to suit a wider public, American as well as British, and to meet the needs of the average family as well as the librarian and specialist. Continuous revision on an organized basis and the *Britannica book of the year* were introduced in 1938. The 1958 issue was uncom-

Some Major Encyclopaedias

promisingly attacked by Professor Einbinder in his *The myth of the Britannica* (1964) for its errors and slanted treatment. Some faults have since been rectified.

THE NEW ENCYCLOPAEDIA BRITANNICA (15th ed. 1974. 32 vols), also known as BRITANNICA 3, claimed to represent 'a revolution in encyclopedia making' by dividing the set into three parts: a *Propaedia* (outline of knowledge), a schematic study guide and introduction to the Macropaedia; a 10-volume *Micropaedia* (ready reference and index-references to lengthier articles in the Macropaedia); and the 19-volume *Macropaedia* itself (knowledge in depth), truly impressive for both scholarship and extended treatment in its 4,207 entries. The 50-page article, 'Rome, Ancient', has five sections, a detailed contents list, marginal subheadings and an appended annotated bibliography of 2.5 columns. At times, however, the monographic treatment becomes daunting. Thus, individual articles on Western European national literatures are abandoned for a monolithic 'Literature, Western' (Vol 10, pp 1086–1264), subarranged under periods, *then* countries. Last of all are given the initials of all 82 contributors, plus a bibliography of 7.5 columns, in five sections. This is surely carrying synthesis too far for easy identification, and also putting severe pressure on the indexing capabilities of the Micropaedia. In his *Encyclopedia ratings* (5th ed, 1982), Walsh estimates *Britannica 3*'s index entry to text words ratio as only 1:184, against the 11th edition's 1:60. Coloured maps *in situ*, with gazetteers facing, are excellent, but too many of the column-width coloured illustrations are little more than double postage-stamp size.

The average user of *Britannica 3* is likely to be confused by the two A–Z sequences of entries. Thus, 'Montgomery' and 'Piaget' appear only in the quick-reference Micropaedia, whereas 'Wellington' and 'Plato', given brief, basic treatment in the Micropaedia, are allotted substantial articles in the Macropaedia, to which the user is referred, together with any other mentions. The Micropaedia thus acts as a filter, a quick-reference fact-index in ten volumes, always to be consulted first—admirable training for the reference assistant but irritating to the user conditioned to a more traditional approach. In any case, the 'fact-index' is neither revolutionary nor new. The French *Encyclopaedia universalis* (1st ed, 1968–1975, 20

General Encyclopaedias

vols) exploited the device earlier. One reviewer concludes that while the 15th edition of the *Britannica* 'should be purchased for its detailed coverage of the contemporary world, it will not entirely replace any printing of the Britannica since 1970'.[9]

ENCYCLOPEDIA AMERICANA (International ed. Danbury, Conn.: Americana Corp., 1980. 30 vols) was first published in 1829–1833, being then largely based on the Brockhaus *Konversations-Lexikon* of 1827–1829. The latest overhaul was in 1919–1920; annual or more frequent revision began in 1936. Its 30 million words compare with the Britannica's 42 million. While the scope is international, there is evident concentration on US themes, especially history, places and personalities. As in the *Britannica*, lengthier articles are documented, signed and sectionalised, with a prefatory list of headings. Features include a factual approach to science and technology, and provision of double-page-spread maps of all US states, Canadian provinces and major countries, backed by gazetteer indexes. The index volume musters c 350,000 entries. The *Americana* makes comparatively few concessions to a colour-conscious age, although its 23,000 illustrations are well placed. This is a well-established, 'no-nonsense' US encyclopaedia for adults and secondary school sixth-formers. The *Americana annual* has appeared since 1923.

COLLIER'S ENCYCLOPEDIA (New York: Macmillan Educational Corp., 1981. 24 vols), first published 1949–1951, is both easier to consult and read than *Britannica 3* and more attractive than the *Americana* to adults and teenagers for its visual appeal and fluent narrative style. Like the *Americana*, it has double-page-spread maps plus gazetteers, but with a less detailed text than its two rivals—21 million words. A feature of the set is undoubtedly Vol 24, which includes 184 pages of classed bibliography, with over 11,000 numbered and very briefly annotated entries, compensating in fact for the lack of references appended to articles. Such an arrangement allows for bibliographies to be updated *en masse* without undue resetting of the text of Vols 1–23, but advantage is infrequently taken of this opportunity. The very detailed index—c 400,000 entries—gives an index entry to text ratio of about 1:50. *Collier's yearbook* is one of the better encyclopaedia annuals.

Some Major Encyclopaedias

CHAMBERS' ENCYCLOPAEDIA (New rev ed. London: International Learning Systems Corp., 1973. 15 vols), first published 1859–1868, has passed through the hands of several publishers. The 1973 edition, reprinted by Pergamon in 1982, is a patched-up version of the 1967 issue, itself an overhaul of the 1950 edition. While *Chambers'* was for some years regarded as the standard encyclopaedia being published in the UK, it cannot now compare with the *Americana* and *Collier's*, let alone *Britannica 3*, for currency. The latest bibliographical references on Japan are dated 1959, and those on World War II, 1962. Basically, *Chambers'* is well organized and, with a 15 million word text, has greater depth of treatment on, say, historical themes than the *Macmillan family encyclopedia* or *Everyman's*. Vol 15, too, is a good example of its kind, comprising a detailed index with over 200,000 entries (ratio to text words, 1:60); a 44-page atlas by Bartholomew; a gazetteer; list of 3,000 contributors; and a classified list of articles. Yearbooks, varying in title, have appeared regularly since 1952, but they are largely illustrated annual surveys of events, and not supplements to the parent set. The prospect for a revised and updated new edition of *Chambers'* appears to be slim. Cost has been estimated at $10 million.[10]

THE MACMILLAN FAMILY ENCYCLOPEDIA, in 24 volumes,—a reprint of *Academic American encyclopedia*—first appeared in 1980, with a 2nd 'fully revised and updated' edition in 1982; yearbooks are promised. The 20,000 entries, averaging three per page, are of brief or medium length, on *Brockhaus* lines, and nearly 50 per cent carry short bibliographies. Attractive features are the abundant illustrations, one or two per page and 75 per cent of them in colour; the 1,000 coloured maps; and the comprehensive index, with a remarkably high ratio of entries to text—1:36. As a medium-sized multi-volume encyclopaedia it scores in currency and strikes a good balance between the 'academic' and the 'popular' approach. Its US origin needs to be borne in mind. The American edition was online Channel 2000—'the first online encyclopedia made available to the public over videotex'.[11]

EVERYMAN'S ENCYCLOPAEDIA (6th ed. Dent, 1978. 12 vols) was first issued in 1913–1914. With each edition, at acceptable ten-yearly intervals, new features have been added. The 6th edition

General Encyclopaedias

has a larger format; good monochrome illustrations, all well-placed, as opposed to the previously bunched half-tone plates; and is the easiest to handle of the medium-range encyclopaedias. The British slant is apparent in the separate entries given to, say, London, Oxford and Cambridge colleges, to British regiments, and to outline maps of English counties. Longer articles are sectionalized and often documented. On the debit side, articles are not signed, although a list of 350 contributors appears in Vol 1. The biggest drawback is the continued lack of an index. The maps appended to Vol 12 are the only attempt at colour. Within its obvious limits, *Everyman's* has value for desk and family use and is frequently seen in medium to small British public libraries as a third or fourth-string encyclopaedia.

THE NEW COLUMBIA ENCYCLOPEDIA (3rd ed. New York and London: Columbia University Press, 1975. 3052 pp), first published in 1935, is comparable to *Everyman's* in several ways. Both have about 50,000 unsigned articles, although *Everyman's* does list its contributors. The latter has about 8 million words of text, against *The New Columbia's* 6.5 million, concentrated in one weighty volume. Neither has a general index, although cross-references are provided. Both show a national slant. Outline text maps are common to each of them. Illustrations are fairly plentiful in *Everyman's*, but there are fewer in its rival. In both, longer articles, at least, carry bibliographies. *The New Columbia encyclopaedia*, a bargain at $29.50, is undoubtedly the definitive one-volume factual encyclopaedia in English.

Junior encyclopaedias

Colour-consciousness has become particularly apparent in encyclopaedias for young people aged 8 to 17, and for home use many, perhaps most, sets are bought with this age group in mind.

The first choice for children's librarians is often THE WORLD BOOK ENCYCLOPEDIA (Chicago, London, etc: World Book–Childcraft International Inc, 1981. 24 vols), first issued in 1967, and now available on-line from Compuserve. It musters c 5,000 contributors, 16,000 pages, and 30,000 illustrations—one-third in

Some Major Encyclopaedias

colour—plus 2,000 coloured maps in the text. Vol 22 comprises a 150,000-entry index (ratio to text, 1:70), with many cross-references and interspersed 'study guides'. Appended is a list of selected reference books and addresses of sources—virtually all American. To cater for a British as well as an American market, Vols 23–24 are devoted to the British Isles, with entries A–H, I–Z. This does result in slight cross-classification with Vols 1–21, where Northern Ireland is given an entry, while Vol 24 includes articles on 'Irish armed forces' and 'Irish constitution'. This encyclopaedia uses 'an advanced electronic data-processing system'. Annual continuous revision is accompanied by a well-planned *World book year book*.

While *World book encyclopedia* is an all-purpose set, MERIT STUDENTS ENCYCLOPEDIA (New York: Macmillan Educational Corp. 20 vols) is more directly based on US high-school requirements. It is well illustrated and mapped, with signed articles clearly written, and a 150,000-entry index. As we have already noted, it is expensive and rarely seen in British libraries.

For children aged 8 to 12, NEW BOOK OF KNOWLEDGE (New York: Grolier; London: Phoenix International. 21 vols, 10,000 pp) has much to commend it; text-matter runs to 6 million words, the 14,000 articles are mostly signed, and one-third of the 22,000 illustrations are coloured. The 'dictionary index' incorporates ready-reference material, and there is continuous revision plus an adequate yearbook.

The needs of a similar age group are the objective of CHILDREN'S BRITANNICA (Encyclopaedia Britannica International, Ltd. 20 vols, 6576 pp), which has 3 million words. Although the text is couched in simple language and the set sells at only £70, it does not reach the standard of the *New book of knowledge* for wealth of illustrations, and articles are neither signed nor documented. The US version is *Britannica junior encyclopaedia* in 15 vols. The latest issue is dated 1977, with no supporting yearbook. The NEW CAXTON ENCYCLOPAEDIA (Caxton Books, 1977. 20 vols) also has unsigned, undocumented entries, but its 17,000 illustrations are nearly all in colour—an important factor for this age group.

Systematically arranged sets for young people include THE MITCHELL BEAZLEY JOY OF KNOWLEDGE (10 vols of text

General Encyclopaedias

and index) and the out-of-print OXFORD JUNIOR ENCYCLOPAEDIA (1976 printing, 12 vols, plus index-and-ready-reference volume). The former is a joint product of Random House, Inc and Mitchell Beazley. Its subject-volumes feature a series of two-page spreads with well-captioned coloured illustrations—admirable starting points for lower-form school project work. The two-volume illustrated 'fact-index' has an appended grouped bibliography. *Oxford junior encyclopaedia*, designed for the enquiring minds of children aged 11 and upwards, has 12 subject-volumes, each with entries A–Z, largely self-indexing. Deficient in coloured illustrations and devoid of further-reading lists, it lacks a detailed general index. 1974 saw a major rewriting of Vol 4, *Communications*, and Vol 10, *Law and society*, but the only volumes now in print are Vols 3, 5, 8, 10, and 12.

FOREIGN-LANGUAGE ENCYCLOPAEDIAS

'The forefront of encyclopedia progress has passed overseas', concludes the American critic Einbinder in an article appearing late in 1980.[12] He bases this impression on two main counts: 1. the striking visual appeal of such sets as *La grande encyclopédie*, *Encyclopaedia universalis* and the Dutch *Grote Winkler Prins*; 2. depth of treatment of current topics and new devices in presenting information. Thus, *Grote Winkler Prins in 25 delen* (8th ed. Amsterdam: Elsevier, 1979–   ), documented and well illustrated, uses coloured boxed information and also chronological tables, to good effect in biographical articles. It further appends to each volume a chronology of the events of a particular century, eg Vol 2, 2nd century AD. Recent French encyclopaedias, equally lavishly coloured, give prominence to current concepts and controversial issues—thought-provoking as well as factual. Einbinder contrasts with this initiative the patching-up processes of annual revision and the expedient of eye-catching encyclopaedia yearbooks. Perhaps, too, there is something to be said for the continental practice of spreading publication over a period of years—like the supplementary volumes to the *Oxford English dictionary*.

Foreign-language Encyclopedias
German

German encyclopaedias, with their long tradition, tend to pay more attention to Central Europe, whereas their French counterparts are more international and free-ranging, forming a textual basis for the encyclopaedias of other countries to build upon.

MEYERS ENZYKLOPÄDISCHES LEXIKON (9th ed. Mannheim: Bibliographisches Institut, 1971–1974. 25 vols; Vol 26–28, 1980: Supplement, World atlas, and Name index, respectively) began publication in 1857–1860, and the 9th edition is the most recent and comprehensive of German multi-volume encyclopaedias. It includes lengthy contributions as well as short entries, has many small coloured illustrations and is well documented. A feature is the inclusion in Vol 4 and successive third volumes of a cumulative index, Vol 25 providing the complete index.

This Federal Republic set must not be confused with the East German MEYERS NEUES LEXIKON (2nd ed. Leipzig: VEB Bibliographisches Institut, 1971–1974. 18 vols). The latter has 120,000 undocumented entries and 24,000 illustrations, 50 per cent of them in colour and many of them marginal. Vol 16 is the index, and Vols 17–18 form the atlas and gazetteer. It will be recalled that the firm of Meyer openly hailed the coming of National Socialism in 1933 and was liquidated in 1946, the Bibliographisches Institut thereafter operating from two ideologically differing centres, Leipzig and Mannheim.

BROCKHAUS ENZYKLOPÄDIE (17th rev ed. Wiesbaden, 1966–1975. 20 vols and atlas; Vol 22: Addenda; Vol 23: Illustrated German dictionary) was first published in 1798–1808. The 20 main volumes (16,000 pages) carry 225,000 entries, mostly brief, with extended, documented articles on countries, etc. The atlas volume is sensibly in larger format. *Der neue Brockhaus* (6th ed. 1978–1980. 5 vols and atlas), first published in 1936–1938, is both condensation and updating of the *Enzyklopädie*. Revised editions at roughly ten-year intervals are planned.

DER NEUE HERDER (1965–1970. 11 vols) is similarly, a shortened, updated version of *Der grosse Herder* (5th ed. Freiburg, 1953–1956. 10 vols), with emphasis on subjects of Roman Catholic interest. *Der Mensch in seiner Welt*, Vol 10 of the parent work, is

General Encyclopaedias

an example of the growing continental practice of including broad-scope essays. *Der neue Herder*, Vols 8–11, elaborates on that Vol 10 by adding a systematic overview in four parts: *Die Natur*; *Das Leben*; *Der Mensch*; *Die Technik*.

None of the foregoing German sets is cheap, but for home use there is the admirable *dtv Lexikon* (Munich: Deutscher Taschenbuch Verlag, 1967–1968. 20 vols), a paperback octavo condensation of *Brockhaus*, with 100,000 carefully edited entries. It is particularly strong on European history and geography, and is supported by good illustrations. It sells in 1983 at about £40.

French

The pride taken by the French in their language, its precision of vocabulary and syntax, is reflected not only in the extensive French-language dictionaries but also in the encyclopaedias. GRAND DICTIONNAIRE UNIVERSEL DU XIXe SIÈCLE (Paris: Larousse & Boyer, later Administration du Grand Dictionnaire Universel, 1886–1890. Reprinted Kraus) was the first French multi-volume encyclopaedia to be designed for a wide public. It combines a dictionary, giving definitions and examples of usage of words, with extensive articles on subjects occasioned by those words, as necessary. Although it is still of value as a source of historical and biographical data, its illustrations are scanty and bibliographies slight. Nevertheless it created a Larousse housestyle, much as did the first *Brockhaus*.

LA GRANDE ENCYCLOPÉDIE (Paris: Lamirault, 1880–1892. 31 vols) has been compared to the 9th edition of the *Britannica* for its scholarly signed articles and valuable bibliographies. The set is rich in biographies, particularly of minor personages not mentioned in other encyclopaedias; in historical aspects of subjects; and as a gazetteer of France as it then was.

GRAND LAROUSSE ENCYCLOPÉDIQUE (1960–1964. 10 vols. Suppléments. 1968, 1975), with nearly 190,000 entries, continues the Larousse practice of combining dictionary and encyclopaedia. Definitions, backed by quotations, are given of 450,000 words, spanning the French language from the seventeenth century

Foreign-language Encyclopedias

onwards. Where appropriate, encyclopaedic treatment follows definition. Thus 'Agriculture' is allotted 16 columns. A feature is the inclusion of grouped bibliographies, limited very largely to books in French, placed at the end of each volume and linked with the text by cross-references. The set is generously furnished with 31,458 illustrations, including 232 colour plates. Most black-and-white illustrations appear on outer margins of pages. The 1968 and 1976 supplements cover 23,000 entries, updating entries being asterisked and bibliographies appended to each volume.

LA GRANDE ENCYCLOPÉDIE (Larousse, 1971–1978. 20 vols and index. Supplement. 1981) complements the earlier set of the same name by stressing twentieth-century achievements. It comprises numerous short entries with c 8,000 lengthy signed articles. The French slant emerges in the space given to French, as opposed to foreign, cities. The 14,000 illustrations are allowed an ample setting, thanks to a broad page. The index claims 400,000 entries, that for 'Cuivre ou Cu' extending to half a column, set solid. *Atlas général Larousse* (1976) is a separate volume, with 184 pages of maps, a 54,000 placename gazetteer and a statistical section. *GE*'s popularity with a wide range of public is ascribed by Einbinder to the dearth of public libraries in France and to its value as a working tool for students who need to obtain their baccalauréat as a stepping stone to a career.

The latest of the polyonymous Larousse family of multi-volume encyclopaedias is the GRAND DICTIONNAIRE ENCYCLOPÉDIQUE LAROUSSE (1982–   ), with its promised 180,000 entries in 10 vols. Compared to *La Grande encyclopédie* of 1971–1978, *GDEL* would appear to be yet another updated condensation. The format is less generous, using a three-column page plus marginal illustrations and smaller illustrations and type. Thus, the article on Algeria in *La Grande encyclopédie* covers pp 380–405 of Vol 1, whereas in *GDEL* it occupies pp 285–94. Each volume of the latter (Vols 1–3 (1982): A–Doucte) has c 2,500 illustrations and 250 maps, all in colour. So far there are no bibliographies.

ENCYCLOPAEDIA UNIVERSALIS (2nd ed. Paris: Encyclopaedia Universalis, 1982. 20 vols), first published in 1968–1975, with an annual *Universalia* since 1973, breaks with the Larousse tradition in several ways and invites comparison with *Britannica 3* in its arrangement. Vols 1–16 form a sort of Macropaedia, being entitled 'Corpus alphabétique' in the 1968–1975 edition. Vols 17–18, 'Symposium. Perspectives. Analysis', consist of documented contributions on current themes, eg 'Informatique et sciences humaines', Vol 18, pp 39–53. Vols 19–20, Thesaurus, Index, resemble a Micropaedia in having numerous short entries, each rarely longer than 750 words, plus references, as necessary, to Vols 1–16. A four-column page of small print is a feature of these two volumes. The layout of Vols 1–16 is of particular interest: articles begin at the head of a column, definitions being conspicuously separated from the extended commentary that follows in smaller type. In the case of controversial issues, eg euthanasia, pros and cons are given, with headed sections. The article on the conquest of space, in Vol 6, runs to over 30 pages, with 22 coloured illustrations and 1.5 columns of bibliography.

Single-volume encyclopaedias have the advantage of being less costly to produce, maintain and buy. LE PETIT ROBERT 2: DICTIONNAIRE UNIVERSEL DES NOMS PROPRES, ALPHABÉTIQUE ET ANALOGIQUE (5th rev and updated ed. Paris: Société du Nouveau Littré-Le Robert, 1981. xxiii, 1992 pp), with a previous edition (1974) in 4 vols, has c 60,000 brief entries for proper names occurring in history, geography, the arts, letters and sciences. Being up to date, it includes names not to be found in other encyclopaedias and has 4,000 small illustrations, plus 200 maps—admirable, therefore, for quick reference.

The systematic approach to knowledge is well exemplified in the ENCYCLOPÉDIE DE LA PLÉIADE series (Paris: Gallimard, 1955–   ), now comprising 24 titles (38 vols) of mutually exclusive monographs, each with its own editor, numerous contributors and detailed index. Titles range from *Histoire de la philosophie* (1969–1974. 3 vols), through *Ethnologie régionale* (1972) and *Jeux et sports* (1967. 1628 pp) to *La France et les français* (1972). Some titles have achieved more than one edition, although the solid text matter makes for concentrated reading rather than quick reference.

Foreign-language Encyclopedias
Italian

ENCICLOPEDIA ITALIANA DI SCIENZE, LETTERE ED ARTI (Milan: Istituto Giovanni Treccani, latterly Rome: Istituto della Enciclopedia Italiana, 1929–1939. 56 vols. Appendice 1, 1938; 2, 1948–1949; 3, 1961, 2 vols; 4, covering 1961–1978, 1978–1981, 3 vols) is a major encyclopaedia of high standard, perhaps the outstanding encyclopaedia of the twentieth century, for its lengthy, authoritative articles, the fine-quality illustrations, as a piece of book production, and for its acceptable method of updating. The complete set, so far, totals 42,422 pages, with 12,400 illustrations (220 in colour). All articles are signed. In the main 56 volumes the humanities are particularly well covered, eg 'Inghilterra': 67 pages on history, language, ethnology and folklore, art, music, and literature; 10 double-pages of photogravure; maps and illustrations in text. Bibliographies are extensive and include periodical articles. The celebrated contribution 'Fascismo', Vol 14, pp 847–84, has a section 'Dottrina' by Mussolini, but this does not reflect the general political stance of the encyclopaedia. Vol 24, the index, has about 400,000 entries; the excellent maps are by Touring Club Italiano. The Supplements, increasingly international in scope, also pay more tribute to scientific and technical achievements, eg the article on artificial satellites in Appendice 4, Vol 3, pp 274–83, has 8 pages of colour plates, 7 diagrams and a 22-line bibliography.

The Istituto della Encyclopedia Italiana, Rome, has also produced a shorter *Lessico universale italiana* (25 vols, 1969–[80?]), with brief, undocumented articles, but production and plates are of the Istituto's usual high standard.

GRANDE DIZIONARIO ENCICLOPEDICO UTET (3rd rev and enlarged ed. Turin: Unione Tipografico-Editrice Torinese, 1962–1973. 20 vols), first published in 1933–1940, also resembles the *Enciclopedia italiana* as a piece of book production, but treatment is again on a reduced scale. A feature is the 200,000-entry index, accompanied by an atlas of 78 general maps (the work of Istituto Geografico de Agostini), plus 30 pages of historical maps.

General Encyclopaedias

Spanish

ENCICLOPEDIA UNIVERSAL ILUSTRADA EUROPEO-AMERICANA (Barcelona: Espasa, 1903–1933. 80 vols in 1981; 10 vols of Apéndice; annual supplements 1–21, 1934–1982), known as 'Espasa' and the largest of twentieth-century encyclopaedias, has over a million unsigned articles, combining the functions of an encyclopaedia, a language dictionary—giving French, Italian, English, German, Catalan and Esperanto equivalents of terms—gazetteer and biographical source-book. Major subjects are treated at length and are well documented. Vol 21, devoted entirely to Spain, is revised at ten-yearly intervals, emphasis throughout 'Espasa' being clearly on the Iberian Peninsula and Latin America. The 21 annual supplements pose a problem to the researcher, because of failure to provide some form of cumulative indexing and the time-lag in production. The latest *Suplemento*, dated 1982, covers 1977–1978.

GRAN ENCICLOPEDIA RIALP (Madrid: Ediciones Rialp SA, 1971–1976. 24 vols) is more manageable than the 'Espasa'. It carries 15,000 articles by 3,000 contributors worldwide, and its 20,000 pages are particularly strong on the history, geography, literature and arts of Spain and Hispanic America. As a major Spanish encyclopaedia, it is more up to date and better pictorially than the 'Espasa', having over half of its 20,000 illustrations in colour. But its index is insufficiently specific and lacks references to the illustrations. Accompanying the index in Vol 24 are an atlas, gazetteer and list of contributors.

Portuguese

VERBO: ENCICLOPÉDIA LUSO-BRASILEIRA DA CULTURA (Lisbon: Editorial Verbo, 1963–1976. 18 vols) has signed and documented articles, mainly on Portugal and Brazil, but not neglecting other parts of the world. Some of the many small illustrations are in colour. A feature is the use of UDC schedule terms for headwords of articles.

Foreign-language Encyclopedias

The GRANDE ENCICLOPÉDIA PORTUGUESA E BRASILEIRA (Lisbon and Rio de Janeiro: Editorial Enciclopédia) is in two area-parts. Portugal is the concern of Vols 1–40 (1936–1960), part of Vols 39–40 forming the Apendice. Like the 'Espasa', this set aspires to provide both language dictionary and encyclopaedia. Articles are unsigned and infrequently documented. Part 2, on Brazil, is slow in appearing. Since 1967 only Vols 1–2, A–Geisel, have appeared.

Russian

Of the earlier Russian encyclopaedias, the ENTSIKLOPEDIYA SLOVAR' [Encyclopaedic dictionary] (Moscow: Granat, 1910–1948. 74 pts), straddling the period of the 1917 Revolution, is important for its coverage of nineteenth-century Russian literature, for lives of earlier Russian Socialists, and for Lenin's article on Karl Marx in Vol 28 (1915).

The first BOL'SHAYA SOVETSKAYA ENTSIKLOPEDIYA [large Soviet encyclopaedia] (Moscow: Sovetskaya Entsiklopediya, 1926–1947, 66 vols) was compiled on a grand scale, with lengthy signed and well-documented articles. Thus, the entry on the Volga (Vol 12, columns 672–710) has nine sections, each with a bibliography, plus text maps. The 2nd edition appeared in 1950–1958 (51 vols; 2-vol index, 1960), with an updating *Ezhegodnik*, or yearbook, 1957– . Compared with the earlier edition, it stresses economic, industrial and technical aspects of Soviet achievement. We are now in the Stalin era, and this edition claims to be purged of the gross theoretical and political errors of the previous set. In reflecting official Soviet thinking of the time, the publishers delayed until 1957 the issuing of Vol 40, which carried the article on Stalin. Vol 50, *U.S.S.R.* (1957), is a comprehensive work of reference on the Soviet Union, with sections on political structure, economy, history, geography and scientific developments. It was translated into English as *Information S.S.R.* (Oxford: Pergamon Press, 1962. xii, 982 pp), with I. R. Maxwell as general editor. Vol 51, a supplement, has many biographical entries—some for persons included for the first time, others whose reputations had been rehabilitated. The two-volume index (1575 pp) carried 200,000 entries.

The 3rd edition of the *Bol'shaya* (Moscow: Izdat. Sovetskaya Entsiklopediya, 1969–1978. 30 vols) has 100,000 entries and represents a more factual approach than the 2nd edition, while maintaining its ideological stance. The US Declaration of Independence is briefly dismissed as the product of a bourgeois revolution; the entry on Glasgow concentrates on the strikes that occurred there. National emphasis is also marked. Thus, 'Azerbaidzhanskaya SSR' occupies Vol 1, columns 716–75, with 25 sections, 5 illustrations, 8 tables, 3 maps and half a column of bibliography. Vol 30 includes a list of contributors. Book production shows an improvement on the 2nd edition: type is clearer and paper is white instead of greyish. But photographs are still of inferior quality.

THE GREAT SOVIET ENCYCLOPEDIA: A TRANSLATION OF THE THIRD EDITION OF THE BOL'SHAYA SOVETSKAYA ENTSIKLOPEDIYA (New York: Macmillan; London: Collier-Macmillan, 1973–1982. 30 vols) is a volume-for-volume version of the original. Because entries per volume are taken from the Russian, the English translation of headwords, and therefore articles, sets up a different A–Z order. While two-thirds of the translation of Vol 1 contains articles under the letter 'A', the remainder is otherwise: we begin with 'Aalen Stage' and end with 'Zulu War'. Thus each translated volume is obliged to have its own A–Z sequence. To help reference to particular articles, interim indexes are provided. The latest (1981) is to Vols 1–25, the final, complete index now being due. Maps and photographs have been omitted from the translation—a drawback, since the original contained a number of World War II Soviet-front campaign maps, for instance. The translation is thorough[13] and the quality of book production high. The text is certainly to be valued as a consistent statement of the Soviet point of view.

REFERENCES AND CITATIONS

1. *The Encyclopedia Americana* New York: Grolier, 1980. Vol 10, 332.
2. Katz, William A. *Introduction to reference work*, Vol 1: *Basic information sources*. 4th ed. New York: McGraw-Hill, 1982. 186.

Further Reading

3. *Times literary supplement* 3555, 10 April 1970. 412.
4. *Wilson library bulletin*, **47** (6), February 1973. 539.
5. *RQ*, **21** (1), Fall 1981. 87.
6. Katz, William A. *op. cit.* 182.
7. Brewer, Annie M. *Dictionaries, encyclopedias and other word-related books, 1966–1974*. Detroit, Michigan: Gale, 1975. 1–25.
8. Katz, William A. *op. cit.* 170.
9. Cole, Dorothy Ethlyn 'Britannica 3 as a reference tool: a review'. *Wilson library bulletin*, **48** (10), June 1974. 825.
10. Kister, Ken 'Encyclopedia publishing: an update'. *Library journal*, 15 April 1978. 823.
11. Bendig, Mark W. 'The encyclopedia online: Channel 2000 and the *Academic American encyclopedia*'. *RSR*, **10** (2), Summer 1982. 25–6.
12. Einbinder, Harvey 'Encyclopedias: some foreign and domestic developments'. *Wilson library bulletin*, **55** (4), December 1980. 257–61.
13. Grimsted, Patricia Kennedy 'Détente on the shelves?' *Wilson library bulletin*, **48** (10), January 1975. 728.

SUGGESTIONS FOR FURTHER READING

History

The standard work is R. L. Collison's *Encyclopaedias: their history throughout the ages: a bibliographical guide, with extensive historical notes to the general encyclopaedias issued throughout the world, from 350 BC to the present day* (2nd ed. New York & London: Hafner, 1966). Three of the eight chapters concern 'Diderot and the Encyclopédistes', 'The Encyclopaedia Britannica' and 'Brockhaus', whereas *Enciclopedia italiana* and the *Bol'shaya sovetskaya entsiklopediya* receive only one page apiece. Appendix 4: 'List of encyclopaedias not mentioned in the text'.

Collison's article 'Encyclopaedias' in *The new Britannica* of 1974 is wide-ranging, with a handy list of national encyclopedias, although on the *Britannica* itself no reference is made to Einbinder's *The myth of the Britannica*, 1964. The article in the 11th edition of the *Britannica*, Vol 9, pp 369–82 is also worth studying.

The whole of *Cahiers d'histoire mondiale/Journal of world history*, **9** (3) 1966, is given over to encyclopaedias, with contributions by specialists. 60 pages deal with 'Eastern encyclopaedias' alone, and a concluding article discusses 'New problems: internationalism, information storage and retrieval, and encyclopedias'. Three more recent contributions on encyclopaedias in antiquity and in the Middle Ages are by Sidney J. Jackson: 'Towards a history of the encyclopedia from Amenemope of Egypt to the

General Encyclopaedias

collapse of Greece', in *The Journal of library history*, **12** (4), Fall 1977, 342-58, with 64 references; his 'Towards a history of the encyclopedia, from Jerome to Isidor', in *International library review*, **19** (1), January 1981, 3-16, with 90 references; and Francis J. Witty's 'Medieval encyclopedias: a librarian's view', in *The Journal of library history*, **14** (3), Summer 1979, 274-96.

Lists of encyclopaedias

One of the fullest listings appears in the British Museum *General catalogue of printed books* under the heading 'Encyclopaedias': Vol 61, 1960, columns 592-669; *Ten-year supplement, 1956-65*, 1968, Vol 14, columns 43-85; *Five-year supplement, 1966-1970*, 1973, Vol 7, columns 975-94; and *Five-year supplement, 1971-1975*, 1978, Vol 4, columns 1184-98.

Like *Dictionaries, encyclopedias and other word-related books*, edited by Annie M. Brewer (2nd ed, 1978; 3rd ed, 1982; suppt 1983. Detroit: Gale. 3 vols), G. A. Zischka's *Index lexicorum/Bibliographie der lexikalischen Nachschlagwerke* (Vienna: Hollinek; New York and London: Hafner, 1959) is international. But it has the advantage of being briefly annotated and of covering the period from the fifteenth century onwards. Entries for items considered important are asterisked. Sheehy's *Guide to reference books* (9th ed. Chicago: ALA, 1976; Supplements, 1980, 1982) and Walford's *Guide to reference material* (Vol 3. 3rd ed, 1977; 4th ed, due 1984) provide annotated entries for selected general encyclopaedias. Mlle L.-N. Malclès' *Les sources du travail bibliographique*, Vol 1 (1950), devotes Chapter 8 to encyclopaedias, concentrating on the history of French encyclopaedias, but including a list of encyclopaedias of 17 other countries, with 21 references. This chapter is updated in her *Manuel de bibliographie* (3rd ed, 1975), pp 155-61, and in *Ouvrages de référence pour les bibliothèques publiques*, by Marcelle Beaudiquez and Anne Bethery (Paris: Cercle de la Librairie, 1978 ed, items 1-33).

Language groups

K. F. Kister provides excellent leads for the purchaser of an English-language encyclopaedia in his *Encyclopedia buying guide: a consumer guide to general encyclopedias in print* (3rd ed. New York and London: Bowker, 1981). This gives a critical and comparative assessment of 36 adult and junior sets in five categories, with Appendix C 'Encyclopedias of the United Kingdom'—making the barest reference to *Everyman's encyclopaedia* (not marketed in the USA), and Appendix D, an annotated bibliography. Kister's guide to encyclopaedias is updated at short intervals.

Further Reading

James P. Walsh, author of *Anglo-American general encyclopedias: an historical bibliography, 1703–1967* (Bowker, 1968), has produced a handy concise folding chart, *Encyclopedia ratings*, (Croydon: Reference Books Research Publications) now in its 5th edition, 1982. It compares 20 sets, adult and junior, under eight heads, plus a column for comment.

The leading reviewing source for English-language multi-volume sets is the 'Reference and subscription books review' section of the twice-monthly *Booklist*, compiled by the ALA's Reference and Subscription Book Committee. The valuable series of three articles on 'Encyclopedias: a survey and buying guide' in the *Booklist*, 1 December 1978–1 February 1979, appeared as a 40-page booklet in 1979 as *Purchasing an encyclopedia: 12 points to consider*. Encyclopaedia yearbooks and supplements were reviewed in the 15 March 1981 *Booklist*, pp 1049–54, and lengthy appraisals of *World book encyclopedia* and *Academic American encyclopedia* in 1 May 1979 and 1 July 1981 issues respectively.

Eleven German encyclopaedias are succinctly surveyed in *German language and literature: select bibliography of reference books*, by L. M. Newman (University of London, Institute of Germanic Studies, 1979. pp 76–7); and Hans-Joachim Koppitz's *Grundzüge der Bibliographie* (Munich: Verlag-Dokumentation, K. G. Saur, 1977) provides background data under the leading German publishing houses, on pp 130–2.

The article on encyclopaedias in both *La grande encyclopédie* (Vol 7, 1973) and *Encyclopaedia universalis* (1980 ed. Vol 6, pp 180–5) is concerned only with Diderot's *Encyclopédie*.

Twenty-five Spanish, Portuguese and Latin American encyclopaedias are given entries, usually annotated, in Abel Rodolfo Geoghegan's *Obras de referencia de América Latina* (Emprenta Crisol, 1965). More recent is the section, on pp 72–8, of *Latin American bibliography*, edited by L. Halliwell (SCONUL, Latin American Group, 1978). The *Humanities* volumes, published in alternate years, of the well-annotated *Handbook of Latin American studies* (University of Texas Press) records national encyclopaedias.

Russian and Soviet encyclopaedias are authoritatively surveyed by J. S. G. Simmons in Vol 1, *General bibliographies and reference books*, of the *Guide to Russian reference books* by Karol Maichel (Hoover Institution, 1962). This contribution is briefly updated in J. S. G. Simmons's *Russian bibliography, libraries and archives* (Twickenham: Anthony C. Hall, 1973), items 201–9, with appendix notes on the Granat encyclopaedia of 1910–1948.

Encyclopaedias: future trends

Warren F. Preece, editor of the *New Britannica* (1974), envisages in two articles, 'Notes towards a new encyclopedia' (*Scholarly publishing*, 12 (1),

General Encyclopaedias

October 1980, 13–30; **12** (2), January 1981, 141–57), an 'Encyclopaedia 21'. This would treat subjects on a global pattern, rid of national slants—a 'United Nations of knowledge'. Tied up with this concept would be the use of video discs instead of pages, operating on a colour TV set.

Already the full text of the latest edition of the *Encyclopaedia Britannica*, the *Britannica book of the year* and its associates, the *Yearbook of science and the future*, and the *Medical and health annual* can be searched online, but only by subscribers to Mead Data Central's Lexis or Nexis services. 'Libraries, schools and individuals will not be offered access to the file'. (*Advanced technology libraries*, 10 (9), September 1981, 3; quoted in *CABLIS*, No 66, October 1981, 9.)

5
Subject Encyclopaedias

Denis J. Grogan

For many readers the term 'reference book' immediately suggests 'encyclopaedia', inasmuch as they will often turn first to a general encyclopaedia when they seek information. Within a particular subject field, however—say physics or economics or the theatre—a searcher's first step is often much less confident. Yet here too there are available hundreds, even thousands, of subject encyclopaedias, offering in most disciplines an obvious first place to look things up.

Virtually every subject area of any significance now has its own encyclopaedia (though the student should note that they may not always be described as such). Typically, they are handy single-volume compilations, often designed for the home or the office-desk or the work-bench. Many are planned as 'one-stop' reference tools, aiming to answer as many queries as possible without having to refer the searcher elsewhere.

Harvey, P. (*ed.*) THE OXFORD COMPANION TO ENGLISH LITERATURE. 4th ed. Oxford: Clarendon Press, 1967.

This was the earliest of the now extensive series of Oxford Companions (all of which are actually subject encyclopaedias) and a model of its kind. Though its reputation stands high with academics and literary critics, it is not designed primarily for specialists: fifty years or so ago the compiler made clear in the preface to the first edition that it was for 'ordinary everyday readers of English literature'.

Scarcely an article exceeds half a page, and the majority are much less; with the extensive system of cross-references this allows the user very speedily to run to earth his quarry. As well as the expected articles under authors, titles, and subjects, there are brief entries for hundreds of characters from literature, and for thousands of allusions which contain a proper name: actual celebrities as well as mythical characters, such as John Wesley, Dick Turpin, and Rumpelstiltzkin; and places both real and imaginary, such as Grub Street, Xanadu, and Pisa.

For its specific purpose it aims to be self-sufficient: there are no bibliographies to suggest further sources to consult and there is no index.

Considine, D. M. (*ed.*) VAN NOSTRAND'S SCIENTIFIC ENCYCLOPEDIA. 6th ed. New York: Van Nostrand Reinhold, 1983.

With its well over two million words from some two hundred specialist contributors, this work has a well-deserved reputation as 'the world's most consulted one-volume science reference'. Now also available in two-volume format, it may well for many users fulfil its claim to 'obviate the need for your having a multi-volume work in your library, home or office'.

Covering engineering, mathematics, and medicine as well as science, it is illustrated with over 2,500 diagrams, graphs, and photographs, virtually one for each page. This sixth edition, like the fifth, departs from the practice of previous editions by appending brief bibliographies to a small number of the major articles. A more radical change is the consolidation of many of the short entries, 'thus yielding more concentrated information in fewer localities', and reducing the number of articles from 16,500 to 7,300. Providing some compensation for the searcher are over 9,500 cross-references, 'essentially an abridged alphabetical index incorporated within the regular pages of the book'.

The range of subjects covered is astonishing: indeed it is scarcely credible some of the specialized topics that have now given birth to their own weighty encyclopaedias: T. de Dillmont *Encyclopedia of needlework* rev ed (New York: Toggitt, 1960) and W. M. Levi *Encyclopedia of pigeon breeds* (Jersey City: TFH Publications, 1965) are two examples, each with nearly eight hundred pages. Even larger are Q. D. Bowers *Encyclopedia of automatic musical instruments* (Vestal, New York: Vestal Press, 1972) and R. W. Fairbridge *The encyclopedia of oceanography* (New York: Reinhold, 1966) with over a thousand pages apiece.

ROLE AND CONTENT

As has often been said, the real task of an encyclopaedia is to provide 'first and essential facts' only: **first**, meaning those obvious details that any enquirer would want to know, and **essential**, in the sense of those intrinsic facts without which it is not possible to perceive the nature of the topic under discussion. Obviously, therefore, all encyclopaedias have to be selective to some extent, and so it is quite unfair to judge any example solely by the amount of information between its covers: it is no task for an encyclopaedia to attempt to exhaust its topic. Indeed, for many subjects 'completeness in a moderate compass', as the *Oxford companion to English literature* (see above) puts it, is impossible. There is a more important criterion to apply in assessing whether a work warrants the accolade of 'encyclopaedia': historically and etymologically such works were intended to encompass the whole circle of learning. This of course has not been feasible in a strictly literal sense for generations, but it is scarcely possible to allow the description of 'encyclopaedia' to a work that does not at least aim for **comprehensiveness**. This must not be confused with completeness: a comprehensive work is one with a coverage of its field that is all embracing, though its depth may vary according to circumstances.

Lichine, A. LICHINE'S ENCYCLOPEDIA OF WINES AND SPIRITS. 4th ed. London: Cassell, 1979.

By a wine-grower and former wine merchant, this volume is designed to be world-wide in its coverage and claims that it is 'the most comprehensive, authoritative book in its field'. Most of it is

Subject Encyclopaedias

taken up by the 487-page alphabetical sequence of entries, but this is preceded by ten chapters on the history of wine, serving wine, spirit-making, etc, and is followed by 137 pages of appendices covering, for example, containers and measures and a comparative table of spirit strengths. It provides a speedy, accurate, and concise response to queries such as 'What are all the various sizes of champagne bottles called? What is a bumper? How is sake served in Japan?'

Although comprehensiveness is a prerequisite for an encyclopaedia this does not of course prevent overweening compilers and publishers of patently inadequate works using the term on their title-pages. The prudent librarian must remain on the alert for such sharp practice and continue to judge all such works by their fruits.

Multi-volume encyclopaedias

No library user can remain unaware for long of another quite distinct category of subject encyclopaedia, the great multi-volume compilations increasingly found in the major disciplines, matching in many respects *New Britannica* and *World book* and *Americana* and *Italiana* in the general field.

Sills, D. L. (*ed.*) INTERNATIONAL ENCYCLOPEDIA OF THE SOCIAL SCIENCES. New York: Macmillan and Free Press, 1968. 17 vols (and biographical supplement, 1979).

The eight million words of this standard work have been written 'for social scientists themselves, students of the social sciences, and for professionals from other fields who seek information about a topic in the social sciences'. It casts its net far wider than many might imagine: history is included, for example, and so is geography (other than physical geography); statistics is covered too, and much of psychology and psychiatry. Education as such is not included, though there are some articles on relevant educational topics.

This is clearly a scholarly work, with the articles often extending to a dozen pages or more. The extensive bibliographies following the articles are not merely suggestions for further reading but also provide the formal documentation for the article itself.

Though the editors feel that the subject matter 'does not easily lend itself to alphabetical treatment', they did eventually choose that arrangement as the most useful to readers. Although they have grouped many specific articles under broader general titles, they have also supplied many hundreds of cross-references from alternative headings and from within the articles themselves, and they have provided an exhaustive 40,000-entry index to the 1,716 articles.

ENCYCLOPEDIA OF WORLD ART. New York: McGraw-Hill, 1959–1968. 15 vols.

An outstanding example of a work deliberately planned as 'a major historical synthesis covering the arts of all periods and countries'. Further lofty aims are to be 'factually complete within the limits of possibility', and to be intelligible to an audience without previous specialized preparation. Understandably, illustrations figure prominently: in addition to thousands of line drawings in the text, a good half of each volume is taken up by half-tone plates.

In facing the dilemma of how to arrange the material the editors found that 'None of the usual plans of classification or exposition can be followed rigidly without doing violence to the autonomy and the individuality of one aspect or another of the many-faceted world of art'. They concluded that the best arrangement was 'a series of separate but co-ordinated monographs, presented in alphabetical order without regard to their content'. Detailed access to the contents of the thousand or so long articles is provided by a 20,000-entry index volume, and each is supplied with an extensive scholarly bibliography of sources, including both books and periodical articles.

These are obviously something more than quick-reference works: some have seen in such comprehensive works an extension of the usual role of the encyclopaedia beyond 'first and essential facts' only. They may still be alphabetically arranged, but they appear to have taken on to some extent the role of a treatise, assimilating all of the literature in a particular field and presenting an authoritative

Subject Encyclopaedias

synthesis of the whole of existing knowledge. In the words of its editor-in-chief the 16-volume *Encyclopaedia Judaica* (Jerusalem: Keter, 1971), for instance, was planned to encompass 'the totality of Jewish knowledge and scholarship'; the 9-volume *Enciclopedia della spettacolo* (Rome: Maschere, 1955–1965) is described by Walford as the 'definitive encyclopaedia of staged entertainment'.

Some of them can even lay claim to the further historical function of summarizing the achievements of their particular discipline at a particular point in time. A work of this nature, therefore, preserves an important archival value long after its specific content has become outdated: it remains, in the words of the honorary editor of the *International encyclopedia of the social sciences*, 'a historical document of its time'.

ARRANGEMENT

What above all marks out a reference book from other works is the way it is arranged: it must be deliberately designed for ease of consultation rather than for continuous reading. And it is by its arrangement, as much as by its content, that an encyclopaedia stands to be judged. It is not sufficient that the information provided is comprehensive and fundamental: it must also be easy of access. The usual method is alphabetical by subject: it is instructive to note how the two great encyclopaedias just described both arrived at an alphabetical arrangement, though starting from opposite premises.

Of course, setting out articles in alphabetical order inevitably separates related topics, and some encyclopaedia compilers have therefore come to a different conclusion. Among the multi-volumed general encyclopaedias, for instance, *Encyclopédie française* (21 vols), the *Oxford junior encyclopaedia* (13 vols) and the *Joy of knowledge* (10 vols) are all arranged **systematically** by subject. Readers are commonly surprised by this; yet historically the systematically arranged encyclopaedia was the first in the field by many hundreds of years. Among subject encyclopaedias too, one occasionally encounters a systematic rather than an alphabetical

Arrangement

arrangement, eg A. Bachmann *An encyclopedia of the violin* (New York: Appleton, 1925); *Encyclopaedia of Ireland* (Dublin: Figgis, 1968); *Larousse encyclopedia of world geography* 2nd ed (London: Hamlyn, 1967). Obviously, in all such cases a detailed subject index is essential if the content is to be readily accessible.

MATERIALS AND TECHNOLOGY: A SYSTEMATIC ENCYCLOPEDIA. London: Longmans, 1968–1975. 8 vols.

Printed in Amsterdam, this is a much revised English version of a six-volume Dutch work, highly respected for fifty years. It is an interesting example of a subject encyclopaedia where the compilers have deliberately arranged their materials in systematic order. They claim that this is an advantage to the reader because it 'ensures that related subjects are dealt with in proximity with each other rather than separated by the random vagaries of the alphabet'. It describes the sources, manufacture, processing and use of natural and synthetic products, specifically 'materials in industry and commerce'. It attempts to include 'all substances bought and sold by volume, weight, or area'. It can provide immediate response to enquiries such as 'What exactly is copra? When was ice-cream invented? Can you tell me how synthetic rubies are made?'

The chapters are contributed by specialists and each is furnished with select references for further reading, including research reports and articles in periodicals as well as books. The systematic arrangement means that each volume can stand on its own (and indeed the publishers make them available separately), eg Vol 7 on 'Vegetable food products'. Each has its own subject index, and these are all combined in the general index to the complete work in Vol 8. This final volume also includes a 54-page appendix of short accounts updating chapters in earlier volumes.

Other non-alphabetical arrangements are more rare. Reference books of an encyclopaedic kind can be found arranged chronologically, particularly in the field of history, eg R. B. Morris *Encyclopedia of American history* 6th ed (New York: Harper, 1981), but some would argue that such a work thereby disqualifies itself as an encyclopaedia.

Subject Encyclopaedias

Langer, W. L. (*ed.*) AN ENCYCLOPEDIA OF WORLD HISTORY. 5th ed. London: Harrap, 1972.

This is an outstanding example of the genre, and deservedly successful, with over a million copies sold of the first four editions. Scholarly and authoritative (the editor was formerly Coolidge Professor of History at Harvard), it ranges from prehistoric man to 1 January 1971.

It describes itself as 'a handbook of historical facts, so arranged that the dates stand out while the material itself flows in a reasonably smooth narrative'. Obviously 'the backbone of the book is chronology', and within the main time groupings, eg the Middle Ages, there are divisions by period, eg the later Middle Ages, then further subdivisions by area, eg the British Isles, subdivided finally into England, Scotland, Ireland. Quite rightly, the 25,000-entry index takes up 200 pages—about an eighth of the total. A two-volume edition (New York: Abrams, 1973) has the same text but is enhanced by over two thousand illustrations.

More commonly, perhaps, such works describe themselves as what they are, eg R. L. Storey *Chronology of the medieval world, 800 to 1491* (London: Barrie and Jenkins, 1973), and its companion volumes; S. H. Steinberg *Historical tables, 58 BC–AD 1978*, 10th ed (London: Macmillan, 1979).

INDEXING

Many compilers of subject encyclopaedias assume that if their works are alphabetically organized, they are thereby self-indexing. This is by no means the case, as the editors of the great general encyclopaedias have realized for years. The better subject encyclopaedias, particularly the multi-volume works, make great efforts to provide full analytical indexes as well as setting out the individual articles in alphabetical order.

McGRAW-HILL ENCYCLOPEDIA OF SCIENCE AND TECHNOLOGY. 5th ed. New York: McGraw-Hill, 1982. 15 vols (and supplements).

Indexing

The only major English-language encyclopaedia covering the whole field of science and technology, this widely used work shows signs of extensive revision for its latest edition, with an extra 1,500 pages and a total of 3,500 expert contributors. The editors claim that 'Each article is designed and written to be understandable to the nonspecialist'. Individual users can obviously form their own opinions on that.

Quite outstanding are the illustrations: with 15,250 for the 12,400 pages, it is obvious that very few pages lack some graphic adornment. The bibliographies appended to many of the articles are scholarly and up to date, referring the reader to periodical articles as well as books.

The 'Analytical index' making up the last volume contains, we are told, each important term, concept and person mentioned throughout the 14 text volumes. As 150,000 entries are required to index the 7,700 articles, the user is up to nineteen times more likely to find the topic he wants if he consults the index first, rather than the main alphabetical sequence.

Such an index is even more necessary with works such as the *Encyclopedia of world art* (see above), which has deliberately adopted a monographic approach, with several of the articles in the main alphabetical sequence extending to fifty pages or more; as its preface concedes, 'At the same time, the advantages for reference of the dictionary-index form are appreciable, and in recognition of this fact, the fifteenth volume of this encyclopedia is devoted to a full and thorough index of analytical character'.

Though only in one volume, a work such as P. Hartnoll *The Oxford companion to the theatre* 3rd ed (London: Oxford University Press, 1970) suffers by comparison from the absence of an index, since it too has chosen the long article approach for many topics. The user who looks up Christopher Marlowe, for example, will certainly find a page devoted to him under his name in the main alphabetical sequence, but he is not likely to find the account of similar length within the 15-page article on England.

Most encyclopaedia indexes combine names (personal and place) and subjects in one alphabetical sequence, but occasionally the student will encounter separate name and subject indexes as in J.

Subject Encyclopaedias

Thewlis *Encyclopaedic dictionary of physics* (see below). Some works also provide an alternative approach in the form of a systematically arranged index: under each of the headings and subheadings in the groupings chosen are listed the individual articles on the topic, eg the 26-page 'Classification of articles' in the index volume of the *International encyclopedia of the social sciences* (see above); the 33-page 'Topical index' grouping the 7,700 article titles of the McGraw-Hill *Encyclopedia of science and technology* (see above) under about a hundred broad subject headings.

In the absence of indexes, an extensive and carefully worked out system of cross-references can provide a partial substitute, but completely adequate examples are rare. Usually the searcher himself is left to provide the link between related subjects, or to guess the heading under which minor subdivisions of the topic have been subsumed.

Scholes, P. A. THE OXFORD COMPANION TO MUSIC. 10th ed. London: Oxford University Press, 1970.

For forty years this has been one of the most popular of the Oxford Companions, and justly so. Much of its appeal derives from the characteristic style of its first editor, which, since his death in 1958, has been worthily maintained by his successors.

It is aimed not only at the 'experienced and well-instructed professional musician' (who has always made full use of the work), but also at 'the younger musician, the concert goer, the gramophonist, or the radio-listener'. The compilers tell us 'It is believed that in no article of the book can a technical term be met with of which an explanation is not speedily available by turning to that term in its own alphabetical position'. The absence of bibliographies has attracted criticism, but the extensive illustrations are perhaps a surprising feature.

Earlier editions used to describe themselves on their title-pages as 'self-indexed'. There is no index as such, and the method of referencing used as a substitute is worthy of study: 'the larger articles are divided into numbered sections and their separate facts are scrupulously indexed, by means of article and section number, in their alphabetical positions throughout the volume'. Furthermore, 'Abundant cross-references are given in the body of almost every considerable article and also of many a smaller one, and frequently at the end of an article will be found a list of further allusions, elsewhere in the book, to the subject of that article.'

TREATMENT

A distinction that the student will be familiar with from his examination of general encyclopaedias (and perhaps from what has gone before in this chapter) is that between the short article and long article approaches. As the preface to the *Encyclopedia of world art* (see above) explains: 'A sharp and clear distinction is drawn between the aims of a monographic encyclopedia and an analytical dictionary index'.

Edwards, P. (*ed.*) THE ENCYCLOPEDIA OF PHILOSOPHY. London: Collier-Macmillan, 1967. 8 vols.

A milestone in the literature of its subject, this major work does not hesitate to claim comprehensiveness: 'We believe that there is no philosophical concept or theory of importance that is not identified and discussed.' A thoroughly scholarly work for the specialist, with extensive bibliographies that are often annotated and evaluative, it nevertheless claims that most articles are 'sufficiently explicit to be read with pleasure and profit by the intelligent non-specialist'.

The editors have deliberately opted for an approach quite distinct from that of the great standard work J. M. Baldwin *Dictionary of philosophy and psychology* (New York: Macmillan, 1901–1905) where 'the great majority of articles were exceedingly brief'. Here the articles are 'of ample length'. Indeed, 'Some of the longer articles . . . are in effect small books, and even the shorter articles are usually long enough to allow a reasonably comprehensive treatment of the subject under discussion'. This has permitted what would be regarded as departures from normal encyclopaedia practice insofar as the editors have encouraged the expression of individual and even controversial views from contributors, and a number of articles embody original research.

Subject Encyclopaedias

Benet, W. R. THE READER'S ENCYCLOPEDIA. 2nd ed. New York: Crowell, 1965.

Deservedly popular, and claimed as the only encyclopaedia of world literature in a single volume, this is an archetypal quick-reference book. It sets out to answer as many as possible of the questions that might be asked by the intelligent and curious reader or writer. With 25,000 entries in the space of 1,126 pages, this is obviously a short article encyclopaedia, but it ranges well beyond pure literature, with entries, for example, for celebrated musicians, artists, and philosophers.

Characteristic of many subject encyclopaedias is the inclusion of substantial information outside the basic alphabetical sequence of the text, commonly displayed in tabular or chronological form. *The Oxford companion to classical literature* (see below), for instance, devotes thirty pages to a date chart of classical literature; a table of Greek and Roman weights and measures; plans and illustrations of Greek and Roman houses, theatres, and temples; and ten pages of maps; N. Wilding and P. Laundy *An encyclopaedia of Parliament* 4th ed (London: Cassell, 1971) has no less than 34 appendices listing the holders of various offices over the years; in H. Osborne *The Oxford companion to art* (Oxford: Clarendon Press, 1970), a bibliography of over 3,000 items follows the alphabetical sequence. If the subject matter is appropriate, illustrations and maps may indeed make up a substantial portion of the work.

THE INTERPRETER'S DICTIONARY OF THE BIBLE. New York: Abingdon Press, 1962. 4 vols (and supplement, 1977).

Despite its title 'dictionary', the editor claims that 'these volumes travel far in the direction of a Bible encyclopaedia'. It is clearly intended as a comprehensive reference book on the Bible, the Apocrypha, and other non-canonical books, including the Dead Sea Scrolls. Its target is the preacher, the scholar, the student, the school-teacher, and the general reader: particular care has been taken to avoid technical language, and erudite references and exhaustive footnotes have been excluded. Nevertheless, the 7,500 articles maintain a high standard of scholarship, with distinguished contributors coming mainly from the United States, but with a fair

Use

representation also of European and Israeli scholars. Each important article has a select bibliography.

They will furnish an immediate response to questions such as 'What exactly was the widow's mite? Can you find me something on the Holy Sepulchre? Is it true that John the Baptist was not the inventor of baptism?'

In justification of its subtitle, 'an illustrated encyclopedia', a tenth of the space is devoted to more than 1,000 black-and-white illustrations; 163 maps; many charts, especially chronological; 24 pages of full-colour maps; and many colour illustrations.

USE

As with the general encyclopaedias, the primary use of subject encyclopaedias is by the enquirer (or librarian) in search of specific facts. The first words of the preface to L.-A. Bawden *The Oxford companion to film* (London: Oxford University Press, 1976) plainly states its aim 'to answer any query which may occur to the amateur of film in the course of reading or film-going'. As user surveys have shown, these fact-finding queries make up the bulk of requests received by libraries of all kinds, and many of them are satisfied from the appropriate subject encyclopaedia. This has been called the 'everyday' approach to information, because the need usually arises in the course of day-to-day activity, and may occur regularly and frequently.

Encyclopaedias are also of value for the 'something on . . .' type of enquiry, another common category. These have been described as material-finding queries, as opposed to fact-finding queries, and they also frequently arise on an 'everyday' basis. The editor of *Van Nostrand's scientific encyclopedia* (see above) explains that 'many users of the book not only seek detailed data on numerous subjects, but also expect well-organized overviews so that any subsequent researching of periodicals and specialized shelf literature can be pursued in the most workmanlike and time saving manner'. Where the enquirer is seeking an introductory, outline, or merely concise account sufficient to enable him to come to grips with a subject that is new or unfamiliar, he may need to go no further than a good

Subject Encyclopaedias

subject encyclopaedia. But even for the more demanding enquirer hoping to make a detailed study of a topic, it can often provide a convenient starting point.

Similarly, the librarian can also usefully turn first to a subject encyclopaedia as a stepping stone to a more extended search. Not only should it help to get the topic clearly in focus at the outset, but it will often suggest further paths to explore. Indeed, for the beginner, it is a good rule of thumb to open a search with the encyclopaedia, unless a more obvious starting point suggests itself. This role as 'launch pad' for a more extended search is the second of the two primary uses of the encyclopaedia, both general and subject.

The thrust for such further exploration of the topic under scrutiny is sometimes provided by the short bibliographies found at the end of the articles. These are only rarely complete bibliographies of course—merely guides to further reading—and they are perhaps the exception rather than the rule in the bulk of the single-volume works. The major multi-volume specialist encyclopaedias, on the other hand, include bibliographies as a matter of course.

Cross, F. L. and Livingstone, E. A. (*eds.*) THE OXFORD DICTIONARY OF THE CHRISTIAN CHURCH. 2nd ed. London: Oxford University Press, 1974.

An outstanding example in a field well supplied with encyclopaedias, and far and away the best single-volume work, this aims 'to bring together, in a concise and handy form, as large a body of information as possible'. Addressed not just to 'professionals', or even Christians, but to the educated public as a whole, it nevertheless maintains the highest scholarly standard. F. L. Cross, the original editor, was for 24 years Lady Margaret Professor of Divinity at Oxford, and wrote about half the articles himself. The remainder are by some 250 very eminent scholars, but 'in order to secure maximum uniformity it was agreed at the outset that all contributions should be subject to such editorial modification and reconstruction as seemed desirable, and that anonymity should be preserved'.

The compilers rightly claim that the bibliographies appended to some 4,500 of the 6,000 articles form 'a notable constituent' of the

Level

work itself. Compiled independently of the articles, and by no means merely lists, they are frequently descriptive and evaluative, and attempt 'to record the principal items of primary and permanent interest'. The compilers are justly proud of their achievement: 'It is believed that the *Dictionary* will put the student of Church history in possession of a larger body of bibliographical material than any other work of similar compass'.

The appropriate subject encyclopaedia is often a good source to try for narrow or specialized topics that have not yet grown to warrant a whole book of their own. The many biographical entries, for example, in the work just described remind us that enquirers often seek information about people. Like the general encyclopaedias, many (though not all) subject encyclopaedias are valuable sources of biographical information, particularly for minor figures, about whom they may be the only convenient source. The editor of *The encyclopedia of philosophy* (see above) claims, for instance: 'We have also made it a special point to rescue from obscurity unjustly neglected figures, and in such cases, where the reader would find it almost impossible to obtain reliable information in standard histories or in general encyclopaedias, we have been particularly generous in our space allotments'.

Students should note, however, that some encyclopaedias exclude such details as a matter of policy: the ten-volume *International encyclopedia of higher education* (San Francisco: Jossey Bass, 1977), for example, 'decided that no biographical information would be included because it would be impossible to determine, on an international basis, the names of those who ought to be recognized'. Biography is omitted from the McGraw-Hill *Encyclopedia of science and technology* (see above) because it is 'a work *of*, not *about* science'.

LEVEL

An important distinction between subject and general encyclopaedias is that the former are much more obviously aimed at readers of differing levels of attainment. While it is probably the case that most subject encyclopaedias are written for the moderately well informed, there are many important titles designed for the specialist.

Hammond, N. G. L. and Scullard, H. H. (*eds.*) THE OXFORD CLASSICAL DICTIONARY. 2nd ed. Oxford: Clarendon Press, 1970.

The best one-volume encyclopaedia in its field, it makes plain its comprehensive embrace: 'all fields of ancient Greek and Roman civilization'. Describing itself as 'a compendium of modern scholarship', it is basically a work for the specialist, with extensive bibliographies, including original sources and papers in learned journals. The preface draws attention to P. Harvey *The Oxford companion to classical literature* (Oxford: Clarendon Press, 1937) as a work more suited to 'the ordinary reader': all the Greek names, for example, are transliterated.

Thewlis, J. (*ed.*) ENCYCLOPAEDIC DICTIONARY OF PHYSICS. Oxford: Pergamon, 1961–1964. 9 vols (and supplements).

Clearly a major work, now thoroughly tested in use, it covers not only physics proper, but to a greater or lesser extent a large number of subjects in which physics is applied, eg astronomy, physical metallurgy, photography. Enquiries that this work could answer are: 'How are mirrors silvered? Can you find me something on the use of echo-sounding in fishing? I am looking for details of the official tests for watches'.

Contributed by some 3,000 specialists, the 15,000 entries include both long and short articles (though none are more than 3,000 words), with a limited number of diagrams, many reproduced from the original papers. The 50,000-entry subject index in Vol 8 employs the useful practice of indicating, by a volume number in bold type, that the article referred to is over 500 words.

Although 'not written primarily for specialists', the articles are claimed in the foreword to be 'of graduate or near graduate standard'. Nevertheless, experience has shown that the general arrangement and indexing do permit access to much of the work's content for intelligent users of limited scientific background.

Level

It is most important in examining a subject encyclopaedia to ascertain its level carefully. The compilers, and even more so the publishers, in their understandable anxiety that the fruits of their labours should be frequently consulted, are not always reliable guides here. They sometimes lay claim to a more extensive potential readership than is feasible, and it occasionally becomes necessary for such claims to be modified. The preface to the first volume of one of the encyclopaedias considered earlier describes it as suitable for a 'layman with only slight technical knowledge'; some years later the preface to the final volume put it: 'anyone who has studied physics and chemistry to sixth form level will have little difficulty in following the text'. The book-jacket of A. Ralston and E. D. Reilly *Encyclopedia of computer science and engineering* 2nd ed (London: Van Nostrand Reinhold, 1983) claims that it 'meets the needs of everyone in its field, including the layperson, the non-specialist in computer science and related technology, and the specialist requiring detailed elaboration of a subject related to his or her profession'. In the work itself, however, the editors are more modest: 'a basic reference work for non-specialists who need elaboration of subjects in which they are not expert'.

Subject encyclopaedias are frequently the targets for criticism on level; in particular they have been castigated as of little use to the specialist. The articles do not go into sufficient depth for his purposes, and the form in which the information is published inevitably prevents it from being thoroughly up to date. Some of this is unfair, and the critics clearly expect too much. The plain facts of economics frequently dictate that a particular discipline can support no more than one encyclopaedia; the compiler must then choose to direct his efforts at satisfying the limited number of experts in the field, at the expense of the probably more numerous non-specialist users, or, as is usually the case, he may pitch his level at that of the intelligent layman, to the annoyance of the specialist. If he tries for the cake *and* the halfpenny he runs the risk of losing both.

The better editors frankly acknowledge this, and often take the trouble to explain their particular approach. Those who consult the *International encyclopedia of the social sciences* (see above) are advised that 'We have not attempted to make every article useful to the reader without prior knowledge of the subject'. The reader of H. Osborne *The Oxford companion to art* (Oxford: Clarendon Press, 1970), on the other hand, is informed in the first sentence of the preface that the work 'has been designed as a non-specialist introduction to the fine arts'. Furthermore, 'individual articles are not intended to be more than introductory'. That this approach need not necessarily lead to trivialization is implied by the later claim: 'The articles have been prepared by experts for readers who are accustomed to tackling specialized reading in other fields. They are neither popular in tone, nor do they assume specialized knowledge in their own field'.

Those who seriously try for the double invariably find a difficult task on their hands. The editor of one of the well-known titles described earlier tried to explain his attempt this way: 'An effort has been made to customize descriptions in terms of their innate simplicity or complexity, keeping in mind the probable background and experience profile of the reader who may be seeking information on a given topic'.

Perhaps the ideal of an encyclopaedia as a tool of equal value to the layman and the expert is as much a dream as the encyclopaedia encompassing the whole of knowledge. This is worth bearing in mind before accepting criticism; it is important for the student to examine each work with care and to measure its achievement against the demands made on it and the uses to which it is put. It is a well-known fact that many of those who come to libraries with 'everyday' queries are seeking information in a subject area peripheral to their primary interest: they are in effect non-specialists in those fields. Many subject encyclopaedias have been carefully designed for precisely such needs; Peter Gray *The encyclopedia of the biological sciences* 2nd ed (London: Van Nostrand Reinhold, 1970), for example, aims 'to provide succinct and accurate information for biologists in those fields in which they are not themselves experts'.

Neither must it be forgotten that an important role of the encyclopaedia, in all disciplines, is to explain its subject to the average intelligent layman, because it is often to an encyclopaedia of the subject that the ordinary curious enquirer turns first. This is where the encyclopaedia editor has the chance to play his part, in the words of Lowell A. Martin, an American librarian and a professor

Level

at Columbia University, as 'a mediator, between the world of scholars on the one side and the individual seeking information on the other, between those who know something and those who seek to know'. In science and technology, in particular, this role as mediator is vital, so dependent is our society on achievements made in these fields. The editor's introduction to J. R. Newman *The international encyclopedia of science* rev ed (London: Nelson, 1965) takes care to explain that 'the needs of the common reader—the student, the teacher, the non-specialist—have been our measuring rod'.

Hey, D. H. (*ed.*) KINGZETT'S CHEMICAL ENCYCLOPAEDIA. 9th ed. London: Baillière, 1966.

A widely used example of a handy quick-reference encyclopaedia regularly revised for fifty years but now sadly out-of-print. The work of a team of specialist contributors, mainly UK academic chemists, it is nevertheless not written for the professional chemist. Its original editor hoped it would be useful to 'all classes of the community'. The current foreword, by a former President of the Chemical Society, explains further that 'sometime or other every one of us is confronted with some chemical problem about which we would like information. The educated man of the present age cannot afford to accept the view that we are condemned to choose between two cultures.' As one might expect, the articles are all short; in those cases where bibliographies are supplied they are brief and confined to books.

A small number of encyclopaedias for the layman, paradoxically, are highly specialized works. The explanation lies in the fact that certain specialist fields have also become the province of the amateur enthusiast. This is sometimes made quite explicit. A. Hellyer *The Collingridge encyclopedia of gardening* (London: Hamlyn, 1976) tells us it is for 'the vast number of gardeners and plant lovers who nowadays are educating themselves towards almost professional standards of excellence'.

THE FOCAL ENCYCLOPEDIA OF PHOTOGRAPHY. Rev ed. London: Focal Press, 1969.

Subject Encyclopaedias

The 'desk edition' of this work is a striking example of just what it is possible to accomplish between the covers of a single modest-sized volume: 2,400 articles, containing 1.7 million words, plus 1,750 black-and-white illustrations. Long and short articles are used as appropriate; the short bibliographies are invariably of books only, cited without dates of publication. Extensive cross-references compensate for the lack of an index. Despite the technical nature of much of the content, its claim to be written in 'plain readable commonsense English' is well founded.

CURRENCY AND ACCURACY

The common charge that encyclopaedias are rarely up to date needs examining with care. As compilations of accepted and digested information, they cannot be at the frontiers of knowledge in every respect, but it is reasonable to look critically at their general performance. The better single-volume encyclopaedias appear in regularly updated editions, and some of the multi-volumed works arrange for supplementary volumes, often on an annual basis, eg the McGraw-Hill *Yearbook of science and technology* serves among other things to bring up to date selected subjects in the *Encyclopedia*.

In certain subject fields, of which law is the most obvious example, the consequences of relying on superseded information are so serious that special arrangements are often made to update the various reference tools and loose-leaf encyclopaedias are frequently encountered, eg *Atkin's encyclopaedia of court forms in civil proceedings* 2nd ed (London: Butterworth, 1961–   ). In theory it is a most effective and flexible method: in practice, it is cumbersome, and misfiled or even missing pages are far from unknown.

Accuracy in matters of fact, on the other hand, is an area where it is only fitting to expect the highest standards. Amid the thousands of subject encyclopaedias in our libraries, there are some that are worthless, and a larger number that are unreliable in some degree. Some years ago a very experienced librarian advised: 'Do not rely on encyclopaedic works; suspect every statement and do your best to verify it'. It is indeed a sound practice to double-check where

Exploitation

possible, not only in areas where there may be room for opinion, but also in matters of fact. Sheehy warns that 'as the immediate profits from cheap work are often large and as many buyers do not discriminate between good and poor encyclopedias, unscrupulous publishers will sometimes utilize hack writers or reprint, with only slight changes, out-of-date material'.

EXPLOITATION

One of the librarian's most important tasks is to maximize the resources at his disposal. Mention was made at the beginning of this chapter of the enquirer's uncertainty at the start of a subject search. The way libraries are obliged to display reference books might well contribute to this lack of awareness. A regular library user could scarcely avoid noticing the great general encyclopaedias, grouped together as they usually are on clearly indicated shelves. Subject encyclopaedias, on the other hand, are placed by most library classification schemes according to the subject, and are thus not only dispersed throughout the library but even within their own subject area have to compete for recognition with all the other books on the topic. Some libraries, of course, arrange for an *ad hoc* sequence of purely reference books, or even more specifically of quick-reference books. Yet even here the subject encyclopaedia has to sit cheek by jowl with guides to the literature, dictionaries, handbooks, directories, yearbooks, and all the other categories of reference tools.

Confused terminology provides a more fundamental explanation for a user's uncertainty; the plain fact of the matter is that many important subject encyclopaedias are called something else. *The Oxford companion to French literature*, Brewer's *Reader's handbook*, the *Merck index of chemicals and drugs*, are not only long-established and world-famous; they are also transparently encyclopaedias. This is no mere pedant's quibble; a searcher can go sadly astray if he passes over the *New Grove dictionary of music and musicians* or Macquoid and Edwards' *dictionary of English furniture* or Julian's *A dictionary of hymnology* or Thomson's *dictionary of banking*, because their titles suggest they may be restricted to the definition of terms. He would in fact be denying himself the most important *encyclopaedias* in their respective fields.

'Dictionary', in fact, is the most frequently misapplied ascription. In theory, of course, the distinction is crystal clear; it is neatly demonstrated in the two companion volumes by Peter Gray. In *The encyclopedia of the biological sciences* (see above) he explains: 'This is an encyclopedia, not a dictionary. That is, it does not merely define the numerous subjects covered but describes and explains them.' In his twin work *The dictionary of the biological sciences* (London: Reinhold, 1966) he explains: 'It was the infeasibility of indexing *The encyclopedia of the biological sciences* in a manner that would permit enough individual words to be found that led me to the conviction that a separate dictionary was a necessity'.

In practice, the distinction is often blurred, with much overlapping and even merging. Indeed in certain subjects for most practical purposes the differentiation no longer has any significance. The terms are often used interchangeably, sometimes within the same work: the Royal Horticultural Society *Dictionary of gardening* 2nd ed (Oxford: Clarendon Press, 1956) is subtitled 'a practical and scientific encyclopaedia of horticulture'. There are works which seek to be both: *The interpreter's dictionary of the Bible: an illustrated encyclopedia* (see above) defines terms (giving pronunciation, etymology, variant spellings) as well as describing and explaining them.

There are works which strive to be neither: A. Bullock and O. Stallybrass *The Fontana dictionary of modern thought* (London: Fontana/Collins, 1977) claims that it 'steers a middle course between an ordinary dictionary and an encyclopaedia'. There are also works which genuinely are both: E. J. Labarre *Dictionary and encyclopaedia of paper and paper-making* 2nd ed (Amsterdam: Swets and Zeitlinger, 1952) and its *Supplement* (1967).

We can also find examples of a hybrid known as an 'encyclopaedic dictionary'. But even here there is confusion; despite its double-barrelled title, R. I. Sarbacher *Encyclopedic dictionary of electronics and nuclear engineering* (London: Pitman, [1960]) is a pure-bred defining dictionary; on the other hand, even though the title was chosen 'only after a great deal of discussion', J. Thewlis

Further Reading

Encyclopaedic dictionary of physics (see above) is a plain straightforward encyclopaedia. J. Franklyn and J. Tanner *An encyclopaedic dictionary of heraldry* (Oxford: Pergamon Press, 1970), however, represents a genuine blend, as its preface makes clear for us: 'it is manifest that we are aware of the significance of the words constituting our title'.

What is equally manifest is that others are less aware; the distinguished editor of one Oxford Companion tells us in his preface that it 'is a handbook, not an encyclopaedia'; yet it plainly is a subject encyclopaedia, as both Walford and Sheehy confirm. Some may not specifically describe themselves as any particular kind of reference work at all: *Halsbury's laws of England* is an encyclopaedia, and is indeed described as such by Walford, but all its title page says is 'a complete statement of the whole law of England'. Most distracting of all are those works calling themselves encyclopaedias, but which are nothing of the kind. T. Corkhill *A concise building encyclopaedia* (London: Pitman, 1951) is simply a defining dictionary; F. F. Clough and G. J. Cuming *The world's encyclopaedia of recorded music* rev ed (London: Sidgwick & Jackson, 1966) is a discography, as its Introduction makes evident in the first line; '*Modern plastics' encyclopedia* (New York: Plastic Catalog Corp) is a yearbook and directory issued as a supplement to the American technical journal *Modern plastics*; R. Clarence '*The Stage' cyclopaedia* (London: The 'Stage', 1909) is a bibliography of plays, as its subtitle makes clear; Robson, Lowe, Ltd *Encyclopaedia of British Empire postage stamps* (London: Lowe, 1948–   ) is really something else; Walford describes it as a catalogue.

SUGGESTIONS FOR FURTHER READING

Each of the works described in this chapter has an entry with a full bibliographical citation and a descriptive annotation in Walford (including the *Concise* edition) or Sheehy, and in most instances in both. In choosing what to write about them, therefore, I have assumed that the student will also read carefully what Walford and Sheehy have to say on each item.

Furthermore, all except two or three of the largest multi-volumed works are among those selected by A. J. Walford and C. A. Toase *Basic stock for the reference library* 4th ed (London: Library Association, 1981) and accepted as a standard by the Department of Education and Science to

Subject Encyclopaedias

indicate 'a minimum reference stock for the smallest size of library authority'. It is hoped, therefore, that they will be within the reach of every student, for there is no substitute for the discipline of personal acquaintance with reference books.

As a reference book, none of the titles here is without fault. There is no such work known to me. What can be said about them all, however, is that they are broadly satisfactory for the purpose for which they were designed, some of them eminently so. Their faults, of course, users should be aware of, but more important are their virtues, and it is on these that I have tried to concentrate in my comments.

ADDENDA

While this work was in the press there appeared D. Arnold (*ed.*) *The new Oxford companion to music* (Oxford: Oxford University Press, 1983) in two volumes, 'a very different book from the old one-volume work' by Scholes, described above. Curiously, however, it does not seem to be a replacement: the Scholes edition is still in print six months after the publication of the new work, which advertises the availability of the old edition on its book-jacket.

In September 1983 there was also published a fourth edition of P. Hartnoll *The Oxford companion to the theatre*, referred to above.

6
Biographical Reference Works

Barrie I. MacDonald

What is biography? *The concise Oxford dictionary* definition is 'the written life of a person'. It can be described more fully as the recreation of a person's life, drawing upon memory, and written and oral evidence. 'The aim of biography', wrote Sir Sydney Lee, editor of the *Dictionary of national biography*, 'is the truthful transmission of personality'. Certainly the ideal biography should not be merely a narrative of the events of a life, but should also give the flavour of personality, as well as the person's achievements, in relation to the period in which he/she lived, and the events in which he/she participated. It should above all be accurate, balanced and objective. The biographer, wrote Virginia Woolf, 'chooses; he synthesizes; in short, he has ceased to be the chronicler; he has become the artist'.[1] The 'attraction of biography for the reader is two-fold: it appeals to our curiosity about human personality, and it appeals to our interest in factual knowledge, in finding out "what exactly happened" '.[2]

Broadly speaking, biography can be divided into two categories: individual biography, at its best the highly creative and interpretive literary form described by Virginia Woolf; and collected biography, now usually intended for reference purposes, which is the subject of this chapter.

BIOGRAPHICAL REFERENCE PROCESS

Requests for biographical information are among the most frequent enquiries a librarian will receive. Many will be straightforward enough to be answered from such standard sources as *Chambers biographical dictionary* or *Who's who*; others will require sound knowledge of biographical reference works, the biographical resources of non-biographical works, and the various bibliographical guides to biography; and will result in lengthy searches.

Most important in the reference process is the initial interview, during which the librarian will clarify the enquiry by asking questions which establish an understanding and a common objective with the enquirer. Firstly, any supplementary information the enquirer has about the subject will enable the librarian to assess which reference works are likely to contain the required information. Is the subject living or dead? What nationality is he/she? For what achievements is he/she known? To what profession or occupation does he/she belong? The less that is known of the subject (sometimes only the name) the more steps in the search the librarian will need to follow: from the general encyclopaedias and biographical dictionaries; through national, international and specialized current and retrospective biographical dictionaries to the bibliographical guides and indexes to biography. This initial process of assessing which reference works are likely to contain an entry for a particular person requires experience and a knowledge of reference material. An interesting project to automate this first stage in the biographical search has been undertaken at the University of Chicago Library.[3]

Other essential points to know before undertaking the enquiry are the amount, level and type of information required. These will enable the librarian to decide which sources are most suitable. It would, for example, be inappropriate to supply *Chambers biographical dictionary* rather than the *Dictionary of national biography* to an academic wanting a long, scholarly article with full bibliography on Queen Elizabeth I, whereas for a twelve-year-old schoolgirl wanting an outline biographical sketch on 'Good Queen Bess', *Chambers* or the *McGraw Hill encyclopaedia of world biography*, and not *DNB*, would offer the right level and length.

Not all enquiries will be for complete biographies of people;

Assessment of Biographical Reference Works

some will be for selected, often obscure, details. Did George III speak with a German accent? In which leg was Byron lame? Which museums have works by Leonardo da Vinci? What does Jane Austen's autograph look like? How tall is Prince Charles? Thorough knowledge of biographical sources will enable a quick decision to be made as to which of the sources with entries for these persons is likely to contain that particular fact. For example, of all the entries for Prince Charles in *Burke's peerage*, *Debrett's peerage and baronetage*, *International who's who* and *Current biography*, only the latter would give his height. Denis Grogan gives many useful examples of biographical reference enquiries.[4]

Reliability and accuracy of even the most authoritative reference works can occasionally be in doubt; therefore potentially questionable facts, such as birthdates, should be double-checked in as many sources as possible. Enquirers and trainee librarians should be warned of inaccurate works, perhaps with a note attached to the book. A problem with current biographical works is the currency of the information in even the latest edition, such works as *Who's who* being already out of date when published, due to the delay between compilation and publication; they should therefore be kept up to date by regular amendment, from newspaper coverage of appointments, honours, awards and obituaries. Thorough preparation for enquiry work, by considered stock selection, updating and correction of reference books, and compilation of information files and specialist indexes, is as essential as reference skills in enquiry work. Herbert Woodbine, editor of *The Library Association Record* from 1936 to 1944, wrote 'there are no geniuses in reference work, but that experience does, time after time, show the way to the solution of a problem'[5]—this is never more true than of biographical reference work.

ASSESSMENT OF BIOGRAPHICAL REFERENCE WORKS

The following points are some of the criteria for assessing biographical reference works:

1. **Purpose.** The title or preface will normally indicate the pur-

Biographical Reference Works

pose of the work; whether it is intended to be general, international, national or specialized in scope; and, within those categories, retrospective or current.

2. **Authority.** An important point in assessing the value of biographical dictionaries is their authority, as indicated by the sponsoring body (often a university or learned society), author, or contributors. Reputable publishers, such as Europa (London), Who's Who Verlag (Munich), or Marquis (Chicago), also guarantee authority.

3. **Coverage.** Is the work comprehensive within its chosen area, as, for example, *The medical directory* for British medical practitioners; or highly selective, eg *Who's who in the theatre*. The more specific the chosen area of the work, the more likely it is to be comprehensive.

4. **Selection policy.** The criterion for selection is particularly important with current works; whether it is solely by merit, as decided by the publisher or editor, as with *Who's who*; or by application, subscription to the work, or even payment, as with 'vanity' publications.

5. **Sources of information and method of compilation.** Many current 'Who's whos' use the questionnaire method of compiling the entries, whereby each biographee writes and later corrects his/her own entry; in other cases the publisher researches the material; both methods have advantages and disadvantages. For the national retrospective biographical dictionaries, it is preferable that contributors use original sources in writing articles.

6. **Frequency of publication.** An important consideration for current works is whether they are annual, biennial or irregular, and therefore how up to date is the information. If the work is irregular, and claims to be a new or revised edition, check it against the previous edition. If the work is retrospective, does it have regular supplements to update the main set?

7. **Accuracy and reliability.** These are mostly established through experience, though routine examination of the work, and reviews in the professional press, may help.

8. **Arrangement.** Most biographical dictionaries are arranged alphabetically, some having classified indexes; those works

Biographical Dictionaries

arranged by subject area or in chronological order can be all the more useful in providing an alternative approach to biography.

9. **Format and style.** The material should be presented in a clear and easy-to-use format. The style of entry varies from the quick reference sketch used in current 'Who's whos', through the outline biographies of *Chambers biographical dictionary*, to the lengthy narrative articles of the national biographical dictionaries.

10. **Indexes and cross-references.** Alphabetically arranged works are self-indexing, though classified indexes in such works, as with the *Dictionary of American biography*, can be useful. Classified or chronologically arranged works must have alphabetical name indexes. Adequate cross-references are important, especially to works including foreign names.

11. **Special features.** Bibliographies, tables, diagrams, portraits, and autographs, can greatly enhance the reference value.

12. **Comparison with similar works.** After examining a new work using these criteria the librarian can then compare it with similar works for duplication, and assess its value relative to comparable established reference works.

BIOGRAPHICAL DICTIONARIES

Louis Shores defines a biographical dictionary as 'essentially a directory of notable persons, usually arranged alphabetically by surname, with biographical identification that ranges from brief outline to extended narrative'.[6] There are three broad categories of biographical dictionaries: **general or universal**, containing persons from all countries; **national, area or local**, for persons from a specified continent, country, region or town; and **specialized**, for persons from specific classes, occupations, professions, or subject areas. Most works within these categories will be either retrospective or current.

Biographical Reference Works

UNIVERSAL BIOGRAPHICAL DICTIONARIES

General biographical dictionaries

Chalmers, A. THE GENERAL BIOGRAPHICAL DICTIONARY. New ed. London: Nichols, 1812–1817. 32 vols; Liechtenstein: Kraus, reprint 1976.

Michaud, J. F. BIOGRAPHIE UNIVERSELLE ANCIENNE ET MODERNE. Nouvelle ed. Paris: Desplaces, 1843–1865. 45 vols; Graz: Akademische Druck- und Verlagsanstalt, reprint 1964.

Hoefer, J. C. NOUVELLE BIOGRAPHIE GÉNÉRALE. Paris: Didot, 1852–1866. 46 vols; Copenhagen: Rosenkilde & Bagger, reprint 1963–1969.

These multi-volume works are probably the highest regarded general biographical dictionaries. *The general biographical dictionary*, after several earlier editions, was edited and revised by Alexander Chalmers for publication from 1812 to 1817. It contains more than 8,000, often lengthy, articles with footnote references to other sources. Although universal in coverage, it has a stated bias to British and Irish biography. The earlier and more authoritative of the two French works, the *Biographie universelle ancienne et moderne*, was originally published by Jean François and Louis Gabriel Michaud, of the Royalist printing house in Paris. Alphabetically arranged, its signed articles are scholarly, often very long, and with some sources of further reading. Said to have a Roman Catholic and Royalist bias in its first edition, later corrected, its articles sometimes show a lack of objectivity; Henry VIII, for example, is described as 'ce tyran voluptueux'. Articles on English persons generally are less satisfactory, and a French bias is evident in the length of articles. The 'rival' *Nouvelle biographie générale*, started in 1852 under Johann Hoefer's direction, was originally intended as a complement to the publisher's *Encyclopédie moderne*; many of its articles are taken from that and other Didot publications, as well as pirated from Michaud, for which the publisher was promptly sued.[7] The articles, though shorter and less scholarly than

Universal Biographical Dictionaries

Michaud, are better presented with more bibliographical references. It is, overall, a more comprehensive work.

For the majority of libraries, the most accessible and comprehensive general biographical sources, apart from the general encyclopaedias, will be the single-volume dictionaries:

CHAMBERS BIOGRAPHICAL DICTIONARY. Rev ed. Edinburgh: Chambers, 1974.

WEBSTER'S BIOGRAPHICAL DICTIONARY. Latest ed. Springfield, Massachusetts: Merriam, 1980.

The entries in these two works are necessarily short, but their comprehensive coverage often provides quick verification of a person's dates and brief outline of his life. They can be useful as a starting point for a biographical enquiry, by giving some idea of the period, nationality and occupation of a person, of whom little was known initially. *Chambers biographical dictionary*, first published in 1897, now contains over 15,000 entries, plus a supplement of new biographies. The sketches contain a pronunciation guide for unusual names, dates, brief outline of the person's life and works, and occasional bibliographical references. Subject indexes cover 'Art and architecture', 'Explorations', 'Nicknames', and other useful topics. *Webster's biographical dictionary* is very comprehensive, with over 40,000 brief biographies; it also contains pronunciation guidance, and at the end useful lists of world leaders and monarchs. Rather better than either for important contemporaries is: B. Jones and M. V. Dixon *Macmillan dictionary of biography* (London: Macmillan, 1981) which has 7,000 short, well-written entries with bibliographical references.

Two general works are useful biographical sources, despite not having recent editions: J. Thomas *Universal pronouncing dictionary of biography and mythology* (5th ed. Philadelphia: Lippincott, 1930), known as *Lippincott's biographical dictionary*, lists both real and mythological persons in one alphabetical sequence; and *The new Century cyclopedia of names* (New York: Appleton-Century-Crofts, 1954) which contains more than 100,000 entries, about one-third of which are biographical, for literary and

Biographical Reference Works

mythological characters, as well as real persons, and excellent appendices of lists of world rulers and heads of state.

Some general biographical dictionaries are intended primarily for study purposes, or younger readers:

THE McGRAW-HILL ENCYCLOPAEDIA OF WORLD BI-OGRAPHY. New York/London: McGraw-Hill, 1973. 12 vols.

'Designed to meet a growing need in school and college libraries', this work contains 5,000 illustrated, clearly arranged, signed, short biographies. The coverage is broad, with the Third World well represented, and contemporary, as well as historical, personages. It has a 'study guide' volume of biographees listed within a structured, curricula-related, subject and historical outline, with indexes of biographees and subjects. Similar single-volume works are: *Purnell's encyclopaedia of famous people* (Maidenhead: Purnell, 1980), which has over 1,000 illustrated, outline biographies; and *Who did what: The Mitchell Beazley illustrated biographical dictionary* (London: Mitchell Beazley, 1979), whose 5,000 entries briefly list 'the essential achievements of the people who shaped our world'.

Current universal biographical dictionaries

Most libraries will have at least one of the following current international biographical dictionaries, offering short uniform sketches for quick reference. They are useful because, if the nationality of the person is not known, they save searching through numerous national 'Who's whos' which, even if a full selection was available, would not be as up to date:

THE INTERNATIONAL WHO'S WHO. 1935–   . 47th ed, 1983–1984. London: Europa, 1983. Annual.

THE INTERNATIONAL YEAR BOOK AND STATESMAN'S WHO'S WHO. 1953–   . 1983 ed. East Grinstead: Thomas Skinner Directories, 1983. Annual.

Universal Biographical Dictionaries

WHO'S WHO IN THE WORLD. 1st ed, 1971–1972; 6th ed, 1982–1983. Chicago: Marquis, 1982. Irregular.

The international who's who contains over 15,000 entries, representing world-wide coverage of heads of state, government and military officials, diplomats, and prominent persons from the law, business, arts, sciences and the professions. The entries, arranged alphabetically, give name, title, date of birth, nationality, education, profession, career, present position, honours, publications, and address. Entries are compiled and checked by the biographee. Lists of the world's reigning royal families, with biographies of each monarch, and the year's obituaries precede the biographies. A reliable work that is a first source for internationally known contemporaries. *The international year book and statesman's who's who* is a general reference work on international and national organizations, and countries of the world; its third part is a biographical section containing over 6,500 entries. Biased towards government officials, politicians and military officers, with only about one-third overlap with the previous work. A relatively new work, broader in coverage than the previous two, is *Who's who in the world*, published by Marquis, the American biography specialists. The entries, similar to those in the previous works, reflect American origin by also including biographees' 'civic and political activities', 'religious and political affiliation', and 'lodges and social clubs'. Entries, though initially compiled from biographees' own data, are often rewritten by Marquis staff.

Two American periodical publications provide popular biographical articles that help bring to life 'Who's who' entries:

CURRENT BIOGRAPHY. 1940– . New York: H. W. Wilson. Monthly; annual cumulation.

'THE NEW YORK TIMES' BIOGRAPHICAL SERVICE. 1970– . New York: Arno Press. Monthly.

Current biography contains lively articles on about 350 international celebrities annually; mostly statesmen, politicians, writers, performers, and sports personalities. The entry, usually two or three pages in length, with recent photograph, contains full names, birthdate, and address, followed by a chatty article quoting liberally from the biographee and others, including useful personal information unlikely to be found elsewhere, such as height and colour of eyes. The entry concludes with bibliographical references, mostly newspaper and periodical articles. Biographees check the entry before publication. Each monthly issue carries a cumulative index for the current year; the annual volume, which reprints the year's articles in one alphabetical sequence, also contains a cumulative index to all preceding volumes of the decade, a professions' index and obituaries of the year. A *Current biography cumulated index, 1940–70* (New York: H. W. Wilson, 1973) has appeared. *'The New York Times' biographical service* offers between 100 and 150 photomechanically reproduced biographical articles, interviews, and obituaries from the newspaper in each monthly issue. Published in loose-leaf format with a monthly, six-monthly and annual index, its coverage is international, although biased towards Americans. It is particularly useful on people currently in the news, and can rectify omissions in reference books.

NATIONAL OR AREA BIOGRAPHICAL DICTIONARIES

Today the standard pattern of biographical dictionaries for most countries is a retrospective dictionary of deceased notables, and one or more quick-reference 'Who's whos' for important contemporaries.

Retrospective

Most important within this category are the 'official' national biographical dictionaries, usually multi-volume works of unimpeachable authority, containing lengthy, scholarly articles, researched from original sources, and including substantial bibliographies. They are the most authoritative source of biography of a nation's eminent predecessors. Such works, seen as symbols of national prestige, are today established as part of a new nation's 'coming of age':

National or Area Biographical Dictionaries

DICTIONARY OF NATIONAL BIOGRAPHY. London: Smith, Elder, 1885–1901. 63 vols; reissue: 1908–1909. 22 vols; 2nd–8th SUPPLEMENTS, 1901–1970. Oxford: Oxford University Press, 1912–1981.

This fine achievement of Victorian ambition, perseverance, and attention to detail, is the most important reference work of English biography, and the pioneer of national biographical dictionaries. It was initiated by the original publisher, George Smith, whose heirs presented it in 1917 to the Oxford University Press, which has published it and the various supplements ever since.[8] Sir Leslie Stephen, the first editor and a major contributor, who supplied 820 of the original 29,120 biographies, was succeeded by Sir Sydney Lee in 1888. The work covers notable persons from Great Britain, Ireland, and the Colonies, including America during the Colonial period, from the early Britons to the present century, including legendary figures such as Cymbeline and King Arthur. The original work is revised by *Corrections and additions to the Dictionary of National Biography, cumulated from the Bulletin of the Institute of Historical Research, University of London, covering the years 1923–63* (Boston: G. K. Hall, 1966). The basic work is updated through decennial supplements, each containing a cumulative index of twentieth-century biographies. The lengthy, signed articles, researched where possible from original sources and private papers, were written by specialist contributors, including such notables as Wilkie Collins and James Ramsay MacDonald. Entries have extensive bibliographies, and portraits and memorials are often indicated. A micrographic edition of the basic set, plus the supplements to 1960, is now available as *The compact edition of the Dictionary of National Biography* (Oxford: Oxford University Press, 1975. 2 vols, with reading glass). The *Concise dictionary of national biography* (Oxford: Oxford University Press, 1953 and 1982. 2 vols), originally the *Index and epitome*, contains brief versions of all entries in the full set up to 1970, and is, therefore, both an index to the work and abstract of its articles, as well as a biographical dictionary.

The national biographies of Germany, France, Italy, and the United States are similar in scope to *DNB*, on which they are modelled, offering long, well-researched, signed articles with bibliographies, arranged alphabetically. Germany has two overlapping sets; the *Allgemeine deutsche Biographie* (Leipzig: Duncker und Humblot, 1875-1912. 56 vols) containing 23,000 biographies for persons who died before 1899; and the *Neue deutsche Biographie* (Berlin: Duncker und Humblot, 1953-   ) which is currently updating the earlier work with persons who died between 1899 and 1953. The French and Italian national biographical dictionaries are still in progress: the *Dictionnaire de biographie française* (Paris: Letouzey, 1929-   ); and the *Dizionario biografico degli italiani* (Rome: Istituto della Enciclopedia Italiana, 1960-   ). The *Dictionary of American biography* (New York: Scribner, 1928-1937. 21 vols); *Supplements* 1-6, 1935-1960 (New York: Scribner, 1944-1980) was initiated by the American Council of Learned Societies. The term 'American', widely interpreted, includes persons born in the United States or the older colonies, naturalized Americans, and those identified with America through association or contribution. The dictionary and its supplements, bringing it up to date, contain approximately 17,000 signed biographies by such notable contributors as Carl Sandburg; the Index volume consists of six indexes: to biographees; contributors; contributors' articles; birth-places of biographees; occupations; and 'distinctive topics' covered. The *Concise dictionary of American biography* (New York: Scribner, 1964) abridges the biographies of the original work, and is a useful quick-reference biographical dictionary.

Not all national biographical dictionaries adopt alphabetical arrangement; some more recent projects have opted for a chronological approach. The *Australian dictionary of biography* (Melbourne: University Press, 1966-   ; *Vol 1-2: 1788-1850.* 1966-1967; *Vol 3-6: 1851-1890.* 1969-1976; *Vol 7-8: 1891-1939, A-Gib.* 1979-1981), is a truly national project, supported by the Australian National University. The selection, from convict settlers to politicians and administrators, is very egalitarian. A person is placed in the period when he did his most important work; if that overlaps two periods the earlier is chosen. When completed, a general index volume to the estimated 7,000 biographies in the set will be prepared. A similar chronological arrangement is adopted by the *Dict-*

National or Area Biographical Dictionaries

ionary of Canadian biography (Toronto: University of Toronto Press, 1966–   ) in which each volume covers a specified period from AD 1000 to the present. Persons are placed in the volume for the period when they died. Selection, as in the Australian work, is very wide, from pioneers and fur-traders, to Governors-General. Canada being a bilingual country, there are English and French parallel editions. Each volume contains excellent historical introductions to the period covered, putting the biographies in context. Name, occupation, and geographical cumulative indexes are being published. The advantage of the chronological approach is its historical perspective; the works become historical as well as biographical, reflecting Carlyle's view that 'History is but the essence of innumerable biographies'.

There are extensive works for many countries that are not the 'official' national biographies, but because of their scope and comprehensiveness are as highly valued:

Boase, F. MODERN ENGLISH BIOGRAPHY. Truro: Netherton, 1892–1921. 6 vols; London: Frank Cass; reprint 1965.

Frederic Boase researched his monumental work from *The Times, Illustrated London News*, local newspapers, transactions of learned societies, and church registers. It contains over 30,000 short biographies—a greater coverage of national and local celebrities for 1850–1900 than *DNB*. Great trouble was taken in checking, at Somerset House, exact birth and death dates. Portraits in books, periodicals and newspapers are listed. Four other works supplement *DNB* for British and Irish biography: R. Chambers *A biographical dictionary of eminent Scotsmen* (new ed. Glasgow: Blackie, 1855. 5 vols); *The dictionary of Welsh biography down to 1940* (London: Honourable Society of Cymmrodorion, 1959); J. S. Crone *A concise dictionary of Irish biography* (2nd ed. Dublin: Talbot Press, 1937); and H. Boylan *A dictionary of Irish biography* (Dublin: Gill and Macmillan, 1978). Two similar works exist for the United States, both comprehensive and offering lengthy articles with portraits and autograph facsimiles: *Appleton's cyclopaedia of American biography* (New York: Appleton, 1888–1900. 7 vols; Detroit: Gale; reprint 1968), now largely superseded by *DAB*; and the *National cyclopaedia of American biography* (permanent series, 1892–   ;

current series, 1930–   , New York: White), which in 74 volumes by 1982 had included in both its series full biographies for over 66,000 Americans, both living and dead, with a cumulated index volume. Each volume of the *Dictionary of African biography* (New York: Reference Publications Inc, 1977–   ), sponsored by the Encyclopaedia Africana, covers a couple of countries, with an authoritative history, followed by short, signed biographies; the two volumes issued so far, of the projected twenty, cover Ethiopia, Ghana, Sierra Leone, and Zaire.

Another type of retrospective national biographical dictionary is the 'Who was who', consisting of entries removed from the 'Who's who' on the biographees' death:

WHO WAS WHO, 1897–1980. London: Black, 1920–1981. 7 vols; *Who was who: a cumulated index 1897–1980.* London: Black, 1981.

WHO WAS WHO IN AMERICA, 1897–1981. Chicago: Marquis, 1942–1981. 7 vols; *Historical volume, 1607–1896.* 1963; *Index 1607–1981.* 1981.

These bridge the gap between the current *'Who's who'* and the older retrospective national biographies, and often include people not included in *DNB* or *DAB*. *Who was who* contains biographical sketches, basically unchanged since the last inclusion in *Who's who*, with the date of death added, but in some cases edited and updated. *Who was who in America* has added a historical volume covering the period 1607 to 1896 to pre-date the main set of removed entries from *Who's who in America*; later volumes add the place and name of the cemetery where the person was buried, as well as the death date.

Obituaries from newspapers, periodicals and yearbooks are invaluable biographical material. Many quality newspapers and periodicals, including the *New York Times*, *The Times* and *Illustrated London News*, have their own indexes for research purposes:

THE NEW YORK TIMES OBITUARIES INDEX, 1858–1968. New York: The Times, 1970; *New York Times obituaries index, 1969–79.* Glen Rock, New Jersey: Microfilming Corporation, 1980.

National or Area Biographical Dictionaries

OBITUARIES FROM 'THE TIMES', 1951–75. Reading: Newspaper Archive Developments, 1975–1979. 3 vols.

The *New York Times Obituaries Index* is a straightforward index to over 350,000 obituary notices from 1858 to 1979, later obituaries being included in the *New York Times biographical service* (q.v.). *Obituaries from 'The Times'* is both an index to all the newspaper's obituary notices, and a collected biography containing a selection of those for the major national and international figures who died during the period 1951–1975, reprinted without rewriting, and therefore representing the contemporary view of the subject before later reassessment.

The annual obituary (1980–   . New York: St Martin's Press; London: Macmillan, 1981–   ) contains in each annual volume over 400 illustrated, specially written, evaluative obituaries for internationally prominent persons dying during the year, arranged chronologically by death date, with alphabetical, professions' and obituary writers' indexes, which cumulate in each edition. Many general yearbooks, like *The annual register* (1758–   . London: Longman), also contain useful obituaries.

Finally a category of works which offer different, often highly specialized, approaches to retrospective biography. Interesting examples answer specific questions—'What did they look like?' 'What did their signature look like?' 'What did their contemporaries say about them?' and 'Who was it who gave their name to that word?'. G. Uden *They looked like this* (Oxford: Blackwell, 1965) and its companion volume, *They looked like this (Europe)* (Oxford: Blackwell, 1966) aim to 'give eyewitness accounts of the physical appearances of the great figures of history' by selecting extracts from contemporary diaries, letters, and journals. The finding of reproductions of the signatures of historical personages, often a slow process, is now made easier by R. Rawlins *Four hundred years of British autographs* (London: Dent, 1970) which gathers together 1,000 facsimile autographs of monarchs, statesmen, politicians, and the famous from all fields of endeavour, with brief biographical details and descriptions of the autograph, its date and source. *The Penguin dictionary of biographical quotation*, edited by J. Wintle and R. Kenin (Harmondsworth: Penguin Books, 1981), contains

Biographical Reference Works

10,000 'good' contemporary, or later, quotations about 1,300 notable deceased Britons and Americans. C. L. Beeching *A dictionary of eponyms* (London: Bingley, 1979) is arranged alphabetically by eponym, eg Biro, Bowler Hat, Dow-Jones Index, Sandwich, Yale Lock, etc, each entry giving a biography of the person whose name is now a commonly used word, with a description of its use.

Current

The standard current biographical dictionary in most countries is the 'Who's who', a regularly published collection of biographical sketches of important people from all walks of life, often compiled from information from the biographee:

WHO'S WHO. 1849–   . 1983 ed. London: Black, 1983. Annual.

This notable 'first', the model for all later 'Who's whos', began in 1849 as a slim handbook of the titled and official classes, containing only lists of names; it changed to its present format of alphabetically arranged, biographical sketches in 1897. The coverage is primarily British and Commonwealth citizens, though some international figures from other countries are included. It represents a broad spectrum of achievement in politics, central and local government, the armed forces, commerce, industry, the professions, and the arts, as well as those with hereditary titles. Selection is by the publisher solely according to merit, and once included, the entry normally remains until the biographee's death, so inclusion is of considerable prestige. The entries are compiled initially from information supplied by the biographee, and then subsequently updated by the biographee annually checking and revising the entry. This method usually results in accurate, up-to-date entries, but has to rely on the vagaries of the biographees—birth dates, education and early career being items often omitted. The entry usually contains full names, title, honours with dates received, current position, birth-place and date, parents' names, marital state, and name of spouse and number of children, education, career, publi-

National or Area Biographical Dictionaries

cations, recreations, address, and clubs. Late information on biographees, received since the press date, is listed in a pink supplement at the beginning.

Modelled on *Who's who*, the following works have the same arrangement and type of entry, with slight variations in scope, frequency of publication, and method of compilation. The term 'Who's who' itself has become completely international: *Who's who in France* (1953–   . 16th ed, 1983–1984. Paris: Lafitte, 1982. Biennial), despite its title, is in French, for example. *Who's who in Germany* (1955–   . 8th ed, 1982–1983. Munich: Who's Who Verlag, 1983. 2 vols) contains biographies, in English, for West Germany, compiled through personal interviews, rather than the questionnaire method, which the publishers found unsatisfactory for their national and subject 'Who's Who Guides'; these also include, amongst others, *Who's who in Austria* (10th ed, 1982) and *Who's who in technology* (2nd ed, 1983). The German language 'Who's who', *Wer ist wer?* (1905–   . 22nd ed, 1983. Frankfurt: Schmidt-Römhild, 1983. Irregular) contains 40,000 biographies of West Germans, some Swiss and Austrians.

Almost as long established as *Who's who* itself is *Who's who in America* (1899–   . 42nd ed, 1982–1983. Chicago: Marquis, 1982. 2 vols, biennial). It currently includes 75,000 notables from the United States, Canada and Mexico, and contains indexes of biographees deleted in the latest edition due to retirement or death, and those appearing in the Marquis companion regional volumes. It has, in common with other 'Who's whos', planted fictitious biographies, to check pirating by rivals who might unwisely reprint its material, including the 'ghost' entries, and thereby be proved guilty of infringement of copyright. *Who's who in Australia* (1906–   . 23rd ed. Melbourne: Herald and Weekly Times, 1980. Triennial) contains in addition to its 12,000 biographies, lists of Australian Nobel Prize winners and recipients of honours and titles. Special features such as these, or photographs, are useful in 'Who's whos'. Illustrated works are becoming more usual: an early example, *Who's who in Canada* (1907–   . 1982–1983 ed. Toronto: International Press, 1982. Annual), has photographs for two-thirds

Biographical Reference Works

of the biographees, unlike its more traditional and authoritative rival the *Canadian who's who* (1910–   . Vol 17. Toronto: University of Toronto, 1982). Finally a variant on the usual alphabetical arrangement—a classified work—the *India who's who* (1969–   . 12th ed, 1980–1981. New Delhi: INFA Publications, 1980. Annual) has biographical sketches arranged by profession, with an alphabetical index.

Another type of area 'Who's who' is that which covers a continent, or group of countries linked geographically, racially or culturally:

WHO'S WHO IN EUROPE. 4th ed, 1980–1981. Brussels: Servi-Tech, 1980. Irregular.

This work contains over 42,000 persons from all 28 countries of Europe, except Turkey, in one alphabetical sequence; French is used, except for titles of biographees' publications, which are in the original language. Another work for a continent, the *Africa who's who* (1st ed. London: Africa Journals Ltd, 1981), covers all Organization of African Unity states, and South Africa and Zimbabwe.

WHO'S WHO IN THE ARAB WORLD. 1965–   . 6th ed, 1981–1982. Beirut: Publitec, 1981. Irregular.

A general reference work containing an outline of the Arab world, surveys of 20 Arab countries from Algeria to the Yemen, excluding Iran and Lebanon, and a 'Who's who' of 4,000 prominent figures, in this group of nations linked by religion, race and cultural background. Two similar works use English as the 'lingua franca': *Dictionary of Scandinavian biography* (2nd ed. Cambridge: International Biographical Centre, 1976), which covers the five geographically and historically linked countries of Denmark, Norway, Sweden, Finland and Iceland; and *Who's who in the Commonwealth* (1st ed. Cambridge: International Biographical Centre, 1982), which covers this 'important group of nations, larger in both area and population than the USA, USSR, or China'.

A final category of area biographical dictionary is the local 'Who's who', limited in coverage to a region, local administrative

Specialized Biographical Dictionaries

unit, or town. In Victorian Britain, local and civic pride found expression in the illustrated county biographical works, such as *Norfolk notabilities* (1893) and *Suffolk celebrities* (1893); and the later series of town and county 'Who's whos', *Who's who in Cheltenham* (1910) and *Who's who in Berkshire* (1936).[9] Now almost non-existent in Britain, except for occasional examples such as *The Birmingham Post year book and who's who* (34th ed, 1982–1983. Birmingham: The Post, 1982), local 'Who's whos' still exist in the United States, where such works as *Who's who in New York* (1960) and *Who's who in California* (1976) have appeared, as have the Marquis series of regional companion volumes to their *Who's who in America* (q.v.); *Who's who in the West* is an example.

SPECIALIZED BIOGRAPHICAL DICTIONARIES

Specialized biographical dictionaries are probably the largest and most diverse group of reference books discussed in this chapter, covering almost every subject, occupation, profession, and type of publication. I can, therefore, only indicate a few main types and subject areas.

Retrospective

Collected biographies of special groups of persons have a long history, extending back to Greek literature, an early example, Diogenes Laertius' *Lives of eminent philosophers*, of the third century AD, establishing the genre of 'short lives' with bibliographies. By the eighteenth and nineteenth centuries, such specialized collections as Samuel Johnson's *Lives of the poets* (1779–1781) were an established literary form, and many appearing then, such as Alban Butler's *Lives of the saints* (1756–1759) and Samuel Smiles' *Lives of the engineers* (1862), are still standard works. From these developed the scholarly biographical dictionaries, for various subject areas, that we have today:

Thieme, U. and Becker, F. ALLGEMEINES LEXIKON DER

Biographical Reference Works

BILDENDEN KÜNSTLER VON DER ANTIKE BIS ZUR GE-GENWART. 1st ed. Leipzig: Englemann & Seeman, 1907–1950. 37 vols.

Bénézit, E. DICTIONNAIRE CRITIQUE ET DOCUMEN-TAIRE DES PEINTRES, SCULPTEURS, DESSINATEURS ET GRAVEURS . . . 1st ed. 1911–1923; 3rd ed. Paris: Grund, 1976. 10 vols.

DICTIONARY OF SCIENTIFIC BIOGRAPHY. New York: Scribner, 1970–1980. 16 vols.

The German and French works are the most comprehensive biographical dictionaries for the visual arts. Thieme/Becker, with its complementary volume, H. Vollmer *Allgemeines Lexikon der bildenden Künstler des XX. Jahrhunderts* (Leipzig: Seeman, 1953–1962. 6 vols), is the more comprehensive of the two, containing approximately 50,000 entries. The alphabetically arranged articles, the longer of which are signed, give brief personal details, followed by a narrative of the artist's life and works, with an exhaustive bibliography. Bénézit has 'a narrower view of the visual arts' than Thieme/Becker, architects, photographers, and designers being poorly represented.[10] Despite a European bias, Oriental artists are included. The entries contain brief personal details with an outline of the artist's life, followed by a list of museums with works represented; the sale prices fetched at auctions and art galleries; and occasional sketchy bibliographies. As their coverage is inevitably selective, both these works are primarily retrospective. There is no comparable work for artists in English; *Bryan's dictionary of painters and engravers* (4th ed. London: Bell, 1903–1904. 5 vols; Port Washington: Kennikat Press, reprint 1964), with 20,000 entries, is neither as comprehensive nor as up to date. An example of a similar work for scientists is the *Dictionary of scientific biography*, an authoritative work sponsored by the American Council of Learned Societies. It contains over 5,000 biographical essays on scientists from more than sixty countries; these essays include brief personal details, followed by signed articles including quotations, diagrams, and formulae illustrating the subject's work, and a bibliography of

Specialized Biographical Dictionaries

original and secondary sources. A supplement and index volumes have been issued.

Subject dictionaries and companions can be useful sources of biographical information, despite the often short entries. Described by Walford as 'the standard one volume encyclopaedia for the theatre', the *Oxford companion to the theatre*, edited by Phyllis Hartnoll (4th ed. London: Oxford University Press, 1983), contains a large proportion of biographical entries giving short outlines of the careers of actors, playwrights and directors. A similar work is J. R. Taylor *Penguin dictionary of the theatre* (London: Penguin Books, 1970). Both works are part of uniform series covering most subjects.

Current

Firstly, current biographical dictionaries for those working within broad categories of occupation—the 'arts' or 'sciences':

WHO'S WHO IN ART. 1927–   . 20th ed. Havant: Art Trade Press, 1982. Irregular.

WHO'S WHO IN AMERICAN ART. 1935–   . 15th ed. New York: Bowker, 1982. Biennial.

AMERICAN MEN AND WOMEN OF SCIENCE. 1906–   . 15th ed. New York: Bowker, 1982. 8 vols. Triennial.

WHO'S WHO IN SCIENCE IN EUROPE. 1967–   . 3rd ed. Guernsey: Francis Hodgson, 1978. 4 vols. Irregular.

Who's who in art aims to produce a comprehensive list of living artists in Britain, but is actually limited to those who want to appear: mostly art teachers, though some professional artists. The entries include art qualifications, type of work, art college attended, exhibitions, work in permanent collections, publications, signature, and address. Rather broader in scope is *Who's who in American art*, covering American and Canadian artists, art historians, critics, teachers, and museum personnel. Similar works for the 'arts' are: *Who's who in the theatre* (1912– . 17th ed. Detroit: Gale, 1982. Irregular), described as 'the portable memory of the British theatre', with its detailed biographies and useful lists and indexes; *International authors and writers who's who* (1934– . 9th ed. Cambridge: International Biographical Centre, 1982. Irregular); and the *International who's who in music and musicians' directory* (1935– . 9th ed. Cambridge: Melrose, 1980. Irregular). The mammoth *American men and women of science*, in its latest edition, contains over 150,000 American and Canadian scientists in universities, industry, foundations, and government projects at home and abroad. The criteria for selection are: achievement in the particular science; important published research; or position. The entry contains birthdate; area of specialization; education and degrees; career to date with current position; detailed information on research; publications; and mailing address. Available online from Lockheed Dialog and Bibliographical Retrieval Services 1982– , it is published in two sections: physical and biological sciences, and social and behavioral sciences; both having discipline and geographical indexes. The 50,000 entries in *Who's who in science in Europe* are less detailed, with little information about past career or publications. It now covers scientists from Eastern and Western Europe working in universities, research establishments, and industry.

Current biographical dictionaries for the professions—traditionally the Church, the Law and Medicine—but nowadays most occupations for which qualifying examinations are necessary, such as architecture, engineering, and even librarianship, are of a standard type, giving general information about the profession, as well as brief biographies of its members:

CROCKFORD'S CLERICAL DIRECTORY. 1858– . 88th (possibly the final) ed, 1980–1982. London: Oxford University Press, 1983. Irregular.

THE BAR LIST OF THE UNITED KINGDOM. 1977– . 1983 ed. London: Stevens, 1983. Annual.

Specialized Biographical Dictionaries

THE MEDICAL DIRECTORY. 1845–   . 139th issue, London: Churchill, 1983. Annual.

Professional directories, as in these for the 'learned' professions, rarely give personal details in the biographical entries, only such information relevant to the profession, such as qualifications, career, and professional publications. *Crockford's*, the standard reference work of the Anglican clergy, has information on how to address the clergy, a biographical section, and indexes of parishes of the Church of England. The biographies of the clergy give only name, birthdate, education, degree, dates of ordination, and career outline, with Church positions held. The biographical entries for barristers in *The Bar List*, which replaced *The Law List* (1841–1976), are even briefer, giving only name, degree, Inn of Court and date when called to the Bar, address and Circuit. *The medical directory*, in addition to lists of Health Authorities, medical schools, and hospitals in Britain and Ireland, contains short biographies of qualified members of the medical profession, giving degrees, medical school attended, current post, previous positions, and professional publications.

Collected biographies of writers often contain essay-type entries, with critiques and full bibliographies:

Vinson, J. CONTEMPORARY NOVELISTS. 3rd ed. London: Macmillan, 1982.

CONTEMPORARY AUTHORS. 1962–   . Vol 106. Detroit: Gale, 1982; *New revision series*. 1981–   . Vol 7, 1982; *Permanent series*. 1975–   . Vol 2, 1978.

Contemporary novelists covers over 500 notable living writers, mostly British and American. Each entry includes a brief biographical sketch, a full bibliography, critical studies of his/her work, comments from the author, and a signed critique from an authoritative contributor. Companion volumes in this useful series are: *Contemporary dramatists* (3rd ed, 1982) and *Contemporary poets* (3rd ed, 1980). As writers now 'move more rapidly from one area of communication to another, the medium is less significant than the communicator', so the American *Contemporary authors* aims to be a current source on over 70,000 writers from all media,

Biographical Reference Works

including the press, broadcasting, and films. Biographical entries include personal details, career, checklist of writings, work in progress, comments from the author, and further sources of biography and criticism. Similar works, though more retrospective in coverage, are: *Twentieth century authors*, edited by S. J. Kunitz and H. Haycraft (New York: H. W. Wilson, 1942; *First supplement*, 1953), and its companion volumes *World authors* 1950–1970 and 1970–1975, edited by J. Wakeman (1975 and 1980), which contain short essays with photograph and bibliography. There are increasing numbers of 'Who's whos' of writers in particular genres, examples being: B. Doyle *Who's who of children's literature* (London: Hugh Evelyn, 1968), and B. Ash *Who's who in science fiction* (London: Elm Tree Books, 1976).

'Who's whos' for British politicians illustrate the varying, but equally valid, approaches that biographical dictionaries can have to the same material:

DOD'S PARLIAMENTARY COMPANION. 1832–   . 1983 ed. London: Dod's, 1983. Annual.

'THE TIMES' GUIDE TO THE HOUSE OF COMMONS. 1880–   . June, 1983 ed. London: Times Books, 1983. Irregular.

Roth, A. THE MPs' CHART. 1980 ed. London: Parliamentary Profiles, 1979. Irregular, with updating service.

Dod's parliamentary companion contains illustrated biographical sketches for members of both Houses of Parliament, concentrating on their parliamentary career. *'The Times' guide to the House of Commons*, issued after each British General Election, gives brief biographies for both the successful and unsuccessful candidates for each parliamentary constituency, together with voting figures, arranged by constituency with a name index. Entries for the successful candidates—the MPs—have photographs. Andrew Roth's *The MPs' chart*, designed to give 'instant insight into the place, position and character of individual MPs', gives, in addition to standard biographical information, details of political outlook and 'traits', the latter providing such irreverent, quotable thumb-nail sketches as 'Iron Maiden in blue chiffon' for Margaret Thatcher.

Specialized Biographical Dictionaries

Biography and lineage of members of the British royal family and aristocracy are contained in several long-established genealogical works:

BURKE'S GENEALOGICAL AND HERALDIC HISTORY OF THE PEERAGE, BARONETAGE AND KNIGHTAGE. 1826– . 105th ed. London: Burke's Peerage, 1970; 4th impression, 1980. Irregular.

DEBRETT'S PEERAGE AND BARONETAGE. 1769– . 1980 ed. London: Debrett's Peerage, 1979. Irregular.

DEBRETT'S HANDBOOK. 1982– . London: Debrett's Peerage, 1981.

Burke's peerage has full heraldic details of each member of the royal family, the royal lineage, biographies and lineage of peers, baronets and knights. *Debrett's peerage* does not give such complete lineage as *Burke's peerage*, but has useful sections on orders of knighthood and chivalry, names of chiefs and clans of Scotland, and advice on forms of address for titled persons. *Debrett's handbook*, which succeeds *Kelly's handbook to the titled, landed and official classes* (1880–1977), contains, in one alphabetical sequence, brief biographies for those with hereditary and honorary titles, MPs, senior government officials, businessmen, and those prominent in public and social life 'who both create and spend wealth'; it includes many people not included in *Burke's*, *Debrett's*, or *Who's who*. Biography and lineage of world royalty and aristocracy are covered by: *Annuaire de la noblesse de France et de l'Europe* (1843– . 89th vol. Neuilly-sur-Seine: La Nobiliaire, 1960. Irregular), and its English edition *Royalty, peerage and nobility of the world* (91st vol. London: Annuaire de France, 1976); *Burke's royal families of the world*: Vol 1 *Europe and Latin America*; Vol 2 *Africa and the Middle East* (London: Burke's Peerage, 1977; 1980.); the *Almanach de Gotha* (1763–1944. Gotha: Perthes); and the *Genealogisches Handbuch des Adels* (1951– . Limburg: C. A. Starke, in progress).

Lists of members of societies and academies, exhibitors in art

Biographical Reference Works

exhibitions, and of university and public school alumni, can be useful sources of biographical information. *The biographical memoirs of the Fellows of the Royal Society* (1955– . Annual), continuing the *Obituary notices of Fellows of the Royal Society* (1932–1954), contains lengthy biographical essays, with portraits and complete bibliographies. Lists of exhibitors include: A. Graves *The Royal Academy of Arts: A complete dictionary of contributors and their work from its foundation in 1769 to 1904* (London: Henry Graves, 1905; Bath: S. R. Publishers and Kingsmead Reprints, 1970), its supplement *Royal Academy exhibitors 1905–1970* (Wakefield: E. P. Publishing, 1973–1982. 6 vols); and M. Bradshaw *Royal Society of British Artists: Members exhibiting, 1824–1962* (Leigh-on-sea: F. Lewis, 1973–1977. 5 vols). Notable examples of historical lists of ex-students of universities are: J. Foster *Alumni oxonienses: The Members of the University of Oxford, 1500–1714/1715–1886* (Oxford: Parker, 1891–1892, 4 vols/1888, 4 vols; Liechtenstein: Kraus Reprint, 1968); and J. and J. A. Venn *Alumni cantabrigienses: A biographical list of all known students, graduates and holders of office at the University of Cambridge to 1900* (Cambridge: Cambridge University Press, 1922–1954. 10 vols; Liechtenstein: Kraus Reprint, 1974). Similar lists exist for some British public schools, an example being the *Rugby School Register 1675–1921* (Rugby: The School, 1901–1929. 5 vols).

Finally, not all biographical enquiries will be for people who actually existed; some will concern characters from folklore, mythology, or fiction. Written by a foremost authority on British and Irish folklore, Katharine Briggs, the *Dictionary of fairies, hobgoblins, brownies, bogies and other supernatural creatures* (London: Allen Lane, 1976; new ed. Penguin Books, 1977) gives 'biographies', with quotations and bibliographies. Many classical and mythological dictionaries give information on characters from Greek and Roman mythology, as does: M. Grant and J. Hazel *Who's who in classical mythology* (London: Hodder, 1979). For finding out who particular fictional characters are, and which book they appear in, W. Freeman *Dictionary of fictional characters* (London: Dent, 3rd ed, 1973) is an invaluable source, from which one progresses in many cases to a readers' guide or companion to a particular author's works, offering popular outlines of the characters: G. Leeming *Who's who in Thomas Hardy* (London: Elm Tree Books, 1975) is an example. Specifically for characters in children's fiction is M. Fisher *Who's who in children's books* (London: Weidenfeld, 1975).

BIOGRAPHY PERIODICALS

Current biographical articles are sometimes published initially in periodical form, as with *Current biography* (q.v.) or *'The New York Times' biographical service* (q.v.). Some specialized periodicals exist, such as *The celebrity bulletin* (1952–   . London: Celebrity Service Ltd. Twice weekly), a service for the media, which lists 'celebrities' visiting London, and where they are staying. Other biography periodicals can be found listed in *Ulrich's international periodicals directory*.

BIOGRAPHY. Honolulu, Hawaii: Biographical Research Center/ University Press of Hawaii. Vol 1, No 1, Winter 1978–   . Quarterly.

An academic journal offering 'a forum for all well-considered biographical scholarship', with lengthy articles, reviews of individual and collected biographies, and an annual bibliography of 'lifewriting'.

BIBLIOGRAPHICAL GUIDES AND INDEXES TO BIOGRAPHY

Collected biographies

This category contains bibliographical guides and indexes to the contents of general, national, and specialized biographical dictionaries, which are invaluable as short cuts to lengthy biographical searches. In some cases, these guides may refer to rather obscure sources not immediately available; however they can prove useful

Biographical Reference Works

for identification of the subject of a search, and for giving further sources for the researcher:

Brewer, A. BIOGRAPHY ALMANAC. Detroit: Gale, 1981.

Hyamson, A. M. A DICTIONARY OF UNIVERSAL BIOGRAPHY OF ALL AGES AND ALL PEOPLES. 2nd ed. London: Routledge; Detroit: Gale, reprint 1981.

Riches, P. M. AN ANALYTICAL BIBLIOGRAPHY OF UNIVERSAL COLLECTED BIOGRAPHY. London: Library Association, 1934; Detroit: Gale, reprint 1980.

Most libraries should have these bibliographies, which list alphabetically the names of biographees, with dates and brief identifying description, and then collected biographical works which contain entries for them. The *Biography almanac* is a guide to over 20,000 'newsmakers from Biblical times to the present' in 325 biographical dictionaries, including the *Dictionary of American biography* and the *International motion picture almanac*. Hyamson contains over 100,000 biographies appearing in 24 collected biographies and general reference works, including the *Annual register*, *Dictionary of national biography* and *Allgemeine deutsche Biographie*. In Riches, the 'Analytical Index', in Part 1, contains 56,000 name entries, with reference to over 3,000 English-language collected biographies; Part 2 contains full bibliographical details for all the works analysed, and chronological and subject indexes of biographees. An older, though still useful, guide is: L. B. Phillips *Dictionary of biographical reference* (London: Low, 1889; Detroit: Gale, reprint 1981).

Similar indexes to the sources of biography are currently appearing:

Lobies, J.-P. INDEX BIO-BIBLIOGRAPHICUS NOTORUM HOMINUM Osnabruck: Biblio Verlag, 1972– .

ESSAY AND GENERAL LITERATURE INDEX. 1900– . New York: H. W. Wilson, 1934– . Six-monthly, annual, and five-year cumulations.

Bibliographical Guides and Indexes to Biography

BIOGRAPHY AND GENEALOGY MASTER INDEX. Detroit: Gale, 1980. 8 vols.

Index bio-bibliographicus, a massive work appearing in fascicules, and estimated to be completed within ten years, is both a bibliography of some 2,000 collected bibliographical works from all countries and languages, and an index to their contents. The *Essay and general literature index* analyses the contents of collected essays and miscellaneous works, published mainly in Britain and the United States. The 1982 edition indexed over 4,000 essays and articles, many of them biographical, arranged in one alphabetical sequence of authors, titles, and subjects, followed by a list of books indexed. The *Biography and genealogy master index*, originally the *Biographical dictionaries master index* (1975), locates more than 3,000,000 entries, for mostly contemporaries, in 350 British, American and Canadian current biographical dictionaries; to be supplemented annually. For deceased subjects the companion work, *Historical biographical dictionaries master index* (Detroit: Gale, 1980) covers over 300,000 entries in 35 American historical sources, such as *Who was who in America*. Similar indexes to specialized biographies exist, such as several Gale 'spin-offs' from the *Biography and genealogy master index*, including the *Theatre, film and television biographies master index* (Detroit: Gale, 1979); and the *Index to literary biography* by Patricia P. Havlice (Metuchen, New Jersey: Scarecrow Press, 1975).

Individual biographies

Bibliographical details of individual biographies can, of course, be traced in the various national bibliographies and 'in-print' services, though some specialized bibliographies exist:

BIOGRAPHICAL BOOKS 1950–1980. New York: Bowker, 1980.

Computer-produced from all Bowker databases, this lists information on 42,000 individual biographies, autobiographies, letters and diaries, of over 17,000 persons, published or distributed in the United States since 1950; with vocation, author, and title indexes.

Biographical Reference Works

Catalogues to general or specialized libraries can also be useful bibliographical guides to individual biography:

National Maritime Museum CATALOGUE OF THE LIBRARY. Vol 2: BIOGRAPHY. London: HMSO, 1969. 2 vols.

Royal Commonwealth Society BIOGRAPHY CATALOGUE OF THE LIBRARY by Donald H. Simpson. London: The Society, 1961.

These two handsomely produced library catalogues are invaluable sources of biography within their subject areas. The National Maritime Museum Library catalogue covers naval and maritime biography; Part 1 contains a list of collected biographies, navy lists, individual biographies, autobiographies and journals; Part 2, the reference index, contains 15,000 names with brief description and dates, from 21 collected works, including *DNB*, Boase, and James Ralfe's *Naval biography of Britain*. The Royal Commonwealth Society Library catalogue has an alphabetical sequence of 6,500 persons born in, or actively associated with, the countries of the Commonwealth, giving brief identifying details and references to books and periodicals in their stock, followed by country and author indexes. The *British Museum general catalogue of printed books* is primarily an author catalogue; however it does list books about an author, as well as those by him. The *British Museum subject index of the modern works added to the Library, 1881–1960* does not have entries for individual biography under specific names; however, there are general subject headings for Biography, Autobiography, Portraits, etc, and subheadings such as Music: Composers, though only collected works would be listed.

Guides to specific types of biography are important:

Matthews, W. BRITISH DIARIES: AN ANNOTATED BIBLIOGRAPHY OF BRITISH DIARIES WRITTEN BETWEEN 1442 AND 1942. Berkeley: University of California Press, 1950.

This excellent source for biography researchers is a chronological listing of published and unpublished diaries. The entries are usually annotated, and it has an author index. William Matthews, an enthusiast of the diary and autobiography, has also published *Amer-*

Bibliographical Guides and Indexes to Biography

ican diaries (1945), *Canadian diaries and autobiographies* (1950), and *British autobiographies* (1955).

Portraits

Searching for portraits can be a difficult part of biographical research, and although many encyclopaedias and biographical dictionaries contain references to portraits, and even reproduce them occasionally, the librarian will need to use the guides to tracing portraits, including indexes and art gallery catalogues:

ALA PORTRAIT INDEX. Washington: Library of Congress, 1906; New York: Burt Franklin, reprint 1964.

This index contains references to approximately 120,000 portraits of over 40,000 people in books and periodicals, but not to original paintings, unless reproduced. The entry includes a brief identifying description, followed by works containing a portrait of the person.

Catalogues of portrait collections in art galleries, museums, and academic or professional organizations are useful sources. Two good examples are: the *National Portrait Gallery: Concise Catalogue, 1856–1969; 1970–1976* (London: The Gallery, 1970; 1977), which contains over 3,000 entries, giving details of sitter, portrait, and artist; and *The Royal College of Physicians of London: Portraits* (London: J. & A. Churchill, 1964), and *Portraits: Catalogue II* (Amsterdam: Elsevier/Excerpta Medica, 1977), which have photographs and complete documentation of about 300 portraits.

Periodical literature

BIOGRAPHY INDEX. 1946– . New York: H. W. Wilson. Quarterly, annual, and three-year cumulations.

This currently analyses 2,600 periodicals, newspapers, collected and individual biographies, diaries, and letters. International in scope, though an American bias. Each entry contains brief personal details of the biographee, followed by citations, with portraits and illustrations indicated. It has an index of professions. The general

Biographical Reference Works

periodical indexes, *British humanities index*, and *Readers' guide to periodical literature*, also have biographical references, as do the specialized indexes *Art index* and *Music index*.

Primary sources

The librarian will often need to direct an enquirer to primary, as well as secondary, sources. Much valuable biographical material, such as correspondence, diaries, and private papers, is still only in manuscript—stored in archives and record repositories. The Royal Commission on Historical Manuscripts *Record repositories in Great Britain* (London: HMSO, 7th ed, 1982) lists over 180 repositories, such as government and parliamentary archives, national and other libraries, and local record offices, where provision is made for regular use by researchers. Some published guides give locations in Britain for correspondence and papers of certain individuals, eg the 'Index of persons' issued as part of the *Guide to the reports of the Royal Commission on Historical Manuscripts, 1870–1911; 1911–1957* (London: HMSO, 1914; 1966); locations for newly acquired manuscripts are listed in the Royal Commission on Historical Manuscripts *Accessions to repositories and reports added to the National Register of Archives* (London: HMSO, 1957–   . Annual). A useful, though selective, guide to biographical manuscript sources, P. Hepworth *Select biographical sources* (London: Library Association, 1971) is intended as a pilot project for a larger, more comprehensive location register of correspondence, diaries, and private papers stored in British archives.

Subject bibliographies

Slocum, R. B. BIOGRAPHICAL DICTIONARIES AND RELATED WORKS. Detroit: Gale, 1967; *Supplement*, 1972; *Second Supplement*, 1978.

This massive work, the standard subject bibliography of biographical dictionaries, contains over 12,000 entries in its three volumes. International in scope, it is organized into three main

Further Reading

sections—universal biography, national or area biography, and biography by vocation—with author, title, and subject indexes.

Walford and Sheehy, of course, also have extensive annotated lists of collected biographies, as do some of the bibliographical guides and indexes described earlier in this section.

REFERENCES AND CITATIONS

1. Woolf, V. The new biography. *Collected essays.* London: Hogarth Press, 1967. Vol 4, 231.
2. Shelston, A. *Biography.* London: Methuen, 1977. 3.
3. Weil, C. B. Automatic retrieval of biographical reference books. *Journal of Library Automation*, 1 (4). December 1968. 239-49.
4. Grogan, D. Books about people. *More case studies in reference work.* London: Bingley, 1972. 149-213.
5. Woodbine, H. Reference libraries. *Library Association Record,* **39** (3). March 1937. 119-20.
6. Shores, L. *Basic reference sources.* Chicago: American Library Association, 1954. 99.
7. Christie, R. C. Biographical dictionaries. *Quarterly Review,* **157**. January 1884. 187-230.
8. 'George Smith and the DNB'. *The Times Literary Supplement.* 24 December 1971. 1593-5.
9. Hanham, H. J. Some neglected sources of biographical information: county biographical dictionaries, 1890-1937. *Bulletin of the Institute of Historical Research,* **34**. 1961. 55-66.
10. Houghton, B. Bénézit, E. Dictionnaire critique et documentaire des peintres, sculpteurs, dessinateurs et graveurs. 3rd ed. 1976. *Library Review,* **26** (4). 1977. 334-7.

SUGGESTIONS FOR FURTHER READING

Edel, L. Biography: a manifesto. *Biography,* 1 (1). Winter 1978. 1-3.
Ellman, R. *Golden codgers: biographical speculations.* London: Oxford University Press, 1973.
Garraty, J. A. *The nature of biography.* London: Cape, 1958.
Gittings, R. *The nature of biography.* London: Heinemann, 1978.
Katz, W. A. Biographical sources. *Introduction to reference work.* 4th ed. New York: McGraw-Hill, 1982. Vol 1: *Basic information sources.* Chapter 8.
Maurois, A. *Aspects of biography.* Cambridge: Cambridge University Press, 1929.

Biographical Reference Works

Roberts, A. D. Biographical works of reference. *Introduction to reference books*. 3rd ed. London: Library Association, 1956. Chapter 13.

Staveley, R. *et al.* Biographical records. *Introduction to subject study*. London: Deutsch, 1967. Chapter 20.

Wynar, B. Biography. *Introduction to bibliography and reference work*. 4th ed. Littleton, Colorado: Libraries Unlimited, 1967. Chapter 6.

7
Directories and other Business Publications

Malcolm J. Campbell

'The basis of all good reference work is the expert exploitation of a well-selected collection of yearbooks and directories.' Collison's statement,[1] sweeping as it may sound, should easily be accepted by British librarians as incontestable. The key role played by directories is by no means universally established, however. For example, Coman, writing in 1976,[2] said 'British libraries stock directories very heavily. This is occasioned by the many overseas connections of British firms. With the rise of so many multinational companies in the US, there should be a similar demand for the information available in directories in this country'. A similar comment was made in New Zealand.[3] Another motive for providing a collection of directories is given by Lamb:[4] 'those who use them are not as a rule familiar with the use of books as sources of information . . . they are the ground bait for potentially good library users'. Certainly a thorough knowledge of the library's stock of directories, and its **exploitation** (as Collison observed), is essential to all who venture into reference work.

So what precisely is a directory? The *ALA glossary of library terms*[5] says it is 'a list of persons or organizations, systematically arranged, usually in alphabetic or classed order, giving addresses, officers, functions and similar data for organizations'. Henderson's definition, only slightly modified through nine editions of *Current British directories*[6], runs: 'any work which enables a searcher to

Directories and other Business Publications

locate, identify or obtain information about a person or organisation; or which provides the searcher with a list of persons or organisations in a particular industry, trade or group, or in a particular place'. Certainly both of these would exclude from consideration press guides, which are about neither persons nor organizations. Bibliographies too are excluded; thus 'directories' of directories are misnamed (a common sin).

For the purpose of this chapter it is proposed to include 'annuals' and 'yearbooks' where they contain directory-type material, though by no means all do. The idea of a directory has a respectable antiquity, since, from the beginnings of recorded time, man has felt the need to make orderly lists of people, organizations and things. The results of censuses as mentioned in the Bible, if published, would have constituted directory tools of the time, and the *Domesday book* is surely a directory of a kind.

What follows is an examination of some of the categories of directory available, with examples. It should however be remembered that much such material may be concealed in works classified elsewhere, just as many a directory contains useful statistical and other data which might be overlooked without a thorough examination of its contents. Furthermore, much mockery has been made of some of the unlikely subjects given directory treatment (*viz* Beachcomber's *List of Huntingdonshire cabmen*, selections from the fictional pages of which provoked breakfast-time chuckles for *Daily Express* readers over many years, later reaching an even wider audience through Sir Michael Redgrave's elegant readings on television). But all such guides have a value for *somebody*, especially to those with something to sell to groups and individuals with special interests. A Sunday newspaper reviewer[7] once admitted to a misjudgment in having poured scorn on the idea that a directory of *Booksellers in India, Pakistan and Sri Lanka* could be of any possible use to anybody. Librarians would not fall into that trap, but should have their answers ready when challenged as to the relevance of *Wisden's cricketers' almanack* or *The golfer's handbook* in their commercial departments.

By their very nature, directories become out of date virtually on publication—people, enterprises, and organizations appear and disappear, change location and name constantly. It is common, there-

Topographical Directories

fore, for publication to be annual, and where this is so, date and periodicity are not mentioned in the descriptions which follow. Also, directories themselves appear and disappear, and change their publishers and contents, so no more can be claimed here than that descriptions are reasonably accurate at the time of writing.

TOPOGRAPHICAL DIRECTORIES

Typically, directories of cities, towns, even sometimes villages, carry alphabetical and classified listings of businesses, private residents, and streets and their occupants in order of house numbers. In the United Kingdom, Kelly's have been pre-eminent in this field and, in their time, covered a large part of the country in this way. Their county directories, which additionally provided historical information and enabled one to determine the resident families in country seats, did not survive World War II. Afterwards, there was a gradual decline in the number of towns and cities covered by Kelly's until 1976, since when only the directory for London was published.

The history of KELLY'S POST OFFICE LONDON DIRECTORY is well documented[8] (as indeed are earlier national and provincial directories[9]). Features additional to those already mentioned are sections locating prominent buildings; Court and national and local government listings; and a set of maps to which the streets section provides the key. Most recent editions have dropped, regrettably, the ecclesiastical and legal sections, which might have been thought to have proved their worth over the years. An earlier, more understandable loss, was that of the listing of private residents, the need for which was reduced by the growth of telephone ownership, with consequent comprehensive listing of private residents in the telephone directory itself. In its final form the section had constituted a rather random gathering of the elect, and its passing will be mourned by few.

The demise of the Kelly's series outside London has not, of course, left the provinces totally devoid of directory coverage. There have always been national rivals ready to fill some gaps, and local publishers, often with newspaper connections, as well as

Directories and other Business Publications

others, prepared to record the current condition of a locality. Contents vary widely; for example, many chambers of commerce list their members alphabetically and/or in classified order. *Bray's Exeter street directory* and its companion for Exmouth (Exeter: Exe Publishing Company, 1980, 1981) list streets with residents, etc, together with official information, organizations and so on, but no separate listing of businesses, and only the Exmouth directory has an alphabetical list of residents. In Scotland the Post Office directory of Glasgow is of a comprehensiveness equal to the best of Kelly's; Belfast and Dublin are well served too.

Recent newcomers to the scene are *Thomson local directories* which, with some additional features, are similar in scope to the 'yellow pages' of telephone directories, for the compilation of which Thomson's formerly were responsible. The first editions of these have been heavily criticized by Peter Marshall[10] for a number of shortcomings, and it remains to be seen whether subsequent revisions will render them more reliable as a reference tool.

Overseas, the need for topographical directories is well recognized. Major centres in West Germany, for instance, are covered by extensive volumes such as the BERLINER-STADTADRESSBUCH (Berlin: Adressbuch Gesellschaft). In France, Paris has its BOTTIN DE LA RÉGION PARISIENNE (Paris: Didot-Bottin). Many of the cities of the USA are thus served, with, typically, a classified section; an alphabetical listing of residents and businesses; a streets list with business and residential occupants; and a *numerical* listing of telephone numbers with subscribers' names, a feature unknown in the United Kingdom. In New Zealand there are two parallel series of directories of places, overlapping, but not duplicating each other, in their content: UNIVERSAL BUSINESS DIRECTORIES, published by UBD Ltd of Auckland, and WISE'S POST OFFICE DIRECTORIES (Auckland: Wise's Publications).

Few libraries could afford many overseas topographical directories, but it is well for librarians to remember their existence and attempt to familiarize themselves with their availability at an alternative location. The uses to which they will generally be put will be obvious. One, it is to be hoped, not to be repeated, was the loan by London's Guildhall Library to the Royal Air Force

Telephone Directories

during the 1939–1945 war of a certain German city directory, to facilitate its more accurate destruction.

TELEPHONE DIRECTORIES

Listings of telephone subscribers are almost universal in extent, and are still a relatively inexpensive means of building up a comprehensive bank of data on corporate bodies and individuals in foreign countries. This is especially so where classified or 'yellow' pages are included—though they are not always yellow in colour. Not all countries publish telephone directories, or at least they may be virtually unobtainable beyond their own borders. Neither is their appearance always the regular and frequent occurrence to which some of us are accustomed. Easier and cheaper availability, as well as more frequent updating would be facilitated by widespread acceptance of the microfiche form, as presently marketed by Bell and Howell for most of the USA. British Telecom have been testing reaction to the possibility of issuing the UK series in this way; it is to be hoped that they realize that sales would be considerable overseas.

Close examination is recommended before using an unfamiliar directory, as content and arrangement can vary considerably. British users of American directories, for example, should bear in mind that names prefixed by 'Mac', 'Mc', 'M', etc, follow all the other 'M's in sequence. Scandinavian languages have letters additional to the Roman alphabet, and their order is not always obvious. Some Arabic directories have Roman as well as Arabic listings, but their notions of alphabetical order are not always so helpful. Otherwise, the almost universal employment of Roman script makes the use of most telephone directories, after diligent study, comparatively easy, but those from Greece and Japan will remain an enigma to those unfamiliar with their respective alphabets.

Occasionally, as for Paris, a listing in street order is provided, in addition to the alphabetical and classified sections. The rarity of this highlights another difficulty, caused by the abbreviation of the

Directories and other Business Publications

various forms of appellation for 'street', 'road', etc, but familiarity soon follows recourse to the appropriate dictionaries.

A further complication sometimes arises from the order of places within sets of telephone directories. Where, as for example in Holland, this is alphabetical throughout, there is no problem. French towns and villages are easily found after determination of the appropriate *département*. For some countries, indexes are built into one or all of the volumes; elsewhere, as in Germany, Italy, the UK and USA, these may be separately purchased. For zip and post codes, separate listings may again have to be referred to; the US is covered in one handy volume, but a multi-volume series is published for Britain.

International listings of telephone subscribers would generally be too large or too selective to be feasible. Both the formerly useful *International yellow pages* and the Sodemac *Common market telephone directory* are no longer published, but a relative newcomer should be noted:

EURO PAGES: DIRECTORY OF EXPORTERS FROM BELGIUM, WEST GERMANY, FRANCE, ITALY AND THE NETHERLANDS. Published by an international consortium including British Telecom.

The above is the title of the edition available in the UK; this does not include coverage of UK companies; these would be contained in editions for the other five countries, published in their own languages. Arrangement is classified, with an index to products. The series is distributed free to 268,000 companies and public bodies in the European Community. The UK edition contains names, addresses and telephone numbers of 130,000 companies.

TELEGRAPHIC ADDRESS AND TELEX DIRECTORIES

The use of telegraphy has to a large extent been superseded by the telex network, which provides at both ends a printed record of question and answer. One long-standing reference book which has adapted itself to this change is:

General Business Directories

MARCONI'S INTERNATIONAL REGISTER. New York: Telegraphic Cable and Radio Registry.

Coverage is world-wide, and the principal arrangement is alphabetical in columns, with telex numbers, answerback code, and cable address. A classified section is followed by an index of cable addresses.

For some years many unscrupulous operators have become rich through the promotion of dubious international listings of telex subscribers, and their products should be avoided, as should the payment of money for an entry; but of the highest repute, and fully comprehensive in coverage, is:

JAEGER AND WALDMANN WORLD TELEX. Darmstadt: Telex-Verlag Jaeger and Waldmann. 4 vols annually, with quarterly supplements.

Two volumes arrange entries alphabetically within countries, one for Europe, the other for the rest of the world. The third volume is classified by activity, and the fourth is a consolidated answerback code index. Apart from its obvious use as a telex number reference, *Jaeger and Waldmann* constitutes probably the most extensive world-wide directory available, since larger organizations of all kinds have come to accept telex as almost as essential for communication as the telephone.

Within national boundaries, directories of telex subscribers are published by providers of the service. In the United Kingdom, for example, this is British Telecom. In the United States, a number of networks prevail, and for full coverage, listings published by Western Union, ITT, RCA and TWX are required.

GENERAL BUSINESS DIRECTORIES

Any general directory purporting to be of world-wide scope will be highly selective in its coverage of companies listed. However, there are some, in addition to the aforementioned *Jaeger and Waldmann*, which are worthy of note:

Directories and other Business Publications

PRINCIPAL INTERNATIONAL BUSINESSES: THE WORLD MARKETING DIRECTORY. New York: Dun & Bradstreet.

Some 50,000 larger enterprises are listed, under 133 country headings; with address, sales volume, number of employees, Standard Industrial Classification (SIC) number, activities, and chief executives. There are classified and alphabetical sections; and notes are given in English, French, German and Spanish. It is expensive for a one-volume work, but, by virtue of its comprehensive geographical range, this source is worthy of consideration where little can be provided in the way of directories for individual overseas countries. Moody's Investors Service of New York are a subsidiary of Dun & Bradstreet; they publish *Moody's international manual*, which gives more extended financial and other data on 3,000 corporations and multinationals in 95 countries. It is updated with fortnightly News Reports.

Of universal scope, and detailing corporations of a particular type, is:

WORLD DIRECTORY OF MULTINATIONAL ENTERPRISES. 2nd ed. London: Macmillan, 1982. 2 vols.

This contains detailed profiles of about 500 multinationals with annual turnover exceeding $1 billion. The barest minimum information is given on vastly more companies in:

BOTTIN INTERNATIONAL. Paris: Didot-Bottin.

Industrial, commercial and professional concerns are here classified within countries and towns. Some town plans are included, as are trade indexes in English, French, German and Spanish, together with a geographical index. A sister publication, *Bottin Europe*, is classified by product, then country, with a further country-by-country section including descriptions, in French and English, of towns and cities, followed by lists of service establishments such as banks, advertising agencies, insurance companies, etc.

MAJOR COMPANIES OF EUROPE. London: Graham and Trotman. 2 vols.

Here the first volume is devoted to the countries of the European

General Business Directories

Community, the rest being placed in Volume 2. For each company, directors and executives are named, with the concern's activities, affiliations, financial data, etc. Also from Graham and Trotman come similar 'Major companies' works covering the Arab world, the Far East, Nigeria, and Argentina, Brazil, Mexico and Venezuela.

Europe is also served by *Jaeger's Europa-Register* (Darmstadt: Deutscher Adressbuch-Verlag) and the two-volume *ABC Europ Production* (Darmstadt: Europ Export Edition). *Owen's commerce and travel and international register* (London: Owen's Commerce and Travel) covers Africa, the Near and Middle East, South East Asia and the Far East. Africa receives more detailed treatment in *Slam trade year book of Africa*. Published in Madrid is *Ibar Anuario-Comercial Ibaramericano*, most useful for its coverage of Latin America, but including also Spain, Portugal and the USA.

In the *West Indies and Caribbean year book* (Toronto: Caribook) there is a heavier emphasis on textual description of component territories and their services, followed by classified listings of commercial and industrial activity. Much more attention has been focused on Arabic countries in recent years, but of long standing is the *Arab directory: Le guide arabe* (Beirut: Halabi), which is in Arabic and English languages, giving general information country by country, followed by listings of concerns by subject.

An important series indicating company relationships should be mentioned, since, under four separate titles, they cover a large part of the industrialized world:

WHO OWNS WHOM (UK AND REPUBLIC OF IRELAND EDITION): A DIRECTORY OF PARENT, ASSOCIATE AND SUBSIDIARY COMPANIES. London: Dun & Bradstreet. 2 vols, plus quarterly supplements.

Parent companies are listed, with their subsidiaries and associates in separate sequences, for the UK and Eire. There is also a listing of consortia and their members. Vol 2 consists of subsidiaries and associates alphabetically, indicating their parents. *Who owns whom (Australia and the Far East)*, *Who owns whom (North America)*

Directories and other Business Publications

and *Who owns whom (continental edition)* follow a similar pattern. Full addresses and other data are not given.

A range of directories of a different nature is the Kompass series. Though of fairly consistent content and format, each is published independently by its own national Kompass publishing concern—in the case of the UK, a subsidiary of the IPC organization:

KOMPASS: REGISTER OF BRITISH INDUSTRY AND COMMERCE. East Grinstead: Kompass Publishers. 2 vols.

The first volume classifies over 28,000 manufacturers and suppliers, to a reasonable degree of particularity, within 33,000 products and services (the classification is common to the series). Vol 2 gives fuller details—address, directors, capital, number of employees, bankers, products, etc, within county and town or city. Beyond certain basic information, firms may pay for extended entries (thus length of entry does not necessarily reflect importance of the concern). Member companies of the Confederation of British Industry are indicated, in the alphabetical index, with a dagger sign.

The KOMPASS range has been generally established in territories where nothing of comparable scope already existed, or through absorption of one such directory if it did exist. Not all of those once published survive, and for North America two major classified directories still dominate:

THOMAS REGISTER OF AMERICAN MANUFACTURERS. New York: Thomas Publishing Company. 17 vols.

Earlier volumes are arranged in alphabetical subject order, corporations being listed within subjects by state and town. There is a trade names register, and an alphabetical listing of some 85,000 enterprises, with address, products, directors and executives, and a coded indication of size of capital. Vols 12 to 17 consist of a collection of trade catalogues.

MACRAE'S BLUE BOOK. Hinsdale, Illinois: MacRae's Blue Book Company. 5 vols.

General Business Directories

Arrangement is similar to *Thomas*, but the scale of the work is smaller; the price is consequently lower.

For the United Kingdom, the directory giving the barest information on the largest number of companies is the long-standing:

KELLY'S MANUFACTURERS' AND MERCHANTS' DIRECTORY. Kingston upon Thames: Kelly's Directories.

This has changed its character over recent years, consisting now of alphabetical and classified listings of UK companies with addresses, etc. It was formerly of some significance for its international coverage, but this is now reduced to a minor classified exporters section, a large proportion of the entries in which are for British firms in fact.

Another alphabetical listing, but with more extended entries, is:

KEY BRITISH ENTERPRISES. London: Dun & Bradstreet. 2 vols.

Here are descriptions of about 20,000 public and private companies in primary, manufacturing and distribution industries, transport and communications, with address, branches, activities, UK and overseas sales turnover, directors, capital structure, SIC number, trade names and numbers employed. There are indexes of products, business activities and locations. Dun & Bradstreet (the parent company is in New York), publish in a number of countries a range of broadly similar works, including *Dun & Bradstreet million dollar directory* and *Dun & Bradstreet middle market directory* for the USA, *Canadian key business directory*, and *Australian key business directory*. Much of the output from this source is sold on a confidential basis and is not available to public libraries.

THE STOCK EXCHANGE OFFICIAL YEAR BOOK. London: Macmillan.

Formerly published by Thomas Skinner Directories, this standard record of all enterprises listed on the London and Federated Stock Exchange has seen some changes since Macmillan took it over. Chief of these is the arrangement, now in a straightforward alphabetical sequence instead of by broad categories corresponding to the arrangement of the *Stock Exchange daily list*; subscribers to

Directories and other Business Publications

the latter are now left without a quick key to the finding of a company's daily share price listing. Directors, history, capitalization, accounts and dividends, etc, are given. There are alphabetical and classified indexes, and a section indicating parents with principal subsidiaries/affiliates. New is a 'late news' supplement, and a record of companies removed from the previous edition. The companion *Register of defunct and other companies* has ceased its annual publication; there is now a listing of these (dating only from 1963, however) available on microfiche or microfilm from the Companies Registration Office. Most British and many overseas libraries with any interest in company financial data will need to keep an up-to-date edition of the *SEOYB*—and indeed a file of back copies for reference. It may be noted that similar compilations exist for publicly quoted concerns in many other countries, though not always officially linked with indigenous stock exchanges. For example, the multi-part *Handbuch der Deutschen Aktiengesellschaften* for West Germany, the various Moody's *Manuals*, and Standard & Poor's works covering North America, are independently produced.

POOR'S REGISTER OF CORPORATIONS, DIRECTORS AND EXECUTIVES. New York: Standard & Poor. 3 vols.

The first volume gives briefer details than *Standard & Poor's corporation records* (described later with updating company services), but of rather more enterprises; and the second comprises an alphabetical guide to directors and executives, with their appointments, addresses and education. About 70,000 are listed, and coverage is of Canada as well as of the United States. Vol 3 lists corporations by SIC number and geographically. The British equivalent of Vol 2 of *Poor's register* is the *Directory of directors* (East Grinstead: Thomas Skinner Directories). These works give the barest relevant business facts of the subjects' lives; biographical directories of the 'who's who' type exist for many sectors of business and geographical areas, and are discussed in Chapter 6.

Straightforward listings of businesses within individual countries, with no details other than addresses, telephone and telex numbers, are common. For the UK, *Kelly's manufacturers' and merchants'*

Individual Trades Directories and Buyers' Guides

directory has been described. *Stubbs' buyers' guide* (London: Dun & Bradstreet—it is announced that the 1983 edition is likely to be the last) and *Kemp's directory* (London: Kemp's Group. 3 vols) are well known in this country, as is *Sell's directory of products and services* (Epsom: Sell's Publications). Each has virtues of its own, and differing arrangements, offering various approaches to the problem of finding details of enterprises and the goods they offer. There is not room here to describe the many such publications existing for other territories, but they will be of primary importance in reference libraries with commercial sections.

INDIVIDUAL TRADES DIRECTORIES AND BUYERS' GUIDES

The range of industries and trades well documented by directories and buyers' guides is so enormous that all but the largest libraries need to adopt some yardstick of selection. There are five principal factors which will govern this process:

1. The money available.
2. The space available.
3. Relevance to the activities and interests of the clientèle for whom the library is intended.
4. Changing national and international circumstances. In recent years, for example, directories on every aspect of petroleum and natural gas have proliferated. At the same time, there is very much more available in the form of aids to identifying elements of the Arab market, than there was prior to 1974. Conversely, the importance of the UK textile industry has declined from its former eminence, so there are now fewer directories relating to it than was once the case.
5. Quality and value for money. Choices may need to be made between several works covering the same subject field.

It is possible here to describe only a few of the more important works in one or two subject sectors, as an indication of what might be available. Local requirements differ and those selected should

Directories and other Business Publications

not necessarily be regarded as essential to the stock of all libraries. Naturally, first claim on resources will generally be on directories relating to the country in which the collection is situated, but consideration has to be given also to those of international range, if not guides restricted to individual overseas territories.

For companies engaged in mining operations there are several to choose from, including the *E & MJ international directory of mining and mineral operations* (New York: McGraw-Hill) and *World mines register* (San Francisco: Miller Freeman)—notably detailed for the Americas. Worthy of special mention is:

FINANCIAL TIMES MINING INTERNATIONAL YEAR BOOK. London: Longman Group Ltd.

Some 4,000 companies are detailed, with capital structure, profits, dividends, three years' share record, accounts, subsidiaries and directors.

Similar in scope, and similarly formerly known as 'Walter R. Skinner's ...', is *Financial Times oil and gas international year book* (with its companion *Financial Times who's who in world oil and gas*), a helpful feature for some purposes being their arrangement of companies alphabetically, regardless of country of origin, which the user may not always know. Others to be noted in this subject field are the works of Pennwell Books of Tulsa, Oklahoma (formerly the Petroleum Publishing Company)—*Worldwide refining and gas processing directory, Worldwide petrochemical directory, Offshore contractors and equipment directory, USA oil industry directory, Canadian oil industry directory* and a number of regional petroleum industry volumes. These are highly comprehensive in their content.

Another former *Walter R. Skinner* title is:

FAIRPLAY WORLD SHIPPING YEAR BOOK. London: Fairplay Publications.

All aspects of the industry are covered: shipowners, builders, repairers, engine-builders, salvage and towage services, and marine insurers. Details include directors and executives, financial capitalization and results, and affiliations. Of comparable scope is the *International shipping and shipbuilding directory* (Tunbridge Wells:

Individual Trades Directories and Buyers' Guides

Benn Brothers). The problem of choice is further confused by the existence of the *Directory of shipowners, shipbuilders and marine engineers* (Sutton, Surrey: IPC Industrial Press). The Fairplay publication has a greater emphasis on financial descriptions of concerns, but otherwise the contents of the three are so similar (and each is an excellent example of what a directory should be) as to cause surprise that a market exists for them all.

The chemical industry is another well served by directories of international scope. One which includes more than 10,000 corporations from about 95 countries is *Worldwide chemical directory*. This is published by Chemical Data Services, now an IPC subsidiary, of Sutton, Surrey, whose range includes *Chemical company profiles* for both the Americas, and for Africa, Asia and Australasia. Individual countries are covered too in a range of *Chemfacts* surveys of individual countries of Western Europe; these, at upwards of £40 each, would perhaps be too expensive for purchase in their entirety by any but the most specialized library. The success of this series perhaps accounts for the disappearance of some publications formerly noted in the chemical field; but one which has not is the *Directory of chemical producers: Western Europe* (Menlo Park, California: SRI International), which has a companion volume for the United States.

The foregoing examples of international directories could be extended to include many more devoted to one country, but even as they stand they may serve to illustrate the kind of choice which has to be made in selecting for coverage of a particular activity. This frequently involves the decision whether to seek minimum detail on the largest possible number of concerns, or more extended information relating to finance, personnel, etc, on a more selective basis. Where resources are modest, the first course is to be recommended, coupled with an awareness of larger collections to which requests for more detail may be directed.

Periodicals form the subject matter of Chapter 9, but should not be overlooked as a potential source of directory materials. *Toy trader yearbook* is a work published separately from its parent

Directories and other Business Publications

journal; *Chemical week buyers' guide*, however, is a special issue received as part of the *Chemical week* subscription. With the weekly *Estates gazette* comes a monthly supplement consisting of a comprehensive directory of estate agents, auctioneers, surveyors, valuers and property companies. The classified advertisements in *Men's wear* are arranged in such a way as to constitute a weekly 'mini-directory'.

A good deal may be missed if journals are simply placed on display unopened, since useful occasional items of long-term reference value may be missed, such as the frequent guides in *The Banker* (UK) to companies in various financial sectors—for example, overseas banks in London, New York, etc.

TRADE NAMES SOURCES

Directories of manufacturers frequently carry a section listing trade names pertaining to the activity concerned—that in *Benn's hardware directory* is an excellent example. For some subjects there are guides solely to trade names and their owners, eg the *Watchmaker, jeweller and silversmith directory of trade names and punch marks* (London: IPC Consumer Industries Press). Branded chemicals and pharmaceuticals abound in such numbers that they require bulky volumes of their own, including W. Gardner's *Chemical synonyms and trade names* (8th ed. London: Technical Press. 1978) and G. C. Hawley's *Condensed chemical dictionary* (10th ed. New York: Van Nostrand & Reinhold, 1981).

Drugs and chemicals are excluded from the British one-volume directory of trade names:

UK TRADE NAMES. 7th ed. East Grinstead: Kompass Publishers, 1982.

No library which receives any volume of brand name enquiries (a staple of the reference library diet) could afford to be without this, but the introductory notes should be studied carefully for excluded categories, such as, for example, food, drink and tobacco brands, and lapsed registrations. In respect of the latter, it will be found helpful to retain earlier editions on file, since by no means

Trade Names Sources

all enquiries relate to trade names in current use. A still more extensive source emanated during the period from 1958 to the late 1970s from the Patent Office itself, which supplied certain libraries with details, on paper slips, of new registrations. These occupy many catalogue card drawers now, but the service has in any case ceased, and at the time of writing it still remains to be seen whether some commercial concern will find it a viable proposition to come forward to fill the gap in some way. As a last resort the Patent Office itself may be able to help—but only in regard to names registered there.

In the USA, as well as the listings already mentioned in *Thomas register* and *MacRae's blue book*, there has since 1975 been a Gale publication in two volumes, *Trade names directory*, updated by *New trade names* supplements. For other territories it is worth noting that in some general directories (including some in the *Kompass* series) brand names appear in the alphabetical index of companies. Otherwise, directories entirely devoted to a country's trade names are rare, though *Brand names of Japan* (Tokyo: Chamber of Commerce and Industry) may still be found of some use, notwithstanding that it is now twenty years old.

No source of this category of information may be said to be in any way complete, and it is, therefore, as well to be acquainted with as many as possible, especially those already in one's own library stock. The CBD series (*Current British directories*, etc) which are described later, make the tracing of directories within their scope containing lists of trade names, comparatively easy, by way of their subject indexes. One service on an international scale is that of Compu-mark of Antwerp and Intermark Index of Zurich. *Répertoire alphabétique et phonétique des marques internationales* is a seven-volume listing in five product groups of trade marks listed in the weekly *Les marques internationales*, a record of registrations with the World Intellectual Property Organisation. The set is updated with cumulative quarterly supplements. Coverage is of 24 countries—none English-speaking.

Directories and other Business Publications
SOME 'NON-TRADE' DIRECTORIES

While it is true, as has been intimated earlier, that *any* listing of persons, corporations or organizations may be put to some commercial use, there are numerous categories of directory the primary purpose of which is by no means related to business. One which may be said to be aimed primarily for the aid of those needing help, but which also serves a valuable purpose for those individuals and corporate bodies with cash to spare for a good cause is:

THE CHARITIES DIGEST. London: Family Welfare Association.
Of very long standing, having survived a change of title and publisher, this presents details of about 1,000 charities, arranged by category. Similarly indispensable is the *Directory of grant-making trusts* (Tonbridge, Kent: CAF Publications, alternate years); here no less than 2,200 trusts are described, covering England, Scotland and Wales, with alphabetical, geographical and subject indexes. Of wider scope, but necessarily more selective, is the *International foundations directory*, published by Europa and now in its second edition. Another source of data on aid sources, but not confined to the charitable, nor even the financial, is the *Social services year book* (London: Longmans). National and local government services, those concerned specifically with children, health and community relations, counselling agencies and voluntary bodies, are just some of the topics within its range.

Education, and in particular higher education, is another field well served by directories; and one directory which few libraries could afford to be without is:

COMMONWEALTH UNIVERSITIES YEAR BOOK. London: Association of Commonwealth Universities. 4 vols.
Arranged alphabetically within countries, universities are fully described, with lists of staffs of faculties and departments, in the first three volumes. Vol 4 is devoted to indexes. It is published annually, whereas the equivalent source for the rest of the world appears only every three years. This is the *International handbook*

of universities and other institutions of higher education (London: Macmillan, for the International Association of Universities). A one-volume work, it is not able to present the depth of detail afforded by its Commonwealth counterpart. The United States, of course, has no lack of such guides, of which perhaps pre-eminent is *American universities and colleges* (12th ed. Hawthorne, New York: Walter de Gruyter, 1982, for the American Council on Education). It has a companion *American junior colleges*. For very much briefer entries, but with a coverage that is truly staggering, one should not forget *The world of learning* (London: Europa. 2 vols). Here, country by country, are included not only universities and colleges, but schools of art and music, libraries and archive collections, learned societies, research institutes, museums and galleries.

From higher education to the career search is a logical progression, and here again there is no lack of guidance at all levels. Prominent in this field is the Careers Research and Advisory Centre (CRAC), the catalogue of which contains a number of careers guides, typical of which is:

GRADUATE EMPLOYMENT AND TRAINING. Cambridge: Hobson's Press.
This details opportunities offered by 2,500 employers, with a supplement on postgraduate study facilities. Similar in its scope, but of a bulkier size is '*GO*'—*graduate opportunities*, which is offered free to final-year students in universities, polytechnics and colleges of higher education. Incidentally, the descriptions of activities of many of Britain's larger employers contained in these and other such guides should not be overlooked in the search for company information; often they are more readable, and for some purposes, more to the point, than the more obvious sources.

PROFESSIONAL REGISTERS AND MEMBERSHIP LISTS

Authority to practise a profession is commonly conditional upon inclusion in a register maintained by some governing body. The

Directories and other Business Publications

published forms of these registers constitute directories in themselves, and their official standing gives them an importance which cannot be ignored by public libraries of even modest size. Thus, for instance, in Great Britain, nobody should have to travel far to find a copy of the *Medical register* (London: General Medical Council. 2 vols), giving address, qualifications and registration number of 115,455 medical practitioners. Even so, few libraries could be without the similarly two-volume *Medical directory* (Harlow, Essex: Churchill Livingstone) which, though unofficial, gives fuller information in a 'who's who' type format, and includes, with effect from the 1982 edition, qualified doctors not now on the Register, by virtue of the work they do on retirement from practice. There is also a geographical list and details of hospitals and their staff.

Parallel professional lists for overseas territories can be of value, though in the case of a large country like the United States, such works will themselves be large and correspondingly expensive. Medical practitioners there are listed in the *American medical directory* (American Medical Association), in two large volumes.

For the legal profession in North America there are a number of guides, the most comprehensive of which is:

MARTINDALE-HUBBELL LAW DIRECTORY. New Jersey: Martindale-Hubbell. 8 vols.

Extensive details of lawyers and legal practices have the added refinement of an indication of their professional ability. In addition, digests of the laws of the States and Provinces of the United States and Canada are given, and those of 52 other countries.

There is no British equivalent of *Martindale-Hubbell*, and since the demise in 1976 of the long-established *Law list*, it is necessary now to use both the *Solicitors' diary, almanac and legal directory* (London: Waterlow) and the *Bar list* (London: Stevens) for lists of practitioners of both branches of the profession. Reference to sadly-lost standard works prompts the hope that reports that the current edition of *Crockford's clerical directory* might be the last will be proved premature. It is surely unthinkable that such a quirky source of serendipitous amusement should vanish altogether

Information Source Indicators

or at best be reduced to the format of computer tape or floppy disc?

Looking beyond the professions, it is hard to think of any human activity which does not boast its societies, associations, institutions, clubs, fraternities and so on. Very many of these produce lists of members, not all of which find their way into guides to directories as such. Here will be found useful the *Directory of British associations* (7th ed. Beckenham, Kent: CBD Research, 1982); its companion *Directory of European associations* (Part 1: National industrial, trade and professional associations. 3rd ed, 1981; Part 2: National learned, scientific and technical associations, 2nd ed, 1979); and, for North America, *Encyclopedia of associations* (Detroit: Gale Research) which is annual in three volumes, with an updating service. These, in their detailed descriptions of organizations, include publications produced, among them lists of members, which in some cases may not be available for sale to non-members.

INFORMATION SOURCE INDICATORS

Since even the largest libraries cannot hope to be in the position of being able to answer every question that may come their way, a wide range of directories signposting specialized sources of information will soon prove its value. The works on associations just mentioned would form an essential part of such a collection. Organizations of all kinds are also an important feature of the Europa series of encyclopaedic guides to many aspects of national and international life—economic, cultural, political and so on:

EUROPA YEAR BOOK . . .: A WORLD SURVEY. London: Europa Publications. 2 vols.

Lists and descriptions of 1,650 international organizations are followed by treatments of individual countries. In addition to textual and statistical data, there are listings of government, political parties, the press, publishers, commercial and industrial organizations, and educational institutions. Of similar content on a regional basis, with additional 'who's who' sections, are *The Middle East*

Directories and other Business Publications

and *North Africa*, *The Far East and Australasia* and *Africa south of the Sahara*. From the same publisher, *The world of learning* provides, in addition to educational listings already mentioned, libraries and other information sources. Fuller descriptions of libraries, on an international scale, are given in *Internationales Bibliotheks-Handbuch—World guide to libraries* (6th ed. Munich, Germany: K. G. Saur Verlag, 1982).

From the R. R. Bowker Company comes *Subject collections in European libraries* (2nd ed. New York, 1978), while for North America there are many guides, notably the same publisher's *American library directory*. The *Directory of special libraries and information centers* (7th ed. Detroit: Gale Research, 1982) is highly comprehensive, with subject, geographic and personnel indexes. There is a quarterly updating service. A more detailed treatment of the subject specialization content of this directory is contained in the five-volume *Subject directory of special libraries*, of which a sixth edition was published in 1982. Bowker are again the source of *Subject collections: A guide to special book collections*, but this has not been revised since 1979. These titles include coverage of the United States *and* Canada, which is true of many North American directories.

Many of the states of the USA have guides to their library resources. In the United Kingdom, the Reference, Special and Information Section of the Library Association has issued a series, *Library resources in . . .*, currently covering nine regions of the country. Co-operative groupings of libraries of all kinds from time to time publish lists of their members, eg *HATRICS* in Hampshire, *NANTIS* for Nottinghamshire, and *SINTO* (Sheffield Interchange Organisation). The *Libraries, museums and art galleries yearbook* (Cambridge: James Clarke) includes the most comprehensive detailing of public and special libraries in the UK and Eire, but, despite its name, the 1978–79 edition is the latest published. A new edition, to be entitled the *Libraries yearbook 1982/83*, will exclude museums, art galleries and stately homes.

Aslib is an organization grouping libraries and information units with specialist interests, including some in the public sector

Information Source Indicators

(roughly corresponding to the Special Libraries Association in the USA).

ASLIB DIRECTORY. London: Aslib. 2 vols. Vol 1: Science, technology and commerce, 5th ed, 1982; Vol 2: Medicine, social sciences and the humanities, 4th ed, 1980.
Considerable detail is given for each collection, including specializations, which are fully indexed.

Similar compilations to those mentioned exist for many other countries and may serve to identify valuable overseas contacts.

Government departments can (?should) be information sources, and they are generally well documented. In the UK their libraries are described in the *Guide to Government Department and other libraries* (British Library, Science Reference Library, alternate years) and, for the USA, Mildred Benton has compiled both the *Roster of federal libraries* and *Federal library resources*, but these are now somewhat out of date. Over 5,000 sources in Congress itself are included in *Washington information directory* (Washington, DC: Congressional Quarterly) which is a guide to US federal government departments.
In Britain the *Civil Service year book* (London: HMSO), which has undergone several title changes in a long life, and *Whitakers almanack* are well enough known, and serve most purposes, though *Vacher's parliamentary companion* (London: A. S. Kerswill, quarterly) may also be needed. A guide to the contact points in the Department of Trade and Industry and its ancillaries is provided periodically in the weekly *British business*. Invaluable for its coverage of both non-departmental government and non-government bodies is *Councils, committees and boards: A handbook of advisory, consultative, executive and similar bodies in British public life* (5th ed. Beckenham: CBD Research, 1982).
For Germany, the *Taschenbuch des öffentlichen Lebens* (Bonn: Festland Verlag) includes societies and institutions and many other aspects of public life, as well as government departments, and *The Times of India directory and year book* (Bombay: Times of India Press) also is a similarly comprehensive volume. There is no uni-

versal standard form for this type of publication, but they are well worth tracking down as the basis for an overseas directories collection.

COMPANY REPORTS, CARD SERVICES, ETC

The essential sources of companies' financial information are the documents which are required to be filed with each country's national or regional registering authority. In England and Wales this is the Companies Registration Office in Cardiff, with a London search facility (Scotland and Northern Ireland have their own Registrars); in the United States, registration is by State, with the Securities Exchange Commission wielding federal authority over stock exchange dealings. G. P. Henderson's *European companies: A guide to sources of information* (3rd ed. Beckenham: CBD Research, 1972) is an indispensable aid in identifying the procedures within European countries for registration, etc, and how best to secure company information.

Company annual reports are produced primarily to satisfy legal requirements and to inform shareholders, who are entitled to receive copies. Others, including interested libraries, may generally obtain them only as a courtesy. They can occupy a great deal of space and staff time. Selection may be necessary, and could be on the basis of size, products, or local interest. For business purposes a five-year file will usually be sufficient, though where local interest is a factor, permanent retention may have to be considered.

This is a field where the microfiche form offers a manageable and convenient means of publication. Disclosure Inc, of Bethesda, Maryland, can supply over 100,000 SEC-filed reports in this way, and in Britain *The Financial Times*, as well as acting as agents for Disclosure, operates the Mirac service covering the 5,000 or so quoted companies' reports. Searchers at the London and Cardiff offices of the Companies Registration Office will also, for most purposes, be handed (for £1), fiches, which may be taken away for consultation, or used to provide a hard-copy print-out. The lack of a postal service was remedied in 1983.

The *CRO directory of companies* represents a positive benefit

Company Reports, Card Services, etc

resulting from reorganization of the Registrar's records, coupled with computerization. From 1981 a quarterly listing, alphabetically, of all current (900,000 or so) registered companies has been available on microfiche or microfilm, giving registration number, name, registered address, accounting reference date and date of last filed accounts. Optionally, weekly updates may be purchased, with changes of name and/or address, as well as more recent filings of accounts. While it is true that the registered office address is not always that from which the main operations of a company are performed, this recent development represents a considerable advance on the situation in this field a few years ago. A parallel service, listing companies dissolved since 1963, has already been described.

For most libraries, sufficient company financial detail can be obtained through regular updating services, which digest the information into a handy form. Extel Statistical Services perform this role admirably in the United Kingdom and indeed, though less completely, for some overseas territories:

EXTEL BRITISH COMPANY INFORMATION SERVICE. London: Extel Statistical Services. Loose-leaf.

An annual 'card' is issued, following the company meeting, with directors' names, activities, capitalization data, balance sheets, profit-and-loss accounts, subsidiaries, etc. Through the year, updating news cards are issued as necessary. Over 7,000 quoted companies are covered, and figures over a ten-year period are given in the companion *Extel analysts card service* for 1,500 of them; a further 2,250 unquoted companies are the subject of a separate service.

A one-volume reference with further-digested data on 700 of the larger quoted concerns is the *Extel Handbook of market leaders*, published twice a year. The *Extel book of new issues of public companies* should also be noted, since it contains details of prospectuses, rights issues, and other means by which British and Irish companies have raised capital during each year.

Extel card services covering overseas countries are necessarily selective rather than comprehensive, but give detail similar to the British quoted service for corporations in North America, Europe,

Directories and other Business Publications

Australia, Singapore and Malaysia. Before leaving the products of this prolific source, the newer *Extel unlisted securities market service* should be noted, covering companies subject to this section of the (UK) Stock Exchange's operations. Overseas, for some 1,000 Canadian firms, the *Financial Post corporation service* uses updating news cards in conjunction with a booklet giving basic data. The *FACtS* card service from Financial Analysis (Pty) covers Johannesburg-quoted concerns, and the *Irish Independent* and *Wardleycards* similarly treat companies in Eire and Hong Kong.

Two US organizations offer competing comprehensive coverage of North American enterprises:

STANDARD & POOR'S CORPORATION RECORDS. New York: Standard & Poor. 6 vols. Loose-leaf.

Updates are issued quarterly, and main entries following the receipt of annual reports are supplemented by additional news items as announced through the year. These latter are not gathered with the principal entry, which factor, coupled with the fact that the order is not alphabetical, makes use of the indexes at the beginning of each volume obligatory.

Moody's Investors Service Inc of New York (a Dun & Bradstreet subsidiary) issue data in a series of *Manuals* for each sector: Industrial; OTC (Over-the-counter) industrial; Bank and finance; Municipal and government; Public utilities; and Transportation. Each is supplemented by updating services in loose-leaf binders, and again retrieval via the indexes is essential. Like Extel, both Standard & Poor and Moody produce a range of further aids to investors.

European quoted companies have their card services too, notably those issued by the DAFSA and Hoppenstedt concerns for France and West Germany. Also from DAFSA comes *Informations internationales*, which presents on loose sheets of two or more pages, financial profiles of over 700 corporations in Europe and the USA. Recently revamped, it now gives more detail on each company, in both English and French, German having been dropped along with the former Hoppenstedt connection.

Loose-leaf and card services are naturally somewhat expensive,

Company Reports, Card Services, etc

at least in terms of most public libraries' budgets, but it is well to be aware of their existence and, if at all possible, of alternative locations where they may be consulted. They are not normally to be found in bibliographies and booklists. One guide, in addition to Henderson's *European companies* and *Financial directories of the world* is Mary M. Grant's *Directory of business and financial services* (7th ed. New York: Special Libraries Association, 1976), which is arranged by title, with indexes of subjects and publishers.

Another form of presentation of data from company reports is tabulation of key ratios in such a way as to make comparisons of size and performance an easy matter. *The Times 1000*, and similar listings by *Fortune* and *Forbes* magazines are of this kind, as are the series of *Largest companies in* . . ., (such as *France's 30,000 largest companies*), which also cover Austria, Belgium and Luxembourg, Denmark, The Netherlands, Finland, Italy, Norway and Sweden. In uniform format, and detailing varying numbers of companies, they are produced indigenously but published under the Dun & Bradstreet umbrella. Outside the series, but similar in approach, is *200 largest* (Belgrade: Ekonomska Politika). Rankings lists abound, generally in periodicals, but are not properly the concern of this chapter, since addresses—a minimal requirement of a 'directory'—are not usually given.

Two London organizations which competitively present data in tabulated form are Jordan's and Inter-Company Comparisons. Both treat quoted and unquoted enterprises in volumes devoted to particular sectors, such as brewing, furniture, pharmaceuticals and so on. Jordan's also publish *Britain's top private companies* (the 'Top 2000' and the 'Third 1000' in separate volumes); *Britain's top quoted industrial companies*; *Britain's top 1000 foreign owned companies*; and *Scotland's top 500 companies*. A package deal is offered to libraries wishing to subscribe to the entire Jordan's series. Other organizations have lately adopted the Jordan's and ICC approach, notably Clifton Data Research Services, of St Albans, Hertfordshire, which, however, have dropped treatments of individual business sectors to concentrate on the new *Clifton company guide*, covering over 3,000 industrial and commercial enterprises.

Directories and other Business Publications

It is noteworthy that so very much more is accessible, in published form, about companies than was the case twenty years ago. In part, this is due to changed legislation on disclosure, but it is also a reflection of demand, to which some response on the part of public libraries is called for. Those with limited funds for expensive hard-copy services, for which there is only occasional recourse, will now be able to access a large part of their needs through the medium of a Prestel terminal, since a number of the publishers mentioned here act as information providers (for a price) to that service.

DISCOVERING DIRECTORIES

It has been possible in this chapter to indicate examples of only some types of directory, and the reader will need to look elsewhere for more complete guides to what is available. Means must also be found of keeping abreast of new titles and new editions as they appear. Thus, while British libraries will find a useful aid to selection in the A. M. Allott and A. E. Bagguley *Basic business directories: A select annotated list of 100 titles* (London: The Library Association Reference, Special and Information Section, 1974), its age, pending any new edition, compels caution in its use. More up to date is the annual *The top 1000 directories and annuals: A guide to the major titles used in British libraries* (Reading: Alan Armstrong & Associates Ltd). In fact, over 1,500 titles are listed alphabetically, with separate listings of new titles of the last eighteen months, and by month of issue, by publisher, and by subject. Mostly covering UK titles, but with some from overseas, there is a monthly updating *New editions* service.

Undoubtedly pre-eminent in the field of directory bibliography is the firm of CBD Research Ltd of Beckenham, Kent. Works listed are each, as far as possible, physically examined by the former-librarian compilers, ensuring a high degree of accuracy. *Current British directories*, published every three years, is the foundation-stone of the series, being first produced in 1953 by G. P. Henderson while he was still employed in London's Guildhall Library. His *European companies* has been mentioned already, and the second edition of *Current European directories* was published in 1981. I. G. Anderson was editor of *Current African directories* in 1972, and a companion volume on Asia and Australasia appeared in 1978.

The CBD range on this subject has not embraced the North (or South) American continents. Examination of Bernard Klein's generally unsatisfactory *Guide to American directories* (11th ed. New York: B. Klein Publications, 1982) will quickly reveal the difference in approach, presentation and depth of indexing. Fortunately there is now a very much more acceptable alternative in the form of *Directory of directories* (Detroit: Gale Research) which reached its second edition in 1983 and is updated by a supplementary service. It describes 7,000 directories, as fully and accurately as one would expect from this publisher.

On an international scale (though with a North American emphasis), are *Irregular serials and annuals: An international directory* (8th ed. New York: Bowker, 1984) and the less informative *Trade directories of the world* (New York: Croner Publications), which is a loose-leaf monthly updating service commenced in 1952. Two other international guides, to specific subject areas, were formerly published by Francis Hodgson of Guernsey; the third edition of *Directory of scientific directories* was published in 1979 by Longmans, and *Financial directories of the world* in 1982 by Vallancey International of Hong Kong. Arrangement of each is geographical, then by subject, with full indexes. Their scope is wider than their titles suggest, as there is, for example, considerable coverage of information sources, such as library directories. *Transnational corporations: List of company directories and summary of their contents* was published in New York by the UN Centre on Transnational Corporations in 1977. Here 282 directories are listed in alphabetical order, with a country index; a new edition would be welcome.

To keep a running check on newly available titles and new editions, several sources are recommended, in addition to the new Alan Armstrong and Gale services mentioned above. *Public affairs information service bulletin* (New York: PAIS; weekly, with cumulations) has a heading 'Directories' which should be checked

Directories and other Business Publications

regularly as a valuable source, especially of out-of-the-way items appearing within periodical issues. The annual volume of the companion *PAIS: Foreign language index* also lists a selection. Another aid is *Export Magazine* (The Hague: Stichting Voorlichtling over Buitlandse Markten), each issue of which contains a list of accessions to the library of the Dutch Ministry of Economic Affairs, arguably the largest single collection of (*inter alia*) directories in the world.

Appropriate libraries' accessions lists, often available free, provide helpful checklists on what is new; notable is that of the UNCTAD/GATT International Trade Center in Geneva, but there are a number of others worth scanning on receipt.

The above resources are mentioned primarily as aids to the identification of directories published other than in the parent country. Indigenous works are listed on publication in *British national bibliography* and its overseas equivalents (the Commonwealth Secretariat published in 1977 *Commonwealth national bibliographies: an annotated directory*), but these are by no means infallible. Work with directories has much of the spice associated with that of the detective, and this element extends to the business of tracking down the tools of the trade themselves.

REFERENCES AND CITATIONS

1. Collison, R. L. *Library assistance to readers.* 5th ed. London: Crosby Lockwood, 1968. 106.
2. Coman, E. T. Jnr. Review in *College and research libraries*, **37**, September 1976. 473–4.
3. Dailey, L. Directories as a special collection. *New Zealand libraries*, **38** (5), October 1975. 271–5.
4. Lamb, J. P. *Commercial and technical libraries.* London: Allen & Unwin *and* The Library Association, 1955. 128.
5. Thompson, E. H. (ed.) *ALA glossary of library terms.* Chicago: American Library Association, 1943.
6. Anderson, I. G. (ed.) *Current British directories.* 9th ed. Beckenham, Kent: CBD Research, 1979.
7. Smith, G. Slow sellers of '77. *The Sunday Times*, 1 January 1978. 35.
8. Goss, C. W. G. *The London directories 1677–1875.* London: Dennis Archer, 1932.
9. Norton, J. E. *Guide to the national and provincial directories of*

Further Reading

England and Wales, excluding London, published before *1856*. London: Royal Historical Society, 1950.
10. Marshall, P. Thomson's local misdirectory. *Refer: Journal of the RSIS*, **2** (1), Spring 1982.

SUGGESTIONS FOR FURTHER READING

Campbell, M. J. (ed.) *Manual of business library practice*. London: Bingley; *and* Hamden, Connecticut: Linnet Books, 1975 (new edition in preparation). (Chapter by G. P. Henderson on directories and company information sources.)

Daniells, L. M. *Business information sources*. University of California Press, 1977.

Grogan, D. *Case studies in reference work*. Hamden, Connecticut: Shoe String Press; *and* London: Bingley, 1967. (Chapter on yearbooks and directories.)

8
Newspapers and other Material on Recent Events

Geoffrey Whatmore

It is a matter for regret that current information, an essential part of the fabric of modern living, is one of the more difficult aspects of reference work. Possibly because of their ever-increasing flood, always changing and seldom between hard covers, reports of recent events, new facts and statements are often elusive even a few weeks after publication. The weakest point is the information gap between their first announcement and the incorporation of contemporary data in published abstracts, indexes and digests. Not only facts, but much of the debate—the polemics and protests that influence the decision-making process—are lost altogether if published, as much of it is, via the press and broadcasting media. The bibliographic tools in the field, though good of their kind, are insufficient, especially in Britain and Europe, where the market for such publications is limited. The lack of a good summary of contemporary events in Britain is keenly felt, for although major political and international affairs, and business and finance are reasonably well covered, developments in the arts and entertainment, much sociology, crime and current biography are much more difficult to locate.

Broadcasting Reference

BROADCASTING REFERENCE

It used to be taken for granted that the main source for current events was newspapers, but an increasing number of people derive most of their awareness of the affairs of the day from radio and television. The spoken word presents obvious difficulties for later retrieval, but some world radio news can be referred to again via a new computer service:

WORLD REPORTER. London: BBC/Datasolve, 1982– .

Initially the database comprises the text of (a) output from the BBC's External Services' News, broadcast overseas from London, and (b) the *Summary of world broadcasts* (see below). This is the first British computerized full-text general background news retrieval service. Additional information includes data from *The Economist*.

The teletext news services of Ceefax and Oracle, now becoming familiar as current awareness facilities, have no retrospection, and are thus not to be regarded as reference tools.

Television news, even more ephemeral than radio, is not available for retrospective reference in Britain, but in New York the CBS television news bulletin scripts are marketed, by the Microfilming Corporation of America, with a quarterly and annual index. In addition, Vanderbilt University (Nashville, Tennessee) issues *Television news index and abstracts*, a guide to the Vanderbilt Television News Archive, a collection of video-tape cassettes of the evening news broadcasts for each of the three major US television networks.

The radio output of a large part of the rest of the world is covered by:

SUMMARY OF WORLD BROADCASTS. Caversham: British Broadcasting Corporation, 1947– .

The BBC Monitoring Service listens to, and reports on, foreign radio broadcasts from more than 100 countries in over 50 languages. Transcripts in English of this material are published daily, except Sundays, in four parts: for the USSR, Eastern Europe, the Far East, and the Middle East and Africa. Each part is supplemented by its own *Weekly economic report*. The summaries are designed as a current awareness service but, from the librarian's point of view, the lack of an index inhibits their use for reference. The *Summary of world broadcasts* which is also available on-line as part of the news database, *Nexis* (Dayton, Ohio: Mead Data Central), is partnered by the US equivalent, the daily *Foreign broadcast information service*, published via the US Department of Commerce; between them they cover the world, including China and Latin America. Both are additionally available in microfiche format and, as we have seen, as computer databases.

NEWSPAPERS

Though newspapers are incomparably the richest source for current information, the deliberate lack of formality and order in the presentation of stories makes it hard to use them retrospectively, as anyone who has had to search for an item vaguely remembered knows. This is why it is worth while for the media, heavily dependent on recent facts, to establish expensive libraries of classified press cuttings for their own use.

The rest must make the best use they can of back issues, microfilmed sequences, news digests, and, in Britain, of two national newspaper indexes, those of *The Times* and *The Financial Times*. Still widely regarded as a 'paper of record', though it is not, a complete run of *The Times* from its first issue in 1785 is published on 35 mm roll film by Research Publications of Reading (formerly Newspaper Archive Developments). This, and a file of the local newspaper, ideally with a partial index if staff levels permit, is likely to be the total long-term resource in many libraries. (Great effort has been put during the last decade into the indexing of local newspapers; more than 600 such indexes, admittedly variable in quality and scope, are now known to exist). Other national newspapers, unless on microfilm, are seldom retained for more than a few weeks and, as a consequence, important leading articles and features in such papers as the *Guardian* or *The Daily Telegraph* are elusive.

The newspaper publishers themselves vary in the length of time

Newspapers

for which they hold back issues: about five years by *The Daily Telegraph*, a year or more by *The Financial Times*, and much shorter periods by many others. Bound or microfilmed sequences (not necessarily of all editions) are retained for record, but the publishers do not encourage viewing by the general public.

Apart from local storage, the only comprehensive collection of newspapers in the United Kingdom is the British Library's Newspaper Library at Colindale in North London. The Newspaper Library holds final editions of British and many overseas newspapers, both currently published and historic. Its twice-yearly *Newsletter* serves as a platform for all those interested in newspapers and news information. Pre-1801 national English newspapers are held in the Department of Printed Books at Bloomsbury. More than half a million volumes and parcels of newspapers are stored at Colindale, and about 5,500 volumes and parcels are added each year. With the exception of *The Times* and *The Sunday Times*, UK newspapers cannot normally be consulted until they are bound, so the access gap for news persists: in the case of national newspapers, a few months, and in the case of UK provincial papers, up to two years. In spite of this, a library of newspapers presents the best source there is for assessing the *Zeitgeist*, the life of the times as seen through the eyes of contemporaries.

Librarians and bibliographers are gradually becoming more aware of the cornucopia which is buried in the sequences of old newspapers, national and provincial. This is evidenced by, amongst others, the efforts of the Standing Conference of National and University Libraries (SCONUL). Their *World list of national newspapers*, compiled by Rosemary Webber and published by Butterworths in association with the Social Science Research Council, contains in excess of 1,500 national newspapers from 120 countries, with their locations in libraries in the British Isles. SCONUL's work towards improving access to newspaper sequences continues, since the first supplement to the *World list* has now appeared.

The Newspaper Library collection is the best starting point for the identification of older newspaper titles, whose contents are listed by P. E. Allen for the British Library in eight volumes, under the title of *Catalogue of the Newspaper Library, Colindale*. Though this is limited to the Newspaper Library holdings, it is more up to date than the long-established *Times tercentenary handlist of English and Welsh newspapers, magazines and reviews* (London: The Times, 1920), which was based principally on the holdings of the British Museum and the Bodleian. The earliest flowerings of the English provincial press are listed in G. A. Cranfield's *A handlist of English provincial newspapers and periodicals, 1700–1760* (rev ed, Cambridge University Press, 1961) and in *A census of British newspapers and periodicals, 1620–1800*, by R. S. Crane and F. B. Kaye (Chapel Hill: University of North Carolina Press, 1927). The *New Cambridge bibliography of English literature*, Vols 2 and 3, is a further source not to be overlooked. Public library local collections have, over many years, collected and cared for early newspapers of their town, and their catalogues are an essential source. Devoted care by scarce staff is often given to the preservation for posterity, in classified order, of press cuttings about local matters. Only a few local histories of the press have been written, not all of them published, one such being Leary's *History of the Manchester Periodical Press*, a manuscript bound and preserved in Manchester Reference Library. In some cases titles are known but no copies remain. I once had the great pleasure in Chetham's Library, Manchester, of unearthing from a chest a single copy of the *Manchester Weekly Courant*, a newspaper listed in the *New Cambridge bibliography* as 'no copies traced'.

Microfilm is the only practical format for long-term storage of bulky perishable material like modern newsprint. The miniaturized format is now generally accepted, as shown by the Library of Congress annual, *Newspapers in microform* (Washington: 1973 to date), which lists thousands of US and foreign titles, increasing yearly. An important microfilmed collection of early newspapers is *Early English newspapers 1622–1820*, based on the Burney Collection in the British Library, and filmed by Research Publications Inc. The collection is available in the UK from Research Publications Ltd of Reading. More English publishers than is generally realized hold their back issues on microfilm. In addition to *The Times*, *The Financial Times*, *The Daily Telegraph*, *Daily Express*, *Guardian*, *Daily Mirror* and many provincial newspapers may be purchased in this form. The permanent retention by public libraries

Newspaper Indexes

of a greater number of newspaper titles in the form of microfilm spools would go some way to overcoming the relatively poor public access to back issues of newspapers. As a paper[1] by the County Librarian of Devon has it:

> 'One of the most important resources of the local studies library is the file of local and regional newspapers, frequently dating from the late eighteenth century, which often provide the only contemporary reference to an event or personality of some historical interest. The heavy use made of the original hand-copy files, coupled with the inbuilt deterioration of newspapers manufactured from mechanical wood-pulp, has long led a number of public libraries to microfilm, often as a joint venture with the newspaper company concerned and occasionally neighbouring authorities with appropriate sharing of costs'.

Though no specifically British catalogue is published, lists of microfilmed newspapers are issued by the microfilm companies, Kodak, Bell & Howell, University Microfilms, and by the English company, Research Publications (part of the International Thomson Organisation). The British Library Newspaper Library issues a sale list of its microfilm holdings. The Mansell catalogue, *Microforms in print*, includes many newspapers on roll film.

NEWSPAPER INDEXES

The existence of only two indexes among nine national daily newspapers in Britain leaves a substantial reference void unfilled; but for major and syndicated news stories *The Times index* can be used to identify dates, thus allowing the researcher to locate articles, not only in *The Times*, but also in other newspapers. Some feature articles in newspapers, and in the weekly journals of opinion, are picked up by the *British humanities index* (Library Association) and the American *Social sciences index* (H. W. Wilson), though the time lag and scarcity of back issues renders these references less effective than they might be. Not to be forgotten are the quarterly

Newspapers and other Material on Recent Events

indexes to *The Economist* and *The Listener* which make the retention of back issues of those publications so much more valuable.

Attempts have been made over the years to achieve the dream of a full index to the news. One of them was *Curtice's index to 'The Times'*, *the London morning and evening papers, one hundred and twenty weeklies and thirty one provincial newspapers*, published in 1893 as a quarterly, but it had a short life. Edward Curtice's dream survives as Romeike and Curtice's press cutting agency. The dream is given substance today by computer typesetting, when the residual text stored in electronic form can be made available for automatic retrieval or re-publication via computer technology. We deal with the impact of the news databases in a later section.

With the recent arrival of *The Financial Times* index there are two British newspaper indexes to consider, plus a major American one, among others. These are:

THE TIMES INDEX. Reading: Research Publications, 1790– .

THE INDEX TO THE FINANCIAL TIMES. London: Financial Times Business Information, 1981– .

THE NEW YORK TIMES INDEX. New York: New York Times Company, 1851– .

The 'official index' to *The Times* was commenced in 1906, and before that an index was independently published under the title of *Palmer's index to 'The Times' newspaper*; this went back to 1790. Work is now going on to index back to 1785. The volumes for 1785 and 1786 are published. The two indexes were in competition from 1906 until June 1941, when *Palmer's* ceased publication. From 1974 *The Times index* includes, in the same sequence, references to items in *The Sunday Times* and its colour magazine; *The Times Literary Supplement*; *The Times Educational Supplement*; and *The Times Higher Education Supplement*. Since the beginning of 1977 the index has appeared monthly, with annual cumulations; a substantial improvement over the previous two-monthly and quarterly publications. With the suspension of publication by *The Times* and its sister publications from 1 December

Newspaper Indexes

1978 to 17 November 1979, the continuity of *The Times index* was preserved by indexing *The Daily Telegraph* and *Sunday Telegraph* in the same sequence. This was regarded as a poor substitute by *Times* people, but the only way to avoid a disastrous gap in the record. An index to the *TLS* in two volumes from 1902–1939 is published by Research Publications; it is to be followed by a further sequence covering 1940–1980. It is a compliment to describe *The Times* as a plain man's index, for it contains only a modest number of cross-references, and assumes some intelligence on the part of the user. Material is indexed from several aspects, under personal name, subject, country, or locality, using specific headings. For names (so important for news) it is very good. As with all other indexes prepared while news is still developing, the twin problems of consistent treatment and changing emphasis have not entirely been solved. Nevertheless, the microfilm of *The Times*, together with its printed index (hard covers) makes a powerful reference tool for contemporary information. The years 1790 to 1905 (*Palmer's index*) are in 65 volumes, followed by the Kraus reprint 1906 to 1967 in 118 volumes. Later volumes are also available.

The appearance from 1981 of *The Financial Times* index in monthly issues with annual cumulations is a most welcome event. Although it obviously has a substantial overlap with *The Times index* it does not rival so much as complement *The Times'* coverage. While its strength is company financial and industrial news, the *FT index* also carries the key to the international and arts features of the newspaper. The arrangement of the index is unusual in that it is divided into three sections: Corporate (Companies); Generals; and Personalities. The latter is a valuable feature since it provides reference to industrialists, company chairmen, etc, for whom biographical information is often lacking elsewhere. The lay-out of the Generals Section is really a classified one by country (with a huge section on the United Kingdom), which follows the pattern of some of the news digests. International items go under the appropriate subject heading. Thus, 'Energy' and 'Oil' are only lightly dealt with at these headings and the rest has to be sought under country, without references. Nevertheless, once the arrangement is grasped, the index provides an almost unique source on a major aspect of news. Like *The Times*, the *FT index* may be used in association with microfilm spools of the newspaper.

The New York Times index is surely one of the great indexes of the world. It is published semi-monthly, appearing on just a few library shelves in Britain about three months after the latest entry in it, which is slightly slower than *The Times index*. With computer-aided production, it is able to cumulate annually into a massive volume of 1,900 or so three-column pages. It should be noted that it is subject-orientated, and that personal name and geographic entries are less fully treated. Thus the heading for President Carter (entered as CARTER, JIMMY) started off with 4.5 columns of *see also* references. Statements by the British Chancellor of the Exchequer (under Denis Healey at the time) on economic conditions in the UK, can be traced from page references at his name, but the entries are not informative here. They are given in more detail under 'Great Britain—Economic Conditions', taking up eight columns in chronological order. It might well be said, however, that to cover a year of the *New York Times* in a single volume is a sufficiently large task, and to add detailed biographical entries would make it unmanageable.

In the United States, the larger potential market permits publication of more newspaper indexes; some indeed have come into being in support of sales of microfilmed back issue sequences. At Wooster, Ohio, the microfilm publishers Bell & Howell have established an indexing centre preparing monthly and cumulative annual indexes to a number of leading American newspapers: *Chicago Sun-Times*, *Los Angeles Times*, *New Orleans Times-Picayune*, *St. Louis Post-Dispatch*, *San Francisco Chronicle*, the *Houston Post*, and *Detroit News*, broadly covering the regions of the country. Titles change from time to time. Other US national newspapers publishing indexes include *The Washington Post*, *Christian Science Monitor* 1972–   (monthly), *National Observer*, 1970–   (annual), and *The Wall Street Journal*, 1958–   (monthly). The *Wall Street Journal index* (monthly), with its specialized financial coverage, is taken by certain larger British business libraries. For the US field Anita C. Milner has produced a two-volume guide entitled

News Digests

Newspaper indexes: a location and subject guide for researchers (Scarecrow Press).

Elsewhere, newspaper indexes do not always have the stability that librarians would like. The *Glasgow Herald index*, started in 1906, ceased publication in 1968. The demise of the *Time Magazine index* was a loss to all concerned with current affairs reference. In Europe, the index to *Le Monde* survived only erratically for odd years until 1968, in spite of its appearance in Sheehy.[2]

A particular weakness of newspaper indexes is edition changes. Because newspapers vary their contents and page lay-out between editions, an inquirer using an index with any edition but the final one may fail to locate items, which may not have appeared in earlier editions, or they may have been printed on other pages from those listed. The position is not made any easier by the newspaper practice of not indicating clearly the edition of each paper, so that the reader may not be aware that his is not the final one.

NEWS DIGESTS

More convenient than indexes for a general picture of current affairs are the **news digest services** which, in contrast to indexes which require a two-stage process to find information, provide factual summaries within one set of covers. Three digests of international news may be taken to typify this group, though only one of them is generally to be found in British libraries. These are:

KEESING'S CONTEMPORARY ARCHIVES. Harlow, Essex: Keesing's (Longman Group), 1931– .

FACTS ON FILE. New York: Facts on File, 1940– .

DEADLINE DATA ON WORLD AFFAIRS. Greenwich, Connecticut: DMS Inc, 1955– .

Pre-eminent in Europe and strongly international in scope, *Keesing's* monthly (formerly weekly) loose-leaf summaries are designed to be clipped between hard covers, chronologically, as they arrive. Topics are grouped together—generally geographically—and con-

Newspapers and other Material on Recent Events

sulted via indexes supplied in cumulative outline form each month, and in more detailed analytical form cumulating twice during the year and then annually. Personal name indexes form a separate cumulative sequence. Somewhat controversially, the main index arranges most items, including those in the UK, first by country. In addition, for quick reference, each issue contains a brief summary of the previous month's events, set out in strictly chronological order. Articles are brief, tightly written précis of current developments. A sequential page number and letter provides the link with the index, and may also be used to refer back to earlier items on the same topic. Sources, mostly English language or European newspapers, and official texts, are quoted. Over the years the work has earned the confidence of its subscribers in being as accurate as news ever can be. *Keesing's* has been virtually without competition on this side of the Atlantic since 1931, and back issues are available in microfiche form as well as in hard covers.

Closely similar to *Keesing's* in format is the American *Facts on file* (which commenced in 1940); published weekly, it is indexed twice monthly with frequent consolidations; it uses conventional direct headings. Naturally stronger on American news, *Facts on file* offers a wider, if perhaps slightly lighter coverage, with items on economics and business, sport, obituaries, books, plays, and films. Page references using a grid, dividing the three-column pages into sections, are a helpful invitation to the hurried enquirer.

Deadline data is a weekly card service arranged alphabetically by some 180 country and inter-governmental organization headings. The card format makes for easy update and retrospective reference, at the price of brevity of presentation. Each country 'file' or group of cards consists of five elements: general data, governmental organizations, chief officials, armed forces, and chronology. A computerized subject index is supplied and updated quarterly. In an allied field is *News bank series* (Spring Valley, New York: Arcata Microfilm Corporation), a monthly indexed microfiche service, from 1970 to date, of original articles from 100 American newspapers.

Although it seems to be less widely known at home than it should be, special reference should be made to the British Information Services' monthly *Survey of current affairs*, international in scope with a firmly British approach. The same sectional format is followed each month, with good maps and tables, and a particularly valuable section on documentation, which lists governmental and other official reports, with bibliographical details. Of regional digests, one of the most important to world watchers is the *Current digest of the Soviet press*, published weekly since 1949 by the US International Committee on Slavic Studies. Other regions of the world are covered by a scattering of regular news and factual summaries such as, amongst others, *Asian recorder* (New Delhi, 1955– , weekly); *Asia research bulletin* (Singapore, 1972– , monthly); *Arab report and record* (London, 1966– , semi-monthly); *Africa research bulletin* (Exeter, 1963– , two series, monthly); and *Canadian news facts* (Toronto: Marpep, 1967–). Notwithstanding the EEC, there is nothing specifically for Europe.

Abstracts and other services of news in specialized fields are referred to elsewhere but, because they are based specifically on newspaper items, attention should be drawn to *McCarthy's press services*, which re-publishes daily replica copies of press articles on industrial products and companies. The material is drawn from mainly British daily and regional newspapers, and presented on A4 sheets which, when folded, are filed in A5 card trays. Newspaper stories in the business field are also very briefly indexed by the *Research index* (fortnightly), published by Business Surveys of Dorking, Surrey.

NEWS DATABASES

Although they are not publications in the traditional sense, attention must be drawn to the rapidly growing number of computer databases now marketed, where competition exists among the host suppliers to acquire additional tapes as they become available from the typesetting process.

The pioneer in this field is the NYTIS System (formerly the *New York Times* Information Bank), comprising at present seven databases available to the public. From its inception a decade or more

Newspapers and other Material on Recent Events

ago, the NYTIS database has undergone a number of expansions, and in its current form offers the full text of the *New York Times* news and features (from June 1980), plus summaries ('enhancements') which are updated within 48 hours of publication. Separate databases include abstracts from the *NYT* and 56 other publications. The inclusion of both full text and abstract facilities in the database underlines the debate over the relative value of these two formats for news. Among other database segments are advertising and marketing intelligence, company news, the *Boston Globe*, and *Deadline Data* (referred to earlier).

The NYTIS System is now being challenged in the UK and elsewhere by a number of rival news bases such as the BBC *World reporter* (already described); and *Nexis* (Mead Data Central), which consists of a cluster of full text outputs from 1975, including *The Washington Post*, Reuters, United Press and Associated Press wire services, and, from Britain, *The Economist* and the BBC's *Summary of world broadcasts*, all supplied direct from the operational tapes. As elsewhere, the insatiable demand for business information has led to the establishment of specialized services, such as Textline, providing access to abstracts from the financial columns of British and foreign newspapers. Doubtless, many more can be expected.

Databases of *index* references to the news are similarly proliferating in America, and are available in the UK via various host services. These include Lockheed DIALOG with the indexes to *The Wall Street Journal*, *Christian Science Monitor* and the *New York Times*. The Bell and Howell indexing operation is to be consulted online via the System Development Corporation's ORBIT data retrieval system.

YEAR REVIEWS

With a longer look, and more time at their disposal, annual reviews naturally enjoy a better perspective, summarizing trends in various fields; they are apt to be less effective for detailed reference to highly specific events. Providing the year of search is determined, an array of year reviews makes a strong reference source for events, though single copies are of limited use. (The problem is overcome

Year Reviews

by some publications, which provide each annual volume with a three-year index.) The chronologies, which form a staple section of each publication, fill an obvious need, but since they are seldom indexed, and necessarily selective, the identification of a single item may not invariably be successful. Three major general reviews in English, among others, may be singled out:

THE ANNUAL REGISTER. London: Longman, 1758– .

THE AMERICANA ANNUAL. New York: Grolier, 1923– .

BRITANNICA BOOK OF THE YEAR. Chicago: Encyclopaedia Britannica, 1938– .

The doyen of this group, *The annual register*, which first appeared under the editorship of Edmund Burke, has now established for itself such an aura of academic respectability that it is to be found in practically every reference collection. Through its feature articles, the later volumes are perhaps better for catching the flavour of a year, than for factual reference. Nevertheless its reprints of 'world documents', its six-year world statistical survey, and its obituary section (prepared long before the *Dictionary of national biography* supplements are issued), should form part of the mental card index to sources, which is in every good reference librarian's mind. The main body of each annual volume consists of surveys by specialist contributors, arranged into regions and countries, plus articles on broad issues such as International Organizations, The Sciences, The Arts, Sport, Economic and Social Affairs, and so forth. Apart from a 'books of the year' section, no general bibliographies are provided.

While *The annual register* stands alone as a distinct publication, its coverage is rivalled in North America by year books linked with encyclopaedias. Most are illustrated, with more pages and matter than the British annual and, belying their popular appearance, are wide-ranging and detailed in scope. *Britannica*'s presentation is fairly typical, beautifully printed and presented, taking the form of a large number of articles on the affairs of the year, encyclopaedia-style, plus special sections on biography and chro-

Newspapers and other Material on Recent Events

nology. The *Americana* prefers to group its articles under broad headings—Environment, Religion, Population, and many others. As with all this class of work—indeed any reference book—good indexes and guides to users are vitally important. The *Britannica* is ingenious and conscientious in this respect, providing cross-references in the margin of the text and *see also* references at the end of each article. A cumulative index to five years' earlier volumes is provided in the volumes published after 1965. It should be noted that each of these reviews covers events for the year prior to the date in the title, a point scrupulously noted on the spine of the *Britannica*.

Other annuals, published principally in response to the encyclopaedia publisher's endless quest to keep his main publications up to date and thus saleable, are *The world book year book*, an annual supplement to *The world book encyclopaedia* (Field Enterprises), and *Collier's yearbook* (1939–   ), neither frequently to be seen in Britain. The *Facts on file yearbook* has summarized the year's events as seen through its weekly service, every year since 1940.

An appreciative word may also be expressed in favour of newspapers which, in the dearth of news over Christmas and the New Year, devote several pages to summaries and chronologies of events in the year just concluding. *The Times* and *The Sunday Times* prepare good ones, and the *New York Times* with its *Review* is superlative, though naturally American in its domestic items. To those libraries with space, and the initiative to collect these, go the rewards of a rich and relatively cheap source of reference.

ALMANACS

These indispensable and handy annual volumes have a fascinating history going back to Roger Bacon and Rabelais, but the main purpose today of the English language ones in the general field is not so much for calendar and astronomical data, as for the compendia of current facts of all kinds about the minutiae of modern living and officialdom. There are four worth special mention, one English and three American, all very similar in approach:

Almanacs

WHITAKER'S ALMANACK. London: Whitaker's Almanack, 1868– .

THE WORLD ALMANAC AND BOOK OF FACTS. New York: Newspaper Enterprise Association, 1868– .

INFORMATION PLEASE ALMANAC. New York: Simon and Schuster, 1947– .

READER'S DIGEST ALMANAC AND YEARBOOK. Pleasantville, New York: Reader's Digest Association, 1966– .

Whitaker's is virtually a mini-encyclopaedia, perhaps the archetypal form, still quaintly describing itself on the title page as 'an almanack for the year of our Lord . . .'. The range of information in the 1,200 pages of the complete edition is a triumph of compression which it is impossible, and perhaps unnecessary, to describe in a few lines. Back issues should be retained for the sake of non-repeated items, and for the chronologies, which usually bracket two years, autumn to autumn for the twelve months preceding the year of publication. The index, in the front, has to be good, otherwise the almanac would fail, but it is not utterly without fault. Occasional items, eg the twelve Caesars in the issue to hand, are introduced as space fillers, and these are not invariably indexed. If you are baffled by an inquiry, try *Whitaker's* first.

The principal US almanac, *The world almanac*, is equally venerable, and naturally better on American aspects, though its scope is world-wide. Items dealt with, not to be found in *Whitaker's*, include a personalities section, movies, best sellers, and memorable dates. It is especially good on disasters: storms, kidnappings, oil spills, assassinations, and big fires. The issues from 1868–1973 are available in microform. Both *Whitaker's* and *The world almanac* are essential side by side in any reference collection.

Information please almanac adopts a broadly classified order, dividing its contents into world resources, military strength, world history, brief biographies of American presidents, 'historical and news events from ancient to modern times', and other large matters. It is especially helpful on US sport. A comparative newcomer, the *Reader's Digest almanac*, is a rarity in England, but its coverage of crime (chiefly American), and former American administrations, has often saved the day with the answer to an off-beat inquiry. In England the slim paper-covered *Daily Mail year book* (Associated Newspapers Group, 1900–   ) is by no means to be despised because it is cheap, and although of limited range, makes effective use of its 380 pages, though it could do with a more comprehensive index.

INTERNATIONAL YEAR BOOKS

Statistics of nations, populations and domestic facts, governments and ministers, trade, education, and geographic features are, after home news, amongst the commonest fields of inquiry, and these can be most quickly and conveniently produced from international year books. It is probably for the names of ministers and officials that the volumes are most frequently consulted, but caution should be exercised: politicians rise and fall, and changes are not always announced. A publication a year old (and the information in it is likely to be at least six months old at the time of publication) is not fully reliable. Further, no year book (or newspaper for that matter, on many topics) is a primary source, and it may require cross-checking wherever possible. The following titles are amongst the most important:

THE STATESMAN'S YEAR-BOOK. London: Macmillan, 1864– .

THE EUROPA YEAR BOOK. London: Europa Publications, 1959– .

THE INTERNATIONAL YEAR BOOK AND STATESMEN'S WHO'S WHO. London: Thomas Skinner Directories, 1953– .

Edited with scholarship, the 1,500 compact pages of *The statesman's year-book* are arranged in the latest edition into two sections: international organizations; and the countries of the world in a single alphabetical order, an improvement on the traditional divi-

International Year Books

sion of Commonwealth and the rest, which had in previous editions become somewhat anachronistic. The short bibliography following each country's entry is a boon to the seeker after deeper sources. Taken for granted as it is, and with an unassailable reputation, the *Statesman*'s concerns itself nowadays less with history than with current facts and statistics, heads of government departments (a frequent source of enquiry), defence data (very comprehensive), and commerce and industry.

Europa's two volumes are not, in fact, confined to Europe. Vol I is divided into three major sections: Part 1 deals with international organizations, Part 2 with European countries, and Part 3 with the first few countries, Afghanistan to Burundi, of the alphabetical survey of the rest of the world. Vol II lists the remaining countries of the world from Cameroon to Zimbabwe. Probably no work in the English language is so comprehensive on economic and commercial, as well as political, activities of all the countries of the world. Newspaper titles are included for each nation, and the statistical tables are extensive. *Europa* was preceded by two loose-leaf publications—*Europa* and *Orbis*—until 1958.

Preferring a direct arrangement alphabetically by country, is *The international year book*, which combines international organizations and states of the world with a substantial biographical section between the same covers. Like its competitors, data for each country are given under standard headings and are easy to consult, though for small countries, eg Laos, the entries are very brief. The inclusion of a biographical section puts some pressure on space, and the entries for personalities are less full than those of *International who's who*.

Widely taken in American libraries, where it tends to be preferred to *The statesman's*, is the *Political handbook of the world* (McGraw-Hill), compiled for the Council on Foreign Relations. Though it is generally simpler and less detailed than its British counterparts, its coverage is especially good on South American countries. *The yearbook of world affairs* (London: Stevens, for the London Institute of World Affairs, 1947–   ) collects, annually, articles on international relations, and surveys the literature. Mention should also be made of the Prestel pages concerned with foreign governments, which are more up to date than an annual publication can ever be.

Each of the regions of the world is the subject of at least one annual reference work, eg the *Europa* series. These titles, which follow the style of the *Europa year book*, and expand some of the data contained in it, include *Africa south of the Sahara* (1971–   ); *The Middle East and North Africa* (1948–   ); and *The Far East and Australasia*. Among others, the long-established *West Indies and Caribbean year book* (Skinner 1927–   ) may be mentioned. A useful newcomer is *African year book and who's who*, published by *Africa Journal*, of London. Though numerous Common Market publications are available, a regular annual has yet to appear specially devoted to the European continent, where the nearest thing is the *European yearbook* (1955–   ) published annually for the Council of Europe by Nijhoff. The content is mainly federal in outlook, and comprises articles on European organizations, the texts of basic documents and resolutions, chronologies and bibliographies. Although not a year book, Vol V of the *Encyclopedia of the nations*, entitled *Europe*, is worth a place on the shelves in spite of the last (fourth) edition being distributed in the United Kingdom by the New Caxton Library Service as long ago as 1971—too long for a reliable factual publication about Europe. The passage of time since publication is of less concern in relation to its reproduction of national crests and flags in monochrome at the head of each country section. The Foreign and Commonwealth Office annual, *A yearbook of the Commonwealth*, gives a wide range of data on member countries, plus committees and regional organizations.

Space here precludes specific mention of all the national year books which earn their keep among the stock of the larger reference libraries. Not all countries publish them, some of the states of the Eastern bloc being notable omissions. The United Kingdom's official annual is *Britain: an official handbook*, a work of immense detail and catholicity of choice, published for the Central Office of Information by HMSO. This attempts to provide statistics and useful facts, with names and addresses of official bodies, concerning all aspects of current British life. Its analytical index is a model of its kind, and the work includes a guide to official sources and publications. Amongst foreign national year books, regard should be paid to the *China yearbook*, issued from the Republic; the official *Year book of the Republic of South Africa*, issued by the South Africa Department of Information; and the *Official year book of Australia*, a mainly statistical compilation issued by the Australian Bureau of Statistics. A list of other national year books and their publishers appears in Walford.[3]

PRESS GUIDES

Like the national year books, at least one comprehensive list for the indigenous press is to be assumed as part of the bibliographical resources of most Western countries. The notes which follow leave to Chapter 9 librarians' guides such as *Ulrich*, and concentrate on those works giving advertising rates and editorial information. Two principal lists are published from London:

BENN'S PRESS DIRECTORY. Benn Publications, 1846–

WILLING'S PRESS GUIDE. Thomas Skinner Directories, 1874–

Both have changed publishers over the years, and *Benn's directory* (formerly known as *Mitchell*, and the *Newspaper press directory*), now in two volumes, is much the more detailed. It has a strong appeal to advertisers wishing to know in what specialist publication or regional newspaper to advertise to reach a certain public. Circulations and, for the larger publications, the names of editors and senior managers are given. *Benn* may be consulted also for such useful and sometimes hard-to-come-by information as addresses of broadcasting and press organizations, and it contains in its preface a widely quoted statistical comparison of press publications by category. There is always the problem with newspaper lists of whether to enter direct by title, or to try to meet the convenience of the user with arrangement by location. The *Benn directory* prefers to list all the national newspapers together, followed by the provincial press in order of town, aided by county and title indexes. Overseas newspapers and periodicals, with their London offices, form a separate volume.

Willing's favours a direct alphabetical sequence of titles for UK newspapers and periodicals, with the foreign press arranged under country. A classified index assists British newspaper location by town. Though a conveniently sized desk book, *Willing's* generally gives briefer information than *Benn*. In recent years its coverage abroad has been confined to the principal periodicals of Europe and USA, but the 1982 edition includes Australasia, the Gulf States and the Far East. Both guides attempt to give year of foundation for many titles, but this should be treated with caution, since amalgamations and changes of title can confuse the true date.

Mention should also be made of *British rate and data* (Maclean-Hunter, monthly, 1954–   ) the trade's guide to advertising rates; and of Dawson's *Guide to the press of the world* (1890– , annual, gratis), designed principally to assist wholesalers and bulk purchasers.

The American counterpart of *Benn's press directory* is:

AYER DIRECTORY OF PUBLICATIONS. Bala Cynwyd: IMS Press, 1869–   .

North American newspaper titles are listed by state, and alphabetically by locality within a state; there are appropriate title and classified indexes. Like all the better US current information guides, *Ayer* is comprehensive and well organized on statistical information, providing much useful advertising and circulation data in hieroglyphic and tabular form, plus editors, executives and circulations. *Ayer's* back issues are available on microfilm.

The Editor and Publisher international year book (New York: Editor and Publisher) has, since 1920, provided cheaply, between soft covers, an enormous range of highly compressed world press information, attempting a list of all daily newspapers published in the rest of the world, as well as the press in North America.

The major press guides of European countries, like the English language ones, are often venerable and mostly reliable. Amongst these may be listed: *Annuaire de la presse et de la publicité* (France), *Der Leitfaden für Presse und Werbung* (East and West

References and Source Books

Germany), *Repertorio analitico della stampa Italiana* (Italy). *The press in India* covers the sub-continent. The titles and some US holdings of East European and Russian newspapers are covered by two publications of the Library of Congress: *Russian, Ukrainian and Belorussian newspapers 1917–1953*; and *Newspapers of East Central and South East Europe in the Library of Congress.* Many others are listed in Walford and Sheehy.

For the average British reference library the English language guides, plus perhaps one for each of the principal European countries, are likely to be sufficient. It must be admitted, however, that in spite of these and the help of *Ulrich*, the addresses of new or short-lived newspapers in East European or developing countries can be difficult to come by. Embassies are often helpful, and the International Press Institute in Zurich makes a good point of contact.

REFERENCES AND SOURCE BOOKS

The student who has read this far will not be surprised to learn that the library profession has not produced much in the way of guides to sources for recent events. William Katz' *Introduction to reference work*, Vol 1 (McGraw-Hill), has good sections on modern current events material. Katz' other volume in the field, which he edited with Andrea Tarr, *Reference and information services* (Scarecrow Press) covers 'everything you ever wanted to know about almanacs' among many other current information works and indexes. A remarkable attempt at a comprehensive look at sources for affairs of the day and of the world was *Facts, files and action* by J. Edwin Holmstrom (Chapman & Hall, 1951–1953. 2 parts). Though dated, Part I, in particular, is a *tour-de-force* study of references to business and public affairs and remains well worth reading. *Public affairs information service bulletin* (twice monthly with quarterly and annual cumulations, 1915–   ) provides an up-to-date list of books, periodical articles, government publications, and reports in English, relating to economic conditions and public affairs on a world-wide basis. From 1978 this publication may be consulted as a computer-accessed databank.

Newspapers and other Material on Recent Events

A good compact list of books in print is The Library Association Public Libraries Group Readers' Guide, *The media*, compiled by Barrie I. MacDonald, 1977. This may be supplemented by *Review of sociological writing on the press*, working paper no. 2, prepared for the Royal Commission on the Press by Professor Denis McQuail in 1976. Books and official publications on radio and television in the United Kingdom are listed in *British broadcasting 1922–1982*, a select bibliography edited by Gavin Higgens and published in 1983 by BBC Data.

For the British press, Francis Williams' *Dangerous estate* (Longmans, 1957) is the best history. A more modern approach, challenging traditional attitudes, is *Newspaper history from the seventeenth century to the present day*, edited by George Boyce, James Curran and Pauline Wingate (Constable, 1978). One of the few books on the organization of news and current information, mainly in relation to media libraries, is my own *The modern news library* (London: Library Association, 1978).

The Press Royal Commission Reports, known by names of their Chairmen, are Ross (Cmnd 7700, 1949), Shawcross (Cmnd 1811, 1962) and McGregor (Cmnd 6810, 1977). The annual reports of the General Council of the Press provide a body of 'case law', chiefly concerning complaints over bias, error or intrusion.

The three post-war broadcasting inquiries were Beveridge (Cmnd 8116, 1951), Pilkington (Cmnd 1753, 1962) and Annan (Cmnd 6753, 1977).

The discerning student of the media will be entertained and stimulated by the writings of Marshall McLuhan, especially *Understanding media* (New York: McGraw-Hill, 1964).

REFERENCES AND CITATIONS

1. *Aslib Proceedings*, **29**, Nov–Dec 1977. 11–12.
2. Sheehy, Eugene (*comp.*) *Guide to reference books*. 9th ed. Chicago: American Library Association, 1976. 1st supplement 1980; 2nd supplement 1982.
3. Walford, A. J. (*ed.*) *Guide to reference material*. 4th ed. London: Library Association, 1980– . 3 vols.

9
Periodicals and Serials

Malcolm J. Campbell

The *ALA glossary of library terms*[1] defines a serial as 'a publication issued in successive parts, usually at regular intervals, and as a rule, intended to be continued indefinitely. Serials include periodicals, annuals (reports, yearbooks, etc) and memoirs, proceedings and transactions of societies'. Harrod, in *The librarians' glossary*[2], departs little from this. The use in both instances of 'usually' and 'as a rule'—terms not to be favoured in formulating definitions—indicates the difficulty of precisely specifying just what a serial is.

The ground has been well covered by other writers, notably Osborn[3] who, after an exhaustive survey of the literature, concludes by suggesting that, while dating and numbering are significant factors, a serial is what libraries through 'a common understanding' treat as such. This may appear to be begging the question, but is eminently sensible. Grenfell[4] has an appendix on 'What is a periodical? – or serial?' and Davinson[5] devotes considerable space to definitions of these two terms, noting that they are loosely used for the same purposes, 'periodical' being favoured in the UK, 'serial' in the USA. Certainly it is indicative that while the British Library's Library Association Library catalogue subject index has no entry under 'serials', the *Encyclopedia of library and information science*[6] ignores both 'periodicals' and 'serials'.

A convenient distinction may be to regard 'serial' as a broader generic term embracing 'periodical' within its coverage, the contents of the latter consisting primarily of articles designed to be read as a narrative, as opposed to tables of statistics or other material intended specifically for reference purposes and likely to be placed on a library's shelves with other works on the same subject. Many statistical sources, as well as directories, annuals and yearbooks, are normally serials, but are separately treated in this book, as are newspapers.

The term 'journal' in the UK is virtually synonymous with 'periodical' (though strictly it should include newspapers). 'Magazine', however, has a glossy, more trivial connotation, but this is not the case in the USA.

HISTORY

Periodicals as we know them may be said to date from the great flowering of science and culture seen in England under Charles II and in the France of Louis XIV. It was a time which saw the birth of great institutions gathering together the élite for the purpose of promotion and study of their spheres of interest. In 1665 the *Philosophical transactions of the Royal Society* were first published; consisting of correspondence between the Fellows, they made available for a wider public the means by which scientific discoveries had earlier been communicated on a private basis.

The French *Journal des scavans* (later *Journal des savants*), also founded in 1665, was rather a general literary journal, a form which had its origins in the *Bureau d'Adresse*, which survived only from 1633 to 1642. The *Journal* (like the *Philosophical transactions*) continues today after many vicissitudes and changes of character. It had an Italian imitator in the *Giornale de letterati* (1668–1769), but the first English-language literary journal was *Mercurius librarius, or a faithful account of all books and pamphlets*, established in 1680. *Weekly memorials for the ingenuous* (1681–1683) followed the pattern of the *Journal des savants* and used some of its material. A more familiar literary production was the *Monthly review* (1749–1845), which extended its range to coverage of scientific matters. The weekly, monthly and quarterly literary review flourished

Current Problems and Future Solutions

throughout the eighteenth and nineteenth centuries, and into the twentieth century.

The gentleman's magazine, which appeared between 1731 and 1907, still has significance in reference work, particularly for its antiquarian, topographical and genealogical content. The student should familiarize himself with its bound volumes and indexes. In North America, two short-lived journals inspired by *The gentleman's magazine* were founded in 1741—Benjamin Franklin's *General magazine* and Andrew Bradford's *American magazine*, By 1810, 27 periodicals were said to be appearing in the United States.[7]

The nineteenth century saw the emergence of an increasing number of special-interest periodicals, developments of which, in the television and do-it-yourself age, have largely displaced most of the vehicles for general reading which formerly abounded. In this country picture magazines too have all but disappeared (aside from the Sunday newspaper supplements), a notable survivor being *Illustrated London news* (1842–   ).

CURRENT PROBLEMS AND FUTURE SOLUTIONS

It is unprofitable to attempt to calculate the actual numbers of periodicals published in the world today. There have been many estimates, employing varying criteria as to what constitutes a periodical. Growth on a large scale there certainly is, difficult though this may be to reconcile with some publishers' estimates of the threat of widespread photocopying (which has not gone unchallenged[8]). The situation may be easing, but sheer quantity still presents a problem for the researcher and practitioner in keeping abreast of developments. As authors, they are further faced with long delays between the writing up of their contributions to knowledge, and its actual appearance in print. A variety of alternatives to traditional journal publishing is either currently in use, or projected:

1. **Reports.** Articles or reports published individually or in series. These can be issued as quickly as they can be printed, without waiting for integration with other material into a journal.

Periodicals and Serials

2. **Synopses**. Journals containing synopses of articles, complete texts of which are supplied on demand.

3. **Letters journals**. These consist merely of short communications, more speedily set up and distributed than when tied to major articles.

4. **Microforms**. Current issues sold solely in microfiche form have not yet been widely accepted, but some hard-copy journals include fiche versions for filing purposes. The availability of retrospective files on fiche or film is valued by libraries with limited storage space.

5. **The electronic journal**. A future development is likely to be the storage of articles on computer for retrieval on demand. The full implementation of the Post Office's Prestel system makes this a viable proposition for widespread use, employing as it does an adapted television receiver. Here again the key might be a hard-copy synopsis journal. Public acceptance of Prestel in the home has been slow to take off, however.

6. **Facsimile transmission**. In essence a virtually instantaneous means of supplying photocopies. Many libraries could take advantage of one journal subscription in this way, and unscrupulous use on a large scale might threaten the existence of many journals. However, there is still little sign of a network of library systems linked by a compatible system being established.

On the face of it, the electronic journal would seem to be the answer to all problems. Current and back issues would all be stored for instant retrievability in some remote computer. (A research study on the production of electronic journals was reported to the 1982 Aslib Annual Conference.[9]) Libraries might no longer need to subscribe to periodicals at all—indeed, given the versatility of Teletext, the whole future of libraries and librarians may be called in question. In theory, nobody need move from his own fireside or office desk to discover any known fact. A future without hard-copy periodicals publication seems unlikely, however, and

Types of Periodicals

students may expect to have to study serials management for many years to come. Significantly, there has been little practical change in the picture since the first edition of this book was published in 1980. Malcolm Shifrin has provided a more extended survey of future possibilities in Ross Bourne's *Serials librarianship*.[10]

TYPES OF PERIODICALS

A glance at any press guide will demonstrate that periodicals exist to serve every possible need and interest, from the most depraved to the highest expressions of the human spirit. Within this wide range there are four types which are of importance to the reference function:

1. **Journals published as a commercial venture.** These form the largest group, embracing trade journals, those relating to professional and economic activities, and so on. Their informative purpose is generally and naturally secondary to that of making money, so they must maintain an optimum level of subscription and advertising revenue. Exceptions to this latter means of income-raising exist—charging a proportionately higher subscription rate, and settling for a smaller circulation—their ultimate expression being the newsletter. Here, in a compact format, generally devoid of advertisements, are concentrated hard facts or advice from an apparently well-informed source. Frequently the contents of newsletters are confidential to the subscriber; in this case public libraries at least could not be expected to subscribe to them, eg *Fleet Street letter*.

2. **Learned journals.** Large numbers of these are still published direct by academic and professional institutions, but increasingly the process of production and distribution is passing to commercial publishers. Contributions may be the result of original research, and constitute an important part of the literature of their subject, or they may be merely vehicles for attaining professional or academic prestige. A former king of Norway once said 'if these men must upset what we have been taught to

believe, they ought to keep their opinions to themselves, or publish them in learned periodicals which nobody reads',[11] and certainly it is a fact that an unhealthily high proportion of subscribers are libraries, subject as they are to budget cuts and the temptation of easy photocopying. This and other factors affecting the future of learned journal publishing have been discussed by the Secretary of the Association of Learned and Professional Society Publishers.[12]

3. **House journals.** These serve the function of communicating between a company and its staff, shareholders or the world at large (or a combination of any of these), and are frequently no more than a recitation of the achievements of the firm and its employees. Some, however, carry important contributions to knowledge, and bank reviews for example, may be physically as well as authoritatively of some substance, or lighter-weight reviews of regional economies. Some manufacturing corporations, too, produce important journals, notably in the scientific and technical fields.

House journals are usually free, but librarians should not be tempted on that account to collect them without regard to their consumption of staff time and accommodation. In the UK the British Institute of Management and the British Library (Science Reference Library) have significant collections; D. M. King and M. Thompson have produced a guide, *House journals held by the Science Reference Library*, published by the Library in 1978. Many are listed, too, in *Benn's press directory*, and the *Gebbie Press house magazines directory* (New York: Gebbie Press).

4. **Year's work in ...; Advances in ....** This category of serial often differs rather in format and frequency than in content from what are generally regarded as periodicals, but the terms cover a wide variety of approaches:

THE YEAR'S WORK IN ENGLISH STUDIES. London: Murray, 1921– .

A reprinting of material published during the year under review in periodicals and books, forming a survey of English and, since 1954, American, literature studies.

THE YEAR'S WORK IN MODERN LANGUAGE STUDIES. London: Oxford University Press, 1931– .
Here the year is reviewed by means of specially commissioned articles which have not appeared elsewhere.

ADVANCES IN LIBRARIANSHIP. New York: Academic Press, 1970– .
Six to eight topics are examined by international experts, at greater length than is commonly possible in a monthly or quarterly journal.

Academic Press produce a number of *Advances in* . . ., mostly in the scientific/technical fields, containing a variety of papers from as many hands. Works with titles prefixed in this way may be of a quite different nature, and the Pergamon catalogue for example reveals some which are simply series of works on the same broad topic, or conference proceedings which may not necessarily be annual.

Another form of title begins *Developments in* . . ., eg *Developments in adhesives* (London: Applied Science Publishers, 1977–   ). As with other sectors of periodicals publishing, the *genre* is proliferating, and while mostly such works may be considered as 'state-of-the-art' surveys, prospective purchasers should know the nature of what they are buying before commencing a continuing commitment.

REFERENCE USE OF PERIODICALS

Periodicals serve four main purposes in a reference library:

1. to supply generally the latest possible information on a given subject;
2. they are often the *only* source of material on new subjects;
3. to supply a particular article to a reader who has seen it cited in a book or another journal;

4. to provide an overview of the state of a given discipline at a particular time.

Libraries' policies of selection and retention of periodicals will be governed to a large extent by these factors, in addition to local circumstances and alternative availability. A public library, catering for the widest possible spread of interests, will need to reflect these with a broad range of periodicals of all kinds. Only a small proportion of them will be bound for permanent filing, except in the very largest institutions; Manchester Central Library's complete file of the weekly *Radio Times* must now be of immense value and interest to historians and others, but few libraries could spare space for the preservation of such apparent ephemera. It is fortunate, therefore, that Chadwyck-Healey of Cambridge have produced back issues up to 1980 on 35 mm microfilm, and subsequent issues on 49-frame microfiche.

Academic libraries, on the other hand, will select, for a narrower readership, journals reflecting the concerns of the institution. A far higher proportion will be retained for ever—their users will more frequently pursue cited articles. The same principles apply even more intensely in special libraries, serving companies, research associations, etc. Here needs will by definition be more specialized still, and few journals will be jettisoned before many years of use.

Retention policies have been influenced in recent years, however, by the emergence of the British Library Lending Division, which has enabled libraries of all kinds in the United Kingdom—and indeed to some extent overseas—to view more critically their extensive files of less frequently consulted journals. A listing of *Current serials received* by the BLLD is available, and should be held in all libraries of any size.

CURRENT AND RETROSPECTIVE BIBLIOGRAPHY

Before considering the means by which periodicals may be located, it should be remembered that differing principles obtain in arrangement and description. An example is the treatment of journals issued from corporate bodies—entries under the name of the body, first word of the title, short title, etc. Again, the indiscriminate use of abbreviations in citations may lead to faulty identification of a journal. There are British and American standards governing this,[13] and the subject has received international attention, as well as a listing of about 10,000 abbreviations of titles by Wall[14] and a detailed exposition of problems by Osborn.[15]

Press guides are not within the compass of this chapter (see p 215) but passing reference must be made to *Willing's press guide*, *Benn's press directory* and, from North America, *Ayer directory of publications* and the *Standard periodicals directory*. Sufficient to say here that, although the aims of each pair may appear to coincide, their lay-outs and contents differ, and students should familiarize themselves with these differences.

In the same category, but in a class of its own, since it is truly international, is *Ulrich's international periodicals directory*, published in alternate years by Bowker of New York and now available online from Dialog. The latest two-volume edition has 67,000 entries grouped by subject; an important feature is a note of where items are indexed/abstracted. Its sister publication, *Irregular serials and annuals: An international directory*, appears in intervening years and covers such items as yearbooks, transactions, proceedings and directories. Both are supplemented by *Ulrich's quarterly*. Alternative access to details of 65,000 publishers and corporate authors of 96,000 titles in the two works, arranged by country, is provided by *Sources of serials* (2nd ed, 1981). Gale Research of Detroit publish a four-part *National directory of newsletters and reporting services*, the second edition of which (1981) contains 3,000 entries.

Media guides, such as *BRAD: British rate and data*, and the American *Standard rate and data* series, may also be required. For some countries their equivalents provide the cheapest (sometimes the only) comprehensive keys to periodicals and other advertising media, though published primarily with the needs of advertisers in mind. *EMA: Editorial media and analysis* (London: Bill Gibbs–PNA Group; monthly) names specialist contacts for the receipt of news hand-outs and lists free-lance writers by broad subjects.

For the selection process, however, librarians need more infor-

Periodicals and Serials

mation than can be provided by all-embracing comprehensive listings, and a preliminary check could be made in:

Katz, W. B. and Katz, L. S. MAGAZINES FOR LIBRARIES. 4th ed. New York: Bowker, 1982.
 Helpful and often critical descriptions are given of a wide international range of journals (not simply 'magazines' in their British connotation) within subject groupings. Note particularly the headings 'Free magazines' and 'Abstracts and indexes'.
 Unfortunately there is no direct British equivalent on the scale of Katz and Katz, the nearest being:

Woodworth, D. P. CURRENT BRITISH JOURNALS. 3rd ed. Boston Spa, Yorkshire: British Library Lending Division, 1982.
 Arrangement is by subject, with title and subject indexes; brief descriptions include a note of where each is indexed, but some useful features of earlier editions are excluded from this one.

Periodicals out of the mainstream of commercial publishing are in danger of being overlooked in public libraries, and such guides as John Spiers' *The underground and alternative press in Britain: A bibliographical guide with historical notes*, from Harvester Press in Brighton, will be needed. Regrettably, such aids tend to appear and vanish as capriciously as some of the journals they describe; Spiers itself was last revised in 1977, under the editorship of M. Colwell.

Guides to periodicals within particular ranges of interests abound, such as *Management and economics journals: A guide to information sources*, by V. G. Tega (Detroit: Gale, 1977), constituting No. 33 in that publisher's 'Management information guides' series. Some other examples are E. Johansson *Check list of British official serial publications* (12th ed. British Library, 1983); Y. Messenger *Commonwealth specialist periodicals: An annotated directory of scientific, technical and professional journals published in Commonwealth developing countries* (London: Commonwealth Secretariat, 1977); International Trade Centre, Documentation Service *International trade documentation* (special issues on country and trade periodicals. Geneva: ITC, 1977 and 1978); and A. M. Woodward *Directory of review serials in science and technology 1970–1973: A guide to regular or quasi-regular publications containing critical, state-of-the-art and literature reviews* (London: Aslib, 1974).

Numerous periodicals are now available retrospectively in microform, making necessary a comprehensive bibliography such as *Guide to microforms in print* (London: Mansell; annual) which lists books as well as journals from about 200 publishers, in two volumes, arranged by author/title and subject. Similarly there is need for guidance as to the availability of periodicals in translation, and about 360 of these are included in *Journals in translation* (3rd ed. Boston Spa: British Library Lending Division and International Translations Centre, 1982), which deals with the BLLD's own holdings. Many series of translations, by no means all of which are technical, are issued by the National Technical Information Service of the US Department of Commerce—*Translations on Eastern Europe: Economics and industrial affairs*, for example.

There are two major retrospective sources for historical details of British periodicals:

Watson, G. NEW CAMBRIDGE BIBLIOGRAPHY OF ENGLISH LITERATURE. Cambridge: University Press, 1969–1977. 4 vols and index.

More fully described in the later chapter on bibliographies, this is a revision of the earlier *Cambridge bibliography of English literature*, with more material, but omitting Commonwealth titles.

The Times. TERCENTENARY HANDLIST OF ENGLISH AND WELSH NEWSPAPERS, MAGAZINES AND REVIEWS. London: The Times, 1920. Reprinted, London: Dawsons, 1966.

Chronological listings are given of the London and suburban press from 1620 to 1919, and of the provincial press from 1701 to 1919.

An attempt to provide a similar chronicle for North American publications was not fully accomplished due to the death of its editor:

Mott, F. L. A HISTORY OF AMERICAN MAGAZINES. Cambridge, Massachusetts: Harvard University Press, 1930–1968. 5 vols.

Chronological listings of journals published from 1741 to 1905 are provided in the earlier volumes, for which full indexes are included. Vol 5, however, which was to have covered the years 1905 to 1930 is uncompleted.

Of retrospective guides within specific sectors, a recent example is R. Harrison's THE WARWICK GUIDE TO BRITISH LABOUR PERIODICALS, 1790–1970 (Brighton: Harvester Press, 1977). Apart from the largest general public libraries, such listings will be of most concern to more specialized collections and it would be unprofitable to categorize them here.

LIBRARY CATALOGUES AND UNION LISTS

The next best thing to possession of a required periodical issue in one's own library is to know where else it may be seen. Where a particular article is required, for which a photocopy will serve, a large proportion of such requests in the UK can be met through the British Library Lending Division. However, it may be more expeditious to telephone or telex a not too distant co-operative library which may post a photocopy the same or the succeeding day. In this instance, or for a very specialized item, a union list of periodicals would provide the key. These, and individual libraries' lists of holdings, will also be needed to direct the reader who wishes regularly to see current issues of a periodical, or to consult back files.

The printed catalogue of the British Library Reference Division is still proceeding, and arrangement of periodicals in its predecessor was by place of publication, and that information is not always to hand. Lists of holdings of the Science Reference Library are more conventionally accessible for publications within its scope. These are now appearing within broad subject groupings, such as *Periodicals on agriculture held by the Science Reference Library* and *Periodicals on chemistry* . . . In 1982 a useful *Abstracting and indexing periodicals in the Science Reference Library* appeared in its second edition.

Library Catalogues and Union Lists

Older material will be found in R. T. Milford and D. M. Sutherland, *Catalogue of English newspapers and periodicals in the Bodleian Library, 1622–1800* (1936). Libraries of professional bodies, trade unions, companies, academic institutions, and most large public libraries, produce lists of their periodicals holdings, very often made available at no charge or on an exchange basis. Locality and specialized interest will determine which of these should be obtained.

The usefulness of union catalogues of periodicals as finding-lists for current issues and back copies is well recognized, and there are many to choose from. Varying principles of description can present a problem where recourse to a number of union catalogues is made in reference work, and some proposed standards have been suggested by Koster.[16] In using national and international lists it is important to study their prefatory matter for details of coverage, principles of arrangement, and the meaning of space-saving symbols and abbreviations employed.

As presaged in the previous edition of this book, the long-standing *British union catalogue of periodicals* has ceased publication, though doubtless it will still be used, albeit with caution. It is succeeded by *Serials in the British Library*, on the principle that most requests for loans and photocopies are now channelled through that body's Lending Division. It appears quarterly, with annual cumulations on microfiche.

Other national union catalogues include the *Union list of serials in New Zealand libraries*, first published in 1953 by the National Library Service in Wellington, and the *Union list of current periodicals and serials in Irish libraries*, from the Irish Association for Documentation and Information Service in Dublin. It does appear, however, that the work of compiling national union lists is becoming altogether too unwieldy for larger nations, and localized or specialized listings are now more common, such as the Bibliothèque Nationale's catalogue of periodicals from the seventeenth century to 1939 in the libraries of Paris, and a union list of foreign serials in West German and West Berlin libraries published by Harrassowitz of Wiesbaden. Regional lists have the advantages of encompassing a wider range of libraries, and of giving more detailed accounts of holdings than is possible generally on a national scale.

Periodicals and Serials

The London and Home Counties Branch of the Library Association produced several editions of the *London union list of periodicals*, the last of which, in 1970, demonstrated the weaknesses inherent in low-cost 'home-made' production. LASER (the London and South East regional library cooperative) has continued to gather details of constituent libraries' holdings and will supply information on request, but all efforts to find a means of effecting publication, at least for an acceptable cost, have so far proved unavailing. Other efforts abound, such as the *Union list of periodicals* from the County of Hereford and Worcester Association of Technical Libraries, and the Radcliffe Infirmary's *Union list of periodicals in the Health Service libraries in Oxford*.

Serials holdings in academic institutions are of course considerable, and union lists embrace the component libraries of many universities—Cambridge, Oxford, Edinburgh, and so on. Otherwise, there is an increasing number of attempts to achieve national coverage within a specific subject area, an example being the *Union catalogue of legal periodicals: A location guide to the holdings of legal periodicals in libraries in the United Kingdom* (London: Institute of Advanced Legal Studies, 1978), which includes about 3,500 titles in 114 locations. In 1977, Carol Travis edited *Periodicals from Africa: A bibliography and union list of periodicals published in Africa* for the Standing Conference on Library Materials on Africa (SCOLMA). Sheffield University has produced a *Check list of Japanese periodicals held in British university and research libraries*, but pre-eminent in mining this seam are the London publishers Mansell. Their works include P. Auchterbrie and Y. H. Safadi *Union catalogue of Arabic serials in British libraries*; Brenda E. Moon *Periodicals for South East Asian studies*; G. R. Nunn *South East Asian periodicals: An international union list*; and the same compiler's *Japanese periodicals and newspapers in western languages: An international union list*.

KEYS TO PERIODICALS' CONTENTS

How, given the increasing specialization and compartmentalization of journals, can the busy specialist ensure that he sees all that he should of this output (**current awareness**), avoid wasteful reading in a wide spectrum of journals (**scatter**), and quickly retrieve required data from what could present itself merely as an inchoate mass (**retrospective searching**)? Some part of the answer lies in the use of indexes to the contents of periodicals, and abstracting services which provide a précis of the articles noted.

Most periodicals of any reference value produce indexes of their own, generally at quarterly or annual intervals; the idea had its origins in the *Journal des scavans*. For long-established journals, cumulative indexes covering a number of years can be of great value, as with *The gentleman's magazine*, or *The engineer*, to which an index covering the first hundred years was published in 1956. An aid to tracing indexes of US and Canadian origin is:

Devers, C. M. *et al.* GUIDE TO SPECIAL ISSUES AND INDEXES OF PERIODICALS. 2nd ed. New York: Special Libraries Association, 1976.

Editorial and advertisers' indexes are included, as well as special sections and annual issues. There is a subject index.

Reference to individual indexes can be tedious, and services covering a number of journals will be resorted to for subject enquiries.

The growth of numbers of serials themselves is paralleled in the vast number of indexing and abstracting services now available. *Ulrich* alone currently lists hundreds, and is by no means a complete record of the world's output. Grenfell[18] said in 1965, 'It would assist the librarian in checking the aggregate coverage of his subject if guides to indexing and abstracting services were more plentiful and up-to-date, particularly for the humanities and social sciences'. The Féderation Internationale de Documentation, and the National Federation of Abstracting and Indexing Services, are at present working upon a world inventory in machine-readable form.

In the meantime there is the FID's own *Abstracting services*, though this is now somewhat out of date. More useful is the *International serials catalogue* (Paris: International Council of Scientific Unions Abstracting Board, 1978–1979. 2 vols). This identifies scientific and technical journals abstracted and indexed by member services of the Board. Part 1 is an alphabetical list, Part 2 an index-concordance. Of more general interest is Joseph V. Marconi's *Indexed periodicals* (Ann Arbor: Pierian Press, 1976), which monitors about 11,000 titles indexed in 33 American, Canadian and British services from 1802 to 1973. A study of UK abstracting and indexing services has been published as a British Library Research and Development report.[19]

Indexing and abstracting services are frequently international in scope, as Chandler[20] has noted, since interest in new developments in whatever field transcend national boundaries. However, a service which is encyclopaedic in subject-range faces the accusation of *not* being fully comprehensive—some journals are necessarily excluded—and of undue time-lag between publication of an article and its citation in an index. These questions, and that of which articles to select for indexing within a given periodical issue, were discussed in 1976 by Beletskaya[21] with regard to the Russian *Letopis' zhurnal 'nykh statai (Chronicle of journal articles)*, which at its inception in 1926 indexed 19,856 articles from 206 periodicals, and had grown by 1975 to cover 176,364 articles in 1,892 journals.

Should a library select such indexing/abstracting services on the basis of their coverage of journals actually stocked; or should journals be selected for stock by virtue of their inclusion in indexing and abstracting services held? Perhaps a judicious balance between the two approaches is the only answer.

INDEXING SERVICES

An indexing service is simply a directional aid to material which has been published in serial form within a given period on a given subject, and sometimes by a given author, with sufficient bibliographical detail to identify the issue, and the page or pages on which the item is to be found. An early example is:

Poole, W. F. AN INDEX TO PERIODICAL LITERATURE, 1801–1881. 4th ed. Boston, Massachusetts: Houghton, 1891. 2 vols. Five supplements to 1907. Reprinted 1938, New York: P. Smith.

Indexing Services

This index included 479 United States and British periodicals, with entry by subject and occasionally by title.

A more recent attempt to provide a key to nineteenth-century journal articles is:

Houghton, W. E. WELLESLEY INDEX TO VICTORIAN PERIODICALS, 1824–1900. Toronto: University of Toronto Press; and London: Routledge and Kegan Paul, 1966– .

Instead of producing one continuous sequence, the first volume covers eight major journals of the period; the second volume covers twelve monthlies and quarterlies. A further twenty are to be indexed in the next two volumes, of which the first appeared in 1979.

The most comprehensive of all continuing international periodicals indexes on an international scale is published in Germany:

INTERNATIONALE BIBLIOGRAPHIE DER ZEITSCHRIFTENLITERATUR AUS ALLEN GEBIETEN DER FORSCHUNG. Osnabrück: Dietrich, 1897– .

Now appearing semi-annually, and covering over 8,000 titles, it originated in three separate services, combined into one since 1965. It is popularly known as *Dietrich* or *IBZ*.

Important, but more manageable in size by virtue of its more limited coverage (160 American general and popular journals) is the:

READERS' GUIDE TO PERIODICAL LITERATURE. New York: H. W. Wilson, 1905– .

Articles from 1900 onwards are indexed by subject and author, with some titles. For smaller libraries, entries for a selection of 58 journals are offered in the *Abridged readers' guide to periodical literature*, available from 1935.

The H. W. Wilson Company is possibly the most prolific publisher of periodicals indexes. From the *Readers' guide* has grown an empire to which yet another (*General science index*) was added in 1978.

Humanities index and *Social sciences index* are the result of the splitting, in 1974, of the *Social sciences and humanities index*, which itself was an off-shoot from the *Readers' guide* and *International index to periodicals* (1916–1965). *Education index* was established as a separate entity in 1929. *Index to legal periodicals* commenced in 1908, and has sections devoted to a table of cases and book reviews, in addition to the usual subject and author sequences. Others in the series are *Library literature* (1921–   ); *Art index* (1929–   ); *Bibliographic index* (1937–   ); *Biography index* (1946–   ); *Applied science and technology index* and *Business periodicals index*, which until 1958 were components of *Industrial arts index*; *Biological and agricultural index* (1964–   ), formerly *Agricultural index*. There is not space here to describe each of these fully; the current Wilson catalogue serves this purpose well. Generally they appear monthly or quarterly, and cumulate annually. Some include books and pamphlets, in addition to periodical articles, and English-language material only is indexed, with a natural bias towards North American coverage.

Also from Wilson is *Book review digest* (1905–   ), which condenses about 6,100 reviews per year from 81 periodicals. An author/title index to the years 1905–1974 appeared in four volumes in 1976. *Current book review citations* (1976–   ) is an annual *index* only, to reviews in over 1,000 journals, which in its first year pin-pointed over 55,000 of these.

Britain has no comparable organization, but there are parallels to some of the Wilson services:

BRITISH HUMANITIES INDEX. London: Library Association, 1963–   . Quarterly, with annual cumulations.

Indexes about 350 periodicals and newspapers; some social sciences material is included, as well as the humanities. It grew from *Subject index to periodicals*, 1915–1961, which then split into three parts, *British technology index*, from 1981 retitled *Current technology index*, acknowledging its increasing international coverage (monthly, cumulating annually), and *British education index* (three times a year) being the other products of the division. The last is now published by the British Library, Bibliographical Services Division.

Periodical articles are included in the coverage of the *Annual bibliography of English language and literature*, which appears about four years after the year under review, that for 1977 in 1981, for example. It commenced in 1920 and was for a period published in the United States, but is now issued by the Modern Humanities Research Association in London.

An important specialized service is *Engineering index* (1885–), published since 1920 in New York by the American Society of Mechanical Engineers. This is multilingual, and covers some 3,000 journals. Its monthly appearance is supplemented by a weekly card service on a range of subjects of the subscriber's choosing, containing brief abstracts or annotations of articles. *Engineering index* is now also available online via *Compendex*.

INDEX MEDICUS. Washington: National Library of Medicine, 1960– . Monthly.

The principal medical article indexing service; some 2,300 periodicals are included, but for smaller libraries *Abridged index medicus* is available, covering just 100 journals. Book reviews are separately cumulated into a *Bibliography of medical reviews*. The need to speed up the indexing process in such a comprehensive service led to the development of the computer-generated Medical Literature Analysis and Retrieval System (MEDLARS), which has achieved application far beyond its original purpose.

Other major specialized services include *Index to foreign legal periodicals* (London: Institute of Advanced Legal Studies, 1960–) and *Music index* (Detroit: Information Service, 1949–), encompassing over 300 periodicals. A product of interlibrary co-operation is *Public affairs information service bulletin* (New York: PAIS, 1915–), which covers books, pamphlets, US government publications and reports on the social sciences and its ramifications, as well as articles from about 1,000 periodicals. It appears weekly, with five intermediate cumulations and an annual volume.

A survey of major indexing services should not fail to include those of the Predicasts Corporation of Cleveland, Ohio. Their 'Funk and Scott' indexes are of particular importance in the business field, *F & S Index United States*, formerly *F & S Index of corporations and industries* (1960–), covering newspapers, journals, reports, etc, for activities in that country. A closely classified section on products and industries is followed by an alphabetical listing of references to individual corporations. It is paralleled for the rest of the world by *F & S Index International* (1967–   ) and *F & S Index Europe* (1978–   ) which have an additional geographical section. For the UK alone, *Research Index* (Dorking, Surrey: Business Surveys, 1965–   ) is more modest, again with alphabetical subject and companies sequences. Only about 100 newspapers and journals are indexed, and the format is duplicated typescript, but fortnightly publication ensures speedy accessibility.

There have been a number of attempts to catch up retrospectively with articles on subjects inadequately represented in existing services. An ambitious recent example is Róbert Dán's *Accumulated index of Jewish bibliographical periodicals* (London: Mansell, 1978) which covers the period 1858–1943. In 1982 the Oxford University Press published an *Index to selected bibliographical journals*, covering 1933–1970. Mansell also published, in 1976, B. C. Bloomfield's *An author index to selected British 'Little Magazines' 1930–1939*, with 11,000 entries. Other recent 'retrospectives' include K. I. Macdonald *The Essex reference index: British journals on politics and sociology, 1850–1973* (London: Macmillan, 1975); G. M. Terry *A subject and name index to articles on the Slavonic and East European languages and literature, music and theatre, libraries and the press, contained in English-language journals, 1920–1975* (Nottingham: University Library, 1976), and L. Batty *Retrospective index to film periodicals, 1930–1971* (New York: Bowker, 1975).

Productions of Clover Publications of Stevenage, Hertfordshire, are geared to a wider non-specialized public than is common. *Clover information index* (1975–   ) covers articles on consumer durables (automobiles, do-it-yourself, etc) from popular periodicals. It was joined in 1978 by *Antiques index*, *Popular medical index* and *County magazines index*, which are similarly orientated. Each appears quarterly, the last of the year being an annual cumulation. A more comprehensive North American equivalent to *Clover* is *Consumers' index to product evaluation and information sources*, quarterly from Pierian Press of Ann Arbor, Michigan. *A popular periodical index* has been published since 1973 by Robert M. Bottorf in Camden, New Jersey.

In recent years in the UK alone, additional services have covered alloys, the 'alternative press', anaesthesiology, ecological sciences,

Abstract Services

film, genealogy and rock music. In this way the task of the searcher for leads to specific articles or kinds of data is eased. For the purpose of keeping up to date with writings on a discipline, however, the form is less convenient, so there has grown up a new kind of aid, the presentation of title-pages of journals, which can be comfortably scanned. Special libraries have been doing this for some time, to satisfy the needs of their known clientèle; now some are marketing their product, and commercial concerns also have seen possibilities in the idea.

Contents of current journals and *Contents pages in management*, for example, are compilations of the London and Manchester Business Schools, respectively. In the same subject area, *Management contents* is published by G. D. Searle, Skokie, Illinois; and the *Journal of economic literature* (Nashville, Tennessee: American Economic Association) contains, in addition to index and abstracts sections, one devoted to the contents of current journals. In Britain, the Library Service of the Department of Trade and Industry and its satellites market the weekly *Contents of recent economics journals*, through HMSO. *SCIMP: European index of management periodicals* is a co-operative enterprise by members of the European Business School Libraries Group, supplying data to a computer in Helsinki. It is distributed in the UK by the Manchester Business School Library.

But the reproduction of title-pages has been most seriously undertaken in the United States by the Institute for Scientific Information in Philadelphia. When, in 1974, it commenced weekly publication (with a subject index) of *Current contents: Social and behavioural sciences*, covering about 1,000 journals, it was already producing *Current contents: Agriculture, biology and science*; . . .: *Chemical sciences*; . . .: *Clinical practice*; . . .: *Education*; . . .: *Engineering and Technology*; . . .: *Life sciences*.

ABSTRACT SERVICES

Harrod[22] gives four definitions of the term 'abstract', with an indication of the various types within each, of which the first is the most relevant in the present context. He says an abstract is a 'form

Periodicals and Serials

of current bibliography in which sometimes books, but mainly contributions to periodicals, are summarized: they are accompanied by adequate bibliographical descriptions to enable the publications or articles to be traced, and are frequently arranged in classified order'. An abstract may translate from a foreign language original—an important facility, since a full translation may not be available. Harrod further categorizes five types of abstract:

indicative: containing just enough to direct attention to the importance or otherwise of the original;
informative: a more extended digest, with data from the original, which may in itself give sufficient information for the searcher;
evaluative: pronouncing judgment on the value of the original;
general: covering the full scope of the original for all types of readership;
selective: picking up points of concern to a limited specialized readership—perhaps for the known clientèle of an organization, as current awareness for staff, or in response to a specific enquiry.

An **author** abstract is one prepared by the writer of the article itself; it sometimes appears at its head in the journal in which it is published. A **comprehensive** abstracting service embraces all material within a given subject field, and a **selective** service has in mind the requirements of a particular readership.

There are wide differences in presentation of abstracts, which may be readable pieces of prose, eg the *Anbar* services; numbered key-words, eg the brief abstracts section of the periodical *Ocean energy*, or tabulated quantitative data (*Predicasts* and *Worldcasts*).

The *Anbar* service (Anbar Publications) commenced in 1961, abstracting articles of management interest generally. In 1970–1971 it was split into five distinct parts: *Accounting + data processing abstracts*; *Marketing + distribution abstracts*; *Personnel + training abstracts*; *Top management abstracts*; and *Work study + O & M abstracts*. Each appears eight times a year, and cumulates into the one-volume *Compleat Anbar*. Entries are classified by a unique system and, while each component part is published in conjunction with an appropriate professional body, the entries often contain lively critical comments.

Abstract Services

Predicasts indexes have already been described; their abstracting method is quite different from that of *Anbar*. PROMT is an amalgam from 1977 of the former *Chemical market abstracts* and *Equipment market abstracts*, the former commencing in 1950, the latter (as *Electronic market abstracts*), in 1972. The abstracts, though in narrative form, are not 'designed to be read as literature'. *Predicasts* itself, and *Worldcasts* (Regional and Product), are extended indexes in tabulated form, of forecasting articles, reports, etc, on economic aspects of products, industries, and geographical areas. Columns are allocated to quantities given in the original—for an earlier year, the most current year, and a projection for the future. It is thus possible to compare differing interpretations of likely future trends. The entire Predicasts package is available online via the Lockheed system.

The change of name of *Chemical market abstracts* ended confusion with:

CHEMICAL ABSTRACTS. Columbus, Ohio: American Chemical Society, 1907–   . Fortnightly.

Over 170,000 articles are abstracted each year from more than 12,000 periodicals. Patents and formulae are included, as are short book reviews. Cumulative five-yearly indexes are published, and the service may be purchased in separate subject sections. Related services are *Access*, a five-yearly (from 1969) listing of periodicals abstracted, together with locations in North America and elsewhere, and *Chemical titles* (1960–   ), which is an indexing, not an abstracting, medium.

Of even longer standing is:

SCIENCE ABSTRACTS. London: Institution of Electrical Engineers, 1898–   . Vols 1–5, 1898–1902, reprinted London: Butterworth, 1964.

International in scope, *Science abstracts* was split in 1903 into Series A, *Physics abstracts* (fortnightly from January 1969), and Series B, *Electrical engineering abstracts*, now *Electrical and electronics engineering abstracts* (monthly). A further Series C was added in 1966—*Control abstracts*, retitled in 1969 *Computer and control abstracts* (monthly). Each carries indexes to authors, subjects, bibliographies, books, conferences and patents. Series A and B additionally index reports, and Series C carries a journals index. All are available on microfiche and magnetic tape, in addition to hard copy.

Economic titles/abstracts has been published in various forms since 1953 (until 1977 as *Economic abstracts* and more recently combining with its sister *Key to economic science*) at the Hague by Martinus Nijhoff for the Ministry of Economic Affairs. In a classified order, with subject index, it has a bias towards European material.

Among other long-standing series are *Psychological abstracts* (Washington, DC: American Psychological Association, 1927–   ) and *Biological abstracts* (Philadelphia: Biological Abstracts, 1926–   ), the latter having, since 1962, a companion publication *Biochemical title index*. Of particular significance in our own field is *Library and information science abstracts*, published since 1950 by the Library Association (as *Library science abstracts* until 1968). It appears bimonthly, and covers about 230 periodicals from all parts of the world.

An example of retrospective abstracting is K. S. Warren's *Schistosomiasis: The evolution of a medical literature: Selected abstracts and citations, 1852–1972* (Cambridge, Massachusetts: MIT, 1973). A service relating to a particular period of time is *Historical abstracts 1775–1945*, which has been published quarterly since 1955 by Clio Press of Santa Barbara, California.

The quantity and subject range of abstracting services now available is illustrated by some which have commenced in the UK alone since 1975. Information Retrieval of London has established series covering immunology, applied ecology, oncology, and toxicology. An extensive range issuing from the Commonwealth Agricultural Bureau at Slough includes coverage of cotton and tropical fibres, ornamental horticulture, poultry, protozoology, small animals, sorghum and millets, and tropical seeds. *Inspec*, at the Institution of Electrical Engineers in London, has a series of *Key abstracts* covering communication technology, electrical measurement and instrumentation, electronic circuits, industrial power and control systems, solid state devices, and systems theory.

References

Attempts to keep abreast of the burgeoning abstracts industry, both commencing in 1982 from Gale of Detroit, will be welcomed. They are *Abstracting and indexing services directory*, published three times per year, describing in each issue about 2,000 abstracts, indexes, digests, bibliographies and catalogues in all fields; and *Indexes, abstracts and digests: Guide to books in all languages that identify contents of books, periodicals and other documents in systematic and abbreviated form*, which has 6,000 entries.

Most of the services available will be beyond the means of the general reference library. Before very long, however, it may be that a good deal of such information is obtainable only through the medium of a data terminal or adapted television receiver. Public reference libraries are having to consider the implications inherent in this new situation, not least that of the future for a free information service.

REFERENCES AND CITATIONS

1. Thompson, E. H. *ALA glossary of library terms*. Chicago: American Library Association, 1943. 159.
2. Harrod, L. M. *(comp.) The librarians' glossary*. 4th ed. London: Deutsch, 1977. 903. (A 5th ed by Ray Prytherch was published by Gower in 1983.)
3. Osborn, A. D. *Serial publications: their place and treatment in libraries*. 3rd ed. Chicago: American Library Association, 1980.
4. Grenfell, D. *Periodicals and serials: their treatment in special libraries*. 2nd ed. London: Aslib, 1965.
5. Davinson, D. *The periodicals collection*. 2nd ed. London: Deutsch, 1978. 7–12.
6. Kent, A., Lancour, H. and Daily, J. E. *(eds.) Encyclopedia of library and information science*. New York/Basle: Dekker. Vol 22, 1977.
7. Thomas, I. *History of printing in America*. Albany, New York: The author, 1874. Vol 2, 292.
8. Line, M. B. and Wood, D. N. The effect of a large-scale photocopying service on journal sales. *Journal of documentation*, 31 (4), December 1975. 234–45
   Tongeren, E. Van. The effect of a large-scale photocopying service on journal sales (and a reply from Line and Wood). *Journal of documentation*, 32 (3), September 1976. 198–206.
   Woodward, A. M. *Factors affecting the renewal of periodical subscriptions*. London: Aslib, 1978.

Periodicals and Serials

9. Shackel, B. and Pullinger, D. J. Electronic journals and communication of research.
   Simkins, M. A. The impact of new technology on the information profession.
   Both in *Aslib proceedings*, 35 (2), February 1983.
10. Shifrin, Malcolm. The challenge of non-traditional types of serial. In: Bourne, Ross. *Serials librarianship*. London: Library Association, 1980.
11. Inge, W. R. *Diary of a Dean: St. Paul's 1911–1934*. London: Hutchinson, [1949]. 80.
12. Millson, R. J. Institutions and learned societies as information sources. *Aslib proceedings*, 30 (2), February 1978. 48–54.
13. British Standards Institution. *Recommendations for abbreviations of titles of periodicals* (BS 4148, Part 1: 1970; Part 2: 1975).
    American National Standards Institute. *American national standard for the abbreviation of titles of periodicals*. Washington, DC: ANSI, 1974.
14. Wall, C. E. (*comp.*) *Periodical title abbreviations*. Detroit: Gale, 1969.
15. Osborn, A. D. *Op. cit.* Chapter 18.
16. Koster, C. J. Standard serial citation: bibliographical standards for union catalogues of serials. *Catalogue and index* (21), January 1971. 3–5.
17. Olsen, K. D. Union lists and the public record of serials. *Special libraries*, 61 (65), 1970.
18. Grenfell, D. *Op. cit.* 165.
19. Burgess, G. M., Vickery, A. and Keenan, S. *Inventory of abstracting and indexing services produced in the United Kingdom*. London: British Library, 1978. R & D Report No 5420.
20. Chandler, G. *How to find out*. Oxford: Pergamon, 1963. 33.
21. Beletskaya, Z. G. Letopis' zhurnal 'nykh statai na sovremennom étape. *Sovetskaya bibliografiya* (159), 1976. 3–8.
22. Harrod, L. M. *Op. cit.*

SUGGESTIONS FOR FURTHER READING

Bourne, R. *Serials librarianship*. London: Library Association, 1980.
Davinson, D. *The periodicals collection: its purpose and use in libraries*. 2nd ed. London: Deutsch, 1978.
Osborn, A. D. *Serial publications: their place and treatment in libraries*. 3rd ed. Chicago: American Library Association, 1980.

These are the fullest recent treatments of the subject, and are essential reading for the student. The following titles will also be found helpful:

Further Reading

Houghton, B. *Scientific periodicals: their historical development, characteristics and control.* London: Bingley, 1975.

Brown, C. D. *Serials – acquisition and maintenance.* Birmingham, Alabama: EBSCO Industries Inc, 1972. 201.

Grenfell, D. *Periodicals and serials: their treatment in special libraries.* 2nd ed. London: Aslib, 1965.

Katz, W. A. *Introduction to reference work.* 4th ed. New York: McGraw-Hill, 1982. (Vol 1: *Basic information sources*; chapter on indexing and abstracting services.)

Grogan, D. *More case studies in reference work.* London: Bingley, 1972. (The chapter on periodicals, for practical applications.)

10

Reports and Theses, Conferences and Symposia, Standards, and Patents

C. Peter Auger

Reference material relating to reports, conferences and symposia, theses, standards, and patents places an extra degree of responsibility on the librarian. The reason is that when readers with queries have been correctly introduced to the appropriate sources, they are frequently unable or unwilling to pursue their enquiries with quite the same facility which they show when directed to more conventional, and certainly more familiar works, such as directories, dictionaries, or encyclopaedias. Difficulties for readers arise partly because reference material in these areas is genuinely not easy to use, and partly because it is unfamiliar. In addition, the reference material embodies to a greater or lesser extent information and publications which may be subject to various obstacles, restrictions and constraints, such as the frequent issue of amendments (standards specifications), the requirement to furnish a 'need to know' (research reports), the non-availability of listed publications (conference papers withdrawn before presentation), authors' rights to be consulted (theses), and publication in the form of a legal document (patents). Yet such sources, especially in the fields of science and technology, frequently provide information not obtainable elsewhere, sometimes because it is too new to have reached ordinary channels of publication, and sometimes

Reports

because it is too detailed or specialized to warrant the expense and delay of formal editing and assessment. Thus, the librarian is more likely to be asked for further guidance, and in consequence needs himself to have a good understanding of the material in question.

Many libraries, even when they have definite acquisition policies towards such materials, have tended to shy away from the task of cataloguing, indexing, and arranging the publications involved, and have instead established special collections arranged on some broad fundamental characteristic, with a heavy reliance on specially produced indexes and guides. In some areas, bibliographic control is indifferent or non-existent; documents may therefore appear under more than one identity. Added to this are the problems of great variety in physical format, which prevent collections being shelved alongside other printed material, because for example they are issued as preprints (conference papers), microfiches (reports), typescripts (theses), or merely in draft form with a limited life (standards).

Despite all this heterogeneity, however, the publications under consideration justify their juxtaposition in the present chapter by virtue of one common feature; they are all amenable to treatment as series of publications, wherein each individual item has its own unique identifier, usually in the form of an alphanumeric code (BS 9000; AD 600000; SAE 770047; British Patent 1470959; etc). In this respect they are far in advance of conventional books and journals, which despite the increasing application of International Standard Book Numbers and International Standard Serial Numbers, are likely to continue to be referred to by traditional identifiers such as authors and titles. There is, of course, plenty of scope for rationalization in the alphanumeric codes employed; but, properly used, such shorthand devices eliminate many of the problems associated with identification and acquisition.

REPORTS

The term 'report', in its everyday sense, is well enough understood as indicating an account given, or an opinion formally expressed, after an investigation or consideration. When, however, reports are looked at collectively as a form of literature, then the question of definition becomes a little more difficult. In the context of reference material, reports may be regarded as accounts from government establishments, scientific institutions, and industrial laboratories, about work performed and results achieved, rendered to their clients and sponsors. This is certainly the case with reports in the fields of science and technology, where they are frequently known as research and development (R & D) reports; and in recent years they have spread increasingly to other fields, such as education and economics.

Reports often contain extensive descriptions of experiments, investigations, studies, and evaluations, fully supported by figures, graphs and tables, and of late, computer-derived print-out. Normally reports do not remain silent about the unsuccessful aspects of a project, and since they are written during, or immediately after, the work they describe, they contain results and data on the very latest stages of research in a particular area. They are, therefore, of great importance as a communication medium in those areas of science and technology where progress is being made at a very rapid rate, as for example aerospace, electronics, and nuclear energy. It is no coincidence that such fast-moving subject areas are also of great importance to national governments for reasons of defence and military strength. Consequently many reports start life as documents issued by agencies of the armed services, or by government departments. Indeed the origins of many series of reports, still being issued today, can be traced back to the massive research programmes conducted during World War II.

Much of the world's report literature originates in the USA, and due to the fact that the greater part of this literature is issued on the authority of the government establishments and agencies, that is, with the support of public funds, as many reports as possible are sooner or later made available to the public, subject always to the overriding factor of whether or not national security is involved. When a report is considered unsuitable for public release for security reasons, it is termed 'classified', and strictly speaking, not available to anyone who is unable to demonstrate a 'need to know'.

Reports, even when entirely free from security and distribution restrictions, are still regarded by journal editors and commercial

Reports

publishers alike as unpublished documents, which have not been subjected to the rigours of refereeing or editorial control. Consequently they have tended to go unnoticed in many of the conventional abstracting journals and national bibliographies. Instead it has been the custom, for a great number of years, to publicize the details of newly issued or recently available reports in special announcement journals, the presentation and content of which are quite different from those of other current awareness sources.

The major report announcement medium of this genre, covering a very wide range of disciplines, and embracing foreign as well as United States documents, is:

GOVERNMENT REPORTS ANNOUNCEMENTS AND INDEX (GRA&I). Springfield, Virginia: US Department of Commerce, National Technical Information Service (NTIS). 26 issues per annum.

GRA&I is a highly structured abstracting publication, the format of which has been designed for librarians and technical information specialists. NTIS is the central agency responsible for the dissemination of information about research sponsored by the United States Government.

Each entry in *GRA&I* usually records a document's accession number, corporate author, title, personal author, data, pagination, contract number, report number, and availability. Also included is an abstract, supplemented by a note of the indexing terms used. Indexes to *GRA&I* are issued annually as a set containing several volumes. Abstracts are arranged in accordance with the 22 broad subject field categories which comprise a classification scheme endorsed by the Committee on Scientific and Technical Information (COSATI) of the Federal Council for Science and Technology in 1964.

In addition to the fortnightly issues of *GRA&I*, other means are issued by NTIS to announce the availability of new reports, notably a series of weekly newsletters:

ABSTRACT NEWSLETTERS. Springfield, Virginia: US Department of Commerce, NTIS.

Covering 26 separate subject areas of industrial, technological,

Reports, Theses, Conferences, Symposia, Standards, Patents

and sociological interest. A typical newsletter is that devoted to library and information sciences; it is published in co-operation with the American Society for Information Science/Educational Resources Information Center (ASIS/ERIC) Clearinghouse on Library Information Sciences, and provides news of reports on information systems, marketing and user services, operations and planning, personnel, and reference services.

Whereas *GRA&I* is extremely wide in its subject coverage, there are several announcement journals which concentrate on a narrower, albeit still broad area of science or technology. Inevitably there is a fair degree of duplication of coverage between *GRA&I* and the more specialized journals.

Firstly there is:

SCIENTIFIC AND TECHNICAL AEROSPACE REPORTS (STAR). Washington: US Government Printing Office. 24 issues per annum.

Publications abstracted in *STAR*, which is prepared by the Scientific and Technical Information Office of the National Aeronautics and Space Administration (NASA), include scientific and technical reports issued by NASA and its contractors; other US government agencies; corporations; universities; and research organizations throughout the world. The value of *STAR* lies in its thoroughness of coverage, and its practice of providing information about on-going research projects before they have even reached the report stage. NASA points out that *STAR* should be used in conjunction with its sister publication *International aerospace abstracts (IAA)* (New York: American Institute of Aeronautics and Astronautics. 24 issues per annum) since the latter covers the conventionally published literature in the same field.

Secondly, the increasingly important energy field is covered by:

ENERGY RESEARCH ABSTRACTS (ERA). Washington: US Government Printing Office. 24 issues per annum.

ERA is a comparatively recent title, the first issue having appeared in 1977. It is compiled by the Department of Energy and may be regarded as the successor to *Nuclear science abstracts (NSA)*, an announcement service published in 33 volumes between 1948 and 1976, and still today a reference work of the highest value. *NSA* appeared under the aegis of the United States Atomic Energy Commission (USAEC). *ERA* still devotes a large amount of its coverage to nuclear energy, but its contents reflect DoE's broader charter for energy systems, conservation, safety, environmental protection, physical research, biology and medicine.

For reports in the field of nuclear energy proper, there is still:

INIS ATOMINDEX. Vienna: International Atomic Energy Agency. 26 issues per annum, prepared as part of the Agency's International Nuclear Information System (INIS).

Away from the realms of science and technology, a notable announcement service is:

RESOURCES IN EDUCATION (RIE). Washington: US Government Printing Office. 12 issues per annum.

RIE, formerly known as *Research in education*, is provided by an information network co-ordinated by the Educational Resources Information Center (ERIC).

ERIC comprises a number of clearinghouses in professional or disciplinary associations and university departments, together with a central administrative and processing facility. ERIC acts both as a document provision agency and a bibliographic service, with a heavy emphasis on reports and projects. *RIE* is made up of résumés and indexes. The résumés highlight the significance of each document, and are numbered sequentially with an ERIC document prefix. Indexes cover subjects, authors and institutions.

Research workers in Britain tend to rely heavily on the American announcement journals, but can, when the occasion demands, turn to two publications devoted in the main to British reports. The first of these is:

R & D ABSTRACTS. Orpington, Kent: Department of Industry. 26 issues per annum, compiled and issued by the Technology Reports Centre (TRC) until the termination of its report handling activity in 1981.

R & D abstracts contained details of reports and publications on science and technology which were received at TRC from govern-

Reports, Theses, Conferences, Symposia, Standards, Patents

ment R & D establishments, government supported R & D activities, and other sources in the UK and overseas. Its main readership was regarded as British industry.

The second (and now the main) British source of news about reports is:

BRITISH REPORTS, TRANSLATIONS AND THESES. Boston Spa, Yorkshire: British Library Lending Division (BLLD). 12 issues per annum.

The purpose of *British reports* is to list, like its predecessor *BLL announcement bulletin*, British report literature and translations produced by British Government organizations, industry, universities and learned institutions. The publication has been improved by quarterly keyword indexes, and by annual indexes by author, keyword, organization and report number.

Other countries too have their reports announcement services, notably the Federal Republic of Germany, where the Technical Information Library (TIB) of the University of Hanover Library for several years compiled a quarterly index giving details of reports added to the TIB's collection. In 1978 the index acquired a new title and publisher, viz *Forschungsberichte aus Technik und Naturwissenschaften* (Weinheim: Physik-Verlag, 4 issues per annum).

Although reports can be catalogued in the same way as published literature, using personal and corporate authors for the main entries, they are normally identified by, and filed under, report numbers of one sort or another. Considerable efforts have been devoted to imparting some form of bibliographical control on the reports literature, and in certain areas well known report number series present few difficulties to the users, as for example the AD reports issued by the Department of Defense. AD stems from ASTIA Document, and ASTIA itself stood for the Armed Services Technical Information Agency, the forerunner of the present Defense Technical Information Center.

There are several keys to report numbers and codes, the most comprehensive of which, and indispensible in any library with a reports collection is:

Godfrey, L. E. and Redman, H. F. DICTIONARY OF REPORT

SERIES CODES. 2nd ed. New York: Special Libraries Association, 1973.

The purpose of the *Dictionary* is to identify or provide an association for most of the codes that have been applied to reports. Its coverage is very wide, and it also includes notes which provide guidance on ambiguous codes and on the major reports-issuing agencies. A work which to some extent complements Godfrey and Redman is:

Simonton, D. DIRECTORY OF ENGINEERING SCIENTIFIC AND MANAGEMENT DOCUMENT SOURCES. 2nd ed: Newport Beach, California: Global Engineering and Documentation Services, 1974.

A consolidated cross-index of document initialisms assigned by government and industrial organizations, not only to reports, but also to specifications and standards.

THESES

A thesis may be regarded as a statement of investigation or research, presenting the author's findings and any conclusions reached, and submitted by the author in support of his candidature for a higher degree, professional qualification, or other award. On the basis of this definition it is clear that a thesis has several points in common with a report: both present details of investigations and research; both offer findings and conclusions; both are submitted to an overseeing body (the university in the case of a thesis, the sponsor in the case of a report); and both are unpublished documents.

The thesis often reports investigations of an advanced nature, reflecting the writer's attempt to extend the limits of knowledge in his chosen subject. As such, a thesis can be an important document to other research workers, since it will contain results not available elsewhere, even though such results must be regarded as primarily intended to show a candidate's grasp of a given subject, and the research methodology involved. Many theses ultimately appear, in an amended form, as journal articles or monographs, and are frequently cited in the literature.

Reports, Theses, Conferences, Symposia, Standards, Patents

Since 1950, the standard reference work on information about British theses has been the:

INDEX TO THESES ACCEPTED FOR HIGHER DEGREES BY THE UNIVERSITIES OF GREAT BRITAIN AND IRELAND AND THE COUNCIL FOR NATIONAL ACADEMIC AWARDS. London: Aslib. 2 issues per annum.

The *Index* covers all subject fields, and in Vol 30, published in 1982, included some 8,400 items. The availability of theses varies from university to university, and, usually, readers are required to sign a declaration that no information derived from a thesis will be published or used without the consent in writing of the author.

The British Library Lending Division has, since 1970, been trying to increase the utilization of British doctoral theses by microfilming the theses of those universities which have agreed to participate in an experiment to build up a central collection.

The availability of theses is made known in *British reports . . .*, and xerographic enlargements from the microfilms are made available for loan or retention. About two-thirds of the doctoral theses currently produced in the UK are being made available through BLLD, which from time to time publishes a complete list of the participating institutions.

If the reader wishes to find out about British theses before the start of the Aslib *Index*, he should consult:

Biboul, R. RETROSPECTIVE INDEX TO THESES OF GREAT BRITAIN AND IRELAND 1716–1950. Santa Barbara, California: Clio Press, 1976.

A compilation published in a number of volumes, each of which is devoted to a broad subject area, as for example Vol 5: *Chemical sciences*.

In the United States, where the preferred term is 'dissertation', the principal source of reference is:

DISSERTATION ABSTRACTS INTERNATIONAL (DAI). Ann Arbor, Michigan: University Microfilms International. 12 issues per annum.

DAI began publication in 1938 as *Microfilm abstracts*, became

Conferences and Symposia

Dissertation abstracts in 1952, and changed again in 1969 to its present title. In 1966 the publication was split into two sections: Section A (Humanities and Social Sciences) and Section B (Sciences and Engineering). Section C on Europe was added in 1976.

Each entry in *DAI* comprises the following information: title of the dissertation, author's name, year, awarding institution, and the order number allocated by the publishers: a number which acts as a unique identifier, similar to a report number. A feature of *DAI* is the comprehensiveness of the abstracts, each of which is usually about half a page in length.

An aid to the restrospective searching of dissertation literature is to be found in:

COMPREHENSIVE DISSERTATION INDEX 1861–1972. Ann Arbor, Michigan: Xerox University Microfilms, 1973, with a cumulation covering the years 1973–1977, and annual supplements.

The work consists of 37 basic volumes allocated to a number of broad subject areas, and contains details of over 700,000 doctoral dissertations granted by United States and certain foreign universities.

In Great Britain it is the usual practice for candidates to present their theses in typescript form, only a handful of copies being produced. On the Continent, however, it has long been the custom to have theses printed, sometimes in as many as 200 copies; a procedure which greatly simplifies the establishment of collections by exchange.

Each European country keeps its own records of theses, as for example the *Jahresverzeichnis der Deutschen Hochschulschriften* (Leipzig: VEB Verlag für Buch- und Bibliothekswesen; annual).

CONFERENCES AND SYMPOSIA

Papers made available prior to, or at, meetings and conferences, where they are presented by their authors in person, are usually termed 'preprints' or 'meetings papers'. The practice is especially common in the United States, and many large American societies issue preprints in advance of their meetings, where each paper is customarily identified by a serial code, not unlike a report number. After the meeting or conference has taken place, the papers are reviewed, and all, or a certain proportion, selected for inclusion in a society's permanent records, or the conference organizer's official transactions. Those not selected for such treatment are simply listed, and quite frequently abstracted, cited, and requested. A further complication is that not all the papers promised to a conference organizer and so assigned preprint numbers are actually written up; some may be read and then withdrawn, others simply never presented at all. Nevertheless they sometimes manage to turn up in bibliographies.

The physical forms which conference literature can take include the preprint noted above; the bound conference volume, either available during or shortly after the event; a conference record as part of, or a supplement to, an established journal; conference records issued as part of the reports literature; and conference records in which abstracts only are provided, a practice adopted for example in the United States by the Electrochemical Society.

Generally, the library will want to have access to two main types of information about conferences and meetings: firstly, what events are going to take place, and secondly what form does the official record take. On the first count it is possible to consult:

WORLD MEETINGS. Chestnut Hill, Massachusetts: World Meetings Information Center.

A registry of future meetings in science, technology and medicine in the United States and Canada (since 1963), and outside those countries (since 1968). Each issue lists events due to take place up to two years hence, and entries consist of details of the name, location, and date of each meeting, together with a note of the organizer's name and address. A further series, on the social and behavioural sciences, began in 1971.

A British publication which looks ahead to meetings is:

FORTHCOMING INTERNATIONAL SCIENTIFIC AND TECHNICAL CONFERENCES. London: Aslib. 4 issues per annum.

It provides details of forthcoming conferences in all subject fields

Conferences and Symposia

of science and technology, and meetings included are either international conferences held throughout the world, or British national meetings, such as Aslib's own annual conference.

Once conferences and meetings have taken place, the problem then becomes one of identifying the permanent form in which the proceedings are eventually published. In the United Kingdom the National Lending Library began in 1965 to publish the *Index of conference proceedings received by the NLL*. Subsequently the series was cumulated as the *BLL conference index 1964–1973* (Boston Spa, Yorkshire: British Library Lending Division, 1974), and BLLD has continued to record conference proceedings in its:

INDEX OF CONFERENCE PROCEEDINGS RECEIVED. Boston Spa, Yorkshire: British Library Lending Division, 12 issues per annum.

The *Index* is essentially an internal finding aid for BLLD, and the single-line entries need to be studied with some care if conference details are not to be overlooked. An eighteen-year cumulation covering the period 1964–1981 is available on microfiche.

A United States bibliographic service which also offers to its subscribers a procurement facility for conference proceedings is the:

DIRECTORY OF PUBLISHED PROCEEDINGS. Harrison, New York: InterDok Corporation.

Usually referred to simply as *InterDok*, the publication consists of Series SEMT, providing information on proceedings in the sciences, engineering, medicine and technology, issued 12 times per annum; and Series SSH, covering the social sciences and the humanities, with issues 4 times per annum.

Several other publishers have recognized the need to identify and acquire conference proceedings and individual papers. For example:

Kyed, J. M. and Matarazzo, J. M. SCIENTIFIC ENGINEERING AND MEDICAL SOCIETIES PUBLICATIONS IN PRINT 1980. New York: Bowker, 1981.

A reference work providing a single source of bibliographic control over publications by 303 US scientific and engineering societies

Reports, Theses, Conferences, Symposia, Standards, Patents

and related organizations. The societies are arranged alphabetically by name and full address.

In passing, it should be mentioned that important though it is for the librarian to be able to identify and acquire meetings papers in response to specific requests, members of the scientific and academic communities themselves often express scepticism on the value of such literature, much of which is regarded as shortened or inferior versions of work that is about to be, or has been, published elsewhere.

STANDARDS

Standards may be regarded as formal rules applicable in all sectors of industry and trade, and covering methods of test; terms; definitions and symbols; performance and constructional specifications; codes of practice; and other technical matters. Usually they are prepared by agreement among the interested parties concerned, and are subsequently used to simplify production and distribution, to ensure uniformity and reliability, and to eliminate wasteful variety. Standards can also be considered as constraints which hinder the development of new and improved designs, and so act as an obstacle to scientific and technical progress.

On balance, however, standards must be regarded as vital to the success of any advanced industrial society, and the various collections available, at national and international levels, are ample evidence of the vital contribution they make to the manufacturing and commercial aspects of everyday life.

The average standard is not a lengthy document—usually a pamphlet a few pages in length, with details of methods, measurements, definitions, properties and processes. It invariably has an identifying alphanumeric code which in many cases can acquire an international significance, as for example DIN 31 or BS 1629. Many bodies, from national standards institutions to professional associations, trade societies, government agencies, and individual manufacturers, issue standards. The most comprehensive work, which provides details of this wide range of originators, is the *Directory of engineering . . . document sources*, mentioned above.

Standards

Two other compilations which are broad in scope are both prepared by the National Bureau of Standards. The first is:

Slattery, W. J. AN INDEX OF US VOLUNTARY ENGINEERING STANDARDS. Washington: US Government Printing Office, 1971. Supplements, 1972 and 1975.

This covers standards, specifications, test methods and recommended practices issued by national standardization organizations in the United States. The second is:

Chumas, S. J. DIRECTORY OF UNITED STATES STANDARDIZATION ACTIVITIES. Washington: US Government Printing Office, 1975.

This describes the work of nearly 600 organizations concerned with the establishment of standard practices and their incorporation in codes and specifications.

In the United Kingdom, the official organization charged with the responsibility of preparing and publishing standards and encouraging their use, is the British Standards Institution (BSI). Currently, about 7,000 British Standards are in force, and the publication of new and revised standards averages 500 per annum. The key to BSI's activities lies in the:

BRITISH STANDARDS YEARBOOK. London: BSI.

Issued annually as a definitive catalogue, with annotations, and a comprehensive alphabetical subject index. It is updated by:

BSI NEWS. London: BSI. 12 issues per annum.

A magazine which, in addition to general items on all aspects of standardization, provides information on new standards, revisions, amendments, drafts, and standards withdrawn. A further service which updates the *Yearbook* is the *Sales bulletin* (London: BSI. 6 issues per annum); this lists, in numerical order, new, revised, and amended publications. For ease of reference, successive issues are cumulative.

Although there are a number of bodies in Britain which devise their own standards, most work through BSI. Two examples of these exceptions are the *IEE wiring regulations* (15th ed. London:

Institution of Electrical Engineers, 1981); and the *Heating and Ventilating Contractors' Association Standard DW 142 on duct work* (London: HVCA, 1982). At one time many large industrial companies produced their own standards, but for reasons of economy and consistency, the current trend is again to work through BSI.

Most other industrialized countries have their own national standards organizations, and their publications are widely quoted in the literature.

The German Institute of Standardisation (Deutsches Institut für Normung, abbreviated to DIN) co-ordinates all standardization work in **Germany**. DIN was established in 1917, and details of its 13,000 standards at present in force are listed in the *DIN-Katalog für technische Regeln* (Berlin: Beuth Verlag, annual). New standards, and information on drafts and revisions, are covered by *DIN Mitteilungen* (Berlin: Beuth Verlag. 12 issues per annum).

Because of their world-wide usage, many DIN standards have been translated into English and Spanish. In the case of the English versions, DIN publishes an annual list: *English translations of German Standards* (Berlin: Beuth Verlag); and English translations of German standards, in 23 special technical fields, are also available as a special collection.

France too is active in standardization, and the official body responsible for issuing standards is the French Standards Association (Association Française de Normalisation, abbreviated to AFNOR). Particulars of French standards are given in the *Catalogue des Normes Françaises* (Paris: AFNOR) which is both an index to each AFNOR specification, and a reference source on standards translated into other languages.

In the **United States**, as indicated above, very many bodies are active in preparing standards, and although there is a central organization, the American National Standards Institute (ANSI), its main function is to co-ordinate the publication of standards through a series of committees. For example American National Standards Committee Z39, Standardisation in the Field of Library Work, Documentation, and Related Publishing Practices, has as its secretariat the Council of National Library Associations, and it is composed of representatives from many national organizations.

Standards

Lists of ANSI standards are available from the Institute's headquarters, and news of ongoing activities is contained in *ANSI reporter* (New York: ANSI. 26 issues per annum).

Although the advantages of national standardization programmes are considerable, the ultimate benefits are derived when standards receive international recognition. The Organisation Internationale de Normalisation, Geneva (International Standardisation Organisation, abbreviated to ISO), acts as a selling agent and information centre for the national standards of the member countries, and for its own international standards: namely ISO and International Electrotechnical Commission (IEC) *Standards*. For United Kingdom readers the most convenient guide to work in international standards is the *ISO catalogue*, available from BSI.

In certain areas of standardization, notably metals and alloys, attempts have been made to integrate national standards by means of compilations which compare like specifications, enabling a user to select a national standard which is an equivalent or near equivalent of a standard issued by another body. A recent example is:

HANDBOOK OF COMPARATIVE WORLD STEEL STANDARDS. Tokyo: International Technical Information Institute, 1980.

This permits a rapid comparison of steel standards issued in Great Britain, France, Japan, the United States, the Soviet Union and the Federal Republic of Germany.

Finally, no discussion of standards is complete without reference to the important part they play in government purchasing and matters of national security. In the United Kingdom, two series are commonly used in many branches of industry as well as the armed services and government departments. The first of these comprises documents issued by the Ministry of Defence with the prefix DEF. DEF specifications are available through HMSO, whilst DEF standards (DEF-STAN) are obtained direct from the Ministry itself.

The second series, again from the Ministry of Defence, embraces DTD specifications for aerospace materials and processes. DTD stands for Directorate of Technical Development, now the Directorate of Research Materials, and a complete list is contained in:

Reports, Theses, Conferences, Symposia, Standards, Patents
INDEX OF DTD SPECIFICATIONS. London: HMSO, 1980.

Similarly, in the United States, another widely used series of military specifications, identified by the prefix MIL, is listed in the Department of Defense's:

INDEX OF SPECIFICATIONS AND STANDARDS. Washington: US Government Printing Office; annually with supplements.

The Federal Supply Service of the General Services Administration compiles an:

INDEX OF FEDERAL SPECIFICATIONS AND STANDARDS. Washington: US Government Printing Office.

The individual items in this index reflect the influence of the Administration's tremendous bulk purchasing power.

PATENTS

A patent is an official document setting out in great detail an inventor's solution to a particular problem, and granting that inventor the sole right for a specified period of years to make, use, or sell the invention described. All such inventions must meet certain criteria of novelty, and must be capable of industrial application. Normally the librarian is not concerned with the writing, filing, exploitation and contesting of patents, since these tasks are the province of the inventor himself, the patents engineer, the patents examiner, and the patents agent.

Because, however, patent specifications often disclose technical information at a much earlier date than other literature; because they review and examine the prior art which led up to the invention; and because, taken collectively, they can be indicative of trends in research, no literature search on an industrial topic can be considered complete unless British and foreign patents have been taken into account.

All major countries have a patents system, because it has long been recognized that the protection obtained in return for disclos-

Patents

ure acts as a stimulus to the inventive spirit, and so benefits technical progress in a most positive manner. In the United Kingdom, details of all applications filed, specifications published and patents sealed, are announced each week in the:

OFFICIAL JOURNAL (PATENTS). London: Patent Office. 52 issues per annum.

In addition:

PATENTS FOR INVENTIONS: ABRIDGEMENTS OF SPECIFICATIONS. London: Patent Office.

Mostly illustrated, these are published weekly in pamphlet form, with one pamphlet for each of the 25 groups of divisions which comprise the units of the *Classification Key* (London: Patent Office; revised annually). Together with a separately issued *Reference index*, the *Key* is the principal means for searching for a patent on a specific topic.

For each complete series of 25,000 specifications the appropriate key unit, subject matter index, name index to applicants, and covers for binding into abridgements volumes are supplied. The Patent Office also issues a range of other publications, and in the context of this chapter, one pamphlet in particular is of great usefulness, namely:

PATENTS: A SOURCE OF TECHNICAL INFORMATION. London: Patent Office.

Written for industry, research and development units, universities, polytechnics, inventors, engineers and scientists. It is updated periodically.

A great deal of information on patents can also be determined from specialist patent abstracting and indexing companies, as for example:

WORLD PATENTS INDEX. London: Derwent Publications. 52 issues per annum.

This index is able to indicate, as a result of processing by computer the 11,000 or so patent specifications published each week in

Reports, Theses, Conferences, Symposia, Standards, Patents

the major industrial countries of the world, who has patented what and where.

Derwent, in fact, provides a comprehensive range of patents services, details of which can be found in its brochures and instruction manuals.

Some conventional abstracting services, particularly *Chemical abstracts*, cover patent specifications in a very comprehensive manner, whereas others, for example *Engineering index*, shun them altogether.

A feature of the British patent system (and indeed of many others) is that each patent is assigned firstly an application number, and secondly a patent number, so that the exercise of bibliographical control at all stages during a patent's life is made very simple indeed.

It is customary for inventors, and the companies and organizations which employ them, to file patent applications in leading trading and industrial nations throughout the world, each of which has its own patents system. In the course of time such applications are published as United States, German, Japanese, and so on, patents, thus providing global coverage for an invention. Conversely, many foreign countries file applications with the British Patent Office. Thus, there is a strong international flavour to patents, one manifestation of which is the system of International Classification Marks, by which each British patent has been classified since 1957.

The principles on which the eight main subject sections are organized are revealed in the:

INTERNATIONAL PATENT CLASSIFICATION and its companion volume OFFICIAL CATCHWORD INDEX. Geneva: World Intellectual Property Organisation, 1974.

Further developments in this connection stem from the United Kingdom's greater involvement in Europe. The Patents Act of 1977 was designed firstly to improve the domestic law, and secondly to enable UK and European patent laws to co-exist, for the London Patent Office operates simultaneously with the new European Patent Office in Munich. The latter establishment is responsible for

Conclusion

the *Official journal of the European Patent Office*, the first issue of which came out in December 1977.

An important guide to the international patents scene is:

Bank, H., Fenat-Haessig, M. and Roland, M. (eds.) PATENT INFORMATION AND DOCUMENTATION IN WESTERN EUROPE. 2nd ed. Munich: Saur, 1981.

The work is an inventory, of patent information and documentation services, which describes in great detail the activities of national patent offices and other official and semi-official bodies.

The topic of foreign patents cannot be concluded without reference to the practice of some patent offices of publishing, after a relatively brief interval, full details of the patent applications they have received; this is in marked contrast to the long period customary in the United Kingdom between the filing of a patent and the publication of the detailed specification. It is therefore possible for the foreign version of a British patent to be made public overseas before the complete and final English-language specification is available in London.

Consequently certain countries' specifications are regularly scanned with considerable interest as sources of advance information. Especially valuable in this context are the *Offenlegungsschriften* published by the Deutsches Patentamt, Munich.

CONCLUSION

All the categories of reference material described above demand a considerable amount of study and application if the user is to be able to make full and effective use of the resources which individually and collectively they have to offer. Reports call for an understanding of the world of research and development contracts; theses require an insight into methods of awarding higher degrees; conference papers necessitate an appreciation of scientists' eagerness to enhance their public reputations; standards depend on an appreciation of the diversity of standardization bodies; and for patents a grasp of the concepts of intellectual property is essential.

The observations made and the examples quoted are but an

Reports, Theses, Conferences, Symposia, Standards, Patents

indication of the sort of information these forms of reference material have to offer. The literature which describes and explains their characteristics and value in detail is both extensive and specialized. The following suggestions for further reading must therefore be considered simply as first steps towards the users' acquiring a deeper understanding.

SUGGESTIONS FOR FURTHER READING

Auger, C. P. *Use of reports literature*. London: Butterworths, 1975. (Information sources for research and development).

Chitty, G. M. *NTIS: Concept of the Clearing house 1945-1979*. Springfield, Virginia: US Department of Commerce, 1979 (PB-300 947/9GA).

Davinson, D. *Theses and dissertations as information sources*. London: Bingley, 1977.

Drubba, H. Conference documentation – general overview and survey of the present position. *International Associations*, 28 (8-9), Aug-Sept 1976. 383-7.

Holloway, A. H. et al. *Information work with unpublished reports*. London: Deutsch, 1976.

Liebesny, F. *Mainly on patents: the use of industrial property and its literature*. London: Butterworths, 1972.
(Information sources for research and development).

Morehead, J. *Introduction to United States public documents*. 2nd ed. Littleton, Colorado: Libraries Unlimited, 1978.
(See especially Chapter 4: Non-depository publications, which deals with the report literature.)

Woodward, C. D. *BSI – The story of standards*. London: British Standards Institution, 1972.

11

Maps, Atlases, and Gazetteers

Harold Nichols

One can imagine the concept of a map for route finding being appreciated by prehistoric man, drawing with a stick in loose earth. Later, man would record ownership of property, or rights based on land, by drawing a sketch plan on a more permanent material. Cartography developed through the need to note routes for practical commercial purposes, with sea routes on charts for navigators and explorers; others had similar needs for military campaigns and sieges. After the industrial revolution, even more detailed, accurate maps were needed properly to exploit the resources of a country. Large-scale plans, which allow boundaries to be accurately recorded, were needed for a variety of ownership uses; the assessment of land rents, mineral rights, tithes, and the planning of land, as with Enclosure Acts in England; the settlement of farmers in the opening up of new countries, as happened in the USA and Canada; leading to all the modern civil engineering uses of maps.

The modern map requires a scientific base, surveyed by a national organization, and in most countries the national survey produces the data for making national maps, which serve also for other map-makers. Until recently this topographic information has been disseminated in map form as printed or manuscript sheets, but the map is now often produced in microform and the data are increas-

Maps, Atlases, and Gazetteers

ingly available on magnetic tape in digitized, machine-readable form to create a computer-generated map when required.

Topographic maps represent an area of the earth's surface by showing all possible surface features within the limitations set by scale, and the need to add labels such as place-names and other information represented by conventional signs. The cartographer also produces topographic base maps, to which are added data on a subject which has a geographic distribution. Such maps are **distribution** maps or, since they have a special subject, **thematic** maps. The thematic data are obtained from special surveys or published statistical sources, and the cartographer uses various devices, symbols, flow lines, colours, etc, to show the distribution of this quantitative or qualitative information.

To use **general** maps, the minimum facts which must be understood are conventional signs, scale, representation of relief, and the method of locating a required sheet in a uniform series. In providing an information service, a librarian must be conversant with the types of information for which a map may be a source, so that appropriate maps are acquired, and arrange that the retrieval system for current maps relates to locations, scales and subject matter rather than to publisher, in order to be most useful for enquiries. One of the common uses is in tracing locations of settlements, of physical or political features, and of man's environment. A map is not a photograph of the earth's surface but rather an edited version; it may omit some locations, such as entrances to potholes, and add others not visible on the ground, like administrative boundaries. Once a location is known, an enquirer may wish to establish a route, comparing the advantages of different routes by the classification of roads or the steepness of gradients. Even a general map can exhibit specialist emphasis, one being designed for a walker, another for the motorist. In highland regions of Britain, not all maps will note the existence of deer fencing, which offers a frustrating obstacle to the walker. Tourism requires camping maps, lake and inland waterway maps, maps of historical sites, archaeology, forests and woodlands, state parks, and many more. Commercial users are not often distinguishable in their needs from the ordinary traveller. Though the one may wish to check political boundaries, ports, railways, and roads in a remote country for

Selection

arrangements in exporting heavy machinery, the traveller may be equally demanding in seeking the best road route to Singapore. Maps must not be lost to information use because they are unrecorded, being printed in books, periodicals, reports, and government publications. These should be selectively catalogued or indexed, as are map supplements to journals and books. Recently H. W. Wilson & Co introduced references to the existence of maps in the articles indexed in the firm's periodical indexes.

The geographer's use of maps will not often require the aid of the librarian for interpretation, although the more complicated requirements of the user call for a greater range of maps. Geographers and planners, in particular, need to take measurements from maps. These may be of distance, direction, area, or height. In atlases the geographer hopes to see scales used which facilitate the comparison of measurements for different regions, on different plates. In all practical uses of a map, the date of evidence shown is important, and cataloguing must inform the potential user of this date, if known. For a thematic map, the relevant date will be that of the statistics used, not the date of the topographic base. Early maps are acquired in a library for a different purpose. Here the date of printing, together with the surveyor and others involved in production, is important because early maps are kept to illustrate the development of map-making, or the work of a particular cartographer.

SELECTION

National and commercial publishers produce 'map series', where the map is divided for convenience into many sheets. A librarian may choose to buy only those sheets which, at a useful scale, cover a part of a country, perhaps a tourist region, and have coverage of other areas at a smaller scale, but every library information service should have world coverage on the scale of 1 : 1M.

INTERNATIONAL MAP OF THE WORLD. 1 : 1M (IMW).
This is produced co-operatively in a uniform format, with the

Maps, Atlases, and Gazetteers

sheets issued by the appropriate national surveys of the world coordinated by the UN Cartographic Office.

Larger scales should be available for selected areas, probably 1 : 100,000 in a public library for road maps of popular foreign countries, and 1 : 50,000 sheets for student use and for areas of holiday interest, in the latter case in an edition designed for recreation use. With thematic maps and **street plans** little general guidance can be given, but acquisitions should be based on experience of the map types that are published throughout the world, and on a perceptive knowledge reflecting users' requirements. The librarian should, however, buy just a little more adventurously. Information about maps of regions of particular interest to a library is enhanced if the library receives the catalogues of map producers concerned with that region and, wherever possible, buys direct from the publisher. The various official national surveys prepare sales catalogues, as do commercial firms, and a file of these catalogues and brochures should be maintained. In most countries the official survey is national, but some official maps are prepared by the different states in federal countries such as Australia and West Germany, and by specialist organizations. Nichols[1] gives information on a number of them.

GEO KATALOG. Stuttgart: Geo Center. Annual. 2 vols.

The sales catalogue of the major retailer, and wholesaler, listing maps and atlases in print. It is supplemented monthly by *Geo Kartenbrief*. Vol 1 covers maps, atlases, guidebooks for recreation and tourism and maps published by commercial firms. Maps are listed under countries within continents, apart from Germany and the Alps which commence the volume. Vol 2 is loose-leaf and concerned with the publications of national surveys. Index maps are provided for map series in both volumes, allowing individual sheets to be identified if they are to be bought selectively. Entries are in German, but a list of abbreviations used shows the English meanings.

Winch, K. L. INTERNATIONAL MAPS AND ATLASES IN PRINT. 2nd ed. London: Bowker and Stanford, 1976.

Winch also provided a means of identifying maps and atlases

Selection

published all over the world, but it is out of date and should be thought of only as providing a possible English-language access to up to date information in *Geo Katalog*. Entries, giving all necessary bibliographical information, are arranged by continents and countries according to the area classification of UDC.

Some current national bibliographies record maps, and for UK and Eire publishers and agents, excluding O.S. sheet maps in series, the Publishers' Association, Book Maketing Council, Map and Guide Group produced *Catalogue of maps and guides* in 1982, but for librarians selecting from current maps produced in many countries, a major map library's additions list is an aid.

American Geographical Society. CURRENT GEOGRAPHICAL PUBLICATIONS. 10 per annum.

This covers all forms of publication; the maps section is arranged according to the AGS map classification scheme, based on area.

Bodleian Library, Map Section. SELECTED MAP AND BOOK ACCESSIONS. Monthly.

Sheet maps and atlases are listed under countries grouped within continents. As a library in receipt of legal deposit accessions, entries might occasionally include, say, a child's picture atlas, but as a major map library, there are entries for maps from all over the world.

These, and similar lists, identify new maps over a very wide range, and a librarian regularly consulting them will be made aware of the great variety of maps produced by commercial and institutional publishers everywhere. Bibliographical searching in libraries is not necessarily for the acquisition of new materials, but sometimes for the identification of older published maps. Retrospective searches of a file of current bibliographies will occur, but some major map collections' catalogues are available:

British Library. CATALOGUE OF PRINTED MAPS, CHARTS AND PLANS. London: British Museum, 1967. 15 vols. TEN YEAR SUPPLEMENT, 1965–1974. 1978.

This catalogue provides brief descriptive notes for entries, and, where possible, includes the date of survey. The arrangement is by specific place-names; regions, alphabetically arranged, with general or thematic subdivisions.

American Geographical Society. INDEX TO MAPS IN BOOKS AND PERIODICALS. Boston, Massachusetts: G. K. Hall, 1967. 10 vols. SUPPLEMENT, 1971; SECOND SUPPLEMENT, 1976.

This index has 176,000 entries alphabetically by subject and geographical area. Map titles and scales are given, with full citation of the book or article in which the map appears.

GENERAL MAPS

The Ordnance Survey is the official map-producing agency for Great Britain, excluding the Isle of Man and Channel Islands. There is a separate Ordnance Survey of Northern Ireland. Descriptions of the various map series are in the Ordnance Survey *Map catalogue* (annual); new issues and reprints are listed monthly in *OS publication report*. Index maps, to identify sheets, are available for each scale. All OS maps use a system of co-ordinates, the National Grid, which provides a unique reference number for any place, whatever the scale of the OS map consulted. On larger scales, greater precision is obtained from the greater number of digits that are definable. The National Grid may be considered as a series of squares, superimposed on the map of Britain, whose sides are respectively parallel with, and at right angles to, a central meridian. These basic squares have 100 km sides, or grid lines, and are identified by pairs of letters (originally numbers). The grid lines are printed on OS maps, their number and spacing changing according to scale so that, for any point on a map, it is possible to read rectangular co-ordinates which are measured in metres, first eastwards and then northwards, from the SW corner of the sheet, and thus from the SW corner of the 100 km grid square containing the point. Harley[2] should be consulted on the National Grid, and its use practised.

OS topographical sheets appear in several map series:

General Maps

Routeplanner 1:625,000, covering the country on two sheets printed back to back.

Routemaster 1:250,000. Motoring map, nine sheets printed on both sides; relief shown.

Landranger 1:50,000. Standard map series comprising 204 sheets available in coloured or outline editions. Content includes tourist information, visible antiquities, public rights of way.

Pathfinder 1:25,000, the larger scale useful for walkers, planners, and educational needs.

Outdoor leisure maps, based on the *Pathfinder* mapping, cover popular tourist areas, eg South Devon.

The prime duty of the Ordnance Survey is the maintenance of the basic scale surveys of the country for planning and industrial needs. This information is published on large-scale printed plans, but also in microform and print-outs from microfilm, and as magnetic tapes recording digitized map data which can be used to plot a map at a scale required by the user. *1:10,000*, the largest scale covering the whole country; all enclosure boundaries shown in rural areas, all streets named; some town plans, eg Central London, produced individually. *1:2,500*, not produced for moorland and mountain areas; all physical boundaries accurate; area measurement details. *1:1,250* sheets cover urban areas. At local OS offices, master survey drawings at 1:1,250 and 1:2,500 are updated by local surveyors, and microfilmed for distribution to OS microfilm agencies. These agents can supply *Survey information on microfilm* as print-outs, microfilm copy cards or transparencies. Regulations concerning the copying of Ordnance Survey maps have appeared in the *Library Association Record*[3], and OS leaflets are available, eg *Copyright-business and internal use*.

Access to any sheet maps in series should always be by the use of index maps which readily identify a required sheet. Index maps to series are available from the OS and other publishers to be displayed for reader use. The cataloguing of the individual sheets of a map in series is unnecessary for most libraries, and unproductive. When cataloguing a map published in many sheets and individual maps, the specialist manual[4] interpreting the AACR2 for use with maps should be used.

Maps, Atlases, and Gazetteers

The US Geological Survey provides general purpose maps of different scales for the USA, although some maps which are published by the USGS in the National Topographic Map Series are prepared by other Federal bodies, like the Coast and Geodetic Survey. There is no centralized preparation of cadastral plans, ie large scale maps showing property boundaries. Notes on topographic maps are given in *Publications of the Geological Survey*, 1879–1961 and 1962–1970 and annual supplements. *New publications of the Geological Survey*, monthly, includes new issues and reprints of topographic series. There are national index maps for small scales, and state indexes for larger scale topographic maps.

The USGS topographical map series has sheet boundaries formed by lines of latitude and longitude; such maps are usually known as quadrangle maps. The main series are designated as follows: *7½ minute quadrangle*, where the individual sheets cover 7½ minutes of latitude and longitude on a scale of 1 : 24,000. This series provides detailed planning and recreational information. 'Metropolitan area' maps consist of several quadrangles at 1 : 24,000, and cover selected conurbations. The *15 minute quadrangle* series has a scale of 1 : 62,500, the *30 minute quadrangle* a scale of 1 : 125,000; the other scales are 1 : 250,000; 1 : 1M. There are State maps in base, topographic and shaded relief editions, and a national park series at various scales.

THEMATIC MAPS

Geological

In Britain, the Ordnance Survey issues Geological Survey maps on behalf of the Institute of Geological Sciences, and *OS map catalogue* lists sheets on scales from 1 : 250,000 to 1 : 50,000. Some 1 : 25,000 and 1 : 10,560 sheets are also published. New sheets are listed in Geological Survey *Geological report*, quarterly; and *HMSO sectional list 45* lists *Memoirs* and *Explanations*, texts to accompany different sheets. To obtain a true indication of the geology of a district it may be necessary to have two geological maps for the same area. These are from the two editions of the Survey, the

274

Thematic Maps

'Drift' and 'Solid', which are particularly required in the north, where glacial flow has caused surface movement, making superficial rock deposits. Superficial deposits, along with outcrops of regular strata, are shown on the 'Drift' edition, whilst 'Solid' demonstrates main strata. In some areas the geological sheet combines the features of the two editions.

The United States Geological Survey publishes Geologic Quadrangle maps (1 : 24,000 and 1 : 62,500), mineral resource maps and charts, hydrological investigation atlases on differing scales, accompanied by *Bulletins* and other texts. Geological maps are included in the USGS publications catalogues, and in the state indexes to geological mapping, which include maps by other bodies as well as the USGS.

Land use maps

Land use maps, which show in detail how areas are being used at a certain time, have a long history. *Second land use survey of Britain* began in 1960 to prepare 1 : 25,000 sheets giving 18 categories of agricultural use. Coleman,[5] director of the Survey, has described the purpose of land use planning, and included portions of published maps. Closely allied are soil maps, where the soil's structure, particularly in relation to agriculture, is shown; and land classification or capability maps, which indicate the potential of land areas. Special maps of this nature come from a variety of sources; in Canada, the Department of Environment, Lands Directorate, produces land capability maps; in Britain, soil maps are from Soil Survey of England and Wales and, separately, of Scotland.

Charts

Charts are, historically, marine maps giving depths of soundings and other information, such as lights and port plans. Now, there are also aeronautical charts, with an emphasis on route-finding by physical features, stressing relief, rivers, etc, not place-names. Marine charts covering the world are produced by the Ministry of Defence (Admiralty), Hydrographic Department, and listed in the annual *Catalogue of Admiralty charts* . . ., and by the US Defense Mapping Agency, Hydrographic Center, *Catalog of nautical charts*. Charts of inland lakes, rivers and canal maps are made by other bodies. The International Civil Aviation Organisation *Aeronautical chart catalogue* has international charts, on scales from 1 : 1M to 1 : 250,000, which conform to ICAO standards. Aeronautical charts have value in libraries for their portrayal of physical geography.

Road maps

Road maps and general maps designed for tourist use are particularly the province of the commercial publisher seeking to show information not on official maps. Bartholomew publish a *National map* series at 1 : 100,000, which has contours at metric intervals, and seeks to satisfy consumer needs in that, for example, caves are located. Kompass *Wanderkarten* 1 : 50,000 are recommended for walking or climbing in central Europe, whilst Michelin; Touring Club Italiano; Mair; Bartholomew; Cappelen; and Rand McNally are well known for smaller-scale editions, excellent for tourists. With some exceptions, the main map publishers in each country are more probably accurate and up to date in mapping tourist information for their own country than any foreign publisher is likely to be.

ATLASES

Atlases are the quick-reference books of cartographic information. They provide a summary topographical knowledge of a country or continent on small-scale maps. Their contents are arranged in a logical manner for consultation, which is facilitated by an index. Though geography students require them for other reasons, this quick-reference facility is their main value in a general library. Modern atlases are of many types, but all exhibit an editorial policy

Atlases

in the style and graphic character of the plates, which is seen in colouring and lettering, as well as factual content, although different scales and projections will be used within one atlas, as thought necessary. Many atlases contain more than maps and index, but it must be said that for a library, the added illustrations, tables and diagrams, and often the very small-scale thematic maps in a general reference atlas, are not useful. The information they provide should be supplied more effectively from more specialized sources.

Libraries require:

(a) major world atlases for general reference use;
(b) atlases to assist school and undergraduate geographers;
(c) national atlases which map one country for many topographic and specialist themes;
(d) regional atlases covering a recognized area of a country and usually of a broad subject type;
(e) atlases devoted to maps showing the distribution of data relevant to one theme;
(f) road atlases for the motorist.

Although there are atlases in which map plates are folded to be accommodated in the volume, normally the volume size determines plate size; the larger the plates, the larger the scales which can be used. Atlases usually number the verso and recto of an opening as two plates, but maps are often printed across the opening, and the format should allow the double plate to be reasonably flat, with the printing at the fold clearly visible. The main point to examine in assessing the suitability of a general atlas is that it is up to date; all recent name changes, boundaries, and major roads should be included. This is decided by checking known changes and known areas. The scales used on different plates should be chosen to allow a student to make comparisons of areas and distances, with ease. The atlas index must cover all the names used on the plates, with a suitable reference system, as well as alternative forms. Sheehy[6] notes a number of points to examine in studying an atlas. These can be usefully read by students, but the paramount requirements of information needs may cause the application of these considerations to be modified. Valuable review articles[7] appear, at intervals,

Maps, Atlases, and Gazetteers

in periodicals; and reviews of individual atlases and maps are given in many cartographic and geographical journals: *Geographical journal* (in the 'Cartographic notes' pages), *SLA Geography and Map Division bulletin*, and *Bulletin of the Society of University Cartographers* are particularly to be noted.

GENERAL REFERENCE ATLASES

THE TIMES ATLAS OF THE WORLD. Comprehensive ed. Rev. London: Times Newspapers, 1980.

The world atlas with which others are compared. The 244 map pages are derived from the five-volume *Mid-century edition*, with new plates added, using scales from 1 : 515,000 for West European countries like The Netherlands and Switzerland, to 1 : 5.5M for Mexico, and Central America. Continental scales are smaller, eg USSR 1 : 15M, but these are supplemented by plates of larger scale, such as Leningrad; Urals 1 : 5M. Following the first publication in 1967, there have been six revised editions to 1980, revisions which have included, for example, increased provision for China. The index has some 210,000 names, normally in the Permanent Committee on Geographical Names/Board on Geographic Names (PCGN/BGN) form (see p 288), and geographical co-ordinates as well as the plate map-grid reference. World thematic maps, and a glossary of geographical terms, are included.

THE INTERNATIONAL ATLAS. Rev ed. Chicago: Rand McNally, 1980.

A very good atlas, it is an example of the value of co-operative publishing for highly expensive ventures. The associated publisher in Britain is G. Philip. As an international venture, the publishers try to get away from the idea that atlases 'devote a major share of their contents to the country or region in which they are published, reflecting a prime concern of their audience'. This is correct, but it is not entirely lost in *The international atlas*, where, however, the policy has led to more uniform scales for different parts of the world, but not necessarily the largest scales to be found in general atlases for these areas. The homeland bias can be desirable; educational atlas publishers provide an emphasis on maps of the nation where the atlas is to be marketed, and this is needed by the schools. In *The international atlas*, most countries are covered at 1 : 3M for Europe and North America, with 1 : 1M for key regions in each continent, and 1 : 300,000 for major conurbations. This atlas gives a pictorial impression of relief, by hill shading and altitude tints. The index has 160,000 entries.

There are numerous **secondary** atlases. These are usually required in variety by students, not necessarily studying geography. Revised editions are issued, at frequent intervals, by well-known publishers like G. Philip, and old editions should be replaced unless they are discovered to have some useful maps not retained in a revision. Repeated publication of a title should mean an adequate atlas, and choice will often depend on personal taste, but one example can be noted for details of interest:

THE WORLD ATLAS. 12th ed. Edinburgh: John Bartholomew, 1981.

Originally *Edinburgh world atlas*, it is perhaps popular because of the extensive contour layer colouring. In common with a growing number of atlases, a location of plates index map is given, as well as a listing of plates. There is quite a high proportion of world distribution maps; the general maps are on a scale of between 1 : 4M and 1 : 12.5M, but Europe is at 1 : 3M, and the UK at 1 : 1.25M. This atlas uses, to index places, a special system of co-ordinates, 'Bartholomew's hour system of geographical co-ordinates'.

NATIONAL ATLASES

National atlases are normally produced by governments or academic institutions, the better to appreciate an overview of the national environment. They can cover many topics, usually in the areas of physical environment, industrial resources, socio-economic factors, demography, etc. Data derived from a census may be a primary source of information for such an atlas.

Maps, Atlases, and Gazetteers

NATIONAL ATLAS OF THE UNITED STATES OF AMERICA. Washington: US Geographical Survey, 1970.

This atlas contains 765 maps with special subject maps at scales 1 : 7.5M, 1 : 17M and 1 : 34M. These thematic maps cover physical, historical, economic, socio-cultural subjects; and administrative maps, eg areas of postal zip codes. The general maps showing place-names, rivers, road and rail, but not relief, cover the country at 1 : 2M, whilst the 27 largest cities are mapped at 1 : 500,000. The index has 41,000 entries, with populations. Some of the maps have been available separately, as have other sections, including the text pages 'Mapping and charting' which, whilst dealing with cartographic techniques in general, have examples and descriptions of all the *National topographic map* series.

NATIONAL ATLAS OF CANADA. 5th ed. Ottawa: Department of Energy, Mines and Resources, 1981.

The 270 maps on scales from 1 : 10M to 1 : 50·5M, but mostly of 1 : 15M or 20M, cover many aspects of physical, human, and economic geography. Industry maps reflect the importance of forest products, non-ferrous metal, and other industrial minerals. Several maps are concerned with the exploration of Canada, and territorial evolution from 1667.

Britain as a whole does not have a national atlas, although sheet maps and atlases, which were of a type relevant to such an atlas, have been produced in the past.

ATLAS OF THE ENVIRONMENT. Vol 1. London: Department of the Environment, 1977– .

Loose-leaf volume with a first issue of 16 maps, many based on statistics from the 1971 census; and most are new editions of maps originally prepared for the Department's *Desk atlas*, an atlas of planning maps which grew to 143 sheets. Maps are mostly 1 : 2M, with explanatory notes.

NATIONAL ATLAS OF WALES. Cardiff: University of Wales Press, 1981– .

A bilingual atlas which, when completed in 1984, will consist of

National Atlases

over 200 thematic maps on scales of 1 : 500,000 and 1 : 1M, displaying the physical, political, cultural, economic, industrial, land use, demographic, and communications environments of contemporary Wales, with some historical elements.

ATLAS OF THE SEAS AROUND THE BRITISH ISLES. Lowestoft: Ministry of Agriculture, Fisheries and Food, Directorate of Fisheries Research, 1981.
Shows a range of physical, chemical, biological and geological information, including fishery grounds, oil and gas fields, sources of pollution, in 75 coloured charts and text.

Many thematic atlases are devoted to a region within a nation, and are probably created by a local institution. University of Sheffield, Department of Geography, *Census atlas of South Yorkshire* (1974), offers computer and laser graphic mapping, using 1971 census figures, for 35 selected population characteristics in over 2,700 enumeration districts.

Other thematic atlases are on a world basis, and range from smaller-scale atlases from commercial publishers, to major scholastic atlases with the co-operation of experts from many countries:

OXFORD REGIONAL ECONOMIC ATLASES is a series from Oxford University Press, which covers a number of continental areas. Some editions have a very small plate size, but the series is well used for geographical study and teaching.

CLIMATIC ATLAS OF EUROPE. 1970; ... OF SOUTH AMERICA. 1975; ... OF NORTH AND CENTRAL AMERICA. 1979; Budapest: Cartographia, WMO and Unesco.
The first volumes of a world climatic atlas which the World Meteorological Organisation has prepared to make climatological observations, collected around the world over several decades.

WORLD ATLAS OF AGRICULTURE. Novara: Istituto Geografico Agostini, 1969– , prepared by the International Association of Agricultural Economists, is a loose-leaf atlas of land use throughout the world, with a descriptive text for all major areas.

Maps, Atlases, and Gazetteers
Road atlases

Road atlases must be thought of as a category on their own. Like road maps, they are mostly produced by private publishers and motoring organizations who seek to emphasize the anticipated needs of motorists in general, and touring motorists in particular. Commercial motorists and lorry drivers can be critical of the lack of information, such as sites of service stations, restaurants, low bridges, etc. Useful comments on road mapping can be read in articles by motoring or travel journalists, and currently O'Donoghue, Murphy and Stephenson[7] provide a conspectus. Although motorists might be expected to possess road maps, such maps are commonly used in libraries, sometimes to plot a very long route, and sometimes to select an atlas before buying one.

HISTORICAL ATLASES

Maps produced before 1850 are considered 'early maps', and naturally reflect contemporary knowledge. If a modern map-maker using current cartographic knowledge allied to historical evidence, prepares a map of a geographical/historical period (say the extent of the Roman Empire) this is an historical map. The maps can only represent known data, and are dependent on historical research for facts which can be recorded. Archaeological discoveries contribute to the making of the maps concerned with prehistory. D. and R. Whitehouse *Archaeological atlas of the world*. (London: Thames and Hudson, 1977), shows some 5,000 sites on 103 maps, with a text and bibliography for each section, contributing to the knowledge which can be applied to historical maps.

SHEPHERDS HISTORICAL ATLAS. 8th rev ed. London: G. Philip, 1976.
    A classic in this field, with 200 coloured maps and extensive index, it covers history from 1450 BC to the mid-twentieth century AD. The same publisher has another well-regarded name in Muir's *Historical atlases*, eg Ramsay Muir *Atlas of ancient, mediaeval and modern history* (rev ed. London: G. Philip, 1982).

Early and Local Maps

Lobel, M. D. (*ed.*) ATLAS OF HISTORIC TOWNS. Vol 1. Oxford: Lovell Johns, 1968; Vol 2. London: Scolar Press/Historic Towns Trust, 1975.

Specialized and detailed plans on scales of 1:2,500 and 1 : 5,000 illustrate, with texts, the development of historically important British towns. The volumes are planned as part of an international series initiated by the International Commission for the Study of the History of Towns.

EARLY AND LOCAL MAPS

The study of early maps by many collectors, and the interest in early maps which is generally evident, would suggest that all libraries should pay attention to the history of cartography. An early map may be studied as an artefact or for its content, by the historian of an area. In the latter case it should be remembered that an early map may not be completely trustworthy. It is, of necessity, a selective record: what the map-maker included or omitted may make a significant difference to the apparent truths in a map, and so the reasons for drawing it should be understood, if possible. Printed maps and atlases of the sixteenth and seventeenth centuries are highly decorative, attractive as collectors' items, and therefore expensive. Many university and city libraries possess copies bought for special interests or received as gifts, but a selection of examples to illustrate the subject can be built up, with care, by buying facsimile atlases and original maps extracted from damaged volumes. It is necessary to identify correctly detached plates and atlases, and an outstanding bibliographical tool is:

Koeman, Ir C. ATLANTES NEERLANDICI. Amsterdam: Theatrum Orbis Terrarum, 1967–1972. 5 vols.

It is a bibliography of atlases and pilot books published in The Netherlands before 1800, which covers the period of the major flowering of early cartography, with map-makers like Ortelius, Mercator, Blaeu, Jansson, and others. Koeman describes over 1,000 editions of atlases, arranged alphabetically under cartographer or publisher, with indexes by author, by year of publication, by all cartographers, engravers, etc, and by geographical names which provide an index to the individual plates. The bibliographical description includes signatures, page numbering, and notes of the text pages to aid in identifying detached maps.

The published catalogues of the British Library, Map Library; Library of Congress, Map Division; New York Public Library, Research Libraries; and National Maritime Museum, Greenwich, are all valuable in the study of early atlases.

In 1579 Christopher Saxton issued an atlas of England and Wales, which consisted of maps of each county area, and the county became the unit of the printed small-scale map of England and Wales until the nineteenth century. County maps are popular, but not very important for local historical evidence before the larger scale of 1 inch to 1 mile was used for new surveys of the late eighteenth century. These maps could show changes resulting from industrial development.

Skelton, R. A. COUNTY ATLASES OF THE BRITISH ISLES, 1579–1850. Vol 1. London: Carta Press, 1970.

This work provides the descriptive bibliography of atlases up to 1703; the description of individual maps, and of the bibliographical history of the atlas, is the most extensive in any bibliography. Atlases are entered under date of publication, arranged chronologically. Until a later volume is prepared to cover later atlases, it is necessary to supplement the work with Thomas Chubb's *The printed maps in the atlases of Great Britain and Ireland, 1579–1870* (reprint, London: Dawson, 1966).

Many bibliographies of county maps have been compiled. These are obviously of the greatest value for maps of the counties concerned, but they are of assistance in studying other areas, as they tend to reflect the publishing pattern of every other county, particularly for those maps which appeared in atlases. Two outstanding examples are P. D. Harvey and Harry Thorpe *Printed maps of Warwickshire, 1576–1900* (Warwick: Warwickshire County Council/University of Birmingham, 1959) and D. Hodson *Printed maps of Hertfordshire, 1577–1900* (London: Dawson, 1975). There are similar cartobibliographies which concern other countries, and an-

Early and Local Maps

other outstanding example is James Clements Wheat and Christine F. Brun *Maps and charts published in America before 1800* (New Haven/London: Yale University Press, 1969).

Early local maps are often manuscript, and drawn to show property boundaries or areas. Extant estate maps, frequently of lands in one ownership, date from the early sixteenth century and were either working documents for estate management or, if more decoratively finished, status symbols. Some early local maps were made to illustrate the facts in a legal dispute, and they are often to be found in national record offices along with other plans of local interest. The Public Record Office and Scottish Record Office have published catalogues of map holdings, and there is a *Guide to cartographic records in the National Archives* (Washington: US Government Printing Office, 1971). For countries colonized by Europeans, there are, from the seventeenth century, maps and rivercharts made by explorers, usually printed in Europe for official reports and other publications. Catalogues of national libraries show many examples. Many local plans and planning maps have been produced to satisfy legal requirements. From the mid-eighteenth century, enclosures in England and Wales were enabled by acts of parliament, and a map accompanied deposited awards which, if they still exist, are in the PRO or local record office. Similarly the commutation of tithes produced plans of parishes and townships for many areas. In Europe, from the sixteenth century, town plans evolved from the early 'bird's eye views'. Plans were frequently drawn for military needs, but they became common in the eighteenth century often by inclusion in topographical books, and later they were published to accompany street directories. The uses in local research of these and many other classes of map have been well described by J. B. Harley.[8]

There is an increasing scholarly interest in the history of maps of a local or regional nature because they are a source of evidence for so many different studies. Research in this subject will be assisted by Peter Eden (ed.) *Dictionary of land surveyors and local cartographers of Great Britain and Ireland 1550–1850* (Pts 1–3, Supplement. Folkestone: Wm Dawson, 1975–1979), which contains the name, date, counties for which work is extant, types of map made, and brief biographical details known, for some 10,000 surveyors. It must not be forgotten that the classification 'early local map' includes superseded editions of the appropriate sheets of the national survey on all scales. In Britain, Harley and Phillips[9] have written notes on the early Ordnance Survey maps for every scale, some larger than any scale in use today.

GAZETTEERS

The gazetteer is the reference book first used in attempting to locate a place, whether a settlement, a physical feature, or a man-made feature, such as the name of an administrative district. The word was originally used to describe a writer for a gazette, an official newspaper report. The change of use of the word to mean an alphabetical list of geographical names, which includes some means of identifying their location, appears to have followed the publication *Gazetteer's or Newsman's interpreter* by Lawrence Echard in 1703, to which he added a second volume in 1704 with the title *The Gazetteer*. It is misleading to define a gazetteer as a geographical dictionary; that phrase should be restricted to a dictionary devoted to the specialist terminology of geography and allied studies. The gazetteer is basically a listing of places, with sufficient information to identify their location, but most gazetteers add more information about a place; notes on industry, matters of tourist interest, population, and facts concerning local administration.

As with all reference works, the gazetteer providing international coverage is less comprehensive and probably less informative about the places within one country than is a gazetteer devoted to that country alone. The sum of a number of national gazetteers offers much more than an international gazetteer can offer, but the international gazetteer is often the first to be consulted, because it is sometimes not known which country contains the required place. The initial lack of information may also apply to the spelling, particularly if the place is in a foreign country and one which does not use the Latin alphabet. This difficulty is aggravated when the enquirer has seen the place-name written in a transliterated form different from the form used in the gazetteer. The same difficulty occurs when names have been anglicized, eg the Irish Dúnchaoin being written as Dunquinn. The gazetteer listing is arranged alphabetically, and is therefore dependent on the spelling; so the user must attempt to find the one required by trial with variant possible spellings. Gazetteers do use references from well-known variant spellings.

Seltzer, L. E. (*ed.*) COLUMBIA LIPPINCOTT GAZETTEER OF THE WORLD. New York: Columbia University Press, 1962.

One of the larger world gazetteers, with 130,000 entries, and this is a field where width of coverage is all important. It shows locations by reference to country; province; and distance and direction to a significant town; and includes brief descriptive and historical information. A user can assess the value of such a gazetteer by checking the entries for places which are known. It will sometimes be found that when a gazetteer seeks to extend the information supplied beyond that of location alone, the additional facts are sadly out of date.

WEBSTER'S NEW GEOGRAPHICAL DICTIONARY. Springfield, Massachusetts: Merriam, 1976.

With less than 50,000 entries, this is much smaller than *Columbia Lippincott*, but it has the virtue of providing pronunciations for place-names. This work has a bias to USA which, of course, can be of value. In spite of the title, it is a gazetteer, not a dictionary of geography.

THE TIMES INDEX-GAZETTEER OF THE WORLD. London: The Times, 1965.

With around 345,000 entries, this is the largest gazetteer of the world available, and therefore normally the first one would use to identify locations. Places are located by their co-ordinates of latitude and longitude and, for those entries (more than half), which are mapped in *The Times atlas, Mid-century edition*, there are also grid references applicable to these maps. No additional information is provided. This gazetteer is a reminder that atlas indexes can in themselves be used as basic gazetteers and, just as world gazetteers tend to give emphasis to the countries of particular interest to the citizens of the country where the gazetteer is published, the similar bias of a world atlas can be successfully used, through its index, to identify places of little significance. The names in a gazetteer, and the names on atlas maps are inevitably only a selection, and compilers make slightly different selections for lesser names, and may provide different transliterations, or more up-to-date changes of name. When tracing information, one should always be aware of this possibility.

Encyclopaedias might be considered as incorporating gazetteers, because so many entries are of place-names. A national encyclopaedia is of particular value as a source for information on a place in that country. **National gazetteers** are published throughout the world, but for the general purposes of English language users, transcribed gazetteers are desirable, whenever possible, for foreign scripts. There are two organizations which, in concert, have a programme for establishing standardized forms of transliteration and transcription of geographical names throughout the world, and for publishing series of national gazetteers. They are the United States Board on Geographic Names; and the Permanent Committee on Geographical Names for British Official Use, usually known as BGN and PCGN. The gazetteers they have produced are listed in Walford and in Sheehy. In spite of these two bodies working in agreement on systems, difficulties can still arise due to the lack of an accepted standardized spelling in the country of origin.

National gazetteers from different countries can, of course, differ greatly. As always, width of coverage for the basic gazetteer facts for location is of prime importance, but some provide very full information:

Honet, A. and Cleeren, R. DICTIONNAIRE MODERNE GEOGRAPHIQUE, ADMINISTRATIF, STATISTIQUE, DES COMMUNES BELGES. Brussels: Imprimeries Dewarichet, 1968.

This is a good example of the wide range of information which might be provided in a gazetteer, probably, as in this case, by the use of a large number of symbols.

Mason, O. (*comp.*) BARTHOLOMEW GAZETTEER OF BRITAIN. Edinburgh: John Bartholomew, 1977.

Gazetteers

'Includes references to inhabited places and physical features in England, Scotland, Wales and Isle of Man. Entries show the names of places and features arranged in alphabetical order, and each entry includes a locational reference to the set of maps incorporated in the book, as well as a National Grid reference. In addition, the relationship to a nearby place is provided in both miles and kilometres.' This gazetteer has about 40,000 entries, which means that . . .

GAZETTEER OF THE BRITISH ISLES. Reprint. Edinburgh: Bartholomew, 1970.
. . .with 90,000 entries, is more comprehensive and should be retained. The latter, however, is otherwise less useful, in that National Grid references and new names resulting from local government reorganization are not included.

National gazetteers can be readily identified in Walford and Sheehy, updated by current geographical bibliographies. Atlas indexes, gazetteers of counties or states, post office guides, lists which are derived from, or are, indexes to place-names in census reports, should be noted within this general heading. Such publications, along with guide-books and other useful works observed and recorded by the alert librarian, are all used when appropriate for gazetteer information. The following examples may serve to show the types of material available:

ATLANTE INTERNAZIONALE. INDICE DEI NOMI. Milano: Touring Club Italiano, 1968.

GAZETTEER OF CANADA. ONTARIO. Ottawa: Department of Energy, Mines and Resources, 1966.

General Register Office, Scotland. INDEX OF SCOTTISH PLACE NAMES FROM THE 1971 CENSUS . . . Edinburgh: HMSO, 1975.

AYER DIRECTORY OF PUBLICATIONS. Philadelphia: Ayer Press. Annual.

Maps, Atlases, and Gazetteers

Brief notes, administration, industry, on 8,000 towns of USA and Canada where newspapers and periodicals are published.

Another factor to be considered in a quest for a place-name is that the name may have been superseded, or may refer to a place no longer in existence. There should, therefore, be some selective retention of old gazetteers, and even guide-books, for information on districts which have been destroyed or radically changed. Those historical atlases which have a good index are of value here, but of more significance are the retrospective gazetteers, which are specialized, and so more comprehensive for their topic. Enquiries concerning early place-names may arise in connection with their appearance in early documents, sometimes in abbreviated form, and in a Latin or vernacular form no longer used.

Ellis, H. J. and Brickley, F. B. (*eds.*) INDEX TO THE CHARTERS AND ROLLS IN THE DEPARTMENT OF MANUSCRIPTS, BRITISH MUSEUM. London: British Museum, 1900–1912. 2 vols.

Indexes place-names and religious houses named in manuscripts acquired up to 1900, and identifies these early names with the modern spelling.

Darby, H. C. and Versey, C. R. DOMESDAY GAZETTEER. Cambridge: Cambridge University Press, 1975.

An example of a period gazetteer derived from a major manuscript source.

Local historians and family historians are regular users of older national gazetteers. Nineteenth-century registration districts, for example, may have names which are unfamiliar in today's topography. In Britain, there are a number of publications which are of permanent value for historical use:

Lewis, S. A. TOPOGRAPHICAL DICTIONARY OF ENGLAND . . . 7th ed. London: Lewis, 1848–1849. 4 vols.

This is the most frequently recommended, and it does provide quite extensive contemporary descriptions and historical notes for a town or village.

Gazetteers

THE PARLIAMENTARY GAZETTEER OF ENGLAND AND WALES . . . Glasgow: A. Fullerton, 1844. 4 vols.
Provides another good listing and much statistical information.

ENGLISH PLACE-NAME SOCIETY. Volumes are published on a county basis, although national coverage is not yet complete. Names are arranged alphabetically by civil parish within their wapentakes, or hundreds, according to the region, but there are alphabetical indexes. As well as settlement names, parish, street, and field names are given, with many historical forms shown by citing from dated records. The primary concern of the Society is with the origin and meaning of the names, but locations at parish level are given by the OS National Grid reference. An example:

Mills, A. D. THE PLACE-NAMES OF DORSET. English Place-name Society, Vol LII, Pt 1. Cambridge: Cambridge University Press, 1977.
Here one discovers that 'Pidele' of the Domesday Book, 1086, is now Tolpuddle (National Grid reference SY 793945) within Puddletown Hundred, one field name in the parish being 'Dogs plot'.

Gazetteers, atlases, and sheet maps are all sources of geographical types of information. Each is an obvious source of a particular aspect of information, and they will often be used together for a study or a specific item of information. On the other hand, many other books, not necessarily of a reference nature, might be used for a geographical enquiry. The enquirer is not concerned that the answer was obtained from a particular type of reference source, only that the answer is accurate and up to date. So it must always be recognized that maps may be included in textbooks and periodical articles, as well as in atlases; that places are written about or identified not only in gazetteers, but in geography texts, guidebooks, travel books, sociological works, etc, which are usually indexed. Sometimes a thematic map, where the sources of the data used are cited, can act as a clue to the possible publication of more up-to-date and more detailed statistics. Because of their format, maps tend to be considered as things apart in a library, even physically distant in a university library, where the map collection is commonly in the geography department rather than in the main library. This is unwise; a map collection is yet another strand in the net of resources available for providing study material and specific information in the library.

REFERENCES AND CITATIONS

1. Nichols, Harold. *Map librarianship.* 2nd ed. London: Bingley, 1982. 46–65.
2. Harley, J. B. *Ordnance Survey maps.* Southampton: Ordnance Survey, 1975. 24–29.
3. Reproductions of Ordnance Survey maps. *Library Association Record,* **77** (5), May 1975. 111, 128.
4. Anglo-American Cataloguing Committee for Cartographic Materials. *Cartographic materials: a manual of interpretation for AACR2.* London: Library Association, 1982.
5. Coleman, Alice. Land use planning—success or failure. *Architects Journal,* **165** (3), 19 January 1977. 94–134. Land use survey maps. 111–16.
6. Sheehy, E. P. *Guide to reference books.* Chicago: American Library Association, 1976. 587.
7. Stephenson, R. W. Atlases of the Western hemisphere: a summary survey. *Geographical Review,* **62** (1), January 1972. 92–119.
   Murphy, Mary. Atlases of the Eastern hemisphere: a summary survey. *Geographical Review,* **64** (1), January 1974. 111–139.
   O'Donoghue, Y. Some recent British atlases. *British Book News,* August 1977. 584–9.
8. Harley, J. B. *Maps for the local historian: a guide to British sources.* London: National Council of Social Service, 1972.
9. Harley, J. B. and Phillips, C. W. *The historian's guide to Ordnance Survey maps.* London: National Council of Social Service, 1964.

SUGGESTIONS FOR FURTHER READING

Lawrence, G. R. P. *Cartographic methods.* London: Methuen, 1979.
   Useful for a basic understanding of maps.
Thrower, N. J. W. T. *Maps and man.* Englewood Cliffs, New Jersey: Prentice-Hall, 1972.
   Can be read for the wider appreciation of maps in relation to Western culture.
Hodgkiss, Alan. *Understanding maps, a systematic history of their use and development.* Folkestone: Wm Dawson, 1981.

Further Reading

A most informative, well-illustrated and readable work.

Nichols, Harold. *Map librarianship*. 2nd ed. London: Bingley, 1982.

Covers current, early and local maps in separate sections.

British Standards Institution. *Bibliographical references to maps and charts*, BS 5195. London: BSI, 1975–1977. Pt 1: References to maps in accessions lists. Pt 2: References in books and articles.

Harley, J. B. *Ordnance Survey maps: a descriptive manual*. Southampton: Ordnance Survey, 1975.

A student will find particularly valuable the 40 plates of sections of OS maps, and conventional signs used.

Hydrographic Office. *Symbols and abbreviations used on Admiralty charts*. Chart 5011, Book ed 3. Taunton: Ministry of Defence, 1976.

Lock, C. B. Muriel. *Geography and cartography*. London: Bingley; Hamden, Connecticut: Linnet, 1976.

A reference handbook which can be consulted for information on map publishers, individual atlases, periodicals.

International Federation of Library Associations and Institutions. Joint Working Group on the International Standard Bibliographic Description for Cartographic Materials. ISBD (CM). *International standard bibliographic description for cartographic materials*. London: IFLA International Office for UBC, 1977.

12
Government Publications

James G. Ollé

Fifty years ago, Arundell Esdaile, eminent bibliographer and Secretary of the British Museum, said that the periodical had added 'a new terror to research'. Since then librarians and library users have been faced with several other new terrors: research reports, conference proceedings, microforms and the growing, thriving paraphernalia of information technology. To these one could add official publications. But although extensive collections of official publications are a fairly recent feature of many libraries, official publications themselves are not. It is here that one perceives a notable difference between the growth of library resources in Britain and America. In Great Britain, notwithstanding that its own official publications originated in the seventeenth century, and were quite numerous by the eighteenth century, the demand for them, outside Westminster and Whitehall, was fairly small until the 1950s. This was partly because of the late development of universities and polytechnics in Britain, and partly because there has been no British counterpart to the long-standing, nationwide depository system which has given to many public and academic libraries in the USA substantial collections of official publications and has encouraged the appointment of specialist librarians to look after them.

This striking difference in the status of official publications in the libraries of the two countries is reflected in the literature of librarianship. Even a cursory examination of the references under the heading 'Government Publications' in *Library literature* shows that the majority are American. Until a decade ago it was possible to put in a single pamphlet box all the literature on official publications published in Britain. This has changed. It is now generally recognized that most official publications are unique sources of information, and that many are of vital importance. It has also been realized that, over the years, they have generated complicated bibliographical problems, the unravelling of which has called for considerable labour on the part of librarians and academics.

One may learn about official publications, as one may learn about the other printed sources of information dealt with in this manual, by plunging into them. This method is not recommended. Official publications represent a spreading jungle of documents. A few signposts are absolutely necessary for their exploration. The preference given to British government publications in this chapter is not altogether due to the British origins of this book. It is also recognition of the fact that there is interest in these publications in many parts of the world, particularly in the USA.

BRITISH GOVERNMENT PUBLICATIONS

The term 'British government publications' is often used as though it were synonymous with 'HMSO publications'. It is not, and it never has been. Today, so many documents are published directly by British government departments and institutions that it has been calculated that less than 30 per cent of them are published, or even stocked, by Her Majesty's Stationery Office. It is probably unnecessary to point out that the Patent Office and the Ordnance Survey are massive publishers in their own right. (Their publications are dealt with elsewhere in this volume.) This causes no difficulty. The demarcation is clear-cut and easily recognized. What must be remembered is that every government department, institution, advisory board and nationalized industry acts, to some extent, as its own publisher. It should be remembered also that although some of their publications may be slight, ephemeral and perhaps gratuitous, this is by no means true of them all. As we

Government Publications

shall see later, the sheer number and the potential value of non-HMSO official publications have caused so much concern that steps have had to be taken to list them and make them more readily available. But among government publishers HMSO remains of paramount importance. This is because HMSO alone has the authority to publish on behalf of Parliament. As the guardian of Crown Copyright, HMSO allows commercial publishers to reprint Parliamentary publications, but their initial publication remains its own privilege and responsibility.

The singular importance of HMSO publications, coupled with their large number (about 7,000 titles a year), are reasons enough for studying them as a separate class of published sources of information, but there are others. The more involved one is with HMSO publications, the more evident it becomes that they deserve all the attention they have received, in recent years, in books, articles and special courses. In this area of British publishing, few paths are straight.

Government publications cannot be divorced from the departments, etc, which produce them. They are firmly linked to the machinery of government, which is not constant. Serials and series change their names and departments; reports that were Parliamentary may become Non-Parliamentary; publications which were HMSO may become non-HMSO. HMSO's catalogues are of restricted value. They announce publications; they do little to explain them. The need for the unofficial textbooks on, and bibliographies of, British government publications we now have is real.

In most British libraries at least one member of the staff should be familiar with the main features of HMSO publications.

I have heard that it is a cardinal maxim in the training of HMSO's enquiry officers that they must never say, off the cuff, in answer to even the most recondite enquiry, that 'HMSO does not publish anything on that subject'. They could be wrong. HMSO's publications cover many more topics than the public realizes. The government's interests, which are linked with its responsibilities, and the vast amount of expert knowledge and experience it can draw upon to minister to them, have given birth to a remarkable range of publications, varied both in form and subject; publications which deserve exploration, even though they may not invite it.

Parliamentary Publications

There are three ways by which the scope and importance of HMSO's publications may be appreciated. The most agreeable is to contrive a visit to one or other of the Government Bookshops, which HMSO administers, where the display of HMSO publications is more elaborate than any you will find in a library. The second way is to browse through a recent issue of HMSO's *Monthly Catalogue* and its 'Monthly selection' inset. The third method, for the most resolute, is to spend a few hours with the unique *Guide to British government publications* which has become available since the first edition of this manual was published. This is such an important addition to the growing literature about British government publications that it deserves a paragraph to itself.

Rodgers, Frank. A GUIDE TO BRITISH GOVERNMENT PUBLICATIONS. New York: H. W. Wilson, 1980.

Governments take little trouble to explain their publications. As agents for the legislature and the government departments, the central government publishers, such as HMSO, feel it is not their business to. Guides to government publications, where they exist, are usually unofficial. This excellent guide to British government publications is not only unofficial but an American work from an American publisher. It is not the only aid to the use of our government publications which has come from the USA. Rodgers has explained, with a wealth of administrative and bibliographical detail, the present pattern of our government publications. Unless there are radical changes in the machinery of government, this welcome guide should not require much revision for a while.

PARLIAMENTARY PUBLICATIONS

A point which soon becomes evident when one uses HMSO's lists and catalogues is that British government publications have an official classification unrelated to subjects. Its basis is the origin, the administrative history, of the publications. The starting point is two broad divisions: Parliamentary Publications and Non-Parliamentary Publications. Parliamentary Publications are those directly related to the activities of Parliament: what Parliament

Government Publications

considers, what it says and what it does. The more important types of Parliamentary Publications are listed below. They are all either series or serials.

HOUSE OF LORDS PUBLICATIONS

Journal
Official reports of the Parliamentary debates (Hansard)
Papers and bills

HOUSE OF COMMONS PUBLICATIONS

Journal
Official report of the Parliamentary debates (Hansard)
Bills
Papers
Weekly information bulletin

PAPERS PRESENTED TO PARLIAMENT BY COMMAND

Command papers

ACTS AND MEASURES

Public general acts
Local and personal acts
Measures of the General Synod of the Church of England

If Scotland and Wales ever have their own Assemblies, the Parliamentary Publications will increase. For the position in Northern Ireland, which formerly had its own Parliament, but now has only an Assembly for consultative purposes, see the section on the government publications of Northern Ireland below.

In the above table, all the major series and serials which make

Parliamentary Publications

up the Parliamentary Publications class are listed separately. But to explain them, it is more convenient to divide them into four groups, as follows:

(a) Journals and Hansard
(b) Lords papers, Commons papers, and Command papers
(c) Bills, acts of Parliament and measures
(d) House of Commons weekly information bulletin

(a) Journals and Hansard

The *Journals* of the two Houses are the official and permanent annual record of their proceedings. As their main use outside Westminster is for historical research, they are seldom found except in academic libraries.

The *Official reports of the Parliamentary debates*, commonly known as *Hansard* (in honour of their first publisher), are a complete and reliable record of what is said in Parliament. They are far more informative than the parliamentary reports in the press. There are two series, one for each House. Both are published daily while Parliament is in session. Later they are cumulated into bound volumes which incorporate any corrections deemed necessary. There are weekly, volume and sessional indexes.

The section of the Commons *Hansard* devoted to its daily ritual called Question Time is worth remembering, as it includes useful information, some of it statistical. A good deal of trouble and expense is devoted to providing answers to Members' questions. Note that *Hansard* includes written as well as oral answers.

Hansard does not, however, include the reports of the several Standing Committees of the House of Commons. These are the important committees which consider the details of Bills. The reports of their debates are published separately by HMSO.

As will be noted later, the demand by historians for back runs of *Hansard* and the *Journals* has led to the publication of complete sets of them in microform.

What happens at Cabinet meetings is not revealed officially, or in detail. This does not prevent press speculation and discreet 'leaks'

Government Publications

to the media. But there is neither a *Journal*, nor a *Hansard*, for the meetings of the Cabinet and its Committees.

(b) Lords papers, Commons papers and Command papers

The best-known of these series is the Command Papers, but the House of Commons Papers are also both numerous and important. They include returns printed by direction of the House; reports and accounts required under the provisions of certain Acts; the Minutes of Proceedings of Standing Committees; and the reports of the Select Committees of the House.

The number of Select Committees has increased over the past decade. They now include Committees on Expenditure, Overseas Development, Nationalised Industries, Race Relations and Immigration, and Science and Technology. Designed to strengthen the influence of Parliament over the executive, the Select Committees have no powers, except to report, and they are often denied the information they need to do that effectively. Increasingly, however, their reports are given publicity by the media.

The House of Lords Papers, which do not form a separate series, are fewer in number, and of less importance.

A Command Paper is so called because it is presented to Parliament by a minister, by command of the sovereign. It may be a treaty, a statement of government policy, or a report. If the latter, it could be a serial report, or the *ad hoc* report of a Royal Commission or departmental committee.

Many of the Command Papers emanate from the Foreign and Commonwealth Office. Treaties and exchanges of notes may be important, but to most people they are of much less interest than the reports of investigating commissions and committees, which are often headline news. Reports of this kind are commonly referred to by the names of the respective chairmen. For example, the Department of Trade *Report of the Committee to consider the law on copyright and designs* (Cmnd 6732, 1977) is known as 'The Whitford Report', after Mr Justice Whitford, the chairman of the Committee.

Although the reports of Royal Commissions are always pub-

Parliamentary Publications

lished as Command Papers, the evidence submitted to them appears among the Non-Parliamentary Publications. For peculiar administrative reasons, the reports of departmental committees may be published either in the Command Papers series, or as Non-Parliamentary Publications.

House of Commons Papers and House of Lords Papers are numbered serially within the parliamentary session. Command Papers, on the other hand, are numbered in series of indefinite length, one series being distinguished from another by a prefix taken from the letters of the word Command. The present Cmnd series, which is the fifth, began in 1956.

(c) Bills, acts and measures

A Bill is a draft of a proposed Act of Parliament. It may be Public, Local, or Personal. Local Bills, which are numerous, are promoted by local authorities, nationalized industries and other corporate bodies. Often they are concerned with transport matters, eg the *Merseyside Metropolitan Railway Bill*, which became the *Merseyside Metropolitan Railway Act 1975*. Personal Bills, now rare, concern individuals.

Public Bills are published by HMSO. Local and Personal Bills are published by their promoters. A Public Bill, if it is not thrown out, is likely to be reprinted several times, with amendments, on its way through Parliament.

A Public Bill which has passed both Houses and received the Royal Assent becomes a Public General Act (sometimes called a Statute). Public General Acts are first published separately and then in annual bound volumes called *Public General Acts and Measures*, as they include the Measures passed by the General Synod of the Church of England. (Up to 1971, 'Measures' meant the 'Measures of the National Assembly of the Church of England'.)

In recent years, there have been numerous complaints, even within the legal profession, on the difficulty of finding out what Statutes and parts of Statutes, on a given subject, are currently in force, notwithstanding the publication, by HMSO, of an annual subject index and an annual chronological table of Statutes, indi-

Government Publications

cating which are in force. To help matters, in 1972 the Statutory Publications Office inaugurated a loose-leaf edition of current Public General Acts called *Statutes in force*. For this edition, the Acts have been reprinted, in their latest amended form, as booklets, which are filed in loose-leaf binders in subject groups, eg Agriculture, Road Traffic. *Statutes in force* and the bound volumes of the *Public General Acts* are compiled by the Statutory Publications Office. Local Acts and Personal Acts, unlike the Bills from which they are derived, are also published by HMSO, but not in collected volumes.

Up to 1962, Acts of Parliament were cited rather awkwardly by the years of the sovereign's reign covered by the relevant parliamentary session, but since 1963 the numbering has been within the calendar year, eg the *New Towns Act 1975* c 42. (c, sometimes written as ch., means 'chapter' within the Statute Book.)

(d) Weekly information bulletin

Since 1978 HMSO has published, while Parliament is in session, a *House of Commons weekly information bulletin*. This useful publication, compiled in the House of Commons Library, provides information on the progress of new legislation and the composition of Commons' committees. It also lists the latest White Papers and Green Papers. For a short period there was also a *House of Lords weekly information bulletin*, but publication of this was discontinued, presumably through lack of demand. It is relevant to mention here that HMSO is now expected by the government to balance its books. It has become a 'trading' department.

POLIS

Some libraries must have up-to-date information on parliamentary activities. Obvious examples, apart from the two parliamentary libraries, are the libraries of the national newspapers and broadcasting organizations. The labour of compiling detailed indexes to the latest Parliamentary Publications is now unnecessary. Since

Non-Parliamentary Publications

October 1980 the House of Commons Library's Indexing Unit has operated a Parliamentary On-Line Information System (devised by Scicon Computer Services Ltd) commonly known by the acronym POLIS. Although it was created primarily for the benefit of the members and staffs of the two Houses of Parliament, POLIS is also available to external users, including government ministries and departments, local government authorities, and trade, industrial and professional associations.

By Spring 1983 POLIS included subject-indexed references to the parliamentary debates; parliamentary questions and answers; the debates of the House of Commons Standing Committees; the Papers and Bills of both Houses; and the Command Papers series. Like most computerized information sources, POLIS is a database, not a databank, ie it provides bibliographical references to published sources of information—in this case the series of Parliamentary Publications published by HMSO.

Full details of POLIS may be obtained from the Computer and Technical Services Section, House of Commons Library, London SW1A 0AA.

NON-PARLIAMENTARY PUBLICATIONS

This term was first used by HMSO in 1923. Previously, these documents had been referred to either as 'Official Publications' or as 'Stationery Office Publications'.

Non-Parliamentary Publications are listed by HMSO according to the departments, institutions, boards, etc, from which they emanate, except for Statutory Instruments, which are always grouped together. Non-Parliamentary Publications may be conveniently reviewed in four groups, as follows:

(a) Statutory Instruments, which, like the Statutes, are primary sources of the law;
(b) the reports of those investigating committees which are *not* published as Command Papers;
(c) most of the numerous statistical series;
(d) a miscellany of advisory and information publications by ex-

perts (not all of them in the government's employ) on many aspects of science, technology, medicine, education and the fine arts.

(a) Statutory Instruments

Statutory Instruments are the most obtrusive part of that complicated body of legal source literature called subordinate legislation. A Statutory Instrument is made by a minister under the authority of a specific Act of Parliament, to which it is a vital, although sometimes only a temporary, appendage. SIs, like Acts, can be of national or local application. The latter may not be published by HMSO.

SIs deal with aspects of legislation too detailed to be incorporated in Acts. As they can be amended, or revoked, at short notice, SIs can be applied to emergencies more conveniently than can Acts. A typical example: SI 1977 No 1057 *The petrol prices (display) order 1977*, made by the Minister of State, Department of Prices and Consumer Protection, in accordance with the provisions of section 4 (3) of the *Prices Act 1974* c 24.

SIs are first published separately. (Almost every issue of HMSO's *Daily list* notifies the publication of several of them.) They are later collected into annual volumes, but these exclude local Instruments, and those which have been revoked.

(b) Reports of committees

Since World War I, a number of reports of departmental investigating committees and working parties which formerly would have been issued as Command Papers, have been issued as departmental Non-Parliamentary Publications. To research workers, whose happy hunting ground is the bound volumes of the Sessional Papers, the alienation of some reports from the Command Papers series is a nuisance. Over the past fifty years, most of the famous reports on educational matters have been Non-Parliamentary.

Not all reports on matters of public interest are government

Non-Parliamentary Publications

reports. *The structure and reform of direct taxation* (the Meade Report) was published by Allen & Unwin for the Institute of Fiscal Studies in 1978.

(c) Statistical publications

Government departments are assiduous in the collection of statistics. The government itself needs them, and has both the authority and the resources to compile them. In the publicity brochures distributed by the Central Statistical Office, there are references to 'The Government Statistical Service', a term not to be found in HMSO's catalogues. This comprises the statistics divisions of all the major government departments, but the only ones which need be mentioned here are the two major collecting agencies, namely, the Office of Population Censuses and Surveys, which is responsible, among other things, for the decennial census in England and Wales; and the Business Statistics Office of the Department of Industry, which compiles an extensive series of *Business monitors* (monthly and quarterly), providing statistics of production within a wide range of industries.

The Central Statistical Office (CSO) occupies a key position in the Government Statistical Service, as it collects statistics from all the statistical divisions of the departments, and digests them in convenient form for general use. It also draws the attention of commerce, industry, and the general public to the existence and value of government statistics, through exhibitions, press announcements, and the widespread distribution of free pamphlets.

The CSO's principal HMSO publications are the *Monthly digest of statistics*, *Annual abstract of statistics*, *Social trends* (annual), *Regional statistics* (annual), and *Economic trends* (monthly).

The major source of information on the government's statistical series, of which there are many, is the detailed CSO *Guide to official statistics* (4th ed, HMSO, 1982), but the more important are listed in a free pamphlet, revised annually, called *Government statistics*, obtainable from: Central Statistical Office, CO: CSO Section, Great George Street, London SW1P 3AQ. The importance of government statistics may also be appreciated if one studies the

Government Publications

annotated bibliography: Committee of Librarians and Statisticians *Recommended basic United Kingdom statistical sources for community use* (3rd ed, Library Association, 1975).

(d) Miscellaneous Non-Parliamentary Publications

In a short space it is impossible to do justice to the variety of HMSO publications which fall under this heading. They include important reference works, such as *Britain: An official handbook* (note the HMSO publications cited in the bibliography) and *A yearbook of the Commonwealth*, and periodicals of unique value such as *British business* (monthly journal of the Department of Trade and Industry) and the *London Gazette*, the medium for official notices.

As to the rest, a random sample of subjects dealt with by HMSO Non-Parliamentary Publications during the Autumn of 1982 gives some support to HMSO's claim that its publications deal with almost every subject under the sun: industrial air pollution, information technology, occupational pension schemes, adult literacy, safety in nuclear power stations, language teaching in junior schools, the government and the press during the Falklands conflict, early musical instruments as works of art, and the history of Kew Gardens.

WHITE PAPERS, GREEN PAPERS AND BLUE BOOKS

These are all colloquial terms. **White Paper** means a statement of government policy. It may indicate the broad lines of a piece of legislation the government has in mind. **Green Paper** means a statement of proposed action by the government published for discussion. HMSO provides the document with a green cover and adds 'Green Paper', in brackets, to the title in its catalogues. Confusingly, not all consultative documents are published as Green Papers. Some are non-HMSO publications. A good example of a Green Paper, published by HMSO, is the Department of Trade *Reform of the law relating to copyright, design and performers'*

Non-Parliamentary Publications

protection: a consultative document (Cmnd 8302, 1981), a follow-up to the Whitford Report on copyright (also a Command Paper) mentioned earlier.

Blue Book, a term of nineteenth-century origin, not much in use today, means a report (of some commission or committee) substantial enough to need protective covers. The traditional colour, not always used now, is blue.

CHANGES IN THE MACHINERY OF GOVERNMENT

These have been frequent over the past forty years. Since 1970, HMSO has noted them briefly in its catalogues. A good case history is transport. Once there was a Ministry of Transport (hence 'the MOT test'). This was absorbed into a new super-ministry called the Department of the Environment, but from this it later emerged as the present Department of Transport. An annual review of changes in the machinery of government is published in *Management in government*, the quarterly journal of the Management and Personnel Office. This is now an HMSO publication.

HMSO LISTS AND CATALOGUES

The coverage of HMSO publications by the *British national bibliography*, although not arbitrary, is selective. For economic reasons it cannot be otherwise. Many libraries therefore acquire HMSO's official lists and catalogues. The most important are the *Daily list*, the *Monthly catalogue*, the *Annual catalogue*, and the *Sectional lists*.

In the *Daily list* the main divisions are 'Parliamentary Publications' and 'Non-Parliamentary Publications', but in the *Monthly catalogue* (oddly entitled the *Monthly catalogue of books*) and the *Annual catalogue*, the second group is called the 'Classified List'. This does not mean that it is a subject classification; merely that in this section the Parliamentary and Non-Parliamentary reports of each department are brought together. A Command Paper is entered under 'Command Papers' in the Parliamentary section and

Government Publications

again under the name of the relevant department in the Non-Parliamentary section.

Statutory Instruments appear in the *Daily list*. The classified monthly and annual lists of them, prepared by the Statutory Publications Office, are published by HMSO, but not as part of its own catalogue service. The *Daily list* is now available on Prestel a day before the printed copies reach subscribers.

The *Monthly catalogue* and the *Annual catalogue* are now produced by a computer-based indexing system. This has brought about many changes in the 'Classified list' which librarians have not welcomed. Speedy publication of these catalogues is still awaited, but details of all HMSO publications available will probably be obtainable soon from an online database.

The *Sectional lists*, of which there are now about three dozen, are lists of HMSO publications (and selected international organizations' publications for which HMSO is the British agent) currently in print. Most of the lists are departmental, eg *Sectional list 26 : Home Office*. HMSO has never published a comprehensive catalogue of its publications in print.

HMSO also publishes several auxiliary serial lists, primarily for its own use, but available free to libraries that need them. The most useful is the weekly *List of Non-Parliamentary Publications sent for printing*. There is no comparable list of forthcoming Parliamentary Publications, as these are usually printed and published at short notice. In a rather casual way ministers sometimes announce that a White Paper, or the report of some investigating committee, is due to be published 'shortly', 'next week' or whatever.

HMSO's sales service

The average bookseller is little concerned with HMSO publications, but in most of the larger cities of the UK one bookseller has been appointed as official agent for HMSO. In London and six provincial cities (Birmingham, Bristol, Manchester, Edinburgh, Cardiff and Belfast) HMSO has its own 'Government Bookshops', which sell HMSO publications over the counter and through the post. For an advance annual subscription a library can obtain all HMSO's major

Non-Parliamentary Publications

publications automatically as published. This 'Selected Subscription Service' has become rather expensive, but it saves the time and labour of frequent ordering.

Standing Committee on Official Publications

The Standing Committee on Official Publications (SCOOP), a Sub-Committee of the Reference, Special and Information Section of the Library Association, was formed in 1971 to provide helpful liaison between HMSO and its major customers. Until 1982 the Committee was known as the HMSO Services Working Party. Although there have been no major changes at HMSO as a result of this Committee, there have been welcome improvements in HMSO's services, including some changes in its catalogues. The activities of SCOOP are reported regularly in *Refer*, the half-yearly journal of the Reference, Special and Information Section.

Non-HMSO publications

Since World War II, there has been a massive growth in the number of non-HMSO official publications. In addition to the many published directly by government departments, there are many others published by the nationalized industries and the extraordinary number of Councils, Committees and Boards in the public sector which are in some way linked with the central government, eg the British Council, the Milk Marketing Board.

Having no responsibility, save in a few instances, for the distribution of any of these publications, HMSO excludes the vast majority of them from its lists and catalogues. By the late 1970s the proliferation of non-HMSO publications, the difficulty of discovering what had been published, and obtaining titles that were known, and wanted, had become regular talking points at meetings of librarians concerned with reference and information services. Fortunately, this problem has recently been dealt with by a commercial publisher, Chadwyck-Healey Ltd, Cambridge. With the co-operation of most of the departments and institutions acting partly, or entirely, as their own publishers (with the obvious exceptions of the Patent Office and the Ordnance Survey), Chadwyck-Healey has been able not only to publish a comprehensive list of non-HMSO publications, but to provide microfiche copies of most of those listed. Details of the serial catalogue are as follows:

CATALOGUE OF BRITISH OFFICIAL PUBLICATIONS NOT PUBLISHED BY HMSO. 1980 to date. Cambridge: Chadwyck-Healey, 1981 to date. Bimonthly; annual cumulations.

In support of this we now have, for the first time, a detailed directory of all the publishers of British official publications, with brief information on what they publish and how they publish:

Richard, Stephen. DIRECTORY OF BRITISH OFFICIAL PUBLICATIONS: A GUIDE TO SOURCES. Mansell Publishing, 1981.

The scope of non-HMSO publications is almost as wide, in subject and form, as HMSO publications. It includes a surprising number of serials, including some very useful ones distributed free, eg *British Library news*, monthly. There are also advisory booklets on subjects as various as education, export opportunities, food and nutrition, fair trading, employment protection, and the prevention of accidents at work and at home. Notable among the producers of non-HMSO publications are the Central Office of Information (which publishes a number of advisory pamphlets on behalf of the other government departments) and the nationalized industries.

Old British government publications

The demand for these has risen steeply since World War II, partly because many people have cultivated a taste for historical research, more specifically because there is now boundless interest in the political, social, and economic life of the nineteenth century.

HMSO is obliged to keep some of its publications in print, and it maintains stocks of others for which there is an appreciable

Non-Parliamentary Publications

demand. HMSO will also supply photocopies of out-of-print Parliamentary Publications and Statutory Instruments in its own files. But this does not afford much help to research libraries which need complete or extensive runs of Parliamentary Publications for the past two hundred years. Thanks to the diligence of scholars, the initiative of reprint publishers, and the helpful co-operation of HMSO, this problem has been largely overcome. The only major difficulties now are the reluctance of some readers to use microtexts, and the considerable cost of purchasing all the reprint series now available.

Access to old government publications was not the only problem. Their bibliographical control was imperfect and confusing. The credit for dealing with this hazard lies with bibliographers on both sides of the Atlantic.

As this chapter is not designed specifically for research workers, it is unnecessary to name and describe all the reprint series and retrospective bibliographies of British government publications which now exist, but some acquaintance with those listed below, most of which are fairly widely held in university libraries, will prevent would-be researchers from being denied help which it is easy to provide. But first, it is necessary to explain that, in some research libraries, there are sets (originals or microtexts) of the House of Commons Sessional Papers.

The House of Commons Sessional Papers

At the beginning of the nineteenth century, a Speaker of the House of Commons devised a scheme for binding the House of Commons Bills, House of Commons Papers, and the Command Papers, published within each session, in four classes—namely, Bills; Reports from Committees; Reports from Commissioners; Accounts and Papers. Within each class, the documents were arranged in alphabetical order by subject. This system survives, although, as from the session for 1969–1970, it has been modified. There are now only two classes: Bills, Reports, Accounts; and Papers. There is no obligation to use this system (which is controlled by its own contents lists and indexes), and most libraries ignore it and arrange Parliamentary Papers numerically within their respective series.

RETROSPECTIVE BIBLIOGRAPHIES

SALE CATALOGUES

ANNUAL CATALOGUES OF BRITISH GOVERNMENT PUBLICATIONS 1894–1970. Cambridge: Chadwyck-Healey, 1974–1975. 7 vols.

This reduced facsimile reprint includes the annual catalogues from 1894 to 1970, and the quinquennial indexes to them from 1936 to 1970.

CUMULATIVE INDEX TO THE ANNUAL CATALOGUES OF HER MAJESTY'S STATIONERY OFFICE PUBLICATIONS 1922–1972. Compiled by Ruth Matteson Blackmore. Washington, DC: Carrollton Press, 1976. 2 vols.

This is published as companion to the microfilm edition of HMSO publications issued by the Historical Documents Institute (see below), but can be used with other collections of these publications.

INDEXES TO THE SESSIONAL PAPERS

As mentioned earlier, the House of Commons Sessional Papers have their own indexes, which include a series of decennial cumulations, and an excellent half-century cumulation:

House of Commons. GENERAL INDEX TO THE BILLS, REPORTS AND PAPERS PRINTED BY ORDER OF THE HOUSE OF COMMONS AND TO THE REPORTS AND PAPERS PRESENTED BY COMMAND, 1900 TO 1948–1949. HMSO, 1960.

Retrospective Bibliographies

FORD INDEXES AND BREVIATES

These well-known bibliographies, compiled by Professor P. G. Ford, Mrs G. Ford, and their associates at Southampton University, are systematically arranged under subjects, and well indexed. The bibliographies called breviates include abstracts of the reports listed. All the Ford bibliographies are selective, but the selection has been shrewdly based upon the known needs of students:

Ford, P. and Ford, G. SELECT LIST OF BRITISH PARLIAMENTARY PAPERS, 1833–1899. Oxford: Blackwell, 1953. Shannon: Irish University Press, 1969.

Ford, P. and Ford, G. A BREVIATE OF PARLIAMENTARY PAPERS, 1900–1916. Oxford: Blackwell, 1957. Shannon: Irish University Press, 1969.

Ford, P. and Ford, G. A BREVIATE OF PARLIAMENTARY PAPERS, 1917–1939. Oxford: Blackwell, 1951. Shannon: Irish University Press, 1969.

Ford, P. and Ford, G. A BREVIATE OF PARLIAMENTARY PAPERS, 1940–1954. Oxford: Blackwell, 1961.

Ford, P., Ford, G. and Marshallsay, Diana. SELECT LIST OF BRITISH PARLIAMENTARY PAPERS, 1955–1964. Shannon: Irish University Press, 1970.

Marshallsay, Diana and Smith, J. H. (*eds.*) FORD LIST OF BRITISH PARLIAMENTARY PAPERS, 1965–1974. Nendeln, Liechtenstein: KTO Press, 1979.
Series in progress.

INDEXES OF CHAIRMEN

The reports of Commissions, Committees, Working Parties and Tribunals are often referred to by the names of their respective

Government Publications

chairmen. In addition, there are occasional reports from individuals; these are known by the names of their authors. A quick way of identifying such reports, other than the most recent, is to refer to the series of 'chairmen and authors indexes' published by the Library Association on behalf of its Reference, Special and Information Section:

Richard, Stephen. BRITISH GOVERNMENT PUBLICATIONS: AN INDEX TO CHAIRMEN OF COMMITTEES AND COMMISSIONS OF INQUIRY. Vol I: 1800–1899. London: Library Association, 1982.

Richard, Stephen. BRITISH GOVERNMENT PUBLICATIONS: AN INDEX TO CHAIRMEN AND AUTHORS. Vol II: 1900–1940. London: Library Association, 1974; reprinted 1982.

Richard, Stephen. BRITISH GOVERNMENT PUBLICATIONS: AN INDEX TO CHAIRMEN AND AUTHORS. Vol III: 1941–1978. London: Library Association, 1982.

REPRINTS

HISTORICAL DOCUMENTS INSTITUTE SERIES

THE CONTROLLERS LIBRARY COLLECTION OF HMSO PUBLICATIONS 1922–1977. Arlington, Virginia: United States Historical Documents Institute; Inverness: Historical Documents Institute.

This is a microfilm series based on HMSO's own file of its publications.

READEX MICROPRINT CORPORATION SERIES

The Readex Microprint Corporation, New York, has reissued, by its unique method of microproduction called Microprint, almost

Northern Ireland

complete sets of the *Journals*, *Hansard* and the *House of Commons Sessional Papers*.

IRISH UNIVERSITY PRESS SERIES

The former Irish University Press published between 1967 and 1972, in about one thousand volumes, handsomely bound in half leather, facsimile reprints of many important nineteenth-century government reports, selected with the help of Professor and Mrs P. G. Ford. For full details of this series see the classified *Catalogue of British Parliamentary Papers in the Irish University Press 1000 volume series and area studies series 1801–1900* (Dublin: Irish Academic Press, 1977). This includes an abstract of every Paper in the series.

SCHOLARLY RESOURCES SERIES

HOUSE OF COMMONS SESSIONAL PAPERS OF THE EIGHTEENTH CENTURY. Compiled and edited by Sheila Lambert. Wilmington, Delaware: Scholarly Resources, 1975–1976. 147 vols.

A splendid edition of all the House of Commons Bills and Papers of the eighteenth century known to be extant, reproduced in facsimile. Vol I includes a long introduction by the editor and a list of the Papers for 1715–1760. Vol II is a list of the Papers for 1761–1800.

NORTHERN IRELAND

From 1921 to 1972, the province of Northern Ireland had its own Parliament, commonly referred to as Stormont. During that period there was a pattern of Parliamentary and Non-Parliamentary Publications for Northern Ireland similar to that for the United Kingdom, although the number of publications was, of course, very much smaller. But in 1972 the Northern Ireland Parliament was

Government Publications

abolished. Since then the province has had direct rule from Westminster. In 1982, as a step towards devolution of powers, Northern Ireland was allowed to have an elected Assembly. It first met in November 1982. As its functions are purely monitorial and consultative its future is uncertain.

The official publications emanating from Northern Ireland have always been published and distributed by HMSO Belfast, which issues monthly and annual lists of them. The main HMSO lists and catalogues do not include them.

There is a retrospective bibliography of the Parliamentary Publications of Northern Ireland. It is on similar lines to the Ford breviates:

Maltby, Arthur. THE GOVERNMENT OF NORTHERN IRELAND 1922–1972: A CATALOGUE AND BREVIATE OF PARLIAMENTARY PAPERS. Dublin: Irish University Press, 1974.

UNITED STATES GOVERNMENT PUBLICATIONS

In terms of variety, number of titles, and sales, HMSO claims to be the largest publisher in the British Commonwealth. By the same token, the Office of the Superintendent of Documents, Washington, DC, can claim to be the largest publisher in the world. The printing of Congressional and departmental documents is the special responsibility of the Government Printing Office (GPO). In 1895, the Office of Superintendent of Documents (SUDOCS) was created, within the GPO, to handle efficiently their cataloguing, sale and distribution.

James Bennett Childs has called the USA 'the classical land for government publications'. The production of government publications in the USA is certainly enormous (SUDOCS handles nearly three times as many new titles each year as HMSO). This provides a great challenge for American librarians, one they can hardly ignore, owing to the elaborate depository system for federal documents.

There is also considerable interest in British government publi-

United States Government Publications

cations in the USA. This is hardly matched by the interest taken in US government publications in Britain, which is concentrated in comparatively few libraries, among them the British Library Official Publications Library, London; the British Library of Political and Economic Science, London School of Economics; and the libraries of the provincial universities which support research in the social sciences. Elsewhere, the demand for US government publications is either small or non-existent. The acquisition of US government publications by British libraries is a perennial source of difficulty. HMSO ceased to be the British agent for them some years ago.

To British observers, the most striking thing about US government publications is not the bulk of them, but the Federal Depository Library System mentioned earlier. This is administered by SUDOCS, and through it, nearly 1,200 American libraries receive free copies of these publications, excluding those intended specifically for official use. The depository system was strengthened, in the 1960s, by the establishment of a small number of regional depository libraries, which are obliged to receive and retain one copy of all the publications nominated for deposit. The other depository libraries are allowed to select the classes of publications they require.

Official catalogues of US government publications

The major source of information on US government publications is the *Monthly catalog*. Its bibliographical details are as follows:

Superintendent of Documents. MONTHLY CATALOG OF UNITED STATES GOVERNMENT PUBLICATIONS. Washington, DC: Government Printing Office. January 1895 to date. (This is the current title. It has changed several times since 1895.)

Although it is quite a substantial publication, the *Monthly catalog* does not list all federal publications. Like the HMSO catalogues, it has block exclusions, notably patent specifications and maps, but some items are excluded only because they are non-GPO documents which have not been reported to SUDOCS.

Since July 1976, the production of the *Monthly catalog* has been computerized, and compiled according to the Anglo-American code. The *Catalog* is arranged under the names of the federal departments and the independent agencies in alphabetical order. Each issue is thoroughly indexed in four separate sequences: author, title, subject, and series/report, which cumulate half-yearly (January to June), and annually. Index references are to the serial entry numbers, not to the pages of the *Catalog*. There is an annual, separately published *Serials supplement*.

Although a poll of subscribers to the *Monthly catalog* showed that most of them approve of the recent changes to it, two defects remain: it is not a prompt record of what has been published, and it is not as complete as it should be.

In addition to the *Monthly catalog* there is a free, annotated list, *Selected US government publications*, formerly fortnightly, now monthly. Also, since January 1978 there has been a complete and up-to-date catalogue of all publications currently offered for sale by SUDOCS. This is the bimonthly *GPO sales publications reference file* (PRF), which is published in microfiche.

Various subject bibliographies of US government publications are available from SUDOCS on request.

Among the unofficial, selective sources of information on new US government publications are 'Views and over-views on/of US Documents' in the quarterly *Government publications review* (for details of this publication see under 'Further reading' below) and 'Government publications' in *RQ*, the quarterly journal of the ALA Reference and Adult Services Division.

The major US government publications of reference value are listed in the *Guide to reference books* (9th ed, by Eugene P. Sheehy; Chicago: American Library Association, 1976), which also includes a comprehensive list of retrospective bibliographies of US government publications. Beginning with the period 1970–1971, there has been a more thorough listing of the reference works in the annotated biennial bibliography called *Government reference books* (Littleton, Colorado: Libraries Unlimited).

United States Government Publications

The range of US government publications

US government publications have a basic structure which is roughly comparable to that of British government publications, but this is not readily apparent in the *Monthly catalog*, the arrangement of which resembles that of the 'Classified List' in HMSO's *Monthly catalogue*. The various writers on US government publications define their basic structure in various ways. In its simplest form it consists of the following groups:

1. Congressional Publications.
2. Publications of the Presidency.
3. Departmental and Agency Publications.
4. Publications of the Judiciary.

Group 1 is comparable to British Parliamentary Publications, and Group 3 to British Non-Parliamentary Publications.

1. CONGRESSIONAL PUBLICATIONS

These include:

(a) The daily *Congressional record*, which includes a remarkable body of miscellaneous material, in addition to the edited reports of the debates of the Senate and the House of Representatives.
(b) The *Journals* of the Senate and the House, published at the end of each session.
(c) A miscellany of 'Papers', as they would be called at Westminster, published in four series, *Senate reports*, *House reports*, *Senate documents*, *House documents*. All these are known collectively as 'The serial set'.
(d) *Hearings*, ie the transcripts of testimony given to Congressional Committees.
(3) Congressional *Bills* and *Laws* (otherwise known as *Statutes*). Many Bills are introduced to Congress; few become Laws. Those that do are first published separately ('slip laws'), and later in sessional volumes called *Statutes at large*. As in the UK,

Government Publications

there are public laws and private laws, and in addition to this primary legislation there is secondary legislation, ie Presidential proclamations and executive orders.

(f) Congressional reference works, among them the *Official Congressional directory*.

2. PUBLICATIONS OF THE PRESIDENCY

Orders, proclamations and other Presidential documents emanate from the White House Office, the Executive Office of the President, and other sources. This is not a clear-cut group.

3. DEPARTMENTAL AND AGENCY PUBLICATIONS

The range of publications issued by the eleven departments (Agriculture; Commerce; Defense; Health, Education and Welfare; Housing and Urban Development; Interior; Justice; Labor; Transportation; the Treasury; the Department of State) and the numerous agencies defies summary. Many of the topics represented, from agriculture to zoology, can be matched by HMSO, but, at their best, HMSO's Non-Parliamentary Publications are more attractive. The departmental publications of both countries include periodicals, reference works, subject series, and a wealth of statistics. In the USA, as in Britain, there are frequent changes in the machinery of government, but in the USA there is a useful official reference aid which helps in this matter, the *United States Government Manual*, published annually.

4. PUBLICATIONS OF THE JUDICIARY

This group, normally of interest only to law librarians, includes the publications of the Supreme Court and other federal courts.

Further Reading

INFORMATION EXCLUDED FROM BRITISH AND US GOVERNMENT PUBLICATIONS

Neither British nor American government publications reveal all the information about the activities of their respective governments and government departments, which the public may wish to have. In Britain, this is partly remedied by the enterprise of investigative journalists, public announcements by ministers, or discreet but intentional 'leaks' to the media. Unpublished information of historical interest is made public, selectively, under the thirty-year rule, by the deposit of documents at the Public Record Office. But whether the information released is new or old, the provisions of the much criticized Official Secrets Act 1911 must be observed. Although there have been several government promises, in recent years, to 'liberate the practice relating to official information' (to quote from a Queen's Speech on the opening of Parliament), the White Paper (Cmnd 7285) published in July 1978 on the government's proposals to amend the Official Secrets Act does not promise very much change.

Not surprisingly, therefore, there have been many references in the British Press to the benefits of the US federal Freedom of Information Act 1974.

It should be remembered, however, that on both sides of the Atlantic, a good deal of unpublished official information has not been withheld because it is 'classified', but only because it was not regarded as worth publishing. Such information is probably obtainable, in some form or other, on request.

SUGGESTIONS FOR FURTHER READING

Government publications in general

The following articles are recommended as they are by a former official of HMSO who has personally investigated the official publications of many countries around the world:

Cherns, J. J. Government publishing: an overview. *IFLA journal*, 4 (4), 1978. 351–9.

Government Publications

Cherns, J. J. What is the role of government publishers? *State librarian*, **27** (2), July 1979. 16–19.

For recent developments in government publishing at large, and informed articles on all aspects of government publications, see the file of:

Government publications review. New York and Oxford: Pergamon Press, 1974 to date. Bimonthly.
The accent is on American official publications, but there are occasional references to British government publications.

British government publications

There is an introductory textbook which is concise and up to date:

Butcher, David. *Official publications in Britain*. London: Bingley, 1983.

Although it is now in need of revision, the following advanced textbook remains useful for its thorough coverage of Parliamentary Publications:

Pemberton, John E. *British official publications*. 2nd ed. Oxford: Pergamon Press, 1973.

For a good explanation of Statutes and Statutory Instruments see:

Way, D. J. Primary sources of legal literature. In: Moys, Elizabeth M. (ed.) *Manual of law librarianship*. London: Deutsch, 1976. Chapter 3.

There is a considerable literature on British Parliamentary procedure. The following book is particularly recommended, as it is readable as well as authoritative:

Taylor, Eric. *The House of Commons at work*. 9th ed. London: Macmillan, 1979.

This is supplemented, at various points, by:

Walkland, S. A. and Ryle, M. *The Commons today*. 2nd ed. London: Fontana, 1981.

Government publications of the USA

Morehead, Joe. *Introduction to United States public documents*. 2nd ed. Littleton, Colorado: Libraries Unlimited, 1978.

Further Reading

There have been several textbooks on US government publications. This one is lucid, systematic and reasonably up to date.

Government publications of other countries

Although government publications exist the world around, not many countries have authoritative manuals on their official publications. This is being remedied, slowly but surely, by the Pergamon Press (publisher of the *Government publications review*), which is also publishing a series called 'Guides to official publications' edited by John E. Pemberton.

Access to suppressed government information

The case for 'open government' in the UK; in particular, the case for a Freedom of Information Act comparable to the federal freedom of information legislation in the USA, is argued in the following symposium:

Secrecy, or the right to know? London: Library Association for the Freedom of Information Campaign, 1980.

13

Statistics as a Reference Resource: statistical publications and sources

Angela M. Allott

Statistics are of value, importance and use to all sections of the community. For virtually every facet of life, the appropriate statistical data provide an authoritative basis for its analysis, evaluation, and development. Statistics are produced, collected, collated and processed on behalf of both official and non-official organizations and groups. The results are stored in printed or computer format and then prepared for dissemination and retrieval through conventional publications or via new technology. A certain percentage of existing statistics is restricted to closed user groups, or made accessible on a need-to-know basis to approved outsiders, or made available on request as a free or pro-rata service from the originating source.

THE STATISTICS COLLECTION

Whereas all kinds of libraries have publications which contain statistics, reference librarians should consciously provide a statistics collection of specifically statistical publications relevant both to the area in which they are working and to their users. In addition to acquiring the publications purely concerned with statistics, they

Guides to Statistics: General

should keep in mind the statistical aspect of all subjects. For special and government libraries, the statistics collection is an integral part of their essential stock.

The professional librarian needs to know what statistics exist; where to buy or borrow them; and, preferably, how to use them on behalf of his clientèle. From the vast array of statistical publications, he must have some familiarity with at least the main international, national, regional and local series; a knowledge of the subject compilations; and an acquaintance with the leading statistical collections and centres of excellence in the United Kingdom.

The statistics collection within the library is used both by the staff on behalf of the user through the library's information enquiry service, and by individual statistics users themselves. The latter, when they consult statistical publications and tables in the subjects of their concern, of necessity rely on the professional expertise of the librarian for the selection and organization of the collection. Anyone responsible for a statistical collection must be alert to the problems and challenges involved in keeping it vital and up to date. The librarian must also advise, and liaise with, other sections of the information service in his organization on the availability of statistics, whether to the other departments of the local authority; other branches of a public library system; or to, and for, the subject specialists in academic and special libraries.

To serve all these needs and requirements, the librarian has to have three responses: first, to know what statistical series exist, who issues them, and their availability; second, to select and acquire the publications of most use to the existing and potential client groups, and to form these into an organized, coherent and accessible collection; third, through both staff and user education and training, to obtain maximum benefit from this essential but expensive special resource.

GUIDES TO STATISTICS: GENERAL

As books about statistics are nearly as numerous as the statistical series themselves, only an indication of typical examples can be given. They fall into two main types. There are those answering the question 'Who issues what?', which list or describe the statistical publications issued by governments, organizations, societies, etc, covering all subjects and areas at every level. Secondly, there are those answering the question 'What has been issued on what subject by whom?', which are arranged on a subject basis.

The guides and bibliographies cannot lead the librarian or statistics user to all possible sources of statistics, but they can indicate the most likely and the most useful. These, in turn, lead to more and more detailed sources. It is up to the librarian to choose wisely.

Statistical data are liable to change. Although all bibliographies and guides aim to be correct when they are produced, they inevitably become less so with the passage of time. This is true of books, serial publications, or specialist articles. To catch the state-of-the-art for statistical sources is like freezing a frame from a film, where one knows that as soon as time and motion is added, the picture will change.

INTERNATIONAL STATISTICS: GENERAL GUIDES

Guides to international statistics share a similar pattern of provision as those for other categories of statistics, but they are on a grander scale. They range from expensive reference works and ongoing bibliographical listings to scholarly monographs and simple introductory pamphlets.

The major influence in international statistics is the United Nations. As long ago as 1968, a resolution of the Economic and Social Council urged the Secretary General to take steps 'to ensure the development of an integrated and co-ordinated statistical programme based on longer term planning . . .'. To achieve this, international standards for statistics were needed, and they are listed in *UN directory of international standards for statistics*[1] (including a bibliography of methods). The UN DIRECTORY OF INTERNATIONAL STATISTICS, VOLUME 1[2] is comprehensive for its own publications, and has excellent coverage of the other main international statistics-issuing bodies. An important development is described in it under 'Data banks of economic and social statistics'. This gives an inventory of databases by subject

International Statistics: General Guides

and by organization. There are technical descriptions of the individual files, and there is a summary of the availability of machine-readable data, arranged by organization. In the second volume (in preparation) the organization of the Statistical Office of the UN and of other international bodies will be described, plus information on the standards, concepts, definitions and classifications for statistical use worldwide.

UNDOC,[3] dealing as it does with all kinds of UN publications, includes the full range of statistical titles. It has an index, in UN reference number order of documents, and a subject index. UN statistical publications have an identifying abbreviation as part of their reference number. UNDOC indicates the status of each document, and so unpriced or restricted items, as well as 'normal' published/priced ones, can be identified. The *UN publications catalogue*[4] is free from all UN publications Sales Offices. Each of the ten specialized UN agencies, such as Unesco, FAO, ILO, etc, has its own bibliographical arrangements for its publications, in addition to the general UN system. All issue free lists of current titles publicly available.

The Congressional Information Service has introduced, from January 1983, the INDEX TO INTERNATIONAL STATISTICS (IIS).[5] It covers statistical publications by the UN; European Communities; Organisation for Economic Co-operation and Development; Organization of American States; and 30 other intergovernmental organizations. All types of publications containing statistics are listed, whether periodicals, annuals, series, or monographs. There are subject and title indexes. In addition to its ordinary subscription service, the IIS offers an optional microfiche service of the full text of publications covered. The UK agent for IIS is Thompson, Henry Ltd, Sunningdale, Berkshire.

The LA/RSS *Recommended basic statistical sources: international*[6] is an example of a select listing of useful titles. It is the result of the initiative and continuing co-operation of the Committee of Librarians and Statisticians. Joan Harvey's *Sources of statistics*,[7] though mainly concerned with UK statistical publications, includes the outstanding international titles too. Though

The Statistics Collection

dated, as is G. A. Burrington's *How to find out about statistics* (London: Pergamon, 1972), both are compact and straightforward introductions to the literature of statistics.

SMIL[8] is the foremost publicly available collection of statistics from overseas countries in the UK, and its information and enquiry service is an important part of official assistance to exporters. SMIL publishes several guides to the statistics of overseas countries; these include its free publication *National statistical offices of overseas countries*.[9]

SISCIS: SUBJECT INDEX TO SOURCES OF COMPARATIVE INTERNATIONAL STATISTICS,[10] compiled by F. C. Pieper, is an unique reference tool. It is a subject-arranged index which indicates in which international statistical publication comparative statistics can be found. It has a useful checklist of titles of the key international statistics, mainly official, but with most important non-official items as well. It is comprehensive, and a most important asset to any statistics collection.

Wasserman's and O'Brien's STATISTICS SOURCES: A SUBJECT GUIDE TO DATA ON INDUSTRIAL, BUSINESS, SOCIAL, EDUCATIONAL, FINANCIAL AND OTHER TOPICS FOR THE UNITED STATES AND INTERNATIONALLY[11] has long established its usefulness. It concentrates mainly on US and Canadian publications, but it does contain some international statistical publications.

INTERNATIONAL STATISTICS: ECONOMIC, GEOGRAPHICAL, POLITICAL, TRADE GROUPINGS — GUIDES

Whereas international statistical publications reflect a global view, increasingly the world is divided into smaller groups of nations based on geographical, political, trade and economic interests. Each of these categories is further sub-divided or cross-divided by other points of reference, eg developed/developing nations, socialist nations, etc. These different combinations are reflected in the various statistical compilations and publications mentioned below.

Joan Harvey's series of continent-based guides, STATISTICS AFRICA;[12] STATISTICS AMERICA;[13] STATISTICS ASIA AND AUSTRALASIA;[14] STATISTICS EUROPE,[15] deal comprehensively with the statistical sources and resources for all the countries of the area. They are impressive reference books, well organized bibliographically, and well produced. For each group/country, eg European Communities or France, the information provided includes details of the central statistical office and important organizations that collect and publish statistics; the principal libraries in that country where statistical collections may be consulted by the public; the libraries/information services in other countries where these publications can be consulted; the principal bibliographies of statistics; the major statistical publications arranged in standard categories, ie general, production, agriculture, etc. All the volumes contain indexes for titles and subjects.

The Organisation for Economic Co-operation and Development (OECD) issues, every two years, with regular supplements, a free *Catalogue of publications.*[16]

European Communities statistics are well documented but there is no single guide to them. Details of the current publications available are included monthly in the *Publications of the European Communities*,[17] which appears as an insert to the *Bulletin of the European Communities*, as well as being made available as an offprint. The annual cumulation is slow to appear. *New European books* (monthly from Alan Armstrong and Associates), covers sales items, including some statistical publications, from the EC. *Eurostat news*[18] has, in addition to its news items and comments, a helpful supplement listing all titles currently available, indicating frequency of publication. *Eurostat index*,[19] now in its 2nd edition (1983) is compiled by Anne Ramsay, of the Newcastle Polytechnic European Documentation Centre. It is an alphabetical keyword index to sources of statistics contained in the Eurostat series. She has also produced *How to find out about the statistics of the European Communities*,[20] one of the Association of UK European Documentation Centre libraries' 'How to. . .' pamphlet series. The

The Statistics Collection

UK EDCs all stock the majority of EC statistical publications. Apart from the specifically statistical guides, many of the major bibliographical guides to the EC, such as John Jeffries' *Guide to the official publications of the European Communities* [21] have useful chapters on EC statistics.

NATIONAL STATISTICS: GUIDES

In every country the government has to have an involvement with statistics and the United Kingdom is a typical example. In common with all developed countries, the UK has a comprehensive Government Statistical Service (GSS), as well as many non-official statistics-issuing bodies. The GSS is provided for the Government by specialist staff employed in the statistics divisions of individual departments, and the statistics are made available through Central Statistical Office, CSO/HMSO publications. In addition, mirroring the wider trend in official publishing, each government department independently issues statistics publications and offers further information and advice. This dual CSO/departmental approach complicates the task of tracing official statistical publications, and contradicts the widely held impression that all government statistics are published by HMSO.

Changes in official statistical publications have been brought about since 1980 with the implementation of the reform recommendations of the White Paper [Cmnd 8236],[93] which followed the Rayner scrutiny of all the government statistical services.[32] These cost-saving exercises are the most significant developments in the reorganization of the GSS since its foundation in 1941 and its massive expansion in the 1960s and 1970s. In the 1980s librarians have to be aware of all these changes, alterations and modifications in relation to statistical publications. Typical users' adverse reactions to the post-Rayner situation were those voiced at the meeting of the Royal Statistical Society of 10 June 1981, as reported in *Journal of the Royal Statistical Society, Series A (General)*, Vol 145, Part 2, 1982, pp. 195–207.

The statistics currently published by the GSS, the government departments, together with the statistics produced by their predecessors in earlier ministries, form a complex resource. The guides and bibliographies which are the keys to the tracing of the publications are complex too. They cover both current and historical statistics.

NATIONAL STATISTICS: GENERAL GUIDES

The UK, USA and foreign publications mentioned below illustrate the main types of general guides.

Central Statistical Office, GUIDE TO OFFICIAL STATISTICS[22] is official, exhaustive, authoritative, well produced, a major contribution to the bibliography of UK statistics. It rightly won a Library Association Besterman medal as an outstanding bibliography when its first edition was issued in 1976. Although dealing with official statistics, CSO's *Guide* helpfully also mentions non-official statistics where they either complement or take the place of official ones.

GOVERNMENT STATISTICS: A BRIEF GUIDE TO SOURCES,[23] is an annual free pamphlet, giving the major titles and series. It is an easily obtained, easily used listing of current statistical publications from HMSO. By its few judicious footnotes it alerts librarians to the fact that certain publications are available only from specific addresses in Scotland, Wales and Northern Ireland (and less frequently, in England) and thereby introduces them to the idea that all is not centralized through HMSO.

The LA/RSS RECOMMENDED BASIC UNITED KINGDOM STATISTICAL SOURCES FOR COMMUNITY USE[24] is a highly select list of titles, chosen by experts to help the ordinary non-expert librarian build up a balanced and representative stock. The LA/RSS UNION LIST OF STATISTICAL SERIALS IN BRITISH LIBRARIES[25] was a very handy listing of the statistical resources of *c* 300 libraries. Although the financial cutbacks of the last five years have altered the holdings of every kind of library—academic, public, special, research, etc, the union list can still indicate a likely library rather than a certainty. A new edition would be a boon.

G. F. Lock's GENERAL SOURCES OF STATISTICS[26] is Vol 5 of *Reviews of United Kingdom statistical sources*[27] which succeeded the pioneering SOURCES AND NATURE OF THE STATISTICS OF THE UNITED KINGDOM[28]. Unlike other volumes in the same series which are subject based and mainly current, Lock's book is a general overview and covers some historical statistics. His short account of how the GSS came into being is particularly useful and informative.

STATISTICAL NEWS,[29] like its counterparts in other countries, is an updating, current awareness journal produced by the Central Statistical Office. Besides short items of news, details of new, altered, changed or deleted statistical series or titles, there are special interest articles on all aspects of statistical publications, eg 'Disseminating statistics—the CSO experience',[30] by H. P. Lumsden; 'Information technology policy in the United Kingdom',[31] by A. R. D. Norman and D.A.T. Rayfield; 'Rayner review of the Government Statistical Service';[32] 'Developments in local authority comparative statistics',[33] by Chris Griffin.

In the USA, amongst the many guides to statistics, the *American statistics index*[34] covers exclusively official government publications, whereas the *Statistical reference index*[35] concerns itself with non-official titles. *Statistics Canada*[36] is an example of the free catalogues of current titles usually available from all national statistics-issuing bodies.

The Statistics and Market Intelligence Library[8] (SMIL) is primarily concerned with export and marketing information. Its useful occasional series, *Sources of statistics and market intelligence*, covers various countries, eg Iran,[37] Germany,[38] Saudi Arabia.[39] Norway's counterpart of the UK Central Statistical Office has issued an informative, *Guide to Norwegian statistics*,[40] with the text in English as well as Norwegian.

Regional and Local Statistics: Guides and Sources

Certain countries, with more than one official language, eg Canada, Switzerland, issue all their publications in parallel languages.

Language is important in relation to statistics. Although the statistics themselves, ie the actual numbers in the series or tables, are generally thought to be universally understood, there are associated language problems when using foreign statistical publications. The digits may be understood but the footnotes, warnings, exceptions, references, etc, may be incomprehensible. Where any language other than the 'home' language is used, it usually has English or French subtitles. This language problem is probably less acute for international statistics than for national ones, since an internationally agreed selection of languages is built into their publishing programmes, and they use agreed international classification schemes. The many UN efforts towards the standardization of statistics nomenclature, classification and presentation, and the encouragement of national standards bodies to adopt them, should diminish the difficulties of using the statistics of other countries. The UN's statistical development programme aims at better cooperation, and, as the 1968 resolution said 'contributing to the efficiency of national statistical systems in both developed and developing countries . . .'.

REGIONAL AND LOCAL STATISTICS: GUIDES AND SOURCES

Whereas international and national statistics are unambiguous terms, 'regional' and 'local', when applied to statistics, may be interpreted in several ways. 'Regional' may refer to areas as large as Europe; or, as in Balachandran's *Regional statistics*,[41] to the 'regions, states, towns, etc' of the USA. 'Regional' statistics for the nation groupings have already been considered in earlier paragraphs.

In the UK 'regional' is often applied by Government to the accepted divisions of England into eight standard regions plus Scotland, Wales, and Northern Ireland. There are specific statistical annuals/periodicals for Scotland, Wales and Northern Ireland but,

The Statistics Collection

apart from the data in the *Annual abstract of statistics*,[42] there is no separate general statistical title for England. As it is not always clear from the title of a publication whether its coverage is total for the UK, for England, Wales and Scotland, minus Northern Ireland; for England and Wales together; or for England alone; care must be taken when recommending or using it.

Much information on the general sources of regional statistics is included in the Central Statistical Office's *Guide to official statistics*,[22] with more specialized sources being included in publications such as CSO's *Regional accounts*.[43] *Regional trends*[44] contains statistical tables, together with some informative comment, lists of sources, and definitions. The *Scottish abstract of statistics*[45] has its list of sources, and the *Scottish economic bulletin*[46] is an example of a publication which has statistical tables as well as authoritative articles on varying aspects of Scottish statistics. The *Northern Ireland annual abstract of statistics*[47] has been issued since 1982; it succeeds the *Digest of statistics, Northern Ireland*. Collett's *Northern Ireland statistics: a guide to principal sources*[48] supplements the coverage in the *Guide to official statistics*,[22] and updates A. T. Park's 'Northern Ireland government statistics'.[49] From An Foras Forbartha, Dublin, comes J. V. Curtin's *A guide to regional statistics*.[50]

Local Statistics: Guides and Sources

Improved community information depends to a certain extent on the proper appreciation and exploitation of statistical data. In the UK, units smaller than the standard regions—in descending order: counties, towns, parishes, electoral wards—have been subjected to complex statistical analysis by computer. Every aspect of local life: politics, industry, education, health, employment, leisure, libraries, etc, can benefit from the resulting data. Although many of the titles mentioned in earlier sections contain sources of local statistics, it is necessary for details of the more intensive treatment of the figures, to consult more specialized publications. There is no totally comprehensive guide to all the available local statistics.

The major sources of local statistics are the census reports. Every

Regional and Local Statistics: Guides and Sources

ten years, (with a few exceptions) from 1801 to 1981, the census (an attempt to present an accurate picture of the state of the country at a given moment in time) has been held. Increasingly sophisticated questions have produced the responses that form the raw material for statistical analysis by Government, by researchers, and by other interested bodies. Decisions based on the seeming evidence of these statistics affect all our lives. Historically, the census has been the most important information source for local statistics. The OPCS/General Register Office Edinburgh, *Guide to census reports: Great Britain 1801–1966*[51] provides a comprehensive listing of all the reports, etc. It is based on, and is a development of, the earlier *Census reports of Great Britain 1801–1931: guides to official sources, no. 2*. After a lapse of one hundred years, the original census records are made available to the public, and they become an essential historical resource for a locality.

More than any other census, the 1981 census has been analysed, scrutinized, summarized, explained and documented. The Office of Population Censuses and Surveys (OPCS) keeps the public well informed on all aspects of the census, including the progress of the publication programme. Through OPCS Monitors[52] and *Population trends*,[53] the information in and about the census is disseminated. One of the OPCS Monitors is a special USER GUIDE CATALOGUE,[54] which lists all the guides to census material. In it, a *Cross-classification of England and Wales by user guide numbers*, is a handy aide memoire. The geographical units (region, county, district, electoral ward, parish, community, enumeration district, special enumeration district) are listed, and then cross-matched with other divisions/aspects (new towns, city centre, inner city, partnership areas, regional health authorities, area health authorities, health districts, towns, parliamentary constituencies, European parliamentary constituencies) so that librarians and other statistics users can choose the most appropriate census user guide. OPCS *Monitor Cen 82/4*, November 1982, reported that the detailed reports for every county in England and Wales had been issued in the County report series, and that the national reports publications had begun. OPCS *Monitor Cen 58*[55] gave a useful summary and review of local authorities statistics. OPCS *Population trends*[53] contains statistical tables, comment and news on the census, information on other OPCS surveys and projects, and details of publications.

Whereas in earlier years only printed versions of census statistics were issued, modern census results are available as magnetic tapes with computer access, on microfilm and microfiche, as well as in conventional published format. The major depository for census data records, current and retrospective, is at the Social Science Research Council (SSRC) Data Archive Unit, University of Essex. Its *Data archive bulletin*[56] reports on all aspects of censuses, including developments relating to SSRC holdings of the 1981 Small area statistics (SAS). Local authorities are making intensive use of SAS records on behalf of all their departments, including libraries. Certain local authorities have a positive policy of promoting the use of census results, eg West Midlands County Council *First census results for the wards of the Birmingham partnership.*[57]

The Chartered Institute of Public Finance and Accountancy (CIPFA) *Local government trends*,[58] CIPFA *Local government comparative statistics*,[59] and CIPFA *Community indicators*,[60] are non-government statistics relating to local authorities. All contain detailed notes, definitions, sources of statistics, and introductory guides to their use, as well as the basic statistical tables.

Many local authorities regularly issue collections of statistics relating to their own areas, and all these publications indicate the diverse sources of the statistics used, whether they have been extracted from official national publications, or developed from local databases. The format and level of these statistical compilations depends on the target audience, eg Greater London Council issues *Annual abstract of Greater London statistics*;[61] as well as the more popular free handout, *London facts and figures.*[62] Other examples are *South Yorkshire statistics*,[63] *Abstract of Birmingham statistics*,[64] *Greater Manchester – facts, figures and finance.*[65]

A major review of the secondary analysis of British data sets, with special emphasis on the population census both currently and historically, is *Secondary analysis in social research: a guide to data sources and methods*,[66] by Catherine Hakim. Though a non-official guide, it has authoritative standing, as the author was formerly with OPCS.

SUBJECT-BASED GUIDES AND BIBLIOGRAPHIES

In addition to the sources of information already discussed, containing details of who issues which statistics, there are many subject-based guides and bibliographies. These vary in scope, purpose, complexity, and treatment. As the same statistics may have relevance in many different subject areas, there is much cross-classification, and details of statistics appear in a variety of information publications. Population statistics, for example, are of basic importance to national and local government; to health and education authorities; to planners, politicians, and librarians; to industry and commerce; to advertisers and marketing managers, etc; each interest group identifies and uses the statistics differently, and the subject guides reflect these variations.

The intellectual level of the subject guides ranges from introductory pamphlets to specialist books or articles. The treatments vary from total or partial, to historical or contemporary. The subject guides also differ in frequency and manner of publication. They may appear as Press Notices, issued as needed by ministries, in a single statistical series; as monthly/quarterly publications updating a group of statistical sources on related subjects; as annual supplements to statistical series, with explanatory notes and details of changes in a particular subject; as one-off expensive specialist monographs; as regular editions of standard subject guides to statistics; as ongoing series of subject guides, etc.

All the guides—already referred to in earlier sections of this chapter as identifying the statistics issued by international, national, regional and local bodies—also contain much information from a subject point of view. Only the merest indication of the wide range of specialized subject-based guides to statistics can be given here. The highly selective list of titles below has been chosen to illustrate most of the points mentioned above.

International

UN DIRECTORY OF INTERNATIONAL STATISTICS, VOL. 1.[2]

The Statistics Collection

Section III is in subject order.

Pieper, F. C. (*comp.*) SISCIS: SUBJECT INDEX TO SOURCES OF COMPARATIVE INTERNATIONAL STATISTICS.[10]

Wasserman, P. and O'Brien, J. (*eds.*) STATISTICS SOURCES: A SUBJECT GUIDE TO DATA ON INDUSTRIAL, BUSINESS, SOCIAL, EDUCATIONAL, FINANCIAL AND OTHER TOPICS FOR THE UNITED STATES AND INTERNATIONALLY.[11]

Ramsay, Anne (*comp.*) EUROSTAT INDEX.[19]
A detailed key-word subject index to the statistical series published by the Statistical Office of the European Communities, with notes on the series.

US Bureau of the Census GUIDE TO FOREIGN TRADE STATISTICS.[67]
Contains a description of foreign trade statistics, etc.

National and Subject

US Bureau of the Census DIRECTORY OF FEDERAL STATISTICS FOR LOCAL AREAS: A GUIDE TO SOURCES.[68]

US FACT FINDER FOR THE NATION.[69]
Pamphlets on census material by subject. Various dates.

US Bureau of the Census. 'Guide to sources of statistics', *Statistical abstract of the United States 1981*, Appendix IV, pp 946–984.[70]
Simple listing of main statistical sources of the tables, alphabetical order for subjects.

Central Statistical Office GUIDE TO OFFICIAL STATISTICS.[22]

Foster, Pamela BUSINESS STATISTICS INDEX.[71]

Subject-based Guides and Bibliographies

REVIEWS OF UNITED KINGDOM STATISTICAL SOURCES. VOL. 1.[27] For example Vol 13: *Wages and earnings*.

The '*Reviews*. . .' follow the earlier publication *Sources and nature of the statistics of the United Kingdom*.[28] The General editor of '*Reviews*. . .' is W. F. Maunder on behalf of the Royal Statistical Society and the Social Science Research Council.

WHOLESALE PRICE INDEX: PRINCIPLES AND PROCEDURE.[72] (*Studies in official statistics*, No. 32)

CHANGES TO THE WHOLESALE PRICE INDEX. Department of Industry Press notice, 14 April 1983.

'Retail prices index: annual revision of the weights'.[73] *Employment gazette*.

'The unstatistical reader's guide to the retail prices index.'[74] *Employment gazette*.

An introductory account of RPI; RPI weights are reviewed annually using the latest results of the Family expenditure survey.

Department of Employment FAMILY EXPENDITURE: A PLAIN MAN'S GUIDE TO THE FAMILY EXPENDITURE SURVEY.[75]

Available only on request to Department of Employment (Stats A6), Level 1, Caxton House, Tothill Street, London SW1H 9NF, or Tel. 01 213 3806.

Copeman, H. THE NATIONAL ACCOUNTS: A SHORT GUIDE.[76] (*Studies in official statistics*, No. 36)

Updates and supplements *Studies in official statistics*, No. 13 'National accounts statistics: sources and methods'. London: HMSO, 1968. The guide explains the National Income and Expenditure 'Blue Book'.[198]

Johnson, Fred INCOME DISTRIBUTION.[77] Open University Second Level Course: Statistical sources.

The Statistics Collection

Bell, D. and Greenhorn, A. (eds.) A GUIDE TO FINANCIAL TIMES STATISTICS.[78]

An excellent guide to a specific source. It is essential reading for all FT perusers, but its price (£9.50) is rather high for its 56 pages. If it were made available in paperback, or as part of the FT annual subscription, it would be much more widely available and more frequently consulted.

Chinn, M. (ed.) STATISTICS FOR CONSUMERS: A GUIDE TO THE STATISTICS COLLECTION IN THE LIBRARY OF THE CONSUMERS' ASSOCIATION.[79]

Industrial Aids Ltd PUBLISHED DATA ON EUROPEAN INDUSTRIAL MARKETS.[80]

Includes references to 2,000 market research reports, and a guide to other sources of information, such as statistics, etc.

Cyriax, G. (ed.) WORLD INDEX OF ECONOMIC FORECASTS: A GUIDE TO SOURCES OF ECONOMIC FORECASTS.[81]

Mort, David THE FORECASTING BUSINESS: A REVIEW OF THE OUTPUT OF THE MAJOR FORECASTING ORGANISATIONS.[82]

Ardern, Richard OFFSHORE OIL AND GAS: A GUIDE TO SOURCES OF INFORMATION.[83]

Office of Population Censuses and Surveys OPCS CENSUS 1981, MONITOR SERIES.[52]

Covers all aspects of information concerned with collecting, disseminating, distributing, and analysing data from the 1981 Census.

POPULATION TRENDS.[53]

Includes details of recent publications; special articles on topics relating to population and census studies; tables of statistics.

'William Farr, 1807–1883: his contribution to present day vital and health statistics.'[84] *Population trends.*

Subject-based Guides and Bibliographies

National Health Service: Department of Health and Social Security STEERING GROUP ON HEALTH SERVICES INFORMATION: A REPORT ON THE COLLECTION AND USE OF INFORMATION ABOUT HOSPITAL CLINICAL ACTIVITY IN THE NATIONAL HEALTH SERVICE.[85]

The Korner report: it suggests changes in the collection of certain statistics.

Central Statistical Office STATISTICAL NEWS.[29]

Gives a comprehensive account of current developments in British official statistics, plus special articles on current matters with a useful subject index.

Griffin, Chris 'Developments in local authority comparative statistics'.[33] *Statistical news.*

Sellwood, Roger and Griffin, Chris 'New developments in statistics at CIPFA'.[86] *Statistical news.*

'Public records: possible amendments to the Statistics of Trade Act'.[87] *Statistical news.*

'Statistics of Trade Act 1947: [possible amendments]'.[88] *Employment gazette.*

The Wilson Committee report [Cmnd 8204] and the Government's response to it in the White Paper 'Modern Public Records' [Cmnd 8531] affect the so-called 'statute-barred' records; reactions to possible amendments were requested by the Director of Statistics, Department of Industry.

MARKET AND STATISTICS NEWS: A MONTHLY REVIEW OF BUSINESS INFORMATION.[89] Warwick University.

News items, general comments with special articles, plus a useful list of additions to the statistics collection at Warwick University.

Walter, Clare 'European Trade Associations statistics: Part II—Germany, Netherlands, Norway, Portugal, Spain, Sweden, and Switzerland'.[90] *Market and statistics news.*

The Statistics Collection

Titcombe, J. M. and Connerton, L. (*comp.*) GERMANY (FRG) STATISTICAL SOURCES.[38]

Broad subject arrangement with subject and title indexes. One of a series of SMIL bibliographies.

Incomes Data Service (IDS) MANPOWER INFORMATION.[91]

Useful introduction to the scattered sources of manpower statistics. One of IDS publications which complements its regular data series.

STATISTICS AND MARKET RESEARCH: A GUIDE TO CURRENT PERIODICAL ARTICLES.[92] Birmingham Public Libraries.

NON-OFFICIAL STATISTICAL PUBLICATIONS AND SOURCES

The awareness of the importance of non-official statistics has been growing in recent years in the UK. The problems of their identification, availability, bibliographical control and dissemination have also been noticed. In the aftermath of the White Paper on the *Government Statistical Services*,[93] the implementation of its recommendations, and the effects of the Rayner reports[32,94] on each ministry's statistical service, non-official statistics have become more important to both statistics users and to librarians. There is no agreed description of what constitutes a non-official statistic, but a working definition might be 'figures collected and issued on a regular basis, but not published by central government'.

There is, as yet, no authoritative listing of non-official statistical titles. Many are helpfully included in the CSO *Guide to official statistics*[22] when they supplement existing official statistical series, or when they are identified as being the sole source of statistics on a particular subject. Libraries have collected non-official statistics on a less than comprehensive basis for many years, with each librarian developing expertise in subjects of special local concern. They are difficult to trace bibliographically because they are not always recorded in the major sources, eg *British national biblio-*

Non-official Statistical Publications and Sources

graphy[95] (BNB); but increasingly they are being included in the British Library Lending Division *British reports, translations and theses*.[96]

Equally incomplete is knowledge of the holdings in UK libraries of such titles, because there is no union list—nor can there be until these non-official statistics are identified, listed and made available in a systematic manner. Fortunately, Leona Siddall's *Survey of non-official statistics and their role in business information*[97] should be a major step forward to a more orderly control of such publications and resources, at least in this one subject area. She has systematically identified the statistics-collecting bodies and their publications; considered the bibliographical problems; and recommended practical courses of action to improve their accessibility and more effective use. The non-official statistics of other broad subject fields could be surveyed in a similar manner.

Very helpfully, non-official statistics cover subjects which other statistics cannot cover. The organizations which collect and disseminate these statistics are varied. They range from Chambers of Commerce, research associations, trades unions and trade associations, to national and local societies, local and regional authorities, banks, firms, market researchers, etc. It is even possible to include online services in the category of non-official statistics producers.

Non-official statistics do not have the built-in authority of official ones and, although not generally contentious, it is not unreasonable to bear in mind their origins and any known limitations or prejudices of their parent bodies. Non-official statistics can be unique statistical sources or they can complement or supplement official statistics. Sometimes they are presented more simply than official statistics, sometimes in a more complex way.

The following titles are examples of guides which list non-official statistics plus typical non-official statistics publications:

Birmingham Public Libraries STATISTICS AND MARKET RESEARCH: A GUIDE TO CURRENT PERIODICAL ARTICLES.[92]

A current awareness service. Of the journals scanned, 9 are official, 47 are trade and commerce journals containing non-official

The Statistics Collection

statistical information, eg *Building Societies Association bulletin, Metal bulletin, Petroleum Times price report,* etc.

Warwick Statistics Service MARKET AND STATISTICS NEWS.[89]

A current awareness service. Special articles on relevant topics, eg European Trade Associations statistics, Pt. I, February 1983; Pt II, March 1983.[90] Of the associations listed for Federal Republic of Germany, these non-official statistics-collecting/issuing bodies have the following pattern of dissemination:
- four restrict statistics to members only;
- two either do not publish or do not circulate their statistics;
- seven issue statistical yearbooks;
- five have annual reports with significant statistical sections;
- five issue a selection of statistical publications;
- two issue journals, quarterly or fortnightly, which include statistics.

This shows that non-official statistics are of limited accessibility, and persistence is needed to trace and use them.

Statistics and Market Intelligence Library GERMANY (FRG) STATISTICAL SOURCES.[38]

It is useful to contrast the information in SMIL's pamphlet with that in the previous reference.

Christian Economic and Social Research Foundation ANNUAL REVIEW OF CHIEF CONSTABLES' REPORTS: PART ONE. DRINK OFFENCES.[98]

Supplements: Home Office *Offences of drunkenness*.[99]

Building Societies Association A COMPENDIUM OF BUILDING SOCIETY STATISTICS.[100]

'Draws heavily on figures published in a variety of not always easily accessible sources'. Used in conjunction with *Report of the Chief Registrar*.[101]

London and Cambridge Economic Service THE BRITISH ECONOMY: KEY STATISTICS, 1900–1970.[102]

Economic trends:[195] annual supplement, 1983, recommends these 'Key statistics' to readers who require earlier figures. Though out of print, copies are still available for consultation in many libraries.

Department of Employment and the Manpower Society IMPROVING MANPOWER INFORMATION.[103]

Of the 11 sets of information identified as being needed by firms planning changes, 7 categories involved the use of local statistics, both official and non-official.

Greater London Council, GLC Industry and Employment Committee STATUS OF LONDON UNEMPLOYMENT STATISTICS: DISCUSSIONS.[104]

Incorporated Society of British Advertisers. ISBA AREA INFORMATION 1982: POPULATION, DEMOGRAPHIC PROFILES, PRESS READERSHIP AND CIRCULATION, RETAIL OUTLETS, INDEPENDENT LOCAL RADIO.[105]

HISTORICAL STATISTICS: PUBLICATIONS AND SOURCES

Generally, the titles mentioned so far have referred to current statistics, and the importance of being 'up to date' has been stressed. But all present-day figures stand on the foundation of earlier statistics, and the latter put the former into historical perspective.

Historical statistics, and commentaries on them, have their own pattern of publication and provision at every level—national, international, and subject based. They range from general coverage to extreme specialisms. As far as can be traced, there is no single comprehensive bibliography of all historical statistics, but each interest area has its specialist bibliographies and guides, eg 'International bibliography of historical demography',[106] 1978 to date, in *Annales de démographie historique,* or *Bibliography of index numbers,*[107] edited by W. F. Maunder.

Inherent in compilations of historical statistics is the attempt to make comparisons meaningful, in relation to present-day records, by some reference to a standard base. This is a very difficult aspect of statistical analysis, and it involves, in addition to the careful application of statistical techniques, an understanding of the historical, social, economic, political, and geographical circumstances of the collection of the original data. The actual lack of availability of statistics; the loss of comparability through problems of definition, variable quality, changes in boundaries, or alterations in industrial classifications; variations in the original purposes for which the statistics were collected, etc—all these affect the reliability of historical statistics, and confuse their interpreters. B. R. Mitchell has a cautionary comment: 'All one can do is be careful and keep a firm rein on credulity without going to the other extreme of stultifying total scepticism'. His other comments in *International historical statistics, Africa and Asia*[108] are informative and enlightening. Even more than for current statistics, it is imperative to read and heed the numerous footnotes, caveats, special references, etc, when consulting historical statistics.

To answer the common, everyday UK enquiries (eg the prices of petrol, bread, the average wages 50 years ago compared with those of 1984) with a mere statistic, index number or quantity of money, converted into decimal currency, can in itself be a little misleading, unless the social context of the comparison is understood. The 'instant answer' compilation can be useful, eg H. E. Priestley's *The what it cost the day before yesterday book from 1850 to the present day*,[109] but one must consult the more academic volumes to sustain an argument or understand the historical relevance. One must try to avoid an unrealistic effect being left in the enquirer's mind.

Increasingly since 1945, retrospective surveys, economic and social science projects are treating historical statistics in more sophisticated ways. For future historians and economists, the improved current statistics now being collected, the mirror of society in the late twentieth century, will provide fuller data—assuming that the physical life of modern records, printed publications, magnetic films, microforms, etc, is as long and enduring as it is now presumed they will be.

It is possible to mention only a few titles to show the range of international, national, and subject historical statistics. The national

Historical Statistics: Publications and Sources

pattern of the UK is typical, but each country is special in its relationship with the past.

International

UN DEMOGRAPHIC YEAR BOOK: HISTORICAL TABLES.[110]

OECD MAIN ECONOMIC INDICATORS: HISTORICAL STATISTICS, 1960–1979.[111]

Mitchell, B. R. EUROPEAN HISTORICAL STATISTICS, 1750–1975.[112]

Mitchell, B. R. INTERNATIONAL HISTORICAL STATISTICS: AFRICA AND ASIA.[108]

Anderson, M. (*comp.*) INTERNATIONAL MORTALITY STATISTICS, 1901–1975.[113]

OECD CONSUMER PRICE INDICES: SOURCES AND METHODS AND HISTORICAL STATISTICS: SPECIAL ISSUE.[114]

National

Mitchell, B. R. and Deane, P. ABSTRACT OF BRITISH HISTORICAL STATISTICS.[115]

Mitchell, B. R. and Jones, H. G. SECOND ABSTRACT OF BRITISH HISTORICAL STATISTICS.[116]

US Bureau of the Census HISTORICAL STATISTICS OF THE UNITED STATES: COLONIAL TIMES TO 1970.[117]

The Statistics Collection

Finlayson, J. HISTORICAL STATISTICS OF AUSTRALIA: A SELECT LIST OF SOURCES.[118]

Urquhart, M. C. and Buckley, K. A. H. (*eds.*) HISTORICAL STATISTICS OF CANADA.[119]

Department of Employment BRITISH LABOUR STATISTICS: HISTORICAL ABSTRACT 1886–1968.[120]

Lee, C. H. BRITISH REGIONAL EMPLOYMENT STATISTICS, 1841–1971.[121]

Chapman, Agatha L. and Knight, Rose WAGES AND SALARIES IN THE UNITED KINGDOM, 1920–1938.[122]

London and Cambridge Economic Service THE BRITISH ECONOMY: KEY STATISTICS 1900–1970.[102]

Munby, Denys INLAND TRANSPORT STATISTICS OF GREAT BRITAIN, 1900–1970, Vol 1: RAILWAYS, PUBLIC ROAD TRANSPORT, LONDON TRANSPORT.[123]

Business Statistics Office HISTORICAL RECORD OF THE CENSUS OF PRODUCTION, 1907 to 1970.[124]
For every historical statistical subject, eg production, *see also* articles such as Leak, H. 'Census of production and distribution';[125] Lomax, K. S. 'Production and productivity movements in the UK since 1900';[126] Stafford, J. 'Development of industrial statistics'[127] in *Statistical news*; Browning, H. E. 'The census of production'[128] in *Statistical news*.

'ALTERNATIVE' STATISTICS: PUBLICATIONS AND SOURCES

The vast majority of statistics used and quoted, with or without acknowledgement, with or without modification, are those issued by official bodies, governments, etc. The naïve approach to statis-

'Alternative' Statistics: Publications and Sources

tics takes all figures at their face value, disregarding the historical, social and political context in which they are collected and disseminated. But increasingly statistics are being used and interpreted according to the users' economic, social and political viewpoint. The Open University publications, *Statistics in society, 1983*, are a helpful introduction to the more critical evaluation of statistics.

There is a growing collection of publications, the compilers of which not only analyse and criticize the 'official' data, but also tend to question its essential veracity, query its methodology, and distrust its ostensible purpose. These changes affect libraries in their information-giving role. Public libraries, reflecting as they do their communities and serving the potential and observed needs of those communities, must take into account these alternative statistics, and include them in the stock, just as they do for the wider range of all other general subjects, books and journals. In the sphere of commerce and industry, which affects academic, public and special libraries, there are publications containing alternative statistics. *Social audit* (London) reports present data on the social, environmental and safety accountability of companies. Campaigns for improved safety in relation to asbestos, lead, agricultural chemicals, etc, have all resulted in publications quoting official statistics in a critical way.

Radical statisticians now offer alternative publications and provide alternative forums for discussion of statistics. Where this development is particularly strong is in relation to the emotive issues of the day—unemployment, nuclear power, ethnic minorities, defence spending, poverty, etc.

The Radical Statistics Group, with its sub-interest groups, issues the *Radical statistics newsletter*, and has published titles such as *The unofficial guide to official health statistics*;[129] *The nuclear numbers game: understanding the statistics behind the bomb*;[130] *Reading between the numbers: a critical guide to educational research*.[131] Imaginatively, the Radical Statistics Health Group/Local Radio Workshop issued an audio tape/cassette version of *A better start in life? Why perinatal statistics vary in different parts of the country*.[132]

Pressure groups and special interest groups of every variety issue publications containing statistics to further their causes. Often

The Statistics Collection

these are leaflets or pamphlets, eg *Housing facts and figures*.[133] Committed academics write articles or produce weightier tomes, eg Peter Townsend's *Poverty in the United Kingdom: a survey of household resources and standards of living*.[134] A useful volume for alerting statistics users to the possibility of views other than 'official' ones is *Demystifying social statistics*,[135] edited by John Irvine and others.

If one takes an example of a controversial subject, eg ethnic minorities statistics, it is interesting to compare and contrast 'official' and 'alternative' data. When asked for information on such topics, it is important to be aware of the disagreements and discrepancies between the varying sets of statistics. There is only one point on which all groups are agreed, and that is that the statistics available on UK ethnic minorities are unsatisfactory. The All-party House of Commons Home Affairs Committee, Second Report, 1983: *Ethnic and racial questions in the Census*,[136] said that existing statistical information on the number of black people in Britain is inadequate, being based on sample surveys, local surveys, and on a count in the 1981 Census of people living in households headed by someone born in the New Commonwealth or Pakistan. The resulting figures are inaccurate. The House of Commons Home Affairs Committee recommended that future censuses include a question on race. It is salutory to peruse the columns of Hansard to see how Members of Parliament quote the same official/unofficial figures to support totally opposed hypotheses. As long ago as 1972 there had been concern expressed on the inadequacy of the available statistics, eg Claus Moser 'Statistics about immigrants: objectives, methods and problems'[137] in *Social trends*. Concerned groups, eg Runnymede Trust/Radical Statistics Race Group *Britain's black population*,[138] Chapter 7: 'The politics of statistics'; or the Commission for Racial Equality *Ethnic minorities in Britain: statistical background*[139] (1980), have urged better methods of obtaining reliable information on the statistics of ethnic minorities.

A similar pattern of investigation, publication and discussion occurs on all subjects where statistics are a vital component in the understanding of the current situation. All users of statistics, whether 'straight' or 'alternative', must be aware that, like an earlier belief in the authority of the printed word or the present misconception that 'It must be true, I've seen it on TV', statistics can be manipulated, presented, analysed, modified, suppressed, etc, to back up arguments by commentators on all subjects according to their personal viewpoint. It is this quality for misleading, as much as for informing, for misinformation as much as for enlightening, which gave rise to the tag 'Lies, damn lies and statistics'—a somewhat easier phrase to remember than the four validity tests for statistics used in educational research, posed by Cook and Campbell 'Statistical conclusion validity; internal validity; external validity; and construct validity' (*Quasi experimentation – design and analysis issues for field settings*).[140]

CLASSIFICATION SCHEMES FOR STATISTICS: INTERNATIONAL AND NATIONAL

INTERNATIONAL STANDARD INDUSTRIAL CLASSIFICATION OF ALL ECONOMIC ACTIVITIES (ISIC).[141]

STANDARD INTERNATIONAL TRADE CLASSIFICATION REVISION 2 (SITC REV. 2).[142]

COMMODITY INDEXES FOR THE STANDARD INTERNATIONAL TRADE CLASSIFICATION, REVISION 2 (SITC REV. 2).[143]

GENERAL INDUSTRIAL CLASSIFICATION OF ECONOMIC ACTIVITIES WITHIN THE EUROPEAN COMMUNITIES (NACE).[144]

NOMENCLATURE FOR THE CLASSIFICATION OF GOODS IN CUSTOMS TARIFFS.[145]

COMMON NOMENCLATURE OF INDUSTRIAL PRODUCTS (NIPRO).[146]

The Statistics Collection

EXPLANATORY NOTES TO THE BRUSSELS NOMENCLATURE.[147]

EXPLANATORY NOTES TO THE CUSTOMS TARIFF OF THE EUROPEAN COMMUNITIES.[148]

NOMENCLATURE OF GOODS FOR THE EXTERNAL TRADE STATISTICS OF THE COMMUNITY AND STATISTICS OF TRADE BETWEEN MEMBER STATES (NIMEXE).[149]

Foreman, Lewis 'Sources of statistics.[150]

STANDARD INDUSTRIAL CLASSIFICATION (SIC).[151] Revised 1980.

INDEXES TO THE STANDARD INDUSTRIAL CLASSIFICATION.[152] Revised 1980.

STANDARD INDUSTRIAL CLASSIFICATION. REVISED 1980. RECONCILIATION WITH STANDARD INDUSTRIAL CLASSIFICATION, 1968.[153]

'Introduction of the Revised Standard Industrial Classification'.[154] *Economic trends.*

'Standard Industrial classification – revised 1980'[155] [the new classification compared with 1968 edition; timetable of its introduction in 1983]. *Employment gazette.*

Lockyer, M. J. G. 'Rebasing and reclassifying the national accounts: the reasons and the likely effects'.[156] *Economic trends.*

'Wholesale price index to be rebased'[157] [the Producer Price Index from August 1983]. *British business.*

Perry, John 'Index of industrial production – rebasing and reclassification.'[158] *Economic trends.*

Classification Schemes for Statistics

H. M. Customs and Excise TARIFF AND OVERSEAS TRADE CLASSIFICATION.[159]

H. M. Customs and Excise GUIDE TO THE CLASSIFICATION OF OVERSEAS TRADE STATISTICS, 1983.[160]

The classification schemes for statistics of economic activity, industry and trade are intended to assist in the meaningful analysis and intepretation of the data collected. Abbreviations for these codes proliferate—ISIC,[141] SIC (80),[151] NACE,[144] SITC Rev. 2,[142] CCCN,[145] NIMEXE,[149] NIPRO,[146] etc. Whilst care has to be taken that the correct edition of the classification is used with the current figures, earlier editions also need to be retained.

The UN is the major influence on the classification of international economic and industrial statistics. There is the UN *International standard industrial classification of all economic activities (ISIC)*[141]. Each country has its own classification codes. In the UK, *Standard industrial classification, 1980 Revision (SIC (80))*[151] follows ISIC in its general principles, but there are differences of detail, as ISIC provides a generalized framework for economic structures across the world rather than for a particular country. SIC (80) is now also more comparable to the European Communities NACE.[144]

But here, too, differences still occur. The introduction of the SIC (80) in 1983 coincided with other important changes in the presentation of UK economic statistics, and with the rebasing to 1980 of the main statistical series, eg *National accounts statistics*,[156,161] the *Index of industrial production*,[158] and the *Wholesale price index*.[157] The last named changed its title from August 1983 when it became the *Producer price index (PPI)*.[157]

For international trade statistics, the UN classification is *Standard international trade classification, revision 2 (SITC Rev. 2)*[142]. For Europe the *Customs co-operation council nomenclature (CCCN)*[145] superseded the former *Brussels tariff nomenclature (BTN)*[147] in 1976. In the UK, the *Classification for overseas trade statistics*[159] (with its accompanying *Guide to the classification for overseas trade statistics*)[160] has existed since 1970 as a single, integrated classification for duty purposes, and for import and export

The Statistics Collection

statistics. The classification follows in general SITC Rev. 2,[142] and indicates its relationships with CCCN.[145] The Guide is issued annually in an updated edition. The classification is used in the *Overseas trade statistics of the UK*[162] which indicate the flow of goods into and out of the country and in H. M. Customs and Excise *Statistics of trade through UK ports*,[163] which provides information on the flow of trade through UK ports and UK economic planning regions.

BUILDING THE COLLECTION: CHOOSING AND USING

Having established the existence of statistical publications through using the guides and bibliographies, the next stage is to choose appropriate titles, according to the needs of a particular library, so as to form a viable statistics collection.

The proven needs of individual statistics users and the demands for statistical data via the library's information service will influence the choice of titles and their most useful format. Choosing may be slightly easier in a special, research, or subject-based library, than in a 'general' reference one where the focus is harder to establish. The size and coverage of the statistics collection must equate to the purpose, level and philosophy of the parent organization. In cost-conscious times, a frequently used, well organized collection of carefully chosen 'core' statistics will be more efficient and cost effective, and more acceptable managerially, than an extensive one which proves to be too expensive to maintain in an up-to-date condition.

The same raw data are used by many agencies to produce different statistical tables, and they appear and reappear in many guises. There is much duplication of information between statistical series. Every title, at every level, selected for stock, should be assessed as to whether its quota of 'extra' information justifies the initial purchase price, the cost of processing/cataloguing, and the continuing cost of storage.

Choices have to be made, too, concerning complete standing orders or intermittent ones for regular statistical publications, bearing in mind the burden of having a high proportion of resources mortgaged in advance.

A further facet of choice is that of format—whether to buy the statistical information as printed publications, microfilms, microfiche, and computer tapes—or to access them online or via Viewdata. Here, too, there is much duplication of information, and choosing the appropriate mix of formats is a difficult task, cost having to be balanced against accessibility.

There is no single 'correct' mix of annuals, serials, subjects and formats for the building of a statistics collection. Each library has to establish its own unique combination of resources, blended to suit both its needs and its clientèle.

OFFICIAL INTERNATIONAL AND NATIONAL STATISTICS: CHOOSING AND USING—FORMATS AND TITLES

Formats

International and national statistics are the product of co-operation by different statistics-collecting bodies. All are interdependent. The official national statistical offices collect statistics at public expense from all sectors of the country's life to enable meaningful decisions to be made by government. In turn, these statistics, suitably assigned to agreed international classification numbers, are reported to the relevant international authorities, eg the European Communities, or the United Nations. Collated, reprocessed and repackaged, world-wide, or region-wide tables are published by international statistical offices. Each country is affected by world trends, and reacts to them just as the international scene reflects the aggregate of each nation's statistical record. The resulting publication programmes, international and national, are of daunting complexity. It is from this wealth of statistical titles that choice must be made.

The majority of libraries still obtain the greater part of their statistics in conventional printed form, but the situation is changing. Whereas the more sophisticated statistics users and many libraries welcome the greater freedom which the computer brings to statistics access, there is some expressed concern about the possible loss of public accessibility for the ordinary person if all the data are ever only on computer. As often happens, the US library world is first to alert colleagues to this 'encroaching information gap' in relation to statistics. Marc A. Levin, in 'Access and dissemination issues concerning Federal Government information'[164] in *Special libraries*, discusses the problems against a background of cuts in US government expenditure. The well-known discussion point whether 'government information be treated as an economic good to be dealt with in purely economic terms, or as a social good to be dealt with in social terms, or as a combination of both', is fully aired. The UK situation is discussed by Sir John Boreham.[165] At present, there is still a choice of formats for most statistical series at both international and national levels.

From a library's point of view, computers offer the largest saving in space costs compared with printed publications. The statistics which appear in the printed publications, are held originally on computer databases. Each statistical office has its own programme of computerization and parallel microform and conventional paper format publishing. Full details of the complete databases are available from the individual statistical offices. Information on the other non-book formats is often noted in the published compilations, and mentioned in the relevant guides and bibliographies. For international statistics, for example, the UN *Directory of international statistics*, Vol 1, Pt 2,[2] has an inventory of databases of economic and social statistics. OECD offers magnetic tape subscriptions, and IMF (International Monetary Fund, Washington) provides monthly computer tapes of its statistics. Each national statistical office too is developing a variety of packages. CANSIM *Statistics Canada*[166] is probably one of the most advanced examples. Central Statistical Office (UK) is engaged in a positive marketing campaign for its computer-readable data (Graham Giles 'Improving the dissemination of CSO computer readable data'[167] in *Statistical news*). Post-Rayner developments include more emphasis on the use of computers in the dissemination of statistics (H. P. Lumsden

Official International and National Statistics

'Disseminating statistics – the CSO experience'[30] in *Statistical news*). The Central Statistical Office macroeconomic data bank is marketed through SIA Computer Services. Individual ministries too are promoting the use of their statistical databases, eg OPCS Census data. *The 10% small area statistics* are supplied on magnetic tapes, microfilm, microfiche, and paper copies. HMSO is currently planning to launch a series of *'Business data packages'*[169] on floppy disks, in which previously fragmented data, available in different sources on a particular industry, are to be brought together as a practical working tool.

Online access to statistics, and its use in libraries, is developing at a fast pace. The databases vary from international to purely national ones. The European Community, for example, has its *CRONOS*[170] statistical databank. Via Euronet, some 50 different statistics databases, including the *CSO Macroeconomic data bank*,[168] can be accessed. The range of US statistics databases is very extensive. For example, PTS Forecasts (for the USA File 81, for the rest of the world File 83); PTS Time series (Files 82 and 84), covering production, consumption, price and usage statistics for agriculture, manufacturing industries, etc. as well as general, economic, demographic and national income series, are available on DIALOG. Keeping up to date with details of all the latest developments concerning these data files is now a major task for any librarian providing an online information service. Printed directories, eg European Communities Euronet/Diane *Databases in Europe*[171] exist, but their information is soon superseded. The various services are prolific in their current awareness Newsletters and bulletins, eg *Chronolog*,[172] published by DIALOG, SDC *Searchlight*[173]; and IRS *News and views*[174] from Frascati.

Online searching is a valuable tool for statistics users, but the main problem for the librarian is the question of charging. Where there are separate charges for online searches, the decision as to whether to use online to answer an enquiry, even where it is the most appropriate course of action, becomes more complex. Some libraries have a policy of 'no charges', which simplifies the situation, but puts the cost on to the community in general rather than on to the individual user. Further complications occur where, due

The Statistics Collection

to gaps in existing library resources, online statistics are the only possible source of the answer. It can be argued that online charges are unfair, since the customer is being made to pay for a library's deficiencies of stock, whereas for conventional material a comparatively nominal cost is incurred for reservations. All these factors must be considered when online searching of statistics is evaluated.

Increasingly, for statistics, computer access either online or through special data packages will become the norm rather than the exception. Even now, there is the beginning of a trend; the expectation of the generation brought up to use computers at school and college is that all information will be in that format, or at least in microform, with conventional printed publications being decidedly 'second best'. It is not possible here to date when that trend will become everyday practice.

From the point of view of the economies of storage, microforms too have proved highly advantageous. Many of the printed statistical publications are now available in microfilm and/or microfiche, and the choice of format is left to the librarian. The benefits of microform to the library are space economy, ease of access and duplication, and a greater range of sources for a comparatively lower cost. The use of microfiche/microfilm readers in libraries is now accepted easily by staff and users, being taken as part of the more general spread of microform records in industry and commerce—eg garages having maintenance information in microformat, standards engineers have specifications at hand on microfilm cassettes. The choice of format for a statistical title will be influenced by each library's particular conditions.

At international level, many UN, OECD, etc statistical publications are available in microform, eg UN *Commodity trade statistics*,[175] are on microfiche. As in other countries, UK statistical publications are increasingly being sold in microfilm/microfiche, eg OPCS *Census 1981, Occupation statistics* are in microfiche as well as being available in printed and computer packages. Retrospective statistics are ideally suited to microform dissemination, eg *Official statistical serials on microfiche: catalogue*[176] lists select British official publications containing statistics 1801–1977, including the *Annual abstract of statistics, 1928–1977*.[42] Choosing a certain

Official International and National Statistics

percentage of microform versions of statistical publications is a reasonable option for libraries.

Prestel—the UK viewdata service—also has certain statistical files included in its resources. The nature of viewdata limits the amount of information which appears on the screen in each frame. As a source for up-to-date popular economic statistics, Prestel has many advantages,[177] but the lack of a body with responsibility for overall editorial policy and information input standards for Prestel diminishes the belief in the quality and reliability of the data it displays. As there is no single comprehensive directory of subjects covered by Prestel, gaining access to frames depends more heavily on the inclination of the user to pursue a topic. Nowhere, for example, is it possible to see a single listing of the frame numbers input by different information providers, where similar statistics are available, so that meaningful comparisons can be made as to the value for money per frame, completeness of file, or level of updating. The various surveys and studies, user columns in professional journals, etc, do assist the potential Prestel user, but unlike most computer services and databases, all Prestel information providers do not report alterations and changes to information availability in a regular or planned way. Despite these difficulties, statistics on Prestel are a useful adjunct to any statistics collection. It may also be that where Prestel sets are sited in branch and other outlier work stations, it can introduce new sections of the community to the idea of the availability of 'instant information', and be a useful first step to the later, more sophisticated computer-based systems.

However, online access, computer packages, microforms and Prestel, etc, are still at the stage of supplementing and complementing, not supplanting, the provision of statistical publications in conventional printed format. All formats should be used in conjunction with each other to the benefit of the library's statistics users.

Titles

The following list of titles illustrates the very wide variety of publications available for international and national official statistics.

The Statistics Collection
INTERNATIONAL STATISTICAL PUBLICATIONS

GENERAL

UN STATISTICAL YEAR BOOK.[178]
Updated by UN *Monthly bulletin of statistics, World statistics in brief* (popular version).

UN DEMOGRAPHIC YEARBOOK.[179]
Updated by UN *Population and vital statistics* reports.

WORLD BANK ATLAS.[180]

OECD ECONOMIC SURVEYS.[181]
Annual for each member country; updated by OECD *Economic outlook*,[182] every six months.

OECD MAIN ECONOMIC INDICATORS.[183]
Annual volume; OECD *Main economic indicators*, monthly.

European Communities BASIC STATISTICS OF THE COMMUNITY.[184]
Updated and supplemented by EC's *Eurostatistics*,[185] monthly.

Council for mutual economic assistance CMEA (formerly COMECON) STATISTICAL YEARBOOK.[186]

SUBJECT

International Labour Organisation YEARBOOK OF LABOUR STATISTICS.[187]
Updated by *Bulletin of labour statistics*, monthly and supplements.

UN Food and Agriculture Organisation YEARBOOK OF FOREST PRODUCTS.[188]
Updated by *Timber bulletin for Europe*,[189] every six months.

Official International and National Statistics

Non-official

International Tea Committee, London *Annual bulletin of statistics*,[190] and supplement. Updated by *Monthly statistical summary*.

International whaling statistics,[191] Committee for Whaling Statistics. Sandefjord, Norway: IWC, annual.

The official international statistics show a complex pattern of compilation and distribution, with general economic statistics (issued as annuals, updated by serials, with the occasional more 'popular' condensed versions) and subject series (usually issued annually and updated at varying intervals). There are also non-official international statistics, for specialized topics, compiled by a wide variety of organizations. The most usual languages for international statistics are English, French and Russian. The European Communities have seven official languages.

National statistical publications

UK general

ANNUAL ABSTRACT OF STATISTICS.[42]
Updated by *Monthly digest of statistics*[192] and *CSO Press Notices*. *United Kingdom in figures*[193] (single sheet folder of statistics); *Facts in focus*[194] (popular compilation by Central Statistical Office, published by Penguin.)

Economic trends,[195] monthly with annual supplement; *Economic progress report*,[196] monthly.

Regional trends,[44] annual; *Social trends*,[197] annual.

UK subjects: official, non-official

Finance

National income and expenditure,[198] annual; *United Kingdom balance of payments*,[199] annual; Bank of England *Quarterly bulletin*;[200] *Financial statistics*,[201] monthly; *Inland Revenue statistics*,[202] annual.

The Statistics Collection

Local government financial statistics: England and Wales,[203] annual; CIPFA *Finance and general statistics;*[204] *Capital expenditure of county councils,*[205] published by Society of County Treasurers, annual.

Family expenditure survey,[206] annual; *Household food consumption and expenditure,*[207] annual.

HEALTH, WELFARE AND EMPLOYMENT

Health, personal social services statistics for England,[208] annual; *Health and safety statistics,*[209] annual.

Britain in figures: a handbook of social statistics.[210]

Social security statistics,[211] annual; *Employment gazette,*[212] monthly; OPCS *Labour force survey;*[213] *New earnings survey,*[214] annual.

POPULATION

OPCS *Birth statistics,*[215] annual; OPCS *Local authority vital statistics: England and Wales,*[216] annual; *Population trends,*[53] quarterly.

PRODUCTION

Business monitor, production series; Census of production reports[218] (Business monitor PA series); *UK Mineral statistics,*[217] annual.

UK Chemical industry statistics handbook,[219] annual; *Metal bulletin handbook,*[220] annual; Society of Motor Manufacturers and Traders *The motor industry in Great Britain,*[221] annual.

TRADE AND INDUSTRY

British business,[222] weekly; *Annual retail inquiry*[223]; *Overseas trade statistics of the UK,*[162] monthly; Co-operative Union *Co-operative statistics,*[224] annual.

Official International and National Statistics

Transport

British shipping statistics,[225] annual; Civil Aviation Authority *Annual statistics*;[226] *Road accidents*,[227] annual; *Transport statistics, Great Britain*,[228] annual; *Highways and transportation statistics*,[229] annual.

As the above titles demonstrate, the very wide range of official and non-official statistics for the UK follows a complex pattern of interrelated series. Having collected the statistics, a ministry may issue a Press Notice or Statistical Bulletin, include it in a specialist weekly/monthly periodical or annual. Then it is summarized into a more general annual.

Education

Educational statistics show a further complication since each constituent part of the UK collects and processes its own statistics. As the statistics become more specific, so the form of dissemination varies more widely. All the following titles need to be consulted to check the statistics available:

Department of Education and Science *Statistical bulletin*,[230] irregular.

Scottish Education Department *Statistical bulletin*,[231] irregular.

Department of Education for Northern Ireland *Statistical bulletin*,[232] irregular.

Education statistics for the United Kingdom,[233] annual.

Statistics of education in Wales,[234] annual.

University statistics, 3 vols,[235] annual.

Statistics of Education.[236] Five sets of tables—schools; school leavers and examinations; further education; teachers in service; finance and awards.

The official and non-official available statistics for the UK are indicative of the kinds of statistical series and publications issued by most countries of the world. All have general statistical abstracts yearbooks, specialized annuals, and serials. The quantity of foreign publications purchased for a statistics collection will depend on the needs of the library's users, but, in general, the widest selection possible should be provided.

BUILDING THE COLLECTION: MAINTAINING THE STOCK

Once the statistics collection has been established, the professional librarian has the task of maintaining it. This involves the selection of new titles, and a continuing assessment of existing serials; the monitoring of developments (through planned current awareness of publications relating to statistics and their continuing availability); the training of all staff and, additionally, the statistics users; and the physical organization of the stock—its classification, cataloguing, binding and allocation. Lastly, there is the awareness of, and use of, the major national statistical collections.

Monitoring developments in statistics publications involves checking, on a continuing basis, for alterations, deletions, additions, amendments, etc, to individual tables within the statistical series; as well as responding to changes of title, format, frequency, availability, price, publisher, etc, of the publications themselves. *Statistical news* [29] *(UK)* and its foreign counterparts from official statistical offices[9] are useful current awareness aids, which provide news items; subject articles; and details of forthcoming developments and alterations to existing titles and tables. The more general journals, eg *British business*,[222] *Employment gazette*,[212] *Economic trends*,[195] etc, all have significant information on the state of the art for statistics in their subject fields. The statistical journals, eg *Monthly digest of statistics*,[192] *Financial statistics*,[201] etc, and their explanatory notes and methodologies, indicate the changes as these relate to individual tables. All major changes affecting statistical series in different ways, such as in their collection, distribution, and dissemination (eg the recent adoption of the revised classification scheme, SIC (80)),[151–155] must be noted. In this way librarians and statistics users are alerted to possible discrepancies of interpretation, comparability, historical files, differences

Building the Collection

of criteria for inclusion/exclusion, index weightings, etc. All these efforts to keep up to date have only one objective—the better and more intelligent use of the statistics collection.

The librarian has to keep not only himself and his staff, but also the library users currently informed of changes. For the statistics users, the librarian must ensure that, for example, statistical publications within the collection clearly indicate changes in relationship to earlier or later series, to alternative sources, or to the cessation of their availability. Unless suitably annotated, for example, to show that it has now ceased, it is misleading to have the *British labour statistics yearbook*[237] (1976) on the shelf, as the 'latest' copy. It is equally important to show when the format has changed or the publisher is different, eg Home Office *Offences relating to motor vehicles, England and Wales* is now issued as a Home Office Statistical bulletin;[238] or that *Time rates of wages and hours of work*[239] is now published by the Department of Employment, not by HMSO. Occasionally, the title of a publication is kept, but the policy for its contents has changed, eg Department of the Environment *Digest of environmental pollution and water statistics*[240, 241] has kept the same title but curtailed the coverage.

The pace of change in statistical publications has accelerated in the post-Rayner era in the UK, and also increasingly in the Reagan years in the USA. Privatization or de-officializing of statistics is an added complication (eg *Imported timber*,[242] Business Monitor PM 476, ceased publication with the June 1980 issue, but the data are still available from the Timber Trade Federation of the UK in its *Annual*[243]), and care must be taken to draw attention to the altered source and the new publisher. Earlier in this chapter, the development in the UK of non-HMSO departmental statistical publications has been commented on, a trend paralleling the growth of other non-HMSO departmental publications. The greater number of non-official statistics, already mentioned in an earlier section of this chapter, also increases the need for the professional librarian to be aware of the widely differing sources of contemporary statistics, but it is a difficult area to monitor or control. Many titles which were formerly free are now priced.

Increasingly, statistics are available in non-book format, and the librarian has to familiarize himself with the ever changing pattern,

The Statistics Collection

eg *Seminar on online access to statistics, 25th March, 1982*. Papers by Geoffrey Hamilton[244] and Maria Collins[245] have helped the professional to update his knowledge.

Sometimes there are physical problems as well as textual ones when changes occur. Where formerly they were separate publications, tables are issued now as part of a series, ie statistical bulletins, so it is necessary to decide whether to bind or shelve these as a continuation of the original titles, or to treat them as part of a serial, with annotations as to previous format. Many library systems are organized to treat books and serials differently for storage purposes, and for cataloguing or classification. By some means, the variations and changes must be recorded, so that statistics users may easily find historical and current series. Where resources so allow, duplication of titles may be the best solution, eg one set of Department of Education and Science *Statistical bulletins*[230] (at present still unpriced) treated as a serial, with individual extra copies of the Bulletins filed with the monographs they update, eg *DES Stat. Bull. 11/83* updates information in *Education statistics for the UK 1983*.[233]

In-house training of library staff in the case of statistics is essential, and an appreciation of the range of local, regional, national and international statistical publications must be fostered to improve the service to users. At professional level, there is fruitful co-operation through the long established Committee of Librarians and Statisticians, which has members from the Royal Statistical Society and from the Library Association. Increasingly there are seminars on statistical subjects—such as those arranged throughout the UK on the Census 1981 statistics by the Office of Population Censuses and Surveys, and the many joint meetings held locally on the use of SAS (*Small area statistics*)[246] arranged by local authorities. The CBI and the Industrial Marketing Research Association have established statistics working parties and groups.

However, no statistical collection exists in total isolation; it is always part of the wider information resources available locally, regionally, and nationally. The librarian running a statistics collection should be aware of these, and contact and use them. Locally the co-operative schemes, such as Ladsirlac, SINTO, NETWORK, HATRICS, etc, have an important role in identifying resources of

The Statistics Collection as a Reference Resource

statistics and encouraging their closer liaison and greater exploitation. The Sheffield Libraries Co-ordinating Committee, working party on official publications,[247] for example, takes a continuing interest in the development and content of the statistical collections in the area's libraries, whether academic, government, special, or public.

Nationally, the UK is fortunate to have many well organized collections. Apart from the major copyright libraries, eg the British Library; the Bodleian Library, Oxford; and Cambridge University Library; and the other university libraries which serve the needs of academic researchers, there are collections more easily available to the general public. The Office of Population Censuses and Surveys has an important reference library in St Catherine's House, Kingsway, London. There its specialist collections of statistical material are available to all interested persons.[248]

The Statistics and Market Intelligence Library[8] in London is part of the government's services to exports. Its collection of international and national trade and marketing statistics is the most extensive in the UK, and highly experienced government librarians provide an efficient information service.

At Warwick University, the major statistics collection is used and developed by the Warwick Statistics Service, which offers research and consultancy facilities and provides seminars and other training sessions.

THE STATISTICS COLLECTION AS A REFERENCE RESOURCE: SOME CONCLUSIONS

The statistics collection in a library only becomes a living information resource when actively developed, carefully maintained, and effectively exploited by both the professional and non-professional staff on behalf of the users. Its continued usefulness is in direct relation to the standard of trained professional care bestowed on it, and to the level of resources allocated to it. As the importance of the statistical aspects of subjects becomes more appreciated by all sections of the community, the quality of service from the

The Statistics Collection

library's statistical collection should at least keep pace with that interest or, by anticipation, be ahead of its development.

The continuing changes, in content and presentation, in traditional statistical publications; the variations in the compilation and dissemination of statistics; and the developing impact of computerization on the availability and manipulation of statistics—all these problematic factors have to be taken into account by the librarian responsible for the administration and organization of a statistics collection. At every level—international, national, official, non-official—and for every subject, statistical publications are acknowledged as major information tools. But with limited money, staff cuts, etc, the delicate balance between the desirable, the essential, and the possible, has to be struck when keeping the collection going.

Ironically, the post-Rayner developments in the UK and the somewhat similar Reagan situation in the USA have brought the whole subject of statistical publications and their availability into the professional limelight. Statistics users and librarians have had to consider the provision of statistical information more deeply and more urgently than was previously the practice.

As a result of these extra attentions, the provision of statistics information may well improve. Now every reference librarian should be actively aware of statistics as a vital resource. Developing a well ordered collection, and providing an efficient service of statistical information—these are challenging and rewarding tasks for the energetic librarian.

REFERENCES

1. United Nations *Directory of international standards for statistics*. New York: United Nations, 1960.
2. United Nations *Directory of international statistics, Vol 1*. New York: United Nations, 1981.
3. United Nations *UNDOC: current index*. New York: United Nations. Ten per annum, plus cumulative volumes.
4. United Nations *United Nations publications: a reference catalogue*. New York: United Nations. Annual.
5. Library of Congress *Index to international statistics*. Washington:

References

Congressional Information Service. Monthly, with annual cumulations.
6. Library Association (LA) and Royal Statistical Society (RSS) *Recommended basic statistical sources: international.* London: LA, 1975.
7. Harvey, Joan M. *Sources of statistics.* 2nd ed. London: Bingley, 1971.
8. Statistics and Market Intelligence Library (SMIL), 1 Victoria Street, London, SW1H 0ET, Tel. 01 215 5444/5, Telex 8811074.
    The major UK statistics library, part of the services to export, of the Department of Trade and Industry.
9. Department of Trade and Industry, Library Services *National statistical offices of overseas countries.* London: Statistics and Market Intelligence Library. Annual.
10. Pieper, F. C. (ed.) *SISCIS: subject index to sources of comparative international statistics.* Beckenham: CBD Research Ltd, 1978.
11. Wasserman, P. and O'Brien J., (eds.) *Statistics sources: a subject guide to data on industrial, business, social, educational and financial and other topics for the United States and internationally.* 6th ed. Detroit, Michigan: Gale Research Co., 1980.
12. Harvey, Joan M. *Statistics Africa: sources for social, economic and market research.* 2nd ed. Beckenham, Kent: CBD Research Ltd, 1978.
13. Harvey, Joan M. *Statistics America: sources for social, economic, and market research.* 2nd ed. Beckenham, Kent: CBD Research Ltd, 1980.
14. Harvey, Joan M. *Statistics Asia and Australasia: sources for market research.* Beckenham, Kent: CBD Research Ltd, 1974.
15. Harvey, Joan M. *Statistics Europe: sources for social, economic, and market research.* 4th ed. Beckenham, Kent: CBD Research Ltd, 1981.
16. Organisation for Economic Co-operation and Development (OECD) *Catalogue of publications.* Paris: OECD. Biennial.
17. *Publications of the European Communities.* Luxembourg: Office for official publications of the European Communities. Annual, with monthly updates in *Bulletin of the European Communities.*
18. European Communities *Eurostat news.* Luxembourg: Office for official publications of the European Communities. Quarterly.
19. Ramsay, Anne *Eurostat index: a detailed keyword subject index to the statistical series published by the Statistical Office of the European Communities.* 2nd ed. Edinburgh: Capital Planning and Information, 1983.
20. Ramsay, Anne *How to find out about the statistics of the European Communities.* Newcastle upon Tyne: the Association of EDC Libraries, 1982.
21. Jeffries, John *Guide to the official publications of the European Communities.* 2nd ed. London: Mansell, 1981.

The Statistics Collection

22. Central Statistical Office *Guide to official statistics.* 4th ed. London: HMSO, 1982.
23. Central Statistical Office *Government statistics: a brief guide to sources.* London: HMSO, Annual.
24. Library Association (LA) and Royal Statistical Society (RSS) *Recommended basic United Kingdom statistical sources for community use.* 4th ed. London: LA, 1983.
    (Resources in Economic Statistics No. 5)
25. Library Association (LA) and Royal Statistical Society (RSS) *Union list of statistical serials in British libraries.* London: LA, 1972.
26. Lock, G. F. *General sources of statistics.* London: Heinemann for the Royal Statistical Society and the Social Science Research Council, 1976.
    (Vol 5 in the series 'Reviews of United Kingdom statistical sources')
27. Maunder, W. F. (*ed.*) and others *Reviews of United Kingdom statistical sources, Vol 1–* .London: Pergamon Press on behalf of the Royal Statistical Society and the Social Science Research Council, 1974– .
    (Vols 1–5 were published by Heinemann Educational Books.)
28. Kendall, Maurice George (*ed.*) *Sources and nature of the statistics of the United Kingdom.* 2 vols. London: Oliver and Boyd, 1952–1957.
29. *Statistical news.* London: HMSO for the Central Statistical Office. Quarterly.
30. Lumsden, H. P. 'Disseminating statistics – the CSO experience'. *Statistical news*, No. 58, August 1982. 1–2.
31. Norman, A. R. D. and Rayfield, D. A. T. 'Information technology policy in the United Kingdom'. *Statistical news*, No. 59, November 1982. 1–4.
32. 'Rayner review of the Government statistical service: summary of a special meeting of the Royal Statistical Society on 10 June 1981'. *Statistical news*, No. 54, August 1981. 1–4.
33. Griffin, Chris 'Developments in local authority comparative statistics'. *Statistical news*, No. 54, August 1981. 24–25.
34. *American statistics index*: a comprehensive guide and index to the statistical publications of the US Government. Washington: Congressional Information Service. Annual, with monthly supplements.
35. *Statistical reference index: to current American statistical publications from sources other than the US government.* Washington: Congressional Information Service. Monthly, with quarterly and annual cumulative supplements.
36. Canada, Information Department *Statistics Canada: catalogue.* Ottawa: Queens Printer. Annual.
37. Department of Trade, Library Services *Iran, statistical sources.* Rev ed. London: Statistics and Market Intelligence Library, 1977.
    (Sources of Statistics and Market Intelligence No. 3)

References

38. Department of Trade, Library Services *Germany (FRG), statistical sources.* London: Statistics and Market Intelligence Library, 1980. (Sources of Statistics and Market Intelligence No. 10)
39. Department of Trade, Library Services *Saudi Arabia and the Gulf States.* Rev ed. London: Statistics and Market Intelligence Library, 1979.
(Sources of Statistics and Market Intelligence No. 7)
40. Norway, Statistisk Sentralbyra *Veiviser i Norsk statistikk: guide to Norwegian statistics.* 2nd ed. Oslo: Statistisk Sentralbyra, 1980.
41. Balachandran, M. (ed.) *Regional statistics: a guide to information sources.* Detroit, Michigan: Gale Research Co, 1980.
42. Central Statistical Office (CSO) *Annual abstract of statistics.* London: HMSO. Annual.
43. Central Statistical Office *Regional accounts.* London: HMSO, 1978. (Studies in Official Statistics No. 31)
44. Central Statistical Office *Regional trends.* London: HMSO. Annual.
45. Scottish Office *Scottish abstract of statistics.* Edinburgh: HMSO. Annual.
46. *Scottish economic bulletin.* Edinburgh: HMSO for Scottish Office. Two per year.
47. Northern Ireland Office *Northern Ireland annual abstract of statistics.* Belfast: HMSO. Annual.
Before 1982, the title concerned with Northern Ireland was 'Digest of Statistics, Northern Ireland'. Belfast: HMSO. Two per year 1954–1981.
48. Collett, R. J. *Northern Ireland statistics: a guide to principal sources.* Belfast: Queen's University, Department of Library and Information Studies, 1979.
49. Park, A. T. 'Northern Ireland government statistics'. *Statistical news,* No. 2, August 1968, updated by [48]. 12–14.
50. Curtin, J. V. *A guide to regional statistics.* Dublin: An Foras Forbatha, 1972.
51. Office of Population Censuses and Surveys (OPCS) *Census 1801–1966 Great Britain: guide to census reports.* London: HMSO, 1977.
52. Office of Population Censuses and Surveys (OPCS) *OPCS Census 1981, Monitor series.* London: OPCS. Irregular.
OPCS has issued very full information on the 1981 Census via its *Monitors.*
53. *Population trends.* London: HMSO for the Office of Population Censuses and Surveys. Quarterly.
54. Office of Population Censuses and Surveys (OPCS) *OPCS Census 1981, user guide catalogue.* London: OPCS.
55. Office of Population Censuses and Surveys (OPCS) *Great Britain – summary and review: local authorities, CEN 81. Census Monitor 58.* London: HMSO for OPCS, December 1982.

The Statistics Collection

56. Social Science Research Council (SSRC) *SSRC data archive bulletin.* Colchester: Essex University for SSRC. (Now ESRC.) Three times per year.
57. West Midlands County Council *Census report – West Midlands Council No. 2: First census results for the wards of the Birmingham partnership.* Birmingham: West Midlands County Council, 1982.
58. Chartered Institute of Public Finance and Accountancy (CIPFA) *Local government trends.* London: CIPFA. Annual.
59. Chartered Institute of Public Finance and Accountancy (CIPFA). *Local government comparative statistics 1981.* London: CIPFA, 1981.
60. Chartered Institute of Public Finance and Accountancy (CIPFA). *Community indicators.* London: CIPFA.
61. Greater London Council (GLC) *Annual abstract of Greater London statistics.* London: GLC. Annual.
62. Greater London Council (GLC) *London facts and figures.* London: GLC. Annual.
63. South Yorkshire County Council (SYCC) *South Yorkshire statistics.* Barnsley: SYCC. Annual.
64. Birmingham City Council. *Abstract of Birmingham statistics.* Birmingham: Central Statistical Office. Annual.
65. Greater Manchester County Council (GMCC) *Greater Manchester – facts, figures and finance.* Manchester: GMCC. Annual.
66. Hakim, Catherine. *Secondary analysis in social research: a guide to data sources and methods.* London: Allen and Unwin, 1982.
67. United States, Bureau of the Census *Guide to foreign trade statistics.* Washington: Bureau of the Census. Annual.
68. United States, Bureau of the Census *Directory of federal statistics for local areas: a guide to sources.* Washington: Bureau of the Census, 1978.
69. United States, *Fact finder for the nation.* Washington: Bureau of the Census. Irregular.
70. United States, Bureau of the Census 'Guide to sources of statistics' in *Statistical abstract of the United States, 1981.* Washington: Bureau of the Census, 1981. 946–984.
    Example of 'sources of statistics information' usually contained in annual compilations.
71. Foster, Pamela *Business statistics index.* Hartlepool: Headland Press, 1983.
72. Central Statistical Office *Wholesale price index: principles and procedures.* London: HMSO, 1980.
73. Department of Employment 'Retail prices index: annual revision of the weights'. *Employment gazette*, March, 1983, 115–117.
74. 'The unstatistical reader's guide to the retail prices index'. *Employment gazette*, October 1975. 971–978.
75. Department of Employment *Family expenditure: a plain man's guide*

References

to the *Family Expenditure Survey*. London: Department of Employment, 1983.
76. Copeman, Harold *National accounts: a short guide*. London: HMSO for the Central Statistical Office, 1981. (Studies in Official Statistics No. 36)
77. Johnson, Fred *Income distribution prepared for the [Statistical Sources] course team*. Milton Keynes: Open University, 1975. (Second-level course, 'Statistical Sources', Unit 12.)
78. Bell, David and Greenhorn, Alan, (eds.) *Guide to Financial Times statistics*. 2nd ed. London: Financial Times, 1982.
79. Chinn, M. (ed.) *Statistics for consumers: a guide to the statistics collection in the library of the Consumers' Association*. London: Consumers' Association, 1978.
80. Industrial Aids Ltd *Published data on European industrial markets*. 2nd ed. London: Industrial Aids Ltd, 1983.
81. Cyriax, George (ed.) *World index of economic forecasts: a guide to sources of economic forecasts*. Farnborough: Gower Press, 1978.
82. Mort, David *The forecasting business: a review of the output of the major forecasting organisations*. Coventry: Warwick Statistics Service, 1981. (Warwick Statistics Service, Occasional Review No. 2)
83. Ardern, Richard *Offshore oil and gas: a guide to sources of information*. Edinburgh: Capital Planning Information, 1978. (CPI Information Reviews No. 2)
84. 'William Farr 1807–1883: his contribution to present day vital and health statistics'. *Population trends*, No. 31, Spring 1983. 5–7.
85. Department of Health and Social Security (DHSS) *Steering group on health services information: a report on the collection and use of information about hospital clinical activity in the National Health Service*. (Korner report). London: HMSO for DHSS, 1982.
Also 'Korner review of Health services information: a progress report', *Statistical news*, No. 60, February 1983.
86. Sellwood, Roger and Griffin, Chris 'New developments in statistics at CIPFA'. *Statistical news*, No. 59, November 1982. 12–16.
87. 'Public records: possible amendments to the Statistics of Trade Act'. *Statistical news*, No. 60, February 1983. 35–36.
88. 'Statistics of Trade Act, 1947: [possible amendments]'. *Employment gazette*, February 1983. 77.
Wilson committee report and the Government response.
89. *Market and statistics news: a monthly review of business information*. Warwick: Warwick University, Warwick Statistics Service. Monthly.
90. Walter, Clare 'European Trade Associations statistics: part II'. *Market and statistics news*, March 1983. 10–16.
91. Incomes Data Service (IDS) *Manpower information*. London: IDS, September 1977.
(IDS Study 154)

92. *Statistics and market research: a guide to current periodical articles.* Birmingham: Birmingham Public Libraries. Monthly.
93. *Government statistical services.* London: HMSO, 1981. (Cmnd 8236).
   The White Paper giving the Government's response to Sir Derek Rayner's 'Report to the Prime Minister' on the statistical services.
94. Rayner, Sir Derek *Review of government statistical services: Report to the Prime Minister.* London: Cabinet Office, 1980.
95. *British national bibliography.* London: British Library Bibliographic Services Division. Weekly, with cumulations.
96. *British reports translations and theses.* Boston Spa: British Library Lending Division. Monthly.
97. Siddall, Leona. *Survey of non-official statistics and their role in business information.* Warwick: Warwick University, Warwick Statistics Service, 1983.
   Research project.
98. Christian Economic and Social Research Foundation *Annual review of Chief Constables' reports: part one. Drink offences.* London: CESRF. Annual.
99. Home Office *Offences of drunkenness, England and Wales.* London: Home Office. Annual.
   Issued as a Home Office Statistical Bulletin; available from H.O. Statistical Department, Tolworth Tower, Surbiton, Surrey.
100. Building Societies Association (BSA) *A compendium of building society statistics.* 2nd ed. London: BSA, 1979.
101. Registry of Friendly Societies *Report of the Chief Registrar.* London: Registry of Friendly Societies. Annual.
102. London and Cambridge Economic Service *The British economy: key statistics 1900–1970.* London: The Times for the London and Cambridge Economic Service, 1973.
103. Department of Employment and the Manpower Society *Improving manpower information*: [working party report]. London: Manpower Society, 1974.
   (Manpower Society Report No. 1)
104. Greater London Council, GLC Industry and Employment Committee *Status of London unemployment statistics: discussions.* London: GLC, 1980.
105. Incorporated Society of British Advertisers *ISBA area information, 1982.* London: ISBA, 1982.
106. 'International bibliography of historical demography' in *Annales de démographie historique.* London: International Statistical Institute. Annual.
107. Maunder, W. F. (*ed.*) *Bibliography of index numbers: an international team project.* Rev ed. London: Athlone Press for the International Statistical Institute, 1970.

References

108. Mitchell, B. R. *International historical statistics: Africa and Asia.* London: Macmillan, 1982.
109. Priestley, H. E. *The what it cost the day before yesterday book – from 1850 to the present day.* London: K. Mason, 1979.
110. United Nations *Demographic yearbook: historical tables.* New York: UN, 1981.
111. Organisation for Economic Co-operation and Development (OECD) *Main economic indicators: historical statistics 1960–1979.* Paris: OECD, 1980.
112. Mitchell, B. R. *European historical statistics 1750–1975.* 2nd ed. London: Macmillan, 1980.
113. Anderson, Michael (*comp.*) *International mortality statistics 1901–1975.* London: Macmillan, 1981.
114. Organisation for Economic Co-operation and Development (OECD) *Consumer price indices: sources and methods and historical statistics: special issue.* Paris: OECD, 1980.
115. Mitchell, B. R. and Deane, P. *Abstract of British historical statistics.* Cambridge: Cambridge University Press, 1962. (Department of Applied Economics, Cambridge University Monograph No. 17)
116. Mitchell, B. R. and Jones H. G. *Second abstract of British historical statistics* Cambridge: Cambridge University Press, 1971. (Department of Applied Economics, Cambridge University Monograph No. 18)
117. United States, Bureau of the Census *Historical statistics of the United States: Colonial times to 1970.* Washington: Bureau of the Census, 1976.
118. Finlayson, J. *Historical statistics of Australia: a select list of sources.* Canberra: Australian National University, 1970.
119. Urquhart, M. C. and Buckley, K. A. H. (*eds.*) *Historical statistics of Canada.* London: Macmillan, 1965.
120. Department of Employment *British labour statistics: historical abstract 1886–1968.* London: HMSO for the Department of Employment, 1971 o/p.
    Microfiche edition available.
121. Lee, C. H. *British regional employment statistics 1841–1971.* Cambridge: Cambridge University Press. 1979.
122. Chapman, Agatha L. and Knight, Rose *Wages and salaries in the United Kingdom, 1920–1938.* Cambridge: Cambridge University Press, 1953. (Studies in the National Income and Expenditure of the United Kingdom, No. 5)
123. Munby, Denys *Inland transport statistics of Great Britain 1900–1970, Vol I Railways, public road transport, London transport.* Oxford: Oxford University Press, 1978.
124. Business Statistics Office *Historical record of the Census of Production 1907–1970.* London: HMSO for the Business Statistics Office, 1979.
125. Leak, H. 'Census of production and distribution' in *Sources and*

The Statistics Collection

nature of the statistics of the UK, Vol 1. London: Royal Statistical Society, 1952. 1–16.

126. Lomax, K. S. 'Production and productivity movements in the UK since 1900'. *Journal of the Royal Statistical Society Series A*, Vol 122, 1955. 185–220.
127. Stafford, J. 'Development of industrial statistics'. *Statistical news*, No. 1, May 1968, 7–10.
128. Browning, H. E. 'Census of production'. *Statistical news*, No. 5, May 1969, 1–8.
129. Radical Statistics Group *The unofficial guide to official health statistics*. 2nd ed. London: Radical Statistics Group, 1981.
130. Radical Statistics Group *The nuclear numbers game: understanding the statistics behind the bomb*. London: Radical Statistics Group, 1982.
131. Radical Statistics Group, Education Group *Reading between the numbers: a critical guide to educational research*. London: Radical Statistics Group, 1982.
132. Radical Statistics Group, Health Group. *A better start in life? Why perinatal statistics vary in different parts of the country*. London: Radical Statistics Group/Local Radio Workshop, 1980.
Available as an audio tape cassette.
133. Schifferes, Steve (*comp.*) *Housing facts and figures*, 3rd ed. London: Shelter, 1980.
134. Townsend, Peter *Poverty in the United Kingdom: a survey of household resources and standards of living*. London: Penguin, 1979.
135. Irvine, J. et al. (eds.) *Demystifying social statistics*. London: Pluto Press, 1979.
136. Eden, Sir John (Chairman) *Ethnic and racial questions in the Census*. London: HMSO for the House of Commons, Home Affairs Committee, 1983.
137. Moser, Claus 'Statistics about immigrants: objectives, methods and problems'. *Social trends*, No. 3, 1972. 20–30.
138. Runnymede Trust and Radical Statistics Race Group *Britain's black population*. London: Heinemann, 1980.
Chapter 7 is 'The politics of statistics'.
139. Commission for Racial Equality *Ethnic minorities in Britain: statistical background*. London: The Commission, 1980.
140. Cook, Thomas and Campbell, Donald T. *Quasi experimentation – design and analysis issues for field settings*. Chicago: Rand McNally, 1979.
141. United Nations *International standard industrial classification of all economic activities (ISIC)*. New York: United Nations, 1968.
142. United Nations *Standard international trade classification Revision 2. (SITC REV 2)*. New York: United Nations, 1975.
143. United Nations *Commodity indexes for the standard international*

References

trade classification Revision 2 (SITC Rev 2). 2 vols. New York: United Nations, 1981.
144. *General industrial classification of economic activities within the European Communities (NACE).* Luxembourg: Office for official publications of the European Communities, 1970.
145. Customs Co-operation Council (CCC) *Nomenclature for the classification of goods in customs tariffs (Brussels Tariff Nomenclature).* 5th ed. Luxembourg: Office for official publications of the European Communities, 1976.
146. *Common nomenclature of industrial products (NIPRO).* Luxembourg: Office for official publications of the European Communities, 1975.
147. Customs Co-operation Council (CCC) *Explanatory notes to the Brussels nomenclature.* 3 vols. Brussels: CCC, 1966.
148. *Explanatory notes to the customs tariff of the European Communities.* Luxembourg: Office for official publications of the European Communities, 1971.
149. *Nomenclature of goods for external trade statistics of the Community and statistics of trade between member states (NIMEXE).* Luxembourg: Office for official publications of the European Communities. Annual.
150. Foreman, Lewis 'Sources of statistics' in Palmer, Doris *Sources of information on the European Communities.* London: Mansell, 1979. 129–157.
151. Central Statistical Office *Standard industrial classification (SIC) revised 1980.* London: HMSO for CSO, 1979.
152. Central Statistical Office *Indexes to the standard industrial classification, revised 1980.* London: HMSO for CSO, 1981.
153. Central Statistical Office *Standard industrial classification, revised 1980: Reconciliation with standard industrial classification, 1968.* London: CSO, 1980.
154. 'Introduction of the revised standard industrial classification'. *Economic trends*, March 1983. 97–99.
155. 'Standard industrial classification – revised 1980'. *Employment gazette*, March 1983, 118–120.
156. Lockyer, M. J. G. 'Rebasing and reclassifying the national accounts: the reasons and the likely effects'. *Economic trends*, March 1983. 104–107.
157. 'Wholesale price index to be rebased'. *British business*, 15 April 1983. 79–83.
158. Perry, John 'Index of industrial production – rebasing and reclassification'. *Economic trends*, March 1983, 100–101.
159. H. M. Customs and Excise *Tariff and overseas trade classification in the United Kingdom of Great Britain and Northern Ireland.* London:

The Statistics Collection

HMSO for Customs and Excise. Annual.
Two volumes, looseleaf.

160. H.M. Customs and Excise *Guide to the classification for overseas trade statistics, 1983*. London: HMSO for Customs and Excise. Annual.

161. Central Statistical Office *National accounts statistics: sources and methods*. London: HMSO, 1968.
(Studies in Official Statistics No. 13)

162. *Overseas trade statistics of the UK*. London: HMSO for the Department of Trade. Monthly.
Annual supplements contain more detailed information.

163. H.M. Customs and Excise *Statistics of trade through UK ports*. London: HMSO for Customs and Excise. Quarterly/annual.

164. Levin, Marc A. 'Access and dissemination issues concerning Federal Government information'. *Special libraries*, **74** (2) April 1983, 127–137.

165. Boreham, Sir John 'Official Statistics in troubled times: the changing environment for producers and users'. *Statistical news*, No. 64, February 1984. 1–3.

166. CANSIM: Canadian Socio-Economic Information Management System.
[CANSIM] 'A multi purpose shared data bank—CANSIM' Ottawa: Canadian Conference in Information Science, 1979. pp 25–31 of *The Proceedings.*
Seventh Conference: 'Sharing resources, sharing costs'.
Available via *Statistics Canada* or commercial bureaux.

167. Giles, Graham 'Improving the dissemination of CSO computer readable data'. *Statistical news*, No. 59, November 1982. 5–6.

168. *CSO data bank*. London: SIA Computer Services, Ebury Gate, 23 Lower Belgrave Street, SW1W 0NW.

169. *Business data packages*. London: HMSO, to start 1984.
New service from HMSO. Computerized manipulation of statistics. Full details from HMSO.

170. 'CRONOS – Eurostat data bank now accessible via Euronet/Diane'. *Eurostat news*, 4th Quarter, 1980. 7–11.

171. European Communities, Euronet/Diane *Databases in Europe*. Luxembourg: Office for official publications of the European Communities. Annual.

172. *Chronolog*. Palo Alto, California: DIALOG Information Retrieval Service. Monthly.

173. *Searchlight*. Santa Monica: SDC Information Services. Bi-monthly.

174. *News and views*. Frascati: IRS.ESRIN. Monthly. Informative news bulletin for IRS users.

175. United Nations *Commodity trade statistics*. New York: United

References

Nations. Quarterly and annual.
Available in microfiche format.

176. *Official statistical serials on microfiche: catalogue*. Cambridge: Chadwyck-Healey, 1982.
177. Datastream International. Datatrack service of charts and displays of economic indicators; and Datasolve Henley business forecasts.
178. United Nations *Statistical year book/Annuaire statistique*. New York: United Nations. Annual.
179. United Nations *Demographic yearbook*. New York: United Nations. Annual.
180. *World Bank atlas: population per capita, product and growth rates*. Washington: World Bank. Annual.
181. Organisation for Economic Co-operation and Development (OECD) *Economic surveys*. Paris: OECD. Annual.
    Each country in OECD has its own annual economic survey.
182. Organisation for Economic Co-operation and Development (OECD) *Economic outlook*. Paris: OECD. Six-monthly.
183. Organisation for Economic Co-operation and Development (OECD) *Main economic indicators*. Paris: OECD. Monthly, and annual volumes.
184. European Communities, EUROSTAT *Basic statistics of the Community*. Luxembourg: Office for official publications of the European Communities. Annual.
185. *Eurostatics – data for short-term economic analysis*. Luxembourg: Office for official publications of the European Communities. Monthly.
186. Council for mutual economic assistance (CMEA) *Statistical yearbook of member states . . .* Moscow: 'Statistika', *or* London: IPC Industrial Press Ltd. Annual.
    CMEA, formerly COMECON, is the organization covering trade in Eastern Europe.
187. International Labour Office (ILO) *Yearbook of labour statistics*. Geneva: ILO. Annual.
188. United Nations Food and Agriculture Organization *Yearbook of forest products*. Rome: FAO. Annual.
    Also available in computer readable form.
189. *Timber bulletin for Europe*. Geneva: Food and Agriculture Organization of the United Nations. Six-monthly.
190. International Tea Committee *Annual bulletin of statistics*, and supplement: *Monthly statistical summary*. London: ITC. Monthly.
191. Committee for Whaling Statistics *International whaling statistics*. Sandefjord, Norway: Committee for Whaling Statistics. Annual.
192. *Monthly digest of statistics*. London: HMSO for the Central Statistical Office. Monthly.

The Statistics Collection

Updates and supplements information in the UK. Annual abstract of statistics.
193. Central Statistical Office *United Kingdom in figures.* London: HMSO. Annual.
Free single sheet.
194. Central Statistical Office *Facts in focus.* 5th ed. Harmondsworth: Penguin, 1980.
195. Central Statistical Office *Economic trends.* London: HMSO for Central Statistical Office. Monthly with annual supplements.
196. *Economic progress report.* London: Central Office of Information for the Treasury. Monthly.
197. Central Statistical Office *Social trends.* London: HMSO for CSO. Annual.
198. Central Statistical Office *National income and expenditure.* (Popular title: 'Blue Book'). London: HMSO. Annual.
Includes a section updating 'National accounts statistics: sources and methods'.[161]
199. *United Kingdom balance of payments.* (Popular title: 'Pink Book'). London: HMSO for the Central Statistical Office. Annual.
200. *Quarterly bulletin.* London: The Bank of England. Quarterly.
201. *Financial statistics.* London: HMSO. Monthly.
202. Board of Inland Revenue *Inland revenue statistics.* London: HMSO for the Board. Annual.
203. Department of the Environment and Welsh Office *Local government financial statistics: England and Wales.* London: HMSO. Annual.
204. Chartered Institute of Public Finance and Accountancy (CIPFA) *Finance and general statistics.* London: CIPFA. Annual.
Earlier titles: 'Financial, general and rating statistics'; 'Return of rates . . .' issued by Institutes of Municipal Treasurers and Accountants.
205. Society of County Treasurers *Capital expenditure of county councils.* Reading: Society of County Treasurers. Annual.
206. Department of Employment *Family expenditure survey . . .* London: HMSO for the Department of Employment. Annual.
Quarterly results appear in *Employment gazette* as available; summary results are given in *Employment gazette* several months before publication of the final report.
207. Ministry of Agriculture, Fisheries and Food *Household food consumption and expenditure: annual report of the National Food Survey Committee.* London: HMSO for the Ministry of Agriculture, Fisheries and Food. Annual.
Quarterly reports appear in *Food facts*, issued by MAFF, and in *British business*, issued by the Department of Trade.
208. Department of Health and Social Security (DHSS) *Health and personal social services statistics for England.* London: HMSO for the DHSS. Annual.

References

209. Health and Safety Executive *Health and safety statistics.* London: HMSO for the Health and Safety Executive. Annual.
   Volumes issued for 1975 to 1980. For 1981 onwards, new arrangements are planned by the Health and Safety Executive (News release 257, 28 September 1983).
210. Sillitoe, Alan Frank *Britain in figures: a handbook of social statistics.* 2nd ed. London: Penguin, 1973.
211. Department of Health and Social Security (DHSS) *Social security statistics.* London: HMSO for the DHSS. Annual.
212. *Employment gazette.* London: HMSO for the Department of Employment. Monthly.
213. Office of Population Censuses and Surveys (OPCS) *Labour force survey.* London: OPCS. Biennial.
   Surveys in 1973, 1975, 1977, 1979, 1981. OPCS Monitor LFS 83/1 and P.P1 83/1 issued 22 February 1983 enlarges Chapter 5 of the 1981 survey.
214. Department of Employment *New earnings survey, parts A–F.* London: HMSO for the Department of Employment. Annual.
   More detailed information on the Survey results are available on application to the DE at Orphanage Road, Watford.
215. Office of Population Censuses and Surveys (OPCS) *Birth statistics.* London: HMSO for OPCS. Annual. (FMI series).
   Quarterly statistics of live births in OPCS Monitor series FMI.
216. Office of Population Censuses and Surveys (OPCS) *Local authority vital statistics: England and Wales.* London: HMSO for OPCS. Annual.
217. *UK mineral statistics.* London: HMSO. Annual.
218. Department of Trade and Industry, Business Statistics Office *Reports on the census of production . . . pursuant to Statistics of Trade Act, 1947.* London: HMSO for the Business Statistics Office. Annual. (Business Monitors PA series)
219. Chemical Industries Association *UK chemical industry statistics handbook.* London: Chemical Industries Association. Annual (now ceased).
220. *Metal bulletin handbook, Vol 1: Prices; Vol 2: Statistics.* Worcester Park: Metal Bulletin Books. Annual.
   1981 (and earlier) issued as a single volume: original title '*Quin's metal handbook and statistics*', *1914–* .
221. Society of Motor Manufacturers and Traders (SMMT) *The motor industry.* London: SMMT. Annual.
222. *British business.* London: HMSO for the Department of Trade and Industry. Weekly.
   Formerly 'Trade and Industry'. Regular statistics section plus features, e.g. statistics contact points. Penultimate page contains list of statistical series, regularly updated.

The Statistics Collection

223. Department of Trade, Business Statistics Office *Annual statistics on retail trades*. London: HMSO for the Business Statistics Office. Annual.
(Published as Business Monitor SDA 25)
224. Co-operative Union *Co-operative statistics*. Manchester: Co-operative Union. Annual.
225. General Council of British Shipping (GCBS) *British shipping statistics*. London: GCBS. Annual.
Earlier issues published by Chamber of Shipping of the United Kingdom.
226. Civil Aviation Authority (CAA) *Annual statistics*. London: CAA Library. Annual.
Monthly statistics also available from CAA Library, 45–59 Kingsway, London WC2B 6FE.
227. Department of Transport *Road accidents, Great Britain*. London: HMSO for the Department of Transport. Annual.
Road accidents and casualties in Great Britain Quarterly. Available from 5TCG4, Department of Transport, Room B2.40, Romney House, 43 Marsham Street, London SW1P 3EB.
228. Department of Transport *Transport statistics, Great Britain*. London: HMSO for the Department of Transport. Annual.
229. Chartered Institute of Public Finance and Accountancy (CIPFA) *Highways and transportation statistics*. London: CIPFA. Annual.
Earlier title: 'Highway statistics issued by the Society of County Treasurers'.
230. Department of Education and Science *Statistical bulletin*. London (Elizabeth House, York Road, SE1 7PH): The Department. Irregular.
See also separate statistical bulletins for Scotland and Northern Ireland.
231. Scottish Education Department *Scottish statistical bulletin*. Edinburgh: Scottish Education Department. Irregular.
For example No 6/A2/1982: *Education provision for the under 5s.*
232. Department of Education for Northern Ireland *Statistical bulletin*. Bangor (Rathgael House, Balloo Road, BT19 2PR): Department of Education for Northern Ireland. Irregular.
233. Department of Education and Science *Education statistics for the United Kingdom*. London: HMSO for the Department of Education and Science. Annual.
234. Welsh Office *Statistics of education in Wales*. Cardiff: Welsh Office, E & SS Division. Annual.
235. University Grants Committee *University statistics, 3 vols*. Cheltenham: Universities' Statistical Record for the University Grants Committee. Annual.

References

Before 1980 included in *'Statistics of education, Vol. 6: Universities'*. London: HMSO. Annual.

236. Department of Education and Science *Statistics of Education*. (Five sets of statistical tables: schools; school leavers and examinations; further education; teachers in service; finance and awards).
  Not HMSO; only available from DES, Room 337, Mowden Hall, Staindrop Road, Darlington DL3 9DG, in the form of loose sheets of statistics, complete sets, individual sets or separate tables.
237. Department of Employment *British labour statistics yearbook* London: HMSO, 1969–1976. Annual.
  No longer published. Check with DE, Orphanage Road, Watford, for latest information.
238. Home Office *Statistical bulletin*. Surbiton, Surrey: Home Office. Periodic.
  Many previously separate annual publications are now issued in this format, e.g. *Offences relating to motor vehicles, 1981–* .
239. Department of Employment *Time rates of wages and hours of work*. London: Department of Employment. Annual.
  Loose-leaf format.
240. Department of the Environment *Digest of environmental pollution and water statistics*. London: HMSO for the Department of the Environment. Annual.
  Last complete edition, No. 3, 1980; continued as a curtailed publication of the *same* title. For fuller tables, obtain supplementary volumes direct from DOE *not* HMSO.
241. *Digest of environmental pollution statistics*. No. 1, 1978; No. 2, 1979. London: HMSO for the Department of the Environment. Annual.
242. *Imported timber*. London: HMSO for Business Statistics Office. Monthly.
  (Business Monitor PM 476)
  Last issue June 1980. For later information see [243].
243. Timber Trade Federation of the UK *Annual*. London: Timber Trade Federation. Annual.
  Contains information similar to that formerly published in [242].
244. Hamilton, Geoffrey 'Access to statistics: a survey and a call for action' in *Proceedings of the 30th Annual Study Group 16–18 April 1982*. 40–58. London: Library Association for RSIS, 1982.
245. Collins, Maria 'Online access to statistics' in *Proceedings of the 30th Annual Study Group, 16–18 April 1982*. 59–66. London: Library Association for RSIS, 1982.
246. *Small area statistics (SAS)*.
  Issued on magnetic tape, microfilm and paper. Available from: Office of Population Censuses and Surveys, Census Customer Services (England and Wales), Segensworth Road, Titchfield, Fareham, Hants

The Statistics Collection

Po15 5RR. Ditto (Scotland) from: General Register Office, Ladywell House, Ladywell Road, Edinburgh EH12 7TF.

247. Sheffield Libraries Co-ordinating Committee (SLCC) *Annual report.* Sheffield: Registrar's Department, The University of Sheffield, Western Bank, Sheffield S10. Annual.
248. Office of Population Censuses and Surveys *Libraries in the United Kingdom holding census volumes.* London: OPCS, 1980.

FURTHER READING

Berman, Laurie 'Towards a slimmer statistical service'. *British Business*, 27 February 1981. 412–415.

Dean, Andrew *Wages and earnings.* Oxford: Pergamon Press for the Royal Statistical Society and the Social Science Research Council, 1980.
(Vol 13 in *Reviews of United Kingdom statistical sources*, edited by W. F. Maunder)

Dewdney, John C. *The British census.* Norwich: Geo Abstracts, 1981. (Concepts and Techniques in Modern Geography No. 29)

Dowdeswell, P. 'New developments in statistical computing in the Departments of the Environment and Transport – the DISC project'. *Statistical news*, No. 59, 1982. 18.

Fielding, A. 'Official statistics of education in the United Kingdom: a description of sources and an appraisal'. *Review of public data*, 9, 1981. 57–58.

Houghton, Bernard and Wisdom, J. C. *Non-bibliographic online databases: an investigation into their uses within the fields of economic and business studies.* London: British Library, 1981.
(BL Research and Development Reports No. 5620)

Hutchinson, D. 'The use of statistics in government decision-making with particular reference to reports of Royal Commissions'. *Bias*, 8 (2), 1981. 179–223.

Mort, David 'Statistical information – a problem area'. London: Library Association for RSIS, 1982. In *Proceedings of the 30th Annual Study Group 16–18 April 1982.* 33–38.

Nora, Simon and Minc, Alain. *The computerization of society: a report to the President of France.* London: MIT Press, 1980.
Databanks are discussed on pp 79–81.

United Nations *International trade statistics: concepts and definitions, Revision 1.* New York: UN, 1982.

14
Local Studies

Chris E. Makepeace

The mid-twentieth century has witnessed a tremendous growth of interest in the history of local communities which, according to Galbraith, is 'no less important than that of the state, and one which, just because it has received less expert attention, is no less difficult'.[1] This growth has been reflected in the use made of local material in libraries and record offices and in the increased number of publications reflecting the many aspects of local life. Unfortunately, the use of the word 'local history' is misleading, as local collections will include material on all aspects of the community and 'not merely a single class, industry, or section of it'.[2] A more suitable designation is, therefore, 'local studies', which more accurately reflects the subject field.

To enable all aspects of the community to be fully studied, it is necessary to collect and preserve a wide range of material: historic and contemporary; printed and manuscript; book and non-book; primary and secondary sources. For a local studies collection to be truly representative, it should contain as much as possible on the area, irrespective of its format. (It must be remembered that archival and manuscript material may be housed in separate departments, as such material often requires specialist treatment and care.) Although the sources for the history of one area are similar to those for another, the actual coverage will vary, depending on the amount

Local Studies

of material that has been collected by previous generations and the ability of libraries to acquire material to complete their holdings.

Those involved in work on a particular locality will often need to consult a wide range of material. One of the first historians to demonstrate the importance of using all available sources of information was:

Hoskins, W. G. LOCAL HISTORY IN ENGLAND. 2nd ed. London: Longman, 1972.

When this book was first published in 1959, it was regarded as an important step forward in the study of the history of a community, as it drew attention to the many sources which could be used, and, by implication, the type of material which should be housed in a comprehensive local studies collection in the library. Although Hoskins does not go into detail about the origins of the sources he mentions, he shows their use by means of carefully chosen examples. There is a useful bibliography of general material which the local historian might need to consult, and which should be accessible to a local studies collection.

A more detailed account of sources that can be used is in:

Stephens, W. B. SOURCES FOR ENGLISH LOCAL HISTORY. 2nd ed. Cambridge: Cambridge University Press, 1981.

The author of this book claims that it is not a general bibliographical guide, but 'an introduction to the detailed history of a region . . . or local area'.[3] After an introductory chapter in which he refers to many of the general sources of information which should be the basis of the background material in a local studies collection, Stephens chooses six subject areas, such as religion and education, and discusses the various types of source material which can be consulted. Most of the sources mentioned are either manuscript or printed and, with the exception of maps, non-book material is ignored; this may result in some important sources being overlooked. There are relatively few examples illustrating the information that these sources give. Although there is no bibliography, there are copious footnotes which can provide the basis for further reading.

Local Studies

Stephens' lack of information on the content and use of various sources in the above book does not apply to:

Stephens, W. B. TEACHING LOCAL HISTORY. Manchester: Manchester University Press, 1977.

Although intended for teachers involved in local history teaching, this book indicates the various sources that can be used when working on an area, and gives examples of their use and the type of information that can be gleaned from them. There is no bibliography, but the notes at the end of the work constitute an extremely useful list of material that can be consulted when research is undertaken.

The following deals with sources for a particular period:

Rogers, A. APPROACHES TO LOCAL HISTORY. 2nd ed. London: Longman, 1977.

Rogers concentrates on the sources available for the study of mid-Victorian England, and shows how they can be used to provide a framework within which local historians can work, and the categories of material they might expect to find in either a library or record office. Like Stephens, Rogers deals with specific subject areas, but he does not restrict the sources he refers to solely to printed and manuscript material; he includes non-book material as well. The book is well illustrated with photographs and copies of documents referred to in the text. These are supported by examples drawn from many parts of the country, illustrating the use to which the sources can be put, a feature which enhances its interest and usefulness. The chapter notes, as in Stephens, form the basis for further reading as there is no bibliography.

Rogers' book was originally published to accompany a radio series on local history. More recently, a television local history series resulted in the publication of:

Ravensdale, J. R. HISTORY ON YOUR DOORSTEP. London: BBC, 1982.

This well illustrated publication takes certain themes, such as the history of a house; archaeology; the village; and the common, and shows how a variety of sources can be used to build up a picture

Local Studies

of a locality. Not only does it refer to printed and manuscript sources; it also encourages the reader to go out into the field to look for information and evidence. There is an extensive bibliography as well as many useful footnotes in the text. In some cases, in order to draw attention to the material housed locally, local libraries published their own leaflets to go with the series. One such library was Essex Local Studies Library, whose *History on your Essex doorstep*[4] not only refers to local material, but gives an indication of the type of material to be found in a county local studies collection.

Another book which encourages the reader to 'look around' for evidence and information is:

Dunning, R. LOCAL HISTORY FOR BEGINNERS. Rev ed. Chichester: Phillimore, 1980.

Dunning restricts the number of sources he considers in this book, so as not to overwhelm the beginner. He looks at the sources (excluding maps) that can be used for a number of broad subjects, such as transport, or the parish church. His book, he claims, is 'for the beginner who is looking for material near at hand . . . the sources dealt with . . . have been deliberately limited . . . to give a fair coverage . . . and to demonstrate that an important part of local studies involves working out of doors . . .'.[5]

Two pamphlets which provide useful information on sources in general are:

Humphreys, D. W. and Emmison, F. G. (*comp.*) LOCAL HISTORY FOR STUDENTS. London: Standing Conference for Local History, 1966.

Iredale, D. DISCOVERING LOCAL HISTORY. Aylesbury: Shire Publications, 1977.

The pamphlet by Humphreys and Emmison is aimed at students who are involved with local history projects; it indicates the types of sources they may need to consult, and the information that may be found in them. Iredale's book, on the other hand, is intended for someone 'wanting to discover, though not necessarily to write, local history'.[6] He indicates the type of material that should be consulted, and the type of further research that might follow once a specific item of information has been obtained.

A different approach to sources is to be found in:

Iredale, D. LOCAL HISTORY RESEARCH AND WRITING. Chichester: Phillimore, 1980.

This book has two distinct sections: research techniques and sources of information. Unlike some of the previous books, Iredale looks at the various types of source, such as maps or church records, describes their origins, and the information that can be abstracted from them. In addition, there is a useful bibliography, a list of addresses of national and provincial organizations which might be helpful, and the addresses of local record offices. It is a pity that the publishers did not take the opportunity to revise this list when it was reprinted in 1980.

A similar list of addresses has been compiled by:

Standing Conference for Local History. INFORMATION FOR LOCAL HISTORIANS: DIRECTORY OF NATIONAL ORGANISATIONS. London: Standing Conference for Local History, 1975.

This is an alphabetical list of national organizations whose activities might be of assistance to local historians. The entries give the name, address and telephone number of the organization; its sphere of activity; and publications. Although the list is now eight years old, and some of its information is incorrect, it is still a useful reference tool.

It is important that a local studies collection should have a list of addresses of not only local societies, but also local groups or branches of national societies and record offices. Sometimes, these are compiled by the library, as in the case of *A directory for local historians in the County Palatine of Lancaster*,[7] which lists local and regional societies, record offices in the north-west, and has a comprehensive subject index. Alternatively, some of this information may have been commercially published by bodies such as the Federation of Family History Societies, whose *Record offices: how to find them*[8] includes location plans as well as other data on the location of record offices in England and Wales.

Local Studies

Although material in a local studies library will relate to a specific area, it is important that certain general historical works are accessible to enable research to be placed in its correct context. Useful lists of important general works can be found in:

Library Association, County Libraries Group. SOURCES OF LOCAL HISTORY. 4th ed. London: Library Association, 1971.

Hale, A. T. LOCAL HISTORY HANDLIST. 5th ed. London: Historical Association, 1982.

These two booklists are very similar in format and content, listing general background works under specific subject headings and excluding items on specific places. The main distinction between them is that the *Local History Handlist* includes entries for periodical articles. Used together, these lists offer a valuable guide to the general works which should be accessible to the local studies library and to its readership and staff.

The wide range of sources that need to be consulted in local studies work is only one of the problems which faces the librarian. Others are discussed in:

Carter, G. A. A. J. HOBBS' LOCAL HISTORY AND THE LIBRARY. 2nd ed. London: Deutsch, 1973.

Lynes, A. HOW TO ORGANISE A LOCAL COLLECTION. London: Grafton, 1974.

Nichols, H. LOCAL STUDIES LIBRARIANSHIP. London: Bingley, 1979.

Local history and the library was originally published in 1962, but has been revised and updated to take account of the rapid growth in interest in local studies. Carter examines some of the problems associated with local studies librarianship, such as the relationship with archives and the range of material used in local studies collections. The scope of the book is such that it can be used to advantage by both the experienced and the newly qualified librarian involved in the local studies field.

Both Lynes and Nichols concentrate on the librarianship of local studies rather than on the sources and their various problems, which is the main feature of Carter's work. However, throughout the text, there are references to the general works that relate to different types of material. Both authors have included bibliographies, although that by Nichols is more extensive and arranged according to chapter.

Bibliographies are the usual means of tracing what has been published either in book form, or as articles. However, it is often easier to trace older local studies material than that which has been more recently published, since bibliographical tools, such as *BNB*, do not record all that is published because copies are not sent to the British Library; this is often because the publisher, who may also be the author, is ignorant of the law relating to legal deposit. It is, therefore, essential for librarians engaged in local studies work to visit local bookshops and newsagents regularly, and to scan local newspapers and periodicals for reviews and brief news items referring to histories of churches, etc. Many local publications have a circulation that is limited to the area or community to which they relate. In many cases, the local studies library will be the only place where a copy will be preserved for posterity. Some local items do get recorded in national publications such as the *Agricultural history review*,[9] *Urban history yearbook*,[10] the *Annual bibliography of British and Irish history*,[11] and the *Antiquaries Journal*,[12] which contains a useful accession list of material added to the library of the Antiquaries Society and analytical entries for periodical literature. The most important of the periodicals listing local publications is:

THE LOCAL HISTORIAN.[13] London: British Association for Local History,[14] 1952– . Quarterly.

The Local Historian was started to assist local historians 'to progress more surely and swiftly and to achieve more reliable results'.[15] Although a large portion of each issue is devoted to articles on various aspects of local history, often dealing with sources that might be consulted, there is also a substantial bibliographical section containing reviews and lists of recently received books, many of which are not recorded in *BNB*, or if they are,

Local Studies

this occurs very much later than when they were published. *The Local Historian* is, therefore, both an important bibliographic tool and an important source of information on key materials.

Most local history bibliographies that have been and are compiled relate to specific localities or areas and not to the whole country. An important exception to this is:

Anderson, J. P. THE BOOK OF BRITISH TOPOGRAPHY. 2nd imp. Wakefield: E.P., 1976.

Originally published in 1881, this bibliography contains over 20,000 entries for local items in what was then called the British Museum Library. The bibliography includes general topographical works, directories, guide-books, and society publications, but no analytical entries for periodicals. The contents are arranged in two basic groups: thematic and topographical. The thematic section deals with topics such as railways and guides, whilst the topographical section lists works, on individual counties, in alphabetical order of county. After the general works on each county, there are titles on individual towns. Although Anderson's work was published over a century ago, it contains many important nineteenth century and pre-nineteenth century works which might not be found locally.

More recently, the Department of Printed Books at the British Library has published a reader's guide to sources of information on English places,[16] which lists some of the more general sources which can be consulted when tracing local material. The authors point out that many of the items listed will also be found in other major libraries in the country. This list provides a very short, but useful list of the general topographical and bibliographical works that can be consulted.

Most local studies bibliographies follow one of two formats, established in the nineteenth century: a subject approach or an alphabetical by author approach. Either arrangement has advantages and disadvantages, so it is on content and coverage that their value must be judged. For example, the *Bibliotheca Lincolniensis*[17] has a subject arrangement and includes entries for specific periodicals, whereas the *Bibliotheca Staffordiensis*[18] has an alphabetical arrangement, does not include analytical entries for periodical articles, and has few cross-references under towns to other entries; this leaves the user with the feeling that something may have been overlooked.

The same two basic arrangements are also to be found in modern local studies bibliographies. For example, the *Handbook of local history: Dorset*[19] has a subject approach, whilst *A bibliography of the history and topography of Cumberland and Westmorland*[20] follows the alphabetical approach. In both cases, however, the subject field covered is much larger than that of nineteenth-century bibliographies; analytical entries are included, and in the case of the Cumberland and Westmorland bibliography, there is very adequate cross-referencing between entries.

A third approach has been adopted by:

LANCASHIRE BIBLIOGRAPHY. Manchester: Joint Committee for the Lancashire Bibliography, 1961–   . 10 vols.

The first five volumes of this bibliography list specific types of material, such as directories or Acts of Parliament. The next four cover specific historical periods, such as the Stuarts, whilst the last volume adopts a subject approach. This bibliography is also a finding list, for in addition to the bibliographical details, each entry lists those libraries in pre-1974 Lancashire which have copies. As with other bibliographies, manuscript and archival material is omitted, except in the volume covering parish registers where both manuscript and microfilm material has been included. For this type of bibliography to be successful, it is essential that there should be a good index; the user can then adopt either a subject or a location approach.

A major problem with any printed bibliography is that it is out of date as soon as the type is set. This applies to local history bibliographies as much as to other subject bibliographies. The problem of updating can be solved by the issue of supplements, but unless these are incorporated in a revised edition, or are cumulated in some way, the bibliography becomes unwieldy and difficult to use; the *East Anglian bibliography*,[21] for example, has many parts and no cumulative index.

Despite the existence of so many local history bibliographies, there is only one listing of them:

Local Studies

Humphreys, A. L. A HANDBOOK TO COUNTY BIBLIOGRAPHY ... RELATING TO THE COUNTIES AND TOWNS OF GREAT BRITAIN. 2nd imp. London: Dawson, 1974.

This bibliography of local history bibliographies was published in 1917. Although many more have been published since that time, Humphreys' listings provide many useful entries, including not only bibliographies, but also articles of a bibliographical nature. The work is arranged by county, with general bibliographies listed first, followed by bibliographies of towns.

Dividing the country into rural and urban areas, there is relatively little published bibliographical material on the rural areas, whereas the urban historian has a wealth of material to work from. It is unfortunate that the only series which covers most of the country—the *Victoria county histories of England*[22]—does not include a bibliographical volume for each county; Essex is the one exception.[23] For the rest of the country it is necessary to use the copious footnotes to create a bibliography.

For the urban historian there are two good bibliographies:

Gross, C. A. BIBLIOGRAPHY OF BRITISH MUNICIPAL HISTORY. 2nd ed. Leicester: Leicester University Press, 1966.

Originally published in 1900, the new edition has a new introduction, but no new entries. The bibliography is divided into three sections: archival material and general works; general works on urban history; histories of individual towns. Gross realized that many important contributions to urban history appeared in articles in periodicals and journals, so these were included in the entries, a feature which increases the bibliography's usefulness and importance. The index enables entries for specific places, which do not appear under the entry for the town, to be easily traced.

Martin, G. H. and McIntyre, S. A BIBLIOGRAPHY OF BRITISH AND IRISH MUNICIPAL HISTORY. Leicester: Leicester University Press, 1972.

This is the first volume of a series of bibliographies on urban history. It deals only with general works, not works that relate in their entirety to specific towns. There are five main sections, in-

Local Studies

cluding a good one on bibliographies and guides to libraries and record offices. The sections are sub-divided, where necessary, into sub-sections, to achieve clarity when used. A comprehensive index enables the user to trace entries where the scope notes indicate that a particular town is referred to.

The publications of local societies contain much information that is useful to local studies work, but it can be difficult to trace specific entries unless there is a cumulative index. A useful guide to some of these publications is:

Mullins, E. L. P. A GUIDE TO THE HISTORICAL AND ARCHAEOLOGICAL PUBLICATIONS OF SOCIETIES OF ENGLAND AND WALES 1901–1933. London: Institute of Historical Research, 1966; Athlone Press, 1968.

The guide lists the contents of 6,560 volumes published between 1901 and 1933, the first year which *Writings on British history* covers comprehensively. The societies are listed alphabetically, and under each society are listed the contents of the volumes published between the given dates. The compiler has included both the well-known and the less well-known societies, which increases the comprehensiveness and usefulness of the work. The index enables the user to trace entries which might otherwise have been overlooked, as the publishing society is not one which publishes on a specific area or topic.

In addition to locally orientated bibliographies, there are national ones, not only for history, but also for specific subject fields, which may contain entries on local areas, of which the local studies library ought to be aware. For example, there are many local entries in Bonser's bibliographies on Roman[24] and Anglo-Saxon[25] Britain and in the now discontinued Council of British Archaeology's *Archaeology bibliography*.[26] The most important of these general bibliographies is the six-volume series:

OXFORD BIBLIOGRAPHY OF BRITISH HISTORY. Oxford: Oxford University Press, 1951–1977. 6 vols.

When this series was started in 1951, local entries were not included, but as the series progressed, so the policy changed, and a section dealing specifically with local history was introduced.

Local Studies

This section has also been introduced in the earlier published volumes as they have been revised. In addition to the entries in the local history section, there are many local entries to be found elsewhere in the bibliography; these can be traced through the index.

As the amount of printed material increases, it becomes more difficult to compile comprehensive bibliographies of what is published in both book and article form. This difficult task is attempted by:

WRITINGS ON BRITISH HISTORY 1901– . London: Cape/ Institute of Historical Research, 1937– . 24 vols.

This series aims to provide an exhaustive list of all British history publishing for a given year. The volumes fall into three groups. The first group, covering the years 1901–1933, were published retrospectively, and excluded certain categories of material which were adequately listed elsewhere. The second, covering 1933–1939, is a series of single volumes for each year; these are comprehensive in their coverage. The final group covers the years from 1940 to the late 1960s and consists of a single volume for several years. The series is an invaluable aid to historians, both national and local, as it includes many entries for items which might have been overlooked. Each volume includes a section on bibliographies and guides, as well as a useful index which enables all relevant entries to be traced.

A similar work is:

BIBLIOGRAPHY OF HISTORICAL WORKS ISSUED IN THE UNITED KINGDOM. London: Institute of Historical Research, 1957– . 5 vols.

This series is not intended to rival *Writings on British history*, but to provide, for the quinquennial conference of Anglo-American historians, a five-yearly list of what has been published, mainly in book or pamphlet form. From its inception, it has included a section on local history publications, including those not recorded in *BNB*.

Theses, especially those submitted for higher degrees, form an-

Local Studies

other important source of information on any locality, as topics and aspects of the locality, which are not covered in any other publication, are investigated. It is, therefore, important that the local studies library has either a list of those relating to its area, or preferably, copies of relevant theses. It can be difficult tracing what has been submitted and what is being researched, but information can be traced by using:

Jacob, P. M. HISTORY THESES 1901–1970. London: Institute of Historical Research, 1976.

HISTORICAL RESEARCH FOR UNIVERSITY DEGREES IN THE UNITED KINGDOM. London: Institute of Historical Research, 1971–   . Annual. 2 vols. per annum

History theses lists theses completed between 1901 and 1970 and brings together information previously dispersed in several sources. The entries are divided into broad historical periods and then sub-divided into subjects, including one on local history. Information given includes the name of the author; the title of the thesis; date of submission; the university at which it was submitted; and information required to trace a copy. The index enables entries for particular areas or subjects to be easily traced in the main body of the work.

Historical Research for university degrees covers theses after 1970, and is in two parts. The first lists theses submitted during the year covered, and indicates how copies can be traced. The index enables a subject, place and author approach to be adopted. The second lists theses in progress, with the author's name, title of thesis, and university, but there is no index, so that specific entries are difficult to trace.

Printed sources of information, such as books, pamphlets, articles and theses, are mainly secondary sources. It is important for the local studies librarian to be aware of the primary sources and to have a good knowledge of printed primary sources such as newspapers, transcripts, and directories.

Manuscript and archival sources are perhaps the most difficult, as many libraries do not have archival material and, consequently,

Local Studies

the staff do not gain experience in their usage and content. It is important to remember that there are three possible locations for archival material—national, private and local:

1. **National records**, mainly found in the Public Record Office, are often overlooked by the amateur local historian, although they contain much important material. The guide to the Public Record Office[27] merely lists the type of record and the period it covers. It does not give any information on how the records came into existence, or on their potential use. This has been partially remedied by a series of leaflets, dealing with particular subjects,[28] which mentions the relevant printed guides, the indexes, and various categories of material. Further information on the origins of national records can be found in *An introduction to the use of public records*,[29] but the only way to discover the contents of many of the state papers is to consult the published calendars, such as those for the State Papers Domestic.[30] It is not necessary to travel to the Public Record Office to consult all national records, because some have been published as transcripts. A useful guide to these transcripts is:

Morton, A. and Donaldson, G. BRITISH NATIONAL ARCHIVES AND THE LOCAL HISTORIAN: A GUIDE TO OFFICIAL RECORD PUBLICATIONS. London: Historical Association, 1980.

Dealing with records in both the Public and Scottish Record Offices, this pamphlet concentrates on those archives where there is either a published transcript or a published calendar. In addition to giving a brief account of why some of the documents came into existence, there is a brief outline of the format of the calendar, which will be of assistance to those unfamiliar with their arrangement. There is also a useful appendix of the lists and calendars of national records which have been published by either the Public Record Office, HMSO, or one of the transcribing societies.

2. **Private records** can also be important sources of local information. Until 1869, the full extent of archival material in private or institutional collections was not known. In that year, the Royal Commission on Historic Manuscripts was established to investigate

and report on these collections. Since its establishment, many reports have been issued, but the *Guide to the reports*[31] gives little information on the contents of the collections investigated, so it is necessary to refer back to the main report on the collection.

Supplementing the reports published by the Royal Commission, some organizations have published lists of their own holdings or undertaken the compilation of location lists for a particular type of record. Warwick University, for instance, published a guide to its Modern Records Centre,[32] which contains records from many parts of the country. Although not specifically collecting records, but arranging for their safe deposit, the Manchester Studies Unit, Manchester Polytechnic, has surveyed certain types of record and published a directory of their locations. For example, the guide to the location of trade union records in Greater Manchester is extremely useful for researchers of trade union and labour history.[33]

Difficulty can be experienced in trying to trace particular records. In order to assist with this, the National Register of Archives was established in 1945 to co-ordinate the production and distribution of archive calendars, to advise individuals and institutions where they could deposit their archives, and to assist researchers in tracing particular archival collections.[34]

3. **Local records** are usually to be found in the local county record office, which is probably the most important of the archive repositories for the local historian, and the one with which the local studies librarian needs to be most familiar. It is essential that the local studies collection has a copy of the most recent guide to the local record office, together with calendars for the collections found there, and annual reports, as the latter often contain information on newly deposited material. Guides to record offices, in addition to listing collections, often give a brief account of the origins of the material and the periods covered, but nothing on the information that may be found in the record. A useful guide to the type of material found in record offices is:

Emmison, F. G. and Smith, W. J. MATERIAL FOR THESES IN LOCAL RECORD OFFICES AND LIBRARIES. 2nd ed. London: Historical Association, 1980.

Local Studies

Although it does not claim to be comprehensive, this pamphlet acts as a reasonably good indicator. However, as each record office mentioned has provided material for inclusion at its own discretion, the user must be careful not to assume that, because a particular type of material is not listed, it is therefore not available.

To discover the information which can be gathered from the study of certain types of archival material, it is necessary to consult one of the works published on archives, such as:

West, J. VILLAGE RECORDS. 2nd ed. Chichester: Phillimore, 1982.

By using the records of the Worcestershire village of Chaddesley Corbett, West explains the origins of the documents used, and the information contained in them. After each different type of document, West lists published transcripts for the whole country. The value of this book is further enhanced by the inclusion of photographs of original documents and transcripts of the text, so that the reader is able to become familiar with the handwriting and phraseology. There is also a useful glossary to help with the meaning of unfamiliar and archaic words, and an extensive bibliography, which has been updated for the new edition.

A similar work is:

West, J. TOWN RECORDS. Chichester: Phillimore, 1983.

This is a companion volume to *Village records* in that it deals with the records of towns and cities. Each chapter is devoted to a specific source or type of records, such as gild records, town maps and plans, census returns and directories. After describing the origins of the source and giving examples drawn from many areas, each chapter has a list of further reading and a section in which the published records are listed alphabetically by town. In the case of those sources which appear in printed form, such as newspapers, the main ones for each town are listed and the dates covered.

Emmison, F. G. ARCHIVES AND LOCAL HISTORY. 2nd ed. Chichester: Phillimore, 1978.

In some respects, this book is not as useful as *Village records*, for, although Emmison briefly describes the type of record found in a county record office, he does not list the transcripts that are available, nor does he explain the use of the record, leaving the reader to work this out from the examples at the end of the book. There is, however, a useful section dealing with general matters such as the use of record offices and archives in general.

In addition to works dealing with archives in general, there are several which deal with specific types of document, such as title deeds,[35] quarter sessions records,[36] tithes,[37] and local taxation;[38] whilst others deal with the sources required to answer a particular type of enquiry, such as the dating of houses.[39] This type of work, which is usually in pamphlet form, can be very useful, as it includes a lot of detail on the content of the record concerned, its uses, and standard phrases which occur.

Another important book is:

Tate, W. E. THE PARISH CHEST. 3rd ed. Cambridge: Cambridge University Press, 1969. Reprinted 1983.

Parochial administration was the main form of local government prior to the nineteenth century, and as a result, there is much information on local government to be found in parish records, particularly on such subjects as poor relief and highway maintenance. Tate describes the origins of the records and, with the help of carefully chosen examples, indicates the information they contain and their modern use by historians. Like West, Tate includes a glossary, and an extensive bibliography on the subject.

It is not always necessary to visit the record office to look at some classes of material, as they have been transcribed and published. An important guide to these publications is:

Mullins, E. L. R. TEXTS AND CALENDARS: AN ANALYTICAL GUIDE TO SERIAL PUBLICATIONS. London: Royal Historical Society, 1958–1983. 2 vols.

This guide was compiled from the serial publications in the library of the Royal Historical Society, and relates to organizations which specialize in publishing either calendars or transcripts of original documents or archival material. It is divided into sections according to the type of publisher; national bodies like the Public Record Office; national societies such as the Camden Society; En-

Local Studies

glish and Welsh provincial societies; and finally, a section listing those volumes not in the Society's library. Under each major heading, the societies are listed alphabetically with their publications in chronological order and, where necessary, with an explanatory note on the contents. The index enables individual places, persons and types of document to be traced irrespective of publisher.

Some information on these publications after 1971 is to be found in:

Youings, J. LOCAL RECORD SOURCES IN PRINT AND IN PROGRESS. London: Historical Association, 1972–1977. 2 vols.

These two volumes, covering the years 1971–1972 and 1972–1976, cannot be regarded as a supplement to *Texts and calendars*, as they do not cover the same wide field as the earlier work. They are, nevertheless, a useful guide for a period where there is no detailed listing. Like Mullins, Youings divides the entries into type of publishing body and lists those volumes published during the period under review. There is also a section which lists forthcoming publications. Unfortunately there is no index and, therefore, it is difficult to trace entries for specific areas or types of material.

The use of original material can create problems for the amateur historian as well as for the local studies librarian, especially when encountering strange dates, words and unfamiliar handwriting for the first time. Useful in helping to unravel the mysteries of **dating** is Cheney's *Handbook of dates for students*,[40] which includes the modern equivalent for the saints' days and regnal years, used for dating by our predecessors. Some of this information, together with much other useful information, is also to be found in:

Richardson, J. THE LOCAL HISTORIAN'S ENCYCLOPEDIA. Rev ed. New Barnet: Historical Publications, 1975.

This work is divided into eighteen sections, covering topics ranging from agriculture and architecture to heraldry, Latin words and dates. In addition, there are useful sections listing important dates such as those for market charters, the founding of schools, and the building of railways. It is essential to use the index if full use is to be made of this reference tool, as some entries may be overlooked because they are not in the obvious place.

Local Studies

A more comprehensive list of Latin words is to be found in:

Gooder, E. A. LATIN FOR LOCAL HISTORY. London: Longman, 1975.
The major part of this book deals with grammar, but there are short practice pieces, drawn from actual documents, at the end of each section. There is also a section of formulae frequently used in documents, and an extensive word list.

Handwriting can also present problems, but helpful in overcoming this is:

Emmison, F. G. HOW TO READ LOCAL ARCHIVES 1550–1700. London: Historical Association, 1973.
This pamphlet is arranged so that the reproduction of the document and its transcript are opposite each other. Under the transcript there is a note on the peculiarities of the handwriting and phraseology so that the example, the transcript and notes can be easily studied without having to refer back to another page.

Periodicals, both currently published ones and ones which have ceased publication, may contain articles which are of interest to a particular locality. Local periodicals are obvious sources, but national ones, like the *Illustrated London News*[41] or the specialist ones like *The Builder*,[42] are often overlooked. Many current periodicals are listed in Woodworth's *Guide to current British journals*,[43] which gives details of frequency and whether they are indexed or abstracted and, if so, where this information is available. For older periodicals which have ceased publication, it is necessary to check the older bibliographies, but a useful starting point is the library's own holding of periodicals.

Akin to periodicals are **newspapers**, both local and national, weekly and daily. These contain not only news items, but also official announcements, editorial comment, features and advertisements, all of which are of value to the local studies collection, as they provide information on the local community. National papers, although often publishing several editions, rarely have regional editions or variations.[44] Local papers, on the other hand, can cause problems by publishing different editions for different localities, and if they are daily papers, they may have considerable differences between editions. It is, therefore, important to ensure that the library takes, or has access to, the various editions either by taking each edition, or arranging for access to files held by the newspaper itself.

Since newspapers were first published, there have been a great many, some lasting for only a few issues, others for many years. A useful list of newspapers that have been published is:

THE TIMES TERCENTENARY HANDLIST OF ENGLISH AND WELSH NEWSPAPERS, MAGAZINES AND REVIEWS. London: The Times, 1920.

This list is based on the holdings of the British Library and is divided into London and suburban newspapers, and provincial newspapers. The entries are arranged chronologically and, within each year, alphabetically, each entry giving, in addition to the title, the place and duration of publication. There is a title index enabling entries for papers beginning with the town's name to be traced, but little cross-referencing to those papers where the town's name does not come first.

Copies of many newspapers and periodicals have been deposited at the British Library, with the result that the holdings there can be used as a check list. A full list of these is to be found in:

British Library. CATALOGUE OF THE NEWSPAPER LIBRARY. London: British Library Board, 1975. 8 vols.

This series falls into two distinct sections: places and titles. The first volume deals with London newspapers, whilst the second covers individual places in the provinces. Under each town, there is a list of newspapers and periodicals published there, copies of which are in the British Library. The last four volumes list, alphabetically, titles of various newspapers. Thus it is possible to use both a locational and a title approach when using this catalogue.

Another useful guide is:

Wiles, R. M. FRESHEST ADVICES: EARLY PROVINCIAL

Local Studies

NEWSPAPERS IN ENGLAND. Ohio: Ohio State University Press, 1965.

Wiles begins with a lengthy introduction on the history of the English provincial press before 1750, before listing all newspapers and periodicals published before that date. The entries are arranged under town rather than year, which increases its usefulness to the local historian and librarian.

However, both lists mention only those papers found in large collections, whereas many libraries have their own runs of local papers, some of which were never sent to the British Library. Consequently, to trace which library has which paper, it is necessary to consult the various regional lists that have been compiled, such as *Newspapers first published before 1900 in Lancashire, Cheshire and the Isle of Man*,[45] which provide a comprehensive list of holdings in libraries and newspaper offices in the region, together with notes on where they may be consulted.

Just as national archives contain much local information, so also do the **records of Parliament**. There are three useful guides to the material which the local historian might need to consult:

Bond, M. F. GUIDE TO THE RECORDS OF PARLIAMENT. London: HMSO, 1971.

Bond, M. F. THE RECORDS OF PARLIAMENT: A GUIDE FOR GENEALOGISTS AND LOCAL HISTORIANS. Canterbury: Phillimore, 1964.

Ford, P. and G. A GUIDE TO PARLIAMENTARY PAPERS. 3rd ed. Shannon: Irish Universities Press, 1972.

Parliamentary papers not only include public and private Acts of Parliament, but also the reports of Royal Commissions, Sessional Papers, and information that has accrued as a result of evidence presented to various Parliamentary committees investigating bills laid before both Houses, and the implementation of Acts of Parliament, such as Enclosure Awards. Bond's *Guide to the records of Parliament* is the first comprehensive guide to the records of Parliament, both manuscript and printed, which are housed in the

Local Studies

Palace of Westminster. Its value lies in the fact that it is a complete listing of material, some of which is to be found nowhere else; and in the bibliographies and notes found at the end of each section. The other two works are more general in character in that they explain the origin of the main forms of Parliamentary paper which may be encountered; brief notes on their use; and an explanation of the complex numbering system adopted for many Parliamentary papers. Neither book, however, gives any information on which libraries have substantial holdings of these papers, nor do they provide a list of those which the local studies library might find useful. For this information it is necessary to consult:

Powell, W. R. LOCAL HISTORY FROM BLUE BOOKS. London: Historical Association, 1962.

This pamphlet deals only with sessional papers; how and why they were compiled; and their system of numbering. In addition, there is a list of libraries with extensive holdings of Parliamentary papers, and a second list, under broad subject headings, of sessional papers which the local historian might need to consult in the course of research.

Directories, irrespective of whether they are street, trade, commercial or telephone directories, are another important source of local information, containing not only lists of names, addresses and businesses, but also general information on such matters as postal times and churches; and advertisements, which can provide useful information on local firms—information which may not be found elsewhere. The most difficult period for local directories is the early nineteenth century, when several towns were included in a general directory for a particular region. However, from the mid-nineteenth century, directories usually covered either a town and its environs, or a particular county. A useful guide to the early directories is:

Norton, J. E. GUIDE TO THE NATIONAL AND PROVINCIAL DIRECTORIES OF ENGLAND AND WALES . . . PUBLISHED BEFORE 1856. London: Royal Historical Society, 1950.

This begins with an informative account of how the directories were compiled, and then lists 878 directories excluding London.[46] The contents are based on the holdings of major libraries, resulting in the omission of a number of directories held only by small libraries. Each entry has a full bibliographical description enabling different editions to be identified. The index only lists counties and not individual towns. To establish which places are in which directory, it is necessary to consult one or more of the local published lists such as those for the West Midlands[47] or Lancashire.[48]

Directories are one of the sources which genealogists can consult when researching family history. The increased popularity of this subject has been partially due to the increased availability of sources through the medium of microfilm, particularly films of parish registers and census enumerators' returns. Its popularity has made it necessary for the local studies librarian to be aware of the sources genealogists use, and the methods of undertaking genealogical research. There are many books on the subject, such as Hamilton-Edwards *In search of ancestry*,[49] Willes *Genealogy for beginners*,[50] and Camp *Tracing your ancestors*,[51] which explain the various sources that can be used and the way to undertake searches. Other helpful books are:

Currer-Briggs, N. (*ed.*) A HANDBOOK OF BRITISH FAMILY HISTORY: A GUIDE TO METHODS AND SOURCES. Flitwick: Family History Services, 1979.

This useful book deals with the various types of sources that can be used in genealogical research, together with information on their scope and the periods for which they are useful. It includes material in the various national repositories, and details of local record offices, their addresses and opening hours. There is also a short bibliography of works not only relating to genealogy, but also to local history and some of the printed sources and guides.

Steel, D. DISCOVERING YOUR FAMILY HISTORY. London: BBC, 1980.

This was originally prepared to accompany a BBC series on genealogy. After an introduction which looks at certain families, the book goes on to examine specific types of sources, such as newspapers, periodicals, and illustrations, as well as the more conventional genealogical material. It contains lists of useful addresses and an extensive bibliography.

Smith, F. and Gardner, D. E. GENEALOGICAL RESEARCH IN ENGLAND AND WALES. Salt Lake City: Bookcraft, 1956–1966. 3 vols.

This wide-ranging series looks not only at the various types of record that can be used, but also at the problems posed by handwriting and Latin. It also has a section on techniques which the authors consider essential for any proper genealogical search. It does not include lists of published or microfilm registers, so for this information it is necessary to consult:

THE NATIONAL INDEX OF PARISH REGISTERS. London: Phillimore, 1968.

When this series is completed, it will consist of thirteen volumes listing all the available parish registers. The first three volumes form an introduction to the various types of register that exist, together with information on ancillary sources such as monumental inscriptions[52] and wills[53] that can be used in genealogical research. The remaining volumes divide the country into regions, then counties, and finally into parishes, under which the registers are listed. There is no information as to where the registers may be consulted, but this can be found in the Society of Genealogists' two-volume *Parish register copies*,[54] the first volume of which lists the Society's own holdings, and the second, those of libraries and record offices.

For more general information there is:

Pine, L. G. THE GENEALOGIST'S ENCYCLOPEDIA. Newton Abbot: David and Charles, 1969.

This encyclopedia provides a general background to the subject, dealing with such subjects as heraldry, the clan system and sources of information, both in England and abroad, for genealogical research.

Census enumerators' returns and **census reports** are also important sources of local information. The difference between them is that the enumerators' returns are not available for 100 years after

Local Studies

the census, and that they contain personal details of the inhabitants, including names, ages, addresses, occupations and places of birth; whereas the reports are purely statistical, giving total populations, densities per acre and per house, and other information which is compiled as a result of studying the enumerators' returns when they are first returned. Many libraries have acquired copies of the censuses for the years 1841–1881. A list of which libraries have copies, and the areas covered, is to be found in:

Gibson, J. S. W. CENSUS RETURNS 1841–1881 ON MICRO-FILM: A DIRECTORY OF LOCAL HOLDINGS. 4th ed. Plymouth: Federation of Family History Societies, 1982.

The basic arrangement of this directory is by county, but under each county are listed the libraries and record offices which have microfilm holdings of the census enumerators' returns together with the dates held and areas covered.

The accuracy of the information in the census depends to a large extent on the way it was carried out. A valuable account of the way in which the censuses were undertaken is to be found in the *Guide to census reports: Great Britain 1801–1966*,[55] which also includes examples of the types of form used at various times. For a more general account of the censuses of the nineteenth century and their use, *The census and social structure*[56] provides a very useful account.

It is always difficult to obtain accurate information on population before 1801, but there are means of obtaining a reasonable approximation. The sources used for this are outlined in:

Stephens, W. B. SOURCES FOR THE HISTORY OF POPULATION AND THEIR USES. Leeds: Leeds University Institute of Education, 1971.

Using examples from Yorkshire, Stephens shows the wide range of sources that can be used to gain a relatively accurate picture of the population before 1801. He explains the origin of the sources, and outlines the problems that are encountered by the demographic historians using them. The results of work using these pre-1801 sources, as well as details of analysis of various census returns, can be found in *Local population studies*.[57]

Local Studies

Personal names often form an important part in place-name origins, as many include a personal name coupled with a descriptive element. The English Place-name Society has undertaken much research into the subject and has published detailed information on the place-names of several counties, including field names. A short, but useful work relating purely to place-names is:

Ekwall, E. CONCISE OXFORD DICTIONARY OF ENGLISH PLACE NAMES. 4th ed. Oxford: Oxford University Press, 1974.

This dictionary gives both the derivation of individual place-names, and the meaning of some of the more common elements found in them, such as -ton, -tun and -ham. Each entry has a list of the various existing spellings; the date when they were first used; their meaning; and the language from which they are derived. The dictionary, however, does not include field or street names.

A more detailed work is:

Gelling, M. SIGNPOSTS TO THE PAST: PLACE NAMES AND THE HISTORY OF ENGLAND. London: Dent, 1978.

This volume puts the development of place-names into context in the history of England. It provides a useful background work to the study and derivation of place-names, which is not found in other works on the subject.

Biographical information is also important in local studies. Often, general works like the *Dictionary of national biography*[58] contain few people of local significance, although there are more included in *Modern English biography*.[59] A valuable source for local biographies is the various county biographical dictionaries, many dating from the late nineteenth and early twentieth centuries. A useful introduction to this source is *Some neglected sources of biographical information: county biographical dictionaries 1890–1937*,[60] which lists some of these publications and gives a brief history of their origins.

Although this chapter has concentrated on manuscript and printed sources, much of the stock of a local studies collection consists of non-book materials: maps, illustrations, and ephemera.

Local Studies

The problem with this type of material is that it is very localized and difficult to list. There is, however, one exception—maps.

Maps form an important and well used part of the stock of any local studies collection; the best known are those produced by the Ordnance Survey. However, these are the most recent additions to the range of maps available, for county maps have their origins in the late sixteenth century.

A useful introduction to non-Ordnance Survey maps is:

Harley, J. B. MAPS FOR THE LOCAL HISTORIAN: A GUIDE TO BRITISH SOURCES. London: Standing Conference for Local History, 1972.

This book has its origins in a series of articles in the *Local Historian*,[61] and is intended as an introduction to the subject. It deals with six different categories of maps and includes bibliographical information on them; information on the main maps produced in each category; and an indication of some of the pitfalls for the unwary. There is an extensive bibliography, not only of general cartographic works, but also of publications which list maps for a particular area.

The most widespread of the non-OS maps are the county maps, which were often produced for county atlases. One of the main problems with them is that they were frequently reissued at later dates without any change, except possibly in the imprint. A useful list of these atlases is in:

Chubb, T. PRINTED MAPS IN THE ATLASES OF GREAT BRITAIN AND IRELAND . . . 1579–1870. London: Dawsons, 1927. Reprinted 1974.

Compiled from the maps in the British Library, this bibliography arranges the maps in date order, with subsequent editions under the main entry, and not according to county. This is convenient if a map is being dated, but not if maps of a particular county at a specified time are being sought.

Since Chubb was first published, many additional atlases have been located. Details of these are to be found in:

Local Studies

Rogers, E. M. LARGE SCALE COUNTY MAPS OF THE BRITISH ISLES 1596–1850: A UNION LIST. 2nd ed. Oxford: Bodleian Library, 1971.

This book begins with an introduction on how the large-scale county surveys were made, and the type of information which these maps can give the historian. The maps themselves are listed by county, each entry giving the date of publication; scale and surveyor; and libraries holding copies.

A third method of arranging a map bibliography is that used in:

Skelton, R. A. COUNTY ATLASES OF THE BRITISH ISLES 1579–1850. London: Carta Press, 1970.

The maps in this bibliography are arranged chronologically, thus enabling those of a particular date to be traced easily, but not if a specific county is required, as there is no index. The individual entries are very detailed, enabling different editions of the same map to be identified.

In addition to general lists of maps, there are important lists relating to specific areas. An example is:

Chubb, T. A DESCRIPTIVE CATALOGUE OF THE PRINTED MAPS OF GLOUCESTER 1577–1911. Gloucester: Bristol and Gloucester Archaeological Society, 1912.

The entries in this catalogue are arranged chronologically, each entry giving the full title of the map; its scale; imprint; and information necessary to identify various editions. Many similar lists were produced before 1939, and are listed in Harley.[62]

For Ordnance Survey maps a valuable guide is:

Harley, J. B. THE HISTORIAN'S GUIDE TO ORDNANCE SURVEY MAPS. London: Standing Conference for Local History, 1964.

Harley takes the reader through the various editions of the smaller-scale OS maps before dealing with the larger-scale town plans, which are especially important to the urban historian. Not only does he include a brief history of the OS, but he also carefully dates the main edition of each scale. Instead of listing the larger town plans, he provides maps on which the plans are marked, together with the date of the map.

Maps are the only form of non-book material for which there is any reasonable bibliographical information. However, they constitute only a small part of the non-book material in some libraries. Increasingly, local studies libraries are building up collections of illustrative material, especially **photographs**. Not only can these show changes over a period of time, they can also be used for information on costume, architectural detail, street furniture, advertisements and posters, transport and events. Often several types of information can be found on the same photograph. The most effective way to discover what an illustration can yield is to study it for several minutes, and list the information that is seen.[63] Even modern photographs are important, as towns and villages change rapidly and familiar landmarks disappear. An account of a modern photographic record survey and an assessment of it after 21 years is to be found in the *Manchester Review* in two articles—*The Manchester photographic survey*[64] and *Twenty years of continuous record survey*.[66] Most illustrations collections are local in nature, and hence little attention has been paid to recording where various collections are and what their coverage is. Two publications which have attempted to list the various collections are:

Barley, M. W. A GUIDE TO BRITISH TOPOGRAPHICAL COLLECTIONS. London: Council for British Archaeology, 1974.

Wall, J. DIRECTORY OF BRITISH PHOTOGRAPHIC COLLECTIONS. London: Royal Photographic Society, 1977.

Barley's book concentrates mainly on collections of prints, although he does refer to collections of photographs and postcards. It is arranged on a county basis with individual towns listed. He includes not only collections in libraries, but also those in art galleries. There is also a useful index of illustrations which are not housed in the county they relate to.

Wall's book, on the other hand, relates to photographic collections, and is arranged by subject. This is satisfactory if a subject approach is required, but not if information on what an organization has in its collections is needed.

Within any local studies collection there is a large body of material which it is difficult to categorize. Often it is loosely called **ephemera** or 'miscellaneous', and it includes such diverse items as play-bills, broadsheets, tickets, invitations, election literature, and bill-headings. Ephemera is hard to define, but the Working Party on the Collecting and Recording of Ephemera and Minor Publications did agree on the following definition:

> 'material carrying a verbal message, produced by printing or illustrative processes, but not published in the standard book or periodical form. It has one or more of the following characteristics: often it is produced in connection with a particular event or item of interest and not intended to survive the topicality of its message; it is often available without charge, sometimes on a local specialised or personal basis; it exhibits the widest possible variation, although it is normally printed on paper, textile or similar material; it does not lend itself to standard library processes of acquisition, recording or storage, but it is classifiable; its value can be factual, illustrative, typographical or more broadly aesthetic, or any combination of these depending on the terms of reference of the collection.'[67]

It is not possible to list every type of ephemera, but many examples are to be found in *Printed ephemera*,[68] *Collecting printed ephemera*[69] and *Ephemera of travel and transport*.[70] There are also two books which look at the problems of ephemera and its collection:

Clinton, A. PRINTED EPHEMERA: COLLECTION, ORGANISATION, ACCESS. London: Bingley, 1981.

Rickards, M. THIS IS EPHEMERA: COLLECTING PRINTED THROWAWAYS. Newton Abbot: David and Charles, 1977.

After a general introduction on ephemera and its problems, Clinton looks at the ephemera produced in three distinct fields. He deals with the collecting policies as well as the use to which this material can be put. Rickards' book, on the other hand, is intended

Local Studies

for the private collector, but he does provide a useful indication of where ephemera can be found and the wide range of material that constitutes the subject field.

A source of information which must not be forgotten is **tape recording**. The advent of the cassette recorder has made it possible for libraries to build up collections of reminiscences, sounds, and eye-witness accounts for use by future generations of historians. The case for oral history is put in Thompson's *The voice of the past*[71] whilst the journal of the Oral History Society, *Oral History*,[72] gives an indication of the work that is currently being undertaken.

Often, the amateur can be put off by technical jargon, but this problem has been partly overcome by the publication of:

Howarth, K. AN INTRODUCTION TO SOUND RECORDING FOR THE ORAL HISTORIAN AND SOUND ARCHIVIST. Radcliffe: The Author, 1977.

This booklet introduces oral history and explains, in simple terms, some of the technical side of the work, including sound recording.

Archaeology is another area in which the local studies librarian should be aware of what is being published and what records exist. In many areas, sites and monuments records are being compiled either by museums, archaeological units, or planning departments. These records, which may be in card form or on computer printout, will give not only the locations of sites, but also contain additional information which the archaeologists have collected from many sources, both in the field and from documents. Books like Aston and Rowley's *Landscape archaeology*,[73] and Rogers and Rowley's *Landscape and documents*,[74] often give important information on the interpretation of documents and records which the local studies librarian will find useful in assisting readers.

Archaeologists are increasingly becoming interested in standing buildings as well as remains below ground. This interest is also to be found amongst the general public, especially when it comes to protecting threatened buildings. Useful guides to the law relating

Local Studies

to the protection of buildings are *A guide to historic building law*,[75] and *Historic buildings and planning policies*,[76] which set out in a comprehensible form the current legislation on this subject.

Before anyone can hope to get to know a locality, it is essential that all local guides to sources are fully investigated. The more important guides to these are the books by Stephens, Rogers and Carter, together with the *Local Historian*. The section recommending further reading, at the end of this chapter, mentions relatively few books, and should be taken in conjunction with the bibliography in Carter.

REFERENCES AND CITATIONS

1. Galbraith, V. H. *An introduction to the study of history*. London: Watts, 1964. 35.
2. Everitt, A. *New avenues in English local history*. Leicester: Leicester University Press, 1970. 5.
3. Stephens, W. B. *Sources for English local history*. 2nd ed. Cambridge: Cambridge University Press, 1981. 1.
4. Essex Libraries. *History on your Essex doorstep*. Colchester: Essex Local Studies Library, 1982.
5. Dunning, R. *Local history for beginners*. Rev ed. Chichester: Phillimore, 1980. xi.
6. Iredale, D. *Discovering local history*. Aylesbury: Shire Publications, 1973. 3.
7. Lancashire Library. *A directory for local historians in the County Palatine of Lancaster*. 3rd ed. Preston: Lancashire Library, 1977.
8. Gibson, J. and Peskett, P. *Record offices: how to find them*. 2nd ed. Plymouth: Federation of Family History Societies, 1982.
9. *Agricultural history review*. Reading: British Agricultural History Society. 1953– . 5 per annum.
10. *Urban history yearbook*. Leicester: Leicester University Press, 1974– . Annual.
11. Elton, G. R. *Annual bibliography of British and Irish history*. London: Royal Historical Society, 1976– . Annual.
12. *Antiquaries Journal*. London: Society of Antiquaries. 1921–
13. Formerly the *Amateur Historian*.
14. This body has taken over from the Standing Conference for Local History the responsibility for publishing the *Local Historian*.
15. *Amateur Historian*. Vol 1, No 1. 1.
16. British Library Reference Division. *Reader guide no. 6 English places: sources of information*. London: British Library Reference Division, 1979.

References

17. Corns, A. R. *Bibliotheca Lincolniensis*. Lincoln: Morton, 1904.
18. Simms, R. *Bibliotheca Staffordiensis*. Lichfield: The author, 1894.
19. Douch, R. *Handbook of local history: Dorset with supplement and corrections*. Bristol: Bristol University Extra Mural Department, 1961.
20. Hodgson, H. W. *A bibliography of the history and topography of Cumberland and Westmorland*. Carlisle: Cumberland, Westmorland and Carlisle Archives Committee, 1968.
21. Library Association Eastern Branch. *East Anglian bibliography*. 1960– . Quarterly.
22. A full account of the series is to be found in Pugh, R. B. *The Victoria county history of the counties of England*. London: Institute of Historical Research, 1970. See also Pugh, R. B. The Victoria county histories. *Local Historian*, 13 (1). 15–22.
23. *Victoria county history of Essex: bibliography*. London: Institute of Historical Research, 1959.
24. Bonser, W. *A Romano-British bibliography*. Oxford: Blackwell, 1964. 2 vols.
25. Bonser, W. *An Anglo-Saxon and Celtic bibliography*. Oxford: Blackwell, 1957. 2 vols.
26. Council for British Archaeology. *Archaeology bibliography for Great Britain and Ireland*. London: CBA, 1949– . Annual. This bibliography is to be discontinued and replaced by an enlarged *British archaeological abstracts*, which is also published by the Council for British Archaeology.
27. *Guide to the contents of the Public Record Office*. Rev ed. London: HMSO, 1963–1968. 3 vols.
28. Public Record Office. *Leaflets*. 2 vols. Compiled from individual leaflets.
29. Galbraith, V. H. *An introduction to the use of public records*. Oxford: Oxford University Press, 1963.
30. For a full list of calendars see Mullins, *Texts and calendars*. 16–36.
31. Royal Commission on Historical Manuscripts. *Guide to the reports on collections of manuscripts*. London: HMSO, 1914. 3 vols; and *Guide to the reports of the Royal Commission 1911–57*. London: HMSO, 1966. 4 vols.
32. Storey, R. and Druker, J. *Guide to the modern records centre, University of Warwick Library*. University of Warwick Occasional Publications No 2. Coventry: Warwick University, 1977.
33. *Trade union records of Greater Manchester: a guide to their locations*. Manchester: Manchester Studies, 1981.
34. Ranger, F. The National Register of Archives. *Journal of the Society of Archivists*, 3. 452–62.
35. Dibben, A. *Title deeds*. London: Historical Association, 1971. Cornwall, J. *How to read old title deeds*. Shalfleet Manor: Pinhorns, 1964.

Local Studies

36. Emmison, F. G. and Gray, I. *County records*. London: Historical Association, 1974.
37. Evans, E. J. *Tithes and the tithe commutation act 1836*. London: Standing Conference for Local History, 1978.
38. Beckett, J. V. *Local taxation: national legislation and the problems of enforcement*. London: Standing Conference for Local History, 1980.
39. Harvey, J. H. *Sources for the history of houses*. London: British Records Association, 1974.
40. Cheney, C. R. *Handbook of dates for students of local history*. London: Royal Historical Society, 1970.
41. *Illustrated London News 1842–   .* London.
42. *The Builder 1842–1966*.
43. Woodworth, D. P. *Guide to current British journals*. 2nd ed. London: Library Association, 1977. 2 vols.
44. *The Daily Telegraph*, for instance, has stories in the northern edition printed in Manchester, which do not appear in the edition published in London.
45. *Newspapers first published before 1900 in Lancashire, Cheshire, and the Isle of Man*. London: Library Association—Reference, Special and Information Section North West Group, 1964.
46. Goss, C. W. F. *The London directories 1677–1855*. London: Archer, 1932.
47. Radmore, D. F. and S. *Guide to directories of the West Midlands to 1850*. London: Library Association—Reference, Special and Information Section West Midlands Section, 1971.
48. Horrocks, S. (ed.) *Lancashire directories 1684–1957*. Manchester: Joint Committee on the Lancashire Bibliography, 1968.
49. Hamilton-Edwards, G. *In search of ancestry*. Rev ed. London: Phillimore, 1974.
50. Willes, A. J. *Genealogy for beginners*. 2nd ed. London: Phillimore, 1970.
51. Camp, A. J. *Tracing your ancestors*. Rev ed. London: Gifford, 1970.
52. A useful introduction to monumental inscriptions is Jones, J. *How to record graveyards*. London: Council for British Archaeology and Rescue, 1976.
53. See also *A simplified guide to probate jurisdiction: where to look for wills*. 2nd ed. Plymouth: Federation of Family History Societies, 1982.
54. *Parish register copies*. London: Phillimore, 1971, 2 vols.
55. Office of Population, Censuses and Surveys. *Guide to census reports: Great Britain 1801–1966*. London: HMSO, 1977.
56. Lawton, R. (ed.) *The census and social structure*. London: Cass, 1978.
57. *Local population studies*, 1947–   . Twice yearly.
58. *Dictionary of national biography*. London: Oxford University Press, 1961. 28 vols to 1960.

Further Reading

59. Boase, F. *Modern English biography.* 2nd imp. London: Cass, 1965. 6 vols.
60. *Bulletin of the Institute of Historical Research*, **34**, 1961. 55–66.
61. *Amateur Historian*, **7**, 6–8; **8**, 2, 3, 5.
62. Harley, J. B. *Maps for local historians.* 78–80.
63. Makepeace, C. E. Dating and locating unidentified photographs. In: *Proceedings and papers of 1981 symposium of the European Society for the History of Photography.* Bath.
64. Milligan, H. The Manchester photographic survey. *Manchester Review*, **8**, 1958. 193–204.
65. Makepeace, C. E. Twenty-one years of continuous record survey. *Manchester Review*, **12**, 1972. 43–8.
66. Established at a joint meeting of the Library Association Local Studies Group and the Standing Conference for Local History in November 1977.
67. Interim report October 1979.
68. Lewis, J. *Printed ephemera.* London: Faber, 1969.
69. Lewis, J. *Collecting printed ephemera.* London: Studio Vista, 1976.
70. Anderson, J. and Swinglehurst, E. *Ephemera of travel and transport.* London: New Cavendish Books, 1981.
71. Thompson, P. *The voice of the past: oral history.* Oxford: Oxford University Press, 1978.
72. *Oral History.* Colchester: Oral History Society, 1972– .
73. Aston, M. and Rowley, T. *Landscape archaeology.* Newton Abbot: David and Charles, 1974.
74. Rogers, A. and Rowley, T. *Landscapes and archaeology.* London: Standing Conference for Local History, 1974.
75. Peace, D. *A guide to historic buildings law.* Cambridge: Cambridge County Council, 1974.
76. Peace, D. *Historic buildings and planning policies.* London: Council for British Archaeology, 1979.

SUGGESTIONS FOR FURTHER READING

Bagley, J. J. *Historical interpretations.* Newton Abbot: David and Charles, 1972. 2 vols.

Brunskill, R. W. *Illustrated handbook of vernacular architecture.* London: Faber, 1971.

Brunskill, R. W. *A systematic procedure for recording vernacular architecture.* Vernacular Architecture Group, 1975.
This pamphlet contains useful information on architectural detail. It has also been published in the *Transactions of the Ancient Monuments Society*, **13**, 1965–6.

Brunskill, R. W. *Traditional buildings of Britain.* London: Gollancz, 1981.

Local Studies

Buckley, K. A. *British ancestry tracing.* Sutton Coldfield: The author, 1978.

Burkett, J. and Morgan, T. S. *Special materials in libraries.* London: Library Association, 1963.
Chapters 7 and 8 deal with local history and maps.

Camp, A. J. *Wills and their whereabouts.* Canterbury: Phillimore, 1963.

Carter, G. A. Libraries and local history. *The librarian and book world*, **45** (7–8), Aug/Sept 1956.

Cave, L. C. *The smaller English house: its history and development.* London: Hale, 1981.

Celoria, F. *Teach yourself local history.* London: English Universities Press, 1958.

Child, M. *English church architecture: a visual guide.* London: Batsford, 1981.

Cook, T. G. *Local studies and the history of education.* London: Methuen, 1972.

Crafts Advisory Council. *Conservation source book.* London: Crafts Advisory Council, 1979.
This contains the names and addresses of organizations involved in many aspects of conservation. There is also a section on archives and books. A handy reference tool.

Currer-Briggs, N. and Gambier, R. *Debrett's family historian: a guide to tracing your ancestry.* London: Debrett/Webb and Bower, 1981.

Dymond, D. *Archaeology for the local historian.* London: Historical Association, 1967.

Dymond, D. *Writing local history: a practical guide.* London: Bedford Square Press, 1981.

Eden, P. *Small houses in England 1520–1820.* London: Historical Association, 1976.

Field, J. *Discovering place-names.* Princes Risborough: Shire Publications, 1980.

Field, J. *English field names: a dictionary.* Newton Abbot: David and Charles, 1972.

Finberg, H. P. R. *The local historian and his theme.* Leicester: Leicester University Press, 1952.

Finberg, H. P. R. and Skipp, V. H. T. *Local history: objective and pursuit.* Newton Abbot: David and Charles, 1967.

Fisher, J. L. *A mediaeval farming glossary.* London: Standing Conference for Local History, 1968.

Galbraith, V. H. *An introduction to the study of history.* London: Watts, 1964.

Hall, R. de Z. *A bibliography on vernacular architecture.* Newton Abbot: David and Charles, 1972.
Useful entries, but no place index. It is necessary to check regional entries as well as the general entries.

Further Reading

Harvey, R. *Genealogy for librarians*. London: Bingley, 1982.
Hobbs, J. L. *Libraries and the material of local history*. London: Grafton, 1949.
Hoskins, W. G. *English landscapes*. London: BBC, 1973.
Hoskins, W. G. *Fieldwork in local history*. 2nd ed. London: Faber, 1982.
Hoskins, W. G. *One man's England*. London: BBC, 1978.
Hoskins, W. G. *The making of the English landscape*. London: Hodder and Stoughton, 1955.
Iredale, D. *Enjoying archives*. Newton Abbot: David and Charles, 1973.
Kirby, A. *A guide to historical periodicals in England and Wales*. London: Historical Association, 1970.
Matthews, C. M. *Your family history*. London: Lutterworth Press, 1976.
Mawer, A. *The chief elements used in English place-names*. Cambridge: English Place-name Society. Vol 1, Pt 2. Cambridge University Press, 1971.
Mawer, A. and Stenton, F. M. *An introduction to the survey of English place-names*. Cambridge: English Place-name Society. Vol 1, Pt 1. Cambridge University Press, 1926.
Merseyside Archaeological Society. *Recording vernacular buildings*. Liverpool: Merseyside Archaeological Society, 1981.
Mumby, L. M. *Short guide to records*. London: Historical Association, 1972.
Neuberg, V. E. *The past we see to-day*. Oxford: Oxford University Press, 1972.
Newton, K. C. *Mediaeval local records*. London: Historical Association, 1971.
Owen D. M. *The records of the established Church of England*. London: British Records Association, 1970.
Pannell, J. P. M. *Techniques of industrial archaeology*. Newton Abbot: David and Charles, 1966.
  Contains a useful introduction to the subject and includes a chapter on sources. This is the first volume of a series covering the industrial archaeology of the country on a regional basis.
Parker, V. *The English house in the 19th century*. London: Historical Association, 1970.
Pearce, C. G. and Mills, D. R. Census enumerators' books: an annotated bibliography based substantially on the 19th century census enumerators' books. Milton Keynes, Open University, 1982.
Perry, G. A., Jones, E. and Hammersley, A. *A handbook of environmental studies*. London: Blandford, 1971.
Phillimore Bookshop, Catalogue no. 10 (new series) 1983–1984. Chichester, Phillimore, 1983.
Platt, C. *Mediaeval archaeology in England*. Shalfleet Manor: Pinhorn, 1969.

Local Studies

Despite its title, this is a useful bibliographical work drawing attention to some of the sources mediaeval archaeologists use.

Reaney, P. H. *Origins of English place names*. London: Routledge, 1960.

Riden, P. Local history for beginners. London, Batsford. 1983.

Rogers, A. *Group projects in local history*. London: Dawson, 1977.

A very useful work, well illustrated, with sections by individual specialists. There is a very useful bibliography, and many references in the text.

Smith, A. H. *The place name elements*. London: English Place-name Society, 25 and 26.

Smith, J. F. *A critical bibliography of building conservation history* . . . London: Mansell, 1978.

Very useful, as it contains many entries for local places which might not be recorded elsewhere. There is also an index of places.

Smith, J. T. and Yates, E. M. On dating of English houses from external evidence. *Field Studies*, **2** (5), 1968.

Standing Conference for Local History. *Hedges and local history*. London: Standing Conference for Local History, 1971.

Thirsk, J. *Sources of information on population 1500–1760: unexplored in local records*. Canterbury: Phillimore, 1965.

15

Current General Bibliographies

Richard H. A. Cheffins

Bibliographies are central to all aspects of reference librarianship in all types of libraries, but 'bibliography' is too large a subject to be dealt with in a single chapter. Subject or topic bibliographies are discussed elsewhere, as are retrospective bibliographies, or rather bibliographies of older material, as all bibliographies must be considered retrospective in some sense. Here are considered those serial bibliographies not seriously limited in subject scope and covering, on an on-going basis, the output of a whole country or, in some instances, a larger entity. These are of two types—national bibliographies and trade bibliographies—to be defined later. National bibliographies attempt to list all publications in scope that have been published since the previous issue; some bibliographies issued by the book trade also attempt this (eg *Cumulative book index*), but more usually they aim to list all publications in scope available (ie in print) at the time of publication (eg *Books in print*).

According to this dichotomy, a **national bibliography** could be defined as a bibliography produced primarily by or for the library world rather than the book trade. This, empirically, is not untrue but it is not a satisfactory definition. In *Guidelines for the national bibliographic agency and the national bibliography,* produced for Unesco by the IFLA International Office for UBC as a result of

Current General Bibliographies

the International Congress on National Bibliographies, Paris, 1977, it is stated:

> 'The national bibliography can be defined as the cumulation of the authoritative and comprehensive records of the national imprint of a country, published in printed form (and/or produced in other physical forms, such as catalogue cards, machine-readable tapes) regularly, and with the least possible delay. By *authoritative*, it is implied that the records have been made by a responsible organisation within a country, taking account of all possible national sources relating to authorship, publishing background, production date, etc. By *comprehensive*, it is implied that the records of each publication include [sic] the maximum of information details about that publication which can be required in a wide range of bibliographic activities'.[1]

This is a somewhat theoretical definition and begs some questions; a more pragmatic definition is to be found in British Standard BS5408, 1976—'National bibliography: a bibliography listing comprehensively publications issued, or distributed in significant quantity, in a particular country, and sometimes also publications, wherever issued, in the principal languages of the country. The term nowadays tends to be confined to the systematic listing of material received by legal deposit in a copyright library'. From these definitions, a bibliography may be considered a 'national bibliography' if it is national in scope, issued by a competent authority, comprehensive and up to date, and of sufficient detail to satisfy a wide variety of library uses. In this imperfect world the latter criteria should be considered more as goals than as requirements.

By contrast, the **trade bibliographies** considered here are more easily defined. Given the scope of this chapter, these are the serial bibliographies produced commercially by the book trade and primarily for the book trade (though widely used in libraries) covering the output of one or more countries. Lists of books in print predominate.

NATIONAL BIBLIOGRAPHIES

The records of publications in national bibliographies are usually made from copies received by legal deposit and are increasingly intended for re-use in library catalogues. In the context of Universal Bibliographic Control (UBC), a programme initiated by the International Federation of Library Associations and Institutions (IFLA) and supported by Unesco, the 'responsible organisation' referred to above is usually the national bibliographic agency, a unit normally within the national library with the right of legal deposit. Most printed national bibliographies now available are classified lists as recommended by the International Congress on National Bibliographies—recording monographs, first issues of serials and government publications as a minimum.[2] Other types of material such as maps, music, journal articles or theses may also be included, sometimes in separately issued supplements or in parallel publications.

The ideal printed national bibliography is one that appears promptly, with a complete record of all the recent output of information material in all forms produced in a country, and arranged in such a way and with such indexes as to permit items to be traced by author, subject or title. The International Congress established minimum standards for the presentation, content and arrangement of national bibliographies. Nevertheless, variety in national bibliographies persists because of the great variety in the size of the publishing output and of the bibliographic resources that exist in different countries; some bibliographies are not based on legal deposit, or are not compiled using those standard cataloguing and classification systems which assist the subsequent partial or complete re-use of records by libraries nationally and internationally.

Use

Provided that a national bibliography is current, its primary use is likely to be for **selection**. In public libraries, where new books are in great demand, a weekly bibliography (only practical where there is a large output to cover) is of great benefit to the acquisitions

Current General Bibliographies

department. In other libraries, national bibliographies, native and foreign, may be circulated to all the staff (library or academic) for selection purposes. Libraries may subscribe to a range of national bibliographies—to cover the languages they collect, to learn of new books for ethnic communities served by a public library, or foreign academic books needed in a university library. Unfortunately, few national bibliographies produced in developing countries appear promptly enough to avoid books frequently being out of print by the time selection takes place in a library.

The full cataloguing details usually found in national bibliographies enable the acquisitions staff to submit orders to booksellers confident that the ordering details are accurate. Some national bibliographies also include, at least in the annual cumulations, lists of publishers' addresses, which can be particularly useful for locating minor publishers. In countries where sophisticated automated cataloguing systems are available, it is frequently possible to obtain, at the time of ordering, the catalogue records for national publications as well as those from other selected national databases usually derived from national bibliographies. These records may be in card form, on machine-readable tapes or in microform depending on the type of catalogue preferred.

Cataloguing staff use national bibliographies (printed or machine-readable) either for whole records, that is for cataloguing copy, or for parts of records—for checking headings, classification numbers or forms of transliteration.

Interlibrary loans staff will make frequent use of national bibliographies to verify the bibliographic details of items requested. As the lending library should not be put to the additional inconvenience of such checking, the borrowing library should complete this important task before initiating the request. With the increasing use of ISBN union lists maintained on automated databases on which library locations are also noted, it is often only the ISBN for which interlibrary loans staff will be looking in a national bibliography.

Reference enquiry staff will use national bibliographies to supplement the existing resources of the library—to assist a reader with information about books (not in the library's catalogue) by a specific author or on a specific subject, or on publishing trends in a particular country. Increasingly, with national bibliographies becoming available in machine-readable form, especially where access is via a terminal online, reference staff can tackle more complicated queries, which it would be impossible, or at least very time-consuming, to undertake, using printed sources; for instance a request for a list of recent books translated from Russian to French. Only a computerized system can exploit to the full the details of cataloguing and coding which make up the comprehensive bibliographic record in modern national bibliographies and which can be manipulated to answer complex enquiries.

National bibliographies seldom record the individual contents of the items they list. For example, many national bibliographies list the first issues, title changes, and sometimes the last issues of serials, but not individual articles within them. Ironically, when a national bibliography does include journal articles, these are often *foreign* articles on subjects of national interest. By and large, the secondary information services in their printed abstracting and indexing volumes or online services remain the first-line approach for checking the bibliographic details of serial articles.

The final and enduring use for a national bibliography is to provide the permanent **definitive record** of a country's publishing output. As time goes on, the bibliography in its growing database or, in printed form in its cumulative volumes, becomes an increasingly useful starting point for a literature search for academic research. Also, as more and more countries adopt national bibliographies, as existing bibliographies improve their coverage, and as these bibliographies harmonize their style, format and record content, the elusive goal of UBC draws closer and individual bibliographies become components in a truly universal bibliography.

Coverage

Although the International Congress recommended that each issue of a national bibliography should give details of its coverage, most bibliographies at present give little or no such indication. It is, therefore, difficult to know for certain the range of inclusion and exclusion in many national bibliographies—one may search in vain

Current General Bibliographies

for an item, unaware that the bibliography excludes that category of material. One of the background documents for the Congress, *A survey of the contents of existing national bibliographies* by R. H. A. Cheffins,[3] was a study which includes a ranking list of categories of material in such bibliographies. Although several years old now, its findings are unlikely to have been much altered in the interval. Although many national bibliographies include, in addition to monographs and periodicals, material like maps, theses, and printed music, audiovisual materials such as recorded music, prints and films are seldom included, and categories such as videotapes, cassettes or wallcharts virtually not at all. In part this reflects the demands of the users of national bibliographies—most libraries feel a greater need for the records of books than of wallcharts—but the precise scope of the coverage of national bibliographies has been the subject of much debate recently.[4] It is as well to check whether a country's output of some of these categories is recorded elsewhere either in parallel bibliographies issued by the national bibliographic agency, or even by other organizations (patents, for example, are well controlled bibliographically, but by national patent offices). Some national bibliographies place a restriction on the size of publications recorded (eg nothing under five pages), or exclude items issued free. Because there is no detailed standard for material to be recorded except the recommendations of the International Congress which were for standards of *minimum* coverage only, there will be inconsistencies for some time to come (until the scope of legal deposit has been uniformly widened) between national bibliographies regarding their coverage.

National bibliographies, besides being defective in the coverage of *national* output, may also include material that may strictly be considered out of scope, that is foreign material—material published abroad about the country, by one of its nationals or in its language; publications of countries with which there is some propinquity or historic links; or publications printed in the country, but published abroad. Thus New Zealand's national bibliography includes material published abroad on New Zealand; that of Luxembourg includes works published abroad by Luxembourgeois authors; those of both Germanies attempt to cover all German-language publications, as does that of France for French-language

National Bibliographies

publications; that of Senegal includes publications of nearby Mali; and that of the UK includes publications of the Irish Republic (whose own national bibliography includes Northern Irish publications); and that of Hong Kong includes a multitude of foreign publications printed in Hong Kong.

A recent development has been the rise of **regional bibliographies**, that is, bibliographies covering a group of adjacent countries, not bibliographies of regions within countries—though the latter also exist (eg *Bibliographie du Québec*). The Library of Congress's *Accessions lists* can be considered a form of regional bibliography—taking the place of absent bibliographies or supplementing existing ones. Other regional bibliographies, however, depend on the individual contributions of the countries linked together in such a project. Such countries may co-operate for reasons of linguistic, political, geographic or cultural ties in issuing this type of bibliography. In this way, a greater impact can be made with a substantial regional bibliography rather than several less significant smaller national bibliographies—a rare case of the total being greater than the sum of its parts. The cost of compilation and publication can be shared, and so the burden reduced. There is, however, likely to be some sacrifice in currency. The major regional bibliographies are *The bulletin of Arab publications* (Cairo: ALECSO, 1972–) which covers 18 countries which are members of the Arab League; *Bibliografia Latinoamericana* (Bogotá: CERLAL, 1974–) which is effectively a regional bibliography, though not a co-operative venture of the 18 Spanish-speaking countries of Latin America whose publications are included; and the *CARICOM bibliography* (Georgetown, Guyana: CARICOM Secretariat, 1977–) which covers 13 territories including Barbados, Guyana, Jamaica, and Trinidad and Tobago, whose national bibliographies not only exist in their own right but form components of the *CARICOM bibliography*. A new regional bibliography is the *South Pacific bibliography* which covers 25 territories (22 if the Trust Territory of the Pacific Islands is still considered a single entity) and the indigenous peoples of three more—Australia, Hawaii (part of the USA) and New Zealand. Details of this project were given recently in *International cataloguing*.[5]

Current General Bibliographies
Frequency

As with coverage, there exists considerable diversity in the frequency of national bibliographies. The International Congress on National Bibliographies recommended quarterly issues as a minimum, with annual cumulations. On the other hand, countries with a large publishing output, such as the United Kingdom, the Soviet Union or the Federal Republic of Germany, issue weekly bibliographies with several intermediate and final cumulations—monthly, quarterly, semi-annual, annual, quinquennial, or a combination of these.

Weekly appearance is especially useful in the case of those bibliographies which include **cataloguing-in-publication (CIP) entries**. CIP programmes now operate to a greater or lesser extent in nearly twenty countries including Australia, Brazil, Canada, the Federal Republic of Germany (whose programme also covers Austria and German-speaking Switzerland), Malaysia, the UK, the Soviet Union and the USA, and they are joint ventures between publishers and national bibliographic authorities. They have two objectives—to provide basic cataloguing information to publishers in advance of publication so that this information can be printed in the book concerned, usually on the verso of the title-page (the copyright page); and to enable bibliographic data about new publications to appear in the national bibliography or similar listing, and any associated computerized databases in advance of publication. In the case of the United States, which lacks a national bibliography as such, the CIP data are included in the Library of Congress's MARC services.

CIP entries are created from the preliminary matter for forthcoming titles and other information supplied by publishers, and they are upgraded to full records on receipt of the published item which thereafter supersedes the CIP record in the national bibliography. The advantage of CIP is that it enables bibliographic agencies to avoid the inevitable delays in recording items in the national bibliography, enabling libraries using these bibliographies to select and order works before they have been published and to obtain them soon after publication. Thus libraries can maintain a current and up-to-date stock. CIP entries are usually identified as such in national bibliographies or are issued in separate supplements as is the case with the *Deutsche Bibliographie*.

A large number of national bibliographies are issued annually, due usually to the limited publishing output in the countries concerned or to the limited bibliographic resources of the agencies responsible. In the interest of currency, however, it is to be hoped that quarterly issues with annual cumulations, as recommended by the International Congress, may become the norm, and it is encouraging that several small national bibliographies that have been launched in the wake of the Congress, such as that of Papua New Guinea, have shown that such a programme is perfectly feasible, and even a country as small as The Gambia has managed a semi-annual frequency.

Currency

Closely related to the problems of frequency are those of currency. A constant criticism of national bibliographies has been their poor record of currency. In earlier times, when the compilation of the national bibliography was considered a more leisurely and scholarly activity, the need for prompt knowledge of new material was not as pressing as it is now. In some countries, the infrequent appearance of the national bibliography, coupled with the lack, or poor enforcement, of legal deposit, results in much material being out of print by the time it gets recorded in the national bibliography. Delays of up to six months and sometimes between one and five years in the appearance of records in some national bibliographies are common but, in countries with good bibliographical control, a delay of only a few weeks in the appearance of CIP or full bibliographic records is considered intolerable, and lessens the effectiveness of the bibliography. As has already been mentioned, public libraries especially feel the effects of poor currency in attempting to provide new books to readers. In many instances, librarians prefer to use commercial books-in-print services if available because, being dependent upon publishers' information and not on legal deposit, they appear more quickly and are more comprehensive, if less detailed, than national bibliographies as sources of advance information. So far as many national bibliographies are concerned, therefore, it is advisable, when checking the details of particular publications, to bear in mind the delay in the appearance of records there.

Forms of national bibliographies

All national bibliographies are published in **printed form**. Other forms, or more correctly services, are becoming available, but the printed national bibliography is still, and almost certainly will remain for the foreseeable future, of primary importance because of its ease of use by different kinds of users; its ease of production in countries with few technological resources; and its ready transmission to all parts of the world.

The first by-product of a national bibliography is usually a **catalogue card service** and some countries offer a comprehensive service in this respect. A newer and even more important development has been the availability of current, and sometimes retrospective, national bibliographic records in **machine-readable form**. Ultimately, as more national bibliographies are automated (and the bibliography in its printed form is generated from the larger machine-readable database), records will be available either by exchange or in a network. In the former case, exchange of national bibliographic records is usually aimed at cataloguing services. In the latter case, both the cataloguing and reference value of national bibliographies would be available through sophisticated automated systems.

One example of a co-operative bibliography which is the result of automated bibliographic production is *Books in English*. This is a merging of records for current books in English from BNB and the Library of Congress published in Britain and the United States. By definition, therefore, it excludes other-language books published in those countries and is thus not a full merging. There is some duplication in coverage and some variation in the forms of headings used. Libraries find *Books in English* useful for acquisitions and cataloguing purposes.

National Bibliographies

Countries without national bibliographies

Throughout the last thirty years the number of national bibliographies has steadily grown; this is made clear in successive quinquennial (originally decennial) Unesco surveys.[6] However, some countries continue to lack them, and, to that extent, UBC is still defective. The example which springs most readily to mind is that of the United States. Nevertheless, although a national bibliography in the formal sense as defined above is absent there, various substitutes exist which more than compensate. These include the *National union catalog* (NUC), the *Cumulative book index* (CBI), and the commercial in-print services listed below. Whereas the NUC by its very nature (a union catalogue of the holdings of US libraries) includes material in a variety of languages and scripts, the CBI provides a regular listing of English-language material wherever published (not just that published in the USA) which cumulates regularly. Its dictionary catalogue approach, providing access by authors, titles or subjects, makes it a useful tool which will often be the starting point for enquiries.

There are many gaps in the coverage of the world's publishing output. In the absence, especially in newer countries, of a library infrastructure, legislative backing for the deposit of publications, and, most importantly, a stable publishing and printing industry, a regular national bibliography is difficult to produce, though by no means impossible, as the checklist below will reveal. Sometimes, in countries lacking national bibliographies, their publications are covered in other services, for example by the national bibliographies of former metropolitan countries, or in special publications such as the Library of Congress's *Accessions Lists* for Indonesia, Malaysia, Singapore, Brunei, India and adjacent countries, the Middle East; and East Africa. Overlap is apparent in these services because some of these countries also produce their own national bibliographies. It is the lack of promptness, poor coverage (estimated as low as 40 per cent of output), and the need for a standardized catalogue record at the time that an item is acquired, which have caused the Library of Congress to undertake its own bibliographic control using field offices in the countries concerned. As local resources

Current General Bibliographies

are developed and improved, the need for those offices and the work they do should decline.

Other gaps concern the publications of intergovernmental organizations whose comprehensive recording of their own publications is erratic or sometimes virtually non-existent, as was shown by John Clews in his *Documentation of the UN system*.[7] Although some intergovernmental organizations, such as the United Nations, issue indexes to their publications, these services do not serve the other purposes of national bibliographies, such as the provision of comprehensive records for use in catalogues and the announcement of new material. It should be noted that the country acting as host to an intergovernmental organization may include its publications in its own national bibliography. A notable example is Switzerland, where many intergovernmental organizations have their headquarters.

IN-PRINT SERVICES

The range of materials covered by in-print services is now very large, and the traditional lists of books in print and current serials are being supplemented by services covering the reprint and the micro-publishing trades. This has added a new dimension to the records of the availability of material in hard-copy form with the advent of services bearing such seemingly incongruous titles as 'Microforms in print'.

In-print services are generally run by and for the book trade and therefore only flourish in countries, such as the United States, Britain, France and Japan where the trade is well developed. However, some noteworthy efforts have been made in both Latin America, where the American publisher Bowker issues *Libros en venta en Hispanoamerica y España*; and in Africa, where Hans Zell, the publisher of *African book publishing record*, has started to issue *African books in print*, which is intended to appear regularly with alternating English, African, and French material. There is inevitably some overlap between these services: many American publishers, for example, also publish in Britain and vice versa, and their publications will therefore appear in both (the American)

In-print Services

Books in print and in *British books in print*; while *Les livres disponibles* attempts to cover French-language material in 43 countries, including French-speaking African countries, when it is liable to duplicate *African books in print*.

In-print services are intended as book-selling tools and are therefore less detailed than national bibliographies; they usually provide only a line or two of essential information to facilitate the identification of items. But the usefulness of a listing in which current availability and not recent publication is the criterion for inclusion often makes in-print services the preferred source to national bibliographies for the acquisitions process. In fact the two services are complementary and are often used in combination.

More information about national bibliographies

There now exist perhaps as many as a hundred national bibliographies. Many of these are listed and analysed in Cheffins' *Survey of the contents of existing national bibliographies*,[8] Walford's *Guide to reference material*[9] and Sheehy's *Guide to reference books*.[10] The latter two also cover related bibliographies and in-print services. Unesco's *Bibliographic services throughout the world*[11] includes reports on current bibliographic activities in all member states, and updates the information in the bibliographic handbook of the same title.[12] Pomassl's *Synoptic tables*[13] provides a quick reference tool, though it is now beginning to date. Information on the national bibliographies of the Commonwealth is available in an annotated directory issued by the Commonwealth Secretariat, and recently produced in a revised edition.[14]

A checklist of national bibliographies, related bibliographies, and major in-print services

The following is an extensive, though not exhaustive, list of national bibliographies, other bibliographies serving substantially the purposes of a national bibliography, and major in-print services. They are arranged in a single alphabetical list, in order of country, with

Current General Bibliographies

regional bibliographies (as defined above) inter-filed under appropriate names such as Africa, Arab States, Caribbean Community or Pacific Islands. A few bibliographies too general to be categorized as national or even regional are grouped together at the end of the checklist under the heading 'international', although, strictly speaking, there are no comprehensive bibliographies or in-print services that can be considered truly international. Minimum details only are provided for each entry, and further information should be sought in the reference works mentioned above.

The situation concerning national bibliographies is in a constant state of flux. In general, changes tend to be for the better—new bibliographies being produced and others improved—but some setbacks occur (*see* Uganda below). This checklist, **within its limitations,** aims to be as accurate as possible, but some recent changes of names may have been overlooked, or new bibliographies missed.

Africa
AFRICAN BOOK PUBLISHING RECORD. H. M. Zell (*ed.*). London: Mansell, 1975– . Quarterly; supplement to—

AFRICAN BOOKS IN PRINT: an index by author, title and subject. London: Mansell, in association with Ife University Press, 1975– . Irregular; 3rd ed (2 vols) 1984.

Albania
BIBLIOGRAFIA KOMBËTARE E REPUBLIKËS POPULORE TË SHQIPËRISË: Libri Shqip. Tirana: Biblioteka Komëtare, 1958– . Quarterly.

Algeria
BIBLIOGRAPHIE DE L'ALGÉRIE, 1962– . Alger: Bibliothèque nationale, 1964– . Semi-annual.

Arab states
ACCESSIONS LIST: Middle East. Cairo: Library of Congress Office, 1958– . Monthly.

THE BULLETIN OF ARAB PUBLICATIONS, 1970. Cairo:

In-print Services

Arab League Educational, Cultural and Scientific Organization, Department of Documentation and Information, 1972– . Annual.

Argentina
BIBLIOGRAFÍA NACIONAL ARGENTINA EN CURSO. Buenos Aires: Biblioteca Nacional, 1971– . Semi-annual.

Australia
AUSTRALIAN NATIONAL BIBLIOGRAPHY, ISSN 0004-9816. Canberra: National Library of Australia, 1961– . Semimonthly with rolling four-monthly cumulations (January–April and January–August on microfiche, and January–December on microfiche and in hard copy).

Supplemented by *Australian government publications*, 1952– ; *Australian films*, 1959– ; *Current Australian serials*, 1963– ; and *Australian maps*, 1968– ; all currently issued by the National Library of Australia.

Austria
ÖSTERREICHISCHE BIBLIOGRAPHIE: Verzeichnis der österreichischen Neuerscheinungen, 1945– . Wien: Verband der österreichischen Buchhändler/Österreichischen Nationalbibliothek, 1946– . Semi-monthly, with quarterly and annual indexes.

Bangladesh
BANGLADESH NATIONAL BIBLIOGRAPHY. Dhaka: Directorate of Archives and Library, 1972– . Annual.

Barbados
NATIONAL BIBLIOGRAPHY OF BARBADOS. Bridgetown: Public Library, 1975– . Quarterly, with annual cumulations.

Belgium
BIBLIOGRAPHIE DE BELGIQUE = Belgische bibliografie. Bruxelles: Bibliothèque royale, 1875– . Monthly, with annual index.

Bénin
BIBLIOGRAPHIE DU BÉNIN, 1976/1977– . Porto Novo: Bibliothèque Nationale, 1978– . Annual (?).

Bolivia
BIBLIOGRAFÍA BOLIVIANA DEL AÑO. Cochabamba & La Paz: Editorial Los Amigos del Libro, 1963– . Annual.

Botswana
NATIONAL BIBLIOGRAPHY OF BOTSWANA. Gaborone: Botswana National Library Service, 1969– . Three issues a year, the final issue being an annual cumulation.

Brazil
BIBLIOGRAFIA BRASILEIRA MENSAL. Rio de Janeiro: Instituto Nacional do Livro, 1967– . Monthly.

Bulgaria
NATSIONALNA BIBLIOGRAFIIA NA NR BULGARIIA. Sofiia: Narodna Biblioteka 'Kiril i Metodii', 1974– . In eight series with varying frequencies, eg *Ser. 1 Bulgarski knigopis* [a continuation of a separate work of that title, 1897– .]. Fortnightly, with annual cumulations.

Cameroons
CAMEROON IMPRINTS: Bulletin du Centre de Diffusion du Livre Camerounais. Yaoundé: Le Centre, 1978– . Quarterly.

Canada
CANADIANA, 1950– . Ottawa: National Library of Canada, 1951– . Monthly, with a single combined issue for July/August; with annual cumulations.

Caribbean Community
CARICOM BIBLIOGRAPHY. Georgetown, Guyana: Caricom Secretariat, 1977–1978. Annual; 1979– . Semi-annual.

In-print Services

China (People's Republic)
CH'UAN-KUO HSIN SHU-MU. Beijing: Acquisition Library of the Bureau of Publication Administration, Ministry of Culture, 1951– . Monthly.

Colombia
ANUARIO BIBLIOGRÁFICO COLOMBIANO 'RUBEN PEREZ ORTIZ', 1951– . Bogotá: Instituto Caro y Cuervo, 1958– . Annual.

Costa Rica
ANUARIO BIBLIOGRÁFICO COSTARRICENSE. San José: Asociación Costarricense de Bibliotecarios, 1958– . Annual.

Cuba
BIBLIOGRAFÍA CUBANA. La Habana: Biblioteca Nacional 'José Marti', 1959/1962– . Annual.

Cyprus
BIBLIOGRAPHY OF CYPRUS: bibliographical bulletin. Nicosia: Library of the Pedagogical Academy, 1960– . Annual.

Czechoslovakia
BIBLIOGRAFICKÝ KATALOG ČSSR: České knihy. Praha: Státní Knihovna ČSR, 1922– . Weekly, with annual cumulations (there are eight other series in the bibliography, with frequencies varying from monthly to annual).

SLOVENSKÁ NÁRODNÁ BIBLIOGRAFIA: Bibliografický katalóg. Martin: Matica Slovenská, 1946– . Monthly, with annual cumulations.

Denmark
DANSK BOGFORTEGNELSE. København: Bibliotekscentralen, 1951– . Monthly, with quarterly and annual cumulations.
    A weekly list is published in the trade journal *Det Dansk Bogmarked*.

Current General Bibliographies

East Africa
ACCESSIONS LIST: Eastern Africa. Nairobi: Library of Congress Office, 1968– . Monthly.

Ecuador
BIBLIOGRAFÍA ECUATORIANA. Quito: Universidad Central del Ecuador, 1975– . Six issues per year, the final issue being the annual cumulation entitled *Anuario bibliografico Ecuatoriano*.

Egypt
EGYPTIAN PUBLICATIONS BULLETIN: a list of publications deposited in the National Library. Cairo: National Library Press, 1956– . Annual.

Ethiopia
ETHIOPIAN PUBLICATIONS: books, pamphlets, annuals and periodical articles published in Ethiopia. Addis Ababa: University of Addis Ababa, 1965– . Annual.

Fiji
FIJI NATIONAL BIBLIOGRAPHY. Lautoka: the Library Service of Fiji; Suva: University of the South Pacific Library, 1979– . Annual.

Finland
SUOMEN KIRJALLISUUS = Finlands litteratur = Finnish national bibliography, 1944/48– . Helsinki: Yliopiston Kirjasto, 1954– . Monthly with annual cumulations.

France
LIVRES-HEBDO. Paris: Éditions Professionelles du Livre, 1979– . (cover title: *Bibliographie de la France: bulletin du livre*). Weekly, with monthly (*Les livres du mois*), and quarterly (*Les livres du trimestre*) supplements.

This supersedes *Bibliographie de la France – Biblio*.

In-print Services

LES LIVRES DISPONIBLES. Paris: Cercle de la Librairie, 1977. 2 vols (author and title).

The Gambia
THE NATIONAL BIBLIOGRAPHY OF THE GAMBIA: current national bibliography. Banjul: National Library of The Gambia, 1978– . (cover title: *The Gambia national bibliography*). Semi-annual, the second issue being the annual cumulation.

Germany (German Democratic Republic)
DEUTSCHE NATIONALBIBLIOGRAPHIE und Bibliographie des im Ausland erschienen deutschsprachigen Schrifttums. Reihe A, Reihe B, Leipzig: Verlag für Buch- und Bibliothekswesen, 1931–1945, 1946– . Reihe C, 1968– . Reihe A (trade publications) weekly; Reihe B (non-trade publications) fortnightly, with quarterly and quinquennial cumulations; Reihe C (dissertations) monthly.

Germany (Federal Republic of Germany)
DEUTSCHE BIBLIOGRAPHIE. Frankfurt-am-Main: Deutsche Bibliothek, 1947– . Reihe A (trade publications) weekly, with monthly indexes, semi-annual and quinquennial cumulations; Reihe B (non-trade publications) fortnightly, with annual indexes; Reihe C (maps) quarterly with annual indexes; *Sofortdienst* (CIP) 1975– , with monthly and quarterly cumulations.
  Published as *Bibliographie der deutschen Bibliothek*, 1947–1952.

Ghana
GHANA NATIONAL BIBLIOGRAPHY, ISSN 0072-4378, 1965– . Accra: Ghana Library Board, 1968– . Annual.

Greece
HELLĒNIKA VIVLA = Greek books, 1975– . Athēnai: 'Manoutios', 1976– . Annual.

Guyana
GUYANESE NATIONAL BIBLIOGRAPHY: a subject list of new books printed in the Republic of Guyana based on the books

and non-book material deposited at the National Library. Georgetown: National Library, 1973–   . Quarterly, with annual cumulations.

Hong Kong
A CATALOGUE OF BOOKS PRINTED IN HONG KONG: being the special supplement No 4 to the Hong Kong Government Gazette. Quarterly.

Hungary
MAGYAR NEMZETI BIBLIOGRÁFIA. Budapest: National Szechényi Library, 1946–   . Semi-monthly, with annual cumulations entitled *Magyar Könyvészet*.

Iceland
ÍSLENZKA BÓKASKRÁ. Reykjavik: Landbókasafn Islands, 1974–   . Annual.

India
ACCESSIONS LIST: India, ISSN 0041-7734. New Delhi: Library of Congress Office, 1962–   . Monthly.

INDIAN NATIONAL BIBLIOGRAPHY, 1957–   . Calcutta: Central Reference Library 1958–   . Monthly, with annual cumulations.

Indonesia
BIBLIOGRAFI NASIONAL INDONESIA. Djakarta: National Bibliographical Centre, 1963–   . Quarterly.

Iran
NATIONAL BIBLIOGRAPHY: Iran publications. Tehran: National Library, 1963–   . Quarterly.

Irish Republic
IRISH PUBLISHING RECORD. Compiled by the School of Librarianship, University College, Dublin. Dublin, 1972–   . Annual.

In-print Services

Also includes Northern Irish publications.

Israel
KIRJATH SEPHER: bibliographical quarterly of the Jewish National and University Library. Jerusalem: Jewish National and University Library, 1924– . Quarterly, with annual indexes.

Italy
BIBLIOGRAFIA NAZIONALE ITALIANA. Firenze: Biblioteca Nazionale Centrale, 1958– . Monthly, with annual cumulations.

Ivory Coast
BIBLIOGRAPHIE DE LA CÔTE D'IVOIRE. Abidjan: Bibliothèque Nationale, 1970– . Annual.

Jamaica
JAMAICAN NATIONAL BIBLIOGRAPHY. Kingston: National Library of Jamaica, 1975– . Quarterly; the final issue of the year is an annual cumulation.

Japan
NOHON SHUHO. Tokyo: National Diet Library, 1955– . Weekly, with annual cumulation: *Zen Nihon shuppanbutsu somokuroku*, 1948/1949– . Tokyo: National Diet Library, 1951– .

NIHON SHOSEKI SOMOKUROKU (Japanese books in print). Tokyo: Nohon Nihon Shoseki Shippon Kyokai (Japanese Book Publishers Association), 1977– . Annual.

Kenya
KENYA NATIONAL BIBLIOGRAPHY, 1980– . Nairobi: Kenya National Library Service, Reference and Bibliographic Department, 1983– . Annual.

Korea (Republic of)
KOREAN NATIONAL BIBLIOGRAPHY. Seoul: Central National Library, 1968– . Annual.

Current General Bibliographies

Latin America
BOLETÍN BIBLIOGRÁFICO: Bibliografía latinoamericana, ISSN 0120-1204. Bogotá: Centro regional para el Fomento del Libro en America Latina, 1973–   . Quarterly.

FICHERO BIBLIOGRÁFICO HISPANOAMERICANO, ISSN 0015-0592. Buenos Aires: Turner Ediciones SRL, 1961–   .

LIBROS EN VENTA EN HISPANOAMERICA Y ESPAÑA, 2nd ed. Buenos Aires: Bowker, 1974. 2 vols. With supplements 1975–   . (published 1978–   .).

Luxembourg
BIBLIOGRAPHIE LUXEMBOURGEOISE. Luxembourg: Bibliothèque nationale, 1946–   . Annual.

Madagascar
BIBLIOGRAPHIE NATIONALE DE MADAGASCAR, 1970/1971–   . Antanarivo: Bibliothèque Universitaire et Bibliothèque Nationale, 1979–   .
Supersedes *Bibliographie annuelle de Madagascar.*

Malawi
MALAWI NATIONAL BIBLIOGRAPHY. Zomba: National Archives of Malawi, 1967–   . Annual.

Malaysia
BIBLIOGRAFI NEGARA MALAYSIA = Malaysian national bibliography, 1967–   . Kuala Lumpur: Perpustakaan Negara Malaysia, 1967–1974. Annual; 1975–   . Quarterly, with annual cumulation.

Mauritius
BIBLIOGRAPHY OF MAURITIUS. Port Louis: Archives Department, 1955–   . Annual.
Supplement in *Annual report of the Archives Department.*

In-print Services

Mexico
BIBLIOGRAFÍA MEXICANA. Mexico: Biblioteca Nacional, 1967– . Six issues per year.

Namibia (South West Africa)
NNB NAMIBISCHE NATIONAL-BIBLIOGRAPHIE = Namibian national bibliography, 1971/1975– . Basel: Basler Afrika Bibliographien, 1978– . Annual (?).

The Netherlands
BRINKMANS CUMULATIEVE CATALOGUS VAN BOEKEN. Amsterdam: Brinkman, 1840–1880; Leiden: Sijthoff, 1881– . Monthly, with annual cumulation.

New Zealand
NEW ZEALAND NATIONAL BIBLIOGRAPHY, ISSN 0028-8497. Wellington: National Library of New Zealand, 1967– . Monthly, with annual cumulations.

Nigeria
NATIONAL BIBLIOGRAPHY OF NIGERIA. Lagos: National Library of Nigeria, 1973– . Monthly, with semi-annual and annual cumulation.

Norway
NORSK BOKFORTEGNELSE, 1814/1847– . Oslo: Norsk Bokhandlerforening/Universitetsbiblioteket, 1848– . Weekly, with monthly, annual and quinquennial cumulations.

Pacific Islands
SOUTH PACIFIC BIBLIOGRAPHY, 1981– . Suva: University of the South Pacific Library, Pacific Information Centre, 1982– . Annual (but may in future be semi-annual).

Pakistan
ACCESSIONS LIST: Pakistan. Karachi: Library of Congress Office, 1962– . Monthly.

Current General Bibliographies

PAKISTAN NATIONAL BIBLIOGRAPHY, 1962– . Karachi: Government of Pakistan Press, 1966– . Annual.

Papua New Guinea
PAPUA NEW GUINEA NATIONAL BIBLIOGRAPHY. Boroko: Bibliographical Services Section, National Library Service of Papua New Guinea, 1981– . Quarterly, with annual cumulations.
Supersedes the University of Papua New Guinea's annual *New Guinea bibliography*, 1967–1980, now discontinued.

Paraguay
BIBLIOGRAFÍA NACIONAL PARAGUAYA, 1971–1977. Asunción: Universidad Nacional de Asunción, Escuela de Bibliotecologia, 1978.

Peru
BIBLIOGRAFÍA NACIONAL. Lima: Biblioteca Nacional, Instituto Nacional de Cultura, 1978– . Monthly (irregular).

Philippines
PHILIPPINE NATIONAL BIBLIOGRAPHY. Manila: National Library, 1974– . Six issues per year, with annual cumulations.

Poland
PRZEWODNIK BIBLIOGRAFICZNY. Warszawa: Biblioteka Narodowa, 1946– . Weekly, with monthly and annual indexes.

Portugal
BOLETIM DE BIBLIOGRAFIA PORTUGUESA. Lisboã: Biblioteca Nacional, 1937– . Monthly, with a separate annual bibliography published by the National Library.

Puerto Rico
ANUARIO BIBLIOGRÁFICO PUERTORRIQUENO. San Juan: Estado Libre Asociado de Puerto Rico, Departemento de Instrucción Publica, 1951-- . Annual.

In-print Services

Romania
BIBLIOGRAFIA REPUBLICII SOCIALISTE ROMÂNIA. Bucureşti: Biblioteca Centrala de Stat, 1952– . Six series with varying frequency, eg *Ser. 1: Cărţi, albume, hărţi*. Semimonthly.

ANUARUL CĂRŢII DIN ROMÂNIA, 1952– . Bucureşti: Biblioteca Centrala de Stat, 1957– . Annual.

Senegal
BIBLIOGRAPHIE DU SÉNÉGAL. Dakar: Archives du Sénégal, 1972– . Quarterly.
Includes publications of Mali.

Sierra Leone
SIERRA LEONE PUBLICATIONS: a list of books and pamphlets in English received by the Sierra Leone Library Board under the Publications 'Amendment' Act (1962). Freetown: Sierra Leone Library Board, 1964– . Annual.

Singapore
SINGAPORE NATIONAL BIBLIOGRAPHY. Singapore: National Library, 1967–1976. Annual; 1977– . Quarterly, with annual cumulations.

South Africa
SANB SUID-AFRIKAANSE NASIONALE BIBLIOGRAFIE = South African national bibliography, 1959– . Pretoria: State Library, 1960– . Quarterly, with annual cumulations.

Southeast Asia
ACCESSIONS LIST: Southeast Asia, ISSN 0090-2341. Jakarta: Library of Congress Office, 1961– . Monthly.

Spain
BIBLIOGRAFÍA ESPAÑOLA. Madrid: Instituto Bibliográfico Hispánico, 1969– . Monthly, with annual cumulations.

Current General Bibliographies

Sri Lanka
ACCESSIONS LIST: Ceylon. New Delhi: Library of Congress Office, 1967– .

SRI LANKA NATIONAL BIBLIOGRAPHY. Colombo: Ceylon National Library Service Board, 1963– . Monthly.

Swaziland
SWAZILAND NATIONAL BIBLIOGRAPHY, 1973/1976– . Kwaluseni: University of Botswana and Swaziland, University College of Swaziland, 1977– . Irregular (two issues published to date).

Sweden
SVENSK BOKFORTECKNING = Swedish national bibliography. Stockholm: Bibliografiska Institutet, 1953– . Monthly, with quarterly and annual cumulations.
A weekly list is published in *Svensk bokhandel*.

Switzerland
DAS SCHWEIZER BUCH = Le livre suisse = Il libro Svizzero. Bern: Schweizerische Landesbibliothek, 1901– . Reihe A (book-trade publications), semi-monthly; Reihe B (non-book-trade publications). Six issues per year; with annual indexes covering both parts.
Schweizer Bücherverzeichnis constitutes a quinquennial cumulation.

Taiwan (Republic of China)
CHINESE BIBLIOGRAPHY. Taipei: National Central Library, 1970– . Monthly.

Tanzania
TANZANIA NATIONAL BIBLIOGRAPHY: a list of publications printed in mainland Tanzania and deposited with the Legal Deposit Libraries in the country, 1969– . Dar es Salaam: Tanzania Library Services Board, 1970– . Annual.
Formerly (1969–1973) *Printed in Tanzania*.

In-print Services

Trinidad and Tobago
TRINIDAD AND TOBAGO NATIONAL BIBLIOGRAPHY. St Augustine: Central Library of Trinidad and Tobago and University of West Indies Library, 1975– . Quarterly, with annual cumulations.

Tunisia
BIBLIOGRAPHIE NATIONALE DE LA TUNISIE. Tunis: Bibliothèque Nationale, 1970– . Semi-annual.

Turkey
TÜRKIYE BIBLIYOGRAFYASI. Ankara: Mille Kütüphane Bibliyografya Enstitüsü, 1928– . Quarterly, with annual indexes.

Uganda
UGANDA BIBLIOGRAPHY. Kampala: Makarere University Library, 1965– . Quarterly (recently irregular).
    Forms part of the *Accessions bulletin* of Makarere University Library since No 55, Jan–Feb 1965.

UGANDA BIBLIOGRAPHY, 1961/1962– . Kampala: Uganda Society, 1963– . Annual (suspended or discontinued since the 1973 (published 1975) issue ?)
    Published in *Uganda Journal* since Vol 27, No 2, 1963.

USSR
KNIZHNAIA LETOPIS': Organ gosudarstvennoi biblioteki SSR. Moskva: Izdatel'stvo 'Kniga', 1907– . Weekly, with monthly supplements.
    There exist the full paraphernalia of national bibliographies in each of the constituent republics of the Soviet Union.

United Kingdom
BRITISH BOOKS IN PRINT: the reference catalogue of current literature. London: Whitaker, 1965– . Annual.
    Since February 1978 BBIP has been available on microfiche, updated and cumulated monthly; Whitaker produces other trade

Current General Bibliographies

bibliographies: *Paperbacks in print*, 1960–   , annual; and Whitaker's *Cumulative book list*, 1924–   , quarterly, with annual and quinquennial cumulations.

BRITISH NATIONAL BIBLIOGRAPHY. London: Council for the British National Bibliography (1950–1973), British Library, Bibliographic Services Division, 1974–   . Weekly, with monthly indexes and four-monthly and annual cumulations, also five multi-annual cumulations covering 1951–1970 for the classified section and 1950–1970 for the indexes.

Also covers the Irish Republic.

USA
BOOKS IN PRINT: an author/title/series index to the Publishers' trade list. New York: Bowker, 1948–   . Annual.

Updated by *Books in print on microfiche*, monthly, and *Books in print on microfiche – quarterly*; online from Dialog and BRS, July 1982–   . Bowker also produces *Publishers' weekly* (see below); and *Paperbound books in print*, annual in December with supplements in May and September; *Publishers' trade list annual*, 1873–   , annual; and *Subject guide to books in print*, 1957–   , annual.

CUMULATIVE BOOK INDEX: a world list of books in the English language. New York: Wilson, 1898–   . Monthly (except August), with intermediate and annual cumulations; also multi-annual (currently biennial) cumulations.

As its subtitle indicates, not confined to US publications.

GUIDE TO REPRINTS, ISSN 0072-8667. Kent, Connecticut: Guide to Reprints Inc, 1977–   . Annual.

PUBLISHERS' WEEKLY. New York: Bowker, 1872–   . Weekly. *American book publishing record* is the monthly, annual and quinquennial cumulation, 1960–   .

Uruguay
BIBLIOGRAFÍA URUGUAYA. Montevideo: Biblioteca del Poder Legislativo, 1962–   . Annual.

In-print Services

Venezuela
ANUARIO BIBLIOGRÁFICO VENEZOLANO. Caracas: Congress de la República, 1977– . Annual (irregular).

BIBLIOGRAFÍA VENEZOLANO. Caracas: El Centro Biblioteca Nacional, 1970– . Quarterly.

Yugoslavia
BIBLIOGRAFIJA JUGOSLAVIJE: knjige brošure i musikalije. Beograd: Bibliografski Institut FNRJ, 1950– . Monthly 1950–1952, semi-monthly 1953– .

Zambia
NATIONAL BIBLIOGRAPHY OF ZAMBIA. Lusaka: National Archives of Zambia, 1972– . Annual.

Zimbabwe
ZIMBABWE NATIONAL BIBLIOGRAPHY, ZNB. Harare (formerly Salisbury): National Archives, 1961– . Annual.
   Previously entitled *List of publications deposited in the Library of the National Archives* (1961–1966) and *Rhodesia national bibliography* (1967–1978).

International
BOOKS IN ENGLISH. London: Council for the British National Bibliography (1972–1973), British Library, Bibliographic Services Division, 1974– . Microfiche (formerly Ultrafiche), Semi-monthly.
   An author/title list of books in the English language catalogued for BNB and by the Library of Congress.

CUMULATIVE BOOK INDEX. see *under* USA.

GUIDE TO MICROFORMS IN PRINT. Westport, Connecticut: Microform Review; London: Mansell, 1977– .
   An amalgamation of *Guide to microforms in print* and *International microforms in print*. Author and title listing with a separate subject volume entitled *Subject guide to microforms in print*.

Current General Bibliographies

INTERNATIONAL BOOKS IN PRINT: English-language titles published outside the United States of America and Great Britain. München: Saur, 1979–   . Annual.

INTERNATIONALE BIBLIOGRAPHIE DES REPRINTS = International bibliography of reprints. Hans Dettweiler. München: Saur, 1980. 2 vols.

REFERENCES AND CITATIONS

1. IFLA International Office for UBC. *Guidelines for the national bibliographic agency and the national bibliography*. Paris: Unesco, 1979. (PGI/79/WS/18). p 4, para 4.1.
2. International Congress on National Bibliographies (1977: Paris). *Final report*. Paris: Unesco, 1978. (PGI/77/UBC/3; Conf. 401/Col.11). 10–13.
3. Cheffins, Richard H. A. *A survey of the contents of existing national bibliographies*. Paris: Unesco, 1977. (PGI/77/UBC/Ref.1; Conf. 401/Col. 4).
4. Cybulski, Radostaw, et al. 'Coverage of documents in current national bibliographies'. *International Cataloguing*, 11 (1), January/March 1982.
   This lists in its references well over a dozen papers on this topic that had appeared in the previous decade.
5. Holdsworth, H. 'South Pacific: national and regional bibliographies and the founding of the Regional Bibliographic Centre'. *International Cataloguing*, 10 (3), July/September 1981. 29–30.
6. Collison, Robert L. *Bibliographic services throughout the world, 1950–59*. Paris: Unesco, 1961.
   Subsequent quinquennial surveys were compiled by Paul Avicenne and, since that covering 1970–74, by Marcelle Beaudiquez.
7. Clews, John. *Documentation of the UN system: a survey of bibliographic control and a suggested methodology for an integrated UN bibliography*. London: IFLA International Office for UBC, 1981. (The IFLA International Office for UBC occasional papers; No 8.)
8. Cheffins, R. H. A. *Op. cit.*
9. Walford, A. J. *Guide to reference material*. 3rd ed. London: Library Association, 1977. Vol 3. 17–31.
10. Sheehy, Eugene P. *Guide to reference books*. 9th ed. Chicago: American Library Association, 1976; *Supplement*, 1980; *Second supplement*, 1982.
11. *Bibliographic services throughout the world*. Annual supplement to *General Information Programme – UNISIST bulletin* (Paris: Unesco,

References

January 1979–   ) which was formed by merging the *UNISIST newsletter* with *Bibliography, documentation, terminology* (1960–1978). The annual supplement is largely a continuation of the latter.

12. Collison, R. L. *Op. cit.*
13. Pomassl, Gerhardt. *Synoptic tables concerning the current national bibliographies*. Berlin: Bibliotheksverband der Deutschen Demokratischen Republik, 1975. 22 folding tables. Available from K. G. Saur Verlag, Munich.
14. IFLA International Office for UBC. *Commonwealth national bibliographies: an annotated directory*. 2nd ed. London: Commonwealth Secretariat, 1982 [ie 1983].

16
Bibliographies of Older Material

Geoffrey Groom

Enumerative or systematic bibliography is concerned with the 'listing of the salient bibliographical details about a particular group of books which have some kind of co-ordinating feature'.[1] It can take several forms. A **universal** bibliography would be one not limited by chronological period, place of publication, language, subject or form. In fact, true universality is impossible, and most **general** bibliographies (those not limited by subject) have some other limitation: chronological, geographical, linguistic, etc. A **national** bibliography is the record of the national literature in the widest sense, including books published in the language of that country and all books produced in the country, whatever their language; it may also include books concerning the country. A **trade** bibliography is one issued for or by the book trade of a particular country, limited normally to items published within that country, with an emphasis on information essential to the trade, rather than definitive bibliographical information. A bibliography may be **current**, listing items published currently, or it may be **retrospective**, listing items published in earlier years. It may aim to be **comprehensive**, or it may be **selective**.

This chapter will be concerned with general, universal, national and trade bibliographies, which list books printed in Western languages prior to the middle of the twentieth century. Examples of other types of bibliographies not dealt with here include those

Bibliographies of Older Material

devoted to the writings by or about one author, or listing books on one subject, or printed in one place or at one press, or listing works of one literary form. Each major example will be examined in relation to its coverage or scope—what items it aims to record, and whether it is intended to be comprehensive or selective; its arrangement—whether the entries in it are arranged in alphabetical order (alphabetical order, usually based on authorship or title, is used where there is no logical order of the parts, where the main purpose is the identification of individual titles), or in chronological order (which can reveal the growth of a subject or a literary or bibliographical form and shed light on the relationship between items), or in some classified order. Indexes can provide some variety of approach. Many bibliographies discussed in this chapter are provided with indexes of printers, publishers, and booksellers, and of the places in which they worked, thereby providing a starting point for the study of the history of the book-trade. Consideration will be given to the amount and type of information given in each individual entry, which may vary with the purpose of the bibliography but which will normally include most of the following details—the name of the author, editor, compiler or other issuing body; the title of the work in a full or a shortened form; any edition statement; the place of publication; the name of the publisher, printer or bookseller; the date of publication; and an indication of the format and of the collation of the volume. These are the details which allow the user to identify the book, and to verify its bibliographical elements. Other information given may include the price (important in a trade bibliography); an indication of where copies of the work may be found; details of the bibliographical history of the book; and references to other bibliographical sources in which the book may be listed.

In this chapter, published catalogues of individual libraries, and union catalogues, listing in one sequence the contents of two or more libraries, will be treated as examples of enumerative or systematic bibliography, though strictly speaking, a bibliography will not be limited to the holdings of any particular library or libraries and will include a description which takes into account the details of all extant copies, whereas a catalogue records the details of a specific copy or copies.

Bibliographies of Older Material

Recent developments in the application of computers to bibliography deserve mention here. 'The computer makes it possible to escape the tyranny of print on the page, which disposes information according to a predetermined arrangement capable of answering certain clearly defined questions, but which requires comprehensive indexing in order to serve more than a few simple purposes . . . Access-points to bibliographical descriptions in machine readable form are virtually unlimited and permit multiple/conditional searches . . .'[2] The same author goes on to point to a reliable means of image-conversion into digital form which will render obsolete the necessity for the bibliographer to transcribe title-pages 'so that a machine-readable bibliographic file can contain images of the title-page, specimen pages of text (for typographical analysis) as well as structured data required by cataloguing codes such as AACR2'. The application of computers is thus likely to alter the methodology of enumerative bibliography (previously the creation of traditionally arranged bibliographies in printed form) and its objectives (the uses to which that data provided will be put). Such recent developments will be mentioned where appropriate.

UNIVERSAL BIBLIOGRAPHIES

The published catalogues of the great national libraries constitute the most comprehensive single records of publications of their own countries, but they also contain much foreign-language material, the aim having been to acquire representative collections of the most significant foreign works. In that they record collections embracing many languages and many subjects, and include books dating from the fifteenth to the twentieth centuries, and also rare, obscure and privately printed items not found in trade bibliographies, these catalogues come as close as is possible to achieving bibliographical universality.

British Museum. GENERAL CATALOGUE OF PRINTED BOOKS. Photolithographic edition to 1955. London: Trustees of the British Museum, 1959–1966. 263 vols. Reduced facsimile reprint, New York: Readex Microprint, 1967. 27 vols. Known as GK3.

Three supplements of later acquisitions were published as *Ten year supplement 1956–1965* (1968, 50 vols), *Five year supplement 1966–1970* (1971–1972, 26 vols), and *Five year supplement 1971–1975* (1979, 13 vols). At the end of 1982 the British Library's Reference Division announced the publication of a microfiche edition of the GENERAL CATALOGUE OF PRINTED BOOKS 1976–1982.

These volumes reproduce the 5·5–6 million entries in the Library's own working copy of the catalogue. They record books and periodicals printed in Western languages from the fifteenth century onwards and acquired by the Library from its foundation in 1753 up to 1975. The British Museum Library became the British Library in 1973. It holds one of the world's largest collections of printed books and one of the richest, certainly in the field of the humanities, and for the period before the twentieth century. There are now over 9 million volumes in the Department of Printed Books, excluding the separate Newspaper Library, with a further 2·5 million in the rest of the Reference Division. The *General Catalogue* is said to record over 500,000 distinct editions printed before 1801, with a further 100,000 additional copies. Much of the Library's strength in early and rare printed books comes from its adherence to the canons of nineteenth-century historical and philological scholarship, according to which the earlier texts of a particular discipline, and the typographical antiquities of a particular country, were as indispensable to the scholar as the encyclopaedic coverage of current texts. Just over half the Library's total collections are in English. It holds the leading, but not overwhelmingly dominant, collections of English-language material up to 1850. It was about the middle of the nineteenth century that the enforcement of copyright deposit became more rigorous (the privilege was acquired with the Old Royal Library in 1757) and that Anthony Panizzi began to develop the English-language collections in depth as well as systematically. Panizzi also built up the collection of American imprints in the Library, which is now thought to hold about 16 per cent of all pre-1801 American imprints recorded. There are larger collections of European imprints up to 1900 than in most

Bibliographies of Older Material

major libraries in the countries concerned: French and German publications are particularly well represented.

The arrangement of entries is alphabetical by the name of the author, or by words taken from the title for anonymous works, with cross-references under the names of editors, translators, illustrators, etc. Most corporate bodies are entered under the name of the town or country in which they are located. Entries under the names of authors include not only their works, but also biographical and critical works about them and their works. There are structured entries for some authors, mainly the more important figures in English literature and other important authors, involving the sequence: complete works, smaller collections, special categories (eg letters), all arranged in chronological order by date of publication; single works arranged in alphabetical order of title, with translations, adaptations and books about individual works filed immediately following the individual work; selections and abstracts; doubtful and suppositious works; works edited, translated or with contributions by the author; and finally biographical and critical works about the author and his works. Indexes assist the user in some cases (eg there is an index of Greek titles, with English or Latin equivalents, under Aristotle). Entries under the names of countries (eg England) include official publications (arranged in a useful historical or chronological sequence) and non-official publications, works about the country and other titles having some reference to the country, arranged by subject area. Again, indexes (of sub-headings and titles, in the case of England) are supplied where they are necessary. Similar sequences of entries exist under the names of large towns, such as London. Under the names of sacred books (eg Bible) are entered both editions and translations, and works about the sacred books, and again indexes are provided. A number of collective headings draw together important classes of material, eg Liturgies (arranged by rite, with alphabetical index) and Periodical Publications (arranged by place of publication, then alphabetically by title).

A revision of the letters A–DEZ only had previously been published and then been discontinued. In this revision much bibliographical information, such as pagination and publishers' names, had been added to older entries. But in the remainder of the cata-

Universal Bibliographies

logue (DF–Z) such extra bibliographical information may be wanting in the older entries; the old method of cataloguing books published in series by means of cross-references under the author's name instead of by means of main entries, often lacking dates of publication as well as pagination, is still visible; and out-of-date forms of cross-reference may still be seen. Many of the older entries had, however, been improved by corrections and additions in manuscript, which are reproduced. There is very full cataloguing for some early printed books, such as incunables, sixteenth-century works, and the folios of Shakespeare. In contrast to other library catalogues the use in the British Museum Catalogue of elaborate typographical distinctions between different parts of the entry is most noticeable.

A new photolithographic edition of the British Museum Catalogue, being published commercially, is entitled THE BRITISH LIBRARY GENERAL CATALOGUE OF PRINTED BOOKS TO 1975 (London: Saur, 1979–   , in progress). At the time of writing it has reached the letter 'M' in 220 volumes, and should comprise some 360 volumes when complete. This edition of the catalogue will be known as GK4. It incorporates the entries in GK3 and the three published supplements, and also numerous previously unpublished catalogue entries, into one alphabetical sequence, including thousands of corrections and amendments to the entries. The British Museum cataloguing rules govern all except the very latest entries, and entries for the pre-1900 material between DF and the end of the alphabet remain in the old form and are unlikely ever to be revised. The reduction ratio used in the production of the catalogue has meant that some manuscript alterations (of which many are shelfmarks) are in some cases not very legible.

A recent development is the planned conversion of the *General Catalogue* to machine-readable form, by the use of optical character recognition techniques.

Now in course of publication is THE BRITISH LIBRARY GENERAL CATALOGUE OF PRINTED BOOKS, 1976 TO 1982 (London : Saur, 1983–   , in progress).

Bibliothèque Nationale. CATALOGUE GÉNÉRAL DES

Bibliographies of Older Material

LIVRES IMPRIMÉS: AUTEURS. Paris: Imprimerie Nationale, 1897–1981. 231 vols.

In addition to its comprehensive coverage of French publications (the compulsory legal deposit of new books in France was established by Francis I in 1537, though the rigour with which it has been enforced has been variable, especially before the nineteenth century), the Bibliothèque Nationale is also rich in other Romance-language and classical titles.

Each volume of its published author catalogue from 1 to 186 includes titles acquired up to the date of publication of the volume, which produces a chronologically unbalanced catalogue; from Volume 187 (published 1961) items published up to 1957 only are included. The Catalogue does not include title entries for anonymous works, nor entries for anonymous classics, liturgies, periodicals, society transactions, government publications, and works by corporate authors. Nor does it include entries for works published about an author and his works. Arrangement is alphabetical by the name of the author. In the case of classical authors, the French form of name is preferred. In the case of major authors there is an arrangement similar to that in the British Museum Catalogue (collected works, selected works, single works). There are, for instance, two volumes of the Catalogue devoted to Voltaire: over 5,000 entries, arranged in 12 sub-sections, with 8 indexes (of titles, of translations, of adaptations, etc). Under 'Aristote' there are indexes of Greek and Latin titles. Entries are precise and succinct: bibliographical details given for each item include full name of author, title, place of publication, publisher, date of publication, edition statement, format, pagination, and Bibliothèque Nationale shelfmark. One disappointing feature is that, where the book does not bear a place or date of printing or publication, no attempt seems to have been made to determine this information. The entries under Voltaire are more detailed than those under other authors, and for sets of the complete works of Voltaire the Catalogue spells out the contents of each volume. In addition to its published author catalogue, the Bibliothèque Nationale has published additional catalogues of certain specialized groups of material: there is, for instance, a separate author and anonymous title catalogue of the publications of the French Revolutionary period.

Universal Bibliographies

Both the British Museum and Bibliothèque Nationale catalogues include only works found in their own libraries. The following item is a union catalogue:

NATIONAL UNION CATALOG, PRE-1956 IMPRINTS. A cumulative author list representing Library of Congress printed cards and titles reported by other American libraries. London: Mansell, 1968–1980. 685 vols. Vols 686–754 (1980–1981) constitute a supplement, containing new titles, new editions, added entries and cross-references, and additional locations.

The *National Union catalog, pre-1956 imprints*, lists 'the catalogued holdings of selected portions of the catalogued collections of the major research libraries of the United States and Canada, plus the more rarely held items in the collections of selected smaller and specialised libraries'. At the heart of the *National Union catalog* are the holdings of the Library of Congress, founded in 1800 and now the world's largest library with over 18 million volumes. Since 1870 the Library of Congress has received for deposit a copy of all works copyrighted in the United States, and has in addition acquired significant works published outside the United States (two-thirds of its stock is not American). In addition to the Library of Congress, certain major libraries (University of Chicago Library, Harvard University Library, Yale University Library, the John Crerar Library, and the New York Public Library) have endeavoured to report every catalogued item in their collections printed before 1956. Altogether, more than 700 libraries are represented in the *National Union catalog*.

Though restricted for the most part to works in Western languages (it does not contain material in non-Roman alphabets other than Greek and Gaelic, except those represented by Library of Congress printed cards), the Catalog contains entries for books, pamphlets, maps, atlases, music, and for periodicals and serials only if represented by Library of Congress cards or reported by another library. However, incunabula are poorly represented in it, and *Short-title catalogue* and Wing period books are only included when catalogued on cards and reported to the *National Union catalog*. It is primarily a catalogue of main entries, arranged alphabetically by author or anonymous title, plus necessary cross-ref-

Bibliographies of Older Material

erences and selected added entries (eg for joint authors and editors, and for titles of works published anonymously that have been given a main entry under an author). Under an author, no works about the author are included. In the case of important authors, there is often a classified arrangement of titles, eg collected works, selections, single works, etc. The authority for the form both of main and added entries is almost invariably the *ALA's Cataloguing rules for author and title entries, 1949 edition*. Nevertheless, different works by the same author, and copies of the same work, may remain under different headings. In theory, different editions of the same title are entered separately, as are different issues when these have been noted, though it is almost inevitable that a single record with multiple locations may disguise the existence of different bibliographical entities and that there are duplicate records for the same edition. Under the heading 'Bible' there are some 63,000 entries, representing about 700 languages and dialects, for texts and translations of the Bible and its parts. Each entry reflects the information supplied by the cataloguing library, with Library of Congress cards preferred: the information, therefore, varies, from full entries with very detailed bibliographical information, to very sketchy entries. Alphabetical symbols show the reported location, in the United States and Canada, of copies of the work described. As the Catalog consists of catalogue cards from various libraries photolithographed and reduced in size photographically, legibility is not always good. However, the Catalog is of very great value because of the richness of the collections catalogued and because of the detail of many of the entries.

The other outstanding American library catalogue, contrasting entries which do not appear in the National Union Catalogue, is:

New York Public Library. DICTIONARY CATALOG OF THE RESEARCH LIBRARIES, 1911–1971. New York: New York Public Library, 1979–1983. 800 vols.

The catalogue reproduces about 9 million catalogue cards. The New York Public Library is not officially a national library, but its research collections rank in size, scope and quality next to those of the Library of Congress, the British Museum Library and the Bibliothèque Nationale, and constitute a resource of national and

Universal Bibliographies

even international importance. It is a conglomerate of special libraries covering almost every subject field (with the exception of law, medicine and the biological sciences, theology and pedagogy) and of the greatest significance in the fields of the humanities, fine arts, performing arts, social sciences, science and technology. It contains over 5 million books and other printed material in more than 3,000 languages and dialects. Its Catalog covers the holdings of printed materials of the Research Libraries as developed between 1895 and 1971, including entries for the holdings of three predecessor collections that became part of the Library in 1895. Only parts of the collections of music, dance, theatre, Orientalia, Baltica, Slavonica and Judaica are included. But there is material in all languages, the titles of those in non-Roman alphabets being transliterated. Most of the titles are of the nineteenth and twentieth centuries, though some are earlier. The Catalog duplicates many of the entries in the Library's separately published specialized catalogues. The Catalog is in dictionary form, containing entries under authors, editors, illustrators, titles, forms and subjects, in one alphabetical sequence, and includes analytical entries for parts of books and book-sets and series entries for monographs in series. It is printed from microfilm, reproducing the Library's catalogue cards, with some variation in legibility.

Two older examples of universal, yet selective, bibliography demand mention:

Brunet, J. C. MANUEL DU LIBRAIRE ET DE L'AMATEUR DES LIVRES. 5e éd. Paris: Firmin-Didot, 1860–1865. 6 vols.

Brunet lists rare, valuable, noteworthy, and otherwise remarkable books, irrespective of language or period, but is particularly useful for French and Latin titles. In addition to the usual bibliographical details necessary for identification, Brunet includes bibliographical and critical notes, with mention of copies and prices at auction. Vols 1–5 constitute the main alphabetical sequence of authors and anonymous titles. Vol 6 is a classified list in five main subject classes. A *Supplement* in two volumes, by P. Deschamps and G. Brunet, was published 1878–1880. Brunet is supplemented, especially for German titles, by:

Bibliographies of Older Material

Graesse, J. G. TRÉSOR DES LIVRES RARES ET PRÉCIEUX. Dresden: Kuntze, 1859–1869. 7 vols.

The ideal of a truly comprehensive bibliography of books in Western languages has been approached for one period of time, the period from the invention of printing to the end of the fifteenth century. The products of these early presses are known as **incunabula** or **incunables**. The numbers of incunabula are sufficiently small for them to be studied internationally.

Hain, L. F. T. REPERTORIUM BIBLIOGRAPHICUM, in quo libri omnes ab arte typographica inventa ad annum MD . . . Stuttgart: Cotta, 1826–1838. 4 vols.

Hain's listing of over 16,000 incunabula was based largely on the collections of the Munich Hofbibliothek, greatly enriched by books from the Bavarian monasteries. Items personally examined by him are marked with an asterisk. The arrangement is alphabetical by author, with the items numbered serially. The Hain number is referred to in many later bibliographies of incunabula. The fact that incunabula commonly do not have recognizable title-pages makes identification by number especially useful. For each item Hain supplied a description of sufficient accuracy to make it possible for the first time for books to be identified and checked for completeness against his descriptions. Each entry consists of the name of the author and a brief title; a textual description, with transcripts of the *incipit*, the major section titles, and the colophon; and a collation.

W. A. Copinger published a *Supplement to Hain's Repertorium Bibliographicum* (London: Sotheran, 1895–1902). At the end of Copinger is printed K. Burger's *The printers and publishers of the fifteenth century with lists of their works. Index to the Supplement to Hain*, which serves as a brief chronological record, in alphabetical order of printer's name, of the output of each fifteenth-century press. Burger can be invaluable in tracing a difficult title, and he paved the way for the work of Robert Proctor.

D. Reichling further supplemented Hain and Copinger in his *Appendices ad Hainii-Copingeri Repertorium Bibliographicum: additiones et emendationes* (Munich: Rosenthal, 1905–1914. 7 vols and Supplement). Reichling's work was regarded as more author-

Universal Bibliographies

itative than Copinger's, but it is a difficult work to cope with. Vol 7 has several helpful indexes, including an index of towns and printers, and the Supplement combines in the General Index of Authors the items listed in the preceding parts.

In 1897 M. L. C. Pellechet published the first volume of her alphabetically arranged *Catalogue général des incunables des bibliothèques publiques de France*. After her death L. Polain published (in 1905 and 1909) two further volumes, taking the alphabetical sequence down to 'Gregorius Magnus'. The remainder of the catalogue remained unpublished, but has since been completed by the publication on microfilm of the remainder of Polain's manuscript. This catalogue developed the basic form of entry which has since become universally adopted by bibliographers of incunabula. It remains useful because of the additional information it gives of French incunabula not extensively covered by Hain, and also because it quotes the beginning of the text of the second gathering to aid in the identification of imperfect copies lacking significant leaves at the beginning and end of the book.

Robert Proctor, using the 'natural history method', evolved what we now know as 'Proctor order' (chronologically by country, town and printer, in the order of the introduction of printing) in his:

INDEX TO THE EARLY PRINTED BOOKS IN THE BRITISH MUSEUM FROM THE INVENTION OF PRINTING TO THE YEAR 1500. Pt 1. London: Kegan Paul, 1898. 2 vols.

Proctor's aim was to illustrate the early history of printing by arranging books on typographical evidence in chronological order under their printers. His work was invaluable for his assignment of place and date to works issued anonymously. The entries for individual books in Proctor are the minimum necessary for identification, giving a serial number, the date of printing, the British Museum heading, the name of the printer/publisher, the format, a reference to Hain's work, and a note on the types used.

Proctor's *Index* provided the basis for:

British Museum. CATALOGUE OF BOOKS PRINTED IN THE FIFTEENTH CENTURY NOW IN THE BRITISH MUSEUM. London, 1908–   . In progress.

Bibliographies of Older Material

A photolitho reprint of the first eight parts, issued in 1963, reproduces manuscript amendments to the British Museum copy up to the date of issue of the reprint. The catalogue is arranged in Proctor order. The parts so far published cover Germany, German-speaking Switzerland and Austria–Hungary, Italy, France, French-speaking Switzerland, Holland and Belgium, Spain and Portugal. A part listing English incunabula will follow. The German and Italian sections will need supplementary volumes. Each entry consists of the heading (author, short title, and date); a full bibliographical description, made up of extracts from the title, the *incipit* and the colophon; the collation, bibliographical information applicable to all copies of the edition; and notes applicable to the copy described. The wealth of the British Library's collection of incunabula (it has some 11,000 of an estimated total of 35,000 surviving incunable editions) and the fact that the characteristics of an 'ideal' copy are recorded make this catalogue a very important bibliographical tool.

The following is intended to be a complete author catalogue of all known incunabula:

GESAMTKATALOG DER WIEGENDRUCKE, herausgegeben von Der Deutschen Staatsbibliothek zu Berlin. 2. Aufl. Stuttgart: Hiersemann; New York: Kraus, 1968–   . In progress.

The first seven volumes of the second edition are reprints of those published 1925–1938. With Band 9, Lieferung 1, published 1981, the new edition has reached 'Friedrich III'. Under each author, entries are arranged in chronological order. Each entry consists of a bibliographical note—author's name, short title, place of printing, name of printer and publisher, date, format; the collation; the transcript of the title, caption headings, and colophon; references to other bibliographical sources; and locations of copies. The standard method of description is explained in English, in Vol 8, pp*101–*106.

Except in these last two definitive catalogues of incunabula, it is now thought sufficient, when listing incunabula, to give the standard short title, followed by references to the standard bibliographies and catalogues as listed above, though a full description will be necessary for unique books. This is the method used in:

Universal Bibliographies

Goff, F. R. INCUNABULA IN AMERICAN LIBRARIES: A THIRD CENSUS. New York: Bibliographical Society of America, 1964. Reprinted in 1973 from Goff's annotated copy. New York: Kraus.

Authors are listed alphabetically. In addition to the standard short title and references to the standard bibliographies, details include imprint, format, the location of copies, and a serial number. There is an index of printers and publishers, and concordances to the numbers used in Hain, Proctor, the *Gesamtkatalog*, and earlier US censuses.

The total number of incunabula recorded by Goff totals over 51,000, of which over 12,000 are separate editions, representing approximately one-third of the estimated total of incunabula editions surviving. The United States national holdings are surpassed in number of editions only by those of Great Britain, Germany and France, and in comprehensiveness only by those of Great Britain. Goff is an unequalled source of quick information on incunabula.

Using the entries from Goff's catalogue as a base file, the British Library began in 1980 a project for a short-title catalogue of incunabula in machine-readable form, enriching the base file with records of incunabula not in the USA from catalogues such as its own full-scale catalogue and other incunabula catalogues. By 1982 the file contained some 17,000 records, conflating more information than any other published catalogue or bibliography of incunabula. Publication on microfiche is anticipated, and since the basic record is machine-readable, updating is straightforward. Such a microfiche catalogue will be a guide to descriptions of incunabula in published sources and also a guide to locations.

The Bibliothèque Nationale in 1982 began publication in fascicles of its *Catalogue des incunables*. This will describe its collection of 8,000 editions in 12,000 copies (the third largest) in an alphabetical author arrangement.

The published part of the Pellechet–Polain *Catalogue général des incunables des bibliothèques publiques de France* covered letters A–G. The Bibliothèque Nationale *Catalogue des incunables* therefore begins publication with the letter H. Though limited to the holdings of the one library, it contains many rare French imprints. There are the usual short-title entries, with necessary references.

Bibliographical control on an international scale of sixteenth-century publishing is less well developed than that of fifteenth-century books. The number of books printed increased and the book trade was international. The following work aims to be a comprehensive listing of books printed in Europe during the sixteenth century:

INDEX AURELIENSIS: CATALOGUS LIBRORUM SEDECIMO SAECULO IMPRESSORUM. (Bibliotheca Bibliographica Aureliana, 7&c). Baden-Baden: Foundation Index Aureliensis, 1962–   . In progress.

Alphabetically arranged by author or anonymous title, by 1982 it had reached the heading 'Chytraeus'. For each item it provides a title transcription, place of printing, date, name of printer and publisher, format, pagination, a serial number, location in libraries in Europe and in the United States, and references to bibliographical sources. Indexes of printers and publishers, by town and alphabetically by name, and of personal names, are being provided. The parts of this work seen by the present writer lack any general introduction and explanation.

Because this comprehensive listing of sixteenth-century continental books is far from complete, the following two catalogues are of use:

Adams, H. M. CATALOGUE OF BOOKS PRINTED ON THE CONTINENT OF EUROPE, 1501–1600, IN CAMBRIDGE LIBRARIES. Cambridge: Cambridge University Press, 1967. 2 vols.

Adams excludes English books printed on the Continent, as they appear in the Pollard and Redgrave *Short title catalogue . . . 1475–1640*. His listing contains some 30,000 entries, some 16,000 of which may not be in the British Museum *General catalogue of printed books*. The arrangement is alphabetical by author or anonymous title. Some works appear under two different headings, presumably because Adams has followed the usage of different College library catalogues. The sub-arrangement under author can be difficult to follow, especially in the case of the more prolific authors.

National Bibliographies

Short titles are given, with pagination, signature collation, format, imprint, date, and locations. The signature collations can be very useful in helping to identify a book, but they do tend to dominate the entry and make it difficult to locate other pieces of information. There are indexes of printers or publishers (with even more abbreviated entries in chronological order under each name), and of places of publication (listing in chronological order the printers and publishers who appear in the first index).

National Library of Scotland. A SHORT-TITLE CATALOGUE OF FOREIGN BOOKS PRINTED UP TO 1600. Edinburgh: HMSO, 1970.

In 1925 the general collections belonging to the Library of the Faculty of Advocates, Edinburgh passed into the keeping of the National Library of Scotland, which is now one of the four largest libraries in Great Britain, with holdings of over 3 million items. This Catalogue follows the pattern of the British Museum Library's short-title catalogues of foreign books of the same period, its arrangement being alphabetical by author or anonymous title with no added entries under editors, etc. Titles are shortened with no indication of omissions. Other information given is edition statement, name of editor, etc, imprint, date, format, and shelfmark. As in Adams, there are indexes of printers and publishers, and of places of publication.

From the beginning of the seventeenth century retrospective bibliographical control is best viewed on a national rather than international scale. There was a further steep increase in the number of books published: publication in Latin declined as vernacular literature increased.

NATIONAL BIBLIOGRAPHIES

National retrospective bibliographies are used to identify books of which one knows the country of printing or the language and date of printing, starting from the name of the author or the anonymous title, or possibly the name of the printer, publisher or bookseller.

Bibliographies of Older Material

Great Britain

Since the British Museum Library (or the British Library as it now is) holds the leading collection of English-language material up to 1850 and from about that date the copyright privilege has ensured that it has taken the majority of books published in Great Britain, its *General catalogue of printed books* is the most extensive single listing of British books to be consulted for books of all periods. *The National Union catalog*, too, contains much material published in Great Britain, as do the printed author catalogues, up to the date of their publication, of other large general and research libraries, such as the Bodleian Library, Oxford; the London Library; the Library of the Faculty of Advocates, Edinburgh (its general collections in 1925 became the property of the National Library of Scotland, which has now made its catalogue up to 1974 available in microform); Edinburgh University Library; and the Library of Trinity College, Dublin.

There are also available several catalogues aiming to be comprehensive listings of books printed in Great Britain in earlier centuries. For the earliest period of British book production we can turn to:

Pollard, A. W. and Redgrave, G. R. A SHORT-TITLE CATALOGUE OF BOOKS PRINTED IN ENGLAND, SCOTLAND AND IRELAND AND OF ENGLISH BOOKS PRINTED ABROAD 1475–1640. London: Bibliographical Society, 1926. Known as *STC*.

This work aimed to list all 'English books' ('English' as defined in the title, with the addition of Latin service books, wherever printed, if for use in England and Scotland; and 'books' taken to mean all printed pieces) printed up to 1640, copies of which existed in libraries in Europe and the USA. All entries were not, however, based on an examination of the books themselves, and there was in some cases dependence upon printed catalogues of varying degrees of accuracy. Arrangement is alphabetical by author or anonymous title, the choice of headings following with some modifications the British Museum Library's cataloguing rules. The entries, totalling 26,000, are main entries only, details of editors,

National Bibliographies

translators, etc being recorded within the main entries. The title of each work listed is given in a short form, yet in sufficient detail to identify the work; this is followed by any statement of edition, format, place of publication, unless London, which is omitted if printed in the book, name of printer, publisher, bookseller, date of publication, a reference to the entry of a book in the Stationers' Register,[3] and symbols indicating the locations of a selection of copies in representative libraries in Europe and the USA. Each main entry is assigned a unique number. As a location list, Pollard and Redgrave was supplemented by two works, by D. Ramage and W. W. Bishop:

Ramage, D. A FINDING-LIST OF ENGLISH BOOKS TO 1640 IN THE LIBRARIES OF THE BRITISH ISLES (excluding the national libraries and the libraries of Oxford and Cambridge). Durham: Council of Durham Colleges, 1958.

The work by Ramage lists those *STC* items for which additional locations have been found. It provides over 37,000 locations in some 140 libraries, including some of the newer university libraries and several public and cathedral libraries, though its coverage of the libraries of the British Isles is not complete.

W. W. Bishop, in his A CHECKLIST OF AMERICAN COPIES OF "SHORT TITLE CATALOGUE" BOOKS. 2nd ed. Ann Arbor: University of Michigan Press, 1950, performs a similar service for American libraries.

P. G. Morrison has compiled an:

INDEX OF PRINTERS, PUBLISHERS AND BOOKSELLERS IN A. W. POLLARD AND G. R. REDGRAVE A SHORT TITLE CATALOGUE . . . 1475–1640. 2nd impr. Charlottesville: Bibliographical Society of the University of Virginia, 1961.

A total revision of Pollard and Redgrave has been undertaken, and the first stage of this revision has been completed with the publication of:

A SHORT-TITLE CATALOGUE OF BOOKS PRINTED IN ENGLAND, SCOTLAND AND IRELAND AND OF EN-

GLISH BOOKS PRINTED ABROAD, 1475–1640. 2nd ed, revised and enlarged, begun by W. A. Jackson and F. S. Ferguson, completed by Katharine F. Pantzer. Vol 2: I–Z. London: Bibliographical Society, 1976.

The second volume of the work has been published first, because it is this part that has reached as definitive a stage as is possible in a work of this nature. Vol 1, A–H, is due in a few years' time, and at a later date the Bibliographical Society will publish an index of printers, publishers and booksellers. Also in preparation is a chronological index to the revised edition of *STC*, to provide for each year the author's name or other heading and *STC* number for all items published in that year. The revision has resulted in some 10,000 new entries being added for previously unrecorded works (such as ballads and ephemera), editions and issues. Some items have been re-attributed, and some re-dated, and new information has been added to already existing entries. There are now references to books recorded, but not located. The revision has moved away from the concept of the entries in a drastically abridged form towards making available the 'considerable accumulation of data . . . assembled in order . . . to distinguish between the various editions, issues and variants'.[4] The original *STC* entry numbers have been retained and new works, editions and issues, together with items which have been re-attributed or re-dated, have been interpolated by decimal point into the original number sequence. Many of the original headings have been retained: one reviewer[5] has pointed out that the headings under which some of the anonymous works are listed are not easy to find and that an index of anonymous titles would have been useful. The user should note the 'admirable analytic display of complicated materials'[6] under such headings as 'Liturgies' (where a chart of editions of the Book of Common Prayer gives collations and other identifying features of some 140 editions) and 'London' (including bills of mortality), and the new subject or form groupings under such headings as 'Indulgences' and 'Newsbooks'. There are now up to five locations given in Britain and up to five elsewhere (usually the United States), spread geographically as widely as possible.

The following catalogue was a contribution to the revision of the original *Short-title catalogue* in one particular area:

National Bibliographies

Allison, A. F. and Rogers, D. M. A CATALOGUE OF CATHOLIC BOOKS IN ENGLISH PRINTED ABROAD OR SECRETLY IN ENGLAND, 1558–1640. Bognor Regis: Arundel Press, 1956.

The items listed in this catalogue comprise a very small fraction of the total number of *STC* entries, but they are of disproportionately large historical and literary interest and present intractable problems of surreptitious authorship, printing and circulation. 'Catholic' books are defined as works of authors in communion with Rome, including those in Irish, Scots, Welsh, and service books in Latin. The authors provide a census of all the books they have been able to trace and examine (many of them have survived in only a few scattered copies and were not listed in the original *STC*); a reliable though brief description; and the results of their researches on authorship, printing and date (books printed secretly in England commonly had a false imprint or no imprint at all). The entries in Allison and Rogers are a great advance over the relevant entries in the original *STC*, and the greater knowledge thus provided has been incorporated into the second edition of *STC*. Allison and Rogers provide also an index of identifiable printers, and a list of secret presses; an index of translators, compilers and editors; and a chronological list.

The following catalogue was published as a chronological continuation of the Pollard and Redgrave *STC* and shares some of its features:

Wing, D. G. SHORT-TITLE CATALOGUE OF BOOKS PRINTED IN ENGLAND, SCOTLAND, IRELAND, WALES AND BRITISH AMERICA, AND OF ENGLISH BOOKS PRINTED IN OTHER COUNTRIES, 1641–1700. New York: Index Society, 1945–1951. 3 vols.

Wing's *STC* is an indispensable work of reference, the basic bibliographical tool for the period, but is recognized to be incomplete and imperfect. More books were produced in this period than in the earlier period, and they survive in greater numbers. Wing lists between 80,000 and 90,000 entries. He excludes periodicals. He intended to list only separately issued items, but in some instances he took analytical entries relating to parts of books from old-fashioned catalogues, and treated them as complete books. His is an author and anonymous title catalogue, arranged alphabetically. The choice of headings derives from the Anglo-American Cataloguing Rules. He instructs the user to search for anonymous works under the first word of the title not an article, where he may find a cross-reference to the attributed author. Titles have been given as briefly as possible and, although many of the entries reasonably identify the works they describe, in other cases the brevity of the titles causes difficulty in identification and in tracing a book to its heading in a library catalogue. Wing lists different translations of a work chronologically, but without indicating the name of the translator. He is careful to point out in his preface that when bibliographical differences exist beyond the title-page, without altering the format of the book, they have been disregarded. In other words, he does not claim to distinguish between editions and issues on evidence other than the title-page information and the format. He gives references to a number of standard bibliographical works, including the Term Catalogues,[7] and locations in British and United States libraries (up to five on each side of the Atlantic, with as wide a sweep as possible geographically). Main entries are numbered consecutively within each letter of the alphabet, with the alphabetical letter prefixed to the number, eg E227.

Because it proved to be incomplete, the appearance of Wing's *STC* prompted others to compile lists of works of the period in certain libraries not listed in Wing. P. G. Morrison compiled an *Index of printers, publishers and booksellers in D. Wing's Short-title catalogue . . . 1641–1700* (Charlottesville: Bibliographical Society of the University of Virginia, 1955). Wing himself, in preparation for a revised edition of his own work, published *A gallery of ghosts: books published between 1641–1700 not found in the Short-title catalogue* (New York: Index Committee of the Modern Language Association of America, 1967).

Vol 1 (A1–E2926) of the second edition, revised and enlarged by Wing himself, was published in 1972. Some works and editions had been added, and some revisions and corrections had been made, but the revision was far from comprehensive and not to the high standard of that bestowed on the *Short-title catalogue . . . 1475–1640*. Following the appearance of the first edition, the Wing number had become a standard form of identification for books published in England or in English in the period. In his discussion of numeration in the introductory matter to his second edition of Vol 1, Wing wrote that he had retained 'as far as possible the numbers of my first edition', assigning to additional entries numbers followed by letters, eg A3, A3A, A3B. However the re-arrangement of the numeration hinted at here, resulting from transferred or omitted entries, and new entries taking up the previously used numbers, and this without full explanation, was a cause for criticism.

Wing himself died shortly after the publication of Vol 1 of his second edition, but editorial work on the revised edition has continued, and the editors have provided in Vol 2 of the revised edition (E2927–O1000), published by the Modern Language Association of America, 1982, a complete list of the number changes of Vol 1, giving a correlation of old and new numbers and providing references for those items moved to places in Vols 2 and 3; and they have committed themselves to a further revision of Vol 1, returning to the original numeration. In the revised Vol 2 the ground rules are the same as those laid down by Wing, but more thorough revision has taken place than Wing gave to Vol 1. There has been some revision of the order of listing in major sections, such as 'London', and individual entries have been re-examined. The revised Vol 2 keeps the original Wing numbers, giving brief explanations for entries transferred or deleted, and where entries have been moved or cancelled, the number of the moved or cancelled entry has not been used again. The editors continue Wing's practice of using the phrase 'another edition' to refer indiscriminately either to a book produced from another, setting of type, or to another issue or variant state of the same edition if there are differences on the title-page. They add the abbreviation 'var.' (meaning 'Variant') at the end of some entries to indicate there are variants among the copies, which might result from different settings of type. D. F. McKenzie, in his review of the revised Vol 2 in *The Times Literary Supplement*, 17 December 1982, sees Wing in its present form as 'a bibliographical patchwork', hovering 'uneasily between *STC*, a smaller work of traditional scholarship executed to impeccable standards . . . and *ESTC (Eighteenth century short title catalogue)*, a work eight to ten times the size of Wing, child of a completely new technology, diversely innovative'.[8] The revised vol 3 is scheduled for 1985 and the further revision of vol 1 for 1987/88.

For one part of the Wing period there is an important library catalogue that should be noted:

British Museum, Department of Printed Books. CATALOGUE OF THE PAMPHLETS, BOOKS, NEWSPAPERS AND MANUSCRIPTS RELATING TO THE CIVIL WAR, THE COMMONWEALTH AND RESTORATION, COLLECTED BY GEORGE THOMASON, 1640–1661. London 1908. 2 vols.

Thomason collected as many as he could of the products of the press, other than those in folio, during this period of great historical importance and significant social and political change, though he did concentrate on items printed or sold in London. The 22,000 items have been catalogued in a chronological sequence (an arrangement which has obvious advantages when one is dealing with historical sources), with an author, anonymous title and subject index. The newspapers are listed separately. The items in this Catalogue, other than newspapers, are listed in Wing's *STC*, but the Thomason Catalogue is useful for its chronological arrangement and its fuller entries.

The following work constitutes a revision of some of the material in Wing, and continues the work of Allison and Rogers into this period:

Clancy, T. H. ENGLISH CATHOLIC BOOKS 1641–1700: A BIBLIOGRAPHY. Chicago: Loyola University Press, 1974.

This contains abbreviated entries for English books written by Roman Catholics and published in the Roman Catholic interest, copies of which have been traced, but not all of which have been examined. The work is accurate as far as it goes, though it could well be incomplete: small collections in less important libraries may contain many unknown works which would qualify for inclusion.

A useful supplement to the Pollard and Redgrave and the Wing short-title catalogues for those interested in the history of the provincial book trade up to 1700 is:

National Bibliographies

Clough, E. A. A SHORT-TITLE CATALOGUE ARRANGED GEOGRAPHICALLY OF BOOKS PRINTED AND DISTRIBUTED BY PRINTERS, PUBLISHERS AND BOOKSELLERS IN THE ENGLISH PROVINCIAL TOWNS AND IN SCOTLAND AND IRELAND UP TO AND INCLUDING THE YEAR 1700. London: Library Association, 1969.

This excludes items entered in H. G. Aldis *A list of books printed in Scotland before 1700*; E. R. M. Dix *Catalogue of early Dublin-printed books, 1601–1700*, and in F. Madan's *Oxford books*. Based on the original editions of *STC* and Wing, it is arranged alphabetically by place, listing entries in a chronological sequence under the place, giving an author or title heading, short title, imprint, format and *STC* or Wing number. The bulk of the book is taken up by Cambridge, Dublin, Edinburgh and Oxford, and the entries under six Scottish towns, Dublin, and Oxford to 1680 are supplementary to the entries in the three lists already mentioned.

For British publications of the eighteenth century we have until recently had to make use of the British Museum *General catalogue of printed books* and the *National Union catalog*, and also two older publications by Watt and Lowndes:

Watt, R. BIBLIOTHECA BRITANNICA; OR, A GENERAL INDEX TO BRITISH AND FOREIGN LITERATURE. Edinburgh: Constable, 1824. 4 vols.

Watt aimed to be comprehensive for British authors, and selective for foreign publications. Vols 1 and 2 are arranged alphabetically by author, giving brief information about each work. Vols 3 and 4 form an alphabetical subject index, giving for each work the date and brief title, and referring to the author list. Anonymous titles are listed in Vols 3 and 4.

W. T. Lowndes recognized that Watt's work was incomplete, because his plan was so extensive. In his *Bibliographer's manual of English literature*, first published in 1834, Lowndes aimed to compile a national bibliography, limited to works published in or relating to Great Britain and Ireland, but including as much detail as possible about their publication history, and their contents. H. B.

Bohn produced a new edition of Lowndes' work, in 6 vols (London: Bell, 1857–1864).

There is now a new work we can turn to, which, at the date of its publication, claimed to be the most complete listing of eighteenth-century British books:

EIGHTEENTH CENTURY BRITISH BOOKS. An author union catalogue extracted from the British Museum *General catalogue of printed books*; the catalogues of the Bodleian Library; and of the University Library, Cambridge. By F. J. G. Robinson, G. Averley, D. R. Esslemont, and P. J. Wallis. (Project for Historical Biobibliography, University of Newcastle-upon-Tyne). Folkestone: Dawson, 1981. 5 vols.

This lists books printed in the eighteenth century, wholly or partly in English; or printed in Britain, America or the British colonies; and all translations to or from English. The compilers argue that the holdings of the Bodleian and the University Library, Cambridge, which are added to those of the British Library, are both complementary and supplementary, though it is acknowledged that the catalogue does not fully represent these libraries' holdings of music, maps and ephemera; and that the holdings of the three libraries cannot match the Celtic holdings of the national libraries of Ireland, Scotland and Wales, or the Americana of the *National Union catalog*, which are not included. Though the compilers would argue that what they have produced is a tool for historical research, and not a new bibliography independent of the contributory catalogues, the tool is both difficult to use and could be misleading. The eighteenth-century entries from the British Museum *General catalogue* to 1955 and the supplements covering 1956–1970 were converted into machine-readable form, and to this file were added new entries, new editions and additional locations from the Bodleian and Cambridge catalogues and the British Museum supplement to 1975. The basic order of records is that of the British Museum *Catalogue*, and the entries from the Bodleian and Cambridge catalogues were adjusted to that order, it is claimed. The catalogue shows a failure to ensure adequate alphabetical interfiling of entries. Under each author heading, works held at Oxford, but not at the British Library, are listed after the British

National Bibliographies

Library entries, followed by a sequence of items unique to Cambridge, followed by entries unique to the British Museum third supplement. Thus, there can be up to four sequences of titles under the one author. Because the choice of headings for the same work can differ in the three base catalogues, it was not found possible to bring together all editions of one work under one form of heading. Thus, to ensure that one has found a complete listing of all the editions of a given work held in the three libraries one must check all possible headings. The entry information for each title is very compressed. The compilers claim they have tried to retain the sense of the title within a shortened form. They have used the usual ellipses, but have omitted virtually all articles, prepositions, non-distinctive adjectives, etc. The result is that in many cases the title as given is simply neither intelligible nor recognizable to a user not already familiar with the full title and without access to the source catalogues. The various editions of the title are indicated briefly by date and edition number, place of publication, details of the number of issues, volumes or parts, and format; and location symbols are added. If one compares *Eighteenth century British books* with what will be the eventual outcome of the *Eighteenth century short-title catalogue*, the former will be judged to be more limited in its scope and less full in its coverage and the information it supplies.

The following index was published with the primary intent of forwarding local and cross cultural studies:
EIGHTEENTH CENTURY BRITISH BOOKS. An index to the foreign and provincial imprints in the Author union catalogue. Compiled by F. J. G. and J. M. Robinson and C. Wadham. Newcastle-upon-Tyne: Avero (Eighteenth Century Publications), 1982. It indexes the English, Irish, Scottish, Welsh, European, American and rest of the world imprints in the Author union catalogue.

THE EIGHTEENTH CENTURY SHORT-TITLE CATALOGUE (ESTC), based on the British Library Reference Division, will have a scope as comprehensive as practical considerations will allow. It will include all items printed in the eighteenth century in the British Isles and its dependent countries, in any language, and all items printed in English or other British vernaculars anywhere in the world. Numerous genres normally outside a catalogue of this sort will be included—atlases, hymnals, song-books, slip-songs and ballads, advertisements, sale-catalogues, type-specimens, etc, though the first stage at least excludes newspapers; engraved material such as maps, music, prints, portraits and caricatures; printed forms intended to be completed in manuscript; trade cards, tickets, playbills, concert and theatre programmes, and playing cards. After 1695, printing spread to many towns in the British Isles, and the *ESTC* will record much ephemeral printing not previously recorded. It is likely to record more than ten times as many items as the *STC 1475–1640*. The project has already involved the re-cataloguing of the British Library's eighteenth-century holdings, including items never previously catalogued separately. A limited number of locations in other libraries are already on the file, but these will be considerably augmented as the project moves into its second phase in 1983. The eighteenth-century holdings of over 150 libraries in the British Isles and over 300 in North America, together with many in Europe and Australasia, will be added. New records will be created for titles and editions not held by the British Library. Entries created during the first phase are based on an examination of the books themselves and are very full, so that the risk of faulty matching of entries from other libraries at a later stage will be minimized. *ESTC* will go beyond the short-title cataloguing of Wing and even the second edition of *STC*, and incorporate as far as is practicable detailed information on printing history, imperfections of copies, and full distinctions relating to variants and issues. Cataloguing is by a set of rules close to AACR2 and compatible with MARC. Cataloguing data will comprise author, uniform or collective title, accurate transcription of title and imprint, physical description of an ideal copy (pagination, illustration and format), year of publication (the ascertained date, and not necessarily the date given in the imprint), country of publication, language of publication, cataloguing source and its shelf mark, added entries for additional authors, general notes (on contents and authorship), bibliographical references, locations and copy notes for the cataloguing source copy. Title entries will be included for all anonymous and pseudonymous works as well as works of corporate authorship and for works included in the five genre indexes.

National Bibliographies

There has been built into the *ESTC* record the means whereby, when records are printed out by computer, sequences of an author's works and sequences of editions are presented in an intellectually and historically meaningful order.

A preliminary computer-generated microfiche catalogue of the British Library's eighteenth-century holdings was published in December 1983. This enables the user to determine the corpus of an author's work, and its indexes (by date of publication, place of publication other than London, and by selected genres such as advertisements, almanacs, songs, prospectuses, directories) assist those whose research depends on points of access other than author or title. This preliminary catalogue has over 350,000 entries for some 150,000 separate items, including some 20–25,000 previously uncatalogued items. Once the file has been augmented with the holdings of other libraries a further catalogue will be published, perhaps towards the end of the decade.

The availability of the *ESTC* file through BLAISE (British Library Automated Information Service) in Europe and through RLIN (Research Libraries Information Network) in North America for systematic online interrogation represents a novel benefit, giving indexed access, either online or by computer print-out, to every major field of the bibliographical description either singly or simultaneously, in a way that no multitude of patiently compiled indexes could ever achieve. Possible searches cited have included: all illustrated books about mathematical instruments; or English translations of foreign works on chemistry; or sermons printed in America between 1701 and 1749, but excluding those printed in Boston, New York, and Philadelphia; or all references to a particular individual; or references to a printer or bookseller appearing in the imprint.

The great expansion in the quantity of the printed word produced in the English speaking world in the eighteenth century continued throughout the nineteenth century. Despite the efforts of government (in the form of copyright laws) not even the British Museum Library was able to acquire all the printed books produced in Britain in the nineteenth century. Major factors militating against the formation of a definitive collection included the reluctance of publishers to provide, and of librarians to accept, all the publications, and the continued spread in the provinces of ephemeral presses which ignored or were ignorant of the legal requirements.

Reference may be made to a contemporary trade listing of nineteenth century publications, reasonably comprehensive for works issued from the main publishing centres, but much less complete for provincial presses, and not including periodicals and non-commercial publications:

THE ENGLISH CATALOGUE OF BOOKS. London: Sampson Low, 1864–1901; Publishers' Circular, 1906– .

A retrospective volume, covering 1801–1836, was published in 1914, and a series of cumulations cover periods from 1835 to the middle of the twentieth century. For some periods the author, title and catchword subject entries are in one sequence, for other periods the title and catchword subject listings are separate from the author listings. Bibliographical information provided is basic, and includes price.

In the near future we will have a new tool to use when searching for nineteenth century British books. The *Nineteenth century short title catalogue* (*NSTC*) project, based in Newcastle-upon-Tyne, aims to produce a series of catalogues which will contain entries for the great majority of British books for the period 1801–1918. British books will be defined as all works published in the British Isles, the colonies and dependencies both past and present, including the USA, all books in English wherever printed, and all translations from English. The catalogues will initially include the nineteenth century holdings of The British Library, The Bodleian Library, the National Library of Scotland, the library of Trinity College, Dublin, the University Library, Cambridge, and the University Library, Newcastle-upon-Tyne. A notable aspect of the catalogues will be the large number of items found in libraries other than the British Library, and the exceptionally rich holdings of Scottish imprints in the National Library of Scotland. There will be three series of catalogues, covering respectively the three periods 1801–1815, 1816–1870, and 1871–1918. Each catalogue will be an author union catalogue of its period, but in addition complete and detailed listings by both broad and narrow subject classifications and by place of imprint will be provided, together with partial title

National Bibliographies

indexes. By the use of the subject index, specific publications such as scientific texts, hymn books, novels, material relating to the theatre, plays and playwrights etc can be accurately pinpointed. The imprint index will provide some indication of the development of the provincial book trade as represented in the large libraries. The project is working first and foremost from the in-house and published catalogues of the libraries covered. The policy is to adapt the form and order of the entries of the libraries to that used in the British Museum *General catalogue*. All locations of the same work will be united in a single entry, with cross references from alternative headings. Each entry will include: a reference number; author, including epithet and life span; title (always including the first five words and all proper nouns); subject classification (up to three numbers); edition statement, including place of imprint but not details of printers and publishers; and location symbols. The emphasis will thus be upon creating a basic list of publications, rather than upon the niceties of bibliographical description. Volume 1 (Authors A–C) of the first phase (1801–1815) was published in March 1984, and volumes 2–4 will complete the author sequence, each volume containing a subject index and an index of places of imprint. Volume 5 is designed to follow the practice of the British Museum *General catalogue* in grouping certain works together under the headings Directories, Ephemerides, Periodical Publications, England, Ireland, London, and Scotland, and has a subject index, an index of places of imprint, and a title listing on computer output microfiche: thus this normally difficult to locate material will be accessible by author, subject, place of imprint and title.

The publisher of the *NSTC* is Avero Publications Limited, Newcastle-upon-Tyne, and distribution is by Chadwyck-Healey Limited, Cambridge.

All the *NSTC* records will be held eventually in one computer database so that future updating from other libraries will be possible, together with the facility for on-line access to the expanding resource. A logical extension would be to produce a secondary series of entries from special libraries, with a likelihood of finding items not held in the major collections.

Several retrospective catalogues or bibliographies of books pub-

Bibliographies of Older Material

lished in Scotland, Wales and Ireland are, or will shortly be, available. For Scottish printing up to 1700 we can refer to:

Aldis, H. G. A LIST OF BOOKS PRINTED IN SCOTLAND BEFORE 1700, INCLUDING THOSE PRINTED FURTH OF THE REALM FOR SCOTTISH BOOKSELLERS. Edinburgh: Edinburgh Bibliographical Society, 1904. Photographically reprinted with additions, National Library of Scotland, 1970.

Aldis has a chronological arrangement: under each year, entries are arranged alphabetically by author or title. Aldis's original numeration has been retained, and new entries have been added by using decimal points. There is a proliferation of indexes—of printers, booksellers, and stationers, and of authors and anonymous titles.

For works printed in Scottish Gaelic we should soon be able to refer to Vol 1 of the SCOTTISH GAELIC UNION CATALOGUE, compiled by M. Ferguson and A. Matheson, due to be published in April 1984 by the National Library of Scotland.

This catalogue will include all books printed in Scottish Gaelic or with a substantial amount of Gaelic, and will be in the nature of a finding list, since not all copies of works in the catalogue will have been examined. Vol 1 will include material in libraries in Scotland and in other major British libraries. A later volume is intended to cover material in foreign libraries and private collections. This catalogue will eventually supersede:

Maclean, D. TYPOGRAPHIA SCOTO-GADELICA: OR BOOKS PRINTED IN THE GAELIC OF SCOTLAND, 1567–1914. Edinburgh: Grant, 1915.

Maclean's work was based on information collected by him from librarians, booksellers and private collectors, with some entries based on his own library, but the passage of time has shown it to be unreliable, and it also lacks locations.

The National Library of Wales is due to publish in 1985:

LIBRI WALLIAE: A CATALOGUE OF WELSH BOOKS AND BOOKS PRINTED IN WALES BEFORE 1820.

National Bibliographies

This catalogue has been compiled at the National Library of Wales by E. Rees and most of the entries are based on the Library's collections, while other items have been traced in other libraries and private collections. Entries will be included for works of which no copies survive. It excludes ephemera, almanacs and ballads. The arrangement is alphabetical by author. To distinguish between different writers of the same name, dates or epithets are used, with any bardic name being added. All books by writers with the same name are filed alphabetically by title, ignoring dates and epithets, thus obviating the necessity of knowing the author's credentials before embarking on a search for the title wanted. A separate volume will contain indexes of titles and names, a chronological index, and an index of the book trade. For Welsh books within its period this will be the new authority. There is an older work which might be useful for such books published after 1820:

Cardiff Free Libraries. CATALOGUE OF PRINTED LITERATURE IN THE WELSH DEPARTMENT. Cardiff: Free Libraries Committee; London: Sotheran, 1898.

Books printed in Ireland can be looked for in two catalogues:

Dix, E. R. M. CATALOGUE OF EARLY DUBLIN-PRINTED BOOKS, 1601–1700. Dublin: O'Donoghue; London: Dobell, 1898–1912. 4 vols and supplement.

Cambridge University Library. CATALOGUE OF THE BRADSHAW COLLECTION OF IRISH BOOKS IN THE UNIVERSITY LIBRARY, CAMBRIDGE. London: Quaritch, 1916. 3 vols.

Complementing the national bibliographies of a country are certain bibliographies which list special categories of publications. The bibliography of anonymous and pseudonymous publications in English is:

Halkett, S. and Laing, J. DICTIONARY OF ANONYMOUS AND PSEUDONYMOUS ENGLISH LITERATURE. New and enlarged ed. Edinburgh: Oliver and Boyd, 1926–1962. 9 vols.

Bibliographies of Older Material

Halkett and Laing list only those anonymous and pseudonymous works for which an author has been found. There are several sequences arranged by the first word of the title not an article. Under the title is given some brief bibliographical information, a statement of the author's identity and usually a brief indication of the source of the information (many sources are secondary, such as library catalogues). A revision of Halkett and Laing has been started under the direction of Dr J. R. B. Horden, in which every entry is being revised, new entries are being added, and every attribution is being fully documented. The revision is intended to be published in recognized chronological periods. The first volume of this edition was published in 1980 as *Halkett and Laing, A dictionary of anonymous and pseudonymous publications in the English language, third revised and enlarged edition, 1475–1640*. Under each entry full supporting evidence is given for the attribution to an author. The volume also includes indexes of authors and pseudonyms, and tables of numbers in other standard reference works.

The major retrospective bibliography of English literature is:

Watson, G. (*ed.*) THE NEW CAMBRIDGE BIBLIOGRAPHY OF ENGLISH LITERATURE. Cambridge: Cambridge University Press, 1969–1977. 5 vols.

This constitutes a revision of *The Cambridge bibliography of English literature*, 1940, 4 vols, with Supplement, 1957. The *New CBEL* is a bibliography of literature, not of publications in the wider sense, and it was not found to be practical to preserve in their entirety such non-literary sections of the original *CBEL* as Political and social background, Science, Economics, Law, etc. Also dropped are the original sections on the literatures of certain Commonwealth countries. The *New CBEL* is therefore confined to literary authors native to, or mainly resident in, the British Isles, though no restriction of nationality or language has been imposed on the choice of secondary materials listed. But within the field of English studies, it aims at completeness. The basic division is by period, and Vol 5 is a general index. Within each period, the arrangement is by literary genre. Within each author section are listed bibliographies, collections and selections of the author's

National Bibliographies

works; the canon of the author's work, the primary material, usually in a single chronological sequence; and secondary material, biographies and criticisms of the author. Major authors are treated in greater detail than minor authors. In the provision of bibliographical details in the primary section, the detail of an entry is most intense in the early years of the life of a book, though, in general, details are brief. Later editions of a work are cited only when revised by the author, or containing substantial revisions, or having authorial and/or editorial introductions and apparatus. One writer has enlarged on the chances missed in this bibliography—he thinks that the work could have provided information on the contents and interrelationships of the collected editions and selections, more bibliographical distinctions, at least for an author's early editions, specific details about authorial revision, more details of contemporary translations, etc.[9]

This major bibliography has been reduced to a fifth or less in:

Watson, G. (*ed.*) THE SHORTER NEW CAMBRIDGE BIBLIOGRAPHY OF ENGLISH LITERATURE. Cambridge: Cambridge University Press, 1981.

The basic division by period of the original work has been retained, though sections such as 'Book production and distribution' and 'Literary relations with the Continent' have been left out. All the major authors and many minor ones have been included. Under the individual authors, the canon of the author's work has been retained, but much of the secondary reading has been left out. It could be argued that for the general reader and the student, for whom this *Shorter bibliography* might have been designed, the emphasis should have been in the opposite direction.

One catalogue devoted to one literary genre over a limited period deserves mention:

Foxon, D. F. ENGLISH VERSE 1701–1750: A CATALOGUE OF SEPARATELY PRINTED POEMS WITH NOTES ON CONTEMPORARY COLLECTED EDITIONS. London: Cambridge University Press, 1975. 2 vols.

Foxon lists all separately published verse written in English, as well as verse written in other languages and printed in the British

Bibliographies of Older Material

Isles, between 1701 and 1750. Entries are made under author, or first word of title for anonymous works. Each entry has six sections: heading, title and imprint; collation; bibliographical note; first line; notes on authorship and subject; locations. The description, though brief, is based on an examination of as many copies as possible, and distinguishes the various editions, issues and variants of a writer's works, and thus goes beyond what is normally expected of enumerative bibliography. It is a short-title catalogue with more bibliographical sophistication than *STC* or Wing, possible because the scope is more limited. The indexes in Vol 2 (index of first lines; chronological index; index of imprints; index of bibliographical notabilia; index of descriptive epithets; and subject index) will provide fresh approaches to the study of the verse of the period.

United States of America

American retrospective bibliography is served by the *National Union catalog, pre-1956 imprints*, by the New York Public Library's *Dictionary catalog of the research libraries, 1911–1971*, and by several bibliographies and catalogues covering more limited periods.

The most important general listing of early American publications is:

Evans, C. AMERICAN BIBLIOGRAPHY. A CHRONOLOGICAL DICTIONARY OF ALL BOOKS, PAMPHLETS AND PERIODICAL PUBLICATIONS PRINTED IN THE UNITED STATES OF AMERICA . . . 1639 . . . TO . . . 1800. Chicago: The author, 1903–1934. 12 vols. Completed by Vol 13, 1799–1800, by C. K. Shipton (1955), and Vol 14, Index of authors and titles, by R. P. Bristol (1959)—both volumes published Worcester, Massachusetts: American Antiquarian Society.

In Evans the items are arranged chronologically by year of publication, and then alphabetically by author or anonymous title. Evans often listed anonymous works under the author to whom he attributed a work without providing a cross-reference from the title. Bibliographical information is given in some detail, including when possible locations and price at auction. Evans is a basic authority, though his work contains errors and he was unable to trace some items. Each volume has its own indexes, of authors, classified subjects and printers and publishers, and there is a cumulated index of authors and titles in Vol 14. In Vol 13 Shipton supplied cross-references from titles of anonymous books to the author to whom they were attributed, gave shorter titles but full imprints, and provided indexes of authors and of subjects.

R. P. Bristol went on to compile an *Index of printers, publishers and booksellers indicated by Charles Evans* (Charlottesville: Bibliographical Society of the University of Virginia, 1961); a *Supplement to Charles Evans* (Charlottesville: University Press of Virginia, 1979), and an *Index to the supplement to Charles Evans* (Charlottesville: University Press of Virginia, 1971).

Bristol's *Supplement* adds another 11,000 titles to the 39,000 listed by Evans and Shipton in a chronological arrangement, but even he, it appears, has achieved less than a complete coverage, and he did not see many of the items he describes.

Not all Bristol's additional items are included in the following short-title listing of Evans items:

Shipton, C. K. and Mooney, J. E. NATIONAL INDEX OF AMERICAN IMPRINTS THROUGH 1800: THE SHORT-TITLE EVANS. Worcester and Barre, Massachusetts: American Antiquarian Society and Barre Publishers, 1969. 2 vols.

This lists some 40,000 titles in alphabetical order of author or anonymous title (anonymous items appear under the title and again under the author if known), incorporating corrections and additional items. Very brief titles are followed by place of publication, name of printer and publisher, date, pagination, the location of the copy microfilmed by the Readex Microprint Corporation, and a reference to the serial number of the item in Evans.

The other cornerstone of American retrospective bibliography is:

Sabin, J. A. DICTIONARY OF BOOKS RELATING TO AMERICA FROM ITS DISCOVERY TO THE PRESENT

Bibliographies of Older Material

TIME. New York: Sabin, 1868–1892; Bibliographical Society of America, 1928–1936. 29 vols.

This work, also known by its half-title, *Bibliotheca Americana*, was begun by Sabin but had to be completed by others. It is unfortunately uneven in chronological coverage, and its scope had to be reduced with the passage of time, though it remains the most comprehensive bibliography of Americana. It lists both works published in North and South America, including periodicals, though certain categories of material (such as literature and the natural sciences) are sparsely represented. It is not well organized: perhaps a quarter of the entries treat works printed before 1801, and many of these are hidden away among entries listing later works. Arrangement is alphabetical by author or anonymous title with other entries under place-names. Entries, numbered serially, often include annotations, collations and locations.

J. E. Molnar has compiled an *Author-title index to Joseph Sabin's 'Dictionary of books relating to America'* (Metuchen: Scarecrow Press, 1974. 3 vols).

Publication has now begun of a new guide to works printed in Europe, relating to the Americas:

EUROPEAN AMERICANA: A CHRONOLOGICAL GUIDE TO WORKS PRINTED IN EUROPE RELATING TO THE AMERICAS, 1493–1776. VOLUME 1: 1493–1600. VOLUME 2: 1601–1650. Edited by J. Alden with D. C. Landis. New York: Readex Books, 1980–   .

Vol 3 is to cover the seventeenth century, Vols 4–6 the eighteenth century, with Vol 7 being a cumulative index. Vol 1 lists some 4,000 items, only a quarter of which are entered in Sabin. Vol 2 lists 7,400 items, less than one third of which appear in Sabin. It gives a terse and unencumbered presentation of salient American content as well as identifying details of the books, references to bibliographies, and locations, mainly in US libraries. The chronological arrangement is supplemented by a geographic index of printers and booksellers and their publications, showing the spread of the knowledge of America throughout Europe; an alphabetical index of printers and booksellers and their geographic locations; and an index of authors, titles and subjects.

National Bibliographies

For some time two incomplete and inaccurate catalogues, which do not locate copies, have had to be used as an additional help in tracing American publications of the period 1820 to 1870:

Roorbach, O. A. BIBLIOTHECA AMERICANA, 1820–1861. New York: Roorbach, 1852–1861. 4 vols.

Kelly, J. THE AMERICAN CATALOGUE OF BOOKS, 1861–1871. New York: Wiley, 1866–1871. 2 vols.

The gap between 1800 when Evans stops, and 1820, when Roorbach starts, has now been filled by:

Shaw, R. R. and Shoemaker, R. H. AMERICAN BIBLIOGRAPHY: A PRELIMINARY CHECKLIST FOR 1801(–1819). New York: Scarecrow Press, 1958–1983. 23 vols.

Each of Vols 1–19 covers one year, and within the year arrangement is alphabetical by author or anonymous title. Periodicals and newspapers are included once only. Only the briefest details are given of some items. Items are numbered. Locations are included, where known, otherwise references to other sources are given. There are indexes of authors, of titles, of printers, publishers and booksellers, and a geographical index. The checklist has been compiled from secondary sources and will no doubt be enlarged at a later date.

A continuation of the Shaw and Shoemaker checklist is being compiled to provide fuller coverage than Roorbach. R. H. Shoemaker, assisted in later volumes by G. Cooper, published *A Checklist of American imprints for 1820(–1829)* (New York: Scarecrow Press, 1964–1972), with author and title indexes by M. F. Cooper. Newspapers and periodicals are not included in this series, which is being carried on into the 1830s by various compilers. The preface to the 1831 volume emphasizes that it is meant to be a preliminary checklist of items, based on sketchy and intermediary sources, with few items examined, and providing selected locations. Even so, it will probably list eight times as many titles as are in Roorbach.

Publications of the period 1876 to 1910 were listed in:

AMERICAN CATALOGUE OF BOOKS, 1876–1910. New York: A. C. Armstrong, Publishers Weekly, 1880–1911.

Bibliographies of Older Material

This was a series of trade lists of books in print, based on reports from publishers, nevertheless fairly comprehensive and generally reliable. The basic work listing books in print in 1876, one volume arranged under authors and titles, a second volume serving as a subject list, was supplemented by volumes covering various periods up to 1910.

Later volumes of the *American catalogue of books* were superseded by H. W. Wilson's *Cumulative book index: A world list of books in the English language* (New York, 1898–) and the *United States catalog* (four editions between 1900 and 1928, listing books in print).

The major retrospective bibliography of American literature is:

Blanck, J. BIBLIOGRAPHY OF AMERICAN LITERATURE. New Haven: Yale University Press, 1955–

Seven volumes have been published to date, with one or two to follow. The arrangement is alphabetical by the name of the authors treated. Vol 1 begins with Henry Brooks Adams, Vol 7 ends with Frank Richard Stockton. This work is a selective bibliography of American literary authors which, when complete, will cover 300 authors, from the time of the Revolution up to and including writers who died before the end of 1930. The criterion for inclusion is significance in American, not necessarily world, literature. While it does not pretend to supersede existing author bibliographies, within its own terms of reference it supplements and corrects them, and will serve as the basis for such bibliographies of those authors not so treated already, so accurate and thorough are its descriptions. Under each author are listed, in chronological order, all first editions of primary books (all works of belles-lettres and certain non-literary books) with details of title, imprint, pagination, signature collation, binding, publication history, and locations of copies examined in American libraries. Non-literary works generally, secondary books (contributions), revised editions, books edited, and extracts from a primary book, etc, have shorter descriptions. Then follow selected biographical, bibliographical and critical works. It does not aim to include periodical and newspaper publications, later editions, or translations.

National Bibliographies
France

The author catalogue of the Bibliothèque Nationale serves as the single most extensive retrospective national bibliography; and, especially for the earlier centuries, reference may be had to Brunet's *Manuel du libraire et de l'amateur des livres*.

Another bibliography which covers selectively the publications of several centuries is:

Tchemerzine, A. BIBLIOGRAPHIE D'ÉDITIONS ORIGINALES ET RARES D'AUTEURS FRANÇAIS DES XVe, XVIe, XVIIe ET XVIIIe SIÈCLES. Paris: Plée, 1927–1934. 10 vols.

Arrangement is alphabetical by author. Tchemerzine claims to include facsimilies of over 6,000 title-pages, representing works by some 120 major French authors up to 1800, including most major authors. He includes also detailed title-page transcriptions and bibliographical descriptions.

For works of the fifteenth and sixteenth centuries we can refer to:

British Museum. SHORT-TITLE CATALOGUE OF BOOKS PRINTED IN FRANCE AND OF FRENCH BOOKS PRINTED IN OTHER COUNTRIES FROM 1470 TO 1600 NOW IN THE BRITISH MUSEUM. London: British Museum, 1924.

This catalogue includes many editions not found in the printed author catalogue of the Bibliothèque Nationale, although it represents only a proportion of the publications of the period. There are two sections, Books printed in France, and Books in French printed elsewhere. Arrangement is alphabetical by author or anonymous title, the choice of heading and arrangement of entries within the heading following the British Museum *General catalogue* rules, though some of the more complicated headings have been simplified. Titles have been abbreviated as much as possible by the omission of non-essential words and phrases. Though this catalogue can be used on its own, it is best used in conjunction with the British Museum's *General catalogue*.

Bibliographies of Older Material

Compilation of a comprehensive short-title catalogue of French sixteenth-century books, similar to the Pollard and Redgrave *STC* of English books, has proved difficult. French sixteenth-century books were exported in large numbers throughout Europe, and émigré printers published in French in a number of cities.

Books printed or published in Paris in this period are being listed in:

Moreau, B. INVENTAIRE CHRONOLOGIQUE DES ÉDITIONS PARISIENNES DU XVIe SIÈCLE . . . D'APRÈS LES MANUSCRITS DE PHILIPPE RENOUARD. Paris: Imprimerie Municipale, 1972–   . In progress.

Vols 1 and 2, covering the decades 1501–1510 and 1511–1520, will be followed by volumes covering the remaining decades of the century. Within each year, the order of entries is alphabetical by author or anonymous title, and the description gives the names of any editor, translator, etc, the name of printer and bookseller, the date (day and month), format, and locations. In Vol 1 there is separate numbering for each year, but in Vol 2 the numeration is continuous throughout the volume. In each volume, there is an index of authors and anonymous titles and of printers and booksellers, though there will be a need for cumulated indexes to all the volumes when compilation is finished.

The most comprehensive listing of French sixteenth-century books published outside Paris is:

RÉPERTOIRE BIBLIOGRAPHIQUE DES LIVRES IMPRIMÉS EN FRANCE AU SEIZIÈME SIÈCLE. (Bibliotheca bibliographica Aureliana, 25, etc). Baden-Baden: Libraire Heitz, Editions Valentin Koerner, 1968–1980. 30 parts.

This does not cover books printed or published in Lyon, Strasbourg, Caen and Rouen, which are or will be covered by other publications. Each part and its constituent fascicles cover one or more places of printing or publication. Under each place of printing, arrangement is by printer or publisher and date. Information given includes a full title transcription in cases where books have been examined; full imprint transcription; format; locations in libraries; or sometimes only references to other bibliographies. The

National Bibliographies

final part lists the contents of the previous parts; provides an alphabetical listing of places of printing, with the names of the printers in chronological order, an alphabetical index of printers and publishers, and an alphabetical index of authors and anonymous titles.

An author catalogue of French sixteenth-century books in one particular collection devoted to the history of printing and book illustration is provided in:

Harvard College Library, Department of Printing and Graphic Arts. CATALOGUE OF BOOKS AND MANUSCRIPTS. PART I: FRENCH SIXTEENTH CENTURY BOOKS. Cambridge, Massachusetts: Belknap Press of Harvard University Press, 1964.

This is the type of catalogue in which one might have expected a basic chronological or subject arrangement, with alphabetical indexes. As it is, titles are given in order of publication date under author or form heading. Each entry gives the title, imprint, date, format, notes on the ornamentation, illustration and typography, on the bibliographical status of the text, and on the particular copy described, the collation, and references to other sources. There is a chronological index, a general index, and indexes of artists, printers and publishers, and subjects.

A comprehensive listing of French seventeenth-century books is now in progress:

RÉPERTOIRE BIBLIOGRAPHIQUE DES LIVRES IMPRIMÉS EN FRANCE AU XVIIe SIÈCLE. (Bibliotheca bibliographica Aureliana, 75, etc). Baden-Baden: Koerner, 1978– .

In the seventeenth century the printing of works of general interest became more centralized in Paris, and works printed in the provinces tended to have a more local character. The present writer has seen eight volumes of this work to date. Each volume is treating one town, or grouping together the towns in a region. Under the towns, items are being listed chronologically by date of publication. Some volumes have a table of printers and publishers and an index of authors and anonymous titles. General indexes, referring to all the volumes, will be required when compilation is complete.

Bibliographies of Older Material

One of the richest collections of French seventeenth-century books outside France is described in:

Goldsmith, V. F. A SHORT TITLE CATALOGUE OF FRENCH BOOKS, 1601–1700, IN THE LIBRARY OF THE BRITISH MUSEUM. Folkestone: Dawson, 1969–1973.

It includes books in any language printed within the boundaries of France as they are today, and books wholly or partly in French, wherever published. It is not merely a reproduction of the relevant entries from the British Museum's *General catalogue*, but includes individual entries for a large number of 'Mazarinades' not previously separately catalogued. The choice of headings derives from the *General catalogue*'s rules, but the omission from this catalogue of many of the *General catalogue*'s cross-references creates difficulty, which has only been partially solved by a list of 'Alternative forms of names used in the headings'. The indexes are useful, including a selective index of titles (including anonymous works not easily traced elsewhere), and indexes of translators, editors and annotators, of printers and publishers, and of places, with reference back to the index of printers and publishers.

For publications of the eighteenth, and the beginning of the nineteenth, centuries, we can refer to:

Quérard, J. M. LA FRANCE LITTÉRAIRE, OU DICTIONNAIRE BIBLIOGRAPHIQUE DES SAVANTS, HISTORIENS ET GENS DE LETTRES DE LA FRANCE AINSI QUE DES LITTÉRATEURS ÉTRANGERS QUI ONT ÉCRIT EN FRANÇAIS PLUS PARTICULIÈREMENT PENDANT LES XVIIIe ET XIXe SIÈCLES. Paris: Didot, 1827–1864. 12 vols.

Quérard does not limit himself to 'literary' authors but aims to provide a complete national bibliography from 1700. Under the name of each author, arranged alphabetically, he gives biographical details, and details of the author's works, including title, place of publication, publisher, date, format, price, and sometimes historical and critical notes. Vols 11 and 12 list by real name the authors of anonymous and pseudonymous works, with biographical information and details of the works, thus serving as an index to Quérard's *Superchéries littéraires dévoilées* (see below).

National Bibliographies

This work is continued on the same general plan further into the nineteenth century by:

Quérard, J. M. (*et al.*) LA LITTÉRATURE FRANÇAISE CONTEMPORAINE, 1827–1849. Paris: Daguin, 1840–1857. 6 vols.

The standard French trade bibliography for the rest of the nineteenth and early twentieth centuries is known as Lorenz:

CATALOGUE GÉNÉRAL DE LA LIBRAIRIE FRANÇAISE, 1840–1925, par O. Lorenz (continued by others). Paris: Publisher varies, 1867–1945. 34 vols.

To use Lorenz one does need to have some idea of the date of publication of the book one is looking for, as the division is by chronological period of varying lengths. The volumes for each chronological period consist of a main author and anonymous title listing, and a subject list arranged by broad subjects. Lorenz attempts to include all books published in France, and French books published elsewhere, but excludes periodicals (as does Quérard, whose general plan he follows). Lorenz took most of his information from the *Journal de la librairie*.

G. Vicaire, in his *Manuel de l'amateur des livres du XIXe siècle, 1801–1893* (Paris: Rouquette, 1894–1920. 8 vols), attempted to do for the nineteenth century what Brunet did for earlier centuries. In an alphabetical author arrangement he lists fewer titles than Lorenz, but gives fuller information and annotations, including details of the work's publishing history, its illustrations, and its binding.

The bibliography of anonymous and pseudonymous publications in French is:

Quérard, J. M. LES SUPERCHÉRIES LITTÉRAIRES DÉVOILÉES. 2e édition par G. Brunet et P. Jannet. Suivi du Dictionnaire des ouvrages anonymes par A. A. Barbier. 3e édition par O. Barbier et P. Billard. Paris: Daffis, 1869–1879. 7 vols.

This is supplemented by:

Brunet, G. DICTIONNAIRE DES OUVRAGES ANONYMES (DE BARBIER) SUIVI DES SUPERCHÉRIES LITTÉRAIRES

Bibliographies of Older Material

DÉVOILÉES (DE QUÉRARD): SUPPLÉMENT À LA DERNIÈRE ÉDITION DE CES DEUX OUVRAGES. Paris: Féchoz, 1889.

Quérard lists the pseudonym, initials, etc, under which the book was written, then the author's real name, title and other bibliographical details; Barbier lists the title, the author to whom it is attributed, and bibliographical details.

For students of French literature there is no one retrospective bibliography as broad in scope as the *New Cambridge bibliography of English literature*. The following is a selective and evaluative bibliography, compiled by specialists for advanced students:

A CRITICAL BIBLIOGRAPHY OF FRENCH LITERATURE. Syracuse, New York: Syracuse University Press, 1947– . In progress.

Volumes published to date cover the medieval period, the sixteenth to eighteenth centuries, and the twentieth century. Under period, the basic division is by genre. For each author there is a selective listing of bibliographies, of editions of the works, and of biographical and critical works, with annotations. Each volume has an index.

Other bibliographies of French literature are more limited in chronological scope.

Cioranescu, A. and Saulnier, V. L. BIBLIOGRAPHIE DE LA LITTÉRATURE FRANÇAISE DU XVIᴇ SIÈCLE. Paris: Klincksieck, 1959.

Coverage is wide, including literature and everything touching on literature, but the bibliography is selective in that only the most important writers and some secondary authors are included, and only a selection of editions of their works and of critical works is listed.

Cioranescu, A. BIBLIOGRAPHIE DE LA LITTÉRATURE FRANÇAISE DU DIX-SEPTIÈME SIÈCLE. Paris: Éditions du Centre National de la Recherche Scientifique, 1965–1967. 3 vols.

The seventeenth-century volumes are limited to literature more

References

precisely than the sixteenth-century volume, omitting science, law and medicine, but keeping some theology and some history, geography and travel. Again, it does not aim to list all editions.

Cioranescu, A. BIBLIOGRAPHIE DE LA LITTÉRATURE FRANÇAISE DU DIX-HUITIÈME SIÈCLE. Paris, Éditions du Centre National de la Recherche Scientifique, 1969. 3 vols.

The scope and selectivity of the eighteenth-century volumes is similar to that of the seventeenth-century volumes.

Two bibliographies cover French literary authors of the nineteenth and early twentieth centuries:

Thième, H. P. BIBLIOGRAPHIE DE LA LITTÉRATURE FRANÇAISE DE 1800 À 1930. Paris: Droz, 1933. 3 vols.

Talvart, H. and Place, J. BIBLIOGRAPHIE DES AUTEURS MODERNES DE LANGUE FRANÇAISE, 1801–1927. Paris: Chronique des Lettres Françaises, 1928– . In progress. Vols 1–22, so far published, cover A–Morgan.

Talvart and Place is more selective than Thième, but gives fuller information.

REFERENCES AND CITATIONS

1. Stokes, R. *The function of bibliography*. 2nd ed. Aldershot: Gower Publishing Co, 1982. 17.
2. Alston, R. C. [Review of R. Stokes, *The function of bibliography*, 2nd edition, Aldershot, 1982]. *The Library*, 6th series, **6** (1984). 81.
3. The manuscript of the Register of the Stationers' Company from 1557 is extant and has been microfilmed. *A transcript of the registers of the Company of Stationers of London, 1554–1640* has been edited by E. Arber (London: Arber, 1875–1894. 5 vols), and *A transcript of the registers of the Worshipful Company of Stationers from 1640–1708* has been edited by G. E. B. Eyre, transcribed by H. R. Plomer (London: Roxburghe Club, 1913–1914, 3 vols). The Register of the Stationers' Company was a list of claims to copyright, but nevertheless, for the period before the Civil War, it was the fullest contemporary record of books published.
4. Clough, E. [Review of the second edition, Vol 2, of *A short-title*

Bibliographies of Older Material

catalogue ... 1475–1640]. *Library Association Record*, 78 (11), November 1976. 542.
5. Alston, R. C. in: *Papers of the Bibliographical Society of America*, 71 (3), 1977. 394.
6. Rogers, D. The revision of the STC. *The Times Literary Supplement*, 27 August 1976. 1061.
7. A classified list of new books which appeared quarterly from 1668 to 1709. The Term Catalogues were edited by E. Arber (London: Arber, 1903–1906. 3 vols).
8. McKenzie, D. F. Type-bound typography. *The Times Literary Supplement*, 17 December 1982. 1403.
9. Bateson, F. W. [Letter], *The Times Literary Supplement*, 25 December 1969. 1472.

SUGGESTIONS FOR FURTHER READING

The student should attempt to examine as many as possible of the bibliographies and catalogues referred to in this chapter, and should in particular read the prefaces and introductions to them.

Walford, A. J. *Guide to reference material*. Vol 3. 3rd ed. London: Library Association, 1977; and Sheehy, E. P. *Guide to reference books*. 9th ed. Chicago: American Library Association, 1976. With *Supplement*, 1980, and *Second Supplement*, 1982. Both these works will help the student to trace the retrospective national bibliographies of countries other than Great Britain, the United States, and France.

Malclès, L. N. *Manuel de bibliographie*. 3e édition revue par A. Lhéritier. Paris: Presses Universitaires de France, 1976.
Has an international scope, with emphasis on French-language materials. The section 'Bibliographies générales' (pp 11–168) provides descriptions and evaluations of the more important bibliographies, and is particularly good on the theoretical and historical background.

The German equivalents of Malclès are Totok, W., Weimann, K. H., and Weitzel, R. *Handbuch der bibliographischen Nachschlagewerke*. 4. Aufl. Frankfurt am Main: Klostermann, 1972; and Koppitz, H. J. *Grundzüge der Bibliographie*. München: Verlag Dokumentation, 1977.

Padwick, E. W. *Bibliographical method: an introductory survey*. Cambridge: James Clark, 1969.
Pt 2, Chapter 8 is devoted to bibliographies of incunabula.

Pollard, G. General lists of books printed in England. (Bibliographical

Further Reading

aids to research, 4). *Bulletin of the Institute of Historical Research*, 12, February 1935. 164–74.
A concise and informative summary, dealing with the Stationers' Register, contemporary book-trade lists (including the Term Catalogues) and bibliographies.

Howard-Hill, T. H. *Bibliography of British literary bibliographies*. (Index to British literary bibliography, Vol 1). Oxford: Clarendon Press, 1969.
Lists general and period bibliographies (pp 24–79), regional bibliographies (pp 82–112), and also bibliographies of presses and printing, forms and genres, subjects, and authors.

Tanselle, G. T. *Guide to the study of U.S. imprints*. Cambridge, Massachusetts: Harvard University Press, 1971. 2 vols.
Tanselle discusses in his Introduction and itemizes regional lists, both those covering the US as a whole and those covering sections of the US, genre lists, and author lists.

Hackman, M. L. *The practical bibliographer*. Englewood Cliffs, New Jersey: Prentice Hall, 1970.
Chapter 3, 'Retrospective national and trade bibliography', deals with United States national and trade lists, and includes facsimiles of pages from them, useful for those unable to refer to the bibliographies themselves.

17

Subject Bibliographies

J. David Lee

When does a librarian need to use subject bibliographies? Why does he or she need to know about them? In a reference library, the librarian will sometimes meet the reader who knows what he wants and where it is to be found, but more often the opposite is the case. It is knowledge of sources of information which makes the librarian a professional. Books and similar information-bearing materials are his stock in trade, whether a specific reference or an account of the literature on a subject is to be found. The aim of this chapter is to develop, in a practical way, an appreciation of the subject approach, assuming that author bibliographies have not been able to provide the answer. Whilst no librarian knows all subject bibliographies—over 8,000 have appeared in *BNB* between 1950 and 1981[1]—he must know the main general sources and have a firm idea of the types of bibliography which are likely to exist in a subject, and he must be able to trace them. Some subject bibliographic structures the librarian will learn during his training; others he will develop in his career. It is valuable as well as satisfying to be bibliographically minded.

In this chapter we shall discuss the various types of bibliographies, and then the problems of subject bibliography. Examples, mainly limited to the English language, are drawn from varied fields, and the reader can try applying a bibliographical framework to any other subject. It is the total approach to subject bibliographical apparatus which is stressed here. Other chapters have included bibliographies in their place; this one will sharpen up the approach to the genre.

There is no perfect approach to enquiries as a whole, or to the use of bibliographies, though there may be certain types of enquiry which demand a structured response. In general the librarian needs a firm command of the tools of his trade, and to use his knowledge with flexibility.

Shortly we shall deal with the more important general subject bibliographies, which must be known and understood by all. After these, the groupings are arbitrary, but dictated by a feeling that the difference between selective and comprehensive coverage is a crucial one. These are the categories:

1. general retrospective and current bibliographies with a subject approach, including guides to reference books, and library catalogues;
2. subject bibliographies of a selective nature, including series, handbooks to literatures; 'systematic bibliographies' according to Roberts;[2]
3. subject bibliographies with a claim to be comprehensive;
4. special library catalogues, and guides to libraries;
5. analytical indexes of various kinds, including those to periodicals, government publications, and other materials; concordances.

GENERAL BIBLIOGRAPHIES WITH A SUBJECT APPROACH

In seeking material on a subject where the author is not known, general bibliographies may be the first port of call. *British national bibliography* has, from 1950, given a subject approach to British publications on a classified (DC) basis. The American *Cumulative book index*, from 1928, has given a wider world coverage under alphabetical subject headings. To have the two approaches is useful; they represent a fundamental difference in cataloguing between the two countries. The weekly and monthly trade and reviewing jour-

Subject Bibliographies

nals have a different function, namely as aids to selection, and usually lack a detailed and consistent subject approach, often relying on key-word of title. The *Subject guide to books in print*, published annually by Bowker, is what it says, using subject headings for tracing material. It is supplemented in the *Books in print* supplement. A new work from Bowker, *Subject guide to international books in print 1984* extends the scope.

For works published before 1928, one has mainly to turn to library catalogues (see below), as earlier bibliographies are of little value from the subject angle. The attempts of Watt, Brunet and Lowndes are historically interesting.[3] Older bibliographies are the subject of the previous chapter.

General library catalogues

The large repositories are collections of books on all subjects, and their catalogues are, in a sense, total bibliographies for their national literatures. The British Library (founded 1753) began with author lists, but later came to subjects by both approaches—a classified catalogue from 1824 to 1834 under T. H. Horne, and an alphabetical index, from 1874, under George Fortescue.[4]

The BRITISH LIBRARY SUBJECT INDEX OF MODERN BOOKS ACQUIRED. London: British Library, 1982. 12 vols.

In printed form, edited in recent years by F. J. Hill, this has now reached 1961–1970.

Peddie, R. A. SUBJECT INDEX OF BOOKS PUBLISHED BEFORE 1880. London: Grafton, 1933–1948. 4 vols.

The bibliography to consult for earlier works; it is not limited to the British Library. The supplements in some volumes should not be missed.

LIBRARY OF CONGRESS SUBJECT CATALOGUE has been published quarterly since 1950. It is a current subject bibliography, using Library of Congress alphabetical subject headings. Co-operative cataloguing allows the inclusion of other libraries' materials.

General Bibliographies with a Subject Approach

The LONDON LIBRARY SUBJECT INDEX, listing its books to 1953, is an important and convenient general British source, again using subject headings. Work proceeds on a continuation likely to be published in microfiche form.

In closed-access days, and even afterwards, public libraries such as Westminster, Manchester, Bristol, or Glasgow, produced subject catalogues or class lists. Library catalogues and bibliographies can rarely be confused, and it is a remarkable library which can claim its catalogue to be a bibliography. The Institute of Chartered Accountants added material, not possessed, to make its catalogue—*Historical accounting literature* (1975)—more of a bibliography. Other special library catalogues are dealt with more fully below.

General guides to reference books

To find details of reference books which may help in obtaining information, we have two good guides which try to keep as up to date as possible:

Sheehy, E. P. GUIDE TO REFERENCE BOOKS. Chicago: American Library Association, 1976; Supplements 1980, 1982, 1984.

Walford, A. J. GUIDE TO REFERENCE MATERIAL. London: Library Association. 3 vols.

Sheehy's work is the ninth edition of a classic which, as Kroeger, Mudge and Winchell, goes back to 1902; Walford's is in its fourth edition, 1980–   . Both lists are classified and annotated. Walford is 'intended for librarians, in the building up and revision of reference library stock; for use in general and special library enquiry work; as an aid to students taking examinations in librarianship; and for research workers, in the initial stages of research' (Introduction). Sheehy's aims are almost identical.

The two books are invaluable as aids to what exists and may not be in one's library. Walford's *Concise guide to reference material* (London: Library Association, 1981) should also be acquired by libraries, as it includes more recent material than appears in the main volumes. The older English work by John Minto, *Reference*

Subject Bibliographies

books (London: Library Association, 1929–1931, 2 vols), still has some value.

General guides to reading are not a great help to the reference librarian, but can be used to check on works important at a particular time.[5] The most famous of such guides is:

Sonnenschein, W. S. THE BEST BOOKS. 3rd ed. London: Routledge, 1910–1935. 6 vols.

Containing 150,000 entries, indexed in Vol 6, this is a striking achievement, not superseded in its type. The American *Readers adviser: a layman's guide to literature* (12th ed, New York: Bowker, 1974–1977, 3 vols) has its devotees.

SUBJECT BIBLIOGRAPHIES—SELECTIVE

Bibliographies are likely to be selective. A 'Bibliography of history', so-called, will be either very selective, giving the most useful works, or a colossal project. Where a compiler claims comprehensiveness, it usually means that he is not missing out any aspect of the subject, rather than that he is attempting a complete bibliography. The reasons for selectiveness are obvious: the virtues for readers being that the work appears more manageable, and for the compiler that he is able to bring his work to a conclusion. There are very many selective bibliographies, starting with simple lists of further reading appended to a book or article. These are unpretentious, can be bad, but at best are important.

A glance at *Books in print* or *British books in print* will show under the term 'bibliography' the range of subjects covered, and any attempt here to classify subject bibliographies would be pointless. They have their origin in many different ways. Bookish experts in their field (John Arlott on cricket, A. L. Simon on food) turn their attention to listing books they appreciate. The historian G. R. Elton has given us *Modern historians on British history 1485–1945: a critical bibliography 1949–1969* (London: Methuen, 1970) and, for the Royal Historical Society, edits the *Annual bibliography of British and Irish history, 1975–   * (London: Harvester Press, 1976–   .) Librarians may be experts in the subject of their bib-

Subject Bibliographies—Selective

liography—E. A. Baker and D. J. Foskett's *Bibliography of food: a select international bibliography of nutrition, food and beverage technology and distribution 1936–1956* (London: Butterworth, 1958) was based on the compilers' daily work.

Bibliographies on a modest scale are often issued by libraries as reading lists. Where a library has a particularly strong subject collection, it may feel it has a duty to prepare a special catalogue.

Publishers prominent in the bibliographical field include Mansell, G. K. Hall, Bowker, H. W. Wilson, Gale, Scarecrow, Clio Press, Harvester, Greenwood, Kraus and St Pauls.

Contrasts in selective bibliographies are great. For instance, W. K. Richmond chose a classified (grouped) scheme for the entries in his *Literature of education* (London: Methuen, 1972), but had no subject or even author index. As an educationist he was excellent in criticism of the literature. John Challinor, another subject expert, in *The history of British geology: a bibliographical study* (Newton Abbot: David and Charles, 1971), chose a chronological listing to show the development of the literature of the subject. He did not annotate his lists, but expected a deep reading of the text. Brenda White, a librarian, classified the contents of her *Literature and study of urban and regional planning* (London: Routledge and Kegan Paul, 1974), annotated the entries as an expert user, and provided author and subject indexes. There is a place for variety of approach. A form of selective bibliography, which is treated separately below, is the bibliographical guide or handbook.

Annotation adds much to selective bibliographies if they are to be lastingly useful. In a simple checklist of new material, such as the Elton examples above, or on a new subject, such as computer-aided design, Gulf oil security, privacy, or riverblindness, there is less need, but uniqueness rarely lasts for long. The writing of annotations often causes problems to the newcomer to subject bibliography, in that he is afraid to be critical. The solution can only lie in knowing the material well, and having confidence in that knowledge, bearing the expected reader in mind. There are one or two manuals on annotation.[6] Anne Grimshaw pushes annotation even further in *The horse: a bibliography of British books 1851–1976* (London: Library Association, 1982). The book is se-

Subject Bibliographies

lective but each work is fitted into its place, making the whole a bibliographical history of the subject.

Subject bibliographies in encyclopaedias are often most disappointing. One of the values of encyclopaedias is that they give guidance on reading at the end of each article, but only too often such guidance is outdated and poor. Librarians must consult encyclopaedias early in a search for basic literature, but blind acceptance of what they show must be avoided.

The term **bio-bibliography** is sometimes found. It was first applied to bibliographies which have short notes on the authors, such as the author volumes of Watt,[7] but is now applied to those bibliographies where accounts of the books are mingled with information on the author, his background, and publishing history. Bio-bibliographies, such as F. A. Pottle *The literary career of James Boswell, Esq.* (Oxford: Clarendon Press, 1929) or M. L. Pearl *William Cobbett: a bibliographical account of his life and times* (London: Oxford University Press, 1953), are intended to be read; usually proceed chronologically; and are a great help to collectors.

Subject bibliographies—series

It is helpful to the librarian when organizations and publishers produce series of bibliographies, whose type and standard can be known. The Library Association Public Libraries Group does the *Readers' Guides*, which are meant to intrigue readers as well as to aid stock revision. Topics are general—Women's Movement, and The Unknown are recent examples. It is a pity that more titles are not produced, and that they are not kept in print in revised editions. More annotated than they were at one time, they still do not have author indexes. Library Association Publishing does some more ambitious bibliographies, leaving the smaller areas to sections and branches of the parent body.

Similar small publications come from the National Book League, with the aim of encouraging book purchase. The tendency to limit entries to books in print is irritating, but some unusual subjects have been tackled, often with children in mind, and linked with circulating exhibitions. The Historical Association and Common-

Subject Bibliographies—Selective

wealth Institute are two other bibliography-conscious organizations. War and Peace bibliographies (Clio Press); Current affairs bibliographies (Headland Press); and the Soho bibliographies (Oxford University Press) on authors—Conan Doyle the latest—are three series with common standards. We also have:

How to find out, Pergamon Press's simple series, which students will find useful. Electrical engineering, pharmacy, Canada, Shakespeare are four titles. Deeper is the *Information sources for research and development* series (Butterworth), whose titles often begin *Use of* . . . A comparison of A. R. Dorling's *Use of mathematical literature* (1977) with J. E. Pemberton's *How to find out in mathematics* (1969, 2nd ed) will show the different treatments. Valerie J. Bradfield *Information sources in architecture* (1983) has chapters on aspects of information flow in architecture, as seen by the practitioner, but there are plenty of references to the literature.

The *World bibliographical series* (Clio Press) is now a wide-ranging series, written by experts, which gives sources on all aspects of various countries' culture.

As there is likely to be a common policy and format, bibliographical series have a useful place in library stock, and students should get to know them.

Handbooks to the literature; Bibliographical guides

Bibliographical guides or handbooks are the attempt of the bibliographer to grasp all the sources of information in a specific field, to group and describe them so that readers may not only trace material but also understand the underlying bibliographical structure. The British Library Research and Development Department has a strong interest in encouraging this type of literature.[8] There are excellent examples of the type, some compiled by amateurs, others by professional librarians working daily with the literature:

Kamen, R. BRITISH AND IRISH ARCHITECTURAL HISTORY: A BIBLIOGRAPHY AND GUIDE TO SOURCES OF

Subject Bibliographies

INFORMATION. London: Architectural Press, 1981 is a good example.

Thornton, J. L. and Tully, R. I. J. *Scientific books, libraries and collectors* (3rd ed, London: Library Association, 1971; *Supplement 1969–1975*: Library Association, 1978) is another even more historical example. Music fares well in this field, with V. Duckles' *Music reference and research material: an annotated bibliography* (3rd ed, New York: Free Press, 1974), and the rarer G. Marco *Information on music: a handbook of reference sources in European languages* fills six volumes.

Bibliographical study can be taken a long way. In the music field again, *Music and bibliography: essays in honour of Alec Hyatt King* (Munich, London: Saur, 1980), edited by O. W. Neighbour, is a good example.

Bibliographical guides are often in narrative form, meant to be read, like the reading list at the end of this chapter.

SUBJECT BIBLIOGRAPHIES—COMPREHENSIVE

Comprehensiveness in bibliographies should mean that the compiler has aimed to include all aspects of the subject, and to be complete in tracing all relevant material. Examples of such care are rare, and Roberts[9] is ironical about bibliographers who make the attempt. Success is most likely in a small subject field; one thinks of the bibliographical publications of the Bee Research Institute under the indefatigable Eva Crane.

Loder, E. BIBLIOGRAPHY OF THE HISTORY AND ORGANISATION OF HORSE RACING AND THOROUGHBRED BREEDING IN GREAT BRITAIN AND IRELAND. London: J. A. Allen, 1978.

This bibliography is comprehensive in the sense that the author, producing the work as a Library Association thesis, has tried to include all books on the subject between 1565 and 1973, within a special scheme of classification, making her exclusions known.

Harrison, J. F. C. and Thompson, D. BIBLIOGRAPHY OF THE

Special Library Catalogues

CHARTIST MOVEMENT 1837–1976. Hassocks, Sussex: Harvester Press; Atlantic Highlands, New Jersey: Humanities Press, 1977.
This includes 'all known Chartist items in local and national libraries and archives'. B. Henrey believes her work to be so complete in *British botanical and horticulture literature before 1800* (Oxford: Oxford University Press, 1975, 3 vols) that she wants material not noted in it to be offered to the British Library. Confidence indeed.

METHODIST UNION CATALOG: PRE-1976 IMPRINTS. Metuchen, New Jersey: Scarecrow Press, 1975–   , in progress.
A co-operative work covering 200 libraries throughout the world. In twenty-odd volumes this is comprehensive.

Updating current systems for comprehensive bibliographies are rare. One may mention *Current accounting literature* (London: Mansell, 1971–   , in progress) and, from the same publisher, the *Quarterly Index Islamicus*, supplementing the main Index, which, when cumulated, adds material which never appeared quarterly.

SPECIAL LIBRARY CATALOGUES

Special libraries are likely to have a better stock in their subjects than even the largest general libraries. They try to make up losses, analyse in catalogues their stock of books and periodicals, and take material like 'unpublished' papers, not available elsewhere. At best, their catalogues are virtual bibliographies, current and retrospective, of their subjects and allied fields.

The **printed subject catalogue** or index, such as that done by the Royal Institute of British Architects (2 vols, 1937–1938), is not now economically possible for most libraries, staff-intensive as its editing and presentation is,[10] but a shot in the arm for the form has been provided by photographic reproduction of card catalogues, or library typescript, or by computer output. An example is:

Metropolitan Museum of Art LIBRARY CATALOG. 2nd ed.

Subject Bibliographies

Boston, Massachusetts: G. K. Hall, 1980. 48 vols, with supplement 1982.

This work is one of many similar productions by this publisher, though not all have a subject approach. That classic bibliography:

LONDON BIBLIOGRAPHY OF THE SOCIAL SCIENCES, which began in traditional printed form in 1931, now appears, via computer and still elegant, from Mansell. Vol 40, the 17th supplement covering 1982, appeared in 1983. In effect this is now a useful current bibliography of a wide range of literature taken by the important library of the London School of Economics. The Goldsmiths' Library of economic literature has also produced a four-volume *Catalogue* (London: Athlone Press, 1970–1983).

CATALOGUE OF LEWIS'S MEDICAL, SCIENTIFIC AND TECHNICAL LENDING LIBRARY. London: H. K. Lewis.

The useful printed catalogue of a commercial lending library, its last edition revised to the end of 1972, but with three supplements, the latest covering 1979–1981. The work includes a list of books classified by subject. Books not actually held by the library are listed.

Current accessions lists from special libraries are very useful extensions of their catalogues, as in the case of the Victoria and Albert Museum and the Imperial War Museum libraries. The relation between catalogue and accessions list may cause headaches in double preparation of material, but greater use of text-editing computers is likely to enable the same material to be handled in parallel. The journal of an institution which runs a library is often the medium for library accessions lists as well as reviews:

DR WILLIAMS'S LIBRARY BULLETIN is an example of a journal with varied contents, including classified lists of accessions in its field of religion, adding to the printed catalogues which go back to 1841–1885. This is another library the card catalogue of which has been published by G. K. Hall.

Special Library Catalogues
Guides to libraries

The preparation of guides to libraries is a very active area at present, and this is most useful for all other libraries. When the bibliographical tools at a service point prove inadequate, the reader will need to be directed to specialist libraries which will have current catalogues in card, or other, form, and which may well do specialized indexing, perhaps for selective dissemination of information (SDI) to their own readers. Many special libraries are known to all experienced librarians—Wiener Library, Society of Antiquaries of London, Ryerson Library—but still staff will have to consult directories of libraries. The standard British work is:

ASLIB DIRECTORY OF INFORMATION SOURCES IN THE UK. 5th ed. London: Aslib, 1982–   , in progress, the subject index of which enables specialist sources to be found. Vol 1 includes science, commerce and technology; Vol 2 social sciences, medicine and humanities.

WORLD GUIDE TO LIBRARIES. 6th ed. Munich etc: K. G. Saur, 1983, is another useful source complemented by *World guide to special libraries*, Saur, 1983; and the following three works by R. B. Downs should not be forgotten:

AMERICAN LIBRARY RESOURCES. Chicago: American Library Association, 1951, with supplements 1962, 1972, and 1981.

BRITISH AND IRISH LIBRARY RESOURCES. 2nd ed. Chicago: American Library Association; London: Mansell, 1982.

AUSTRALIAN AND NEW ZEALAND LIBRARY RESOURCES. London: Mansell; Melbourne: D. W. Thorpe, 1979.

These three are particularly strong on indications of where, through catalogues and descriptions, further details of the contents of the libraries can be found. All are indexed.

The Library Association *Regional guides to library resources* began in 1958 and are now mostly past their first edition. They list libraries by area, with an indication of their contents and services.

Subject Bibliographies

The subject specialization schemes, established in the 1950s and 1960s amongst public libraries, have created some good collections, though few have published relevant catalogues.

There are now many subject area lists of special collections. Peter Snow's *The United States: a guide to library holdings in the UK* (Boston Spa, Yorkshire: British Library Lending Division, 1982) does not limit itself to book holdings. B. Penney's *Music in British libraries: a directory of resources* has reached its third edition (London: Library Association, 1981). George Ottley's *Railway history: a guide to 61 collections in libraries and archives in Great Britain* (London: Library Association, 1973) complements the same author's *Bibliography of British railway history*.[11] This list could be extended infinitely, showing clearly that librarians need to know about each other's resources.

CURRENT BIBLIOGRAPHIES

Ideally, current bibliographies are needed to supplement retrospective bibliographies, but they are by no means as common. The current general bibliographies must not be forgotten—*British national bibliography*, *Cumulative book index*, etc. Finding current bibliographies is a hard task for a general librarian, and he may well consult a specialist, who will find it easier. The types of current bibliography to look for are:

1. specific current bibliography of the subject, such as *British catalogue of music*;
2. current subject index to periodicals, of which *British education index* is a good example;
3. journals which review or report the contents of other journals. *Antiquaries' journal*, *Journal of transport history* are examples;
4. library accessions lists, such as the Department of Education and Science's *Educational developments at home and abroad*, a classified monthly list;
5. card schemes, such as the *Architectural periodicals index*, or the *International index to film periodicals*, from the Fédération Internationale des Archives du Film;

Current Bibliographies

6. online computer schemes;
7. current awareness bulletins, which, although they give information, are often based on a printed source. The *Arts documentation monthly* from the Arts Council is one example.

Bibliographical indexes

In this section are noted a few special indexes which perform a similar function to bibliographies in directing the user further, but which in themselves give little information. E. Granger's *Index to poetry* (6th ed, New York: Columbia University Press, 1973; with supplement 1970–1977, 1979), J. H. Ottemiller's *Index to plays in collections: an author and title index to plays appearing in collections* ... (6th ed, Metuchen, New Jersey: Scarecrow Press, 1976), *Index translationum: international bibliography of translations 1948–* (Paris: Unesco, 1949– , in progress) are works of this kind. Some similar indexes which cover illustrations are listed on page 576. These indexes are books which absolutely must be known to the librarian. Some have achieved the status of classics: D. E. Cook and I. S. Monro *Short story index 1900–1949* (New York: H. W. Wilson; with supplements covering every four or five years since).

Concordances should also be mentioned; they take indexing to its logical conclusion by indexing all words or the key-words in a text, or the whole oeuvre of an author. Cruden for *The Bible* is a classic at present offered in thirteen editions in *Books in print*, and Bartlett is the standard for Shakespeare. For the user, the aim is to find a phrase in context, or to check all uses of a word or phrase. Words not actually appearing may even be added to give topical indexing. Computers lead to completeness or nonsense; even the word 'the' is indexable. A standard text will have to be chosen, as in the Oxford Microform Concordances to the novels of Virginia Woolf, which have just reached three volumes. They are most common in literature, but one of the most interesting is that to Freud's works.

Subject Bibliographies
INDEXES TO PERIODICALS

Although periodicals are the subject of Chapter 9, it would be artificial to ignore their indexes here. Indexes to individual journals vary greatly, from little more than author and title lists to really thorough subject indexes cumulated every few years.

ULRICH'S INTERNATIONAL PERIODICALS DIRECTORY. New York: Bowker, annual, the major list of periodicals, is actually arranged by subject headings. Note that the cross-references between these appear at the front of the book.

HISTORICAL PERIODICALS DIRECTORY. Oxford: Clio Press, 1982–   , is to be in five volumes, and is international in scope. It is, like *The Warwick guide to British labour periodicals 1790–1970* (Hassocks, Sussex: Harvester Press, 1977), a list, not an index.

Subject indexes to a range of periodicals developed late in the nineteenth century, a noted pioneer being William Frederick Poole in America, the main development coming through the H. W. Wilson Co.[12]

Gomme, G. L. INDEX OF ARCHAEOLOGICAL PAPERS 1665–1890. London, 1907, and supplements; reprint New York: Burt Franklin, 1973.

Is still important for the classic period of antiquarian literature though it lacks proper subject indexing.

The main British development in periodical indexing was through the:

Library Association SUBJECT INDEX TO PERIODICALS, 1913–   ,[13] in progress as BRITISH HUMANITIES INDEX; and as CURRENT TECHNOLOGY INDEX, which continued from BRITISH TECHNOLOGY INDEX in 1981.

To a reader, an article on a subject may be of at least as much use as a book, and in practice a librarian will often work in the parallel channels of bibliographies for books, and subject indexes to periodicals, to reveal relevant material for the reader. There are

Indexes to Periodicals

also specialized indexes such as *British education index*, 1954– , and the *Index Islamicus*. The *International photography index* (Boston, Massachusetts: G. K. Hall, annual) covers one hundred periodicals. The *Index kewensis*, which began in 1895 in two volumes, has now reached Vol 16 covering 1971–1976 (Oxford University Press). It is an enumeration of the general species of flowering plants, and the works in which they were first published. It has just been put on to a computer.

Speed is important in periodical indexing, and *Architectural periodicals index* (London: RIBA, 1972– , in progress quarterly) is available in card, microform, magnetic tape, or printed forms.

Citation indexes are a particular form of periodical index, in which publications which have been cited are listed, as are those publications which cited them, the inference being that a much cited article has especial value. Citation indexes are largely in the sciences, though since 1978 there has been the *Arts and humanities citations index* (Philadelphia, Pennsylvania, and Uxbridge, Middlesex: Institute for Scientific Information).

Abstracts too, whether indicative (with little detail) or informative (with rather more on content), are a form of periodical index. The abstract is an information-giver which lends itself to circulation among relevant readers, perhaps in partly copied form. Useful lists of abstracts and similar services are:

British Library. INVENTORY OF BIBLIOGRAPHIC DATA BASES PRODUCED IN THE UK. London: British Library, 1976.

EUSIDIC DATABASE GUIDE 1983. Oxford, New Jersey: Learned Information, 1983.
   This lists organizations, with a subject index.

Aslib. ONLINE BIBLIOGRAPHIC DATABASES: DIRECTORY AND SOURCEBOOK. London: Aslib, 1983.
   Two particularly useful indexes are *Research index* (Dorking,

Subject Bibliographies

Surrey: Business Surveys, current, fortnightly), which gives references on the business and company world, and *Clover information index* (Biggleswade, Bedfordshire: Clover Publications, current, quarterly), which is concerned with popular subjects so frequently avoided by more academic bibliographies.

Subject approach to government publications

Although government publications as reference material are covered in Chapter 12, a note on their subject bibliography is needed here. The librarian soon learns that there are current departmental lists of government publications; that they rarely contain inter-departmental listings; and that most lists exclude out-of-print material. He may also wish that they were revised more frequently.

Some government publications on a subject may be traced in the usual current and retrospective bibliographies, but apart from HMSO itself we do not have detailed retrospective listing of its publications. There are cumulations of the HMSO annual lists, but they are of little help from a specific subject point of view.

Not all government publications are published by HMSO, and to add to the lists which some departments publish, we now have COBOP:

CATALOGUE OF BRITISH OFFICIAL PUBLICATIONS NOT PUBLISHED BY HMSO. Cambridge: Chadwyck-Healey, 1982–

The organizations themselves are given in Stephen Richards' *Directory of British official publications: a guide to sources* (London: Mansell, 1981).

Government libraries vary in the help they will provide by telephone to enquirers; details are given in the British Library's *Guide to government department and other libraries* (26th ed. London: British Library, 1984).

For older government publications the academics P. and G. Ford provided valuable aid for subject tracing. Their works, listed on page 313 are among those which all librarians should know, and instinctively turn to, at the right time.

Indexes to Periodicals

Indexes to other material

Most material has some form of subject approach.

Theses for instance may be found through the Aslib *Index to theses 1950/1951–* (London: Aslib, 1953– , in progress) and through *Dissertation abstracts international* (Ann Arbor, Michigan: University Microfilms, 1951– , in progress); the former has only broad subject grouping.

Festschriften are partly controlled by the *Essay and general literature index 1900–1933*, etc (New York: H. W. Wilson, 1934– , in progress), where they are listed analytically under subject headings; but there are also specialist bibliographies for particular fields, such as J. P. Danton and J. F. Pulis *Index to Festschriften in librarianship 1967–1975* (Munich, etc: Saur, 1979), which continues previous work. A new work from the British and Irish Association of Law Librarians, *Index to legal essays* (London: Mansell, 1983), edited by Barbara Tearle, is also to be welcomed.

With theses, availability is important, and the work by D. H. Borchardt and J. D. Thawley, *Guide to availability of theses* (Munich, etc: Saur, 1981), lists this for a wide range of institutions.

Series, and the books in them, are listed in

BOOKS IN SERIES. 3rd ed. New York: Bowker, 1980. The three volumes cover series, authors and titles respectively, and the work is almost terrifyingly full.

For **microforms** there is the

SUBJECT GUIDE TO MICROFORMS IN PRINT. London: Mansell, annual.

Sequels are well covered in

SEQUELS. 7th ed. London: Association of Assistant Librarians, 1982. A volume covering Junior sequels was published in 1976.

Conference proceedings appear in

British Library. INDEX OF CONFERENCE PROCEEDINGS RECEIVED, which monthly and annually follows *Conference index 1964–1973* (London: British Library, 1974). This is under

Subject Bibliographies

key-word headings and cannot be described as perfect in subject approach, although additional headings are inserted. This is also available cumulatively in hard copy, on microfiche and online, in a quite exemplary manner.

The FICTION INDEX is an interesting bibliography which has appeared for many years now, giving the subjects of novels, for those readers who wish to follow a topic fictionally. The problems of preparing such a work have been covered by two of the editors.[14] Four volumes, published by the Association of Assistant Librarians as *Cumulated fiction index*, cover the period from 1945 to 1979.

Enser, A. G. S. FILMED BOOKS AND PLAYS London: Deutsch, 1975.

This is another work which needs continuation from time to time. The present edition covers 1928–1974, and has been supplemented for 1975–1981 (London: Gower, 1982). It aims to show which books and plays have been filmed, and from which sources films have been made. It is a useful work without substitute.

Reviews of research are of great interest to others who intend to pursue it, or who wish to check on results.

British Library. RESEARCH IN BRITISH UNIVERSITIES, POLYTECHNICS AND COLLEGES. London: British Library, 1978– , in progress, is the major British example.

Some bodies, such as the Social Science Research Council, and the National Foundation for Educational Research in England and Wales, produce their own reviews of research. In the librarian's own field, *CABLIS* (current research in library and information science), formerly *Radials bulletin*, quarterly, cumulated in December, and published by the British Library Lending Division, is useful.

Indexes to illustrative materials are covered in Chapter 19. Two listings of material have their own special names—**discographies** cover recordings,[15] and **carto-bibliographies** list maps.[16]

TRACING BIBLIOGRAPHIES: BIBLIOGRAPHIES OF BIBLIOGRAPHIES

Bibliographies of bibliographies are in practice fairly rare, and they are seldom used. They are lists of books which at best will tell you what material might contain details of books which might have information to help you. At the time when you want to know if there is a bibliography of a subject, consult

Besterman, T. WORLD BIBLIOGRAPHY OF BIBLIOGRAPHIES. 4th ed. Lausanne: Societas Bibliographica, 1965–1966. 5 vols.
It is arranged by subject heading, and then chronologically by publication date. The user is told how many items are included in each bibliography listed, of which there are said to be 117,000.

Toomey, Alice F. (*ed.*) A WORLD BIBLIOGRAPHY OF BIBLIOGRAPHIES 1964–1974, New York: Bowker, 1977. 2 vols.
Supplements Besterman from Library of Congress sources.

Hill, T. H. Howard-. BIBLIOGRAPHY OF BRITISH LITERARY BIBLIOGRAPHIES. London: Oxford University Press, 1969–1980. 5 vols of a 7-vol series.
The index of British literary bibliography, which is concerned with material on the bibliographical and textual examination of English manuscripts, books, printing and publishing.

Humphreys, A. L. A HANDBOOK TO COUNTY BIBLIOGRAPHY: A BIBLIOGRAPHY OF BIBLIOGRAPHIES RELATING TO THE COUNTIES AND TOWNS OF GREAT BRITAIN AND IRELAND. Author, 1917; reprinted London: Dawson, 1974.
Still a major local history source; arranged by county, with towns after the general material.

Ritchie, M. WOMEN'S STUDIES: A CHECKLIST OF BIBLIOGRAPHIES. London: Mansell, 1980.

Subject Bibliographies

Eager, Alan. A GUIDE TO IRISH BIBLIOGRAPHICAL MATERIALS. 2nd ed. London: Library Association, 1980.

THE BIBLIOGRAPHIC INDEX, 1937/1942– . New York: H. W. Wilson, 1938– , in progress.

This is the best current bibliography of bibliographies, and should be consulted at an early stage of any serious bibliographical compilation. It will help to reveal 'hidden bibliographies',[17] that is, those in other books and periodicals.

Aslib information has a useful function in listing recent bibliographies, such as those of the House of Commons; and on a wider front *Bibliography, documentation, terminology*, from Unesco, since 1961, lists bibliographies by country. The *Arts library review* now has in each issue a 'bibliographical update', and in general the art library world is very active in this field. In recent years, articles by Vaughan Whibley in *Library Association Record* have helped the librarian to keep up to date generally; the *Library of Congress information bulletin* is also a very useful source.

Libraries with good collections of bibliographies include the national libraries, The Library Association and Aslib, but it is still true to say there is no real public bibliographical centre in the UK. The British Library (Lending Division) has the most impressive array in one place. The Bibliographical Society is not concerned with subject bibliography. *Library and information science abstracts*, founded 1950, has become less 'bibliography-conscious', tying in with Library Association policy which says 'the collection of bibliographies (and of library catalogues) now held is not intended to be exploited for its subject content, but to illustrate the technique of compiling such works, and ranges over the history of their production'.[18] The Library Association does, however, award the Besterman Medal for 'an outstanding bibliography or guide to the literature, first published in the UK during the preceding year'.[19]

Assessment of bibliographies: their limitations

A bibliography is successful if it gives the bibliographical information you are looking for, or if it leads you to it.[20] There are, as

Tracing Bibliographies

we have seen, many types of subject bibliography, and there is no ideal, for bibliography is a network with the mesh less fine than one would wish. J. G. Barrow in his *Bibliography of bibliographies in religion* tells us that he did the work to find out what had not been done. Roberts[21] is interesting on what ideal situation might exist, and Paul Otlet, founder in 1895 of the International Institute of Bibliography, predecessor of the International Federation for Documentation, is only the main idealist who sought total bibliography.[22] The ideal has not been forgotten,[23] but unless expansion of information is backed by resources to exploit it, one cannot be hopeful for it.

There are gaps on the wide front, and there are limitations at a practical level. We must be sure of what we are using when we consult a bibliography. We look for fitness for the purpose, and are grateful when a bibliography's arrangement and structure lead quickly to the information required. Annotation is a great help in assessing the value of what one finds. Assessment of material is a skill which comes with experience, and which the student should be encouraged to acquire.[24] Introductions to bibliographies are not always helpful even when they exist, perhaps because the compiler thinks that although his book will be consulted, his prose will not be read. I suspect that many bibliographers would echo G. H. Martin and S. McIntyre in their *Bibliography of British and Irish municipal history* (Leicester: Leicester University Press, 1972): 'those who seek to compile bibliographies bring their cares upon themselves, and have a duty to conceal them, as best they can, from their readers', and Anne Grimshaw mentions her 'often flagging spirit'. Compilers must remember that users require, from the bibliographies they use, answers to very different questions—from the briefly specific to the very fully descriptive. Sequences in various orders may be called for. Subject arrangement in grouped order, often hidden Decimal Classification, is common, but a more specific subject index is still required, as is the author and title index. The **importance of indexes** cannot be over-emphasized. Summary tables and lists can be structured in different ways; they may for example be arranged by date of publication, or by type of material. A compiler must look for the most suitable forms to help

Subject Bibliographies

his users, and the librarian needs to get these firmly in his mind in each case.

A word on the limitations and faults of subject bibliographies may be helpful, and aid the student in his assessment of them:

1. **Coverage.** The printed bibliography has had to end somewhere, and the more selective the bibliography, the less permanent its value. Continuations and updates are not as common as one would like. D. Keeling *British library history* (London: Library Association, 4 vols published 1972, 1975, 1978, 1983) is an example of the former; D. Kennington and D. L. Read *The literature of jazz* (London: Library Association, 1970, 2nd ed 1980) an example of the latter.[25]

2. **Complementary apparatus** may not be good—author and title indexes for instance. Even a brief subject list should have an author index, as subject bibliographies are also used in a strictly non-subject way, shortcircuiting a longer search through retrospective bibliographies. E. H. Mikhail's *Contemporary British drama 1950–1976* (London: Macmillan, 1976) has no approach to the subjects of the critical articles he lists, and R. de Z. Hall's *Bibliography on vernacular architecture* (Newton Abbot: David and Charles, 1972) incredibly has indexes to neither place nor subject.

3. **Location.** There is often no indication of where a rare item may be found. *The guide to printed books and manuscripts relating to English and foreign heraldry and genealogy* (London: Mitchell and Hughes, 1892), by G. Gatfield, still not superseded, is unhelpful, for not only do manuscripts appear without any indication that they are not books, but no repositories are named for those manuscripts which are thus indicated. A bibliography is, to a reader, only a list; he then needs to see the material, and cannot always ask for it to come to him. One is grateful for works like G. Ottley's *A bibliography of British railway history* (London: Allen and Unwin, 1965; reprinted, London: HMSO, 1983); the *Kent bibliography*; or E. W. Padwick's *A bibliography of cricket* (London: Library Association, 1977), which include some locations.

4. **Errors.** Ghost entries and errors may be carried on from the

Library Problems of Bibliographies

past, if the material is not all seen by the compiler. It is reasonable to include some items not seen, but, as in the case of Baker and Foskett (*op. cit.*) the compiler should say so.

5. **Terminological changes.** This is a particular problem in the case of periodical subject indexes, and a conservative approach on the part of the compiler is understandable where long-scale searches will be expected. Some would argue that a classified approach is more helpful, provided there is a good index to the scheme employed.
6. **Citation practice.** Methods of citing books and articles vary, and a chapter could be written on this alone. The use of computer print-out has not helped, though computers are now subtle enough to differentiate founts and produce a wide range of symbols. Help on citation practice, on which the librarian will often have to assist readers, is given in several booklets.[26]
7. **Up-to-dateness.** To list current material in a comprehensive way is not easy, even in a special library, but some services do try to do this. The *Current technology index* and *Architectural periodicals index* do attempt very fast listing of up-to-date articles. This is easier to achieve in a centralized unit receiving the material, than in a co-operative scheme.

LIBRARY PROBLEMS OF BIBLIOGRAPHIES

Although this book is mainly concerned with reference materials as such, it is worth noting a few problems which subject bibliographies raise in libraries:

CLASSIFICATION

Most classification schemes allow libraries to group bibliographies together, or to scatter them by subject (010 as a class, or suffix 016 in DC). Grouping has an advantage for the librarian and bibliographically conscious user, in that one work does help another. Putting them with subjects, on the other hand, helps the user who

Subject Bibliographies

knows the shelf location of his subject. Whichever practice is followed, the catalogue should allow both approaches to be made.

PUBLIC ACCESS

Public access to bibliographies may clash with the library's own needs. Will a *British Library Catalogue* be on public shelves, or in the bibliographical/inter-library loan department? Where is *BNB* in your library? I use the term 'public' to mean clientèle, for the problem is present in academic and large special, as well as public, libraries.

SPECIALIZED BIBLIOGRAPHIES

More specialized bibliographies are not often found in the smaller units of public or academic library systems. It is a belief of some librarians that smaller libraries need bibliographies more, as their stock is smaller, and they need to know what else exists. I have to regard this view as too idealistic, and on grounds of expense and reader frustration must recommend that the larger or more specialized subject bibliographies should be restricted to the central and regional libraries, where expert staff can use those they know to be appropriate in each case. It is quite common to have a good range of selective bibliographies at small service points, and this is good sense, for it encourages staff and readers alike to venture beyond their immediate stock.

The Library Association[27] has suggested levels of coverage for libraries of various sizes, specifically including bibliographies. This was linked with a programme of organizing resources, 'Access to information', and use was made of the list:

BASIC STOCK FOR THE REFERENCE LIBRARY, now in its 4th ed. London: Library Association, 1981. It includes a long list of bibliographies in DC order.

Library Problems of Bibliographies

BIBLIOGRAPHICAL TRAINING

In certain kinds of library it may be worthwhile to encourage users to interest themselves in bibliographies. Whilst the librarian has a strong interest in bibliographies themselves, a reader in his own sphere will be most grateful for an introduction to the key works in his field—he will rarely know them. I am thinking of the art critic and *Art Index* or Arntzen;[28] the educationist and the *British Education Index*, Richmond, Baron and Kimmance;[29] the technical student and the *How to find out* series.

Such introductions may form part of library orientation courses in colleges, though there is no substitute for a helping hand, in a library, at the right moment.

PRODUCTION OF LIBRARY BIBLIOGRAPHIES

A library should have a policy on whether it produces select bibliographies (booklists) or not—this policy based on its stock, the expected nature of its readers' needs, and unfortunately also, on the number and experience of staff available. Where a library has specialized collections, or is totally specialist, full-scale bibliographies ought also to be considered and done if possible:

Watkins, A. H. THE CATALOGUE OF THE H. G. WELLS COLLECTION. Bromley, Kent: London Borough of Bromley Libraries, 1975; and

Birmingham Public Libraries. A SHAKESPEARE BIBLIOGRAPHY. 7 vols. London: Mansell, 1971.

These are two different but excellent examples, each of which might be seen as extensions of the local collection.

AVAILABILITY OF MATERIAL FOUND

Knowing what exists is one problem; finding it and getting it another, and libraries have been much aware of this at a time of

Subject Bibliographies

financial stringency. Co-operation, as in the Kent bibliography, is a keynote, but it is more likely to occur with special, rather than public, libraries. Law and music are two fields where great efforts have, in effect, been made to share resources. The guides to resources and lists of libraries, etc, within a subject field are important (see pages 508–513, 528–529). Groups such as the British Library Working Party on Provision for Law, and IFLA (Art libraries section), are likely to become more common.

SUBJECT BIBLIOGRAPHY: THE FUTURE

We are in danger, the prophets tell us,[30] of being swamped by our own information, and that if we cannot control it, we cannot use it. The point is not lost on librarians, much of whose business is information. In the library press the phrase 'universal bibliographical control' is bandied about.[31] The pleas of James Duff Brown and L. Stanley Jast[32] have never been heeded, and never will be. We are the victims of, as well as gainers by, our literacy. In these circumstances the librarian may, as bibliographer, seek to encourage the listing of materials and the purchase of those lists. Posts of 'bibliographer' actually exist in libraries. But whether the opportunity to compile comes the librarian's way or not, he can find and interpret those lists which have been produced, and are legion.

An excessive devotion to the bibliography is a form of bibliomania, but an appreciation of its value at the right time is a mark of good librarianship. This knowledge can be encouraged during an educational course, and in early days as a professional, by informal instruction and use by a senior. It is also most helpful if the librarian's interest and knowledge are built upon by giving opportunities for the creation of subject lists.

Whereas bibliographic listing of books in general arises naturally from book production and preservation practices, subject bibliography has to be a more consciously directed occupation. It is one which has been pursued by individuals—at least two of whom, Quérard and Watt, have been labelled 'martyrs to bibliography', and others like Lowndes had terrible lives—but it has been adapted to the team:

References

The MANUAL OF LAW LIBRARIANSHIP. London: Deutsch, for British and Irish Association of Law Librarians, 1976.

This is a work edited by Elizabeth Moys from the combined experience of a large group. The work by Barbara Tearle, already cited, is another.

NORTHERN BIBLIOGRAPHY, 1979–   , covers libraries in the Northern Regional Library system.

The Music Bibliography group is working on computer language for music, and has concerned itself with the content of the *British Music Bibliography*. Elton's work on the basis of other historians, and Keeling's on library historians, have already been mentioned.

Methods also have changed. Bibliographies have been prepared on cards and slips (Watt's still remain at Paisley Public Library), on sheets for printing, and the computer is now extensively used.[33] To those who still find this a strange world, the past and the future may be married by a study of the *London bibliography of the social sciences* and its production,[34] or of the Isis bibliographies.[35] Even local history has succumbed to the computer, covered by a University of York project;[36] and art is one of the busiest spheres in bibliography, as shown in most issues of the *Art library journal*, published by Arlis, which is working within IFLA guidelines.

Whatever the changes through the years, and to come, the aim of subject bibliographers remains the same: to provide a link between the books and other materials on the one hand, and the reader in need of information on the other.

'Bibliography must have a purpose', says J. D. Cowley,[37] 'that purpose being to afford guidance in some branch of literature or record of knowledge and to tell us all there is to be known about it, how it came to be published and how it was intended to be used'. There is much scope left for us.

REFERENCES AND CITATIONS

1. Taylor, P. J. Trends in bibliographic publishing in the United Kingdom, 1974–1978. *Aslib Proceedings,* **32,** 1980. 444–58.
2. Roberts, A. D. *Introduction to reference books.* 3rd ed. London: Library Association, 1956.

Subject Bibliographies

3. Watt, R. *Bibliotheca britannica; or, A general index to British and foreign literature*. 4 vols. London: Constable, etc, 1824; reprint New York: Burt Franklin, 1965. The first two volumes are of authors, the last two contain subjects. Brunet, J. C. *Manuel du libraire et de l'amateur de livres*. 5th ed. Paris: Firmin Didot, 1860–1880. Lowndes, W. T. *The British librarian*. London: Thomas Rodd, 1844. This, unlike his more famous *Bibliographer's manual*, is a subject list, but only on divinity.
4. McCrimmon, B. *Power, politics and print: the publication of the B.M. Catalogue 1881–1900*. Hamden, Connecticut: Linnet Books; London: Bingley, 1981.
5. Such as the works of F. Seymour Smith, L. R. McColvin *Personal library*. London: Phoenix House, 1953; or W. E. Williams *The reader's guide*. Harmondsworth, Middlesex; Penguin Books, 1960. There are many more, over the last 150 years.
6. Savage, E. A. *Manual of descriptive annotation for library catalogues*. London: Library Supply Co, 1906, is better than Sayers, W. C. B. *First steps in annotation*. Association of Assistant Librarians, 1955. Other well-known bibliographers including Wilfrid Bonser and A. W. Pollard have been against annotation, on the grounds that the expert will wish to examine and get to know the literature.
7. Watt, *op. cit.* in note 3 above.
8. Taylor P. J. *Information guides: a survey of subject guides to sources of information produced by library and information services in the UK* British Library Rearch Department report 5440, 1978.
9. Roberts, *op. cit.* in note 2 above, pp 66–7.
10. Even the National Maritime Museum, which produced seven parts of its printed *Catalogue of the library*. London: HMSO, 1968–   , in progress, has decided to continue it on microfiche.
11. This has been reprinted by HMSO, and a supplement covering 1964–1980 is expected in 1984. The hoped-for bibliography of periodicals was not produced. Ottley is, within its limitations, a good example of a comprehensive bibliography, but nonetheless it has had to add missed items of earlier years to its supplement.
12. *A quarter century of cumulative bibliography: retrospect and prospect*. New York: H. W. Wilson, 1923, tells their story entertainingly.
13. On the problems of the *Subject index to periodicals*, see Munford, W. A. *A history of the Library Association 1877–1977*. London: Library Association, 1976.
14. Hicken, M. E. Compiling *Cumulated fiction index 1975–1979*. *The Indexer*, **13** (2). October 1982. 88–9
15. Foreman, L. *Discographies: a bibliography*. Rickmansworth, Hertfordshire: Triad Press, 1973; Gibson, G. and Gray, M. *Bibliography of discographies: classical music*. New York: Bowker, 1978; Allen, D. *Bibliography of discographies: jazz*. New York: Bowker, 1981; and

References

Gray, M. *Bibliography of discographies: popular music.* New York: Bowker, 1983.
16. Lock, C. B. M. *Geography and cartography: a reference handbook.* 3rd ed. London: Clive Bingley, 1976. Nichols, H. *Map librarianship.* 2nd ed. London: Clive Bingley, 1982.
17. A. J. Walford's term.
18. British Library. Library Association Library. *Guide to the Library.* 1977.
19. Winners are listed in the Library Association *Yearbook*, annual, and discussed in the *Library Association Record*, as awarded.
20. Reference Services Division, American Library Association. Criteria for evaluating a bibliography. *RQ*, 11 (4). Summer 1971. 359–60.
21. Roberts *op. cit.* in note 2 above, Chapter 6.
22. On whom *see* Rayward, W. B. *The universe of information: the work of Paul Otlet.* Brussels: IFD, 1975.
23. Pomassl, G. Ten years IFLA Committee on Bibliography 1966–1976. *IFLA Journal*, 3 (4), 1977. 319–26. Reports on IFLA's activities continue to appear in their journal, but do not show great interest in subject bibliography as such.
24. *See* the Needham and Staveley items in the list of Further Reading.
25. The progress of the *Foreign Affairs* bibliographies is interesting. Originally published in the journal, from 1919, they achieved book form in a series of volumes reprinting the original reviews, and then, in 1972, Byron Dexter edited *The Foreign Affairs fifty-year bibliography: new evaluations of significant books 1920–1970*, which took a fresh view of the original literature and its reviews.
26. Royal Society *General notes on the preparation of scientific papers.* 3rd ed. London: Royal Society, 1974; British Standards Institution *Bibliographical references* (BS 1629: 1976); Butcher, J. *Copy-Editing.* 2nd ed. Cambridge: Cambridge University Press, 1981.
27. Library Association Standards for reference services in public libraries. *Library Association Record*, 72 (2), 1970. 53–7.
28. Arntzen, E. and Rainwater, R. *Guide to the literature of art history.* Chicago: American Library Association, 1981.
29. Richmond *op. cit.* on p 507; Baron, G. *Bibliographical guide to the English educational system.* London: Athlone Press, 1965; and Kimmance, S. *A guide to the literature of education.* London: University of London Institute of Education, 1961.
30. Hall, P. *Europe 2000.* London: Duckworth, 1977; Gray, J. and Perry, B. *Scientific information.* London: Oxford University Press, 1975; and Lamberton, D. M. *Economics of information and knowledge.* Harmondsworth, Middlesex: Penguin Books, 1971.
31. Anderson, D. *Universal bibliographic control.* IFLA, Verlag Dokumentation, 1974; and other works and articles.
32. Both men wrote on the need to use bibliographical listing as a means

Subject Bibliographies

of deciding what was no longer useful. Brown, J. D. *A manual of practical bibliography.* London: Routledge, 1906; Jast, L. S. Bibliography and the deluge: I accuse. *Library Association Record,* **38,** 1936. 353-60.

33. Among computerized bibliographical information systems are *British education index; Book review index; Historical abstracts; Art bibliographies modern; Philosopher's index; Comprehensive dissertation index; PAIS.* All are available to be searched through the British Library computer search service, though not without cost. There are links too with the Library of Congress.
34. Jones, S. Production of the *London bibliography of the social sciences* by computer. *Program,* 10 (3), 1976. 103-12.
35. Whitrow, M. The Isis cumulative bibliography 1913-65. *The Indexer,* **13** (3). April 1983. 158-65.
36. Local studies database projects. *Library Association Record,* **85** (6), June 1983. 217.
37. Cowley, J. D. *Bibliographical description and cataloguing.* London: Grafton, 1939. p 179. I should in fairness say that Cowley did not place subject bibliography as such on a high plane, but does devote some space to it. He agrees with other authorities in saying that only subject experts should practise it.

SUGGESTIONS FOR FURTHER READING

There is not a large literature on bibliographies. Collison, R. L. *Bibliographies, subject and national* (3rd ed. London: Crosby Lockwood, 1968) is the main work to read, though Malclès, L.-N. *Bibliography* (1961; reprinted Metuchen, New Jersey: Scarecrow, 1973) is a more continuous work. Krummel, D. W. *Bibliographies: their aims and methods* (London: Mansell, 1984) is wide in scope. The first chapter of Roberts, N. *Use of social sciences literature* (London: Butterworth, 1977) is particularly good, and Hale, B. M. *The social sciences and the humanities* (Oxford: Pergamon, 1970) is wide-ranging. Needham, C. D. and Herman, E. edited *The study of subject bibliography with special reference to the social sciences* (College Park, Maryland: University of Maryland School of Library and Information Services, 1970), which is valuable for the educative approach, and specimen bibliographies. Staveley, R. *Notes on subject bibliography* (London: Deutsch, 1962) is still valuable for its approach, and may be followed by *Introduction to subject study,* by Staveley and others (London: Deutsch, 1967). You may find it hard to read the whole of Downs, R. B. and Jenkins, F. B. *Bibliography, current state and future trends* (Urbana: University of Illinois, 1967), but it has useful parts.

On the practical side, Robinson, A. M. L. *Systematic bibliography* (4th ed. London: Bingley, 1979) is excellent, and Hackman, M. L. *The practical*

Further Reading

bibliographer (Englewood Cliffs, New Jersey: Prentice-Hall, 1970) is quite useful. An unusual and little-known book for non-librarians is Pemberton, J. E. *Undertaking enquiries, part 2: literature search and compiling a bibliography* (Milton Keynes: Open University, Public Administration Block III (2), D331, 1974).

I have avoided the historical in this chapter; however, in addition to the works of Malclès and Collison noted above, Taylor, Archer *A history of bibliographies of bibliographies* (Metuchen, New Jersey: Scarecrow Press, 1955); Besterman, T. *The beginnings of systematic bibliography* (2nd ed. London: Oxford University Press, 1936); and Schneider, G. *Theory and history of bibliography* (New York: Columbia University Press, 1934) may be read. Besterman's facsimiles of old bibliographies are illuminating.

Library and information science abstracts show that the periodical literature on subject bibliography is not large. To gain knowledge of bibliographical structure, I recommend the perusal of handbooks and guides, which can be found from Walford and Sheehy. On the application of bibliographical know-how, Grogan, D. *Case studies in reference work* (London: Bingley, 1967; Oxford: Oxford Microform Publications, 1976) has a chapter devoted to bibliographies, and they are shown in use throughout the book and its successor, *More case studies in reference work* (London: Bingley, 1972).

18
International Official Publications

Lena Partington

It has become commonplace to write of the great increase in the amount of international documentation which we have seen in the past thirty to forty years, and which is available to those prepared to seek it out.

In A. D. Roberts' *Introduction to reference books* (1956), for example, no separate chapter was given over to international official publications. Instead, some references to this documentation were included in the chapter on (British) government publications. But today we are, or should be, made very much aware of the all-pervading involvement of government bodies in every aspect of our lives, by our membership, not only of the United Nations and its many agencies; of the OECD, whose *Economic Survey* of this country is given wide coverage in the press and in TV and radio news bulletins each time it appears; but more especially because we are one of the (currently ten) member states of the European Community. In the current edition of the *Yearbook of international organizations*[1] no less than 14,784 bodies are included and most of these generate some research, supported by public money, the results of which are usually written up in the publications they produce. But if the amount of international documentation is increasing, has there been a corresponding increase in the improvement of material given over to its control? Is there still a long delay in the publication of catalogues? When these tools do appear, are they as comprehensive in their coverage as they might be? Are ISBNs and ISSNs always quoted where available? Could the quality of indexes be improved? I could continue, but these are enough pointers to the kind of detail which we, as librarians and information officers, would like to see in future.

In the following pages I intend noting briefly the more recent publications on international documentation generally, and then listing the basic publications with the catalogues and indexes provided by the:

1. United Nations and its agencies;
2. European Communities;
3. Organization for Economic Co-operation and Development.

Bibliographic control over the range of material emanating from so many different sources is bound to vary. Some international organizations have produced excellent catalogues. Others leave a great deal to be desired.

There are, already, some moves afoot to alleviate matters. The bibliographical work of Theodore Dimitrov, together with the proceedings of the first two World Symposia on International Documentation, provide both a starting point for researchers in the field, and essential reading.

The First World Symposium on International Documentation was held in Geneva in 1972.[2] Shortly afterwards, Theodore Dimitrov, Chief of the Processing Section at the United Nations Library in Geneva, published a handbook on the documentation of international organizations. His updated and much expanded edition of this book, which has appeared in two volumes so far, contains 9,291 entries compared with 2,381 in the earlier handbook. The *World bibliography of international documentation*[3] is arranged as follows:

Vol 1, *International organizations*, consists of two parts
    Part 1 International organizations—activities, structure, information policies
        Nature, structure and activities
        Basic documents of IGOs

International Official Publications

          Secretaries – General
          Policies and research on international documentation
   Part 2 Bibliographic control of international documents
          General methodology
          Building international documents collections
          Cataloguing principles and rules
          Indexing, subject analysis, thesauri, classification schemes
          Library and information science dictionaries
          Current catalogues and indexes of international documentation

Vol 2, *Politics and world affairs*
   Part 1 Multilateral diplomacy and international relations
   Part 2 International periodicals
          Chapter 1 Intergovernmental periodicals – union list
          Chapter 2 Political journals and annuals reviewing international problems
          Appendix 1 Lists of major international conferences organized by the UN General Assembly and the Economic and Social Council, and by Unesco
          Appendix 2 List of international anniversaries, decades, years, weeks and days
          Personal author index   )
          Corporate body index   ) *to both volumes*
          Subject index   )

Further volumes are planned covering economics, human rights and other subjects.

The proceedings of the Second World Symposium on International Documentation entitled *International documents for the 80's, their role and use*[4] acknowledge that the range of documentation already existing has demonstrated the need to generate effective remedies, and goes on to make several recommendations which include:

Bibliographic data produced by international organizations

should be incorporated in a consolidated database, accessible online.

Organizations should follow the international standards for the production of their bibliographic descriptions.

AACR2 should be adopted in cataloguing and bibliographic practices.

A compatible list of descriptors for subject analysis should be used.

Authority lists of international governmental and non-governmental bodies should be made available.

Cataloguing in publication should be practised more broadly. Modern technology should be widely adopted to assist.

Further suggestions covered the improvement of published indexes and catalogues, and better linking of international networks with the systems of depository libraries.

Dimitrov's two most recent works have been published by the New York publishers, Unifo. A publishing house based in this country, with an on-going series in the same subject area, is Pergamon, whose series *Guides to official publications*, prepared under the general editorship of John E. Pemberton, was inaugurated by printing together in one volume a revision and updating of an early attempt to provide a guide to bibliographies of official publications: *Government publications: a guide to bibliographic tools* issued in 1975, and a bibliography of government organization manuals compiled, in 1976, by Vladimir M. Palic of the Library of Congress.[5] This somewhat complicated bibliographic history nonetheless provides a tool which gives comprehensive coverage of earlier material. After an introductory section on government publications in general, Part I of the guide covers the USA (federal government by department), then States, Territories and Local Government alphabetically, current then retrospective works. Part II, pp 151–93, is entitled 'International Governmental Organizations'; this deals with general and specialized bibliographies before listing, with annotations, those bibliographies dealing with the United Nations and its regional commissions; it includes retrospective indexes relating to UN Organizations no longer in existence, or special indexes no longer published; the League of Nations; and other organizations, arranged alphabetically and ranging from the annual reports of the Bank for International Settlements through the European Communities and the OECD, to the bulletin of the World Meteorological Organization. Part III covers bibliographic tools for official publications of individual countries grouped in the following geographical areas: Western Hemisphere, Europe, Africa, Near East and Asia and the Pacific Area.

A work not mentioned by Dimitrov, but which should be of particular interest to students in this country, is *Official publishing: an overview: an international survey and review of the role, organization and principles of official publishing*, by Jack Cherns,[6] formerly an Assistant Controller, HMSO. This monumental work appeared as Vol 3 in the Pergamon Series *Guides to official publications*, and is arranged as follows:

Part 1   Introduction on the scope and importance of official publishing.

Part 2   Takes the form of a survey, which includes chapters on official publishing as it existed in 1976/77—in Australia, Belgium, Canada, Denmark, France, Federal Republic of Germany, Hong Kong, India, Indonesia, Israel, Italy, Netherlands, New Zealand, Norway, Singapore, Sweden, Switzerland, Thailand, United Kingdom, and United States of America. There is also a chapter comparing 'USGPO and HMSO: A contrast in origin and functions'. (See especially Chapter 24, 'International Organizations', pp 326–77.)

Part 3   Review—discusses the growth, framework and machinery of official publishing; accessibility of official information; economics of official information; control and future of official publishing.

Government documents librarians have tackled in various ways the problem of organizing their collections. Examples are provided in the 11th volume in the Pergamon series *The bibliographic control of official publications*, edited by John E. Pemberton.[7] The blurb states that the aim of the book is 'to stimulate progress towards the establishment of a comprehensive system for bibliographic control of official publications and to identify the principles upon which a new and definitive coding scheme could be based'. Chapter 8 is of particular interest here since it is concerned specifically with the classification of the documents of international intergovernmental organizations, in this case a scheme devised at the University of Colorado. Chapter 7 'The development of bibliographic control of official publications in Trinity College Library, Dublin' by John Goodwillie, and Chapter 10 'Bibliographic control of official publications at the Institute of Development Studies, England' by G. E. Gorman and J. A. Downey, are relevant to experience closer to home, together with John Pemberton's own chapter, 'Official publications in a new bibliothecal context', which draws together some recent thinking and illustrates it by setting out the framework of the Warwick scheme.

A periodical which is particularly helpful in keeping this information up to date, and alerting readers to new developments is *Government Publications Review: an international journal of issues and information resources*.[8] The subtitle, acquired in 1982 beginning with Volume 9, is intended to reflect more accurately the coverage of the articles which provide a forum for issues associated with the production, distribution, processing and use of government publications. This periodical should be ranked alongside the works compiled and edited by Dimitrov as essential for the student of international documentation.

Usually each issue of the new-style *Government Publications Review* focuses on a theme. Recent examples include Volume 9, No 3 (May–June 1982), which dealt with statistics of international government organizations (IGOs). An article by Hugh F. Brophy entitled 'Publications of the United Nations Statistical Office', pp 175–84, which 'provides a view of the numerous co-ordination efforts the UNSO is undertaking, suggests several cautions of which users of UN data should be aware, and describes enhancements to publication and database offerings' (author's abstract), is particularly relevant; as is Ella Krucoff's article 'European Community Publications: a statistical abundance' in the same issue on pp 189–93. The following issue of GPR (Vol 9, No 4, July–August 1982) concentrated on technological applications for government document collections.

Beginning with Vol 9, 1982 also, there are six issues per year instead of ten, and Part B, the quarterly acquisition tool, has been discontinued as a separate publication. Instead, the last issue of each volume is given over entirely to 'Notable Documents'. Vol 9, No 6, November–December 1982, for example, includes 534 documents which became available from approximately mid-year 1981 to mid-year 1982. These are listed (two columns to a page) with an abstract for each item. Sections are arranged as follows: US government (depository items), technical reports and non-depository publications, state publications, local publications, Canadian publications, Africa, Asia, Europe and Latin America, and United Nations and other international organizations. There is a category (or subject) index, a contents and an author index for the entire volume. Each section has an introduction, summarizing publishing and distribution trends. Most introductions in this issue note problems of accessibility.

Peter Hajnal, Head of the Government Publications Section, University of Toronto Library, has drawn together in a convenient form several strands currently concerning those involved with the publications of international governmental organizations. In an article 'IGO documents and publications' in GPR (Vol 9, No 2, March–April 1982)[9] he discusses the volume of IGO publishing, the various distribution categories, eg general, limited and restricted, recent developments (publishing in microform, emergence of new organizations) and sources of information about IGO material. There is an appendix with a 49-item bibliography.

UNITED NATIONS

The studies of Luciana Marulli-Koenig,[10] Peter Hajnal, [11,12] and Harry Winton,[13] as well as the guides to its publications prepared

United Nations

by the United Nations itself, eg *United Nations documentation: a brief guide*,[14] which can be kept up to date by reference to *United Nations documentation news*,[15] provide a good introduction to the wealth of material available.

The current catalogue to United Nations documents is *UNDOC: current index*, Vol 1, 1979– [16] prepared by the Dag Hammarskjold Library at UN Headquarters in New York. It is issued ten times a year (monthly except July and August) and is arranged as follows:

(a) Checklist of UN documents and publications received by the Library in alphanumeric order by series symbol and by session. Publications which do not bear a symbol are entered by title under the issuing body. Bibliographic entries are displayed according to the International Standard Bibliographic Description (ISBD).
(b) List of Official Records, eg General Assembly, 35th Session, Economic and Social Council.
(c) List of sales publications, arranged by sales number.
(d) List of documents re-published in the Official Records or elsewhere.
(e) List of new document series symbols.
(f) Language table of documents indexed.
(g) Subject index.
(h) Author index.
(i) Title index.

The documents listed are preserved in the Library, and throughout the world in a network of depository libraries. *UNDOC* is the most important printed product of the United Nations Bibliographic Information System (UNBIS) which is available to non-UN users. A list of terms used in indexing and cataloguing documents and other materials relevant to United Nations programmes and activities is given in the *UNBIS thesaurus*.[17] Among the subjects covered are: political affairs and international relations, disarmament, international trade, economic and social development, agriculture, education, employment, health, housing, industry, science, social issues and technology.

A paper by S. Singh and S. Sobel[18] presented at the Second World Symposium on International Documentation reminds us of the reassessment of the UN Library's documentary information activities which resulted in the development of UNBIS. Its aims were 'to expand the reference and information services of the Library by providing complete bibliographic control of the documents issued and received ... and to establish optimum compatibility with national and international information systems in regard to bibliographic description, subject analysis and approach to information retrieval'. A two-volume *Directory of United Nations information systems*[19] reached its second edition in 1980. Although much has already been achieved, there still remains a great deal to be done. Before Unifo, a commercial publisher, produced *The complete reference guide to United Nations sales publications, 1946–1978*,[20] users seeking UN sales items, for example, had to rely on the UN Sales Section's catalogues, which are not professional tools. *The complete reference guide*, compiled by Mary E. Birchfield and published in two volumes in 1982, provides a full listing of sales items covering 32 years of UN publishing. It is the first catalogue to group in a single, logical order both monographs and series issued by the same UN agency.

The latest cumulative sales catalogue and the first to be produced from a computer-assisted listing of sales publications, was *United Nations sales publications 1972–1977: a cumulative list with indexes*,[21] which linked the sales number with the document series symbol, if one was assigned. At the same time, author, subject and title indexes were included to assist in identification. It is hoped that, with computer assistance, further cumulations will be generated regularly. At the moment, an annual checklist[22] is issued. The intention is to provide current information on prices and availability, and the checklist uses UN sales numbers rather than document series symbols or ISBNs and ISSNs.

UN AGENCIES

At the present time, there are 14 major specialized UN agencies. Most of them prepare their own catalogues of current publications,

UN Agencies

or publish retrospective bibliographies covering their publications for a range of years. The notes on those agencies which follow are, of necessity, very abbreviated. In some instances they have offices in this country, or are interested particularly in the information field.

International Labour Organization (ILO)

The ILO is based in Geneva. Its secretariat, operational headquarters, research body and publishing house is known as the International Labour Office.

Publications and information may be obtained in this country from the International Labour Organization, 96–98 Marsham Street, London SW1P 4LY (Tel: 01-828 6401).

ILO publications and documents available in English and offered for sale in December 1981 are listed in the 'complete' catalogue *ILO Catalogue of Publications in Print 1982*.[23] ISBNs, or in the case of periodicals, ISSNs, are given. 'Complete' catalogues are published from time to time, but details of all new books, editions and reprints are contained in *ILO Publications*,[24] which appears every three months.

International Maritime Organization (IMO)

This is the only headquarters of an UN specialized agency to be located in this country. At the beginning of 1983, the IMO moved into prestigious office accommodation at 4 Albert Embankment, London SE1 7SR (Tel: 01-735 7611). The name of the Organization had been changed from the less streamlined version—Inter-Governmental Marine Consultative Organization (IMCO)—by virtue of amendments to the Organization's Convention, which entered into force on 22 May 1982. A spacious library on the third floor contains not only IMO's own publications and other relevant documents and publications, but also an extensive collection of UN agency and other international organization documentation. The Librarian should be contacted if a visit is contemplated. The

International Official Publications

Publications Sales Section is open from 09.00h to 12.45h and from 14.00h to 17.15h.

A full catalogue of sales publications available[25] was issued in 1982, with a Supplement in 1983.

United Nations Educational, Scientific and Cultural Organization (Unesco)

Unesco, based in Paris, is currently involved in the Universal Availability of Publications (UAP) programme. It is now being recognized that making publications available is as important as bibliographic control. Capital Planning Information is preparing a report to assess the availability of publications in this country. The report will indicate where improvement is needed, and will constitute a model for the general assessment of availability in a developed country. It may well lead to a reassessment of priorities. All the main aspects of availability will be covered, from publication and distribution through acquisition and interlending to retention for future availability.

World Health Organization (WHO)

WHO was established in Geneva as the central agency directing international health work. Despite a wealth of catalogues and bibliographies, care still needs to be taken in identifying some series. For example, the WHO series *EURO Reports and Studies* should not be confused with the European Communities series *EUR Reports*, listed in the excellent *Euroabstracts*.

EUROPEAN COMMUNITIES

It seems almost unbelievable amid the continuing debate about whether this country should remain 'in' or withdraw from the EC that we should already be encountering bibliographical articles such as Kenneth Twitchett's in *British Book News*, March 1983, entitled

European Communities

'Britain and the European Community: the first ten years'.[26] This deals with secondary publications which are not our main concern here, but it is a review article by an authority in the field, which pulls the material neatly together; it is one which it is well worth looking at.

Anyone wanting to keep track of the publications of an intergovernmental organization as complex as the European Community should familiarize himself both with its foundation and its institutional framework, and because a work such as John Jeffries' *A guide to the official publications of the European Communities*[27] sets all this out in detail, at least up to the end of 1979, and links it with the publications issued by each body, I am not dwelling at length on either here.

Background to the Treaties—Primary Legislation

During the 1950s, six countries of Western Europe—Belgium, France, the Federal Republic of Germany, Italy, Luxembourg and the Netherlands—established three Communities with the aim of gradually integrating their economies and of moving towards political unity. The three Communities were in order of their founding:

1. The European Coal and Steel Community (ECSC). Established after the signing of the Treaty of Paris 1951.
2. The European Economic Community (EEC), and
3. The European Atomic Energy Community (Euratom).

The EEC and Euratom were both established after the signing of the Treaty of Rome in 1957. Denmark, Ireland and the UK joined the EC in 1973. Greece became the tenth member in 1981. Portugal and Spain are negotiating for entry, with a target date of 1984.

Community institutions

There are five main institutions:

1. The **Commission** which at present (1983) consists of 14 mem-

bers (commissioners)—two each for France, the Federal Republic of Germany, Italy, and the UK; and one each for Belgium, Denmark, Greece, Ireland, Luxembourg and the Netherlands. The Commission is responsible for drafting policy and implementing decisions, and is organized into twenty departments known as **Directorates-General**. Each commissioner is assigned one or more of the Community's spheres of responsibility. An official *Directory of the Commission of the European Communities*[28] is compiled by the Directorate-General for Personnel and Administration, rue de la loi 200, B 1049 Brussels, and issued three times a year. Two commercial publications of a more general nature published by Editions Delba in Brussels will also be helpful here—*European Communities yearbook*,[29] and its biographical companion *European Communities and other European organizations who's who*,[30] which includes senior civil servants currently working within the EC. *Vacher's European Companion*[31] appears quarterly, and is more likely to provide up-to-date information.

A major source of information on any organization is its annual report. The Commission's report on the activities of the Community as a whole is called the *General report*[32] and is usually accompanied later in the year by several addenda: *Report on social developments*,[33] which covers employment, industrial relations, wages, housing, family problems, health protection, social services and social security with the Community; *Report on the agricultural situation in the Community*;[34] and *Report on competition policy*.[35]

The *Bulletin*[36] gives news and a general overview throughout the year of the activities of the Commission and other Community institutions. There are several supplements to the *Bulletin* which frequently contain the texts of basic policy papers.

2. The **Council**—the ministerial organ of the Community—is composed of representatives of the governments of the ten member states. The Foreign Minister is regarded as his country's 'main' representative in the Council, but membership varies with the subjects under discussion, eg environmental Ministers would be present either alone or with the Foreign Minister when pollution topics are to be discussed. The presidency of the Council rotates at six-monthly intervals between member governments. The Council is

European Communities

assisted by a Committee of Permanent Representatives, and by many expert groups.

At the Summit held in December 1974, the Heads of Government agreed to meet at least three times a year in a Community Council, largely in the political co-operation context. These meetings are normally known as 'European Councils'.

3. The **European Parliament** celebrated its 30th anniversary in 1982, growing from an assembly comprising members designated by national parliaments to the world's first international elected house in June 1979—now with 434 MEPs. When Portugal and Spain join there will be 80 more MEPs, 24 from Portugal and 56 from Spain. The average number of sitting days per year has also been increasing steadily, with the European Parliament dividing its time between Strasbourg, where the majority of the sittings are held, and Luxembourg. *The 'Times' guide to the European Parliament*[37] gives detailed results of the June 1979 election and biographies of all MEPs, with photographs.

The European Parliament Information Office in London is centrally located, close to the House of Commons, at 2 Queen Anne's Gate, SW1H 9AA (Tel: 01-222 0411), and certain prominent MEPs have their offices in the same building. Others have access to offices if they need space in London for meetings. To publicize the work of the European Parliament, the Information Office produces a number of free documents, of which the following are a selection: *European Parliament EP news*,[38] which highlights major events at each parliamentary session; *European Parliament: the week*[39] is a summary of events in more detail; *European Parliament: briefing*[40] is published in advance of the sittings; *European Parliament Digest*[41] indicates proceedings and questions, with a list of COM documents giving the parliamentary committees in which they will be discussed. For details of the publishing patterns of the debates in the European Parliament, reference should be made to Jeffries.[42]

4. The **Court of Justice** is composed of 11 judges, appointed for six years, whose responsibility is to ensure that implementation of the Treaties is carried out in accordance with the law. They are assisted by five advocates-general.

5. The **Court of Auditors** emerged as a new joint institution of the Community in 1979. It is charged with auditing the accounts of the Community and of Community bodies. There are ten members—one for each member state.

Fuller and up-to-date information will always be provided by the European Community information offices in London, Cardiff, Edinburgh and Belfast.

As was to be expected in the few years after this country's accession to the European Community, a spate of bibliographical guides to Community publications appeared. One of the main publishers in this field is Mansell, who was responsible for John Jeffries' *Guide to the official publications of the European Communities*,[43] now in its second edition; Michael Hopkins' *Policy formation in the European Communities*,[44] one of the first guides available in this country; *Sources of information on the European Communities*, edited by Doris M. Palmer;[45] and an index to authors and Chairmen of *Reports of the European Communities 1952–1977* compiled by June Neilson.[46]

The material in John Jeffries's book is arranged according to the institutional framework of the European Communities, beginning with the Treaties which established them and sources of secondary legislation, and continuing through the publications of the Community institutions—Commission, Statistical Office, Council, European Parliament, Court of Justice, Court of Auditors—and the various bibliographic aids available. Michael Hopkins' guide draws attention to primary source material arranged under the broad subject heads of the Directorates-General. Each chapter, eg 'Transport' or 'Environment and consumer protection', begins with a short descriptive essay. A list of key policy documents, with full bibliographical details, follows. Lengthy abstracts are given, and there is a documents index, a subject index, and an author/title index.

The collection of essays edited by Doris Palmer includes 'European Communities legislation—where it is and what it is', by L. S. Adler; 'European Communities material in the British Library, other Depository Libraries and European Documentation centres in the United Kingdom', by J. P. Chillag; and 'Sources of Statistics

European Communities

on the European Economic Community: the Statistics and Market Intelligence Library', by Lewis Foreman.

Many EC reports are often referred to by the name of the author or the chairman who presided over the Committee responsible for the work. But it can be difficult to find further details based on this information alone. There are 2,211 entries in June Neilson's index of published reports. They are arranged by surname in one alphabetical sequence. There is also an excellent subject index extending to nearly 60 pages. I understand that June Neilson intends updating her invaluable index in due course.

Another British librarian, active in this area, is Gay Scott whose guide to sources of information *The European Economic Community* was published by Capital Planning Information in 1979.[47] For some years Mrs Scott has also published in a more specialized field *A guide to European Community grants and loans*,[48] which sets out to provide a detailed description of each fund, an explanation of the purposes for which aid can be given, and the criteria which govern eligibility. Methods of applying for funds are given and, in some cases, examples of successful applications, and analyses of the use made of the funds, are outlined. In the third edition (1982), the section covering alternative energy research and high technology funds has been expanded, reflecting the Community's increasing interest in these fields. A publication available from the European Communities Information Office in London is *Finance from Europe: a guide to grants and loans from the European Community*.[49] This covers nine major points, is free, but is not as comprehensive as Gay Scott's guide. Her company, Euroinformation Ltd, was taken over at the end of 1982 by Eurofi (UK) Ltd, which operates from The Old Rectory, Northill, Near Biggleswade, Bedfordshire SG18 9AH (Tel: 076727 680). Mrs Scott's monthly review of EC COM and other documents ceased publication at the same time, but the House of Commons *Weekly information bulletin*,[50] and *British business*,[51] both published by HMSO, list COM documents regularly, and Eurofi are publishing Giancarlo Pau's annual *Index of COM documents*.[52] First appearing in 1982, covering 1981 COM documents, this guide lists, by keywords and then according to their number, eg COM(81)1 to COM(81)826, the legislative proposals for regulations, directives, decisions and recommendations, and the reports and communications from the Commission to the Council of Ministers and the European Parliament.

COM documents, which form the greater part of the official working documentation of the Commission available to the public, used to be an area of some confusion, but need be so no longer. Giancarlo Pau of the EC Information Office in London, writing in his succinct introduction, states that COM documents 'are intended to have a short life, the principle being that they will quickly become enacted and so part of the law of the Communities. In practice many COM documents remain current for months or even years—particularly those that seek important and far-reaching changes'.

Gloria Hooper, MEP (Greater Liverpool), has asked if this index might be made available to members from all community countries and if the Commission should take responsibility for underwriting its future.

Capital Planning Information also published a detailed key-word subject index, compiled by Anne Ramsay, to the many series produced by the Statistical Office of the European Communities: *Eurostat index*.[53] Appendices consist of a list of titles indexed, addresses of EDC/DEP and EC Information Offices where statistics may be consulted, and addresses of Sales Offices. Once again it is the intention of the compiler to update this work at regular intervals.

A good many of the librarians who prepared these guides are active in the Association of European Document Centre Librarians, which was established in the United Kingdom in 1981 in order to promote the effective exploitation of Community publications, and to act as a channel of communication between EDC/DEP librarians and Community institutions on matters relating to information and publications policy. Major recommendations of the Association include the following:

Librarians should be granted access to bibliographical books, databases and other facilities designed to improve access to Community information.

Although significant improvements have been achieved in the

field of bibliographical control, much remains to be done if sales are not to be lost and valuable material go unread.

The quality of indexing in major Community publications needs to be considerably improved if the information they contain is to be readily and easily accessible.

The Association has produced a series of leaflets on tracing information in EC literature. The series called *'How to find out about . . .'*[54] covers seven topics, including the Court of Justice; Commission documents; statistics; the Official Journal of the EC; and the European Parliament, and costs £0.50 per title. The main means of communication is the *EDC Newsletter*.[55]

The Office for Official Publications of the European Communities in Luxembourg is keen to improve channels of communication between itself and the users of its publications, and with this in mind, published a pilot issue of *EDC/DEP Bulletin*[56] in September 1981.

Where may we obtain up-to-date information about new services? The Official Publications Department of the British Library produced, in 1982, a useful (and free) list: *Alerting services covering European Communities documentation*.[57] This covered commercially published bulletins and information services, then available, which could be used to provide information about new EC documents and publications, and which supplemented the officially published lists. The following services were among those highlighted:

Agence Europe,[58] the invaluable pink daily newsheet which each Saturday includes on its front page details of recent publications, and *European Information Service*,[59] the excellently produced bulletin prepared by Paul Bongers and his staff at the British Sections of the International Union of Local Authorities and the Council of European Municipalities, to inform local authorities of developments within the EC likely to have an impact upon them. Their new address is 12 Old Queen Street, London SW1H 9HP (Tel: 01-222 1636/7). One notable omission from *Alerting services*[60] was the GLC's *European Digest*,[61] which is available at £25.00 per year. *Refer*,[62] the journal of the Reference, Special and Information Section of the Library Association, contains a

ORGANIZATION FOR ECONOMIC CO-OPERATION AND DEVELOPMENT (OECD)

The OECD was formed in 1961 to succeed the Organization for European Economic Cooperation. The change of title marked the Organization's altered status and functions; with the accession of Canada and the USA as full members, it ceased to be a purely European body, while at the same time it added development aid to the list of its other activities. The membership now includes 24 countries—Australia, Austria, Belgium, Canada, Denmark, Finland, France, Germany, Greece, Iceland, Ireland, Italy, Japan, Luxembourg, The Netherlands, New Zealand, Norway, Portugal, Spain, Sweden, Switzerland, Turkey, the United Kingdom, and the United States. Yugoslavia participates in the work of the Organization with a special status. The stated aims of the OECD are to promote economic and social welfare throughout the OECD area by co-ordinating the policies of member countries to this end; and to contribute to the good functioning of the world economy by stimulating and harmonizing its members' efforts in favour of developing countries.

The supreme body of the OECD is the Council, which is composed of one representative for each member country. It meets, about once a week, under the chairmanship of the secretary-general, and once a year at ministerial level. The Council is assisted by an Executive Committee of 14.

Most of the Organization's work is prepared and carried out by specialized committees and working parties of which the Committee for Economic Policy; the Development Assistance Committee; the Energy Policy Committee; the Environment Committee; the Fiscal Affairs Committee; and the Scientific and Technological Policy Committee, are merely a sample six out of the existing 200 or so OECD committees—the vast majority of which produce the results of research carried out on their behalf, annual reports and so on, in an active publishing programme.

Organization for Economic Co-operation and Development

In addition, several other bodies have been set up within the framework of OECD. These include the International Energy Agency; the Nuclear Energy Agency; the Development Centre; the Centre for Educational Research and Innovation; and the European Conference of Ministers of Transport.

The latest issue of OECD's full sales catalogue is entitled *Catalogue of publications on sale as at 1 January 1982*.[63] It is published every two years, but during the interval between the two-yearly editions, it is updated by supplements. The Catalogue opens with a concise description of the membership, establishment, aims and organization of the OECD. Then by grouping most of its publications into the following 14 categories or selections, OECD offers a selective standing order service hopefully tailored to the needs of its customers:

1. General economic problems
2. International development
3. Environment/Quality of life
4. Employment and social affairs
5. Energy policy/supply and disposal
6. Nuclear energy
7. Industry
8. Agriculture/food
9. Fisheries
10. Tourism
11. Inland transport
12. Maritime transport
13. Education
14. Science and technology

This provides an indication of the coverage of OECD publications—emphasizing the economic aspects of all subject areas. OECD periodicals and monographs are also now available on durable microfiche which, provided one's clientèle has access to readers, is a space saver of interest to most libraries. In addition, the OECD maintains an active programme in the sale of magnetic tapes, which is particularly valuable in the case of the statistical series collected. This data is usually more extensive and up to date than that of any published work from the same database but, of course, if tapes are acquired they necessitate access to computer time. Linda Hoffman's general article *Statistical data in machine readable form from international, inter-governmental organizations*[64] sets out very clearly the areas for which OECD tapes are available, the periods covered, and the price at the time of writing which at least provides those able to pursue this line of enquiry with a rough guide on the necessary expenditure.

The annual report of any organization, as we have seen, provides a good overview of the activities. Indeed the OECD's annual report is called *Activities of OECD in . . .* (the year under review)[65] and one of the annexes in it lists the material which has appeared: *OECD publications and documents put on sale in . . .* (the same year). To take an example from the environmental field, in 1980, one of the eight publications of the Environment Policy Committee looked at *Environment policies for the 1980s*.[66] A follow-up document, *The environment: challenges for the '80s*,[67] appeared the next year. Other studies concentrate on the action in particular member states, eg *Environmental policies in New Zealand*,[68] and, of course, economic aspects are always to the fore: *The costs and benefits of sulphur oxide control: a methodological study*.[69] There are very many similar types of study in the other areas of the OECD's interests; of particular relevance here would be the series Information, Computer and Communications Policy (ICCP), but these may be followed up using the catalogues which increasingly include ISBNs, ISSNs and other details. In keeping with the growing practice of other international organizations a commercial publisher—North Holland, in this case—has published for OECD, Hans-Peter Gassman's *Information, computer and communications policies for the '80s*.[70]

How may we obtain these publications?

In this country, Her Majesty's Stationery Office (HMSO) acts as sales agent for UN, EC, OECD, and other international organizations. The government bookshop in London is located at 49

Organization for Economic Co-operation and Development

High Holborn, WC1V 6HB, and there are five other government bookshops in the United Kingdom at the following addresses:

80 Chichester Street, Belfast BT1 4JY.
258 Broad Street, Birmingham B1 2HE.
Southey House, Wine Street, Bristol BS1 2BQ.
13a Castle Street, Edinburgh EH2 3AR.
Brazenose Street, Manchester M60 8AS.

The Cardiff bookshop closed in 1982, but the priced publications of international organizations may be ordered through any bookseller, and a list of those who act as agents for HMSO is given on the cover pages of the monthly catalogue (see below).

Full details of the publications as they become available through HMSO, may be found in *Daily list of government publications from HMSO*[71] under the Agency section headed 'Publications sold but not published by HMSO'. These may also be viewed on Prestel via HMSO lead frame 50040. The monthly cumulation referred to above is entitled *Government publications of . . .*[72] (the month they became available for sale). A checklist of periodical publications issued by international organizations is also included at the back of each issue of the monthly list. An annual cumulation, *International organizations publications*,[73] appears as a supplement to HMSO's Government publications catalogue. The latest edition available at the time of writing is dated 1981, and it contains all items placed on sale by HMSO during 1981. The International Agency Publications Section of HMSO—PC21D—has now moved into the new HMSO Publications Centre at 51 Nine Elms Lane, Vauxhall, London SW8 5DR. The telephone number of the general enquiry point for International Agency Publications is 01-211 3935. Mail orders should be addressed to P O Box 276, London SW8 5DT.

Those working with UN and EC documents may seek help in identifying items in the information offices which both organizations have established in London, and in the case of the EC, in Cardiff, Edinburgh and Belfast as well. It is always sensible to check before you visit, to see whether the offices close for lunch, or regrettably increasingly now on certain days of the week, or have other arrangements which must be taken into account. Most

International Official Publications

publications may be seen at the libraries of these offices and, in many cases, may be borrowed.

UN	United Nations Information Centre 14–15 Stratford Place London W1N 9AF Tel: 01-629 6411
EC	European Communities Information Offices in the UK 20 Kensington Palace Gardens London W8 4QQ Tel: 01-727 8090
	European Parliament Information Office 2 Queen Anne's Gate London SW1H 9AA Tel: 01-222 0411
	4 Cathedral Road Cardiff CF1 9SG Tel: (0222) 371631
	7 Alva Street Edinburgh EH2 4PH Tel: (031) 225 2058
	Windsor House 9/15 Bedford Street Belfast BT2 7EG Tel: (0232) 240708

There is no information centre for OECD publications in this country. Application should be made to:

OECD Publications Office
2 rue André Pascal
75775 Paris Cedex 16
Tel: 524.82.00

REFERENCES

General

1. *Yearbook of international organizations.* 19th ed. Brussels: Union of International Associations and International Chamber of Commerce, 1981. ISSN 0084-3814.
2. International Symposium on the Documentation of the United Nations and other Intergovernmental Organizations, Geneva, 1972. *Sources, organization, utilization of international documentation; proceedings.* The Hague: International Federation for Documentation, 1974. (FID Publications, 506).
3. Dimitrov, Theodore D. *World bibliography of international documentation.* New York: Unifo, 1981. 2 vols. Vol 1: *International organizations*; Vol 2: *Politics and world affairs.* ISBN 0-89111-010-0 (Set).
4. Dimitrov, Theodore D. and Marulli-Koenig, L. *International documents for the 80's: their role and use; proceedings of the Second World Symposium on International Documentation, Brussels, 1980.* New York: Unifo, 1982. ISBN 3-11-008717-0.
Distributed outside US and Canada by De Gruyter & Co, Berlin.
5. Palic, Vladimir M. *Government publications: a guide to bibliographic tools* incorporating *Government organization manuals: a bibliography.* Oxford: Pergamon, 1977. (Guides to Official Publications, Vol 1) ISBN 0-08-021457-6.
6. Cherns, J. J. *Official publishing: an overview: an international survey and review of the role, organization and principles of official publishing.* Oxford: Pergamon, 1979. (Guides to Official Publications, Vol 3) ISBN 0-08-023340-6.
7. Pemberton, John E. (ed.) *The bibliographic control of official publications.* Oxford: Pergamon, 1982. (Guides to Official Publications, Vol 11) ISBN 0-08-027419-6.
8. *Government Publications Review.* Vol 1– , 1973– . Oxford: Pergamon. ISSN 0277-9390.
Acquired subtitle 'An international journal of issues and information resources' with Vol 9, No 1, 1982. Bimonthly.
9. Hajnal, Peter I. IGO documents and publications: volume distribution, recent developments, and sources of information. In: *Government Publications Review*, Vol 9, No 2, March–April 1982, pp 121–30.
Appendix: Sources of information about IGO documents and publications—select bibliography.

International Official Publications

UN and its agencies

10. Marulli-Koenig, Luciana. *Documentation of the United Nations System: co-ordination in its bibliographic control.* Metuchen, New Jersey: Scarecrow Press, 1979. ISBN 0 8108 12339.
11. Hajnal, Peter I. *Guide to United Nations organization, documentation and publishing for students, researchers, librarians.* Dobbs Ferry, New York: Oceana, 1978. ISBN 0 379 20257 8.
12. Hajnal, Peter I. *Collection development: United Nations material.* In: Government Publications Review, Vol 8A, 1981, pp 89–109.
13. Winton, Harry N. M. *Publications of the United Nations System: a reference guide.* New York: Bowker, 1972.
    I understand that Dr Winton was working on a revision of this title *Official Publications of the UN System* to be published by Pergamon, in its 'Guides to Official Publications Series', at the time of his death in 1979.
14. *United Nations documentation: a brief guide.* New York: UN, 1981. (ST/LIB/34/Rev 1)
15. *UN documentation news.* No 1, September 1981. New York: UN Dag Hammarskjold Library.
16. *UNDOC: current index.* Vol 1, January/February 1979. New York: UN Dag Hammarskjold Library. (ST/LIB/SER M/-).
    Continues UNDEX, 1974–1978; and UNDI, 1950–1973. Ten issues per year, plus annual cumulation in 3 vols. (ST/LIB/SER M/CUM 1-).
17. United Nations. Dag Hammarskjold Library. *Unbis thesaurus: list of terms used in indexing and cataloguing of documents and other materials relevant to Unitied Nations programmes and activities.* New York: UN, 1981. (ST/LIB/3M)
18. Singh, S. and Sobel, S. *Unbis compatibility with national and international information systems.* In: International documents for the 80's: their role and use; proceedings of the Second World Symposium on International Documentation, Brussels, 1980. pp 185–92.
19. *Directory of United Nations information systems.* 2nd ed. Geneva: Interorganization Board for Information Systems, 1980. 2 vols.
20. *The complete reference guide to United Nations sales publication, 1946–1978.* Compiled by Mary E. Birchfield. Pleasantville, New York: Unifo, 1982. 2 vols. Vol 1: *Catalogue*; Vol 2: *Indexes.* ISBN 0 89111 011 9.

UN sales catalogues

21. *United Nations sales publications 1972–1977: a cumulative list with indexes.* (ST/LIB/SER B/27).

References

22. *United Nations publications in print: checklist English.* New York and Geneva: UN, 1978.

Agencies

23. *ILO catalogue of publications in print 1982.* Geneva: International Labour Office, 1982.
24. *ILO publications.* Geneva: International Labour Office. ISSN 0378-5904.
   Descriptions of each new item with an abstract in the language of the publication.
25. *Publications of the International Maritime Organization. Catalogue 1982.* London: IMO.
   With a supplement, 1983.

European Communities

26. Twitchett, Kenneth J. Britain and the European Communities: the first ten years. In: *British Book News*, March 1983, pp 148–52. Published by the British Council. ISSN 0007-0343.
27. Jeffries, John. *A guide to the official publications of the European Communities.* 2nd ed. Mansell, 1981. ISBN 0-7201-1590-6.
28. European Communities: Commission. *Directory.* Luxembourg: Office for Official Publications of the European Communities. ISBN 92-825-3159-7.
29. *European Communities yearbook.* 5th ed. 1982–1983. Brussels: Editions Delta. ISBN 2-8029-0031-5.
30. *European Communities and other European organizations who's who.* 2nd ed. Brussels: Editions Delta. ISBN 2-8029-0017X.
31. *Vacher's European Companion*: a diplomatic, political and commercial reference book. A. S. Kerswill Ltd. Quarterly.
32. European Communities. *General report.* Luxembourg: Office for Official Publications. ISBN 92-825-3425-1.
   16th report covers 1982.
33. European Communities. *Report on social developments.* Luxembourg: Office for Official Publications. ISBN 92-825-2877-4.
34. European Communities. *Report on the agricultural situation* in the Community. Luxembourg: Office for Official Publications.
35. European Communities. *Report on competition policy.* Luxembourg: Office for Official Publications.
36. European Communities. *Bulletin.* Luxembourg: Office for Official Publications. ISSN 0378-3693.

Published 11 times a year (one issue covers July and August) in the official community languages and Spanish. Each issue contains a sales catalogue on pale yellow paper.
Supplements to the *Bulletin* are published in a separate series at irregular intervals, eg Supplement 1/82: A new Community action programme on the promotion of equal opportunities for women 1982–1985. ISBN 92-825-2925-8.
37. Wood, David. *The 'Times' guide to the European Parliament*. Times Books Ltd, 1979. ISBN 0-7230-0231-2.
The following items, Nos 13–16, are issued from the European Parliament Information Office in London:
38. *European Parliament EP news*.
39. *European Parliament: the week*.
40. *European Parliament: briefing*.
41. *European Parliament Digest*.
42. Jeffries, J. *Op. cit.*
43. Jeffries, J. *Op. cit.*
44. Hopkins, Michael. *Policy formation in the European Communities: a bibliographical guide to Community documentation 1958–1978*. Mansell, 1981. ISBN 0-7201-1597-3.
45. Palmer, Doris M. (*ed.*) *Sources of information on the European Communities*. Mansell, 1979. ISBN 0-7201-0724-5.
46. Neilson, June (*comp.*) *Reports of the European Communities 1952–1977: an index to authors and chairmen*. Mansell, 1981. ISBN 0-7201-1592-2.
47. Scott, Gay. *The European Economic Community: a guide to sources of information*. Capital Planning Information, 1979. (CPI Information Review, No 3). ISBN 0-906011-043.
48. Scott, Gay. *A guide to European Community grants and loans*. 3rd ed. Euroinformation Ltd, 1982. ISBN 0907304-036.
49. *Finance from Europe: a guide to grants and loans from the European Community*. London: European Communities Information Office.
50. House of Commons. *Weekly information bulletin*. Compiled in the Public Information Office of the House of Commons Library. HMSO. ISSN 0261-9229.
51. *British business*. Weekly news from the Departments of Industry and Trade. HMSO. ISSN 0143-9111.
52. Pau, Giancarlo. *Index of COM documents 1981–   *. Euroinformation Ltd, 1982. ISBN 0-907304-028.
Index for 1982 due to be published by Eurofi (UK) Ltd.
53. Ramsay, Anne. *Eurostat index: a detailed keyword subject index to the Statistical series published by the Statistical Office of the European Communities*. Edinburgh: Capital Planning Information, 1981. ISBN 0906011-159.
54. Association of *European Documentation Centre* Librarians. Series:

References

'How to find out about . . .'. Seven booklets available from Mrs Anne Ramsay, The Polytechnic, Ellison Place, Newcastle upon Tyne.
55. *EDC Newsletter*. Available at £5.00 p.a. from Mrs Anne Ramsay, The Polytechnic, Ellison Place, Newcastle upon Tyne.
56. *EDC/DEP Bulletin*. Luxembourg: Office for Official Publications.
57. BL Official Publications Library. *Alerting services covering European Communities documentation*. Undated, but must have appeared during 1982.
58. *Europe: Agence internationale d'information pour la presse*. Brussels. Usually referred to as 'Agence Europe'.
59. International Union of Local Authorities and Council of European Municipalities (British sections). *European Information Service*. ISSN 0261-2747.
Ten issues per year (£15.00, 1982) plus back-up service.
60. BL Official Publications Library. *Op. cit.*
61. Greater London Council. *European Digest*. Monthly (£25.00, 1983). ISSN 0144-1671.
A well-produced document. The information used in compiling the Digest is derived from Official Community Publications and from newspapers and journals appearing during the month of the Digest. For example, under the heading 'Information' in the issue for November 1982, three items were mentioned:
 1. The electronic supply of documents and electronic publishing.
 2. Satellite television—Eurikon and a report discussed by the Committee of Ministers of the Council of Europe.
 3. The trial viewdata service—Europost, which provides information on Community public supply contracts.
62. *Refer*: journal of the Reference, Special and Information Section (RSIS) of the Library Association. Published twice a year in Spring and Autumn by the Section, and distributed free to members; to others, £2.50 per year (UK). ISSN 0144-2384.

OECD

63. OECD. *Catalogue of publications on sale as at 1 January 1982*. Paris, 1982.
64. Hoffman, Linda M. Statistical data in machine readable form from international, inter-governmental organizations. In: *Government Publications Review*, Vol 9, No 3, May–June 1982. pp 167–74.
65. OECD. *Activities of OECD in . . .* (1981). Paris, 1982. Annual. ISBN 92-64-12310-5.
Appendix to the 'annual report'—*Publications and documents put on sale in . . .* (1981).

International Official Publications

66. OECD. Environment Committee. *Environment policies for the 1980s*. Paris, 1980. ISBN 92-64-12049-1.
67. OECD. Environment Committee. *The environment: challenges for the '80s*. Paris, 1981. IBSN 92-64-12249-4.
68. OECD. Environment Committee. *Environmental policies in New Zealand*. Paris, 1981. ISBN 92-64-12161-7.
69. OECD. Environment Committee. *The costs and benefits of sulphur oxide control: a methodological study*. Paris, 1981. ISBN 92-64-12151-X.
70. Gassman, Hans-Peter. *Information, computer and communications policies for the '80s*. Published for OECD by North-Holland Publishing Co, 1981. ISBN 0444-86327-3.

HMSO catalogues

71. *Daily list of government publications from Her Majesty's Stationery Office*. HMSO. ISSN 0263-743X.
Price £0.05; annual subscription (1983): posted daily £42.50; posted weekly £25.50.
72. *Government publications of* ... (the month they become available). HMSO.
Annual subscription (1983) £10.00 including postage.
73. *International organizations publications*. HMSO. ISBN 011 701 1029. £3.75 for 1981 issue, published 1982. Supplement to *Government publications*.
The latter two items appear under cover title: *HMSO Books Catalogue*.

19

Printed Visual Sources

J. David Lee

This chapter will be concerned more with visual enquiry work and the types of material with which to answer queries, than with a description of great reference works which all students and librarians should know. In visual work we do not have the equivalent of the British Library general catalogues, or the definitive 'last picture' to match the definitive 'last word' of the *OED*.[1] There is no full pictorial inventory of visual source material, ie that which may be seen or imagined. Though illustrated books abound, visual reference work is not a good field for standard works, but it is an interesting one.

VISUAL ENQUIRY WORK

The librarian is asked to provide not only factual information, but also pictures of more visual subjects. Enquirers often wish to see illustrations, and it is our purpose here to give an outline of the printed visual materials which are available to them. The recent handbook *Picture librarianship*[2] did not much concern itself with reference work, and in fact the subject is little covered in the literature of librarianship. Yet illustration enquiries occur often and are important. Whether the enquirer is specific or not in his request,

Printed Visual Sources

he actually *needs* his diagram or picture at least as much as the words which accompany it.

Visual enquiries occur in all kinds of library—public, where loan and photocopy facilities will be available; academic; and the specifically visual, such as college of art, or media libraries. Children, in their school work, are often expected to seek illustrations—from the black rat to Henry VIII. In fact the children's librarian may find visuals for children more easily than the reference librarian is able to do so for their parents.

Problems in visual librarianship include:

(a) Poverty of reference stock. Reference libraries may as a matter of policy have avoided acquiring illustrated books, and have concentrated on the more academic ones. Expensive art books are often deposited in reference collections where an eye can be kept on them, but such collections are seldom going to cater for the day-to-day needs of the visual enquirer.
(b) Lack of specificity. Detailed pictures will often be required, and those the library possesses may not go far enough.
(c) Lack of information. The captioning may be absent, or not full enough.
(d) Poor quality. The reproduction may not be good enough, and detail can be lost. Colour reproduction is fraught with even worse problems if truth to the original is required.
(e) Lack of bibliographical control. Whilst any book on trees will tell you about the main varieties of oak, it is not certain that the pedunculate and sessile oaks will both be illustrated, even if the book's catalogue entry declares that it contains illustrations. Bibliographies and indexes leave great gaps, if they tackle illustrations at all. Indexes to pictures themselves are rare enough; they are discussed later.

Here are some examples of visual enquiries:

– Show me van Gogh's self-portrait without the ear. Have you photos of van Gogh with and without the ear?
– I need a circuit diagram for an audio filter.

Visual Enquiry Work

- What did Buckingham Palace look like before the 1913 alterations?
- Have you a picture of the death of Captain Cook?
- I need a picture of such and such a fashion to make a theatre costume. (Advertisers and designers are particularly visual in their needs.)
- Can you identify this beetle found in my garden, and this strange metal tool my wife dug up? (Many visual enquiries are of this identifying kind.)
- Images *of* an individual.
- Images *by* an individual.

We are visual in many of our requirements, perhaps more so now that television is nearly universal. Pictures are a useful stimulus to thought and feeling—witness the recent development of their use with groups recording old memories. The illustrated book is now regarded as *de rigueur*, except to the most hardened academic. Even quizzes, bane of the reference library, may incorporate pictorial questions. Visual historiography—study of the changing form of something, as in design history—has become academically respectable. Genealogists are urged to add illustrative background to their research.

The librarian may be faced with a request for a known identified illustration, as in the fine arts or philately, or with a request to help illustrate a known topic. These are two sides of the same coin; but that there *are* two sides is a point that should be recognized in stock building. Rarely will staff be asked to illustrate the abstract, though 'mood' pictures may sometimes be wanted.

Is there a special way of tackling the visual enquiry? Are there particular questions in visual cases which must be asked in the reference interview? First, one must recognize that the request *is* visual, and second, one must find out the reason for the request, if this is not breaking confidentiality. In view of the need to supply the most apposite material, questioning is possibly of even more importance than it is in verbal work, though in some cases, absolute accuracy is not quite as crucial as it is in such work, that is, alternatives may be acceptable.

Illustrations provided by the librarian will often be required for others to prepare secondary illustrations—graphics for posters and journals, inspiration to painters. Where direct reproduction is not required, this is often known as 'picture reference'.

SOURCES

From what sources are these enquiries answered, and problems solved? Obviously the specific identification problem is best answered from a detailed book devoted to the subject, and beyond the simple, success will depend on the amount and level of illustrated stock held. Whether one's stock is adequate or not can only be established by recording those enquiries which the library has failed to answer satisfactorily, a good discipline for all types of work. Unfortunately one cannot usually tell whether a book is illustrated from its 'look' on the shelf, nor can one glean much from the cryptic message of the catalogue entry. The book may have 'Illustrated' 'Visual' or 'Pictorial' in its title, but these words may be a selling point rather than an indication of standard. If illustrated books contain graphics of a broad nature, artist-made, they may be of little value to the reference librarian; nevertheless the non-photographic element should not be totally discounted. Artists such as L. Ashwell Wood in the 1930s; some illustrators in *Eagle*, with their analytical drawings; or the wood engravers of nineteenth-century magazines, prove that. Diagrams can often be useful, and a knowledge of graphic as well as scientific symbols is one of the specialisms that the librarian can usefully acquire.

Real objects themselves will not often be at hand, though it is worth remembering nearby museums and galleries which may contain them.

Books and periodicals will be the librarian's main source, but special collections of illustrations the library may acquire include:

- fine prints
- bookplates
- ephemera, including postcards and cigarette cards
- collections of photographs,[3] for instance from a defunct newspaper

The Illustrated Book

- local photographs in general
- lantern slides
- the illustrations collection
- a book arts collection. (In larger libraries there may be a bibliographical collection, important for the study of book illustration as such.)

THE ILLUSTRATED BOOK[4]

Most pictorial enquiries are likely to be answered from the general stock of illustrated books. These will include works with titles like *The complete woodcuts of Iain Macnab* or *All the paintings of Albrecht Dürer*, and many with just a handful of pictures. Mary J. Shapiro's *A picture history of the Brooklyn Bridge* (New York: Dover Books, 1983) exists just to show us 167 prints and photos. There have always been illustrated books, from manuscript days—herbals, bestiaries, histories, religious texts, for instance. With modern technology we are able to have facsimiles easily, if expensively, and there are available some excellent copies of illuminated manuscripts.

The illustration of some books is more decorative than informative, and such books are of interest to us only where they themselves are the objects of study. This would apply to children's fiction too; adult fiction is rarely illustrated.

The value of illustration is shown by the reissue of a standard text in an illustrated edition. A recent example is Celia Fiennes' *Illustrated journeys* (Exeter: Webb and Bower, 1982), where a seventeenth-century text was factually illustrated for the first time ever.

We are going through a period where integration of illustrations with text is aimed at, as printing developments have made this possible. The changes in Penguins for example—from the separate photogravure section found at the centre or end of earlier Pelicans, to the present style where illustrations are found on the same pages as the relevant text—show this well. This is helpful from an indexing, ie information-finding, point of view, as well as for continuous reading, since separate sections of illustrations are rarely indexed.

Printed Visual Sources

Encyclopaedias are not generally of great illustrative value. The function of the illustrations at the junior end is as much to break up solid text and give encouragement as it is to give information. Some adult encyclopaedias are open to criticism, not only for the quality of their booklists, but also for the quality of their illustrations. Katz[5] is interesting on the subject. There is a change in the attitude of some publishers. One old work, still of interest, is:

Mee, Arthur I SEE ALL: THE WORLD'S FIRST PICTURE ENCYCLOPEDIA. London: Amalgamated Press, 1928–1930. 5 vols.

This contains 100,000 pictures, and gives few facts other than the visual.

JOY OF KNOWLEDGE LIBRARY. London: Mitchell Beazley, 1976.

A multi-volume heavily illustrated encyclopaedia making a great effort to get away from the heavily factual. Reminiscent of the part works produced by this publisher and others.

Reference libraries tend to buy the more academic books in addition to true reference books and the selection policy of most reference libraries does not generally include the acquisition of illustrated books in their own right, except possibly for the art section. This is understandable: where do readers' requirements for illustrations end, at least in theory? Most of us like our non-fiction books to have some illustrations, and the reference librarian should not be too high-minded in his search for books of worth. Some librarians have an ambivalent attitude to illustrations, feeling that they can devalue a book. I think this is partly related to the ratio of illustrations to text. If the number of illustrations is small enough, enhancement follows; if it is too large an element, purchase is questionable. And yet contempt even for coffee table books is not wholly justified; some of these have illustrations on a size and scale not found elsewhere. They may make one look, and think. It may be hard to justify buying books of the 'Victorian and Edwardian such and such' type, or 'Coketown old and new', unless they have local relevance. Books such as the Press Association's *Album of a nation: the many faces of Britain* (London: Paddington

The Illustrated Book

Press, 1979) or the nostalgic *Times gone by* (London: Marshall Cavendish, 1977), each relying on the contents of a picture library, are not the sort of book the average reference library would even consider buying.

I have mentioned the practice of putting expensive illustrated books in the reference library only, and cannot recommend this; it should be possible to borrow such books. But there can be value, where there is the right clientèle, for large art histories, books on artists, and *catalogues raisonnés*[6]. It all depends on the actual and potential use. Quite a few books of this type have a second volume containing the illustrations, eg H. R. Hitchcock's *Early Victorian architecture* (New Haven, Connecticut: Yale University Press; London: Architectural Press, 1954). D. S. Neal's *Roman mosaics in Britain* (Gloucester: Alan Sutton, 1981) puts them into a microform supplement, slipped into the book.

Facsimiles have been mentioned, and ought to be considered for purchase, as they can be valuable to students and graphic designers. Also useful to the latter are *'visual archives'*, that is, collections of pictures for the use of graphic artists and others. The best-known are those from Dover Books (Constable). Some quite recherché classics are available, such as Callot's *Etchings* and Thomas Hope's *Costumes of the Greeks and Romans*. Many volumes indicate that reproduction is permissible provided that the number of illustrations used does not exceed a stated number. Two other works of this type are *The Bettmann portable archive* (New York: Picture House Press, 1966) and *The illustrator's handbook*, published in the USA as *The great giant swipe file* (New York: Hart Publishing Co, 1978). Each of these volumes contains over 3,000 illustrations.

One type of book where illustrations are always to be welcomed is the **illustrated biography**. The more pictures here the better, and there are several series of books such as pictorial biographies from Thames and Hudson, with titles '..... and his world', which are particularly noteworthy for their illustrations. An interesting single publication is *Hermann Hesse: a pictorial biography* (St Albans, Herts: Triad Paperbacks, 1979; originally a German publication of 1973), which is a most determined effort to put everything about Hesse into pictures. Presumably the authors of

Printed Visual Sources

books like these have been dissatisfied with the level of illustrations found in other books on their subjects.

Some older works, superannuated textually, may be worth saving for their illustrations; examples include technical works of the Victorian and Edwardian periods, where the clarity of the highly processed photographs makes these interesting and usable to historians and graphic artists. The financial value of such books has risen apace in recent years, as the 'dated' becomes chic. The technical diagrams can also help the reconstruction or use of old machinery, an aid to industrial archaeology.

Old periodicals, such as past issues of *Illustrated London News, Graphic, Punch,* and *Picture Post,* are a ready source of illustrations, but the librarian should beware of infringing copyright in more recent years if reproduction is involved. Some journals, as in the fashion world, are well illustrated; others, like political weeklies, illustrate only to punctuate the text. As with book cataloguing, indexing of periodicals and their articles too rarely indicates presence or value of illustrations.

Another valuable category of illustrated book is the **extra-illustrated book**, including 'grangerized' volumes. Here further pictures are added either by the publisher, so that the work may be sold at a higher price, perhaps to subscribers, or personally by the book's owner. Grangerized books are often concerned with local history, and many record offices and reference libraries have them, but in the nineteenth century the practice was more widespread in books on all subjects. This shows the wish of readers to overcome the limitations of illustrating books; such limitations were not technically solved until the 1890s, and have never been financially overcome. A recent example of the extra-illustrated book is John Nelson *The history of Islington* (London: Sotheby Publications, 1980). This added 79 illustrations to the original 1811 text.

STANDARD WORKS

In general there are no standard works covering 'the visual' as a whole. Things seen are ubiquitous, and it is a bold venture to create

Standard Works

a work like *I see all*, mentioned above. Each subject with visual aspects will have its illustrated standard works which the librarian should get to know. Some obvious examples:

Gibbons, Stanley SIMPLIFIED CATALOGUE: STAMPS OF THE WORLD. London: Stanley Gibbons Publications, annual from 1934.
   Now in two volumes, this contains over 50,000 pictures of stamps, arranged by country and date.

Harris, John and Lever, Jill ILLUSTRATED GLOSSARY OF ARCHITECTURE, 850–1830. London: Faber, 1966.
   Instead of words defining terms, pictures do the job.

Thompson, Philip and Davenport, Peter THE DICTIONARY OF VISUAL LANGUAGE. London: Bergström and Boyle, 1980; Harmondsworth: Penguin Books, 1982.
   Proceeding from Abacus to ZZZZZ, this includes those images which we take for granted, and shows new versions.
   The authors have also done *The ABC of visual clichés*.

UNESCO: CATALOGUE OF REPRODUCTIONS OF PAINTINGS 1860–1973. Paris: Unesco, 1974; CATALOGUE OF REPRODUCTIONS OF PAINTINGS PRIOR TO 1860. Paris: Unesco, 1978.
   These show prints of paintings and, as far as they go, are useful. A fuller, more up-to-date work on these lines would be of great benefit.

HOW THINGS WORK: THE UNIVERSAL ENCYCLOPEDIA OF MACHINES. London: Allen and Unwin, 1967–1971; Paladin, 1972–1974.
   A compilation full of diagrams of all sorts of inventions; indexed, with explanatory text. Originally published in Germany, this is one of the most useful technical books in a non-technical society.

JANE'S FIGHTING SHIPS, JANE'S ALL THE WORLD'S AIRCRAFT and other volumes in the excellent series published by

Printed Visual Sources

Macdonald and Jane (previously by Sampson Low) are valued as much for their illustrations as for their text.

Sports, flags, and numismatics are three areas where illustration is very important. Books on knots, wood samples and deaf and dumb language are amongst those which could not exist without pictures.

Among standard works which might be expected to be fully illustrated, because of their subject, but in fact are not, are Thieme-Becker and Bénézit, the two main dictionaries of artists. The *Oxford history of English art* and the *Pelican history of art* are improving in later volumes, but do depend more on text than illustration. It is worth comparing the *Victoria history of the counties of England* with the Royal Commission on Historical Monuments volumes, and the Pevsner *Buildings of England* series. None is perfect, no doubt on grounds of expense, and the student can consider what he would like to see in them, pictorially. There are many gaps in illustrative coverage. For instance, there is no work showing pictures of all major race-horses, current or historical; or of all British coats of arms, of any period. We have all looked in vain for a butterfly, bird or flower in what seemed to be the right books, and not found a picture. Why not? On the whole the reason is expense, but part of the problem is the pervasive nature of the visual element. When one does find a thorough illustration job, it is worth remembering. For example:

Ross-Craig, Stella DRAWINGS OF BRITISH PLANTS. London: Bell and Hyman, 1948– .

A series of volumes in botanically classified order, of drawings of flowering plants, of excellent quality.

As the subject of symbols is one which librarians are asked about, here is a list of the main works:

Cirlot, J. E. A DICTIONARY OF SYMBOLS. 2nd ed. London: Routledge and Kegan Paul, 1971.

This does not include many illustrations as such, but it is most useful.

Reference Works

Cooper, J. C. AN ILLUSTRATED ENCYCLOPEDIA OF TRADITIONAL SYMBOLS. London: Thames and Hudson, 1978.
   Similar to the works of Cirlot and Hall.

Dreyfuss, Henry SYMBOL SOURCEBOOKS. New York, etc: McGraw-Hill, 1972.
   Symbols listed by the area of use.

Hall, James DICTIONARY OF SUBJECTS AND SYMBOLS IN ART. Rev ed. London: John Murray, 1979.
   An excellent guide to the classic symbols in art, the new edition having a subject index.

Modley, Rudolf HANDBOOK OF PICTORIAL SYMBOLS: 3250 EXAMPLES FROM INTERNATIONAL SOURCES. New York: Dover Publications, 1976.

Shepherd, Walter GLOSSARY OF GRAPHIC SIGNS AND SYMBOLS. London: Dent, 1971.
   A complex, but classic work, aiming to show, in a classified order, symbols and their meaning. Uses a system of precedence of symbols, but is indexed verbally.

Arnstein, Joel THE INTERNATIONAL DICTIONARY OF GRAPHIC SYMBOLS. London: Kogan Page; Century Publishing Co, 1983.

REFERENCE WORKS

Reference books with which the visual librarian will need to be familiar include:

Arlis UNION LIST OF PERIODICALS ON ART, DESIGN AND RELATED SUBJECTS. London: Arlis, 1983.

Printed Visual Sources

Coulson, Anthony J. A BIBLIOGRAPHY OF DESIGN IN BRITAIN 1851–1970. London: Design Council Publications, 1979.

Witt Library A CHECKLIST OF PAINTERS c 1200–1976 REPRESENTED IN THE WITT LIBRARY, COURTAULD INSTITUTE OF ART, LONDON. London: Mansell, 1978.
Includes over 50,000 artists represented in the library's card index.

Kamen, Ruth H. BRITISH AND IRISH ARCHITECTURAL HISTORY: A BIBLIOGRAPHY AND GUIDE TO SOURCES OF INFORMATION. London: Architectural Press, 1981.

Salmi, Markku (*ed.*) NATIONAL FILM ARCHIVE CATALOGUE OF STILLS, POSTERS AND DESIGNS. London: British Film Institute, 1982.

National Portrait Gallery DICTIONARY OF BRITISH PORTRAITURE. 4 vols. London: Batsford, 1979–1981.
Within periods, then alphabetical.

BIBLIOGRAPHY OF MUSEUM AND ART GALLERY PUBLICATIONS AND AUDIO-VISUAL AIDS IN GREAT BRITAIN AND IRELAND 1979/80. Cambridge: Chadwyck-Healey; Westport, Connecticut: Meckler Books, 1980.
It is to be hoped that this work, now in its second edition, will be continued.

It should be emphasized that the above books are not direct sources of illustrations but are handbooks of great help to the visual librarian.

VISUAL COLLECTIONS

To some extent a library can radically increase its visual resources by buying other collections in copied form. Here are a very few examples from an increasing number; apart from the first, the following items are in microform:

Courtauld Institute of Art ILLUSTRATION ARCHIVES: A PHOTOGRAPHIC REFERENCE LIBRARY OF EUROPEAN SCULPTURE AND ARCHITECTURE. London: Harvey Miller, 1977– .
These illustrations are high-class photographs of certain classes of art. Companion texts discussing the works are also now available.

Victoria and Albert Museum THE V AND A MUSEUM COLLECTION: A PHOTOGRAPHIC RECORD. London: Mindata, 1976– .

Alinari PHOTO ARCHIVE. Zug, Switzerland: IDC.
Reproduces on microfiche several major archives of early art photography.

Farm Security Administration AMERICA 1935–1946. Cambridge: Chadwyck-Healey, 1980.
Reproduction, on microfiche, of 87,000 photographs of the FSA and the Office of War Information collections housed in the Library of Congress.

SILVER STUDIO DESIGNS 1880–1963. Haslemere, Surrey: Emmett Microforms, 1983.

There are several publishers here and abroad specializing in such microform collections, whose products, which are of reference rather than reproductive value, are regularly mentioned in *Arlis News-sheet*.

LOCAL HISTORY

Local history is one area of library work where visual enquiries are predictably common, despite David Dymond's gloomy comment that 'the average person's visual awareness is still woefully undeveloped and this is one major reason why local history does not enjoy the public and official prestige it deserves'.[7] Local history enquiries are usually on the lines of 'What did such and such or so and so look like?', and changes in appearance are avidly sought.[8] Answers come from illustrated histories and guidebooks of all dates, and from the illustrations which most libraries acquire by purchase and gift. Local history is a field in which books of illustrations with minimal text abound. They were particularly common in the early days of half-tone and photogravure, when the photographs were current. Now they are part of the nostalgia boom.

Reproduction of local illustrations is often requested; such requests must be treated with care from the points of view of copyright, ownership and courtesy.[9] When material is acquired it is tempting to leave the status vague, but this can cause problems later.

Libraries have taken an active part in local photographic surveys, sometimes in co-operation with local societies,[10] and in some places this still continues.

BIBLIOGRAPHIES AND INDEXES

The library profession pursues the ideal of universal bibliographical control, and one strand of twentieth-century librarianship is the growing grasp of the listing, assessment and purchase of most types of material.[11] It cannot, however, be said that illustrations or even photographs are yet coming within this grasp, even under the heading of audiovisual materials.[12] Illustrated books are covered to a point, but not the pictures they contain. As we have seen, the librarian is lucky if a book's illustrations are included in its own index. Although the Victoria and Albert Museum does care for the book arts, and the British Library possesses millions of illustrations, the fact remains that there is no national illustrations collection. Whether we shall ever achieve control remains to be seen, but we are not on the brink, and it is a fact that even if there were universal or widespread indexing of illustrations, unless it had visual accompaniment, its value would be limited.

Bibliographies and Indexes

Attempts to index illustrations as such have been comparatively few. There is no current bibliography or index which aims to list illustrations for their own sake. The librarian can often hope only that what appears to be a promising book does have the pictures he requires.

The following are some of the more useful and interesting indexes to illustrations:

Abbey, J. R. SCENERY OF GREAT BRITAIN AND IRELAND IN AQUATINT AND LITHOGRAPHY 1770–1860... A BIBLIOGRAPHICAL CATALOGUE. London: Curwen Press 1952.

This, and the same author's *Travel in aquatint and lithography 1770–1860* (1956–1957), constitute one of the great works on topographical illustration.

Adams, Bernard LONDON ILLUSTRATED 1604–1851: A SURVEY AND INDEX OF TOPOGRAPHICAL BOOKS AND THEIR PLATES. London: Library Association, 1983.

Arranged chronologically, though with separate supplement, this analyses over 200 illustrated books and books of illustrations, with full indexes.

Monro, I. and K. INDEX TO REPRODUCTIONS OF EUROPEAN PAINTINGS. New York: H. W. Wilson, 1956.

An earlier work of 1948, with 1964 supplement, covered American paintings.

The following more general indexes may be mentioned:

Appel, Marsha C. ILLUSTRATION INDEX. 4th ed. Metuchen, New Jersey: Scarecrow Press, 1980.

This continues the 2nd and 3rd editions, the set giving coverage of a small number of American journals from 1950–1976, and showing illustrations under subject headings.

Ellis, Jessie Croft INDEX TO ILLUSTRATIONS. Boston, Massachusetts: Faxon, 1966.

Printed Visual Sources

Covers, under subject headings, a small number of books and periodicals. One of several similar works by this compiler.

Havlice, Patricia Pace WORLD PAINTING INDEX. Metuchen, New Jersey: Scarecrow Press, 1977.
Analyses over 1,000 books published 1940–1975, giving titles of paintings, names of painters, and whereabouts of reproductions. Continued in a supplement 1973–1980.

Korwin, Yala H. INDEX TO TWO-DIMENSIONAL ART WORKS. Metuchen, New Jersey: Scarecrow Press, 1981. 2 vols.
Similar to Havlice.

Moss, Martha PHOTOGRAPHY BOOKS INDEX: A SUBJECT GUIDE TO PHOTO ANTHOLOGIES. Metuchen, New Jersey: Scarecrow Press, 1980.
Covers 22 US photographic books from 1945 (some being anthologies), giving photographer, portrait, and subject approaches.

Parry, Pamela Jeffcott PHOTOGRAPHY INDEX: A GUIDE TO REPRODUCTIONS. Westport, Connecticut: Greenwood Press, 1979.
Author has also covered *Contemporary art and artists: an index to reproductions* (1978).

Clapp, Jane SCULPTURE INDEX. Metuchen, New Jersey: Scarecrow Press, 1970. 3 vols.

These books may be used when either a specific picture or a picture to fit a known subject, is required. Most of them are American, and may therefore be of less use in UK libraries. It must be emphasized, however, that there are few UK indexes to illustrations of any sort.

THE ILLUSTRATIONS COLLECTION

Libraries of various kinds, but particularly those connected with education, have created illustrations collections—that is they store,

The Illustrations Collection

usually in vertical or lateral files, folders of pictorial material cut from old books and journals. Some, like *Pictorial Education*, were published for this type of purpose, and others, like *History Today* or *National Geographic Magazine*, are also found useful. The pictures are used for reference and/or loan, and are in a very real sense a supplement to the bookstock from an illustrative point of view. That they are not found universally, or that they have been abandoned, may be due to the following problems:

(a) Dependence on random appearance of the illustrations leaves gaps. There is repetitiousness in the images which turn up, eg the White Tower from the manuscript of Charles Duke of Orleans' poems.
(b) Captioning is often bad in the original, and can be difficult to transfer. Dating may not be given, and plausible fakes and misattributions are common.
(c) The illustrations may be of very poor quality, as they are usually reproductions, and colour is often screened.
(d) There may be other physical limitations, such as the unpleasant surface to be handled which is found in colour supplements.
(e) The material has to be prepared for the file, usually by mounting, and perhaps by heat sealing within plastic material.
(f) The arrangement of the picture file may well follow that of the bookstock, and with the size these collections can easily reach, there may be problems in cataloguing and classification. Decimal classification is commonly found, and there is a real need for good subject indexing. Alphabetical subject headings are also often found. Cross-references should be done in the same file.
(g) The pictures get out of order easily and are often battered.
(h) If the pictures are lent, there are return and loan problems, beginning with the need for carrying folders.

The illustrations collection does still continue in some places, but it is not much in favour, and current literature on it is scarce.[13] An effort to get material—beyond the rather passive approach of the cutting up of old books and magazines—can be made, at com-

Printed Visual Sources

paratively low cost, by trying commercial and other free sources; this is covered well in an article by Anthony Coulson.[14]

More liked today is the space-saving slide collection, part perhaps of an audiovisual set-up. Recent literature tends to be on this topic, and it is not only art slides that are dealt with.[15] Additional problems, however, can be:

(a) Cost of the material.
(b) Technical difficulties of slide making and preparing. One's own slides may be made, at a price.
(c) Limitations of what is available, probably within a small budget.
(d) Captioning is never easy within the small space available, and captioning on separate papers is liable to be lost.
(e) There will be physical deterioration; handling causes problems. Good slide duplicators are not cheap.
(f) Viewing equipment will be needed both in the library and at any other place of use.
(g) Slides are stolen and lost easily.

In most libraries neither the illustrations collection nor the slide library are within the orbit of the reference department, but such resources are worth remembering at the right time.

FURTHER SOURCES: LIBRARY COVERAGE[16]

There are not, as far as I know, co-operative schemes concerned with illustrations, though clearly in the national and regional library network all visual subjects such as art, costume, photography, will be covered, and the books will be available. So also, particularly through the British Library Lending Division, will illustrated periodicals, though beware of photocopies, as the illustrations will not be reproduced as well as the text is.

The librarian may need to go outside his own library system, not forgetting loan and children's collections; and for the *ad hoc* urgent enquiry, libraries outside the usual range may be tackled. There are directories to help him, but he must be aware of the nature of the

Further Sources: Library Coverage

types of collection he may approach, and how far they are likely to be helpful. Visual libraries include:

- local authority education libraries; audiovisual; college; and school libraries;
- other academic libraries, eg art colleges and departments;
- commercial picture libraries and agencies;
- publishers and other closed sources such as Phaidon Press;
- special libraries, such as the National Monuments Record.

Directories include:

Wall, John DIRECTORY OF BRITISH PHOTOGRAPHIC COLLECTIONS. London: Heinemann, for the Royal Photographic Society, 1977.
Rather oddly indexed, but invaluable; based on the National Photographic Record.

Bradshaw, David N. (*ed.*) WORLD PHOTOGRAPHY RESOURCES. New York: Directories, 1982.
Grouped arrangement.

Robl, E. H. (*ed.*) PICTURE SOURCES 4. New York: Special Libraries Association, 1983.
The latest edition of a useful series covering North American picture resources. A British equivalent will be:

Eakins, Rosemary (*ed.*) PICTURE SOURCES UK. London: Macdonald, 1984.
This lists picture sources (not just photographic), and will cover all kinds of organization; it will have detailed subject indexing.

Evans, Hilary and Mary PICTURE RESEARCHER'S HANDBOOK. 2nd ed. London: Saturday Ventures, 1979.
With some classification, this lists commercial picture collections.

Nunn, G. W. A. BRITISH SOURCES OF PHOTOGRAPHS AND PICTURES. London: Cassell, 1952.

Printed Visual Sources

Although old, this should not be discarded by the reference library.

Barley, M. W. A GUIDE TO BRITISH TOPOGRAPHICAL COLLECTIONS. London: Council for British Archaeology, 1974.

There is no national visual source in the UK. Whereas for films there is the National Film Archive, for illustrations, perhaps because of the ubiquity of the visual, and the huge numbers of pictures produced, no such repository exists for pictures or, even more narrowly, for photographs. Some of the picture libraries are very large—the Imperial War Museum claims a stock of five million items, and is still growing; the BBC Hulton Picture Library has nearly nine million. The British Library can truly say that, within books, its picture resources are vast, but the fact remains that there is no one clear resource, and no copyright deposit of pictures as such. On the problems of creating a national photographic archive, see Dr Wall.[17]

Some particularly important sources which should be known to the librarian concerned with the visual are the National Monuments Record, Victoria and Albert Museum Library, Westminster Art Library, and the Witt Library of the Courtauld Institute of Art.

COPYRIGHT

This becomes a real problem to the librarian only when he or she is *using* illustrations in publication or display; nevertheless a good working knowledge of copyright is essential, so that, when needed, advice can be given.[18] The reader may well wonder how far he can use pictures which the librarian has found for him. Basically, illustrations (photographs, designs, works of art, etc), whether original or reproduced are automatically copyright, and their unauthorized use may be an infringement and therefore liable to legal action. The copyright of illustrations can be of long duration. In the case of a photograph taken after 1957 the copyright of the original holder or his successor will last for 50 years from its first publication, which

Picture Researchers

can easily be decades after the photograph's production and the photographer's demise. As for copyright in relation to other European countries, the legislation is a nightmare. In the USA particularly, 'invasion of privacy'—that is the use of photographs of a person without his/her agreement—can be a further problem.

Reproduction from pictures in books is usually technically unsatisfactory because of the likelihood of double screening, and it will often be illegal. Crediting of pictures, which should provide an indication of the copyright owner, is quite good in books; in periodicals the situation is improving, in television it is poor, and in newspapers, dreadful. The ideal is a neat indication of the source—by the side of the picture or in the caption; an acceptable alternative is an illustration credit list either at the front, or at the end of the book. Further information on how the copyright holder may be traced may be obtained from the directories already noted, or from the publisher. The organization BAPLA (British Association of Picture Libraries and Agencies) may ultimately be able to help. It is not the librarian's task to pursue all this to its end; rather, it is his duty to propel the ignorant reader in the right direction. Migration of picture collections, particularly former agencies, is a problem, but one on which BAPLA should be able to help.

PICTURE RESEARCHERS

There is a smallish band of people whose profession is the seeking of pictorial material. They are beginning to get the acknowledgement which they deserve, in books and in other source materials. Some of them have jobs with firms, but many are freelance and may be called upon to provide pictures for books, journals, films, television programmes, audiovisuals, etc. There is no specific accredited training, and such people are rarely professional librarians, though there is no reason (except perhaps a financial one) why they should not be. The professional group of picture researchers is the Society of Picture Researchers and Editors (SPREd); not only does it have a Newsletter—there are also books on the subject of picture research.[19] Colleagues in the United States are more closely linked

Printed Visual Sources

with suppliers of pictures, and are members of the Association of Picture Professionals (ASPP). Curators tend to be in the Picture Division of the Special Libraries Association, which produces an excellent journal, *Picturescope*. The triangle of seeker–provider–user is a complex one, particularly considering the multiplicity of providers.

The librarian who wishes to be competent in the field of visual information should aim to know what the picture researcher knows; having learned the jargon (eg 'landscape/portrait' formats), and details of varieties of rights, he can add to this from his greater knowledge of reference materials. Visual flair, the quality so much admired by the client, can be usefully supplemented by the librarian's professional knowledge. Visual librarians in Britain tend to congregate in the Library Association Audiovisual Group; Aslib Audiovisual Group; and Arlis, which has strong international connections in the art world. All of these bodies publish useful journals,[20] and the last-named also produces a very full *Newsletter*.

Knowledge of basic reproduction processes, both current and historical, in all media, is important. It is sensible to know how an illustration will end up being used so that better provision of an original may be made.[21] Similarly, it is worth finding out which types of client prefer glossy prints and which prefer matt prints. Historical bibliographical knowledge, eg of nineteenth-century lithography, will help the librarian to know the origins and status of pictures.[22] The literature on illustration is extensive.

FUTURE DEVELOPMENTS

It is not easy to see what developments there might be in visual reference work. Sources will become more easily available, by publication in microform and on videodisc,[23] the capacity of which is so great. But such storage does not necessarily lead to ease of finding; there must be first-rate indexing, which has to be verbal. Nor is ease of reproduction in all media from microform and videodisc assured. Equipment for display and use of library materials must be provided. All this, the provision of sources and of equipment, requires adequate finance.

References

Transmission of pictures—television, facsimile transmission—is readily possible, but transference of a screened picture is not as simple and accurate as textual transfer, and the production of hard copy is not satisfactory.

Illustrated books will continue to be produced. We are in a good period for them. Even internationalism helps, for variant texts may be fitted to a set of universal illustrations. Electronic encyclopaedias will still require illustrations, for the need for pictures is still there. One is tempted to think that the printed word is more at risk to the spoken word than is the picture.

Indexing has been mentioned before, and one field in which there has been much development is the indexing of the visual. As an adjunct to art history, the computer has been brought into use to classify visual elements, and enable comparisons to be made. The literature on this is now quite extensive, and is still growing.[24]

If all this seems rarified, and at some distance from the enquiry desk of Coketown's reference library, one must assert that librarianship is one profession, and that all practitioners are linked within it. For those who chose to specialize in the visual, the links will be within an even wider circle.

REFERENCES AND CITATIONS

1. *Das Buch der Köpfe*. Munich: Mosaik Verlag, 1981.
   Embodies a good idea, showing pictures of the faces of famous people. Of worldwide scope, it includes 3000 heads.
2. Harrison, Helen, P. (*ed.*) *Picture librarianship*. London: Library Association, 1981 (Handbooks on library practice).
3. Blodgett, Richard *Photographs: a collector's guide*. New York: Ballantyne Books, 1979.
   Castle, Peter *Collecting and valuing old photographs*. 2nd ed, rev. London: Bell and Hyman, 1979.
   Coe, B. and Haworth-Booth, M. *A guide to early photographic processes*. Westerham, Kent: Hurtwood Press in association with Victoria and Albert Museum, 1983.
   Witkin, Lee D. and London, B. *The photograph collector's guide*. London: Secker and Warburg, 1979.
   These are four books which will be helpful to the librarian acquiring such material.
4. Bland, David *The illustration of books*. 2nd ed. London: Faber, 1962.
   The standard general account.

Printed Visual Sources

Brenni, Vito J. *Book illustration and decoration: a guide to research.* Westport, Connecticut: Greenwood Press, 1981.
5. Katz, William A. *Introduction to reference work.* 3rd ed. New York, etc: McGraw-Hill, 1978.
6. Pacey, Philip (*ed.*) *Art library manual: a guide to resources and practice.* London, New York: Bowker, 1977.
   And references therein.
7. Dymond, David *Writing local history: a practical guide.* London: Bedford Square Press, 1981.
8. Miller, Stuart T. 'The value of photographs as historical evidence.' *Local Historian*, 15 (8), 1983. 468–473.
   Discusses the problems of assessing photographs, and how they were produced.
9. Field, Roy 'The library as publisher.' *Library Association Record*, 81 (8), 1979. 383–385.
10. Gower, H. D. *et al. The camera as historian: a handbook to photographic record work.* London: Sampson Low, Marston, 1916.
    Still has something to offer a library considering this work.
11. *Art Libraries Journal*, 7 (2), 1982.
    Contains papers on the International Seminar on Information Problems in Art History.
12. Covered by *British catalogue of audiovisual materials.* London: British Library (Bibliographical Services Division).
13. Hill, Donna *The picture file: a manual and curriculum-related subject heading list.* Syracuse, New York: Gaylord Professional Publications, 1978.
    Corbett, E. V. *The illustrations collection: its formation, classification and exploitation.* London: Grafton, 1941; Ann Arbor, Michigan: Gryphon Books, 1971.
14. Coulson, A. J. 'Illustrations'. In: Pacey, P. *Art libraries manual.* London, New York: Bowker, 1977 372–388
    The British trades alphabet. Wakefield: BTA, and *Treasure chest for teachers.* Kettering, Northants: Teacher Publishing, are two useful guides to free material in general; and Harvey, Adam (*ed.*) *Where to find photographs of the developing countries.* London: Centre for World Development Education, 1978, has its uses.
15. Irvine, Betty Jo *Slide libraries: a guide for academic institutions, museums and special collections.* Littleton, Colorado: Libraries Unlimited, 1979, is a general guide. *See also* Pinion, Catherine F. 'Audiovisual materials'. In: Taylor, L. J. (*ed.*) *British library and information work 1976–1980.* London: Library Association, 1983. Vol. 2. 118–132.
16. Pacey, Philip 'Art libraries', and Lee, David 'Picture libraries' are two further chapters in Taylor, L. J. *op.cit.*, which show recent developments and provide many further references.

References

17. Wall, John 'Towards a national photographic archive'. *Journal of the Royal Society of Arts*, **131**, 1983. 70–86.
18. Smith, Charles H. Gibbs- *Copyright law concerning works of art, photographs and the written and spoken word.* 3rd ed. London: Museums Association, 1978.
    A useful introductory guide.
19. Evans, Hilary *The art of picture research: a guide to current practice, procedure, techniques and resources.* Newton Abbot, Devon: David and Charles, 1979. Evans, Hilary *Picture librarianship.* New York, London: K. G. Saur, Clive Bingley, 1980. (Outlines of modern librarianship).
20. *Audiovisual Librarian* is published for the first two groups, *Art Libraries Journal* for the third; both quarterly.
21. Butcher, Judith *Copy-editing.* 2nd ed. Cambridge: Cambridge University Press, 1981.
    The standard work on treatment of illustrations, editorially. Among works on how to use pictures, Evans, Harold *Pictures on a page: photojournalism, graphics and picture editing.* London: Heinemann, 1978, is a classic.
22. These are just three works from an extensive literature:
    Bland, David *A history of book illustration.* London: Faber, 1958.
    Evans, Hilary and Evans, Mary *Sources of illustration 1500–1900.* Bath, Somerset: Adams and Dart, 1971.
    Russell, Ronald *Guide to British topographical prints.* Newton Abbot, Devon: David and Charles, 1979.
23. Sorkow, Janice 'Videodiscs and art documentation'. *Art Libraries Journal*, **8** (3), 1983. 27–41.
24. Couprie, L. D. 'Iconclass: an iconographic classification system.' *Art Libraries Journal*, **8** (2), 1983. 32–49.
    This is one development. Note also the work of the Museum Documentation Association, Bildarchiv Foto Marburg, and articles in *Visual resources: an international journal of documentation.* London: Gordon and Breach, 1981– , and *Art documentation*, published by ARLIS/NA.

20
Online Information Retrieval Systems

Bernard Houghton

BACKGROUND

Online access to bibliographic and referral databases was the inevitable technological development of applying computers to the processing of bibliographic information. The computer revolution in documentation evolved rapidly, and its three stages are now clearly discernable:

1. Computers were first employed to assist in the production of better **printed** abstracting and indexing services.
2. The existence of the machine-readable databases from which hard-copy indexes were generated made it possible to run both current-awareness and retrospective literature searches in batch-mode against the database, ie a number of searches or user profiles were run at one time, offline, on the computer at the information centre to which the user addressed his subject request.
3. Users are now able to interact conversationally with the machine-held databases by searching online via remote terminals over national and international communication networks.

An information retrieval services industry has now developed, which in many instances markets both printed and online versions

Background

of the same databases. It is possible that we shall see the demise of some hard-copy secondary services, at least in the fields of science and technology, as the cost of paper and print escalates, and the cost of maintaining and accessing computer-held files of bibliographic data diminishes. Tensions will be inevitable in this industry, as the use of online systems increases, with the inevitable decrease in the sales of hard-copy indexing and abstracting services.

Computer processing of bibliographical information began in 1961, when the American Chemical Society (ACS) introduced the keyword-in-context (KWIC) index *Chemical titles (CT)*, a machine-generated alphabetical subject index covering 600 of the most prestigious journals from the parent publication *Chemical abstracts (CA)*. This development was necessitated by the delays in the publication of *CA*, whose abstracts were appearing increasingly later after the original papers which they summarized. *CT* was then introduced as a stop-gap, giving chemists quicker access to the most important papers in their field, and serving as a partial substitute for *CA*, which covered all the literature when it appeared two or three months later. By the end of the decade, however, the whole range of *CA* publications was being produced from a machine-readable database. In this operation, all of the indexing and abstracting information was taken from the 12,000 source journals in a single process of intellectual analysis before it was input to the database in a single keyboarding operation. Throughout the 1960s, computerization was steadily adopted by other learned societies and governmental agencies in the production of their database, particularly in the sciences and technologies, and by the end of the decade the first stage of a computer revolution was almost complete. The new processing methods gave the secondary services increased flexibility in selecting and repackaging the contents of their databases to meet the changing needs of individuals and groups of research workers.

The advantages of computerization were that secondary services were able to produce an extended range of abstracting and indexing **publications**. They were more timely in publication; they were able to process more bibliographic information and thus increase their subject coverage; and they were equipped with better indexes which cumulated more frequently. In addition, the machine-readable files could be used for both current-awareness and retrospective, state-of-the-art searching. Selective dissemination (SDI) services were introduced by information centres such as the Institution of Electrical Engineers' INSPEC (Information Service in Physics, Electronics and Control) service, and the Chemical Society's UKCIS (United Kingdom Chemical Information Service). These services allowed individual users to run subject profiles of their interests against the database to retrieve, at regular intervals, details of relevant papers dealing with their interests. The same centres also offered retrospective subject searches, which selected all the papers from the database which matched a specific request for information. Both these services were run on computers in batch-mode, but batch searching had intrinsic disadvantages. Firstly, the batching of searches was economical of computer time, but it was inefficient from the user's point of view in that he was forced to endure delays in the receipt of his computer output to his request. The turnaround time in sending the search request to the information centre and the receipt of the output may have been up to three weeks, as the centre had to wait for an adequate number of searches to accumulate before it could run them efficiently in terms of machine time. The user was also forced to search 'blind'; he could not sample the output from the system and assess its relevance to his query before the search had been completed. The searcher also had no personal interaction with the system; the search strategy was formulated by a search analyst at the information centre who interpreted the requester's information need in the language of the system.

ONLINE INFORMATION RETRIEVAL INDUSTRY

Online interaction between the user and the database obviated both of these problems. After a developmental period from 1960 onwards, a three-tiered information retrieval services industry emerged in the early 1970s. The three tiers in this industry are:

1. the database producers;
2. the retrieval service suppliers;

3. information services and information brokers.

1. Databases have been defined in the *Directory of online databases*[1] as collections of related textual and/or numeric data in machine-readable form that are processed for computerized publishing and/or electronic dissemination. They can be divided into two categories, **reference** and **source databases**. Under the initial heading are subsumed both bibliographic and reference databases. Bibliographic databases include online files of abstracting, indexing and cataloguing information, eg *Psychinfo (Psychological abstracts)*; *Magazine index*; and the *MARC* databases. Reference databases include online directories and reference sources such as *Ulrich's periodicals directory* and the *Encyclopedia of associations*. Source or non-bibliographic databases encompass numeric, textual-numeric and full-text databases. Numeric databases include information expressed as numbers, presented in the form tables or 'time-series'. They will usually include a measurement or variable, eg population; production of a commodity; imports; exports, etc; a time-series expressed in years or months; and a geographical region or country, eg timber reserves (gross tonnage) of Norway from 1960 to date; automobiles exported from Japan to the United States and the United Kingdom from 1970 to date. Textual-numeric databases combine statistical information with interpretative textual commentary. Properties databases provide data on the physical, chemical or mechanical properties of materials; and full-text databases hold the complete text of documents, for instance statutes and law reports.

Bibliographic database producers are typically the learned and professional societies who have traditionally undertaken the responsibility of collecting and processing the literature covering their fields, and the various government agencies active in science-based and other industries which have a need to provide an information service in support of their activities. Many of the abstracting and indexing services are long established; *Chemical abstracts*, for instance, dates from 1907, and *Physics abstracts*, now a section of the INSPEC database, from 1898. Before 1961, all these services were produced by traditional typesetting and publishing methods, but the massive growth of the scientific and technical literature, which increased four-fold between 1957 and 1970, with an annual growth rate of 10·6%, compelled the database producers to abandon traditional publishing methods and to turn towards computer-aided production of their databases. The expansion of the information retrieval industry has now resulted in commercial organizations such as Data Courier Inc and Predicasts Inc which produce and market online databases.

2. The machine-readable databases produced by the first sector of the industry are leased from their producers by the retrieval service suppliers, who process them to create standardized tape formats, develop computer software systems to facilitate user interaction with the bases, and load them into their computers to provide online retrieval services. User interaction with the database is effected in information services and libraries by using computer terminals, via standard telephone equipment, over national and international communication networks. A listing of the major service suppliers in the United Kingdom and the USA is given at the end of this chapter.

3. The third link in the online communication chain is the information service provided by commercial and public organizations to give their clients access to online databases. Several commercial services are now available, acting as 'information brokers' for their users, eg carrying out online searches for a fee. More and more academic and public libraries are now making an online facility available to their clients, but practice as to the costing of these services varies widely. Some academic libraries will absorb the costs of online searching in their library budgets, making no direct charge to the user for a search, while others pass the whole or a part of the search costs to the user. In public libraries the costing of online searching presents particular problems—online access is an advanced form of reference service, and reference services such as literature searching have been traditionally available to the user without charge. The cost of staff time, and the expense in the provision and utilization of bibliographical resources incurred in carrying out a manual literature search are largely hidden, when

compared with the more starkly accountable costs involved in online searching. More standard policies for the costing of online access will emerge as the facility becomes more generally used in libraries.

HISTORICAL DEVELOPMENT

Interactive online information retrieval systems were pioneered in the United States by two companies, the System Development Corporation (SDC), and the Lockheed Space and Missile Corporation, now DIALOG Information Services Inc. SDC's involvement in online bibliographic retrieval dates from 1960, when it started work on the Protosynthax system, which gave full-text access to the contents of the *Golden book encyclopedia*. Its first nationwide experimental network was introduced in 1965 under a series of grants from ARPA (Advanced Research Project Agency), a US governmental research agency. Thirteen institutional organizations, such as the Central Intelligence Agency (CIA); the Defense Intelligence Agency; and the Battelle Memorial Institute, were given four hours per day access to a database containing 200,000 references on foreign technological literature.

The development of MEDLINE (Medical Analysis and Retrieval Service On-line) was particularly significant in the acceptance of online systems by a large body of users. The US National Library of Medicine (NLM) started using a computerized system to produce its monthly alphabetical subject index to the world's medical literature, *Index medicus*, in 1963. Subsequently, one-off retrospective literature searches were run against this database in batch-mode. In the Autumn of 1967, the NLM began to investigate the potential of online access, and a contract was signed with SDC, which installed and evaluated its ORBIT (On-line Retrieval of Bibliographical Information Time-shared) system at NLM, using a small database in the field of neurology. A pilot online experimental service offering access to a subset of the *Index medicus* database became operational in June 1970 to 90 medical institutions in the United States, allowing users to search the *Abridged index medicus (AIM)* database, which covered 100 of the most important world medical journals. This project utilized SDC's IBM 360/67 computer, which was linked to the Teletypewriter Exchange Network (TWX), which could be accessed via terminals in the medical institutions throughout the country. A fully developed MEDLINE service giving access to 1,200 journals covered by *Index medicus* was introduced in October 1971, and by 1974 all of the current citations in *Index medicus* were made available in one MEDLINE database over the Tymshare communication network.

SDC's commercial online service was inaugurated in October 1972, when the first two databases, MEDLINE and ERIC (Educational Resources Information Center), were put up on an IBM machine at Santa Monica, California. Three months later a new database, CHEMCON, a file derived from *Chemical abstracts condensates*, was added, and this subsequently became the most heavily used file of the SDC range. More databases were added at regular intervals, and by the end of 1982 the ORBIT retrieval software gave access to about 80 different databases.

Lockheed's online retrieval activity commenced in 1964 with experimental work on their DIALOG system; this started as a self-financed research project, and the development continued under a US governmental research contract as the NASA/RECON system, which is now operational at most NASA (National Aeronautics and Space Administration) centres, and also in Europe at the European Space Agency centre at Frascati, near Rome. The DIALOG system, whose software is almost identical to that used in the original NASA/RECON system, was introduced commercially in 1971. Initially only a limited number of databases were available, but DIALOG has since become the largest of the service suppliers, and by the end of 1982 about 200 databases were available, covering most fields in the sciences and technology, and, in addition, ever increasing areas in the social sciences and humanities.

Online activity in Europe followed in the wake of the American experience. The European Space Agency/Space Development Service (ESA/SDS) RECON system was established at Darmstadt in 1968, using a modified version of Lockheed's DIALOG software, to make NASA's database available to ESA staff in Darmstadt and Paris. The first large-scale, generally available European online service, giving access to a number of databases covering sciences

Historical Development

and technologies of relevance to the space and associated industries, was set up by ESA in 1975, operating from a computer in Frascati. In the same year, the Department of Industry (DOI) introduced its DIALTECH service, enabling UK users to access the ESA/RECON databases by dialling into a mini-computer, located at the Technology Reports Centre in Orpington, which automatically connected them to the ESA computer. Now over thirty databases are accessible via the updated version of RECON, the ESA/IRS service.

The British Library online information facility BLAISE (British Library Automated Information Service) was introduced in April 1977, offering a service from its computer at Harlow. Initially BLAISE gave access to the US National Library of Medicine's MEDLINE files; plus CHEMLINE, an online chemical dictionary file assembled by the NLM in association with the Chemical Abstracts Service; and TOXLINE (TOXicology information onLINE), a collection of toxicological citations containing eight files which can be searched simultaneously. Later in the year, BLAISE made available both the UK MARC file, which covers the majority of British copyright material back to 1950, and the US Library of Congress MARC file which gives access to US and other books from 1966. In 1982 BLAISE divided its service into BLAISE-Link, a link with the US National Library of Medicine, for searching the biomedical and related databases; and BLAISE-Line, which continues to offer the non-medical databases from Harlow, United Kingdom. BLAISE now gives access to about ten databases via its BLAISE-Line and BLAISE-Link services, and also makes available facilities for the online production of catalogues. Other major service suppliers in the United Kingdom are Pergamon-Infoline, with about 16 databases; and the Derwent-SDC Search Service, which gives access to the patent databases produced by Derwent Publications Ltd.

The EURONET/DIANE (Direct Information Access for Europe) service, the planning of which commenced in 1971, finally became operational in 1980. EURONET is the data transmission facility developed by the postal, telegraph and telephone authorities (PTTs) of the EEC countries to provide users within the Community with the means of access to bibliographic and referral online databases. BLAISE and ESA/IRS were among the first service suppliers to the new network, which now gives access to about 370 databases from over forty service suppliers. Data-Star, a Radio Suisse company, has become one of the more significant service suppliers now acting as EURONET hosts. It markets its service, which offers over twenty databases, throughout Europe from offices in Switzerland, the United Kingdom, France and Germany.

TERMINALS AND COMMUNICATION SYSTEMS

Communication is effected with the host computer, the machine into which the service supplier has loaded the databases he is marketing, by using a teletype (hard-copy) or a visual display terminal. Information is transmitted to the computer by typing instructions via the terminal's keyboard, the lay-out of which is almost identical to that of a standard typewriter. The terminal keyboard will, however, have some additional keys and switches for specific online functions, eg, the 'break' key, which allows the user to interrupt the flow of characters being received from the host computer, and the 'baud' switch, which determines the speed at which the terminal's output device operates. Hard-copy terminals generate printed output of the information transmitted from the host via a teletypewriter similar to a telex machine. This information will be printed by either impact or non-impact methods. Impact printers transfer the characters to the paper via a character face which impacts with the paper through an inked ribbon. Non-impact terminals employ chemical, electrostatic, or thermal means to transfer their image onto specially coated paper. Non-impact terminals work at higher character per second (cps) rates than do impact models; they operate at speeds from 30 to 120 cps, while impact terminals are usually limited to 30 cps. Hard-copy terminals normally used for bibliographic online access are 30 cps non-impact models. There are several portable, silent 30 cps terminals on the market, such as the Texas Instruments Silent 700 series, which can be conveniently used in any location where a standard telephone handset and a 13 amp electric socket are to be found (see Fig. 1).

Visual display unit (VDU) or cathode-ray-tube (CRT) terminals

Terminals and Communications Systems

Figure 1. Texas Instruments Silent 700 terminal

output the characters on to a television-like screen, on which each character is represented in a grid of either 5 × 7 or 7 × 9 matrices. A typical display format will present 24 lines of 80 characters with 5 lines to one inch. Display units operate at between 30 and 120 cps. Communication output speeds are expressed in manufacturers' brochures in 'bauds', baud being the number of times the output line changes each second. This represents the presence or absence of one bit, and the signalling time is equal to the number of bits transmitted per second; thus, a machine described as operating at 300 baud will output at 30 cps, and one at 1200 baud will equal 120 cps.

Display terminals are not usually equipped with a line-printer output device; this facility is, however, essential for bibliographic information retrieval, where a permanent copy of the search product will be required. It is, nevertheless, possible for the display terminal to be linked to one or more line-printers, and this is standard practice in libraries and information centres using online systems. In addition, either hard-copy or display terminals can work in conjunction with one or a number of 'slave' monitor screens—display terminals which lack the keyboard necessary for inputting data to interact with a system. Configurations of this nature are useful when demonstrating online systems to groups of potential users, as the physical constrictions imposed by using a single hard-copy terminal would effectively limit an audience to two.

'**Intelligent**' **terminals** offer distinct advantages over conventional teletype or display terminals. By using combinations of their cassette tape and user-definable function keys, it is possible to pre-record frequently used strings of characters necessary for logging-on to various hosts for ease of transmission simply by pressing a single function key. In the same manner, detailed search strategies may also be pre-recorded, thus economizing on online time. The data retrieved from the host computer can also be conveniently recorded on cassette, for subsequent editing and printing out. **Microcomputers** are now increasingly being used for online information retrieval. Their memories can also be used for storing data for logging-on procedures and other functions, and they have the advantage that when they are not being used for online retrieval they are not idle, as their multitude of applications for storing and organizing in-house data in libraries and information centres is becoming apparent.

Information may be transmitted from the terminal to the host computer by direct-dialling into the host, when this is adjacent, and it can be achieved by means of a local telephone call, or, via a national postal, telegraph and telephone (PTT) service in conjunction with a communication network. Communication networks, eg British Telecom's International Packet Switch Stream (PSS/IPSS); Tymshare's Tymnet; or Telenet Marketing's Telenet, permit terminals to be connected to systems such as DIALOG, ORBIT or Data-Star by dialling the nearest node of the network—this will usually mean a local call to the network number. The user will then pay a communication cost from the node to the host of his choice, thus obviating the cost of direct dialling. Initially computer link-ups utilized cables designed to carry the spoken word, but now packet-switching technology employs networks designed for the transmission of discrete packets of fast data signals via special high-grade paths between computers, communication network nodes and terminals. British Telecom's IPSS/PSS is designed for the transmission of data within the United Kingdom, and provision is also made for connection to data networks in other countries. Tymshare's Tymnet became operational in 1970, and is one of the larger international data communications networks, employing over 300 nodes in 25 countries. Billing transactions are made through arrangements with the United States International Record Carriers, who have agreements with the national PTTs, who in turn bill their users.

When the user has dialled into the host computer or accessed the nearest node of a communication network, he will receive a high-pitched whistle over the line and this will indicate that contact has been made with the system. Communication having been effected, he will depress the data button on the telephone if the handset is connected to the communication line by a modem (modulator/demodulator), or place the handset in the cradle of an acoustic coupler if this is used to make the connection. The modem is a fixture separate from the terminal, and is usually rented from the national PTT; while the acoustic coupler is a portable piece of equipment. Some terminals are manufactured with the acoustic coupler as an integral part of the unit. Modems and acoustic couplers are devices which enable signals to be sent between a terminal and a host computer in a format acceptable to both.

INFORMATION RETRIEVAL PRINCIPLES

The process of information retrieval is the obverse of that of information storage, and both consist of three analogous stages. In information storage these steps are: 1. the subject analysis of the information contained in the documents to be input to the system, and the formulation of subject concepts for each document; 2. the translation of the concepts into the indexing language used by the database producer; 3. the entry of the subject concepts into the files of which the database consists.

Online Information Retrieval Systems

The retrieval process entails: 1. the subject analysis of the information requested by the end-user (the individual for whom the search is being run) and the establishment of the basic subject concepts or parameters for the search; 2. the translation of these parameters into the indexing language used by the database being searched, and the expression of the relationships which exist between these parameters in a search strategy; 3. the actual search process in which the terms used in the search strategy are matched against those stored in the database to describe the subject contents of the documents in the database. Where there is coincidence between the terms which have been assigned to a document in the database and those in a search strategy, the document will presumably be relevant to the end-user's information needs.

This matching process is facilitated by creating inverted files from the databases which have been loaded into the service supplier's host computer. Inverted files are organized according to the most likely search parameters, eg the indexing terms which have been assigned to the documents; keywords from the titles and abstracts of the documents; the authors' names, etc; these files will in effect be a collection of subfiles, as the accession numbers of the documents which have a common data element, such as an indexing term or an author's name, will be posted under that element in the inverted file. For example, a section of an inverted file of indexing terms would give:

INDEXING TERM	INFORMATION
DOCUMENT NUMBER	109; 438; 972; 1104; 1309 . . .
	INFORMATION ANALYSIS
	321; 773; 842; 902; 1438 . . .
	INFORMATION CENTRES
	293; 507; 891; 372; 843 . . .
	INFORMATION RETRIEVAL
	114; 189; 344; 562; 976 . . .
	INFORMATION STORAGE
	139; 189; 344; 498; 562 . . .
	INFORMATION WORK
	120; 643; 789; 815; 897 . . .

LH-FSH RELEASING HORMONE
D6.472.709.429
/biosyn /physiol permitted; DF: LHFSHRH
74
X   FSH RELEASING HORMONE
X   LH RELEASING HORMONE

LH RELEASING HORMONE see LH-FSH RELEASING HORMONE
D6.472.709.429

LIBERIA
Z1.58.432.527

LIBIDO
F2.739.794.511
only /drug eff /physiol /rad eff
68
XR INSTINCT
XR MOTIVATION
XR SEX

LIBMAN-SACKS DISEASE see LUPUS ERYTHEMATOSUS, SYSTEMIC
C17.490   C23.205.200.436

LIBRARIANSHIP see LIBRARY SCIENCE
L1.583+

LIBRARIES
L1.346.596+
IM; do not use /educ /instrum /methods; specify geog or other site
CATALOG: /geog /form
XR INFORMATION SERVICES

LIBRARIES, DENTAL
L1.346.596.363
IM; do not use /educ /instrum /methods; specify geog or other site
CATALOG: /geog /form
65

LIBRARIES, HOSPITAL
L1.346.596.463
IM; do not use /educ /instrum /methods; specify geog or other site
CATALOG: /geog /form

LIBRARIES, MEDICAL
L1.346.596.563+
private & public libraries; includes private collections of books; IM; do not use /educ /instrum /methods; specify geog or other site   CATALOG: /geog /form

LIBRARIES, NURSING
L1.346.596.663
IM; do not use /educ /instrum /methods; specify geog or other site
CATALOG: /geog /form
67(65)

LIBRARY ADMINISTRATION
L1.583.363
only /educ /man /stand

LIBRARY ASSOCIATIONS
L1.583.390
only /hist /organ; med libr assoc: do not coord with MEDICINE
CATALOG: /geog /form
XR SOCIETIES

LIBRARY SCHOOLS
I2.783.388   L1.583.430
only /class /econ /hist /organ /stand /trends /supply; specify geog if pertinent
X   SCHOOLS, LIBRARY

LIBRARY SCIENCE
L1.583+
only /hist /man /stand; med librarianship: do not coord with MEDICINE
X   LIBRARIANSHIP

LIBRARY SERVICES
L1.453.639+   L1.583.464+
do not use /educ /methods /util (except by MeSH definition)   CATALOG: /geog /form
76; was NON MESH before 1976

LIBRARY SURVEYS
L1.583.564
only /econ /hist /methods /stand /trends /util   CATALOG: /geog /form

LIBRARY TECHNICAL SERVICES
L1.453.639.570   L1.583.464.570
do not use /educ /methods /supply /util (except by MeSH definition)
CATALOG: /geog /form
76; was LIBRARY TECHNICAL PROCESSES (NON MESH) before 1976

LIBYA
Z1.58.266.513   Z1.630.600

LICE
B1.131.617.564+
/microbiol /parasitol permitted; do not use /drug eff for insecticides: TN 111; sucking lice = ANOPLURA, biting lice = MALLOPHAGA, elephant-lice (= Rhynchophthirina) goes here
PHTHIRAPTERA was heading 1975-79
use LICE to search PHTHIRAPTERA back through 1975
see related
   PEDICULOSIS
X   PHTHIRAPTERA

LICE, PLANT see APHIDS
B1.131.617.412.165

LICENSES see LICENSURE
N3.706.110.510+

LICENSURE
N3.706.110.510+
by the state; differentiate from ACCREDITATION (by the profession); IM; only /hist; various boards can go here; specify geog   CATALOG: /geog /form
X   INSTITUTIONAL PERSONNEL LICENSURE
X   LICENSES
X   LICENSURE, INSTITUTIONAL, PERSONNEL
XU LICENSURE, HOSPITAL

LICENSURE, DENTAL
N3.706.110.510.180
by the state; differentiate from ACCREDITATION (by the profession); IM; only /hist; various boards can go here; specify geog   CATALOG: /geog /form

LICENSURE, HOSPITAL
N3.706.110.510.290
by the state; differentiate from ACCREDITATION (by the profession); IM; only /hist; specify geog   CATALOG: /geog /form
(Aug 77)
see under LICENSURE
X   HOSPITAL LICENSURE

LICENSURE, INSTITUTIONAL, PERSONNEL see LICENSURE
N3.706.110.510+

LICENSURE, MEDICAL
N3.706.110.510.410
by the state; differentiate from ACCREDITATION (by the profession); IM; only /hist; various boards can go here; specify geog   CATALOG: /geog /form

LICENSURE, NURSING
N3.706.110.510.490
by the state; differentiate from ACCREDITATION (by the profession); IM; only /hist; various boards can go here; specify geog   CATALOG: /geog /form
66

LICENSURE, PHARMACY
N3.706.110.510.560
by the state; differentiate from ACCREDITATION (by the profession); IM; only /hist; various boards can go here; specify geog   CATALOG: /geog /form
68

LICHEN PLANUS
C17.462
sometimes called simply 'lichen': check text & its bibliog

LICHENS
B5.513
plant, not skin disease; do not use /anat /embryol /microbiol /parasitol

Figure 2. Extract from MeSH (Medical Subject Headings) thesaurus used for MEDLINE

This arrangement allows the searcher to create the sets of references, a set being all those references in the database which have the data element he seeks in common, which are the basis of an online information retrieval search.

INDEXING LANGUAGES

The main approach to online databases will be the subject approach, and to perform a subject search effectively the searcher will need to have a sound knowledge of the indexing languages used by the databases being searched. Indexing languages employ either controlled or natural language. The terminology used in a controlled language will be embodied in a **thesaurus**, a list of indexing terms available to the indexers to describe the subject content of the documents being input to the database. An extract from the MeSH (*Me*dical *s*ubject *h*eadings) thesaurus used for MEDLINE is given on page 601. A **controlled language** standardizes the indexing terminology used in the database; it enables both indexers and searchers to work more precisely, in that it prevents the same concept being indexed under two or more terms. Language is rich in synonyms, and where these exist to describe a concept, a thing, or a process, the thesaurus will give guidance in the choice of the most appropriate form of subject entry into the database; it will choose a preferred form of name, and refer the searcher from alternatives. It thus aids communication between the indexer and the searcher: it provides them with a common language. The INSPEC thesaurus, for instance, chooses INFORMATION SCIENCE as a preferred term, and refers users from DOCUMENTATION, LIBRARIANSHIP, and LIBRARY SCIENCE.

A thesaurus will not only standardize the terminology within a field; it will also indicate the relationships which exist between its component terms. Under each term in its alphabetical sequence it will display the various types of relationship which the term bears to others in the thesaurus. This helps the indexer and the searcher, in that it may guide them to a more suitable term if they have initially consulted the thesaurus under a term which was, perhaps, too precise or too broad to describe the subject request. The *The-*

saurus of psychological terms, for example, gives the following display under LAWS:

LAWS
- Broader: GOVERNMENT POLICY MAKING
- Narrower: ABORTION LAWS
  GUN CONTROL LAWS
  MARIHUANA LAWS
  MARIHUANA LEGISLATION
- Related: GOVERNMENT
  LEGAL PROCESSES
  LEGISLATIVE PROCEDURE

Natural language bases, such as CHEMCON, SDC's online version of *Chemical abstracts*, dispense with concept indexing, and rely on the terms used by the original authors of the papers in their titles, or the language used by the abstractors to describe the subject content of the papers as the basis of retrieval. The terminology used in natural language is referred to as being either hard or soft. **Hard terminology** infers unambiguous use of language, and this is traditionally used by authors of papers in the physical, exact sciences where nomenclature has been defined and published in glossaries by national and international scientific councils and standardizing bodies. From an information retrieval viewpoint, titles in physics, mathematics, chemistry, etc, are usually 'good'. But as terminology in the social sciences and the humanities is less precise, authors in these fields are much more likely to give **softer**, more amorphous, titles to their papers; and, in addition to not having a well defined vocabulary to use, these authors are more likely than scientists to use fanciful and imaginative titles. 'Looking with the third eye' and 'Grass – the modern tower of Babel' are, for instance, both titles of serious contributions dealing with aspects of drug abuse; and 'The willow wielders' is the title of a book on cricket. Searches on natural language bases in the social sciences and humanities are, therefore, more likely to suffer from recall failure than those in the sciences. Papers will not be retrieved because their titles do not contain the terms chosen by the searcher in his search strategy.

Online Information Retrieval Systems

SEARCH STRATEGIES AND BOOLEAN LOGIC

Search strategies for online retrieval are expressed as Boolean logical statements: the individual parameters which have been identified as defining the scope of the search, and the terms within these parameters are linked by one or more Boolean logical operator. George Boole was a mathematician who devised a method of expressing in symbolic form the relationships which exist between concepts. His three operators, logical product (AND logic), logical sum (OR logic), and logical difference (NOT logic) can be expressed graphically as Venn diagrams. In designing a search, the individual parameters are identified, and the terms necessary to encompass them are selected. The parameters and terms are then joined together by the operators AND, OR and NOT. The initial step will be to analyse the search question into its component parameters:

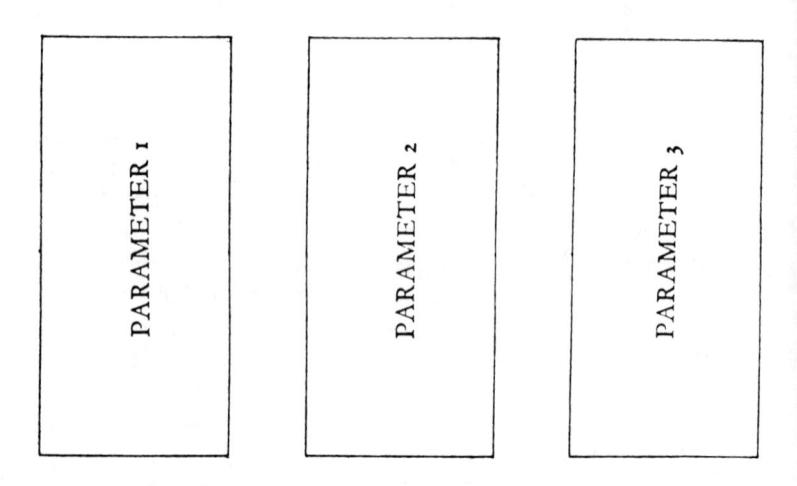

PARAMETER 1	PARAMETER 2	PARAMETER 3

After these subject categories, or facets, have been established, the terminology within each can be filled in by reference to the thesaurus, if the base being searched employs a controlled language; or by natural language terms, if the base is so organized, eg:

Search Strategies and Boolean Logic

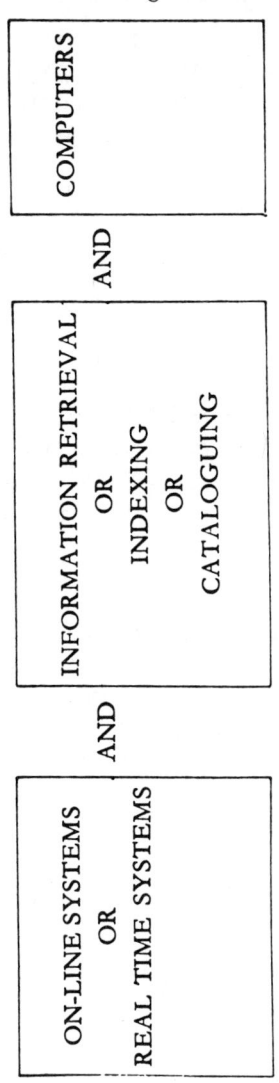

```
┌─────────────────┐
│   COMPUTERS     │
└─────────────────┘
        AND
┌─────────────────────────────┐
│   INFORMATION RETRIEVAL     │
│            OR               │
│         INDEXING            │
│            OR               │
│        CATALOGUING          │
└─────────────────────────────┘
        AND
┌─────────────────────────────┐
│     ON-LINE SYSTEMS         │
│            OR               │
│     REAL TIME SYSTEMS       │
└─────────────────────────────┘
```

Ideally the strategy will be planned by the online searcher in the presence of the end-user, the person who has requested the search. **Venn diagrams** are an effective means of illustrating to the user the logic employed in a search strategy; they are more readily

Online Information Retrieval Systems

(CHILDREN OR YOUNG ADULTS) AND (MENTALLY HANDICAPPED OR BRAIN DAMAGED) AND (READING) AND (TEACHING OR INSTRUCTION OR LEARNING). This would be expressed in a Venn diagram as:

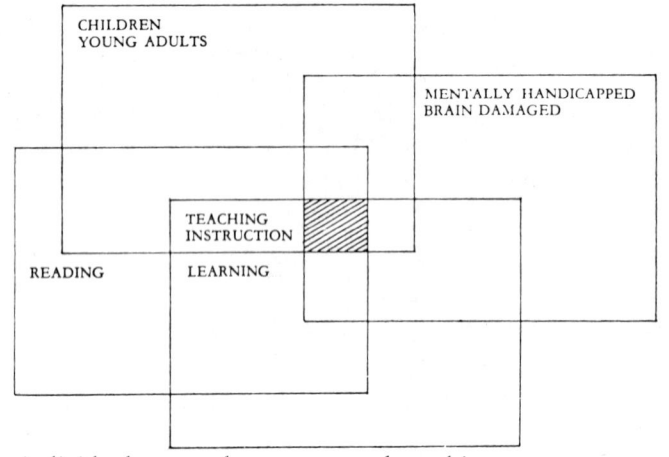

The individual rectangles represent the subject parameters to be ANDed together, and the ORed terms are represented as the horizontal group within each rectangle. NOT logic can also be easily represented by a Venn diagram, as seen below for a search on 'Online information retrieval systems other than MEDLINE'.

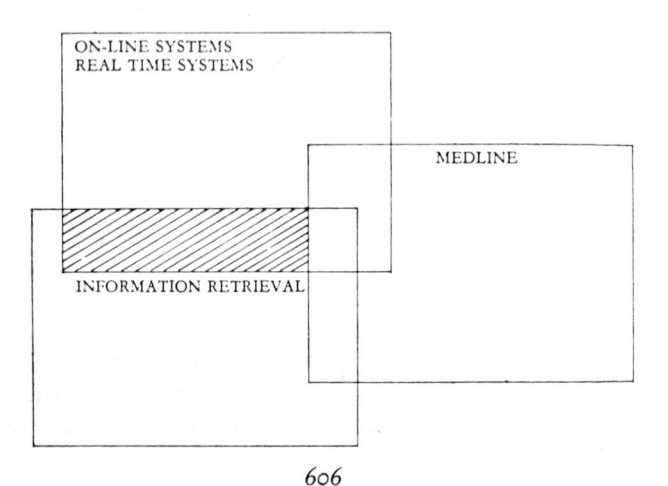

ONLINE INTERACTION

The searcher interacts with the host computer by using the system's command set or command language; these commands instruct the computer to carry out the various operations involved in an online search, such as selecting a set of references, combining two or more sets, printing sets of references over the terminal, etc. Online searching is essentially a cyclic process; the searcher will devise a search strategy, and test that strategy by sampling the relevance of the references online. If the scope of the initial strategy is seen, on the evidence of the references retrieved, to be too broad, he will narrow the scope of the search by inputting an additional limiting parameter; or if the original strategy is proved too constricting, and no references, or only a small number, have been retrieved, he may broaden his search by omitting one of the parameters, or by using broader terminology inside the original parameters. The command set is then the means by which this cyclic, or iterative, interaction is achieved. Command sets will vary from system to-system, but all sets will have basic, common functions which can be conveniently grouped into five categories:

1. General commands: those giving the searcher control over the progress of the search, enabling him, for instance, to interrupt the flow of the terminal's output; to delete a character which has been typed wrongly; to ascertain the cost of the search after a certain period of time has elapsed, etc.
2. Entering and leaving the system: logging-on when beginning the search and logging-off on completion of the search.
3. Choosing a particular file from the range available over a certain system.
4. Performing the actual search, selecting the sets, and manipulating combinations of these sets.
5. Printing or displaying the titles of the references retrieved in a particular set to ascertain their relevance; printing the full references online when relevance has been established; or printing offline if the number of references is excessive.

Differences in the specific commands used to carry out the same function on different systems can be confusing when the searcher is switching from one system to another. On DIALOG, for instance, sets are created by using the SELECT command or its abbreviated form S before the term used, eg SELECT ONLINE or SONLINE. The same operation is carried out on SDC's ORBIT system by simply inputting the term ONLINE. The adoption of a standardized command set by all systems would undoubtedly make searching, over a number of bases offered by different systems suppliers, a less complex process, at least to the inexperienced searcher. Some command languages are, however, almost identical—for instance, those of DIALOG and ESA/RECON, and those of SDC ORBIT and British Library BLAISE. A standardized command set will also be used for access to the bases available on EURONET, no matter which organization is the service supplier. The standardized set was developed by Negus under a feasibility study commissioned by the EEC.[2] A useful *Online command chart* giving comparative summaries of similar capabilities of seven systems, including DIALOG and ORBIT, arranged by OPERATIONS such as file selection, changing files, truncation, logging-off, and 37 other functions, is available from the journal *Online*.

No command can be input to the system until a user cue has been received from the host computer. These cues are given by the system to indicate to the user that it is his turn to contribute to the dialogue which is the essence of online interaction. On DIALOG the user cue is an interrogation mark—?, after which the searcher is required to input a command or instruction, eg:

? SINDUSTRY (c.r.)

When the searcher presses the terminal's carriage return key (c.r.), the message is sent to the host computer over the communication lines. In the above and following examples of online interaction, the searcher's contribution to the dialogue will be underlined. SDC's user cue is SS1/C?, SS2/C?, SS3/C? . . . for successive sets. In answer to the first cue, the searcher would input the first search command to select his base, eg:
SS1/C?
FILE BIOSIS (c.r.)

Online Interaction

where the command FILE is used to select a particular base.

In addition to user cues, the searcher will also be required to answer program messages to achieve interaction. On SDC ORBIT, for instance, after he has identified himself to the system by inputting his USERID and password he will be asked:
ARE YOU AN EXPERIENCED USER? (YES/NO).
If he is new to the system, and unsure of the commands, he will reply NO and will then be given annotated user cues in a tutorial mode which will explain the system in some detail. If he answers YES, he will be given the standard unannotated cues.

On DIALOG the EXPAND command will result in the system giving the user a number of terms from the inverted file above and below the term expanded, with an indication of how many citations have been posted under each term. This facility is useful when the searcher is unsure of the terminology employed by a database, and he does not have access to its thesaurus. On DIALOG, the EXPAND command normally gives a display of twenty terms, with the expanded term sixth in the listing, eg:

? EHISTORICAL CRITICISM (c.r.)

REF	INDEX-TERM	TYPE ITEMS	RT
E1	HISTORIAN	7	
E2	HISTORIANS	190	
E3	HISTORIC	194	
E4	HISTORICA	2	
E5	HISTORICAL	5085	
E6	HISTORICAL CRITICISM	194	9
E7	HISTORICAL DATA	1	
E8	HISTORICAL DRAMA	2	
E9	HISTORICAL GEOGRAPHY	1	
E10	HISTORICAL INFLUENCES	1	1
E11	HISTORICAL LANDMARKS	3	
. . . .	. . . .		
E20	HISTORICAL REVIEWS	1164	6

—MORE—

After the last term has been given, the system message—MORE—will be output. If the searcher requires a continuation of this listing, he will answer the message by typing the command PAGE, or its abbreviation P. If not, he will override the message by selecting one of the terms displayed in answer to his EXPAND command, or input another command.

Sample search

The following example is of a simple but typical search on the ERIC database; the searcher has consulted the *Thesaurus of ERIC descriptors* before going online, and selected the descriptors necessary to circumscribe the three parameters in the search on 'training users for online information retrieval systems'—the training, the online, and the information retrieval aspects. It must be strongly emphasized that although online access is interactive, the search topic should be carefully discussed and analysed with the end-user before going online. When this is done, expensive online costs will be reduced by planning the initial strategy. In this search the SELECT STEPS (SS) command is used, thus inputting the searchstrategy, which incorporates the Boolean operators AND and OR, in a single 'nested' search statement. In addition to giving the number of postings in the final statement, in this case set 5, 77 references, the SELECT STEPS command gives postings for each stage of the search statement. Any combination of these sets could then subsequently be combined by the searcher as he desired, if he wished to amend the initial search strategy. The first five references of the search strategy are online by using DIALOG's TYPE (T) command employing format 6, titles only. From this output, relevance has been established, and three of the references which are of particular interest to the end-user are printed online, using format 2, author, title, bibliographic reference and indexing information, before a request is made that the first fifty references be printed offline in the fullest format, 5—as for 2, but including an abstract of the paper. The search is now completed, and the searcher disconnects himself from the system by typing in the command LOGOFF.

Online Interaction

ENTER YOUR DIALOG PASSWORD
<u>WWWWWWW</u> LOGON FILE 1 WED 25MAY83 7:12:12 PORT09C

**SORTS ARE NOT WORKING IN FILE 1 **
**   FILE 36 IS NOT WORKING   **
**FILES 13 & 710 ARE UNAVAILABLE   **
?NEWS NEWS:
  NEW IMPROVED TYMNET NOW AVAILABLE
  FREE TIME OFFER IN MAY:
    ENVIRONMENTAL BIBLIOGRAPHY (#68)
  NOW AVAILABLE:
    UPI NEWS (FILE 261)
    CHEMICAL EXPOSURE (FILE 138)
  ANNOUNCEMENTS:
    PRICE CHANGE FOR COFFEELINE (#164)

<u>? SS (INFORMATION RETRIEVAL OR INDEXING) AND ONLINE SYSTEMS AND TRAINING</u>
        1   3024 INFORMATION RETRIEVAL
        2   1480 INDEXING
        3   1691 ONLINE SYSTEMS
        4 55949 TRAINING
        5   77 (1 OR 2) AND 3 AND 4
<u>?T 5/6/1–5</u>
5/6/1
EJ271540
    EXPERIENCES IN TRAINING END-USER SEARCHERS.

5/6/2
EJ264814
    EDUCATIONAL RESOURCES—WE DELIVER A COMPUTERIZED DELIVERY SYSTEM FOR ALASKA'S SCHOOLS.

5/6/3
EJ264742
    MIRACLES, MICROCOMPUTERS, AND LIBRARIANS.

5/6/4

EJ261942
THE ONLINE POLICY MANUAL . . . A DOCUMENT THAT FEW HAVE;
BUT MANY CAN BENEFIT FROM (ESPECIALLY LIBRARIANS).

5/6/5
EJ261940
HOW TO TRAIN EXPERIENCED SEARCHERS TO USE ANOTHER SYSTEM.

T5/2/1,3,5
/2/1
EJ271540 IR510681
EXPERIENCES IN TRAINING END-USER SEARCHERS.
HAINES: JUDITH S.
ONLINE: V6 N6 P14–23 NOV 1982
LANGUAGE: ENGLISH
DOCUMENT TYPE: JOURNAL ARTICLE (080); RESEARCH REPORT (143)
DESCRIPTORS: COSTS; DATA COLLECTION; DATABASES; GRAPHS; *INFORMATION RETRIEVAL; *ONLINE SYSTEMS; RESEARCH METHODOLOGY; *SEARCH STRATEGIES; TABLES (DATA); *TRAINING METHODS; *USER SATISFACTION (INFORMATION)
IDENTIFIERS: CHEMICAL ABSTRACTS; *CHEMISTS; DIALOG; EASTMAN KODAK COMPANY; *END USERS

5/2/3
EJ264742 IR510167
MIRACLES; MICROCOMPUTERS; AND LIBRARIANS.
SWANSON, DON R.
LIBRARY JOURNAL; V107 N11 P1055–59 JUN 1 1982
AVAILABLE FROM: REPRINT: UMI
LANGUAGE: ENGLISH
DOCUMENT TYPE: JOURNAL ARTICLE (080); PROJECT DESCRIPTION (141)
DESCRIPTORS: *COMPUTER PROGRAMS; COMPUTER SCIENCE; GRADUATE STUDENTS; HIGHER EDUCATION; *INFORMATION RETRIEVAL; *LIBRARY AUTOMATION; *LIBRARY EDUCATION; LIBRARY

Online Costs

SCHOOLS; *MICROCOMPUTERS; ONLINE SYSTEMS; PROGRAMING; WORD PROCESSING
  IDENTIFIERS: MIRABILIS; UNIVERSITY OF CHICAGO IL

5/2/5
EJ261940 IR510024
  HOW TO TRAIN EXPERIENCED SEARCHERS TO USE ANOTHER SYSTEM.
  JACKSON, WILLIAM J.
  ONLINE; V6 N3 P27–35 MAY 1982
  AVAILABLE FROM: REPRINT: UMI
  LANGUAGE: ENGLISH
  DOCUMENT TYPE: JOURNAL ARTICLE (080); PROJECT DESCRIPTION (141)
  DESCRIPTORS: *CHARTS; COLLEGE LIBRARIES; *DATABASES; HIGHER EDUCATION; INFORMATION RETRIEVAL; *INSERVICE EDUCATION; LIBRARIANS; *ONLINE SYSTEMS; STAFF DEVELOPMENT
  IDENTIFIERS; *COMMAND LANGUAGE

? PR 5/1–50
PRINTED 5/5/1–50 (TO CANCEL: ENTER PR-)
?
LOGOFF
        25MAY83 7:20:37 USER7218
    $1.86 0.124 HRS FILE1* 10 DESCRIPTORS
    $1.24 DIALNET
    $3.10 ESTIMATED TOTAL COST

ONLINE COSTS (as at June 1983)

The costs involved in online searching can be conveniently broken down into: 1. the capital expenditure of acquiring the terminal and a modem or an acoustic coupler, and 2. the costs incurred in the online interaction. Teletype terminals can be purchased for as little as £700, but those manufactured with an in-built acoustic coupler, eg the Texas Instruments Silent 700 series, will cost around £1,200.

Online Information Retrieval Systems

Display terminals will cost about £500 to £600, but the cost of a line printer will be additional—as much as, if not more than, the cost of the terminal. A micro-computer with disc drives and printer will cost a minimum of £2,000, and an intelligent terminal such as the Hewlett Packard 2645A Display Station will be around £3,400. An annual maintenance cost of about 10 per cent of the initial cost of the equipment is essential to ensure on-site maintenance of the hardware used for online retrieval. A modem which will receive data at 300 baud can be purchased for £700, while a portable acoustic coupler costs about £240.

Searching costs can be identified as: 1. communication charges; 2. database charges; 3. offline and online print charges.

1. **Communication charges** involve the cost of the telephone call to the host computer, or to the nearest node of a communication network, if one is being used to access the host. In the United Kingdom, access to most online systems will be made by using British Telecom's PSS/IPSS facilities, which initially will involve the cost of a local telephone call to the nearest node. Current (1983) charges are:

Access time	09.00–13.00 h	13.00–18.00 h	18.00–
Local	1.72	1.29	0.32
Area A	5.16	3.44	1.07
Area B	12.90	9.68	3.22
Area C	10.32	7.74	2.58

After connection has been made with the nearest PSS node, the charge is £0.88 per hour for United Kingdom hosts. IPSS costs for European hosts are £1.32 per hour, and for transatlantic hosts, £4.80. In addition to these costs there is a character transmission charge of £0.88 per kilosegment inside the United Kingdom; £1.20 per kilosegment for European hosts; and £3.00 per kilosegment for transatlantic communication. One segment contains 64 characters, or one half of a packet. The DIALNET leased line between London and DIALOG in Palo Alto, California, was linked into PSS in 1983, and accessing DIALOG via DIALNET is now less expensive than access directly via PSS and IPSS. Telephone charges in the United States and Canada are much lower than those in the United

Kingdom, being between one-third and one-half of those levied by British Telecom.

2. **Database charges** will vary widely from database to database and from system to system, as in many cases the same database will be accessible on two or more systems at different tariffs. DIALOG charges currently vary from the cheapest rates of $25 per hour for ERIC (Educational Research Information Center) and $35 per hour for AGRICOLA (National Library of Agriculture, US Department of Agriculture), to the most expensive $300 per hour for the CLAIMS databases covering US patent specifications. DIALOG's average current database connect charge will be about $65 per hour. SDC's current charges range from $35 per hour for ERIC, to $120 per hour for CIS Index (Congressional Information Service), with a slightly higher average charge than DIALOG. BLAISE charges £27.00 per hour for access to its databases, and in addition the system imposes an annual subscription ('front-end') charge of £40.00 on each of its users. DIALOG, SDC, and most other service suppliers impose no annual system charge; the user pays only for the time he spends searching. Data-Star's connect charges for its databases is about £22.00 per hour without a prior commitment of hours from the user. Like other systems which operate a sliding scale of charges based on the number of hours used per annum, the cost can be reduced considerably if the user elects to search for a pre-specified number of hours each year, eg 60 hours per annum at £18.00, 120 hours at £14.67, and 480 hours at £11.00. In addition to some other service suppliers, Data-Star imposes database royalty charges in addition to database connect time, eg £20.00 per hour for BIOSIS (*Biological abstracts*), £17.33 per hour for *Chemical abstracts* and £3.33 per hour for MEDLINE.

3. **Offline and online print charges**. If the final search strategy has retrieved a large number of citations, it may be deemed more economical to print the search product offline at the system supplier's computer centre, and have the offprints sent by airmail. Offline prints on DIALOG and SDC vary from $0.15 to $0.20 per reference, while BLAISE charges £0.15 per page, with a minimum offline print charge of £1.00. An increasing number of service suppliers are now levying online print charges of the same order as those quoted above. The advent of 1200 baud or 120 cps output

has challenged the previous and unequivocally held view that offline printing was cheaper than printing online, except in cases where the end-user needed his information urgently. A recent study by Boyce and Gillen offers a simple formula to determine an online print cost for comparison with offline charges.[3]

The average time taken to complete a search will vary considerably, depending on the complexity of the end-user's enquiry. A series of 33 enquiries ranging over the sciences, technology, and the social sciences was run over 18 individual databases on DIALOG and ORBIT for staff research projects at Liverpool Polytechnic. These enquiries resulted in 56 searches or 1.7 searches per enquiry. The average length of the searches, not including the time spent by the searcher discussing the enquiry with the end-user, was 14 minutes, with an enquiry taking 24 minutes.[4] In an analysis of 340 searches carried out on MEDLINE and *Excerpta medica* to retrieve drug-related information for health care professionals, the average time per search was 10 minutes on MEDLINE and 15 minutes on *Excerpta medica*, again not including the time spent liaising with the end-user.[5] In the recently completed BIROS survey covering 412 searches made for public library enquiries at the Lancashire Library the average time per search was 18.2 minutes.[6]

BENEFITS OF ONLINE SEARCHING

The advantages of online access are considerable, and it is important that their potential should be appreciated by librarians and information workers.

Their most obvious asset is that they enable the literature to be searched far more **quickly and efficiently** than by manual methods. A search that might previously have taken several hours or even days in a library can now be completed online within, perhaps, ten to fifteen minutes. The tedious and extended process of searching manually through successive annual subject indexes, and following up the references and abstracts in the respective volumes, is obviated. Multi-concept searches which because of their complexity could not be searched manually other than by the laborious sequential scanning of the text of abstracts can now be searched efficiently online.

When searching online the searcher is able to access the whole database in a single operation. Online access ensures **file integrity** of secondary services, as the searcher cannot be inconvenienced by missing or misfiled parts, or the non-receipt of individual issues by a library.

Online searching is more **flexible** than the manual approach; the searcher is afforded more access points per document than are available when he is searching hard-copy indexes. Many online databases give the searcher the facility of searching exhaustively over broad classes or sections of the database; MEDLINE, for example, has the 'explode' capability. If the searcher inputs the instruction:

SS 3
USER:
EXP STEROIDS

he will retrieve all references in the database which have been indexed, with not only the generic term STEROIDS, but also with any individual steroid compound which has been subsumed under the 'steroid tree' in the MeSH Tree structures, the controlled language for the database. As MeSH lists almost 300 steroid compounds, he is then searching this number of headings simultaneously. Other systems use concept or category codes in a similar manner.

The online searcher is also able to search most databases on the free text or the **natural language** used in the titles and the abstracts of the references in the database, in addition to searching the controlled language. New terminology which has not yet been accepted into a thesaurus can thus be used as the basis of retrieval.

Multi-database searching is one invaluable facility peculiar to online systems. During the course of searching a multi-disciplinary topic, a searcher can formulate his search strategy in the most apposite database; complete the initial search in that database, save the search strategy in the system; change databases; and then rerun the original strategy in each of subsequent databases he has chosen, all in a matter of minutes.

Online access to various systems renders the **geographical location** of the searcher irrelevant: a terminal in a room equipped with a standard telephone handset and a 13 amp socket becomes an information centre, with access to millions of references covering virtually all disciplines. The searcher with his passwords to DIALOG, SDC, BLAISE, EURONET and other systems has at his fingertips access to more bibliographic information than can be contained in the largest of reference libraries.

When this above facility is combined with an **online document delivery** service, whereby the original text of a reference that has been retrieved online can be requested after the search has been completed and mailed to the searcher, the enormous potential of online retrieval for reference service and information broking can be realized.

The library manager is not usually faced with '**front-end**' or **subscription charges** for using online databases—he only pays for the time he actually uses online. Thus when he obtains his password to DIALOG, for instance, he immediately gains access to over 200 databases to use as and when he needs them. This, of course, compares very favourably with the in-house provision of hard-copy abstracting and indexing services, where he must place subscriptions for those titles which he deems necessary to meet his readership's needs. Once placed, subscriptions are ongoing, unless a conscious decision is made to cancel them, and these subscriptions are not variables dependent on use.

The results of an online search are presented in a **standardized format** the details of which may be determined by the searcher. Most systems have alternative print formats; for instance DIALOG usually provides about six formats for each of its databases, ranging from title and accession number only, used when sampling the relevance of a set of references online, to the full reference—including an abstract. Other systems, such as BLAISE and ORBIT, allow the user to determine his own print format by allowing him to select the bibliographic data elements he requires in his output. These selectable formats contrast starkly with the inherent difficulties involved in recording the results of a manual search, where

References

the references must be transcribed manually onto cards or into a notebook. In an extended search, mistranscriptions and omissions will inevitably occur, and variant forms of abbreviations for the same journal will be used as the searcher becomes fatigued by the labour and concentration necessary in extended manual searching. The standardized formats available online or offline give the end-user a bibliography tailor-made to his own specification.

A library or an information service with an online searching facility can provide a far wider range of literature-searching services than a library which relies solely on printed sources. Kusak has pointed out that 'when coordinated with the traditional reference service, an online bibliographical retrieval service can bolster the image of librarians, increase their impact within the community they serve, and improve . . . overall reference service in ways not previously anticipated'.[7] In a survey undertaken by SDC covering online users in the United States it was reported that in 52% of the organizations where online searching had been introduced the total number of literature searches had increased. This figure was undoubtedly depressed, because 24% of the organizations covered in the survey had never undertaken any kind of literature searching before the introduction of online.[8]

REFERENCES

1. *Directory of online databases.* Santa Monica, California: Caudra Associates Inc. Quarterly.
2. Negus, A. E. *Study to determine the feasibility of a standardised command set for EURONET: final report of a study carried out for the Commission of European Communities, DGXIII.* London: INSPEC, 1976.
3. Boyce, B. R. and Gillen, E. J. Is it more effective to print on- or offline? *RQ*, **20** (4), Winter 1981. 117–20.
4. Houghton, Bernard and Convey, J. *Online information retrieval in the Polytechnic. Report of a pilot project with the Library Service using online retrieval systems.* Liverpool: Liverpool Polytechnic, 1977.
5. Houghton, Bernard et al. A comparison of Excerpta medica and Medline for the provision of drug information to health care professionals. In: 6th International Online Information Meeting, London, December 1982. pp 115–27. Oxford: Learned Information, 1982.

6. Oulton, A. J. et al. *The online public library.* Boston Spa: British Library, 1982.
7. Kusak, J. M. Integration of online reference service. *RQ*, **19** (1), 1980. 60–3.
8. Wanger, J. et al. *On-line impact study: report of on-line users, 1974–1975.* Santa Monica, California: System Development Corp, 1975.

SERVICE SUPPLIERS

BLAISE
(British Library Automated Information Service)
Blaise Marketing and User Education, 2 Sheraton Street, London W1V 4BH.

DATA-STAR
Data-Star, Willoughby Road, Bracknell, Berks. RG12 4DW.

DIALOG
DIALOG Information Retrieval Service Inc, 3460 Hillview Avenue, Palo Alto, CA 94303. USA.
 UK: P.O. Box 8, Abingdon, Oxford OX13 6EG.

ESA/IRS
ESRIN, Via G. Galilei, 00044 Frascati, Rome, Italy.
 UK: IRS-DIALTECH, Room 204, Ebury Bridge House, 2–18 Ebury Bridge Road, London SW1W 8QD.

EURONET/DIANE
EURONET/DIANE Launch Team, B.P. 777, Luxembourg.

INFOLINE,
Pergamon Infoline Ltd, 12 Vandy Street, London EC2A 2DE.
 USA: Pergamon International Information Corporation, 1340 Old Chain Bridge Road, McLean, VA 22101, USA.

SDC Search Service
System Development Corporation, 2500 Colorado Avenue, Santa Monica, CA 90406, USA.
 UK: Stuart House, 47 Crown Street, Reading RG1 2SG.

A fuller list of service suppliers is given in:

Hall, J. L. and Brown, M. *Online bibliographic databases.* 3rd ed. London: Aslib, 1983.

Journals

FURTHER READING

Hoover, R. E. *et al. The library and information manager's guide to online service*. White Plains, New York: Knowledge Industry Publications Inc, 1980.

Houghton, Bernard and Convey, John. *Online information retrieval systems: an introductory manual to principles and practice*. 2nd ed. London: Clive Bingley, 1984.

Keenan, Stella. *How to go online: guidelines for the establishment of online services in public libraries*. British Library Research and Development Report No 5533, March 1980.

JOURNALS

Specialist journals containing articles and features on all aspects of online interaction include:

Online. Online Inc, 11, Tannery Lane, Weston, CT 06883, USA.
Online Review. Learned Information, Besselsleigh Road, Abingdon, Oxford.
Database. (Online Inc)
The Electronic Library. (Learned Information)

21

Videotex Information and Communication Systems

Peter H. Marshall

DEFINING THE SYSTEMS

One of the most significant developments in online systems in the past few years has been the growth of Videotex systems. The term 'Videotex' has been coined to embrace what were formerly known separately as 'Viewdata' and 'Teletext' systems, and relates to a kind of information system which is capable of using the most basic of equipment, and which can be operated with the very minimum of prior knowledge and skill on the part of the user. (The reader may occasionally have seen reference to the term 'Videotext'. This is merely an understandably erroneous, but nevertheless harmless, anglicization of the internationally agreed term.)

Essential features

The essential features of Videotex are:

(a) *A 25 line × 40 column screen display.* This was chosen to enable manufacturers to design a display character set which would be

Defining the Systems

legible on the screen of even the lowest band-width domestic television.

(b) *'Page mode' operation.* The screen of data fills in exactly the same way in which a page would be typed on a typewriter, commencing at the top left-hand corner and filling each line in turn. The screen is cleared (or emptied) before each new 'frame' of information is transmitted to the user. Thus the frame of 25 lines × 40 characters is the basic unit of information in a Videotex system, and as with the pages in a book, the frame numbers form the basic system of referencing within a database. In viewdata systems each page has a number (eg 42014), and each page may consist of up to 26 frames denoted by a suffixed letter (eg 42014a; 42014b . . . 42014z). As with a book, one starts at the top of the page, and only the 'a-frame' is directly addressable. In present-day teletext systems pages are similarly numbered (eg 119) and the various frames of a page are transmitted sequentially (eg 119/1; 119/2, etc).

(c) *Access to the information without prior knowledge of command language.* The systems are entirely menu-driven and can be operated in their most basic form by selecting from a choice of options using the numbers 0–9, plus, in the case of Viewdata, two special symbols: 'star' (*) and 'square' (#). 'Square' is visually identical with the symbol 'hash' but is in fact quite separate, being represented by a different transmission code. A list of Videotex transmission codes follows as Appendix A.

(d) *A display format* in which the control codes, which determine colour, flashing, character height, graphics, etc, are held in character spaces, and affect the remaining part of the line in which they appear. Thus in a line reading:

*a*KEY*bc6de*TO*s*SEE*s*THIS*s*INFORMATION*f*(15p)

a, *b*, *c*, *d*, *e* and *f*, which of course would appear as blank spaces on the screen, represent the control codes for *Cyan, White, Flash, Cyan, Steady* and *Red* respectively, and *s* repre-

Videotex Information and Communication Systems

sents a normal character space. The line would appear on the screen as:

KEY 6 TO SEE THIS INFORMATION (15p)

with the words KEY...TO SEE THIS INFORMATION in cyan, the figure 6 in flashing white, and the (15p) in red.

Teletext and Viewdata

Reference has already been made to the terms Telextext and Viewdata, and it is important both to distinguish between them, and to appreciate the transitory nature of this distinction.

```
P100    CEEFAX 100   Mon 29 Feb   16:20/41

            CEEFAX

     BBC 1              BBC 2
  News........101   News........201
  Finance.....120   Finance.....220
  Sport.......130   Sport.......230
  Weather and       Features....251
  Travel......151   Fun.........280
  TV, Radio...179   TV, Radio...279

        A TO Z INDEX ......199 and 299
        TELESOFTWARE..........BBC1 700
        Travel news not available today
        because of staffing problems
```

Figure 1. CEEFAX, the BBC teletext service

Defining the Systems

Teletext is at present a non-interactive broadcast system. Pages of information are transmitted 'piggy-back' on standard television broadcast transmissions, and when suitably decoded by special circuitry in the receiver are displayed on the screen as text. Such systems are non-interactive, so the user has no way of communicating with the computer on which the information is stored. When, therefore, the user selects a page of information, he is merely instructing his terminal to intercept that page, when it is next transmitted, and to display it on the screen. It follows that the maximum number of pages which can be handled by a broadcast teletext system is the product of the transmission rate (in frames per second) and the maximum time (in seconds) that the user is prepared to wait for his selected page to appear. If the former is (as at present on the BBC's CEEFAX[1] service) 8 frames per second, and the latter is (say) 15 seconds, then the maximum number of frames the system can handle is 8 × 15 = 120 frames. In practice, the more heavily used frames are transmitted more than once in a complete cycle in order to reduce their access time.

(For the sake of completeness it should be mentioned here that the confusion which exists between the terms 'Teletext' and 'Teletex' is rather more serious than the Videotex/Videotext error referred to above. Teletext is as we have described it here. Teletex is a term widely used to refer to the services such as Telecom Gold, which facilitate the transfer of information between office word-processors as electronic mail; it is entirely different from Teletext, and is at present only of passing interest to those concerned with Videotex.)

Viewdata is by contrast an interactive system, in which the user's terminal is directly connected to the computer via modems and a standard telephone line. This enables the user to request any given frame from the computer, and greatly increases the potential capacity of the system. Prestel,[2] the UK public Viewdata system, currently has a capacity of some 300,000 frames. A further consequence of the interactive nature of Viewdata is its potential for communication services such as electronic mail, of which more later.

Having emphasized this difference, it is equally most important to realize that this is the only essential in which the two systems

```
P   R   E   S   T   E   L                          0a                      0p
Main Index
■■■■■■■■■■■■■■■■■■■■■■■■■■■■■■■■■■■■■■■■■■■■■■■■■■■■■■■■■
1  SPECIAL FEATURE           STOCK EXCHANGE
   London stock market information now
   available on CitiService 0+ 5p
■■■■■■■■■■■■■■■■■■■■■■■■■■■■■■■■■■■■■■■■■■■■■■■■■■■■■■■■■
2  INFORMATION News,Weather,Travel,Sport
   Advice,What's On,Ads,Local,Amusements
3  PRESTEL CITISERVICE & OTHER BUSINESS
   INFORMATION
4  ALPHABETIC INDEXES to subjects & IPs
5  WHAT'S NEW                FEBRUARY 17th
6  MESSAGE, BOOKING & ORDERING SERVICES
   Mailbox,Telex & Teleordering
7  ALL ABOUT PRESTEL Customer Guide
■■■■■■■■■■■■■■■■■■■■■■■■■■■■■■■■■■■■■■■■■■■■■■■■■■■■■■■■■
9  MICRONET 800 Telesoftware,news,views
   & products for microcomputer users
0  HOMELINK Interactive homebanking &
   Teleshopping services
■■■■■■■■■■■■■■■■■■■■■■■■■■■■■■■■■■■■■■■■■■■■■■■■■■■■■■■■■
```

Figure 2. Prestel main index page

differ. The character set, graphics and display are identical, and future developments in cable television, which *will* enable a direct connection between source and user, may well make this distinction a thing of the past.

Further essential features of Viewdata

Further essential features of Viewdata relate to the transmission of the data over telephone lines, and these are:

(a) *1200/75 baud transmission rate*. Data are sent from the computer to the user at a rate of 1200 data bits per second. This is about the fastest speed which ordinary speech-quality telephone

Defining the Systems

lines can manage error free, and it enables the Viewdata receiver screen to fill in under ten seconds. Data sent by the user back to the computer travel at 75 bits per second. This is quite fast enough to cope with human typing speeds, and it enables cheap and rugged modems to be installed in Viewdata terminals.

(b) *Even-parity error checking.* This technicality is included here for the sake of completeness. Even parity is the CCITT standard, and is the most common form of error checking used in European online systems. Suffice it to say here however that there are some online systems which use parity-odd or no-parity checking.

Videotex and conventional online systems

To complete our definition of Videotex it is necessary to describe its relationship with the longer established online systems, often known as teletype-compatible systems (Teletype being the tradename of one of the earliest and most commonly used online terminals), and here we are struck not so much by the differences as the similarities. As far as the transmission of data to the user is concerned, the only differences lie in the essential features listed above, plus the special requirements of graphics and a few of the minor characters in the character set (the 'fringe' characters of the typewriter keyboard). The transmission code which is used for all basic characters is the ASCII (American Standard Code for Information Interchange) character set, which is used almost universally in the computer industry by all manufacturers except IBM. Since therefore the only major differences lie in the way in which the data are held by the computer, namely in hierarchically structured pages, addressed by page numbers, rather than records with terminological indexes, it follows that it should at least in theory be possible to build front-end processors on to existing online computer systems to enable them to function in Videotex mode. This is in fact often possible and is treated in more detail below.

Videotex Information and Communication Systems

Prestel and other Viewdata systems

Similar comments apply to the relationship between Prestel-type (or UK Viewdata) systems and their overseas competitors. Although the UK Viewdata standards have been adopted in many countries, with the result that some 99 per cent of Viewdata terminals in use world-wide are of the Prestel-compatible type, competitors do exist, particularly in France and the French-speaking nations. Here again one must emphasize that the alpha-numeric data are handled in these systems in standard ASCII code, and that it is only in the graphics that the differences occur. A French Videotex or Videotex-compatible service, which uses alpha-numerics only, can be received quite satisfactorily with a current Prestel terminal. Readers requiring visible proof of this are recommended to access Questel,[3] the Paris-based online service in its Videotex-compatible form.

Furthermore, work now in progress on the implementation of a new European standard, promulgated by CEPT (Conférence Européene des Administrations des Postes et des Télécommunications), will ensure full compatibility between Prestel-type systems and the French Teletel system, by incorporating the best features of both, including the high-resolution graphics of which Teletel is capable.

HISTORICAL DEVELOPMENT

Teletext and Viewdata were both developed in the 1970s by the BBC and independent broadcasting companies on the one hand, and the Post Office on the other. Fortunately, agreement was reached over a common character set and display format, and the systems were entirely compatible with all the existing enhancements by the end of 1976.

Teletext was seen by the broadcasting agencies as a natural extension of their existing activities, and has developed two major strengths:

(a) *News services*. The news-rooms of the broadcasting services

Historical Development

operate some 14 hours per day, and are continuously monitoring and editing the news of the day to provide copy for the periodic broadcast bulletins. What more logical step than to provide a continuous news service over the air? After a slow start it can now truthfully be said that broadcast teletext has captured the public imagination. Teletext is permanently on display in every high street television showroom, and a significant proportion of all new television sets sold in the UK now have a teletext capability. Teletext displays can also be seen in many public buildings, including public libraries.

(b) *Subtitling.* Subtitling of television programmes has long been a source of tribulation, particularly in areas of poor reception. With the development of teletext subtitling, in which crisp characters are generated within the television set, indistinct and hard-to-read subtitles are a thing of the past. Subtitling for the deaf has also presented problems in the past, in that the verbiage is unwanted by viewers with normal hearing. Teletext enables subtitles for selected television programmes to be selectively displayed by those who require them.

News flashes. A significant blend of the two uses described above enables the viewer of a teletext television to view news flashes, superimposed over the normal television picture as and when they occur.

Viewdata originally sprang from research conducted at the Post Office Research Centre at Martlesham, aimed principally at developing consumer demand for telecommunications services, with a particular emphasis on off-peak use. Viewdata, which linked the telephone lines to a piece of equipment in regular evening-time use in nearly every home, was seen as a panacea for the problems presented by the diurnal demand curve. Unfortunately, early problems over marketing of both domestic equipment and the information which it carried caused a very slow growth of demand in the domestic sector. Demand in some business and professional areas, such as financial markets, travel trade, and law, was high enough however to secure a sound base for future growth of the

Videotex Information and Communication Systems

system, and the boom in the home computer market has brought the domestic market back to life, with Micronet[4] the principal Prestel database for home computer users (of which more later) now achieving millions of frame-accesses each month.

The strengths developed in Viewdata in recent years are:

(a) *a sophisticated pricing structure* enabling information on different levels of value and accessibility to be manipulated within the context of the same system;
(b) *interactive communication* facilitating the development of on-line ordering, online booking, and direct message services;
(c) *presentation* of computer-based information to a much higher level of user-acceptability than has hitherto been possible.

Each of these points is developed further below.

VIDEOTEX SYSTEMS STRUCTURED

Videotex systems may be structured into a number of tiers which vary from one another, part in respect of the accessibility of the information or communication service carried, and part in respect of its value or price.

1. *Teletext.* Broadcast Teletext is a free, open system. Once the equipment has been obtained and the television licence fee paid, it is available to the user without further charge during the hours when a television picture is being transmitted. Furthermore, there is no way in which the providers of the information can limit the information to a section of would-be recipients if they so wished. Examples: CEEFAX (BBC); ORACLE (IBA).[5]

2. *Viewdata, priced and unpriced.* Viewdata systems such as Prestel are capable of two overlapping pricing structures:

    (a) *A time charge* which is applied to the user for the duration of his search on the system. Approximately 65 per cent of

Videotext Systems Structured

all Prestel pages bear only this charge at present. Example: Government information on Prestel.[6]

(b) *Frame charges* may additionally be applied by the information provider to each frame of information accessed by the user. The current Prestel software provides for frame charges from 0.1p to 50p per frame. Example: Prestel Citiservice.[7]

(c) *CUGs*. An information provider may arrange for his Viewdata frames to be placed within a Closed User Group. This facility restricts access to these frames to those Viewdata terminals which have been registered as within the CUG, enabling the information provider to sell to would-be users an annual subscription for the service, *in addition to or instead of* recovering costs by the use of frame charges. This

```
HOMELINK                    4440a           0p
Nottingham Building
Society

HOMEBANKING INDEX

YELLOW OPTIONS IN ( )
MEMBERS ONLY

KEY
 1  Investments and Savings
 2  Mortgages
(3) Change your PIN or Freeze your a/c
 4  NBS Interest Rates
 5  Towns where Homelink is available
(6) Homebanking Users Guide

            0 HOMELINK MAIN INDEX
```

Figure 3. Home banking via Prestel

facility of course also enables confidential or sensitive information to be limited carefully to certain users. Example: Lawtel on Prestel.[8]

(d) *Gateways*.[9] By the use of a Prestel Gateway, a facility which enables users to access third-party computers through the Prestel computers, the information provider is afforded a still higher degree of security, in that the Prestel computer is used solely as a communication medium, and the data are held entirely on the third-party computer under his control. Example: 'Homelink' home banking service on Prestel.[10]

(e) *Private Viewdata systems*. As an alternative to using a public system like Prestel, an information provider may quite economically offer a private Viewdata service from his own computer. Access to this computer is available from the same terminal from which the user accesses Prestel, by means of dialling an alternative telephone number. This gives the information provider complete control over the nature of the service he wishes to provide, its accessibility and its pricing structure. Example: PA Newsfile.[11]

Examples of current costs are given in Appendix B.

Many companies today use Viewdata systems for their own internal communication requirements, offering no public service at all. An example of such a system is BL Viewdata which enables the British Leyland dealer network to trace models of cars, manufactured by BL, in all the various options of trim and colour in showrooms around the country.

(f) *Viewdata-compatible access to non-viewdata systems*. A further degree of sophistication in the Viewdata access/price structure is offered by the provision, through a Viewdata front-end processor, of information held on another computer. This facility enables services such as bibliographic online retrieval services to be offered to Viewdata users either on the same terms as the equivalent teletype-compatible service, or on different terms and conditions. An example of the former is IRS Dialtech[12] and an example of the latter is POLIS,[13] the Parliamentary On-Line Information Service which substitutes for the minimum billing requirement as-

Communication through Videotex

```
European Space Agency

    IRS

Information Retrieval Service

ENTER-
Prestel mode
```

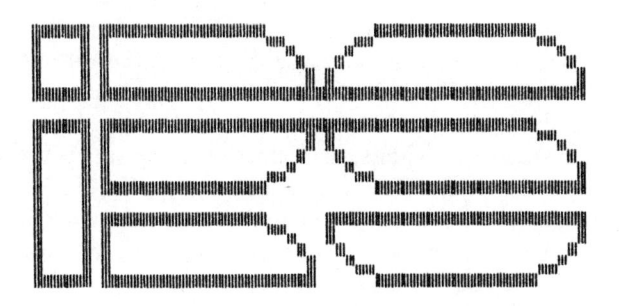

Figure 4. IRS welcome page

sociated with its conventional service a supplementary hourly charge for using its Viewdata computer. Other Viewdata-compatible bibliographic online systems include Questel and Echo.[14]

COMMUNICATION THROUGH VIDEOTEX

One of the reasons for the early slow growth of Viewdata lies in the then undeveloped nature of the communication services to

Videotex Information and Communication Systems

which the medium is eminently suited. It is the development of these services which has given Viewdata, and particularly Prestel, the edge over competing information systems, and again a structure of increasing sophistication may be discerned.

Response frames were available from the earliest times on the Post Office Viewdata Service now known as Prestel, and these enable standard or pre-formatted messages to be sent by users to information providers, on frames specially set up for this purpose. Typical uses are order forms and requests for further information, an example being Bextel, the service edited by the writer,[15] which offers both a book reservation service and a through-the-screen reference enquiry service by these means.

```
P R E S T E L                    7a              0p
    MAILBOX    main index    MAILBOX

       Simpatico    matchmaking service 9

    1  Compose and send your own message

    2  Greetings cards

    3  Standard messages eg "Thank you"

    4  Directory    44  Request an entry

    5  Shared interest groups

    6     How to use MAILBOX

    7  Talk back via MAILBAG

    8  What's New      6 Feb

    9  A-Z of MAILBOX pages              help?
```

Figure 5. Prestel Mailbox message service

Communication through Videotex

Mailbox. Whereas response frames enable only 'user to information provider' messages to be sent, 'Mailbox'[16] on Prestel offers a full 'user to user' service. Not only does this provide a basic electronic mail service to all Prestel users, but it also enables information providers to reply directly to the response frames they receive. Mailbox has been particularly successful in databases which function like an online magazine, and Micronet has regular pages of users' Mailbox messages analogous with the letters pages to be found in most monthlies.

Telex-link,[17] introduced in 1983 as a one-way service, enables

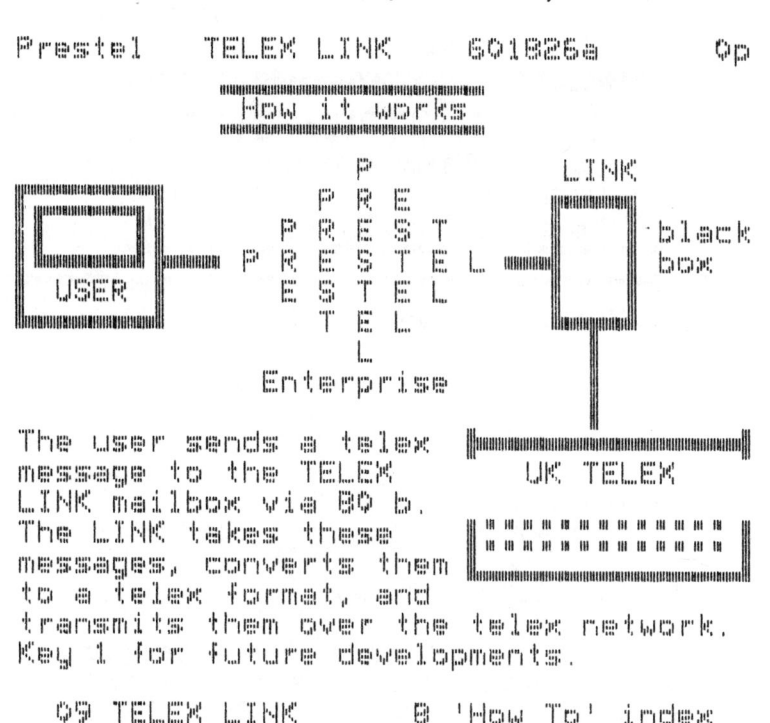

```
Prestel      TELEX LINK      6018264           Op
                      ▒▒▒▒▒▒▒▒▒▒▒▒▒▒▒▒▒▒▒▒
                           How it works
                      ▒▒▒▒▒▒▒▒▒▒▒▒▒▒▒▒▒▒▒▒

                            P                    LINK
                          P R E                ┌────────┐
                        P R E S T              │        │  black
                      P R E S T E L ──────────│        │  box
     ┌──────┐         E S T E L                │        │
     │      │─────────  T E L                  └────┬───┘
     │ USER │              L                        │
     │      │         Enterprise                    │
     └──────┘                                       │
                                                    │
   The user sends a telex        ▒▒▒▒▒▒▒▒▒▒▒▒▒▒▒▒▒▒▒
   message to the TELEX             UK TELEX
   LINK mailbox via 80 b.         ┌──────────────────┐
   The LINK takes these           │ ■ ■ ■ ■ ■ ■ ■ ■  │
   messages, converts them        │ ■ ■ ■ ■ ■ ■ ■ ■  │
   to a telex format, and         └──────────────────┘
   transmits them over the telex network.
   Key 1 for future developments.

       09 TELEX LINK          0 'How To' index
```

Figure 6. Prestel TELEX-LINK

Videotex Information and Communication Systems

telex messages to be sent, for a standard fee, to any UK destination from a Prestel terminal, and this is often cheaper than using a telex machine for the same purpose. Future developments are an extension to destinations abroad, and a return service from telex machine to Prestel terminal.

Tele-ordering Of direct concern to librarians concerned with the implementation of automated book acquisition procedures is the development of Videotex-based tele-ordering or tele-shopping services, and an example already in service on Prestel is the service provided by Watford Technical Books,[18] a sub-IP of Herts 288,

```
WATFORD TECHNICAL BOOKS 28844a        0p
████████████████████████████████████████
            Watford Technical Books
            105 St.Albans Road
            WATFORD   Herts   WD1 1RD
            Telephone 0923-23324
████████████████████████████████████████

Key 1 Subject index to 1,000 titles

    2 How to place your order

    3 How to contact us & where we are

    4 Book news - Feb 11th
         100 Programs for Spectrum

    5 Publishers index

   Books on computing and electronics
   for the professional and hobbyist
   Key 9 Viewfax 258        0 HERTS288
```

Figure 7. Tele-ordering via Herts 288

Communication through Videotex

which provides the means of ordering from a continually changing selection of 1,000 current books on computing. Orders sent to this service are transmitted by the simple means of keying reference numbers from the keyboard, but it is perfectly feasible to integrate such ordering with the formation of an in-house library acquisitions/cataloguing database in such a way that the entry on the library's computer of a draft catalogue entry of a book required for stock causes an order to be transmitted to the supplier. The same catalogue entry is then upgraded for full library use when the book is supplied and added to stock.

Auto-response via Mailbox A particularly interesting feature of Viewdata's communications potential is its ability to return automatic replies to response frames sent by the user.

Suppose a travel agent wishes to book a hotel room via Prestel. It is of course possible to provide him with direct access to the hotel booking computer via a Prestel Gateway. The inherent disadvantage of this scheme however lies in the fact that, to work effectively, the hotel booking computer will need the online capacity to handle the maximum traffic which the Prestel computer can send it throughout the hours that Prestel is available. Instead of arranging a direct online connection through a Gateway, it is equally possible for the travel agent to enter his booking details on a Prestel response frame. Facilities are then provided for the hotel booking computer to retrieve these bookings from the Prestel computer, one at a time in order, process them, and then return to the Prestel computer a message addressed to the travel agent's Prestel Mailbox confirming the booking. The travel agent is then in turn able to retrieve these Mailbox messages at his leisure, the delay to the receipt of this message being related to the amount of traffic being handled when the original response frame was completed, and of course the hours of operation of the hotel computer.

This facility is already used very successfully by Prestel's Telex-Link service, which returns to the user a confirmation of transmission of any telex he sends, or a notification of failure if the would-be recipient's telex machine is out of order.

Community catalogue access One of the consequences of the success of Micronet is the fact that a home or personal computer, fitted with a Micronet adaptor, is now easily the cheapest form of

Videotex Information and Communication Systems

computer terminal; such terminals are now finding their way into homes and schools in increasing numbers.

With the increasing use by public and academic libraries of in-house database catalogue systems which are capable of providing a dial-up online service to external users, it becomes a comparatively simple matter to make the library's catalogue directly accessible online to all local schools and to householders who wish to avail themselves of such a facility.

The writer is at present involved with the implementation of

Figure 8. Telesoftware from Micronet

such a facility, as a pilot trial, using a GEAC computer,[19] and positive results are anticipated during 1984.

Software downloading Perhaps the ultimate in sophistication is provided by the facility of down-loading computer software from the Videotex computer into the terminal. This is now a regular feature of microcomputer-based access to both Teletext and Viewdata, although doubtless still in its infancy. A particularly interesting development is the use of this facility by Micronet to transmit, to users of the BBC Microcomputer, updates of the terminal software used by this computer, to access Prestel. We may well be able to look forward to a time when Viewdata terminals are automatically programmed by the host computer to handle whatever data the computer is about to send, and then automatically reprogrammed for the next use to which the terminal is to be put, and so on.

DISPLAY AND PRESENTATION

We have seen that both Teletext and Viewdata were originally conceived as systems which could be satisfactorily displayed on an ordinary domestic television, and that Videotex displays are now a common feature of high street shop windows. Few people who have seen Videotex fail to comment on the clarity and boldness of the display, and this reaction is equally common amongst computer specialists and those used to working on conventional VDUs. Videotex has already become the 'acceptable face of computing', and with the implementation of the new CEPT standard referred to above, including high resolution 'Picture Prestel', we shall doubtless see further development in the same direction. Contracts for the supply of new computers to enable the development of 'Prestel II', as it is currently known, were signed in early 1984.

EXAMPLES QUOTED IN THE TEXT

1. *CEEFAX*, the BBC teletext service. CEEFAX 1 is transmitted with BBC 1, and has pages numbered from 100 upwards. CEE-

Videotex Information and Communication Systems

FAX 2 is numbered from 200 upwards. Contents on pages 100 and 200; Indexes on pages 199 and 299; Newsreel on page 119; Subtitling on pages 170 and 270; Newsflashes on pages 150 and 250; Telesoftware (automatic transfer of computer programs from the home computer to the user's terminal) index on page 700.
Address: CEEFAX,
        BBC Television Centre,
        Wood Lane,
        Shepherds Bush,
        London W12 7RJ.
        Tel: 01–743 8000

2. *PRESTEL*, the British public Viewdata service.
Address: PRESTEL,
        Telephone House,
        Temple Avenue,
        London EC4Y 0HL.
        Tel: 01–583 9811
General service information from Prestel Customer Service Bureau (Prestel page *5830#) or Freephone 2043.

3. *QUESTEL*, French online bibliographic information service. Available in Videotex-compatible mode via PSS and Euronet.
Address: TELESYSTÈMES/Questel,
        Direction Diffusion de l'Information,
        40 Rue du Cherche Midi,
        75006 Paris.
        Tel: 544.38.13

4. *Micronet*, Micro-ists' database on Prestel. Telesoftware (automatic transfer of computer programs from the host computer to the user's terminal) for downloading; news and magazine pages; Mailbox. Micronet also market the adaptors to enable micro-users to access Prestel (Prestel page *800#).
Address: Micronet 800,
        Telemap Ltd,
        117 Park Road,
        Peterborough PE1 2TR.
        Tel: 0733–63100

5. *ORACLE*, the IBA teletext service. Service on Channel 4

Examples Quoted in the Text

known as 4-Tel. Contents on pages 100 and 400. 4-Tel has a heavy emphasis on back-up to Channel 4 programme material. ITN news pages numbered 200 upwards.
Address: ORACLE,
   Craven House,
   25/32 Marshall Street,
   London W1V 1LL.
   Tel: 01–434 3121
   4-Tel,
   60 Charlotte Street,
   London W1P 2AX.
   Tel: 01–631 4444

6. *Government Information on Prestel* (Prestel page *58#). Co-ordinated by the Central Office of Information.
Address: Central Office of Information,
   Hercules Road,
   London SE1 7DU.
   Tel: 01–928 2345
   (Prestel page *500#)

7. *Citiservice*, Investment and Financial Database on Prestel (Prestel page *881#).
Address: Citiservice,
   Woodsted House,
   72 Chertsey Road,
   Woking,
   Surrey GU21 5BJ.
   Tel: 04862–27431

8. *Lawtel*, legal closed user group on Prestel (Prestel page *251#).
Address: Lawtel Ltd,
   PO Box 6,
   Port Erin,
   Isle of Man.
   Tel: 0624–29391

9. *Gateway*, facility offering access to third party computers via Prestel. The term is not used exclusively by Prestel, and may be found referring to the facility of accessing Prestel or other Viewdata systems via another computer. (Prestel Page *19056#) or

further information from Prestel Headquarters at the above address.
10. *Homelink*, home banking and tele-shopping service on Prestel (Prestel page *444#).
    Address: Homelink,
        Nottingham Building Society,
        Nottingham House,
        5/13 Upper Parliament Street,
        Nottingham NG1 2BX.
    Tel: 0602–419393.
11. *Newsfile*, Private Viewdata service operated by the Press Association.
    Address: Press Association Ltd,
        85 Fleet Street,
        London EC4P 4BE.
    Tel: 01–353 7440
12. *IRS-Dialtech*, bibliographic online service. UK agency of ESA-IRS (European Space Agency – Information Retrieval Service). Available in Videotex-compatible mode via PSS. (Packet switched stream).
    Address: IRS-Dialtech,
        Department of Trade and Industry,
        Room 204 Ebury Bridge House,
        2–18 Ebury Bridge Road,
        London SW1W 8QD.
    Tel: 01–730 9678
13. *POLIS*, Parliamentary On-line Information Service. Provides online indexing of Hansard and other Parliamentary documents. Videotex-compatible access via direct dial to London-based computer.
    Address: Scicon Ltd,
        Brick Close,
        Kiln Farm,
        Milton Keynes MK11 3EJ.
    Tel: 0908–565656
14. *Echo*, online information service provided in Videotex-compatible mode, via PSS and Euronet by the European Communities Host Organisation.

Examples Quoted in the Text

    Address: European Communities Host Organisation,
        15 Avenue de la Faiencerie,
        Luxembourg.
        Tel: 352.20764

15. *Bextel,* local information database, on Prestel, of Bexley London Borough. (Prestel page *42014#)
    Address: Bextel,
        Central Library,
        Townley Road,
        Bexleyheath,
        Kent DA6 7HJ.
        Tel: 01–301 1066 Ext 32.

16. *Mailbox,* Electronic Mail Services on Prestel (Prestel page *7# and *8#).
    Address: Mailbox Manager,
        Prestel Headquarters,
        Telephone House,
        Temple Avenue,
        London EC4Y 0HL.
        Tel: 01–583 9811.

17. *Telex-Link* (as Mailbox)

18. *Watford Technical Books,* online ordering of books on computing via Prestel (Prestel page *28844#).
    Address: Watford Technical Books,
        105 St Albans Rd,
        Watford WD1 1RD.
        Tel: 0923–23324

19. *GEAC Computers,* suppliers of integrated library database systems. Community access for external users.
    Address: GEAC Computers,
        Hollywood Tower,
        Hollywood Lane,
        Cribbs Causeway,
        Bristol BS10 7TW.
        Tel: 0272–509003

Videotex Information and Communication Systems

APPENDIX A

PRESTEL TRANSMISSION CODES

Bits b7 b6 b5 / Row b4 b3 b2 b1	Col 0 (000)	1 (001)	2 (010)	2a	3 (011)	3a	3b	4 (100)	4b	5 (101)	5b	6 (110)	6a	7 (111)	7a
0 0000	NUL		Sp		0			@		P		—		p	
1 0001		Cursor on	!		1		Set verify mode (1)	A	Alphanumeric Red	Q	Mosaic Red	a		q	
2 0010			"		2		Set verify mode (2)	B	Alphanumeric Green	R	Mosaic Green	b		r	
3 0011			£		3		Skip block	C	Alphanumeric Yellow	S	Mosaic Yellow	c		s	
4 0100		Cursor off	$		4		Set programme mode	D	Alphanumeric Blue	T	Mosaic Blue	d		t	
5 0101	ENQ		%		5			E	Alphanumeric Magenta	U	Mosaic Magenta	e		u	
6 0110			&		6			F	Alphanumeric Cyan	V	Mosaic Cyan	f		v	
7 0111			'		7			G	Alphanumeric White	W	Mosaic White	g		w	
8 1000	Active Position Backward (APB)		(		8			H	Flash	X	Conceal Display	h		x	
9 1001	Active Position Forward (APF)		)		9			I	Steady	Y	Contiguous Mosaics	i		y	
10 1010	Active Position Down (APD)		*		:			J		Z	Separated Mosaics	j		z	
11 1011	Active Position Up (APU)	ESC	+		;			K		[		k		¼	
12 1100	Clear Screen (CS)		,		<			L	Normal Height	½	Black Background	—		‖	
13 1101	Active Position Return (APR)		-		=			M	Double Height	]	New Background	¾		¾	
14 1110	Active Position Home (APH)		.		>			N		↑	Hold Mosaics	E		÷	
15 1111			/		?			O		#	Release Mosaics	o		■	

NOTE:

Columns 0 and 1 form the C0 control character set.

Columns 4b and 5b form the C1 set of display attribute control codes.

Columns 2, 3, 4, 5, 6 and 7 form the G0 character set.

Columns 2a, 3a, 4, 5, 6a and 7a form the Mosaic character set. The shaded area represents foreground colour.

644

Appendix B

APPENDIX B
Costs (early 1984)

1. Teletext
Access to teletext services is entirely free once the equipment has been obtained and the television licence fee paid. Teletext televisions currently sell at about £300 to £400 or rent at £120 plus per annum, and the current licence fee is £46 per annum. Some Viewdata terminals will receive teletext services as well.

2. Prestel Access
(a) *Terminals.* Prestel terminals currently retail at £500 to £800 plus VAT, depending on screen-size and degree of sophistication, and are available on rental from about £200 per annum upwards. Alphanumeric keyboards to make full use of Prestel's mailbox facilities cost a further £150 to purchase, or £50 per annum to rent. Screen printers to produce hard-copy print-outs are available to rent from about £150 per annum upwards. Viewdata adaptors to use with existing televisions cost about £100 per annum to rent or some £200 to purchase. Adaptors supplied by Micronet for use with home computers typically cost £50 to £100 depending on the make of computer.

(b) *Standing Charges* are payable to Prestel for each user registration, currently at the rate of £16.50 per quarter for business users and £5.00 per quarter for domestic users.

(c) *Access charges*
 (i) Local call rate telephone charges are payable from about 95 per cent of UK telephone subscribers. For the remaining 5 per cent STD access will be required.
 (ii) Prestel time charges of 5p per minute are payable at peak rate (08.00h to 18.00h Monday to Friday and 08.00h to 13.00h on Saturday). There is no time-based access charge outside these hours or on Bank Holidays.
 (iii) Frame charges levied on each frame by information providers are payable on some 35 per cent of Prestel frames. Charges currently range from 0.1p to 50p per frame and are always pre-announced on preceding frames. Ninety-five per cent of

Videotex Information and Communication Systems

this charge goes to the information provider, a 5 per cent factoring charge being retained by Prestel.

3. Private Viewdata Services
(a) *Terminals*. Exactly the same equipment is needed for a PVS as for Prestel, and the same terminal can usually be used for both.
(b) *Standing Charges and Access Charges* vary enormously with the kind of service. By way of example, 'Norview', the private Viewdata service of Northamptonshire County, is entirely free, whereas PA Newsfile (example 11 above) attracts a standing charge of £600 per annum and a time charge of 50p per minute.

4. Prestel Information Provision
(a) *Terminals*. Exactly the same equipment again may be used, except that a full editing keyboard will be required in place of the alphanumeric message keyboard. This will typically add a further £50 to £100 to the rental charge.
(b) *Standing Charges*. Full costs for information provision on Prestel are £6,000 per annum, plus £5 per annum per frame rented. Each registered Closed User Group is charged at an additional £320 per annum. Information providers are free to resell frames to Sub-Ips at whatever charge they find economic to recover the £5 per annum per frame, and a proportion of the £6,000 per annum which they are paying to Prestel. A typical non-profit charge would be in the order of £20 per frame per annum. A standing charge of £320 per annum is made for each Sub-Ip registration.
(c) *Editing Time Charges*. At the time of writing these are in a state of flux, having been introduced for Sub-IPs but not for information providers. For using the editor, a time-based charge of about twice the normal time-based access charge may be assumed.

BIBLIOGRAPHY AND SOURCES OF FURTHER INFORMATION

This is not the place to attempt an exhaustive professional bibliography on Videotex, and the reader is referred for this purpose to

Bibliography and Sources of Further Information

the excellent coverage of the subject provided by *Library and Information Science Abstracts* (ISSN 0024-2179), published monthly, with annual indexes, by the Library Association. Relevant material appears in the LISA subject classification at classmark ZmNxa. *et seq.*

Technical Manuals

The reader should be aware of two continuously updated loose-leaf manuals:
1. *Prestel Information Provider Manual.*
2. *Prestel Terminal Specification Manual.*

These are available from Prestel Headquarters (address as in example 2), and they provide a wealth of detail about the system.

Current Awareness

BIBLIOGRAPHIES

The best selective bibliography on Videotex for librarians is without a doubt the continuously updated list by Robin Yeates, which appears on Prestel page *420998# *et seq* as part of the LASER (London and South East Library Region) database.

INFORMATION SERVICES AND PERIODICALS

Both LASER (33/34 Alfred Place, London WC1E 7DP. Tel: 01-636 4684) and the VIA (Viewdata Industries Association, 1 Chapel Court, Borough High Street, London SE1 1HH. Tel: 01-407 0270) provide a current information service via Prestel on pages *420# and *808# *et seq* respectively, and both organizations provide message frames for direct through-the-screen communication.

The VIA publishes each month the Newletters *VIA News* and *World Videotex News*, and its other publications include *UK Vi-*

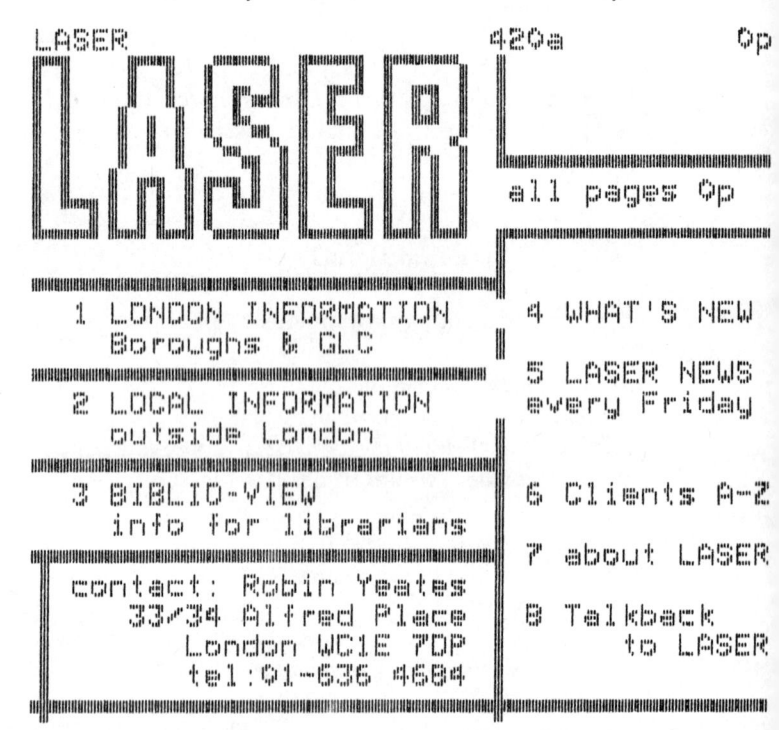

Figure 9. LASER: library information providers on Prestel

deotex Directory, *Videotex Information Providers' Code of Practice*, *Guide to Choosing Private Viewdata Systems*, and *World Systems Addressbook*.

The On-Line Information Centre, 3 Belgrave Square, London SW1X 8PL. Tel: 01–235 1732), although not directly concerned with Videotex, is a useful source of information on that grey area of Videotex-compatible online services. An annual subscription covers both the information service and their monthly newsletter *On-Line Notes* (ISSN 0144–025x).

Another periodical publication of note is *The Prestel Directory*,

Bibliography and Sources of Further Information

```
VIDEOTEX IND ASSOC      BQ842a           0p
PRIVATE VIEWDATA
═══════════════ News Index ═══════════════
Feb 03 RAPPORT joint marketing       11
Feb 06 Bishopsgate for TOPIC         12
Feb 06 Philips in Swiss deal         13
Feb 07 GEC Computers latest deal     14
Feb 08 New motor trade service       15
Feb 17 Rediffusion Computers         16


Update 808 front page ............  9
```

Figure 10. Videotex news from the VIA

published quarterly by Directel Ltd (54 Hagley Road, Edgbaston, Birmingham B16 9PE. Tel: 021-455 6585), which is issued free to all registered Prestel users, and contains subject indexes to the database, a Directory of Information Providers, and a sizeable magazine section.

Most issues of the *Library Association Record* (ISSN 0024-2195), published 11 times a year by the Library Association (7 Ridgmount Street, London WC1E 7AE. Tel: 01-636 7543), contain a feature entitled *What's New on Prestel*, which attempts to keep practition-

649

Videotex Information and Communication Systems

ers up to date with both technical developments in the Prestel system and recent additions to the database.

The best source of impartial information on Videotex terminal equipment is the NRCd (National Reprographic Centre for documentation, The Hatfield Polytechnic, Bayfordbury, Lower Hatfield Road, Hertford, Herts SG13 8LD. Tel: 0992–552341), which publishes in its quarterly journal *Reprographics Quarterly* (ISSN 0306–2880) occasional comparative reviews, as well as news reports of equipment and other technical developments. An annual subscription covers both the periodical and their information service. (It is understood that the NRCd is likely to change its name and move to the main Polytechnic building in Hatfield in 1984. The title of its journal may also change.)

Up-to-date evaluative information on private Viewdata systems is to be found only in (usually expensive) market research reports, which date very fast, and no recommendation can be made here. The reader is advised to consult the LASER and VIA information services for the latest position.

Although these external sources of information can be helpful, the reader is reminded that the key to the appreciation of the Videotex technology is involvement. Screen-based information is radically different from traditional printed material and only by using it can one fully appreciate its potential and limitations. There is a saying that it takes two to tango. So interactive is the Videotex medium that attempting to learn about it from traditional printed sources is, one would suspect, like learning to tango without a partner. It is the characteristic of a good Videotex information system that it teaches one how to use itself. The reader will find that only access to a terminal can provide a satisfactory appreciation of what Videotex can offer; and that every hour at the screen brings a familiarity with Videotex which is never lost.

22

Indexes

K. G. B. Bakewell

Asked on BBC Radio's 'Any Questions' in May 1968 what he would bring into force if he were Prime Minister, Bernard Levin said that he would make it compulsory for publishers of works of non-fiction to supply them with an index.[1] Anybody who has read a number of Mr Levin's book reviews knows how much importance this distinguished reviewer attaches to the index. In 1976 Mr Levin requested the restoration of the death penalty for publishers and authors who produce works without indexes and threatened to come back after his death and 'haunt those criminals who, through cunning, luck, a defect in the law or an abrupt flight from justice, have managed to evade the fate they deserve'.[2] He continued:

'An index is so obviously essential a part of a book that I am amazed not only at the meanness and lack of professionalism displayed by publishers who take no steps to ensure a good and complete index, but even more at the ignorance and lack of pride in their work that makes so many authors indifferent in this matter.'

The writer of an editorial on 'Reference Books' in *The Times Literary Supplement* of 16 October 1970 stated that a reference book is more akin to the index than to any other element of the orthodox book—a way into the material which the reader approaches not by means of a consecutive text but by selecting the particular key he wants—and, like an index, it can be well or badly done. Readers of this volume will know that there are many other kinds of reference book than the 'quick-reference' book to which the writer of this editorial appears to be referring, but *all* such works need a good index if information is to be located. The index to Vol 12 of one major reference book, Arnold Toynbee's *The study of history* (Oxford University Press, 1961) was commended by R. H. Crossman in a review in *The New Statesman*, 19 May 1961; he said 'Begun at the beginning the book is totally unreadable. But a superb index makes it possible to start anywhere and browse forward – or, preferably, backwards.'[3]

A very distinguished librarian once startled me by suggesting that the only books used in any depth by librarians are quick-reference books, which in the main (he said) are self-indexing. This is nonsense. As already indicated, and as is obvious from a study of this book, there is much more to reference service than the use of quick-reference material. And although *some* quick-reference books (such as dictionaries) may be described as 'self-indexing', many others are not. How much less effective works like *Whitaker's almanac*, *The world of learning*, *Directory of British associations* and *The statesman's yearbook* would be without indexes.

Another very distinguished librarian, Lionel McColvin, cared much more about the index. In an excellent paper on the purpose of indexing, he quoted some words spoken by Philip Unwin at a conference of the London and Home Counties Branch of the Library Association in June 1958:[4]

> 'Some reviewers, especially those in one of our most respected weeklies, delight to pounce with governessy righteousness upon any publisher guilty of producing a book without an index. Of course every substantial specialist work must have one but I contend that there are many "general" books to which an index is superfluous. A good list of contents gives an intelligent reader all he needs and an index is not provided for nothing.'

McColvin agreed with Unwin that travel books or volumes of reminiscences might well say so little about so many things that no index is worthwhile. Publishers could, he suggested, save money

Indexes

by not providing an index to such books but they might save even more by not publishing them at all—unless they were so profitable that they could help to pay for indexes for other books which deserved them.

McColvin also explained how he had accepted the advice of somebody who had told him not to provide an index for *The public library system of Great Britain*, the famous 'McColvin Report', because, if he did, everybody would look up what he had said about 'them' and nobody would read the report right through. He later learned that another librarian had passed the published report to one of his staff, saying 'I suppose I'll have to read it but for heaven's sake make an index to it. Fancy charging five bob for the damned thing – and no index'. (Younger readers should perhaps be told that 'five bob' means 25 pence—the exorbitant price charged by the Library Association for a reference book in 1942!)

It is important that librarians, especially reference librarians, should know something about indexes and indexing. Not only do they need to make use of indexes in order to exploit reference material effectively, but they must also be able to judge the quality of the index when selecting reference material, and they may have to compile indexes to library publications such as bibliographies and contributions to local studies. They will also need to maintain their own internal indexes, on cards or perhaps on a microcomputer, to local organizations and activities, previously answered 'awkward' enquiries, etc, and for community information input to Prestel or a private viewdata system.

Definitions and purpose of indexes

Here are three definitions of 'index':

> 'An index is an indicator or pointer out of the position of the required information'.[5]

> 'Just as a map reference is the key to a position on an atlas, so the index should permit one to pinpoint required information in a book'.[6]

'It tells you all that's in the book so that you can get at it quickly'.[7]

These definitions certainly indicate the *main* purpose of an index—to facilitate the speedy location of specific items of information—but there are others, as McColvin has pointed out.[8] The index arranges material in a different way from the main text, bringing together scattered references to a topic. A *good* index indicates what is *not* in the book. It is an aid to selection, and it can limit wear and tear on the book because the reader will not have to flip through the whole text each time a piece of information is sought.

In his message welcoming the formation of the Society of Indexers, Harold Macmillan mentioned yet another value of an index: authors are frequently indebted to indexers for pointing out errors, discrepancies or repetitions that had otherwise escaped detection in the proofs.[9]

The two main purposes of an index—location of specific items of information and rearrangement of text—are brought out clearly in the definition provided in the British Standard on indexing:

'A systematic guide to the location of words, concepts or other items in books, periodicals or other publications. An index consists of a series of entries appearing, not in the order in which they appear in the publication, but in some other order (eg alphabetical) chosen to enable the user to find them quickly, together with references to show where each item is located.'[10]

This definition also brings out the fact that an index does not *have* to be arranged alphabetically, although it often is. Sometimes a classified or numerical index is called for; for instance, *Examples illustrating AACR 2*[11] has an index arranged by rule number; and a secretary in an industrial organization where I was once employed as librarian decided to arrange her correspondence files by the Universal Decimal Classification because she was so impressed by its use in the library.

Indexes

Some early indexes

One of the first book indexes was Alexander Cruden's *Concordance to the Old and New Testaments*, first published in 1737, but Collison[12] and Knight[13] both draw attention to earlier indexes quoted by Wheatley in *What is an index?*. John Marbeck compiled a concordance to the Bible in 1550, and an index was provided to Sir Thomas North's translation of Plutarch's *Parallel lives*, published in 1595. Henry Scobell's *Acts and ordinances of . . . Parliament* (1658) contained 'an alphabetical table of the most material contents of the whole book', preceded by 'an index of the general titles comprised in the ensuing table.'

What an index is not

Two concordances to the Bible have been quoted as examples of early indexes—and certainly such works fulfil a very useful function, enabling us to locate words used in the scriptures. However, in spite of the British Standard definition previously quoted, a modern subject index is emphatically *not* a concordance. There is no point in indexing **words** unless there is something significant in the text about the word indexed; and a good index will index **concepts**, whether or not the word representing those concepts is used in the text. Kathleen Binns has explained how, under pressure from a publisher, she was guilty of turning an index into a concordance by indexing words simply because they were mentioned in the text.[14] She rightly calls such entries, which bulk the index and irritate the reader, 'non-entries'. Stephen Leacock has written an amusing piece about such non-entries:[15] there might be several entries under Napoleon in the index which lead to such sentences as 'wore his hair like Napoleon', 'in the days of Napoleon', 'as fat as Napoleon', 'not so fat as Napoleon', etc.

Nor is an index a contents table—though Valerie Alderson has pointed out that 'indexes' to children's reference books may be little more than chapter headings which should have appeared on the contents page.[16]

Indexes

What should be indexed?

Clearly most non-fiction reference books need an index, but what of fiction books? None can deny the reference value of the four known indexes to Sir Walter Scott's Waverley novels,[17-20] the compilation of one of which has been described by Philip Bradley.[21] Hilary Spurling's index to a more modern classic, Anthony Powell's *A dance to the music of time*,[22] is a valuable reference tool, and there are indexes to other novels.

Newspapers are used extensively in reference libraries as sources of contemporary information. Some national newspapers publish their indexes, notable examples being *The Times*, *Financial Times*, *New York Times*, and *Wall Street Journal*; since 1973, *The Times Index* has also covered *The Times Educational Supplement*, *The Times Literary Supplement*, *The Times Higher Education Supplement*, and *The Sunday Times*. Many libraries maintain their own indexes of local newspapers and some of these have been published.[23] Geoffrey Whatmore has written a very useful guide to newspaper indexing.[24]

Many periodicals are covered by the indexing and abstracting journals described in Chapter 9, but every serious periodical should also publish its own index. Too often this does not happen, or a periodical may publish an index and require its subscribers to request copies rather than receiving it automatically as should be their right; sometimes (as in the case of *Management Today*) an additional charge is made for the index. Often an 'index' to a periodical contains little more than entries under authors and titles of articles. Nowadays an index to a periodical may only be available online; an example is the index to *Management and Marketing Abstracts*, published by Pergamon Press for PIRA (the Research Association for Paper and Board, Printing and Packaging Industries).

Reference librarians may well wish to compile their own indexes to other sources of information, such as reports (all too often published without an index); letters; and illustrations.

Indexes

Cumulative indexes

The following definition of a cumulative index was given in the 1964 British Standard on indexing but dropped from the 1976 revision:

> 'Where a book is published in several volumes, each with its own index, or where a periodical is provided with an index each year or part of a year, and these separate indexes are combined to form an index to the whole series, the product is called a cumulative index.'[25]

An excellent example of a cumulative index which will be well known to all librarians is that compiled by Laurie J. Taylor for Vol 2 of his compilation *A librarian's handbook* (Library Association, 1980), which was awarded the Wheatley Medal for an outstanding index in 1980. It indexes the 1,072 pages of Vol 2 and the unsuperseded pages of Vol 1 of the handbook, published in 1977.

The compilation of cumulative indexes to newspapers and periodicals presents special problems because of changes in terminology and the use of different terms by different contributors. The following entries from the index to the first volume of *The Engineer* (1856) and from *The Engineer Index, 1856–1959* compiled by C. E. Prockter (London: Morgan Brothers, 1964) show some of the changes:

1856	Cumulation
Cranes, for loading and discharging vessels	Cranes, Wharf
Engine, Ritchie's	Locomotive, Railway, Steam
Steamer, the Persia	Merchant ship 'Persia', merchant ship

Doreen Blake and Ruth Bowden have explained some of the problems of compiling the centenary index to *The Journal of Anatomy*

Indexes

(1866–1966), published by Cambridge University Press for the Anatomical Society, for which they were awarded the 1968 Wheatley Medal.[26] It was impossible to use the individual indexes because they lacked uniformity, were incomplete and were sometimes inaccurate. Terminology presented a special problem because there was no nationally agreed anatomical nomenclature until 1895, and since then there have been five!

The long index

Some indexes to be used by the reference librarian are likely to be very long. J. C. Thornton has said 'Scholarly works that embody literary or historical research, or scholarly editions of the collected works of great authors, particularly the great discursive writers such as Samuel Johnson, Coleridge, Hazlitt or Ruskin – these must have long indexes.'[27] It is not only works in the humanities which may need long indexes, however. R. E. Fairbairn's general index to E. H. Rodd's *Chemistry of carbon compounds* (Elsevier, 1951–1962. 5 vols) occupies nearly 700 pages.

E. S. De Beer has pointed out that the longer an index is, the more difficult it is likely to be to use: 'No one imagines that a large index will be all easy going; long entries cannot yield all their secrets at a glance; consultants must do some work.'[28] Part of the art of indexing, however, is to reduce as much as possible the difficulty of using the index, and here such matters as a clear introduction and layout can help. The introduction to De Beer's 600-page index to *The diary of John Evelyn* (Oxford: Clarendon Press, 1955) has a ten-page introduction, which is too long, but in it the user of the index is given some very important information. For example:

1. Abbreviations used in the index are explained.
2. Arrangement of subheadings is not always alphabetical; sometimes it is chronological and sometimes the more important references are placed first.
3. Evelyn's own writings are entered under *Evelyn* and other books are entered under *Books*.

Indexes

4. All clerics, apart from Popes, are entered under surname with cross-references from benefices.
5. Peers are indexed under their family names with cross-references from their titles.
6. Words and phrases are indexed in a single alphabet headed *Words and Phrases*.
7. There are special notes on the entries for members of Evelyn's family.
8. There is a synopsis of subject headings.

De Beer's index to Evelyn's diaries influenced the compilers of another monumental index, that to *The diary of Samuel Pepys* (London: Bell & Hyman, 1983. Vol 11 of *The diary*). Robert C. Latham and his wife Rosalind tried to capture in this outstanding index the flavour of the diary and to make the index acceptable to the amateur (our oft-quoted 'general reader') as well as to the historian.[29] Inevitably there are some very long entries—31 sections, for example, under *Charles II* and several pages under *Parliament*. Asterisks are used to minimize the use of words: under *Meals*, * indicates that Pepys gives the menu; under *Taverns*, * indicates that Pepys ate a meal there; under *Books*, * indicates that Pepys read a book and ** that he comments on it.

How many indexes?

The founder of the Society of Indexers, G. Norman Knight, was a strong advocate of the idea of a book having one index only, and in a letter published in *The Indexer* he quoted H. B. Wheatley ('an index should be one and indivisible, and not broken up in several alphabets') and Sir Edward Cook ('multiplication of indexes is an unmitigated nuisance. It makes reference less easy. One index is the only right plan') in support of his views.[30] The British Standard on indexing states that a single index containing proper names and common nouns in one sequence is generally preferable in books on the humanities, but books on science and technology often have separate indexes of subjects and of authors cited; and goes on to point out that periodicals frequently have separate indexes of au-

Indexes

thors of articles, subjects, titles of books reviewed, and advertisers. 'Separate indexes', says *The Standard*, 'may be useful in providing for specific aspects of the material indexed to be analysed and brought together, eg geographical and other proper names referred to, foreign terms, chemicals and other commodities, numerical and chronological data'.[31]

Clearly, **numerical** and **alphabetical** indexes must be in separate sequences. Clearly too, arrangement can be simplified by division into different alphabets (note, for example, the use of the divided dictionary catalogue in the United States). But I regret very much having provided three indexes (under proper names, titles and subjects) to my *Management principles and practice: a guide to information sources* (Detroit: Gale Research Company, 1977), in accordance with the publishers' policy for their Management Information Guide series, because I frequently find myself consulting the wrong index.

One editor who certainly favoured multiple indexes was R. W. Chapman. His collection of *The letters of Samuel Johnson*, published by Clarendon Press in 1952, contained seven: Samuel Johnson; Persons; Authors (not included in Persons) and Books; Places; Subjects; Johnson's works (a chronological list); and Johnson's English. His collection of *Jane Austen's letters to her sister Cassandra and others*, the second edition of which was published by Oxford University Press in 1952, went one better with eight indexes: Jane Austen's family; Other persons; Places; General topics; Authors, books, plays; Jane Austen's novels; Jane Austen's English; Ships.

How to recognize a good index

This is the title of a useful paper by Geoffrey Hamilton, a former chairman of the Wheatley Medal Selection Committee.[32] His comments are based on the criteria used as guidelines by this Committee.

There should normally be an **introductory note**, which should be clear and concise. It should indicate the scope of the index, any omissions, any unusual features, any abbreviations used, and the

Indexes

arrangement used. See Figures 1 and 2 on pages 665 and 666 for examples of introductory notes used in the index to *The Indexer*.

Obviously the index must be **accurate** and must include all significant items in the text. It should normally be **comprehensive**, though certain limitations on comprehensiveness may be allowable if clearly explained. For example, the introduction to the index to Vol 12 of *The Indexer*, reproduced on page 666, explains that citation references have not been indexed. Sometimes space limitations imposed by the publisher may affect the comprehensiveness of the index.

John L. Thornton has pointed out that many indexes to medical books are unsatisfactory because they are not sufficiently comprehensive;[33] frequently they ignore plates, diagrams, and tables, which often contain useful information not readily accessible via the text and sometimes located several pages away from the text to which they refer; bibliographies and references should be indexed, as should appendices; introductions can be lengthy and informative and should be considered for indexing.

The index should have enough **subheadings** to avoid strings of undifferentiated location references. It is often said that subdivision should be considered when there are more than six location references, but this is an arbitrary figure and sometimes there is no convenient way of subdividing. Usually, however, subdivision *is* possible and is helpful to the user of the index. I once indexed the second edition of a book on economic geography, the first edition of which had been indexed by the author. In the index to the first edition, there were several examples of undifferentiated strings of page references such as the following:

China 5, 9, 10, 11, 12, 17, 40, 52, 54, 60, 63, 66, 68, 71, 75, 76, 89, 95, 100, 101, 103, 105, 107, 117, 123, 125, 127, 128, 136, 137, 140, 141, 142, 156, 166, 180, 194, 203, 211, 242, 260, 264–5, 271, 302, 308, 315, 317, 331

In the index to the second edition, it was quite easy to provide some subheadings:

Indexes

China
  agriculture 17, 40
  animals 95, 100, 101
  fishing 103, 105, 107
  food 52, 54, 60, 63, 66, 68, 71, 75, 76, 89
  forests 117
  fuel and power 180, 194
  manufacturing 203, 211, 242
  minerals 156, 166
  population 5, 9, 10, 11, 12
  settlements 331
  textiles 123, 125, 127, 128, 136, 137, 260, 264–5, 271
  transport and trade 302, 308, 315, 317, 331
  vegetable oils 140, 141, 142

(The book is *Economic geography for professional students* by John Inch, 2nd ed. London: Pitman, 1974).

Accuracy applies to the **arrangement**, whether alphabetical, numerical or some other order, as well as to the location references. If alphabetical arrangement is used, 'word by word' or 'letter by letter' must be chosen and adhered to rigidly; the two systems can result in quite different sequences, as seen in the following brief examples:

word by word	*letter by letter*
air transport	aircraft
aircraft	air transport
All England . . .	Allenby
Allenby	All England . . .
bank holidays	*Banker*
Bank of England	bank holidays
Banker	banking
banking	Bank of England

The British Standard on indexing favours word-by-word arrangement, as does the companion British Standard on alphabetical

Indexes

arrangement, which is currently undergoing revision.[34] In these days of computer filing, the *BLAISE filing rules*[35] are a useful guide; these too favour word-by-word filing.

There should be enough **cross-references** to connect related items in the index:

microforms *see also* aperture cards; COM; microfiche
personnel management *see also* training

In the case of synonyms and alternative forms of name it is often quicker, as well as being more helpful to the user, to make additional entries rather than '*see*' references:

executives 58, 215–9
managers 59, 215–9
London University 75
University of London 75

'*See*' references should, however, be used if there are a large number of subheadings:

executives *see* managers
managers
   recruitment and selection 135–43
   remuneration 175–80
   training 145–55

The **lay-out** of the index is important. The following example shows that 'set out' subheadings are clearer than 'run on' subheadings, although the latter occupy rather less space than the former:

set out
planning
  computer use
  decision making and
  local government
  marketing
  multinationals
  production
  quantitative methods
  top management's role

run on
planning
  computer use; decision making and; local government; marketing; multinationals; production; quantitative methods; top management's role

Some indexes to *The Indexer* have used 'run on' subheadings (see Figure 1 on page 665); the latest index, that to Vol 12, uses 'set out' subheadings (see Figure 2 on page 666).

When sub-subheadings need to be used, there is really no alternative to 'set out'. The following example is taken from the index to the second edition of *Anglo-American cataloguing rules* (1978):

Prefixes, surnames with
  capitalization, App. A.13B
    Dutch language, App. A.37B
    French language, App. A.39C
    Russian language, App. A.46A1
  explanatory references, 26.2D2
  headings, 22.5D
    prefixes hyphenated or combined with surname, 22.5E
  '*see*' references, 26.2A3

A 'run on' version of this would be very confusing:

Prefixes, surnames with
  capitalization, App. A.13B – Dutch language, App. A.37B, French language, App. A.39C, Russian language, App. A.46A1; explanatory references, 26.2D2; headings, 22.5D – prefixes hyphenated or combined with surname, 22.5E; '*see*' references, 26.2A3

Indexes

INDEX

Compiled by K. ATTERTON

Headings and sub-headings are arranged alphabetically word by word.
Titles of books and periodicals are in *italic* type, titles of articles in roman type within quotation marks.

Abbreviations: ASI = American Society of Indexers
AusSI = Australian Society of Indexers
IASC = Indexing and Abstracting Society of Canada/Société canadienne pour l'analyse de documents
Int. Conf. = Society of Indexers' International Conference, 1978
SI = The Society of Indexers, London
TI = *The Indexer*

abstracting and indexing services: Canada, 202, 203; UK, 250
Acts of Parliament, citing, 205-08
AFNOR (Association française de normalisation), 158, 223, 225
Africana MSS, 186
Alabi, Gbade, indexing services, Nigeria, 103
Alderson, Valerie, report, Int. Conf. (*TES*), 103
alphabetization: *ARIST*, 31-32; Australian *Style Manual*, 233-34; Borko and Bernier, 245; OUP, 194; Urdang, 130-31; Wesley, 195: *see also* BSI Recommendations
American Bibliographical Center (ABC-Clio Inc.), 33-42, 46, 108
American Library Association (ALA), 2, 43; Margaret Mann Citation (1978), 148
American National Standards Institute (ANSI), 14, 172; *National Standard for bibliographic references*, 23, 153; *USA standard basic criteria for book indexes*, 16, 19, 20, 23, 28
American Society for Information Science (ASIS, formerly ADI—American Documentation Institute), 24-25, 27, 129n; *Annual review of information science and technology (ARIST)*: vols. 1-10 Cumulative index, 24-32; vols. 12-13, review, 247, 248
American Society of Indexers (ASI): *Directory of courses on indexing*, 12; 'Index specifications' (Bernier), 20n, 23; membership, 7-8, 12; Newsletter, 170; register, 12, 160; SI affiliation, 2, 6, 10-12, 57-58, 109; Society information, 9, 11-12, 55, 123, 172, 187, 251; Wilson award, 58, 160, 172, 201

Anders, E., book reviewer, 183
Anderson, M. D.: *Making an index*, 234; review of *Wills proved at Chester*, letter, 226-27
Andrews, Dr. John S., indexer, *The Evangelical Quarterly*, vols. 1-50, 245
Anglo-American cataloguing rules, 2nd ed., 185; review, 240-41
Anthony, L. J., indexer, *Journal of Documentation* (Aslib), vols. 1-30, 140
architecture index, 181-82
archives: Public Record Office, 163; Rhodes House, 186
ARIST, *see* American Society for Information Science
arrangement, 180; *see also* alphabetization
Ashworth, Wilfred, 'Future perfect' (*Aslib proceedings*), 243n
Asian languages, 63-67; *see also* Chinese
Aslib: Informatics Group, 132, 135; *Journal of Documentation*, 140; SI Int. Conf., 3, 60; thesaurus collection, 204
Association of Assistant Librarians (AAL), 152
Atherton, Pauline, 46; *Books are for use*, 145-48; 'Characteristics of book indexes for subject retrieval in the humanities and social sciences' (with Gratch, B. and Settel, B.), 14-23
Auckland, Edith, President IASC, 203
audio-visual materials, description, 240
Aurora High School Library, 53, 146-47, 148
Austin, Derek W., 203, 244, 248; contributor, *The PRECIS index system*, 52-53, 179; Margaret Mann Citation 1978, 148; *PRECIS: a manual of concept analysis and subject indexing* (BNB), 147, 148

Figure 1 Extract from the index to volume 11 of *The Indexer* (1978-1979) showing a concise introductory note and the use of 'run on' subheadings

665

Indexes

INDEX

Compiled by FREDA WILKINSON

The alphabetical arrangement is word by word.
Added to the page number, n denotes a footnote, F a figure or illustration.
Citation references are not indexed.
The following abbreviations have been used (there are however others which are assumed to need no explanation):

AACR	Anglo-American Cataloguing Rules	IIS	Institute of Information Scientists
ALA	American Library Association	LA	Library Association
ALPSP	Association of Learned and Professional Society Publishers	NFAIS	National Federation of Abstracting and Indexing Services
ASI	American Society of Indexers	PCRC	Primary Communications Research Centre
AusSI	Australian Society of Indexers		
BSI	British Standards Institution	SI	Society of Indexers
IASC/SCAD	Indexing and Abstracting Society of Canada/Société canadienne pour l'analyse de documents	UNISIST	Universal System for Information in Science and Technology

---

Abbreviations of organizations, World guide to (Buttress), 166
ABC-Clio Inc.
  computerized abstracting-indexing service, 131
  publication jointly with ASI and SI, 159
Abstracting and indexing services, Some statistical indicators of UK (East), reviewed, 107
abstracting periodicals articles: workshop at SI conference, 60
abstracts: lecture at NFAIS conference, 209
Ackoff, R.L., on evaluating information systems, 14-15
AFNOR, *see* Association française de normalisation
Agarde, A., indexer of public records, 146
Aitchison, J., and *Root thesaurus*, 224
Aitchison, T.M., appointed Director of INSPEC, 82
Aitken, A.J.: article in *Logophile* on dictionary compiling by computer, 72
Alcock, L., indexer of own archaeological books, 180
Allen and Unwin: indexing of archives, 73-4
alphabet of 24 letters (Middle Ages), 170
alphabetical arrangement in indexes, 171
  experimental studies of retrieval (Hartley, Davies and Burnhill), 149-53
alphabetical listings, 35
alphabetization of prepositions
  in indexes (Wellisch), 90-2; comments on, 128-9, 201-2
  in concordances, 211
Altman, E. (reviser), *Local public library administration*, 230
America: History and Life (AHL), abstracting-indexing service, 131-9 *passim*
American Bibliographical Center: computer-assisted index (ABC-SPIndex), 132, 133F, 136, 139F
American Journal of Archaeology: paper on archaeological indexing, 57; *see also* Dow, S.
American Library Association (ALA)
  ALA filing rules, 222
  ALA glossary, 21
  ALA publications checklist 1980, 166

ALA world encyclopedia of library and information services (ed. Wedgeworth), 202; reviewed, 105-6
ALA yearbook 1980, reviewed, 227-8
and White House conference on library and information services, 95
American National Standards Institute, *Basic criteria for indexes*, 90
American Society for Information Science
and White House conference on library and information services, 94
Annual review of information science and technology: Vol. 13, reviewed, 49; Vol. 14, reviewed, 227
American Society of Indexers (ASI)
  officers, 55, 111, 168, 232
  participation in White House conference on library and information services, 94-5, 97
  Proceedings of the second seminar on freelance indexing, 54, 63; reviewed, 106
  publication jointly with ABC-Clio and SI, 159
  referred to in ALA encyclopedia, 202
Anderson, H., *Coal mining: index*, 31
Anderson, J.D.
  (ed.) *Directory of courses on indexing in Canada and the United States*, 206
  structure in database indexing, 3-13
Anderson, M.D., 114, 154
  Book indexing, 53, 153, 190; alphabetizing prepositions, 128
  index to *Antiquity*, 181, 182
Andrewes, R., on rules for music in AACR 2, 161
Anglo-American cataloguing rules (1967): seminar report indexed by Liverpool students, 191
Anglo-American cataloguing rules (2nd ed., 1978), 46, 48, 224-5; index by K.G.B. Bakewell (Wheatley Medal), 79-80, 92
Examples illustrating AACR 2 (Hunter and Fox), reviewed, 105
Handbook explaining and illustrating AACR 2 (Maxwell), reviewed, 160, 161
Making of a code, The (ed. Clack), reviewed, 160

Figure 2 Extract from the index to Vol 12 of *The Indexer* (1980–1981), showing a concise introductory note and the use of 'set out' subheadings

Indexes

Could indexes replace library catalogues?

Pauline Atherton (now Pauline Cochrane) and her associates at Syracuse University have shown, with their Subject Access Project,[36] that book indexes could be very significant for retrieval generally if more use were made of them. They compared retrieval via key-words taken from contents tables and indexes with retrieval via MARC records and the results indicated that retrieval via BOOKS (the key-word database) was quicker and more effective than retrieval via MARC. Among the benefits claimed for BOOKS were:

1. greater access to books with relevant information;
2. greater precision;
3. less costly online searching;
4. the ability to answer some queries which would not be possible using 'today's catalogue information'.

The important point was made, however, that some effort needs to be made to improve the contents pages and indexes in books to make this kind of retrieval truly effective.

A great deal of information can be retrieved via book indexes which is not apparent from the title or main subject. For example, a glance at the index to *College administration: a handbook*, edited by Ian Waitt (London: National Association of Teachers in Further and Higher Education, 1970) shows that this book contains *significant* information on a variety of topics including European Economic Community training policies, health and safety at work, industrial tribunals, trade unions, unfair dismissal, and the Youth Opportunities Programme.

An article on the Subject Access Project[37] indicated that a major problem was the frequent absence of book indexes, as shown by the following analysis:

books examined	2087
number with index	1147
percentage with index	55

Indexes

In my contribution to a symposium in 1974 on the inadequacies of book indexes,[38] I lamented the frequent tendency to publish books—especially 'readings'—on management, without indexes, and mentioned several titles, varying in length from 175 pages to 1,600 pages, none of which had an index.

This situation is by no means confined to management books. Three popular titles which deserve, but do not have, indexes are: *Ways of escape*, Graham Greene's second volume of autobiography (London: Bodley Head, 1980); *Speak for England*, Melvyn Bragg's 500-page essay on England, 1900–1975, based on interviews with inhabitants of Wigton, Cumberland (London: Secker & Warburg, 1976); and *Akenfield*, Ronald Blythe's portrait of a Suffolk village (Harmondsworth: Penguin Books, 1972).

Indexing societies

In 1957 a retired civil servant, G. Norman Knight, wrote a letter to *The Times* inviting people interested in the formation of a society of indexers to communicate with him. Knight had been a self-tutored free-lance indexer for thirty years, but had never met any other indexers, and was keen to remove the 'intense feeling of solitude' in which the free-lance indexer had to work. Sixty people responded to Knight's invitation to attend a meeting at the National Book League's premises in London—including one gentleman (Dr William Heckscher) who had flown from Utrecht in the Netherlands—and the Society of Indexers was formally constituted. The objectives of the Society were and are to safeguard and improve indexing standards and to secure some measure of uniformity in technique; to promote the professional interests of indexers, and to act as an advisory body on qualifications and remuneration. The British Standard on indexing was produced largely on the initiative of the Society.

One of the Society's outstanding achievements has been the regular publication, since March 1958, of a twice-yearly journal, *The Indexer*. The first two issues of this included a list of books published without an index, arranged alphabetically by publisher, under the heading 'No index – No comment'. From Vol 4, No 3

Indexes

(Spring 1965), extracts from book reviews which referred to the index were included, along with other news items, in a section entitled 'Comments and Extracts' ('Extracts and Comments' from Vol 4, No 4 (Autumn 1965)). Since Vol 7, No 2 (Autumn 1970), the extracts from reviews have been separated out from the other news items, and since Vol 10, No 1 (April 1976), the extracts from reviews have been grouped under such headings as 'No Indexes', 'Inadequate Indexes', 'Satisfactory Indexes', 'Excellent Indexes', 'Unusual Indexes' and 'Superfluous Indexes?'

The Society organized the first National Conference on Indexing in March 1976 and the proceedings of this were published in *The Indexer* 10 (2), October 1976. To celebrate its 21st anniversary the Society organized the first International Conference on Indexing, which was attended by more than a hundred representatives from 16 countries. One of the speakers was the same William Heckscher who had flown from Utrecht to attend the inaugural meeting in 1957; this time he came from the United States. The Society's ailing founder and President, Norman Knight, was able to attend the Conference Dinner and to give his greetings only one month before his death. The proceedings of the conference were published in *The Indexer* 11 (2), October 1978.

Other events in celebration of the Society's 21st anniversary included the publication of a select reading list on indexing[39] and of selections from *The Indexer*.[40]

The American Society of Indexers was formed in 1968 and became formally affiliated to the Society in 1971. The Society is now also affiliated to the Australian Society of Indexers (formed in 1976) and the Indexing and Abstracting Society of Canada/Société canadienne pour l'analyse de documents (formed in 1977), and *The Indexer* is the official journal of all four societies. The parent Society is now an organization in liaison with the Library Association.

Awards for indexers

In 1960 the Library Association instituted the **Wheatley Medal**, so called in honour of Henry B. Wheatley (1838–1917), sometimes

Indexes

referred to as 'the father of British indexing'. It was originally an annual award to the compiler of the most outstanding index published in Britain during the preceding year, but in 1968 the conditions of the award were modified, following a joint meeting of the Society of Indexers and the Library Association Cataloguing and Indexing Group. One of the changes was that indexes published during the preceding *three* years would be eligible for the award, because it was recognized that an index can only be judged by its performance over a reasonable period.

The winner is chosen by a panel consisting of three nominees of the Library Association and three nominees of the Society of Indexers. It says much for the high standards expected for the Medal—and perhaps something for the quality of indexes—that no award was made for the first two years or for four other years. The following are the winners to date:

1960 No award
1961 No award
1962 Michael Maclagan for the index to Michael Maclagen: *'Clemency' Canning* (Macmillan)
1963 J. M. Dickie — J. M. Dickie: *How to catch trout* (W & R Chambers)
1964 Guy Parsloe — Guy Parsloe: *Wardens' accounts of the Worshipful Company of the Founders of the City of London 1497–1681* (University of London, Athlone Press)
1965 Alison M. Quinn — Richard Hakluyt: *The principall navigations, voiages and discoveries of the English nation* (Cambridge University Press/ Hakluyt Society and Peabody Museum of Salem)
1966 No award
1967 G. Norman Knight — Randolph S. Churchill: *Winston S. Churchill*, Vol 2: *Young statesman 1901–1919* (Heinemann)

Indexes

1968	Doreen Blake and Ruth Bowden	*Cumulative index to Journal of Anatomy 1866–1966* (Cambridge University Press/Anatomical Society)
1969	James C. Thornton	M. House and G. Storey (eds.): *The letters of Charles Dickens*, Vol 2: *1840–41* (Clarendon Press)
1970	E. L. C. Mullins	E. L. C. Mullins: *A guide to the historical & archaeological publications of societies in England & Wales 1901–1933* (University of London, Athlone Press)
1971	No award	
1972	No award	
1973	K. Boodson	K. Boodson: *Non-ferrous metals: a bibliographical guide* (Macdonald Technical & Scientific) and
	L. M. Harrod	H. M. Colvin (ed.): *History of the King's works*, Vol 6: *1782–1851* (HMSO)
1974	C. C. Banwell	*Encyclopaedia of forms & precedents.* 4th ed. 24 vols. (Butterworth)
1975	Margaret D. Anderson	Judith Butcher: *Copy-editing: the Cambridge handbook* (Cambridge University Press)
1976	John A. Vickers	G. R. Cragg (ed.): *The works of John Wesley*, Vol 11: *The appeals to men of reason and religion and certain related open letters* (Oxford University Press)
1977	T. Rowland Powel	*Archaeologia Cambrensis, 1901–1960* (Cardiff: Cambrian Archaeological Association)
1978	No award	

Indexes

1979 K. G. B. Bakewell	*Anglo-American cataloguing rules.* 2nd ed. (Library Association)
and	
Annette Surrey	D. G. James (ed.): *Circulation of the blood* (Pitman Medical)
1980 Laurie J. Taylor	L. J. Taylor (comp.): *A librarian's handbook*, Vol 2 (Library Association)
1981 J. Edwin Holmstrom	*Analytical index to the publications of the Institution of Civil Engineers, January 1975–79* (Institution of Civil Engineers)
1982 Peter W. M. Blayney	Peter W. M. Blayney: *The texts of King Lear and their origins. Vol. 1: Nicholas Okes and the first quarto* (Cambridge: Cambridge University Press)

The Society of Indexers established an occasional award for outstanding services to indexing in 1977 and designated it the **Carey Award** in memory of the Society's first President, Gordon V. Carey (1886–1969). So far there have been three recipients of this award, which takes the form of an appropriately worded and beautifully decorated citation: G. Norman Knight in 1977, L. Montague Harrod in 1982, and Margaret D. Anderson in 1983. Appropriately, all three recipients had previously demonstrated their competence as indexers by having previously been awarded the Wheatley Medal, but all three had also done a very great deal to further the cause of indexing.

In 1979 the **H. W. Wilson Company Index Award** was inaugurated for excellence in indexing of an English-language monograph or other non-serial publication published in the United States during the previous calendar year. The award, which consists of a cash prize for the indexer and a citation for the publisher, is presented by the American Society of Indexers on behalf of the well-known index publishers. The first four recipients were:

References

1978 Hans H. Wellisch for the index to Hans H. Wellisch: *The conversion of scripts, its nature, history and utilization* (Wiley)
1979 Linda I. Solow — David Epstein: *Beyond Orpheus: studies in musical structure* (MIT Press)
1980 Delight Ansley — Carl Sagan: *Cosmos* (Random House)
1981 Catherine Fix — Donald Resnick and Gen Niwayama: *Diagnosis of bone and joint disorders* (W. B. Saunders Company)

REFERENCES

1. *The Indexer*, 6 (2), Autumn 1968. 73.
2. Levin, Bernard 'A haunting, I promise, for those who refuse to tell who's who and what's what'. *The Times*, 17 December 1976; reprinted in *The Indexer*, 10 (3), April 1977. 139–41.
3. Quoted in *The Indexer*, 2 (4), Autumn 1961. 141.
4. McColvin, L. R. 'The purpose of indexing'. *The Indexer*, 1 (2), September 1958. 31–5.
5. Wheatley, Henry B. *What is an index?* London: Index Society, 1878. 7.
6. Thornton, John L. 'The use of indexes'. *The Indexer*, 8 (1), April 1972. 17–19.
7. Replies by schoolchildren to the question 'What is an index?' quoted by H. B. King. *The Indexer*, 8 (4), October 1973. 210.
8. McColvin, L. R. 'The purpose of indexing'. *The Indexer*, 1 (2), September 1958. 31–5.
9. *The Indexer*, 1 (1), March 1958. 3.
10. British Standards Institution *Recommendations: the preparation of indexes to books, periodicals and other publications*. Rev ed. London: BSI, 1976. (BS 3700: 1976).
11. Hunter, Eric J. and Fox, Nicholas J. *Examples illustrating AACR 2*. London: Library Association, 1980.
12. Collison, Robert L. *Indexes and indexing*. 4th ed. London: Benn, 1972. 16.
13. Knight, G. Norman *Indexing, the art of*. London: Allen & Unwin, 1979. 18.
14. *The Indexer*, 9 (1), April 1974. 2.
15. Leacock, Stephen 'The perfect index: there is no index, and why'. In: Leacock, Stephen *My remarkable uncle and other sketches*. London:

Indexes

Bodley Head, 1942. 212–15; Leacock, Stephen *The Leacock roundabout*. Garden City, New York: Dodd, Mead & Co, 1946. 420–2; Stevens, Norman (ed.) *Library humor*. Metuchen, New Jersey: Scarecrow Press, 1971. 419–22.

16. Alderson, Valerie 'Towards a scholarly A to Z'. *The Times Educational Supplement*, 19 March 1976. 22.
17. Cornish, S. W. *The Waverley manual: a handbook of the chief characters in the Waverley novels*. Edinburgh: Black, 1871.
18. Rogers, M. *The Waverley dictionary*. Chicago: S. C. Grigg & Co, 1879.
19. Husband, M. F. A. *Dictionary of characters in the Waverley novels*. London: Routledge, 1910.
20. Bradley, Philip *An index to the Waverley novels*. Metuchen, New Jersey: Scarecrow Press, 1975.
21. Bradley, Philip 'A long fiction index'. *The Indexer*, **8** (3), April 1973. 153–7.
22. Spurling, Hilary *Handbook to Anthony Powell's Music of time*. London: Heinemann, 1977.
23. Some are mentioned in Bakewell, K. G. B. 'Analytical cataloguing in British public libraries'. *Library Resources and Technical Services*, **17** (4), Fall 1973. 389–404. Including *Chester newspaper index*, compiled by staff of Chester Public Library and published by the Chester Civic Amenities Committee in two volumes covering 1955–1959 and 1960–1964.
24. Whatmore, Geoffrey *The modern news library*. London: Library Association, 1978.
25. British Standards Institution *Recommendations for the preparation of indexes*. London: BSI, 1964. (BS 3700: 1964).
26. Blake, Doreen and Bowden, Ruth '*The Journal of Anatomy*: index to the first hundred years 1866–1966'. *The Indexer*, **6** (2), Autumn 1968. 48–51.
27. Thornton, J. C. 'The long index'. In: Knight, G. Norman (ed.) *Training in indexing*. Cambridge, Massachusetts: MIT Press, 1969. 86–95.
28. De Beer, E. S. 'The larger index'. *Journal of Documentation*, **12** (1), March 1956. 1–14.
29. Latham, Robert C. and Latham, Rosalind 'Indexing Pepys' diary'. *The Indexer*, **12** (1), April 1980. 34–5.
30. Knight, G. Norman 'Letter to the editor'. *The Indexer*, **3** (3), Spring 1963. 125–6.
31. British Standards Institution *Recommendations: the preparation of indexes to books, periodicals and other publications*. Rev ed. London: BSI, 1976. (BS 3700: 1976). 2 (para 5.1.4).
32. Hamilton, Geoffrey 'How to recognize a good index'. *The Indexer*, **10** (2), October 1976. 49–53.

Further Reading

33. *The Indexer*, **9** (1), April 1974. 8–9.
34. British Standards Institution *Specification for alphabetical arrangement and the filing order of numerals and symbols*. Rev ed. London: BSI, 1969. (BS 1749: 1969).
35. British Library Filing Rules Committee *BLAISE filing rules*. London: British Library, 1980.
36. *Books are for use: final report of the Subject Access Project to the Council on Library Resources*. Syracuse, New York: Syracuse University, School of Information Studies, 1978. (Pauline Atherton, director).
37. Gratch, Bonnie *et al.* 'Characteristics of book indexes for subject retrieval in the humanities and social sciences'. *The Indexer*, **11** (1), April 1978. 14–23.
38. *The Indexer*, **9** (1), April 1974. 1–2.
39. Society of Indexers *A select reading list on indexing*. London: Society of Indexers, 1978.
40. Harrod, Leonard Montague (*ed.*) *Indexers on indexing*. New York & London: Bowker, 1978.

SUGGESTIONS FOR FURTHER READING

Anderson, M. D. *Book indexing*. Cambridge University Press, 1971. (Cambridge authors' and printers' guides).
Most useful pamphlet, full of excellent advice. Replaces the equally useful *Making an index* by G. V. Carey (Cambridge University Press, 1965), now out of print but worth reading if you can find it in a library.

British Standards Institution *Recommendations: the preparation of indexes to books, periodicals and other publications*. Rev ed. London: BSI, 1976. (BS 3700: 1976).
The British indexer's 'bible'.

Collison, Robert L. *Indexes and indexing: guide to the indexing of books and collections of books, periodicals, music, recordings, films and other material, with a reference section and suggestions for further reading*. 4th ed. London: Benn, 1972.
Standard work by the current President of the Society of Indexers.

Collison, Robert L. *Indexing books: a manual of basic principles*. London: Benn, 1962.
Useful, though obviously dated, guide for the beginner. Includes exercises and answers.

Hunnisett, R. F. *Indexing for editors*. London: British Records Association, 1972.

Indexes

Very useful guide. Contains good chapters on terminology, places, persons, subjects, filing and presentation.

Knight, G. Norman *Indexing, the art of: a guide to the indexing of books and periodicals.* London: Allen & Unwin, 1979.
The founder of the Society of Indexers's final contribution to indexing. A first-class comprehensive guide with an exemplary index compiled by the author and Anthony Raven. Also worth reading is the short foreword by the Rt Hon Harold Macmillan.

The issues of *The Indexer* contain many helpful articles (and *see* Ref 40 above). You should also try to examine some of the indexes mentioned in the text and some of those winning the Wheatley Medal or the H. W. Wilson Award.

Index

The index contains entries under authors, organizations, subjects, countries and titles; title entries have, however, been omitted for bibliographical references (except those without authors) and for some works, especially those with non-distinctive titles, which can be traced easily under subject or country (e.g. national bibliographies of certain countries).

The index has been compiled according to British Standard 3700:1976, with a few minor amendments such as the omission of definite or indefinite articles from most titles of publications. British government departments are entered directly under their names.

The arrangements is in accordance with British Standard 1749:1969 so that word by word alphabetization is used, initials file as words, hyphenated words file as separate words. 'Encyclopaedia' and 'encyclopedia' are interfiled, however, as are 'yearbook' and 'year book'.

A page reference followed by 'b' indicates a bibliographical reference and one followed by 'fig' indicates a figure or diagram. Page references in bold type indicate the main treatment of a title.

Index

AACR2 456, 537, 654, 664, 673b11
Abbey, J. R. 577
abbreviations, dictionaries 67
 in citations 227
ABC Europ production 173
Abridged index medicus 237, 593
Abridged readers' guide to periodical literature 235
Abstract newsletters 249–50
abstract services 239–43
 selection of 234
Abstract of British historical statistics 347, 375b115–6
Abstracting and indexing periodicals. . . 230
Abstracting services 233
abstracts 239–43, 517
 currency of 196
 definitions 239–40
 newspapers 208
 reports 249–51
 theses 254–5
abstracts journals
 as subject bibliographies 517
 bibliographies of 233–4, 517
 by computer production 588, 589
 evaluation of 18
 selection policies 234
Academic American encyclopedia 79, 91
 price of 87
academic libraries
 bibliographical provision in 526
 book selection in 426
 cataloguing and classification 27–8
 costs of online searches 592
 language problem in 44
 loan collections 581
 public access 526
 reference material in 7, 14, 20, 25
 subject departments 5

use of UDC 28
 user education 30
Access 241
accessions lists 512, 514
accounting, bibliographies 505, 511
Accounting + data processing abstracts 240
accuracy
 in indexes 661
 of biographical reference works 134
 of encyclopaedias 78, 126–7
 of reference material 9–11, 13
acquisition
 of HMSO publications 308–9
 of illustrated books 568
 of international official publications 554–5
 of reference material 6
ACS 589
Acts and ordinances of . . . Parliament 655
Adams, Bernard 577
Adams, H. M. 468
Admiralty charts 276, 293b
Advances in librarianship 225
advertising rates guides 216
aeronautical charts 275–6
aerospace 250
AFNOR standards 260
Africa (*see also* names of individual countries)
 biographical dictionaries 144, 148
 directories 173, 186
 national bibliographies 436
 news digests 207
 regional bibliographies 186, 214
 statistics 329, 346
 yearbooks 186, 214
Africa south of the Sahara 186, 214
Africa who's who 148
African book publishing record 434, 436

Index

African books in print 434, 436
African year book and who's who 214
Agence Europe 551, 561b58
AGRICOLA data-base 615
Agricultural history review 391, 416b9
Agricultural index 236
agriculture
  atlases 281
  local studies 391
  periodicals 230, 236
Akenfield, no index 668
ALA glossary of library terms 165, 194b5, 219, 243b1
ALA portrait index 161
ALA cataloguing rules 1949 462
Albania, national bibliographies 436
Alden, J. 490
Alderson, Valerie 655, 673b16
Aldis, H. G. 477, 484
Algeria, national bibliographies 436
Alinari 575
Allen, C. G. 71
Allen, D. 530b15
Allen, P. E. 199
Allgemeine deutsche Biographie 142, 158
Allgemeines Lexikon der Bildenden Künstler... 150
Allison, A. F. 473
Allott, A. M. 192
Almanach de Gotha 155
almanacs 210–2
alphabetical indexes 660, 662–3
alphabetization systems 3, 14–15, 56, 662–3
  early use 51
  in encyclopaedias 76, 112–3
Alsted, Johann Heinrich 76
Alston, R. C. 499b2, 500b5
'alternative press' 238
Alumni Cantabrigiensis 156

Alumni Oxoniensis 156
Alvey, J. 75b
Amateur historian 416b13
America
  biographical dictionaires 142, 143, 144, 147, 151, 160
  encyclopaedias of 113
  national bibliographies 450
  retrospective bibliographies 488–92
  statistics 329
American bibliography 488–9, 491
American catalogue of books 491
American Chemical Society 589
American diaries 160–1
American dictionaries 57, 62
  of slang 67
  of synonyms 68
American dictionary of the English language 52
American Geographical Society 271, 272
American heritage dictionary of the English language 62, 63
American history, encyclopaedias 113
American junior colleges 183
American Library Association 17
American library directory 186
American library resources 513
American literature, bibliographies 224–5
American magazine 221
American medical directory 184
American men and women of science 151–2
American National Standards Institute 260–1
American Reference Books Annual 22b
American Society of Indexers 669, 672
American Society for Information Science 250

Index

American statistics index 332, 370b34
American universities and colleges 183
Americana annual 90, **209–10**
Analytical bibliography of universal collected biography 158
Anatomical Society 658
Anbar abstracting service 240
Anderson, D. 531b31
Anderson, I. G. 194b6
Anderson, J. 419b70
Anderson, J. P. 392
Anderson, Margaret D. 675b
  1983 Carey Award 672
  1975 Wheatley Medal 671
Anderson, Michael 347, 375b113
Anglo-American cataloguing rules see AACR2
Annales de démographie historique 345, 374b106
Annan report on broadcasting 218
annotation in subject bibliographies 507, 523
Annuaire de la noblesse de France 155
Annuaire de la presse et de la publicité 216
Annual abstract of statistics 305, 334, 358, 361, 371b42
Annual bibliography of British and Irish history 391, 416b11, 506
Annual bibliography of English language and literature 236–7
Annual catalogues of government publications 307–8
Annual obituary 145
Annual register **209**
  obituaries 145, 158, 209
Annual retail enquiry 362
annual reviews 208–10
Annual review of chief constables' reports 344, 374b98
annuals (*see also* directories) 26

as directories 166
bibliographies of 192
international 212
anonymous works
  bibliographies 485–6
  in French 497–8
ANSI standards 260–1
Antiquaries' journal 391, 416b12, 514
Antiques index 238
antonyms 68
Appel, Marsha 577
Appleton's cyclopaedia of American biography 143
Applied science and technology index 236
Approaches to local history 387
Arab directory 173
Arab report and record 207
Arab world
  biographical dictionaries of 148
  directories of 173
  national bibliographies 436
  news digests 207
  regional bibliographies 429
  telephone directories 169
  union lists of periodicals 232
Archaeological atlas of the world 282
archaeology
  atlases 282
  bibliographies 395
  dictionaries 77
  indexes 516
  role in local studies 415–6
Architectural periodicals index 514, 517
architecture
  bibliographies 509, 524, 574
  glossaries of 571
  illustrations 575
  Victorian 569
archives 162, 398–401, 403
Archives and local history 400
Ardern, Richard 340, 373b83

Index

area biographical dictionaries 140–6
Argentina
　directories of 173
　national bibliographies 437
aristocracy, biographical dictionaries 155
Arlis 573, 575, 584
Arlott, John 506
Arnold, D. 130
Arnstein, Joel 573
Arntzen, E. 527, 531b28
arrangement (*see also* alphabetization systems) of biographical reference works 134–5, 142
　of encyclopaedias 81–2, 112–3
　of indexes 654, 660, 662
　of quotations 72
　of reference material 14–15, 112–3
　of telephone directories 169–70
art and artists
　bibliographies 511–2
　biographical dictionaries of 150, 151, 156
　dictionaries of 65
　directories 183
　encyclopaedias of 111, 115, 118, 572
　indexes to 162, 236
　reproductions of 83
Art bibliographies modern 332b33
art galleries
　bibliographies 574
　catalogues 161
　yearbooks 186
Art index 162, 236, 527
Art libraries journal 529, 586b11, 587b20, 23, 24
Arts documentation monthly 515
Arts library review 522
Ash, B. 154
Asia (see also names of individual countries)
　directories 193
　news digests 207
　statistics 329, 346
　union lists of periodicals 232
Asia research bulletin 207
Asian recorder 207
ASIS 250
Aslib 186–7
　Audiovisual group 584
　Directory 187
　Directory of information sources 513
　Index to theses 254, 519
　Information 522
　list of translators 45
　Online bibliographic databases 517
ASPP 584
assessment *see* evaluation
Association française de normalisation 260
Aston, M. 45, 419b73
Atkin's encyclopaedia of court forms. . . 126
Atherton, Pauline 667, 675b36
Atlantic internazionale 289
Atlantes Neerlandici 283–4
Atlas général Larousse 81
Atlas of ancient, mediaeval and modern history 282
Atlas of historic towns 283
Atlas of the environment 280
Atlas of the seas around the British Isles 281
atlases (*see also* maps) 276–83
　bibliographies of 270–2, 274
　historical 282–3
　of agriculture 281
　reviews of 278
　road atlases 277, 282
　selection of 276–8
Aüchterbrie, P. 232
auctioneers, directories of 180
Audiovisual librarian 587b20
Auger, C. P. 67, 266b

Index

Austen, Jane
  eight indexes to *Letters to her sister* 660
Australasia (*see also* names of individual countries)
  directories 186, 193
  statistics 329
  yearbooks 214
Australia
  biographical dictionaries 142, 147
  CIP programme 430
  libraries 513
  national bibliographies 437
  Nobel Prize winners 147
  statistics 348
  yearbooks 215
Australian dictionary of biography 142
Australian Society of Indexers 669
Austria
  biographical dictionaries 147
  incunabula 466
  national bibliographies 437
Author index to selected British 'little magazines' 238
authority of reference material 12–13
  biographical reference works 134
  dictionaries 57
  of abstracts journals 18
  of encyclopaedias 78
  of periodicals 18
authors
  biographical dictionaries 149, 152, 153–4
  rights in theses 246, 254
autobiographies, bibliographies 160–1
autographs 145
automatic musical instruments, encyclopaedias 109
Ayer directory of publications 216, 227, 289

Bachman, A. 113
Bacon, Roger 210
Bagley, J. J. 419b
Bailey, Nathaniel 51
Baker, E. A. 507, 525
Bakewell, K. G. B. 668, 674b23, 675b38
Balachandran, M. 333, 371b41
Baldwin, J. M. 117
Bangladesh, national bibliographies 437
bank
  reviews 224
  directories 180
Bank, H. 265
Bank of England *Quarterly bulletin* 361, 380b200
Banker, The 180
banking, encyclopaedias 127
BAPLA 583
Bar list of the United Kingdom 152–3, 184
Barbados, national bibliographies 437
Barley, M. W. 413, 582
Baron, G. 531b29
Barrow, J. G. 523
Bartholomew gazetteer of Britain 288
Bartholomew's *national map* series 276
Bartlett, J. 72
Basic business directories 192
Basic statistics 360, 379b184
Basic stock for the reference library 526
Bateson, F. W. 500b9
Batty, L. 238
Bawden, L.-A. 119
BBC (*see also* CEEFAX)
  Hulton Picture Library 582
  Monitoring service 197–8
Beckett, J. V. 418b38
Beeching, C. L. 146
Beletskaya, Z. G. 234, 244b21

Index

Belfast, directories 168
Belgium
  gazetteers 288
  incunabula 466
  national bibliographies 437
Bell, David 340, 373b78
Bell & Howell
  indexing centre 204, 208
  microfilm company 201
  ORBIT 208
Bendig, Mark W. 103b11
Benet, W. R. 118
Bénézit, E. 150, 163b10, 572
Bénin, national bibliographies 438
Benn's hardware directory 180
Benn's press directory **215-6**, 224, 227
Benson, J. 46b
Benton, Mildred 187
Berman, L. 384b
Berkshire, biographical dictionaries 149
Berliner-Stadtadressbuch 168
Bernstein, T. M. 69
Best books 506
Besterman, T. 521, 533b
Besterman medal 331, 522
Bettman portable archive 569
Beveridge report on broadcasting 218
Bextel 634, 643
BGN 288
Bible
  concordances 73, 515, 655
  encyclopaedias 118, 128
  quotations 72
Bibliographer's manual of English literature 477
Bibliographic index 236, **522**
Bibliographic services throughout the world 435, 452b11
bibliographical guides 132, 157-60, 509-10
bibliographical indexes 238

Bibliographical Retrieval Services 152
Bibliographical Society 522
Bibliographie du Québec 429
bibliographies 423-533
  annotation in 507, 523
  American publications 488-9
  atlases 270-2, 283-6
  biography 157-60
  books in series 519
  comprehensiveness in 510, 524
  coverage 427-9
  currency 431-2
  definition of 423-4
  evaluation of 522-5
  forms of 432
  frequency 430-1
  illustrations 576-8
  in-print services 434-5
  indexes to 661
  government publications 312-20
  local studies 391-6
  maps 284-6
  periodicals 18-19, 226-30
  reference materials 15
  statistics 337
Bibliography, documentation, terminology 522
Bibliography of bibliographies in religion 523
Bibliography of British and Irish municipal history **394-5**, 523
Bibliography of British literary bibliographies 501b, 521
Bibliography of British municipal history 394
Bibliography of historical works 396
Bibliography of index numbers 345, 374b107
Bibliography of medical reviews 237
Bibliography of museum and art gallery publications 574
Bibliotheca Americana 490, 491

Index

Bibliotheca Britannica 477, 530b3
Bibliothèque Nationale, Paris
  Catalogue des incunables 467
  Catalogue général 459–60, 493
  periodicals 231
Bilboul, R. 254
bilingual dictionaries 69–71
bills, legislative 301–2
binding of periodicals 7, 17
Binns, Kathleen 655, 673b14
bio-bibliography 159, 508
Biochemical title index 242
Biographical books 159
biographical dictionaries 135–57
  accuracy 133, 134
  conflicting information in 9–10
  evaluation of 14, 133–5
  indexes to 159
  national or area 140–9
  obsolescence of 4
  specialized 149–56
  universal 136–40
Biographical dictionaries 162–3
Biographical dictionaries master index 159
Biographical dictionary of eminent Scotsmen 143
biographical enquiries 9–10
  reference interview 132–3
  sources of information 121, 410
Biographical memoirs of the Fellows of the Royal Society 156
biographical reference works 131–64
  arrangement of 134–5
  evaluation of 14, 133–5
  for local studies 410
Biographie universelle, ancienne et moderne 136
biography
  bibliographies of 157–60
  definition of 131
  dictionaries of 135–57
  illustrations 569–70

periodicals 157, 161
Biography 157
Biography and genealogy master index 159
Biography almanac 158
Biography index 161–2, 236
Biological abstracts 242, 615
Biological and agricultural index 236
biology
  abstracts 242, 615
  dictionaries 128
  encyclopaedias 124, 128
  periodicals 236
Biosis data-base 41, 608
  charges 615
BIROS 616
Birchfield, Mary E. 542, 558b20
Birmingham, statistics 336, 372b64
Birmingham Post year book 149
Birmingham Public Libraries 342, 343, 374b92, 527
Birth statistics 362, 381b215
Bishop, W. W. 471
BLAISE 41, 481, 595–6, 618, 620
  charges 615
  command language 608
  filing rules 663, 674b35
Blake, Doreen 657–8, 674b26
  1968 Wheatley Medal 658, 671
Blanck, J. 492
Bland, David 585b4, 587b22
block-printed books 8
Blodgett, Richard 585b3
Bloomfield, B. C. 238
blue books 307, 406
Blythe, Ronald 668
Board on geographic names 288
Boase, Frederic 143, 410, 419b59
Bodleian Library, Oxford 8, 367, 470, 478, 482
  Catalogue of English newspapers 231
  newspapers in 200

Index

Selected map and book accessions 271
Bolivia, national bibliographies 438
Bol'shaya sovetskaya entsiklopediya 80, 84, 101–2
  Communist viewpoint 80
Bond, M. F. 405
Bonser, W. A. 417b24–5
Book of British topography 392
Book review index 532b33
Book review digest 236
book trade 455
  bibliographies 423, 424
  in-print services 434–5
books
  cost of 6
  limitations for information work 4
Books in English 432, 451
Books in print 423, 435, **450**, 504, 506
books in series, bibliographies 519
BOOKS data-base 667
booksellers 455, 471, 474, 477
  American 489
Booksellers in India . . . 166
Boolean logic 604
Borchardt, D. H. 519
Boston globe 208
Boswell, James 508
botanical literature
  bibliographies 511
  illustration 572
Botswana, national bibliographies 438
Bottin de la région parisienne 168
Bottin Europe 172
Bottin international 172
Bourne, Ross 223, 244b10
Bowens, Q. D. 109
Bowker & Co. 159, 186, 227, 434, 504
Boyce, B. R. 616, 620b3
Boyce, George 218
Boylan H. 143

Bradfield, Valerie J. 509
Bradford, Andrew 221
Bradley, Philip 674b21
Bradshaw, David N. 581
Bradshaw, M. 156
Bragg, Melvyn 668
brand names 180–1
Brand names of Japan 181
Brays's Exeter street directory 168
Brazil
  CIP programme 430
  directories 173
  encyclopaedias 101
  national bibliographies 438
Brenni, Vito J. 586b4
Breviate of parliamentary papers 313
Brewer, Annie M. 74, 87, 103b7, 104b158
Brewer, E. C. 67
Brewer's dictionary of phrase and fable 67
Brewer's reader's handbook 127
Briggs, Katharine 156
Bristol, R. P. 488–9
Bristol Public Libraries 505
Britain: an official handbook 214, 306
Britain in figures 362, 381b210
Britain's black population 350, 375b138
Britannica atlas 81
Britannica book of the year 86, 88, **209–10**
Britannica junior encyclopaedia 93
British and Irish library resources 513
British Association of Picture Libraries and Agencies 583
British autobiographies 161
British book news 17
British books in print 435, 449, 506
British broadcasting 1922–1982 218
British Broadcasting Corporation *see* BBC

685

Index

British business 187, 306, 362, 364, 377b157, 381b222, 384b, 549, 560b51
British diaries 160
British economy 344, 348, 374b102
British education index 236, 517, 527, 532b33
British government publications 314
British humanities index 162, 201, **236**, 516
British Information Services 206–7
British Institute of Management 224
British labour statistics 348, 365, 375b120, 383b237
British Library. Bibliographic Services Division 236
British Library. Lending Division 230, 520, 522
    BLLD announcement bulletin 252
    British reports **252**, 343, 374b96
    Conference index 257
    Current British journals 228
    Current serials received 226
    Gift and Exchange Section 27
    Journals in translation 229
    periodicals retention policies 236
    photocopies provision 230
    Research in British universities 520
    subject bibliographies in 522
    theses 254
British Library. Library Association Library 8
    catalogue 219, 531b18
British Library. Map Library 411
    Catalogue of printed maps 271, 284
British Library. Newspaper Library 8, 199, 457
    Catalogue 199, **404**
British Library. Official Publications Library 317
British Library. Reference Division 8, 199, 367, 457, 482, 517, 519
    Alerting services covering EC documentation 551, 561b57
    Burney collection 200
    English places 392, 416b16
    Serials 231
British Library. Science Reference Library 8–9
    Abstracting and indexing periodicals 230
    House journals 224
    Periodicals on agriculture 230
British library history 524
British library news 310
British Museum. Department of Manuscripts 8, 290
British Museum. Department of Printed Books
    Books printed in France 493, 496
    Books printed in the fifteenth century 465
    Early printed books 465
    General catalogue of printed books 27, 104, 160, 230, **456–9**, 470, 478
    Subject index of modern books acquired 160, 504
    Thomason catalogue 476
British national archives 398
British national bibliography 194, 307, 342, 374b95, **450**, 503, 514
British rate and data 216, 227
British reports, translations and theses **252**, 343, 374b96
British Standards Institution
    Abbreviations of titles of periodicals (BS 4148) 227, 244b13
    Alphabetical arrangement (BS 1749) 662–3, 674b34
    BSI news 259

Index

Glossary of documentation terms (BS 5408) 65
Glossary of terms relating to work study (BS 3138) 54
Maps and charts 293b
Preparation of indexes (BS 3700:1964) 657, 659, 674b25; (BS 3700:1976) 654, 655, 662, 670, 673b10, 674b31, 675b
Sales bulletin 259
Yearbook 259
British technology index 236, 516
British Telecom 598–9 (*see also* PRESTEL)
  Facsimile Directory 21
  telephone directories 169–70
  telex directories 170–1
British union catalogue of periodicals 231
broadcasting
  Annan report on 218
  Beveridge report on 218
  reference materials 197–8, 208
Brockhaus Enzyklopädie 81, **95**
'broken order' 3
Brown C. D. 245b
Brown, James Duff 528, 531b32
browsability effect 43
Brunei, national bibliographies 433
Brunet, G. 463, 497
Brunet, J. C. **463**, 493, 504, 530b3
Brunskill, R. W. 419b
Brussels Tariff Nomenclature 352, 353, 377b156
Bryan's dictionary of painters... 150
Buch der Köpfe 585b1
Buckley, K. A. 420b
Builder 403, 418b42
building, dictionaries 129
buildings 416
Building Societies Association 344, 374b100–1
Bulgaria, national bibliographies 438

Bulletin of labour statistics 360
Bullock, A. 128
Bureau d'adresse 220
Burger, K. 464
Burgess, G. M. 244b19
Burke's peerage 133, **155**
Burke's Royal families of the world 155
Burkett, J. 420
Business data packages 357, 378b177
Business monitors 305, 362, 365, 381b218, 383b242
Business periodicals index 236
business publications
  business information 208
  in loose-leaf form 190–1
  indexes 236, 338, 517–8
  periodicals lists 238
  statistics 305, 343
Business statistics index 338, 372b71
Business Statistics Office 305, 348
  Historical record 375b124
businesses, directories of 172–7, 187, 192
Butcher, David 322b
Butcher, Judith 531b26, 587
Butler, Alban 149

CABLIS 520
cadastral plans 274
California, biographical dictionaries 149
Cambridge
  Alumni Cantabrigiensis 156
  libraries in 468
  University Library 8, 367, 478, 482, 485
Cameroons, national bibliographies 438
Camp, A. J. 407, 418b51, 420b
Campbell, M. J. 195b
Canada
  atlases of 280

Index

biographical dictionaries 143,
  147–8, 161
CIP programme 430
directories 190
encyclopaedias 87
gazetteers 289
land use maps 275
national bibliographies 438
news digests 207
statistics 332, 348
Canadian diaries and
  autobiographies 161
Canadian oil industry directory
  178
Canadian news facts 207
Canadian who's who 148
CANSIM 356, 378b166
Capital expenditure of county
  councils 362, 380b205
card services
  catalogue 432
  company information 188–9
  news digests 206
  of national bibliographies 432
Cardiff Free Libraries 485
careers, directories 183
Carey, Gordon V. 672
Carey Award 672
Caribbean
  directories 173, 214
  national bibliographies 438
  regional bibliographies 429
  yearbooks 173, 214
Carter, G. A. **390–1**, 416, 420b
cartographic materials *see* atlases;
  charts; maps
cartography 283, 285
Cassell's new Latin-English,
  English-Latin dictionary 70
Castle, Peter 585b3
catalogue card services 432
Catalogue des normes françaises
  260
Catalogue général de la librairie
  française 497

Catalogue of British official
  publications not published by
  HMSO 310, 518
catalogues
  of art galleries 161
  of HMSO publications 307–8,
    555
  of libraries 455
  of museums 161
  of periodicals 18–19
  of postage stamps 129, 571
catalogues, union 18–19, 25,
  231–2, 455
cataloguing 27–8
  of maps 273
cataloguing-in-publication *see* CIP
  programmes
Catholic books 473, 476
Cave, L. C. 420b
Cawdrey, Robert 51, 74b4
CCITT 21, 627
CEEFAX 20, 197, 624fig.1, 625,
  630, 640–1
Celebrity bulletin 157
Celoria, F. 420b
Census and the social structure
  409, 418b56
Census atlas of South Yorkshire
  281
Census of British newspapers 200
census reports 334–6
  as local studies sources 408–9
  Guide to census reports 335, 409
Central Statistical Office 305, 330,
  356
  Annual abstract of statistics 305,
    334, 358, 361, 371b42
  Facts in focus 361, 380b194
  Government statistics 305, 331,
    370b23
  Guide to official statistics 305,
    331, 334, 338, 342, 370b22
  National accounts statistics 353,
    377b156, 378b161
  National income 361, 380b198

Index

Regional accounts 334, 371b43
Regional trends 334, 361,
    371b44
Social trends 305, 350, 361,
    380b197
Standard industrial classification
    351, 352, 376b141–3,
    377b151–5
Statistical news 332, 341, 348,
    356, 364, 370b29–33, 373b86–
    7, 375b127–8, 378b165, b167
United Kingdom in figures, 361,
    380b193
Ceylon *see* Sri Lanka
chairmen of committees indexes
    313–14
Challinor, John 507
Chalmers, Alexander 136
Chambers, Ephraim 77
Chambers, R. 143
Chambers' biographical dictionary
    132, 135, **137**
*Chambers' children's colour
    dictionary* 63
*Chambers' dictionary of science
    and technology* 65
Chambers' encyclopaedia 10, 81,
    88, **91**
Chambers of commerce
    membership lists 168
    statistics 343
Chambers' technical dictionary 65
*Chambers' twentieth century
    dictionary* 63, 64
Chandler, G. 234, 244b20
Chapman, Agatha L. 348, 375b122
charges for on-line retrieval 357,
    645–6
Charities digest 182
Chartist movement 510–11
Chartered Institute of Public
    Finance 336, 362, 363,
    372b58–60, 380b204, 382b229
charts 19, 275–6
    Admiralty 276

aeronautical 275
bibliographies of 276
value in reference work 19
*Check list of British official serial
    publications* 228
Checklist of painters 574
Cheffins, R. H. A. 428, 452b3
Cheltenham, biographical
    dictionaries 149
CHEMCON 594, 603
Chemfacts 179
Chemical abstracts **241**, 264, 589,
    591, 594, 603, 615
Chemical company profiles 179
Chemical Industries Association
    362, 381b219
chemical industry
    directories 179
    indexes 127
    statistics 362
    synonyms and trade names 180
Chemical market abstracts 241
*Chemical synonyms and trade
    names* 180
Chemical titles 241, 589
Chemical week buyers' guide 180
chemistry
    dictionary 180
    encyclopaedias 125
Chemistry of carbon compounds
    658
CHEMLINE 595
Cheney, C. R. 402, 418b40
Cheney, F. N. 22b
Cherns, J. J. 321b, 322b, 538
Cheshire, newspapers 405
Chetam's Library, Manchester
    200
Chicago University Library 132,
    461
Child, M. 420b
Children's Britannica 79, 85, **93**
children's literature
    biographical dictionaries 154
    fictional characters 157

Index

children's reference books 79, 85
  biographical dictionaries 138, 157
  dictionaries 60, 63
  encyclopaedias 92–4
  indexes to 655
  Thorndike dictionaries 59
Chicago Sun-Times 204
China (People's Republic)
  national bibliographies 439
  yearbooks 215
  (Taiwan) national bibliographies 448
China yearbook 215
Chinn, M. 340, 373b79
Chitty, G. M. 266b
Choice, 17
Christian Economic and Social Research Foundation 344, 374b98
Christian names, dictionaries 67
Christian science monitor 204, 208
Christianity, encyclopaedias 120
Christie, R. C. 163b7
Chronolog 357, 378b181
Chronology of the medieval world 114
Chubb, Thomas 284, 411, 412
Chumas, S. J. 259
Church of England, biographical dictionaries 152
cinema, encyclopaedias 119
Cioranescu, A. 498–9
CIP programmes 413, 430–1, 537
Cirlot, J. E. 572
citations
  abbreviations of 227
  indexing of 517, 661
  practice 525
Citiservice 631, 641
Civil Aviation Authority 363, 382b226
civil service, directories of 187
Civil Service year book 187

CLAIMS data-base 615
Clancy, T. H. 476
Clapp, Jane 578
Clarence, R. 129
Clason, W. E. 71
classical world
  atlases of 282
  encyclopaedias of 118, 122
  mythology of 156
classification
  Dewey decimal classification 27–8
  in academic libraries 27–8
  of bibliographies 525–6
  of international trade 353
  of reference material 27–8
  of statistics 351–4
  Universal decimal classification 28
Classification for overseas trade statistics 353, 377b159
Classification schemes for statistics 351–4
  publications 376b151–378b163
clergymen, biographical dictionaries 153
Clews, John 434, 452b7
Clifton company guide 191
Climatic atlas of Europe 281
Clinton, A. 414
clothing, directories 180
Clough, E. A. 477, 499b4
Clough, F. F. 129
Clover information index 238, 518
Cobbett, William 508
Coe, B. 585b3
Cole, Dorothy Ethlyn 103b9
Coleman, Alic 275, 292b5
Colindale newspaper library 8, 199, 404, 457
College administration 667
college libraries *see* academic libraries
Collett, R. J. 334, 371b48

Index

Collier's encyclopedia 78, **90**, 91
  bibliography in 82
  Collier's yearbook 90, 210
  index in 84
  maps in 84
  price of 87
  revision policy 86, 88
Collingridge encyclopedia of gardening 125
Collins, Maria 366, 383b245
Collins English dictionary 63, 64
Collison, Robert L.
  Bibliographic services 452b6, 453b12
  Bibliographies 532b
  Dictionaries 74
  Encyclopaedia of librarianship 2, 22b2
  Encyclopaedias 103b
  Indexes and indexing 655, 673b12, 675b
  Library assistance to readers 165, 194b1
Colombia, national bibliographies 439
Columbia Lippincott gazetteer of the world 287
COM 20, 27, 549–50
Coman, E. T. 165, 194b2
command papers 298, 300–1, 307–8
command sets (on-line retrieval) 607–10
Commission for Racial Equality 350, 375b139
Committee on Scientific and Technical Information 249
committees, reports of 304–5
Commodity trade statistics 358 379b175
Common market telephone directory 170
Common nomenclature of industrial products 351, 377b146

Commonwealth
  biographical dictionaries 148, 160
  national bibliographies 435
  yearbook 214, 306
Commonwealth Agricultural Bureau 242
Commonwealth Institute 508
Commonwealth national bibliographies 194
Commonwealth specialist periodicals 228
Commonwealth universities year book 182
communication charges (on-line retrieval) 614–5
communication systems, on-line 596–9
companies
  card services 188–9
  directories 172–7, 188, 193
  information on Ireland 190
  value of microfiche for 188–9
Companies Registration Office 188–9
Directory of companies 188
Compendex 41, 237
Compendium of building society statistics 344, 374b100–1
Comprehensive dissertation index 255, 532b33
comprehensiveness
  in bibliographies 510, 524
  in biographical works 134
  in dictionaries 58–9
  in encyclopaedias 109
  in indexes 661
  of reference material 11, 13
Compton's encyclopedia 84
  index in 84
Compuserve 63
Computer and control abstracts 241
Computer Output Microfilm *see* COM

Index

computer science
  encyclopaedias of 123
Concise building encyclopaedia 129
Concise dictionary of American biography 142
Concise dictionary of Irish biography 143
Concise dictionary of national biography 141
Concise Oxford dictionary 63, 64
Concise Oxford dictionary of English place-names 67, **410**
Concordance to the Old and New Testaments **73**, 655
concordances 51, 73, 515
  of the Bible 72–3, 515, 655
Condensed chemical dictionary 180
conferences 246, 255–8, 265, 519
conflicting information 9–10
Congressional publications 319–20
Considine, D. M. 108
Consultative Committee for Telephony 21, 627
Consumer price indices 347, 375b114
Consumers' Association
  Library guide 340
  Which? 40
Consumers' index to product evaluation 238
Contemporary authors 153
Contemporary dramatists 153
Contemporary novelists 153
Contemporary poets 153
contents lists of journals 239
continuous revision of encyclopaedias 17, 78, 86
Control abstracts 241
Controllers library collection of HMSO publications 314
Cook, Sir Edward 659
Cook, T. G. 420b
Cook, Thomas, 351, 376b149
Cooper, J. 491
Cooper, J. C. 573

Copeman, H. 339, 373b76
Co-operative statistics 362, 382b224
Copinger, W. A. 464
copyright 7, 147, 457, 481, 576, **582–3**
  in US 461, 583
  Reform of the law 306–7
  Whitford report on 300, 307
Copyright Act 1911 7
  infringement of 147, 570
Copyright business and internal use 273
copyright libraries 7–8, 424
  reference material in 7
Corbett, E. V. 586b13
Corkhill, T. 129
Corns, A. R. 392, 417b17
Cornwall, J. 417b35
COSATI 249
cost-effectiveness of reference material 12, 15
Costa Rica, national bibliographies 439
costs
  of encyclopaedias 87
  of on-line searches 592, 613–6
  of periodicals 18
Coulson, Anthony J. 574, 580, 586b14
Council for British Archaeology 395, 417b26
Council for Mutual Economic Assistance 360, 379b186
Council of Europe 214
Councils, committees and boards 187
County atlases of the British Isles **284**, 412
County magazine index 238
county maps 412
Courtauld Institute of Art 574, 575, 582
Couprie, L. D. 587b24
coverage *see* comprehensiveness

Index

Cowley, J. D. 529, 532b37
Crafts Advisory Council 420b
Crane, R. S. 200
Cranfield, G. A. 200
cricket
  bibliography 506, 524
  directories 166
Crockford's clerical directory **152–3**, 184
Crone, J. S. 143
CRONOS data-base 357, 378b178
Cross, F. L. 120–1
cross-references
  in biographical works 135
  in dictionaries 57
  in indexes 663
  in reference material 14
  in subject encyclopaedias 116
Crossman, R. H. 652, 673b3
crossword dictionaries 50, 68
Crouch, W. W. 46b
Cruden, Alexander **72–3**, 515, 655
Cuba, national bibliographies 439
Cumberland and Westmorland
  local studies 393
Cumulated fiction index 520, 530b14
Cumulative book index 423, **433**, 450, 492, 503, 514
cumulative indexes 18, 657
Current African directories 193
current awareness bulletins 44, 233
Current book review citations 236
Current biography 133, **139–40**, 157
Current British directories 165, 192, 194b6
Current British journals 228
Current contents 239
Current European directories 193
Current geographical publications 271
current information 196–218
Current technology index 40, 42, 43, 236, 516

Current serials received 226
Currer-Briggs, N. 407, 420b
Curtice's index to 'The Times' 202
Curtin, J. V. 334, 371b50
Customs and Excise 353, 354, 377b159–60, 378b163
Customs Co-operative Council 351, 352, 353, 377b145, 377b147
Cybulski, R. 452b4
Cyclopaedia; or, An universal dictionary 77
Cyprus, national bibliographies 439
Cyriax, George 340, 373b81
Czechoslovakia
  national bibliographies 439

Dailey, L. 194b3
Daily Express 200
Daily list of government publications 307–8
Daily Mail year book 212
Daily Mirror 200
Daily Telegraph 198–9
  index to 203
  on microfilm 200
Dale, J. H. Van 64
Dán, Róbert 238
Dance to the music of time
  index 656, 674b22
Dangerous estate 218
Daniells, L. M. 195
Danton, J. P. 519
Darby, H. C. 290
Data archive bulletin 336, 372b56
data banks (news services) 197–8, 207–8
data-base producers (on-line services)
  charges 302–3, 615–6
Data Courier Inc. 592
Data-Star 598, 615, 620
Database 621b

693

Index

Databases in Europe 357, 378b180
Datastream International 379b184A
dates and dating
　in local studies material 402
　of houses 401
Davinson, D. 47b, 219, 243b5, 244b 266b
Dawson's guide to the press of the world 216
de Beer, E. S. 658, 674b28
　index to Evelyn's diaries 658–9
de Dillmont, T. 109
Deadline data on world affairs 205–6, 208
Debrett's handbook 155
Debrett's peerage and baronetage 133, 155
defence specifications 212
Demographic yearbook 11, 347, 360, 375b110, 379b179
　code of reliability 11
demography 279, 347
Demystifying social statistics 350, 375b135
Denmark
　biographical dictionaries 148
　national bibliographies 439
Department of Education 363, 366, 382b230, b233, b236, 514
Department of Education for Northern Ireland 363, 382b232
Department of Employment 339, 362
　British labour statistics 348, 375b120; *Yearbook* 365, 383b237
　Family expenditure 339, 362, 372b75, 380b206
　Improving manpower information 345, 374b103
　New earnings 362, 381b214
　Time rate of wages 365, 383b239

Department of Health and Social Security
　Health and personal . . . 362, 380b208
　Korner report 341, 373b85
　Social security statistics 362, 381b211
Department of Industry, Business Statistics Office 305
Department of the Environment 280, 362, 365, 380b203, 383b240–41
Department of Trade and Industry 328, 332, 342, 369b–9, 370b37, 371b38–9, 381b218, 382b223
Department of Transport 363, 382b227–8
Derwent patents services 264, 595
design, bibliography 574
Detroit News 204
Deutsche Bibliographie 441
　CIP programme 430–1
Deutsches Institut für Normung 258, 260
　Katalog für technische Regeln 260
　Mitteilungen 260
Deutsches Wörterbuch 62
Devers, C. M. 233
Developments in adhesives 225
Dewdney, John C. 384b
Dewey decimal classification 27–8
DIALNET 614
DIALOG 41, 152, 208, 227, 241, 357, 593, 594, 598, 616, 618, 620
　command language 608–9
　charges 614, 615
DIALTECH 595, 632, 642
diaries 160–1
　indexes to 658–9
Diary of John Evelyn 658–9
Diary of Samuel Pepys 659
Dibben, A. 417b35

Index

dictionaries 18, 49–75
  abbreviations 67
  art 65
  as encyclopaedias 18, 53, 58
  as quick reference works 53
  bilingual 69–71
  crossword 68
  definition of 49–50
  development of 51–2
  evaluation of 18, 57–60
  place names 67, 410
  quotations 51
  scope of 51–1
  uses 52
Dictionaries: an independent consumer survey 74
Dictionaries, encyclopedias . . . 74, 87, 103b7
Dictionaries of English and foreign languages 74
Dictionary and encyclopaedia of paper 128
Dictionary buying guide 74
Dictionary of African biography 144
Dictionary of American biography 135, 142, 157
Dictionary of American English 62
Dictionary of American slang 67
Dictionary of art terms 65
Dictionary of banking 127
Dictionary of biographical reference 158
Dictionary of books relating to America . . . 488–9
Dictionary of British portraits 574
Dictionary of Canadian biography 143
Dictionary of English furniture 127
Dictionary of eponyms 146
Dictionary of fairies . . . 156
Dictionary of fictional characters 156
Dictionary of gardening 128
Dictionary of historical slang 67
Dictionary of hymnology 127
Dictionary of Irish biography 143
Dictionary of land surveyors 285
Dictionary of modern English usage 68
Dictionary of national biography 42, **141**, 158, 410, 418b58
Dictionary of philosophy and psychology 117
Dictionary of report series codes 252–3
Dictionary of Scandinavian biography 148
Dictionary of scientific biography 150–1
Dictionary of slang 67
Dictionary of the biological sciences 128
Dictionary of the English language 51, 75b3
Dictionary of the social sciences 66
Dictionary of universal biography . . . 158
Dictionary of visual language 571
Dictionary of Welsh biography . . . 143
Dictionnaire critique et documentaire des peintres . . . 150, 163b10
Dictionnaire de biographie française 142
Dictionnaire moderne géographique . . . 288
Diderot, D. 77, 80
Dietrich (IBZ) 235
Digest of environmental pollution 365, 383b240–1
digests, news 205–7
Dimitrov, Theodore 535, 537, 557b3, b4
DIN standards 258, 260
directories
  bibliographies of 192–4
  currency of 166–7
  definition of 165–6

Index

evaluation of 9–20
exploitation of 165
for local studies 406–7
general business 171–7
non-trade 182–3
of companies 188–92
of organizations 185–8
of periodicals 18–19
of trade names 180–1
professional 183–5
selection policies 179
telephone 169–70
telex 170–1
topographical 167–9
trades 177–80
directors, directories 176, 193
Directory of British associations 185, 652
Directory of British official publications 310, 518
Directory of business and financial services 191
Directory of chemical producers 179
Directory of directors 176, 193
Directory of engineering . . . 252, 258
Directory of European associations 185
Directory of Federal statistics 338, 372, 668
Directory of grant making trusts 182
Directory of international standards for statistics 326, 368b1
Directory of international statistics 326, 337, 356, 368b2
Directory of online databases 591, 619b1
Directory of published proceedings 257
Directory of review serials in science and technology 229

Directory of scientific directories 193
Directory of shipowners, shipbuilders and marine engineers 179
Directory of special libraries and information centres 186
Directory of United Nations information systems 542, 558b19
Directory of United States standardization activities 259
disasters 211
discographies 129, 520
Discovering local history 388, 416b6
Discovering your family history 407–8
display terminals 596–9
Disraeli, Benjamin, on statistics 11
Dissertation abstracts 255
Dissertation abstracts international 254, 519
dissertations *see* theses
distribution maps 268
Dix, E. R. M. 477
Dizionario biografico degli italiani 142
Dr. Williams's library bulletin 512
doctors, directories 134, 153, 184
documentation *see* librarianship
Documentation of the UN system 434, 452b7
Dod's parliamentary companion 154
Domesday book 166
Domesday gazetteer 290
donations 27
Dorling, A. R. 509
Dorset 291, 393
Douch, R. 393, 417b19
Douglas, G. H. 75b
Dowdeswell, P. 384b
Downs, R. B. 513, 532b
Doyle, B. 154

Index

drama
  bibliographies of 524
  biographical dictionaries 153
Drawings of British plants 572
Dreyfuss, Henry 573
Drubba, H. 266b
drug information searches, cost 616
drugs, encyclopaedias 127
dtv Lexikon 96
Dublin
  directories 168
  early books 477
Duckles, V. 510
Dun & Bradstreet directories 175
Dunning, R. 388, 416b5
Dutch language dictionaries 64
Dymond, D. P. 420b, 586b7

E&MJ international directory of mining 178
Eager, Alan 522
Eakins, Rosemary 581
Early English newspapers 200
Early printed books 465
East Africa, bibliographies 433, 440
East Anglian bibliography 393
East Germany *see* Germany (German Democratic Republic)
Echard, Lawrence 286
Echo 633, 642
Economic abstracts 242
Economic outlook 360, 379b182
Economic progress report 361, 380b196
economic statistics 344–8, 360
  reports 248
Economic surveys 360, 379b81
Economic titles 242
Economic trends 305, 345, 352, 361, 364, 377b156, b158, 380b195
Economist 17, 202, 208

Ecuador, national bibliographies 440
Edel, L. 163b
Eden, Sir John 350, 375b145
Eden, Peter 285, 420b
Edinburgh University Library 470
Edinburgh world atlas 279
Editor and publisher international year book 216
Editorial media and analysis 227
education
  bibliographies of 507, 514
  directories of 182–3
  encyclopaedias of 121
  indexes of 236, 517, 527
  reports 248, 251, 304
  statistics 363, 366
Education index 236
Educational Resources Information Center *see* ERIC
Edwards, P. 117
Egypt, national bibliographies 440
Eighteenth century British books 478–9
Eighteenth century short-title catalogue 479–80
Einbinder, Harvey 89, 94, 103b12
Ekwall, E. 67, 410
Electrical and electronics abstracts 42, 241
Electrical engineering abstracts 241
electronic journal 222
Electronic library 621b
electronics
  dictionaries 128
  reports 248
Ellis, H. J. 290
Ellis, Jessie Croft 577
Ellman, R. 163b
Elsevier's dictionaries 71
Elton, G. R. 391, 416b11, 506, 529
Emmison, F. G. 399, 400, 403, 418b36

Index

Employment gazette 339, 362, 364, 372b73-4, 380b206, 381b212
employment statistics 348
Enciclopedia della spettacolo 112
Enciclopedia italiana 80, 86, **99**
   bibliographies in 82
Enciclopedia universal ilustrada europeo-americana 80, 86, **100**
Encyclopedia Americana 77, 79, 90, 91, 102b1
   Americana annual 90, **209-10**
   paper used in 85
   price of 87
   revision policy 86, 88
Encyclopaedia Britannica 9, 77, 78, 81, **88-90**, 91
   bibliographies in 82
   continuous revision policy 88
   illustration in 83
   maps in 83
   paper used in 85
   price of 87
   Yearbook 86, **209-10**
Encyclopedia Canadiana 87
Encyclopaedia Judaica 112
Encyclopedia of American history 113
Encyclopedia of associations 185, 591
Encyclopedia of automatic musical instruments 109
Encyclopaedia of British Empire postage stamps 129
Encyclopedia of computer science and engineering 123
Encyclopaedia of Ireland 113
Encyclopaedia of Islam 80
   index in 84
Encyclopaedia of librarianship 2, 22b2
Encyclopedia of library and information science 219, 243b6
Encyclopedia of needlework 109
Encyclopedia of oceanography 109
Encyclopaedia of Parliament 118
Encyclopedia of philosophy 117, 121
Encyclopedia of pigeon breeds 109
Encyclopedia of the biological sciences 124, 128
Encyclopaedia of the nations 214
Encyclopedia of the violin 113
Encyclopedia of wines and spirits 109
Encyclopedia of world art 111, 115
Encyclopedia of world history 114
Encyclopaedia universalis 89-90, 94, **97-8**
encyclopaedias 76-130
   accuracy 78, 126-7
   arrangement of 81, 82, 112-14
   as dictionaries 50
   as gazetteers 288
   bibliographies of 104
   continuous revision of 17
   criteria 77-87
   currency 86
   dictionaries 18, 53
   evaluation of 17
   foreign language 94
   future trends in 105-6
   history of 58, 103-4
   indexing of 84, 114-5
   limitations of subject bibliographies in 508
   level 121-6
   use of 119-21
encyclopaedic dictionaries 63, 64, 116, 122, 128, 129
Encyclopedic dictionary of electronics 128
Encyclopaedic dictionary of heraldry 129
Encyclopaedic dictionary of physics 116, **122**, 129
Encyclopedic world dictionary 64
Encyclopédie, L' 77
   ideological slant 77, 80
Encyclopédie de la Pléiade 82, **98**
Encyclopédie française 112

Index

Energy research abstracts 250–1
Engineer 233, 657
engineering 252, 258
 bibliographies 237
 biographical dictionaries 149
 conferences 257
 dictionaries 67
Engineering eponyms 67
Engineering index 42, 237, 264
English catalogue of books . . . 482
English dictionaries 51–2, 60–4,
  67–8
 abbreviations in 67
 slang 67
 subject 64–6
 synonyms and antonyms 18, 68
 usage of 68
English drama, bibliographies 524
English Duden 69
English encyclopaedias 87–94
English language
 bibliographies 236–7
 dictionaries 51, 62, 63, 64
English literature 477
 bibliographies 236
 encyclopaedias 107–8
 periodicals 224–5
English-Name Society 291
English places 392, 416b16
*English translations of German
  standards* 260
enquiries 426–7
 biographical 9, 132–3
 costs of on-line searches 592,
  613–5
 internal indexes 653
 quick reference 3, 119
 reference process of 30–40
 research 34, 38
 using language dictionaries 53
 statistical information 11
 visual 564–5
enquiry work 16, 133
Enser, A. G. S. 520
Entsiklopediya slovar 101

enumerative bibliography
 definition of 454
 methodology 456
environment
 atlases 280
 OECD activities 554
 statistics 365
 UN agency activities 542–4
ephemera 414
eponyms 67
 dictionaries of 146
ERA 250
ERIC data-base 250, 251, 594
 charges 615
 sample search 610
ESA/IRS 594–5, 596, 620
Esdaile, Arundell 294
Essay and general literature index
  158–9, 519
essays, indexes 159
Essex, local studies 388
Essex reference index 238
estate agents, directories 180
estate maps 285
Estates gazette 180
Ethiopia, national bibliographies
  440
Ethnic and racial questions 350,
  376b136
Ethnic minorities in Britain 350,
  376b139
Euro pages: directory of exporters
  170
Euroabstracts 544
EURONET 357, 595–6, 608, 618,
  620
Europa year book 212–3
 World survey 185–6
Europe (*see also* names of
  individual countries)
 atlases 281
 books of 16th century 468
 biographical dictionaries 148,
  151–2
 directories 168–73, 188, 193

Index

companies 172–3
national bibliographies 468, 490, 493–9
newspapers of 217
patents 263–5
statistics 329–30
yearbooks 212–3
European Americana 490
European Communities 544–52
  Basic statistics 360, 379b184
  Directory of the Commission 546, 559b28
  Bulletin 546, 559b36
  Eurostat index 329, 338, 369b19, 550, 560b53
  Eurostat news 329, 369b18
  Eurostatistics 360, 379b185
  grants and loans 549, 560b48, b49
  Guide 330, 369b21
  How to find out 329, 369b20
  Publications 329, 369b17, 540
  reports 546, 549, 559b332–5
  Who's who 546, 559b29
  Yearbook 546, 559b29
European companies 188, 191, 192
European digest 551, 561b61
European Documentation Centre 550, 560b54–6
European historical statistics 347, 375b112
European index of management periodicals 239
European Information Service 551, 561b59
European parliament 547, 560b38–41
European trade associations statistics 341, 344, 373b90
European yearbook 214
Eurostat index 329, 338, 369b19, 550, 560b53
Eurostat news 329, 369b18
Eurostatistics 360, 379b185
Eusidic database guide 517

evaluation
  of abstracts journals 18
  of bibliographies 522–5
  of biographical dictionaries 14, 133–5
  of dictionaries 18, 57
  of directories 19–20
  of encyclopaedias 17
  of indexes 653
  of newspapers 19
  of periodicals 18
  of reference materials 11–20
Evans, C. 488–9
Evans, E. J. 418b37
Evans, Harold 587b21
Evans, Hilary 581, 587b19, b22
Evelyn, John, index to diaries 659
Everitt, A. 385, 416b2
Everyman's dictionary of abbreviations 67
Everyman's encyclopaedia 78, 81, 85, **91–2**
  atlas 81, 83
  maps in 83
  production costs of 87
  size of 85
Examples illustrating AACR2 654, 673b11
exhibitors, lists of 155–6
Explanatory notes to the Brussels nomenclature 352, 377b147
Explanatory notes to the customs tariff 352, 377b148
Export magazine 194
exporters, directories of 170
Extel British company information service 189–90

F&S indexes 237–8
Facsimile directory 21
facsimile transmission 21, 222, 585
Fact finder for the nation 338, 372b69
FACtS card service 190
Facts, files and action 217

700

Index

Facts in focus 361, 380b194
Facts on file 43, **205–6**
  yearbook 210
Faculty of Advocates, Edinburgh Library 469
Fairbairn, R. E. 658
Fairbridge, R. W. 109
Fairplay world shipping year book 178
fairies, dictionaries 156
Familiar quotations 72
Family expenditure 339, 372b75
  survey 362, 380b206
family history, sources 407–8
Far East
  directories of 173, 186
  yearbooks 214
Far East and Australasia 186, 214
farming *see* agriculture
Federal library resources 187
Féderation international de documentation 233
Ferguson, M. 484
Festschriften 519
fiction
  indexes to 520, 656
  biographical dictionaries 156
fictional characters 156
  in children's literature 157
Field, J. 420b
Field, Roy 586b9
Fielding, A. 384b
Fiji, national bibliographies 440
filing of illustrations 579
Filmed books and plays 520
films
  biographies 159
  catalogues of 574
  encyclopaedias of 119
  periodicals indexes 238, 514
Finance and general statistics 362, 380b204
Finances from Europe 549, 560b49
finance statistics 361–2

Financial directories of the world 191, 193
Financial post corporation service 190
Financial statistics 361, 364, 380b201
financial statistics directories 172
Financial times 188, 199
  Guide to FT statistics 340, 373b78
  Index to 198, 202, **203–4**, 656
  on microfilm 200
Financial Times mining international year book 178
Financial Times oil and gas international year book 178
Financial Times oil and gas international year book 178
Financial Times who's who in world oil and gas 178
Finberg, H. P. R. 420b
Finland
  biographical dictionaries 148
  national bibliographies 440
Finlayson, J. 348, 375b118
Fisher, J. L. 420b
Fisher, M. 157
Fleet Street letter 223
Focal encyclopaedia of photography 50, **125–6**
folklore characters
  biographical dictionaries 156
Fontana dictionary of modern thought 128
food, bibliographies 506, 507, 525
Ford, P. and G. 313, 405, 518
Ford list of British parliamentary papers 313
Forecasting business 340, 373b82
Foreign and Commonwealth office 300
Foreign broadcast information service 198
foreign dictionaries, bibliographies 74

Index

foreign materials, acquisition 26
Foreman, L. 530b15
Forschungsberichte aus Technik und Naturwissenschaften 252
Forthcoming international scientific and technical conferences 256–7
Foskett, D. J. 507
Foster, J. 156
Foster, Pamela 338, 372b71
Four hundred years of British autographs 145
Fowler, H. W. 68
Foxon, D. F. 487–8
France
  biographical dictionaries 142, 147
  incunabula 465, 467–8
  national bibliographies 440, 428
  place directories 168
  press guides 216
  retrospective bibliographies 493–9
  standards 260
France littéraire, La 496
Franklin, Benjamin 221
Franklyn, J. 129
Freeman, W. 156
French dictionaries 64
French encyclopaedias 96–8
French-English dictionaries 70
French language dictionaries 64
French literature
  bibliographies 498–9
  encyclopaedias 127
French standards association 260
Freshest advices: early provincial newspapers 404–5
Freud, Sigmund, concordance 515
Funk and Wagnall's *Dictionary* 62, 63
furniture, encyclopaedias 127

Gaelic books, retrospective bibliographies 484

Galbraith, V. H. 385, 398, 416b1, 417b29, 420b
Galvin, T. J. 47b
Gambia, national bibliographies 431, 441
gardening
  dictionaries 128
  encyclopaedias 125
Gardener, W. 180
Garraty, J. A. 163b
gas, directories 178, 340
Gassman, Hans-Peter 554, 562b70
Gatfield, G. 524
Gazetteer of Canada 289
Gazetteer of the British Isles 289
gazetteers 286–92
  definition of 286
  encyclopaedias as 288
Gazetteer's or newsman's interpreter 286
Gebbie Press House magazines directory 224
Gelling, N. 410
genealogical lists 155
Genealogical research . . . 408
Geneologisches Handbuch des Adels 155
Genealogist's encyclopedia 408
genealogy
  encyclopaedias 408
  for local studies 407–8
  indexes 159
  research into 407
Genealogy for beginners 407, 418b50
General biographical dictionary 136
General council of British shipping 363, 382b225
General industrial classification 351, 377b144
General magazine 221
General Register Officer, Scotland 289

Index

General sources of statistics 332, 370b26
Gentleman's magazine 221
  index 233
Geo Katalog 270
geographic names *see* place names
Geographical journal, reviews 278
geography
  bibliographies 271
  dictionaries 66
  encyclopaedias 113
Geological Survey 274–5
  publications 274
geology
  bibliographies 274, 507
  maps 274–5
German dictionaries 62
German encyclopaedias 95–6
German-English dictionaries 55, 69–70
German Institute of Standardisation 260
German literature, bibliographies 441
Germany (Federal Republic of Germany)
  CIP programme 430
  national bibliographies 428, 441
  statistics 332, 371b38
Germany (German Democratic Republic)
  biographical dictionaries 142, 147
  directories 176, 187, 190
  incunabula 466
  national bibliographies 428, 441
  patents 265
  press guides 216–7
  reports 252
  union list of foreign serials 321
Gesamtkatalog der Wilgendrucke 466
Ghana, national bibliographies 441
Gibbons, Stanley 571
Gibbs-Smith, Charles H. 587b18

Gibson, G. 530b15
Gibson, J. 389, 416b8
Gibson, J. S. W. 409
Giornale de letterati 220
Gittings, R. 163b
Glasgow
  directories 168
  public library 505
Glasgow Herald, index 205
Glossary of documentation terms 65
Glossary of geographical terms 66
Glossary of terms relating to work study 65
Gloucester, maps 412
Godfrey, L. E. 252–3
Goff, F. R. 467–8
Golden book encyclopaedia 593
Goldsmith, V. F. 496
Golfer's handbook 166
Gomme, G. L. 516
Gooder, E. A. 403
Goss, C. W. F. 194b8, 418b6
Gould, J. 66
government department libraries 518
  directories 187
government publications 294–323
  bibliographies 297, 307, 312–20, 518
  British government publications 295–7, 314
  effect of changes in government machinery 297, 307
  information excluded from 321
  non-HMSO publications 309–10
  non-parliamentary publications 303–6
  of Northern Ireland 315–6
  of U.S.A. 316–20
  parliamentary publications 297–303
  problems of 295
  retrospective bibliographies 312–4

Index

statistical publications 305
  subject approach to 518
Government publications 537
Government publications review
  322b, 539–40, 557b8
Government reference books 318
Government reports
  announcements and index 249
Government statistical services 342,
  374b93
Government statistics 305, 331,
  370b23
Gower, H. D. 586b10
Gowers, *Sir* Ernest 68
GPO sales publications reference
  file 318
Graduate employment and training
  183
Graesse, J. G. 464
Gran enciclopedia Rialp 100
Grand dictionnaire encyclopédique
  Larousse 83, 85, 86, **97**
Grand dictionnaire universal 96
Grand Larousse encyclopédique
  78, 81, **96–7**
  bibliographies in 82
  illustrations in 83
Grande dizionario enciclopedico
  utet 99
Grande enciclopedia Portuguesa
  101
Grande encyclopédie 85, 86, 94,
  96, 97
  Atlas général Larousse 97
Granger, E. 515
Grangerised books 570
Grant, M. 156
Grant, Mary M. 191
grants 549
  directories 182
Graphic 570
Gratch, Bonnie 667, 675b37
Graves, A. 156
Gray, J. 531b30
Gray, M. 530–1b13

Gray, Peter 124, 128
Great Britain *see* United Kingdom
Great Soviet encyclopedia 84, **102**
Greater London Council
  Annual abstract 336, 372b61
  European digest 551, 561b61
  London facts 336, 372b62
  Unemployment statistics 345,
    374b104
Greater Manchester County
  Council 336, 372b65
Greece, national bibliographies 441
Greek civilisation *see* classical
  world
Greek-English lexicon 50, 70
green papers 306
Greene, Graham 668
Grenfell, D. 219, 233, 243b4,
  244b18, 245
Griffin, Chris 332, 341, 370b33
Grimshaw, Anne 507–8
Grimsted, Patricia Kennedy
  103b13
Grogan, D.
  Case studies . . . 47b, 75b,
    195b, 533b
  More case studies 47b, 163b4,
    245b, 533b
  Practical reference work 47b
Groot woordenboek der
  Nederlandse taal 64
Gross, C. A. 394
Grosse Duden, der 80
Grosse Herder, der 95
Grosses vollständiges universal-
  Lexicon 76
Grote Nederlandse Larousse
  encyclopedie 78
Grote Winkler Prins 94
Grove's dictionary of music 9, 10
Guardian 198, 200
Guide to American directories 193
Guide to British government
  publications 297

Index

Guide to cartographic records in the National Archives 285
Guide to census reports 335, 409
Guide to current British journals 403, 418b43
Guide to Financial Times statistics 340, 373b78
Guide to foreign trade statistics 338, 372b67
Guide to government department and other libraries . . . 187, 518
Guide to official statistics 305, **331**, 334, 338, 342, 370b22
Guide to parliamentary papers 405
Guide to printed books and manuscripts . . . 524
Guide to reference books 505, 533b
Guide to regional statistics 334, 371b50
Guide to sources of statistics 338, 372b70
Guide to special issues and indexes of periodicals 233
Guide to the classification for overseas trade statistics 353, 378b160
Guide to the historical and archaeological publications . . . 395
Guide to the national and provincial directories 194b9, 406–7
Guide to the records of parliament 405
Guidelines for the national bibliographic agency 423
guides to libraries 26, 29–30
Guides to official publications 537
guides to reference material 12, 16–17, 513
Guyana, national bibliographies 441

Hackman, M. L. 501b, 532b
Haggar, R. G. 65
Hain, L. F. T. 464–5
Hajnal, Peter 540, 557b9, b11, b12
Hakim, Catherine 336, 372b66
Hale, A. T. 390
Hale, B. M. 532b
Halkett, S. 485–6
Hall, J. L. 620b
Hall, James 573
Hall, P. 531b30
Hall, R. de Z. 420b, 524
Halliwell, L. 105b
Halsbury's laws of England 129
Hamilton, Geoffrey 366, 383b244, 660, 674b32
Hamilton-Edwards, G. 407, 418b49
Hammond, N. G. L. 122
Handbook of British family history 407
Handbook of comparative world steel standards 261
Handbook of dates for students . . . 402, 418b40
Handbook to county bibliography . . . 394, 521
handbooks to the literature 509–10
Handbuch der deutschen Aktiengesellschaften 176
Handlist of English provincial newspapers 200
handwriting analysis 403
Hanham, H. J. 163b9
Hansard 298, 299–300, 350
  in microfilm 299
hard terminology 603
hardware, directory 180
Hardy, Thomas 157
Harley, J. B.
  Historian's guide to OS maps 286, 292b9, 412
  Maps for the local historian 285, 292b8, **411**, 419b62
  Ordnance Survey maps 272, 292b2, 293b

705

Index

Harrap's new standard French and English dictionary 70
Harrap's standard German and English dictionary 55, 75b4
Harris, John 571
Harrison, Helen P. 563, 585b2
Harrison, R. 230
Harrison, J. F. C. 510–11
Harrod, L. Montague 675b40
   Librarians' glossary 2, 22b1, 50, **65**, 219, 239, 243b2, 244b22
   1982 Carey Award 672
   1973 Wheatley Medal 671
Hartmann, R. R. K. 75b
Hartnoll, Phyllis 115, 130, 151
Harvard College Library 495
Harvard University Library 461
Harvey, J. H. 418b39
Harvey, Joan M. 327, 329, 369b7, 369b12–15
Harvey, P. 118, 122
Harvey, P. D. 284
Harvey, R. 421b
HATRICS 186, 366
Hawley, C. 180
Havlice, Patricia Pace 578
health, statistics 362
Health and personal social services statistics 362, 380b208
Health and safety statistics 362, 381b209
Heating and ventilating contractors' association standard 260
Heckscher, William 668–9
Hellyer, A. 125
Henderson, G. P. 165
   Current British directories 165, 192, 194b6
   European companies 188, 191, 192
   Financial directories . . . 191, 193
Henrey, B. 511
Hepworth, P. 162

Her Majesty's Stationery Office *see* HMSO
heraldry
   bibliographies 524
   dictionaries 129
Hereford and Worcester association of technical libraries 232
Hertford, maps 284
Hey, D. H. 125
Higgens, Gavin 218
Highways and transportation statistics 363, 382b229
Hill, Donna 586b13
Hillard, J. M. 47b
Historian's guide to OS maps 286, 292b9, 412
Historical abstracts 242, 532b33
Historical Association 508
historical atlases 282–3
Historical biographical dictionaries master index 159
Historical periodicals directory 516
Historical research for university degrees 397
historical statistics 345–8
Historical tables 114
history (*see also* local studies)
   abstracts 242
   atlases 282
   bibliographies 394, 506, 523
   encyclopaedias 113, 114
History of American magazines 229–30
History on your doorstep 387–8
History theses 397
History today 579
Hitchcock, H. R. 569
HMSO 214, 295, 554–5
   lists and catalogues 307–8, 555, 562b71–3
   Monthly catalogue 297, 307
   non-parliamentary publications 303–6
   public bills 301–2

Index

publications 555, 562b71–3
HMSO Services Working Party
  309 (*see also* SCOOP)
Hobb, J. L. 421b
Hodgkiss, Alan 292b
Hodgson, H. W. 393, 417b20
Hodson, D. 284
Hoefer, Johann C. 136
Hoffman, Linda 554, 561b64
Holdsworth, H. 452b5
Holland
  dictionaries 64
  incunabula 466
Holloway, A. H. 266b
Holmstrom, J. Edwin 217
Home book of quotations 72
Home Office 344, 365, 374b99,
  383b238
Homelink 632, 642
Honet, A. 288
Hong Kong
  directories 190
  national bibliographies 429, 442
Hoover, R. E. 621b
Hopkins, Michael 548, 560b44
Horrocks, S. 418b48
horses 572
  bibliographies 507–8, 510
horticulture
  bibliographies 511
  encyclopaedias 125
Hoskins, W. G. 386, 421b
Houghton, Bernard 163b10, 245b,
  384b, 619b4, b5, 621b
Houghton, W. E. 235
house journals 224
*House journals held by the Science
  Reference Library* 224
House of Commons
  biographical dictionaries 154
  Journals and *Hansard* 299
  publications 298
  papers 300, 301
  sessional publications 311, 315

Weekly information bulletin 299,
  302, 549, 560b50
House of Lords
  papers 300, 301
  publications 298
  Weekly information bulletin 302
Household food consumption 362,
  380b207
houses, dating 401
Housing facts and figures 350,
  376b133
Houston post 204
How things work 571
How to find out about the statistics
  329, 369b20
How to find out in mathematics
  509
How to find out series 509, 527
How to organise a local collection
  390–1
How to read local archives 403
How to record graveyards 418b52
Howard-Hill, T. H. 501b, 521
Howarth, K. 415
Hulbert, J. R. 75b
humanities, indexing of books on
  235, 659
Humanities index 235
Humphreys, A. L. 394, 521
Humphreys, D. W. 388
Hungary, national bibliographies
  442
Hunnisett, R. F. 675b
Hunter, Eric J. 673b11
Hurych, J. 47b
Hutchins, M. 47b
Hutchinson, D. 384b
Hyamson, A. M. 158
Hydrographic Office 293b
hymnology, encyclopaedias 127

*I see all: the world's first picture
  encyclopaedia* 568
IAA 250
IBA 20, 630, 640–1

Index

Ibar anuario-comercial Ibaramericano 173
Iceland
  biographical dictionaries 148
  national bibliographies 442
IEE 259–60
Illustrated London News 143, 221, 403, 418b41, 570
illustrations 567, 575, 577
  bibliographies 576–8
  filing of 578–80
  in encyclopaedias 83, 111
  indexes to 577–8, 656
  local studies 575–6
  selection policy 568
Illustrator's handbook 569
ILO *see* International Labour Organisation
IMO *see* International Maritime Organisation
Imperial War Museum
  Library 512
  pictures 582
Imported timber 365, 383b242
Improving manpower information 345, 374b103
in-print services 434–5
In search of ancestry 407, 418b49
in-service training 29
Income distribution 339, 373b77
Incomes Data Service 342, 373b91
Incorporated linguist 73
Incorporated Society of British Advertisers 345, 374b105
incunabula 464–9
  in British Library 459
  in *National Union Catalogue* 461
Independent Broadcasting Authority 20, 630, 640–1
Index Aureliensis 468
Index bio-bibliographicus notorum hominum 158–9
Index kewensis 517
Index Islamicus 517

Index medicus 237, 593
Index of COM documents 549, 570b52
Index of DTD specifications 262
Index of federal specifications and standards 262
Index of industrial production 353, 377b158
Index of printers, publishers and booksellers . . . 471
Index of Scottish place names 289
Index of specifications and standards 262
Index of US voluntary engineering standards 259
Index to Festschriften in librarianship 519
Index to foreign legal periodicals 237
Index to international statistics 327, 368b5
Index to legal essays 519
Index to legal periodicals 236
Index to literary biography 159
Index to periodical literature 234–5
Index to plays in collections 515
Index to poetry 515
Index to theses 254
Index translationum 515
Indexed periodicals 234
Indexer 659, 661, 664–6, 668–9, 673b1–4, b6–9, b14, 674b21, b26, b29–30, b32–3, 675b37–9, 676
  conference proceedings 669
indexers
  societies 668–9
  awards for 669–73
indexes 651–7
  absence of 651–3, 667–8
  accuracy of 661
  arrangement of 654, 660, 662–3
  cross-references in 663
  currency of 196
  definitions of 653–4

Index

importance of 4, 523, 651–3
keyword-in-context 589
layout of 663–4
of chairmen 313–14
of quotations 71, 72
purpose of 652–4
problems of compiling 657–8, 660–4
sub-headings in 663–4
to encyclopaedias 84, 114–16
to fiction 656
to newspapers 19, 198, 201–5, 656
to periodicals 18–19, 233–9, 656
Indexes and indexing 655, 673b12, 675b
Indexing and Abstracting Society of Canada 669
indexing 651–76
and abstracting journals 589, 656
art of 658, 660–4
conferences on 669
British Standard on 654, 655, 657, 659, 662
keyword indexing 601
of encyclopaedias 84, 114–6
of periodicals 656
of reference material 14
of visual material 585
societies 668–9
indexing languages 600, 602–3
indexing services 234–9
reference materials 7, 18
selection policies 234
India
biographical dictionaries 148
national bibliographies 433, 442
press guides 217
India who's who 148
Indonesia, national bibliographies 433, 442
Industrial Aids Ltd. 340, 373b80
Industrial arts index 236
Infoline 620
information bureaux *see* libraries

Information, computer and communications policies 554, 562b70
information explosion 1
Information for local historians 389
information index 133
of subject enquiries 28, 35, 69
Information please almanac 211
Information Retrieval, London 242
information retrieval services 592
information retrieval systems, on-line *see* on-line information retrieval systems
information services 206–7, 592
information sources, directories 185–8
Information sources for research and development series 509
Information sources in architecture 509
Information internationales 190
Inge, W. R. 244b11
INIS Atomindex 251
Inland Revenue statistics 361, 380b202
INSPEC 590, 591
thesaurus 602
Institute of Chartered Accountants 505
Institute of Historical Research 141
Institution of Electrical Engineers 259–60
Wiring regulations 259
institutions *see* organisations
inter-action, on-line 607–10
InterDok 257
internal indexes 653
International aerospace abstracts 250
International affairs, reviews in 12
International atlas 278
International authors and writers who's who 152

Index

International bibliography of specialised dictionaries 74
International books in print 452
International Conference on Indexing 669
International Congress on National Bibliographies 425, 427, 430, 452b2
International Documentation
 First World Symposium 535
 Second World Symposium 536
International documents for the 80s 536, 557b4
International encyclopaedia of higher education 121
International encyclopaedia of science 125
International encyclopaedia of the social sciences 110–1, 112, 116, 123–4
International Federation of Library Associations 423, 425, 452b1, 453b14
International foundations directory 182
international government organisations statistics 539–40
International handbook of universities 182–3
International historical statistics 346, 347, 375b108
International Labour Organisation 360, 379b187, 543
 ILO catalogue 543, 559b23
 ILO publications 543, 559b24
International map of the world 19, **269–70**
International maps and atlases in print 270–1
International Maritime Organisation 543
 Publications 544, 559b25
International mortality statistics 347, 375b113

International motion picture almanac 158
international official publications 534–62
International organisations publications 555, 562b73
International patent classification 264–5
International serials catalogue 233–4
International shipping and shipbuilding directory 178–9
International Standard Book Numbers 247, 426
International standard industrial classification 351, 353, 376b141
International Standard Serial Numbers 247
International Standards Organisation 261
international statistics
 guides 326–30
 indexes to 327
International Tea Committee 361, 379b190
International trade documentation 228
International trade statistics 384b
International whaling statistics 361, 379b191
International who's who 133, **138–9**
International who's who in music 9, 152
International year book and statesman's who's who 138–9, 212–3
international yearbooks 212–5
International yellow pages 170
Internationale bibliographie der Zeitschriftenliteratur 235
Internationale bibliographie des reprints 452
Internationales Bibliotheks-Handbuch 186

Index

Interpreter's dictionary of the Bible
    118, 128
Introduction to sound recordings
    415
Inventory of bibliographic data
    bases 517
Iran
    national bibliographies 442
    statistics 332
Iredale, D. 388–9, 416b6, 421b
Ireland (see also Northern Ireland)
    biographical dictionaries 143
    company information 190
    encyclopaedias of 113
    national bibliographies 429, 442
    retrospective bibliographies 522
    union lists of serials 231
Irish books
    bibliographies 522
    in Cambridge 485
Irish independent 190
Irish University Press
    Catalogue of British
        parliamentary papers 315
Irregular serials and annuals 193,
    227
IRS 632, 633fig.4, 642
Irvine, J. 350, 375b135
Irvine, Betty Jo 586b15
ISBA area information 345,
    374b105
Islam
    bibliographies 511
    encyclopaedias 80, 84
    indexes 517
Isle of Man, newspapers 405
'ISMS 69
ISO standards 261
Israel, national bibliographies 443
Italian encyclopaedias 99
Italian-English dictionaries 70
Italy
    biographical dictionaries 142
    incunabula 466
    national bibliographies 443

press guides 217
Ivory Coast, national
    bibliographies 443

Jackson, W. A. 472
Jacob, P. M. 397
Jaeger and Waldmann world telex
    171
Jaeger's Europa-Register 173
Jahoda, G. 22b, 47b
Jahresverzeichnis der deutschen
    Hochschulschriften 255
Jamaica, national bibliographies
    443
Jane's all the world's aircraft 571–2
Jane's fighting ships 571–2
Japan
    block-printed books 8
    national bibliographies 443
    trade names directories 181
    union lists of periodicals 232
Jast, L. Stanley 528, 531b32
jazz, bibliographies 524
Jeffries, John 330, 369b21, 545,
    548, 559b27
Jewish periodicals, indexes 238
Johansson, E. 228
John Crerar Library 461
Johnson, Fred 339, 373b77
Johnson, Samuel
    Dictionary . . . 51, 75b3
    Letters 75b5, 660
    Lives of the poets 149
Jones, B. 137
Jones, J. 418b52
Jordan's Company Information
    Service 191
Journal des scavans 220
    index 233
Journal of Anatomy, index to
    657–8
Journal of economic literature 239
Journal of transport history 514
Journals see periodicals
Journals in translation 229

Index

Joy of knowledge 82, **93–4**, 112, 568
  index in 84
  size of 85
Judaism, encyclopaedias 112
Julian's *Dictionary of hymnology* 127

Kamen, Ruth 509–10, 574
Katalog für technische Regeln 260
Katz, W. B. 78, 86, 102b2, 163b, 217, 228, 245b 586b5
Keeling, D. 524, 529
Keenan, Stella 621b
Keesing's contemporary archives 43, **205–6**
Kelly, J. 491
Kelly's handbook to the titled, landed and official classes 155
Kelly's manufacturers' and merchants' directory 175
Kelly's Post Office London directory 167, 194b8
Kendall, Maurice George 332, 370b28
Kernig, C. D. 80
Kennington, D. 524
Kent, bibliography 524
Kent, A. 243b6
Kenya, national bibliographies 443
Key British enterprises 175
Key to economic science 242
Keyword-in-context indexes 589
keyword indexing 589
Kimmance, S. 531b29
King, D. M. 224
King, G. B. 47b
King, H. B. 673b7
Kingzett's chemical encyclopaedia 125
Kirby, A. 421b
Kister, K. F. 74, 103b10, 104b
Klein, Bernard 193
Knapp, S. D. 48b

Knight, G. Norman 655, 659, 673b13, 674b30, 675–6b
  founder of Society of Indexers 668–9
  1977 Carey Award 672
  1967 Wheatley Medal 670
Koeman, Ir C. 283–4
Kompass: register of British industry and commerce 174
  Wanderkarten 276
Koppitz, Hans-Joachim 105b
Korea, national bibliographies 443
Korner report 341, 373b85
Korwin, Yala H. 578
Koster, C. J. 244b16
Krummel, D. W. 532b
Kunitz, S. J. 154
Kusak, J. M. 620b7
KWIC indexes 589
Kyed, J. M. 257–8

Labarre, E. J. 128
Labour force survey 362, 381b213
labour relations, periodicals 230
labour statistics 348, 360, 365
Ladsirlac 366
Lamb, J. P. 165, 194b4
Lamberton, D. M. 531b30
Lancashire
  bibliography 393
  directories 407
  local history 389
  newspapers 405
Lancet 17
land use maps 275
landscape records 415
Langenscheidt's encyclopaedic dictionary of the English and German languages 70
Langer, W. L. 114
language dictionaries 54, **60–4**
language problem in reference work 44
language studies, periodicals 225
Large scale county maps . . . 412

712

Index

Larousse, P.
 La grande encyclopédie 85
 Grand dictionnaire encyclopedique Larousse 83, 85, 86
Larousse encyclopedia of world geography 113
LASER 232, 647, 648fig.9, 650
Latham, Robert C. 659, 675b29
Latin America
 directories 173
 encyclopaedias 100
 national bibliographies 429
 regional bibliographies 429
Latin-English dictionaries 70
Latin for local history 403
law 529
 biographical dictionaries 152–3
 British Library Working Party on Provision for Law 528
 directories 184
 encyclopaedias 126, 129
 index 519
 periodicals lists 232, 236, 237
Law list 153, 184
Lawrence, G. R. P. 292b
Lawtel 632, 641
Lawton, R. 409, 418b56
Leacock, Stephen
 index of non-entries 655, 673b15
League of Nations 538
learned journals 223–4
Lee, C. H. 348, 375b121
Lee, Sir Sydney 131, 141
Leeming, G. 157
legal periodicals 232, 236, 237
Leitfaden für Presse und Werbung, der 216
Lessico universale italiana 99
Letopis' zhurnal 'nykh statai 234
letter by letter alphabetization 14–15, 56, 662
letters journals 222
 indexes to 565, 660

Letters of Samuel Johnson, seven indexes to 660
Levi, W. M. 109
Levin, Bernard, views on indexes 651, 675b1, b2
Lewis, S. A. 290
lexicography, bibliographies 55
lexicons *see* dictionaries
Lexis: dictionnaire de la langue française 64
Librarians' glossary 2, 22b1, 50, 65, 219, 239, 243b2, 244b22
Librarian's handbook
 index to 657
librarianship
 definition of 25
 dictionaries 65
 indexing/abstracting services 242, 522
 periodicals 225
 polyglot dictionaries 71
libraries
 accessions 512, 514
 bibliographies produced by 528
 containing US government publications 317
 directories 186–7
 guides to 513–4
 of government departments 518
Libraries in the United Kingdom 384b
Libraries, museums and art galleries' yearbook 186
Libraries yearbook 1982/83 186
Library and information science abstracts 242, 522, 647
Library assistance to readers 165, 194b1
Library Association
 Besterman medal 331, 522
 liaison with Society of Indexers 669
 Library resources series 186
 periodicals indexes 236
 Wheatley Medal 669–72

713

Index

Library Association. Audiovisual Group 584
Library Association. Committee of Librarians and Statisticians 306
Library Association. County Libraries Group 390
Library Association. Eastern branch 393, 417b21
Library Association. London and Home Counties branch 232
Library Association. Public Libraries Group 218, 508
Library Association. Reference, Special and Information Section 186, 309
Library Association Library 8, 219
Library Association record 133, 273, 292b3, 649
library equipment 29
library history, bibliographies 524
Library literature 236, 295
Library of Congress, Washington
  Accessions lists 429, 433
  Catalogue 27
  Classification 28
  Index to international statistics 327, 368b5
  Information bulletin 522
  National union catalogue 433, **461–2**, 470, 488
  newspapers in 217
  Newspapers in microform 200
  photographs in 575
  Subject catalogue 504
  videodiscs in 22
library resources series 186
Library science abstracts 242
library suppliers 26
Libri Walliae 484–5
Lichine, A. 109
Liddell, H. G. 50, 70
Liebesny, F. 266b
Lincolnshire, local studies 392
Linderman, W. B. 48b

Line, M. B. 243b8
Lippincott's biographical dictionary 137
Listener, indexes to 202
literature (*see also* literary forms e.g. drama)
  bibliographies 224–5, 236–7, 486–8, 521
  biographical dictionaries 159
  encyclopaedias 107–8, 118
  handbooks to 509–10
  periodicals 225
Lives of the engineers 149
Lives of the poets 149
Lives of the saints 149
Livres disponibles 435
Lobel, M. D. 283
Lobies, J.-P. 158–9
Local government financial statistics 362, 380b203
Local historian 391–2, 416b15
Local historian's encyclopedia 402
Local history and the library 390–1
Local history for beginners 388, 416b5
Local history for students 388
Local history from blue books 406
Local history handlist 390
Local history in England 386
Local history research and writing 389
local maps 283–6
local organizations and activities
  internal indexes to 653
Local population studies 409, 418b57
local record offices 162, 285, 399
Local record sources in print . . . 402
local studies 385–422
  bibliographies of 391–6
  biographical reference works for 410
  blue books as sources 406
  census reports as sources 408–9

714

Index

directories 406–7
ephemera as sources 414
handwriting 403
illustrations 570, 575–6
indexes of newspapers 198
local records 399–403
maps 411–2
national records 398
newspapers in 200, 201, 403–5
of agriculture 391
Parliamentary papers in 405
periodicals 403
photographs 413, 576
place names 410
private records 398–9
rule of archaeology in 415–6
theses 397
local studies librarianship 390–1
Lock, C. B. Muriel 293b, 531b16
Lock, G. F. 332, 370b26
Lockheed Dialog *see* DIALOG
Loder, E. 510
London
 directories 167
 illustrations 377
 statistics 336, 345
London and Cambridge Economic Service 344, 348, 374b102
London bibliography of the social sciences 512, 529, 532b34
London facts 336, 372b62
London gazette 306
London Library 470
 Subject index 505
London School of Economics 317
London union list of periodicals 232
Longman's dictionary of contemporary English 60
loose-leaf publications
 business information 190-1
 directories 193
 encyclopaedias 126
 news digests 205–6
 statutes 302

Lorenz, O. 497
Los Angeles Times 204
Lowndes, W. T. 477, 504, 530b3
Lumsden, H. P. 332, 370b30
Luxembourg, national bibliographies 428, 444
Lynes, A. 390–1

McColvin, Lionel R. 530b5
 on indexes 652–3, 654, 673b4, b8
 McColvin report 653
McCrimmon, B. 530b4
Macdonald, A. M. 75b
MacDonald, Barrie I. 218
Macdonald, K. I. 238
McGraw-Hill dictionary of scientific and technical terms 65–6
McGraw-Hill encyclopedia of science and technology 77, 114–5, 121
 Yearbook 126
McGraw-Hill encyclopedia of world biography 132, **138**
McGregor report on the press 218
Machine Readable Catalogue *see* MARC
machine readable national bibliographies 432
machines, encyclopaedias 571
McKenzie, D. F. 500b8
Maclean, D. 484
McLuhan, Marshall 218
Macmillan, Harold, on value of index 654, 673b9, 676b
Macmillan dictionary of biography 137
Macmillan family encyclopedia 79, 86, **91**
 index in 84
 revision policy 86
McQuail, Denis 218
Macrae's blue book 174–5
Macroeconomic data bank 357

715

Index

Madagascar, national bibliographies 444
Madan, F. 477
Magazine index 591
Mailbox 634figs, 635, 637, 643
Main economic indicators 347, 360, 375b111, 379b183
Major companies of Europe 172–3
Makepeace, C. E. 419b63, b65
Malawi, national bibliographies 444
Malaysia
 CIP programme 430
 national bibliographies 433, 444
Malclès, L.-N. 17, 104b, 500b, 532b
Mali, national bibliographies 429
Maltby, Arthur 316
management, abstracts and indexes 239
Management and economics journals 228
Management contents 239
Management in government 307
Management principles and practice 660
Managing and marketing abstracts 656
Management today 656
Manchester, statistics 336, 372b65
 trade unions 399
Manchester Photographic Survey 413, 419b64
Manchester Polytechnic
 local studies 399
Manchester Public Libraries 226, 505
Manchester weekly courant 200
Manpower information 342, 373b91
Manual of European languages for librarians 71
Manuel de l'amateur des livres 497
Manuel du libraire **463**, 493

manufacturers, directories 174–5, 180
manuscripts 399, 524
 biographical material 162
 local studies 397–401
maps 267–76
 as local studies sources 411–2
 bibliographies 284–5
 catalogues 284
 early and local 283–6
 general descriptions of 267–9
 in encyclopaedias 83
 selection of 269–72
 value in reference work 19
Maps and charts published in America 285
Maps for the local historian 285, 292b8, **411**, 419b62
Marbeck, John 655
MARC 430
 data-bases 591
 file 595
 retrieval 667
Marco, G. 510
Marconi, Joseph V. 234
Marconi's international register 171
Marculli-Koenig, Luciana 540, 558b10
marine maps *see* charts
Market and statistics news 341, 344, 373b89
Marketing + distribution abstracts 240
Marques internationales, Les 181
Marshall, Peter 168, 195b10
Marshallsay, Diana 313
Martin, G. H. 394–5, 523
Martindale-Hubbell law directory 184
Marxism, Communism and Western society
 bias 80
Mason, O. 288
Masquoid 127

Index

Material for theses in local record offices 399–400
Materials and technology 113
mathematics, bibliographies 509
Matthews, William 160–1
Matthews, C. M. 421b
Maunder, W. F. 332, 345, 370b27, 374b107
Maurois, A. 163b
Mauritius, national bibliographies 444
Mawer, A. 421b
Media 218
media guides 218, 227
Medical directory 134, **153**, 184
Medical register 184
medicine
   abstracts 242
   bibliographies 134, 512
   biographical dictionaries 153
   conferences 256
   directories 184
   indexes to periodicals 237, 238
   reviews 237
MEDLARS 237
MEDLINE 41, 593–4, 595, 606, 616
   charges 615
   'explode' capability 617
   thesaurus 600
Mee, Arthur 568
members of parliament
   biographical dictionaries 154
membership lists of chambers of commerce 168
Men's wear 180
Merck index of chemicals and drugs 127
Mercurius librarius 220
Merit students encyclopedia 79, 88, **93**
Merseyside Archaeological Society 421b
Messenger, Y. 228

Metal bulletin handbook 362, 381b220
Meteorological glossary 65
Meteorological Office 65
meteorology, glossary of 65
Methodist union catalog 511
Metropolitan Museum of Art *Library catalog* 511–2
Mexico
   directories 173
   national bibliographies 445
Meyers enzyklopädisches Lexikon 95
Meyers neues Lexikon 81, **95**
Michaud, Jean Francois 136
microcomputers 639
   internal indexes on 653
   on-line information retrieval 598
microfiche (*see also* microfilm; microform)
   broadcasts on 198
   catalogues on 481
   company reports on 188–9
   incunables catalogues on 467
   Keesings on 206
   statistics on 358–9
   telephone directories on 169
microfilm (*see also* microfiche; microform)
   definition 20
   newspapers on 19, 198, 200–1
Microfilm abstracts 254
microforms (*see also* microfiche; microfilm) 222
   bibliographies of 201, 229
   Hansard on 299
   In print 434, 451, 519
   maps on 267
   newspapers on 200
Microforms in print 201, 229
Micronet 630, 635, 637–8, 640
   Telesoftware 638fig8
Middle East
   directories 185–6
   regional bibliographies 433

Index

yearbooks 214
Middle East and North Africa 185–6, 214
Mikhail, E. H. 524
Milford, R. J. 231
Miller, Stuart T. 586b8
Mills, A. D. 291
Millson, R. J. 244b12
Milner, Anita C. 204–5
minerals, statistics 362
mining, directories 178
Ministry of Agriculture 362, 380b207
Minto, John 505–6
Mitchell, B. R.
   Abstract of British historical statistics 347, 375b115–6
   European historical statistics 347, 375b112
   International historical statistics 346, 347, 375b108
Mitchell Beazley 82, 84, 85, 93–4, 138
Modern English biography **143**, 410, 419b59
Modern historians on British history 506
Modern news library 218
'Modern plastics' encyclopedia 129
Modley, Rudolf, 573
Monde, Le, index to 205
Monro, I. 577
Monthly catalog of United States government publications 317–8
Monthly catalogue of books 307, 308
Monthly digest of statistics 305, 361, 364, 379b192
Monthly review 220
Moody's international manual 172
Moody's Investors Service 190
Moody's Manuals 176
Moon, Brenda E. 232
Moreau, B. 494
Morehead, J. 266b, 322b

Morris, R. B. 113
Morrison, P. G. 471
Mort, David 340, 373b82, 384b
mortality statistics 347
Morton, A. 398
Moss, Martha 578
motor industry statistics 362
Mott, F. L. 229–30
Moys, Elizabeth 529
MPs chart 154
Muir's historical atlases 282
Mullins, E. L. P. 395, 401–2, 417b30
multiple indexes 659–60
Mumby, L. M. 421b
Munby, Denys 348, 375b123
Munford, W. A. 530b13
Muñoz, J. L. 48b
Murfin, M. E. 48b
Murphy, Mary 282, 292b7
Murray, *Sir* James 61
Murray's English dictionary (OED) 61
museums
   bibliography 574
   catalogues of 161
   directories 183
   yearbooks 186
music
   bibliographies 510, 514, 529
   biographical dictionaries 9, 152
   dictionaries 9, 10, 77, 127
   discography 129
   encyclopaedias of 116–7, 129, 130
   in British Library 8
   periodicals indexes 162, 237
Music index 162, 237
musical instruments, encyclopaedias 109
mythology 156

Namibia (South West Africa) 445
names *see* Christian names; place names

Index

NANTIS 186
NASA 250
National accounts 339, 373b76
National accounts statistics 353, 377b156, 378b16
National atlas of Canada 280
National atlas of the United States of America 280
National atlas of Wales 280–1
national atlases 279–81
national bibliographies 423–53
  bibliographies 469–99
  coverage of 427–9
  currency of 431–2
  current 423–53
  definitions of 423–4
  forms of 432
  frequency of 430–1
  in-print services of 434–5
  retrospective 469–99
  use of 425–7
National Book League 508
National Conference on Indexing 671
National cyclopaedia of American biography 143
National directory of newsletters and reporting services 227
National Federation of Abstracting and Indexing Services 233
National Film Archive
  catalogue of stills 574, 582
National geographic magazine 579
  reviews in 17
National income and expenditure 361, 380b198
National index of parish registers 408
national libraries
  reference material in 7–8
National Library of Scotland 8, 469, 470, 482
National Library of Wales 8
National Maritime Museum, Greenwich 160
Catalogue of the library 530b10
  catalogues 284
National Monuments Record 582
National observer, index to 204
National Photographic Record 581
National Portrait Gallery
  catalogue 161
  Dictionary of British portraits 574
national records 398
National Reference Library of Science and Invention *see* British Library Science Reference Library
National Register of Archives 399
National statistical offices of overseas countries 328, 369b9
national statistics 330–3
National Technical Information Service 249
National topographical map series 280
National union catalogue 433, **461–2**, 470, 488
Natural history 76
nautical charts *see* charts
Naval biography of Britain 160
Neal, D. S. 569
Needham, C. D. 532b
needlework, encyclopaedias 109
Negus, A. E. 608, 619b2
Neighbour, O. W. 510
Neilson, June 548–9, 560b46
Netherlands
  atlases 283–4
  national bibliographies 445
NETWORK 366
Neuberg, V. E. 421b
Neue Brockhaus, der 95
Neue deutsche Biographie 142
Neue Herder, der 80, **95–6**
New book of knowledge 88, **93**
New Cambridge bibliography of English literature 200, 229, **486–7**

Index

New Caxton encyclopaedia 85, 93
New century encyclopaedia of names 137
New Columbia encyclopedia 83, 85, **92**
  paper used in 85
New earnings survey 362, 381b214
New Encyclopaedia Britannica 89
New English dictionary on historical principles see *Oxford English dictionary*
New Grove dictionary of music 77, 127
New Orleans times-picayune 204
New Oxford companion to music 130
New Scientist, reviews in 17
New standard dictionary of the English language 62, 63
New Statesman, reviews in 652
New trade names 181
New York
  biographical dictionaries 149
New York Public Library 461
  catalogues 284
  Dictionary catalog **462–3**, 488
New York review of books 12
New York Times
  abstracts from 208
  biographical service 139–40, 145, 157
  Index 19, 41, 43, 202, 204, 208, 656
  Information bank databases 19, 41, 207–8
  obituaries index 144–5
  Review 210
New Zealand
  directories 168
  libraries 513
  national bibliographies 428, 445
  union lists of serials 231
Newcastle-upon-Tyne University Library 482
Newman, J. R. 125

Newman, L. M. 105b
News bank series 206
news databases 207–8
news digest services 205–7
  currency of 196
newspaper cuttings 198
Newspaper history 218
Newspaper indexes 205
Newspaper Library, Colindale 8, 199–200, 404, 457
newspapers 196–218
  abstracts of 208
  bibliographies of 199–200
  evaluation of 19
  indexes 19, 201–5, 656–7
  local studies 403–5
  news databases 207–8
  news digests 205–7
  press guides 215–7
  updating 4
  value of microfilm for 200–1
Newspapers first published before 1900 405, 418b45
Newspapers in microform 200
Newspapers of east central and south east Europe . . . 227
Newton, K. C. 421b
Nexis 198, 208
Nichols, Harold 270, 292b1, 293b, 390–1, 531b16
Nigeria
  directories of 173
  national bibliographies 445
Nineteenth century short title catalogue 482
Nobel Prize winners, Australian 147
nobility
  biographical dictionaries 155
Nomenclature of goods for external trade statistics 352, 377b149
Nomenclature for the classification of goods 351, 377b145
non-parliamentary publications 303–6

720

Index

List 308
Public general acts 301–2
Statutes in force 302
Nora, Simon 384b
Norfolk notabilities 149
Norman, A. R. D. 332, 370b31
North, Sir Thomas 655
Northern bibliography 529
Northern Ireland
  government publications 298, 315–6
  national bibliographies 429
  statistics 334, 363
Norton, J. E. 194b9, 406–7
Norway
  biographical dictionaries 148
  national bibliographies 445
  statistics 332
Nouvelle biographies générale 136
NTIS 249
Nuclear science abstracts 250–1
nuclear science and engineering
  dictionaries 71, 128
  reports 248, 250–1
numerical indexes 654, 660
Nunn, G. R. 232
Nunn, G. W. A. 581

obituaries 19
  as biographical dictionaries 144–5
  in Annual Register 145, 158, 209
Obituaries from The Times 145
Obituary notices of the Fellows of the Royal Society 156
obsolescence of reference material 4
Ocean energy 240
oceanography, encyclopaedias 109
O'Donoghue, Y. 282, 292b7
OECD see Organisation for Economic Co-operation and Development
Offences of drunkenness 344, 374b99

Offenlegungschriften 265
Office of Population Censuses and Surveys 305, 335, 367
  Birth statistics 362, 381b215
  Census 371b50
  Guide to census reports 335, 371b51, 409, 418b55
  Labour force survey 362, 381b213
  Libraries in the UK 367, 384b248
  library 367
  Local authority 362, 381b216
  OPCS Monitor service 335, 340, 371b52
  Population trends 335, 340, 362, 371b53
Official catchword index 264–5
Official journal of the European patent office 265
Official journal (patents) 263
official publications (see also government publications; international official publications)
  bibliographic control 539
  in British Library 8
Official publishing 538, 557b6
Official statistical serials on microfiche 358, 379b176
Official year book of Australia 215
Offshore oil and gas 340, 373b83
oil industry 340
  directories 178
Olsen, K. D. 244b17
on-line information retrieval systems 588–621
  benefits 589–90, 616–9
  charges 357, 645–6
  costs of searches 592, 613–5
  developments in Europe 595–6
  historical development 593–6
  indexing languages 602–3
  interaction 607–10
  retrieval process 599–601

Index

sample search 610
search strategy 601, 604
use of reference material on 73
on-line interaction 607–10
Online 608, 621b
Online review 621b
Open University 349
ORACLE (IBA) 20, 197, 630, 640–1
Oral history 415, 419b72
ORBIT 208, 593, 598, 608–9, 616, 618
Ordnance Survey 35, 272–4, 411
  as publishers 295
  early maps 283
  general maps 272
  geological survey maps 274
  in reference libraries 19
  material in British Library 8
Organization for Economic Co-operation and Development 552–4, 561b65–9
  Catalogue of publications 329, 369b16, 553, 561b63
  Consumer price indices 347, 375b14
  Economic outlook 350, 379b182
  Economic surveys 360, 379b181, 534
  Main economic indicators 347, 360, 375b11, 379b183
  publications in British Library 8
organization of reference materials 14, 25, 29–30
  internal indexes 28, 653
organizations, directories 185
Osborn, A. D. 219, 243b3, 244b15
Osborne, H. 118, 124
Otlet, Paul 523, 531b22
Ottemiller, J. H. 515
Ottley, George 514, 524, 530b11
Oulton, A. J. 620b6
Overseas trade statistics of the United Kingdom 354, 362, 378b162
Owen, D. M. 421b
Owen's commerce and travel and international register 173
Oxford
  Alumni Oxoniensis 156
  early books 477
  Health Service periodicals in 232
Oxford bibliography of British history 395–6
Oxford children's dictionary 63
Oxford classical dictionary 122
Oxford companion to art 118, 124
Oxford companion to classical literature 118, 122
Oxford companion to English literature 107–8, 109
Oxford companion to film 119
Oxford companion to French literature 127
Oxford companion to music 116–7
Oxford companion to the theatre 115, 130, **151**
Oxford dictionary of English Christian names 67
Oxford dictionary of quotations 72
Oxford dictionary of the Christian church 120–1
Oxford-Duden pictorial English dictionary 69
Oxford-Duden pictorial German-English dictionary 69
Oxford English dictionary 52, 54, 55, **61**, 94
  quotations in 72
  quoted 76
Oxford history of English art 572
Oxford illustrated dictionary 63, 64
Oxford junior encyclopaedia 82, **94**, 112
Oxford Microform Concordances 515

Index

Oxford regional economic atlases 281
Oxford Shakespeare concordances 73

Pacey, Philip 586b6, b16
Pacific Islands
　national bibliographies 445
　regional bibliographies 429
Padwick, E. W. 500b 524
paintings
　catalogues 571
　indexes 577, 578
painters 150, 156, 574
PAIS bulletin 193, 217, 237
PAIS foreign language index 194
Pakistan, national bibliographies 445
Palic, Vladimir M. 537, 557b5
Palmer, Doris M. 548–9, 560b45
Palmer's index to 'The Times' newspaper 202
Panizzi, Anthony 457
Pannell, J. P. M. 421b
paper
　dictionary of 128
　used in encyclopaedias 85
Papua New Guinea,
　national bibliographies 431, 446
Paraguay, national bibliographies 446
Parallel lives 655
Paris, directories 168, 169
Parish Chest, The 401
parish registers 408
Park, A. T. 334, 371b49
Parker, V. 421b
Parliament
　biographical dictionaries 154
　directories 187
　encyclopaedias 118
　records of 405
Parliamentary gazetteer of England and Wales 291

Parliamentary On-Line
　Information
　System 302–3, 632, 642
Parliamentary papers 313, 315, 405
Parliamentary publications 297–303
Parry, Pamela Jeffcott 578
Partridge, Eric 67, 75b
Patent information and documentation in western Europe 265
Patent Office 263
　as publisher 295
　trades names register 181
patents 262–5, 428
　abstracts of 263–4
　definition of 262
Patents: a source of technical information 263
Patents for inventions 263
Pau, Giancarlo 549, 560b52
PCGN 288
Peace, D. 416, 419b75–6
Pearce, C. G. 421b
Pearl, M. L. 508
Pearson, H. 84
Peddie, R. A. 504
peerage, biographies of 133, 155
Pelican history of art 572
Pellechet, M. L. C. 465, 468
Pemberton, John E. 322b, 323b, 509, 533b, 537, 539, 557b7
Penguin dictionary of the theatre 151
Penguin dictionary of biographical quotation 145–6
Penney, B. 514
periodicals 219–45
　abstract services 239–43
　bibliographies of 18, 226–30
　biographies in 161
　contents lists in 239
　costs of 6
　definition of 219–20
　evaluation of 18

Index

history of 220–1
  in academic libraries 226
  in public libraries 226
  in special libaries 6, 226
  indexes to 6, 7, 18, 19, 162,
    234–9, 516–7, 656–7, 659–60
  library catalogues of 230–2
  local studies 403
  reference use of 225–6
  selection of 226–30, 234
  subscriptions to 26–7
  union catalogues of 231–2
Periodicals on agriculture 230
*Permanent Committee on
  Geographical Names* 288
Perry, G. A. 421b
Personnel + training abstracts 240
Peru, national bibliographies 446
Petit Larousse 50
Petit Robert, Le 98
petroleum industry, directories 178
Pevsner, *Sir* Nikolaus 572
Phillimore Bookshop 421b
Phillippines, national
  bibliographies 446
Phillips, L. B. 158
philosophy, encyclopaedias 117
photocopiers 30
photocopying 221, 224, 230,
  243b8
photographs 575
  directories 581
  in local collections 413
photography
  encyclopaedias of 125–6
  indexes 517, 578
physics
  abstracts 241, 591
  encyclopaedias 122
Physics abstracts 241, 591
Pictorial education 579
picture libraries 583
Picture post 570
Picture Professionals, Association
  of 584

picture researchers 583–4
Picture sources 581
Picturescope 584
Pieper, F. C. 328, 338, 369b10
pigeons, encyclopaedias of 109
Pilkington report on broadcasting
  218
Pine, L. G. 408
PIRA 656
place names 289, 290, 410
  dictionary of 67, 410
Place-names of Dorset 291
plastics, directory 129
Platt, C. 421b
plays
  bibliography 129
  films 520
  indexes 515
poetry
  bibliographies 487–8
  biographies 149, 153
  indexes 515
Poland, national bibliographies 446
POLIS data-base 302–3, 632, 642
Political handbook of the world
  213
Pollard, A. W. 468, 470–3
Pollard, G. 500–1b
polytechnic libraries *see* academic
  libraries
Pomassl, Gerhardt 435, 453b13,
  531b23
Poole, William Frederick 234–5,
  516
Poor's register of corporations 176
Popular medical index 238
Popular periodical index 238
population statistics 335–6, 337,
  362, 409
Population trends 335, 340, 362,
  371b53
portraits 145, 161, 574
Portugal
  directories 173
  incunabula 466

Index

national bibliographies 446
Portuguese encyclopaedias 100
postage stamps, catalogues of 129, 571
posters, catalogues 574
Pottle, F. A. 508
Poverty in the United Kingdom 350, 376b134
Powell, Anthony, 656, 674b22
Powell, W. R. 406
Predicasts Corporation 41, 237, 240–1, 592
Preece, Warren F. 105b
press cuttings 198, 200, 202
press guides 215–7, 227
Press in India 217
PRESTEL 20, 192, 213, 359, 625, 626fig2, 628, 630–1, 640
  Bextel 634, 643
  Citiservice 631, 641
  costs 645–6
  Directory 648
  Gateways 632, 637, 641
  government information 631, 641
  home computer users 630
  Homelink 632, 642, 631fig3
  homebanking 631fig3
  internal indexes 653
  Lawtel 632, 641
  Mailbox 634fig5, 635, 637, 643
  main index page 626fig2
  manuals 647
  Micronet 630, 635, 637–8fig8, 640
  Tele-link 635fig6, 637
  Tele-ordering 636fig7
price indices, statistics 339, 347, 353
Priestley, H. E. 346, 375b109
Principal international business 172
printed ephemera 414
Printed maps in the atlases of Great Britain and Ireland 284, **411**

Printed maps of Hertford 284
Printed maps of Warwickshire 284
printers 455, 471, 474, 477
  American 489
Prockter, C. E. 657
Proctor, Robert 464, 465
Producer price index 353, 377b157
production statistics 362
professional directories 183–5
proper names, indexing of 659, 660
property companies, directories 180
pseudonymous works
  bibliographies of 485–6
  in French 497–8
psychology
  abstracts 242
  encyclopaedias 117
Psychinfo 591
Psychological abstracts 242
Public affairs information service bulletin 193, 217, 237
Public General Acts 301–2
public libraries
  costs of on-line searches 592–3
  language problem in 44
  local newspapers in 200
  periodicals use in 226
  public access in 526
  reference materials in 5–6, 13, 25
  subject department 5, 32
  use of bibliographies 425–6
  user education in 30
Public library system of Great Britain
  (McColvin report) 652
Public Record Office 321, 398
  catalogue of maps 285
  Guide 417b27
Publications of the Geological Survey 274
Published data on European industrial markets 340, 373b80

Index

publishers 26, 78, 216, 455, 471, 474, 477
  American 489
  in Germany 86
  HMSO as 295–7
  of biographical reference works 134
  of maps 278–9
  producing indexes 651–3
  specializing in dictionaries 58
  specializing in subject bibliographies 507
Pugh, R. B. 417b22
Purnell's encyclopaedia of famous people 138
Puerto Rico, national bibliographies 446
Punch 570

Questel 628, 633, 640
questions in reference process 30–40
quick reference enquiries 3, 41
quick reference works 127
  book indexes in 652
  definition 3
  dictionaries 53
quotations 71–2, 146–7
  dictionaries of 51, 72
  in dictionaries 18, 59

R&D abstracts 251–2
Rabelais, Francois 210
Radcliffe Infirmary, Oxford 232
Radials bulletin 520
Radical Statistics Group 349, 376b129–31
Radio Times 226
railways, bibliographies 514, 525
Ralfe, James 160
Ralston, A. 123
Ramage, D. 471
Ramsey, Anne 329, 338, 369b19–20, 550, 560b53

Random House dictionary of the English language 62, 63, 64
Ranger, F. 417b34
Ravensdale, J. R. 387–8
Rawlins, R. 145
Rayner report 330, 332, 342, 370b32, 374b94
readers
  as index users 651–2, 659
  reference interview with 36–8
  requirements in public libraries 13
Readers adviser 506
Reader's digest almanac and yearbook 211–2
Reader's encyclopaedias 118
Readers' guide to periodical literature 43, 162, **235**
Readers guides 508
Readers Microprint Corporation 314
Reaney, P. H. 422b
RECON 594–5
record offices 389, 570
Record Offices 389, 416b8
Recommended basic statistical sources 327, 369b6
Recommended basic United Kingdom statistical sources 306, 331, 370b24
Record repositories in Great Britain 162
recordings, sound 129, 415
Records of parliament 405
Rees, E. 485
Refer 309, 551, 561b62
Reference and subscription books reviews 22b
reference books
  definitions 2–3
  need of index 651–2, 656
  indexes to children's 655
reference databases 591
reference interview
  biographical enquiries 132–3

Index

training in 29, 36–9
reference librarians 1
  as subject specialists 11, 13
  budgetary control by 6
  desirable qualities in 31–6
  training of 25, 29, 364, 366
  using indexes 653
reference libraries
  definition 2
  development and functions 1–23
reference materials
  authority of 12–13
  acquisition 6
  bibliographies in 15
  conflicting information in 9–10
  comprehensiveness of 13
  cost effectiveness 12, 15
  definition 2, 25–6
  evaluation of 11–20
  guides to 12, 16–17
  in academic libraries 7, 14, 20
  in copyright libraries 7
  in national libraries 7
  in public libraries 5–6
  obsolescence of 4
  organisation of 14
  'reliability' code in 11
  selection of 653
  types of 2–4, 17–20
reference work
  definition and evolution 2, 25–6
  use of indexes in 651–3
reference process 24–48, 32fig1
referral function of libraries 46
Reform of the law 306–7
Regional accounts 334, 371b43
Regional guides to library resources 513
regional planning, bibliographies 507
Regional statistics 305, 333, 371b41
Regional trends 334, 361, 371b44
Register of defunct and other companies 176
Reichling, D. 464–5

'reliability' code in reference material 11
religion, bibliographies 523
Répertoire alphabetique et phonétique . . . 181
Répertoire bibliographique des livres imprimés en France 494–5
Repertorio analitico della stampa italiano 217
Repertorium bibliographicum 464–5
reports 247–52
  abstracts of 249–51
  alternatives to periodicals 221
  definition of 247–8
  indexes to 249, 656
reprints 314–5, 452
reproductions of paintings 571
Reprographics Quarterly 650
Research Association for Paper and Board, Printing and Packaging Industries 656
research enquiries 34, 38, 41, 46
Research in British universities . . . 520
Research in education 251
Research index 238, 517
Research Libraries Information Network 481
Resources in education 251
Rettig, J. 48b
retrieval process, on-line systems *see* on-line information retrieval systems
Retrospective index to film periodicals 238
Retorspective index to theses of Great Britain and Ireland 254
reverse dictionaries 69
Reverse-dictionary 69
Review of sociological writing on the press 218
Reviews of United Kingdom

Index

statistical sources 332, 339, 370b27
revisions of encyclopaedias 17, 78, 86
rhyming dictionaries 50, 56, 66
Richard, Stephen 310, 314, 518
Richardson, J. 402
Riches, P. M. 158
Richmond, K. 507, 527, 531b29
Rickards, M. 414
Riden, P. 422b
Ritchie, M. 521
Road accidents 363, 382b227
road maps and atlases 276, 277, 282
Roberts A. D. 164b, 523, 529b2, 530b9, 532b, 534
Robinson, A. M. L. 532b
Robinson, F. J. G. 478–9
Robl, E. H. 581
Robson, Lowe, Ltd. 129
Rodd, E. H. 658
Rodgers, Frank 297
Rogers, A. 387, 415, 416, 419b74, 422b
Rogers, D. 500b6
Rogers, E. M. 412
Roget, P. M. 50, 56, 68
Roman Catholic books 473, 476
Roman civilisation *see* classical world
Roman mosaics in Britain 569
Romania, national bibliographies 447
Romeike and Curtice's press cutting agency 202
Roorbach, O. 491
Ross-Craig, Stella 572
Ross report on the press 218
Roster of federal libraries . . . 187
Roth, Andrew 154
Rothstein, S. 48b
Royal Academy exhibitors 156
Royal Academy of Arts, The 156

Royal College of Physicians of London: portraits 161
Royal Commission on Historical Manuscripts 162, 399, 417b31
Royal Commissions 300–1
Royal Commonwealth Society 160
royal family, biographical dictionaries 155
Royal Horticultural Society 128
Royal Institute of British Architects 511
Royal Society 156, 220, 531b26
Royal Society of British Artists 156
Royal Statistical Society 331, 370b24 *Journal* 330
Royalty, peerage and nobility of the world 155
Rubinstein, Artur
 specimen enquiry 9–10, 22b3
Rugby School Register 156
Runnyede Trust 350, 375b138
Russell, Ronald 586b22
Russia
 CIP programme 430
 national bibliographics 449
 news digests 207
 newspaper lists 217
Russian encyclopaedias 101–2
Russian, Ukrainian and Belorussian newspapers 217

Sabin, J. A. 489–90
St. Louis post-dispatch 204
saints, biographical dictionaries 149
Salmi, Markku 574
San Francisco chronicle 204
Sansoni-Harrap standard Italian and English dictionary 70
Sarbacher, R. I. 128
Saudi Arabia, statistics 332
Savage, E. A. 530b6
Saxton, Christopher 284
Sayers, W. C. B. 530b

Index

Scenery of Great Britain and Ireland 577
Schifferes, Steve 350, 376b142
Schistosomiasis 242
Schneider, G. 533b
Schnoles, P. A. 116–7, 130
schools, alumni lists 156
science
  abstracts 241–2
  bibliographies of 510, 512
  biographical dictionaries 150–2
  conferences 256–8
  dictionaries 65, 77
  directories 193
  encyclopaedias 108, 114–15, 125
  indexing of books on 659
  periodicals 229
  reports 248
Science abstracts 241–2
science fiction
  biographical dictionaries 154
Science Reference Library *see* British Library. Science Reference Library
Scientific and technical aerospace reports 250
Scientific engineering and medical societies publications in print 257–8
SCIMP 239
Scobell, Henry 655
SCOLMA 232
SCONUL 199
SCOOP 309
Scotland
  biographical dictionaries 143
  early books 477, 484
  foreign incunabula in 469
  gazetteers 289
  statistics 334, 363
Scott, Gay 549, 560b47–8
Scott, *Sir* Walter
  indexes to Waverley novels 656, 675b17–21

Scottish abstract of statistics 334, 371b45
Scottish economic bulletin 334, 371b46
Scottish Gaelic union catalogue 484
Scottish Education Department 363, 382b239
Scottish Record Office
  catalogue of maps 285
sculptures 575, 578
SDC 593, 594, 595, 603, 608, 618, 620
  charges 615
  survey 619
search strategy 40–6, 600, 604
  on-line retrieval 604
  training for 29, 36–9
Searchlight 357, 378b173
Searle, G. D. 239
Secondary analysis in social research 336, 372b65
Secrecy, or the right to know? 323b
Sectional lists 307–8
Securities Exchange Commission 188
Select biographical sources 162
Select Committees 300
Select list of British parliamentary papers . . . 313
Selected US government publications 318
selection of reference material 25, 425–6
  atlases 276–8
  bibliographies 526
  biographical material 134
  indexing and abstracting services 234
  maps 269–72
  periodicals 226–30, 234
  statistical materials 234
Sell's directory of products and services 177
Sellwood, Roger 341, 373b86
Seltzer, L. E. 287

Index

Senegal, national bibliographies 447, 429
Sequels 519
serials 219–45
  definitions 219
  directories 193
  union lists 19, 230–2
Serials librarianship 223, 244b10
series, books in bibliographies 519
sessional papers 304, 311, 315
  indexes 312
Shackel, B. 244b9
Shakespeare, William
  bibliography 527
  concordances 73, 515
Shaw, R. R. 491
Shawcross report on the press 218
Sheehy, Eugene P. 16–17, 60, 104b, 218b2, 277, 292b6, 318, 435, 452b10, 500b, **505**, 533b5
Sheffield Public Libraries 69, 367, 384b247
Shelston, A. 163b2
Shepherd, Walter 573
Shepherds historical atlas 282
Shifrin, Malcolm 244b10
shipping
  directories 178–9
  statistics 363
Shipton, C. K. 488–9
Shores, Louis 78, 135, 163b6
Short title catalgoue 468, **470–1**
  continuation of 473–6
  revisions of 471–3
Short-title catalogue of books printed in France 493
Shorter Oxford English dictionary 49, 61, 74b1
Siddall, Leona 343, 374b97
Sierra Leone, national bibliographies 447
Signposts to the past 410
signatures 145
Sillitoe, Alan Frank 362, 381b210

Sills, D. L. 110–1
Silver studio designs 575
Simkins, M. A. 244b9
Simmons, J. S. G. 105b
Simms, R. 392, 417b18
Simon, A. L. 506
Simonton, D. 253
Singapore, national bibliographies 433, 447
Singh, S. 542, 558b18
SINTO 186, 366
SISCIS: subject index to sources 328, 338, 369b10
Skelton, R. A. 284, 412
SLA geography and map division bulletin 278
Slam trade year book of Africa 173
slang 52, 57, 66
  American dictionaries of 67
  English dictionaries of 67
Slattery, W. J. 259
slide collections 580
Slocum, R. B. 162–3
Small area statistics 366, 383b246
SMIL 328, 332, 342, 344, 367, 369b8–9, 370b36, 371b37–9
Smiles, Samuel 149
Smith, A. H. 422b
Smith, F. 408
Smith, F. Seymour 530b5
Smith, G. 194b7
Smith, J. F. 422b
Smith, J. T. 422b
Social Science Research Council
  Data archive bulletin 336, 372b56
social sciences
  bibliographies 512
  dictionaries 66
  encyclopaedias 110–11, 112
  indexes to 201
  periodicals indexes 201, 235
Social sciences index 201, 235
Social security statistics 362, 381b211

Index

Social services year book 182
Social trends 305, 350, 361, 380b197
Society of County Treasurers 362, 380b205
Society of Indexers 654, 659, 668–70
  Carey Award 672
  conference 669
  formation of 668
  liaison with LA 669
  Select reading list 675b39
  Wheatley Medal 669–72
Society of Motor Manufacturers 362, 381b221
Society of Picture Researchers 583
Society of University Cartographers
  Bulletin 278
  soft terminology 603
soil maps 275
Solicitors' diary, almanac and legal directory 184
Some neglected sources of biographical information 410, 419b60
Somerville, A. N. 48b
Sonnenschein, W. S. 506
Sorkow, Janice 587b23
sound recordings, local studies 415
source databases 591
Sources and nature of the statistics 332, 370b28
Sources du travail bibliographique 17
Sources for English local history 386, 416b3
Sources for the history of population 409–10
Sources of local history 390
Sources of serials 227
Sources of statistics 327, 369b7
South Africa
  national bibliographies 447
  yearbooks 215

South America *see* Latin America
South Pacific
  regional bibliographies 429
South Yorkshire County Council 336, 372b63
Southeast Asia
  regional bibliographies 447
Soviet Russia *see* Russia
Spain
  directories of 173
  incunabula 466
  national biographies 447
Spanish encyclopaedias 100
Speak for England, no index 668
special collections, indexes to 28
special libraries
  accessions lists 512
  catalgoues 511–2
  cataloguing and classification 28
  directories of 186
  loan collections 581
  public access in 526
  reference material in 6–7, 14, 20
  reference work in 25, 32
  user education in 30
Special libraries 356, 378b164
specifications *see* patents; standards
Spiers, John 228
SPREd 583
Spurling, Hilary 674b22
Sri Lanka, national bibliographies 448
Staffordshire, local studies 392
'Stage' *cyclopaedia* 129
Stamp, L. D. 66
stamps, postage, catalogues 129, 571
Standard & Poor's corporation records 176, 190
standard book numbers 247, 426
Standard industrial classifcation 351, 352, 353, 376b141–3, 377b151–5
Standard rate and data 227

731

Index

Standard periodicals directory 227
standards 258–62, 326
  in France 260
  in Germany 260
  in United States 259, 260–1
Standing Conference for Local History 422b
Standing Committee on Official Publications see SCOOP
standing orders
  for directories 19–20
  for periodicals 6
  monitoring of 26
STAR 250
Statesman's year-book 10, 42, **212–3**, 652
Stationers' Company registers 499b3
Stationers' Register 471, 499b3
Statistical bulletins 366, 382b230
Statistical data in machine readable form 554, 561b64
statistical information
  directories 185
  enquiries 10–11
  government publications 305–6
Statistical news 332, 341, 348, 356, 364, 370b29–32, 373b86–7, 375b127–8, 378b165, b167
statistical publications 305–6
  classification schemes 351–4
  selection 354–5
Statistical reference index 332, 370b35
Statistical year book 360, 379b178
Statistical yearbook of member states 360, 379b186
statistics 324–84
  abstracts 334, 358, 361
  bibliographies 337
  definition of 324
  Disraeli on 11
  guides to 325–42
  index 332
  treat with care 11, 212

  international 326–30, 337, 356
Statistics Africa 329, 369b12
Statistics America 329, 369b13
Statistics and Market Intelligence Library see SMIL
Statistics and market research 342, 343, 374b92
Statistics Asia and Australasia 329, 369b14
Statistics Canada 332, 356, 370b36, 378b166
Statistics Europe 329, 369b15
Statistics for consumers 340, 373b79
Statistics in society 349
Statistics of education 363, 383b236
Statistics of trade through United Kingdom ports 354, 378b163
Statistics sources 328, 338, 369b11
statutes 301–2
  in loose-leaf publications 302
Statutes in force 302
  United Kingdom 301–2
statutory instruments 303, 304, 308
Staveley, R. 164b, 532b
STC see *Short-title catalogue*
Steel, D. 407–8
steel, standards 261
Steinberg, S. H. 114
Stephen, *Sir* Leslie 141
Stephens, W. B. 386, 387, 409, 416, 416b3
Stephenson, R. W. 282, 292b7
Stevenson, B. C. 72
stills, catalogue of 574, 582
Stock Exchange
  Daily List 175–6
  Official year book 175–6
  Register of defunct and other companies 176
stock selection 25–7, 133
Stokes, R. 499b1
Storey, R. 399, 417b32
Storey, R. L. 114

Index

street plans 270
Stubbs' buyers' guide 177
Study of history
  index to vol. 12 652
Stych, F. S. 48b
Subject Access Project 667, 675b36–7
Subject and name index to articles on the Slavonic and East European languages and literature 238
subject bibliographies 502–33
  abstracts journals as 517
  annotation in 507–8, 523
  bio-bibliography 508
  general bibliographies 509–10
  library problems 525–8
  limitations in encyclopaedias 508
  publishers specializing in 507
  selective 506–8
  series 508–9
  US government publications 318
subject catalogues of
  of London Library 505
  of public libraries 186
Subject collections 186
Subject collections in European libraries 186
subject departmentalized libraries 5, 32
subject dictionaries 64–6
Subject directory of special libraries 186
subject encyclopaedias 107–30
  arrangement of 112–4
  currency and accuracy 126–7
  exploitation 127–9
  indexing of 114–17
  level 121–6
  role and content 109–12
  treatment of subjects 117–9
  use of 119–21
Subject guide to books in print 504
Subject guide to international books in print 504

subject index
  to London Library 505
  to periodicals 7
Subject index of books published before 1880 504
Subject index to periodicals 236, 516
subscription agents 26
Suffolk celebrities 149
Summary of world broadcasts 197–8, 208
Sunday Telegraph, index to 203
Sunday Times 199, 210
  index to 202
  reviews in 17
Superintendent of Documents 316–7
surnames, dictionaries 67
Survey information on microfilm 273
Survey of current affairs 207
Survey of non-official statistics 343, 374b97
Survey of the contents of existing national bibliographies 428, 435, 452b3
surveyors, directories 180, 285
Swaziland, national bibliographies 448
Sweden
  biographical dictionaries 148
  national bibliographies 448
Switzerland
  incunabula 466
  national bibliographies 434, 448
Sylvester, E. 48b
symbols
  dictionary of 572, 573
  encyclopaedia of 573
  glossary of 573
symposia *see* conferences
synonyms
  American dictionaries of 68
  chemical 180
  in indexes 663

Index

in reference works 14, 42, 57
synoposes, alternatives to
   periodicals 222
Synoptic tables . . . 435, 453b13
System Development Corporation
   see SDC
systematic bibliography, definition
   454

Table alphabeticall, A. 51, 74b2
Taiwan (Republic of China)
   national bibliographies 448
Talvart, H. 499
Tanselle, G. T. 501b
Tanzania, national bibliographies
   448
*Tariff and overseas trade
   classification* 353, 377b159
*Taschenbuch des öffentlichen
   Lebens* 187
Tate, W. E. 401
Taylor, Archer 533b
Taylor, Eric 322b
Taylor, J. R. 151
Taylor, Laurie J. 657
Taylor, 529b1, 530b8
Tchemerzine, A. 493
tea, statistics 361
Teaching local history 387
Tearle, Barbara 519, 529
technology
   bibliographies of 512
   biographical dictionaries 147
   conferences 256–7
   dictionaries 65
   indexes 40, 42, 43, 236, 516
   periodical indexes 236
Tega, V. G. 228
telegraphic addresses
   directories 170–1
telephone directories 169–70
teletext 222, 622, 624–5, 630–9
   costs 645
   history 628
   news services 628–9

subtitling 629
*Television news index and
   abstracts* 197
telex, directories 170–1
*Tercentenary handlist of English
   and Welsh newspapers* 229
Term Catalogues 474, 500b7
terminals, on-line 596
terminology in indexes 42–3, 65,
   525, 600
Terry, G. M. 238
Textline 208
Texts and calendars 401–2
theatre
   biographies 134, 151, 152, 159
   encyclopaedias 115, 130, 151
*Theatre, film and television
   biographies master index* 159
thesauri 600, 602–3
*Thesaurus of English words and
   phrases* 50, 56, 68
theses and dissertations 253–5,
   397, 399–400
   abstracts of 254–5, 519
   author's rights in 246, 254
   availability of 519
   indexes to 254, 519
Thewlis, J. 116, **122**, 128
They looked like this 145
They looked like this (Europe) 145
Thième, H. P. 499, 572
Thieme, U. 149–50
Thirsk, J. 422b
Thomas, D. M. 23b
Thomas, I. 243b7
Thomas, J. 137
*Thomas register of American
   manufacturers* 174
Thomason catalogue 476
Thompson, E. H. 165, 194b5
Thompson, P. 415, 419b71
Thompson, Philip 571
Thomson's dictionary of banking
   127
Thomson local directories 168

734

Index

Thorndike dictionaries 59
Thornton, J. L. 510
Thornton, John L. 658, 661, 673b6, 676b27, 676b33
Thrower, N. J. W. T. 292b
timber, statistics 360, 365
Timber bulletin for Europe 360, 379b189
Timber Trade Federation 365, 383b243
Time magazine, index 205
Time rate of wages 365, 383b239
Times, The 143, 199, 210
   Index 19, 41, 43, 198, **201–4**, 656
   Obituaries 145
   on microfilm 200
   Tercentenary handlist 200, 229, **404**
Times atlas of the world 278, 287
Times educational supplement 202, 656
Times guide to the European parliament 547, 560b37
Times guide to the House of Commons 154
Times higher education supplement 202, 656
Times index-gazetteer of the world 287
Times literary supplement 202–3, 656
   editorial in 651
   reviews in 12, 17, 73, 79
Times of India directory 187
Times tercentenary handlist of English and Welsh newspapers 200, 209, **404**
Titcombe, J. M. 332, 342, 371b38
tithes 401
Title deeds 401, 417b35
Tongeren, e. Van 243b8
Toomey, Alice F. 521
Top management abstracts 240

Top 1000 directories and annuals 192
Topographical dictionary of England 290
topographical information
   bibliography 392
   directories 167–9, 413, 582
   indexes to illustrations 577
Totok, W. 500b
Town records 400
towns
   atalses of 283
   directories 406
   plans of 285
   records 400
Townsend, Peter 350, 376b134
TOXLINE 595
Toy trader yearbook 179
Tracing your ancestors 407, 418b51
trade
   bibliographies 424, 454
   directories 193
   statistics 338, 353–4, 358, 362
Trade directories of the world 193
trade names, directories 180–1
Trade names directory 181
Trade union records of Greater Manchester 399, 417b33
training of reference librarians 25, 29, 364, 366
translating dictionaries 69–71
translations, bibliographies 515
Translations on Eastern Europe 229
translators, Aslib list 45
Transnational corporations 193
transport
   ephemera 414
   statistics 348, 363
Travis, Carol 232
Trésor des livres rares et précieux 464
Trinity College, Dublin 8, 470, 482

735

Index

Trinidad and Tobago
  national bibliographies 449
trusts, directories 182
Tunisia, national bibliographies 449
Turkey, national bibliographies 449
Twentieth century authors 154
Twitchett, Kenneth 544–5, 559b26
Typographia Scoto-Gadelica 484

UBC 423, 425, 427, 433
UDC 28
Uden, G. 145
Uganda, national bibliographies 449
UK *see* United Kingdom
UKCIS 590
UK mineral statistics 362, 381b217
UK trade names 180–1
Ulrich's international periodicals directory 157, 227, 233, **516**, 591
Ulstein, B. 75b
UN *see* United Nations
UN publications catalogue 327, 368b4
UNBIS thesaurus 541, 558b17–8
Underground and alternative press in Britain 228
UNDOC 372, 368b3
  current index 541, 558b16
Unemployment statistics 345, 374b104
Unesco 544, 571
union catalogues 18–19, 25, 231–2, 455
Union list of periodicals on art, design and related subjects 573
Union list of statistical serials 331, 370b25
union lists of serials 19, 230–2
United Kingdom
  CIP programme 430
  directories 167
  encyclopaedias 87–92
  national bibliography 449–50
  national biography 140–1
  statistics 330–3, 350, 354, 361, 362
United Kingdom balance of payments 361, 380b199
United Kingdon in figures 361, 380b193
United Nations
  indexes 434, 538
  publications in British Library 8
  Sales publications 542, 558b20
  statistical publications 326–7, 333, 337, 351, 353, 358, 360, 368b1–4, 376b141–3, 379b175, 379b178–9, 379b188, 384b, 539–40
United Nations documentation 541, 558b14
  News 541, 558b15
United Nations publications in print 542, 559b22
United States
  atlases 280
  biographical dictionaries 142, 143, 144, 147, 151
  CIP programme 430
  directories 168, 173
  government publications 316–20, 537
  incunabula 467–8
  maps 274
  national bibliographies 450
  newspapers in 204
  subject libraries in 5
United States. Board on Geographic Names 288
United States. Bureau of the Census
  Directory of federal statistics 338, 372b68
  Fact finder for the nation 338, 372b69

Index

Guide to foreign trade statistics 338, 372b67
Guide to sources of statistics 338, 372b70
Historical statistics 347, 375b117
United States. Federal Depository Library System 317
United States. Geological Survey 274
United States. Government Printing Office 316
United States catalog 492
United States government manual 320
universal bibliographies 456–69
Universal Bibliographic Control 423, 425, 427, 433
Universal business directories 168
Universal decimal classification 28
Universal etymological dictionary 51
Universal pronouncing dictionary 137
universities
  biographical dictionaries 156
  directories 182–3
  statistics 363
University Grants Committee 363, 382b235
university libraries see academic libraries
University Library, Cambridge 8, 367, 478, 482, 485
University of Chicago Library 132, 461
Unwin, Philip 652
urban planning, bibliographies 507
Urban history yearbook 391, 416b10
Urquhart, M. C. 348, 375b119
Uruguay, national bibliographies 450
USA see United States
USA oil industry directory 178

usage
  of encyclopaedias 119, 127
  of indexes 651–3
Use of mathematical literature 509
user education 26
  in academic libraries 30
  in public libraries 30
  in special libraries 30
  of bibliographies 527
  of statistical material 325
User guide catalogue 335, 371b54
USSR see Russia

Vacher's European companion 546, 559b31
Vacher's parliamentary companion 187
valuers, directories 180
Van Dale, J. H. 64
Van Nostrand's scientific encyclopedia 108, 119
Vanderbilt University 197
Venezuela
  directories of 173
  national bibliographies 451
Venn, J. 156
Venn diagrams 604–6
Verbo: enciclopedia luso-brasileira 100
VIA 647, 650
  news 649fig10
  publications 648
Vicaire, G. 497
Victoria and Albert Museum 575
  Library 512, 582
Victoria county histories 394, 417b23, 572
Video to online 236
videodiscs 22
videotex systems 622–50
  bibliography 646–9
  encyclopaedia on 91
  essential features 622–4
  transmission codes 644

Index

Viewdata 355, 622, 624–7, 630–9
  charges 646
  history 629–30
  internal indexes 653
  Newsfile 632, 642, 646
Village records 400
Vinson, J. 153
violins, encyclopaedias 113
visual sources 563–87
Voice of the past 415, 419b71
Vollmer, H. 150

Wages and salaries 348, 375b122
Waitt, Ian 667
Wakeman, J. 154
Wales
  atlases of 280
  biographical dictionaries 143
  early books in 484–5
  statistics 363
Walford, A. J. 23b, 73, 74, 129
  Guide to reference material 16, 17, 60, 104b, 218b3, 435, 452b9, 500b, 505, 533b
Walkland, S. A. 322b
Wall, C. E. 227, 244b14
Wall, J. 413
Wall, John 581, 587b17
Wall Street journal 204, 208, 656
Walsh, James P. 105b
Walter, Clare 341, 373b90
Wanger, J. 620b8
Wardleycards 190
Warren, K. S. 242
Warwick guide to British labour periodicals 230, 516
Warwick University Statistics Service 341, 344, 367, 373b89
Warwickshire, maps of 284
Washington information directory 187
Washington Post 204, 208
Wasserman, P. 328, 338, 369b11
Watchmaker, jeweller and silversmith directory 180

Watkins, A. H. 527
Watson, G. 200, 229, **486–7**
Watt, R. 477, 504, 508, 530b3, b7
Way, D. J. 322b
Ways of escape, no index 668
Webber, Rosemary 199
Webster, Noah 52
Webster's biographical dictionary 137
Webster's dictionary of synonyms 68
Webster's new collegiate dictionary 64
Webster's new geographical dictionary 287
Webster's new international dictionary 58, **62**, 64
Weekly memorials for the ingenuous 220
Weil, C. B. 163b3
Wellesley index to Victorian periodicals 235
Wells, H. G., bibliography 527
Welsh Office 363, 382b
Wentworth, H. 67
Wer ist wer? 147
West, J. 400
West Germany *see* Germany (Federal Republic of Germany)
West Indies and Caribbean year book 173, 214
West Midlands, directories 407
West Midlands County Council Census report 336, 372b57
Westminster Public Library 505
  Art Library 582
whaling, statistics 361
What is an index? 655, 673b5
What it cost the day before yesterday 346, 375b109
Whatmore, Geoffrey 218, 656, 674b24
Wheat, James Clements 285

Index

Wheatley, Henry Benjamin 659, 669
What is an index? 655, 673b5
Wheatley Medal 669–72
  institution of 669–72
  selection committee 660
  1968 medal 657–8, 671
  1980 medal 657, 672
Which? 40
Whitaker's almanack 10, 187, 211, 652
  as encyclopaedia 211
White, Brenda 507
White, M. D. 48b
white papers 306
Whitehouse, D. 282
Whitford report on copyright 300, 307
Whitrow, M. 532b35
WHO 544
Who did what 138
Who owns whom 173–4
Who was who 42, **144**
Who was who in America **144**, 159
Wholesale price index 339, 353, 372b72, 377b157
Who's who 9, 10, 132, 133, **146–7**
Who's who in America 147
Who's who in American art 151–2
Who's who in art 151
Who's who in Australia 147
Who's who in Austria 147
Who's who in Berkshire 149
Who's who in California 149
Who's who in Canada 147
Who's who in Cheltenham 149
Who's who in children's books 157
Who's who in classical mythology 156
Who's who in Europe 148
Who's who in France 147
Who's who in Germany 147
Who's who in music 9
Who's who in New York 149
Who's who in science fiction 154
Who's who in science in Europe 151–2
Who's who in technology 147
Who's who in the Arab world 148
Who's who in the Commonwealth 148
Who's who in the theatre 134, 152
Who's who in the west 149
Who's who in the world 139
Who's who in Thomas Hardy 157
Who's who of children's literature 154
Wilding, N. 118
Wiles, R. M. 404–5
Willes, A. J. 407, 418b50
Williams, Francis 218
Williams, W. E. 530b5
Willing's press guide **215–6**, 227
wills 408
Wilson, H. W. 201, 235–6, 269, 516
  Index Award 672–3
Wilson Committee report 341, 373b88
Winch, K. 270–1
wines and spirits, encyclopaedias 109
Wing, D. G. 473–6
Wintle, J. 145–6
Winton, Harry 540, 558b13
Wiring regulations 259
Wisden's cricketers' almanack 166
Wise's post office directories 168
Witkin, Lee D. 585b3
Women's studies 521
Wood, David 560b37
Woodbine, Herbert 133, 163b5
Woodward, A. M. 228–9, 243b8
Woodward, C. D. 266b
Woodworth, D. P. 228, 403, 418b43
Woolf, Virginia 131, 163b1, 515
word by word alphabetization 14–15, 56, 662

739

Index

word processors, definition of 20–1
Work study + O&M abstracts 240
World almanac 211
World atlas 279
World atlas of agriculture 281
World authors 154
World bank atlas 360, 379b180
World bibliographical series 509
World bibliography of bibliographies 521
World bibliography of international documentation 535, 557b3
World book dictionary 63
World book encyclopaedia 63, 79, 85, 88, **92–3**
 bibliographies in 82
 Year-book 63, 93, 210
World dictionaries in print 74
World directory of multinational enterprises 172
World guide to libraries 513
World Health Organisation 544
World index of economic forecasts 340, 373b81
World list of national newspapers 199
World meetings 256
World mines register 178
World of learning 183, 186, 652
World patents index 263–4
World reporter 197, 208
Worldcasts 240–1
World's encyclopaedia of recorded music 129
Worldwide chemical directory 179
Worldwide petrochemical directory 178
Worldwide refining and gas processing directory 178
Writings on British history 395, 396
Wynar, B. 164b

Yale University Library 461
Yearbook of forest products 360, 379b188
Yearbook of international organisation 534, 557b1
Yearbook of labour statistics 360, 379b187
Yearbook of science and technology 126
Yearbook of the Commonwealth 214, 306
Year book of the Republic of South Africa 215
Yearbook of world affairs 213
yearbooks 86, 126–7
Year's work in English studies 224–5
Year's work in modern language studies 225
Yorkshire, statistics 281, 336
Youings, J. 402
Yugoslavia, national bibliographies 451

Zambia, national bibliographies 451
Zedler, Johann Heinrich 76
Zimbabwe, national bibliographies 451
Zischka, G. A. 104b